WARS AND SOLDIERS IN THE EARLY REIGN OF LOUIS XIV

Volume 4 – The Armies of Spain 1659–1688

Text and Illustrations by Bruno Mugnai

'This is the Century of the Soldier', Fulvio Testi, Poet, 1641

Helion & Company

Helion & Company Limited
Unit 8 Amherst Business Centre
Budbrooke Road
Warwick
CV34 5WE
England
Tel. 01926 499 619
Email: info@helion.co.uk
Website: www.helion.co.uk
Twitter: @helionbooks
Visit our blog http://blog.helion.co.uk/

Published by Helion & Company 2021
Designed and typeset by Serena Jones
Cover designed by Paul Hewitt, Battlefield Design (www.battlefield-design.co.uk)

Text © Bruno Mugnai 2021
Illustrations © as individually credited
Colour artwork by Bruno Mugnai © Helion & Company 2021
Maps drawn by George Anderson © Helion & Company 2021

ISBN 978-1-913336-43-1

British Library Cataloguing-in-Publication Data.
A catalogue record for this book is available from the British Library.

For details of other military history titles published by Helion & Company
Limited, contact the above address, or visit our website: http://www.helion.co.uk

We always welcome receiving book proposals from prospective authors.

Contents

Spanish Chronology, 1659–1685

1659

January 14	The Portuguese army of Alentejo defeats the Spaniards in the Battle of the Lines of Elvas
January 30	The Spanish army besieges the Portuguese town of Monção. The garrison surrenders on 7 February after a bitter resistance.
February 17	The Spaniards under the Marquis of Viana recapture Salvatierra de Minho
November	The Spaniards besiege Elvas, but are driven off by António Luís de Meneses
November 7	Peace of the Pyrenees between France and Spain

1660

May–June	The Portuguese attempt to seize Valença de Alcántara is repulsed by the Spaniards

1661

November 16	Death of the Spanish prime minister Luís Méndez de Haro
December 14	The Spaniards seize the Portuguese fortress of Alconchel

1662

June 9	Portuguese garrison of Juromenha surrenders to the Spaniards

1663

May 12	The Spaniards under Don Juan of Austria seize Évora
June 8	The Portuguese army under Vilhena and Schomberg scores a resounding victory over the Spaniards at Ameixial-Estremoz
June 24	The Portuguese led by Sancho Manoel de Vilhena and the Count of Mértola retake Évora

1664

July 7	Battle of Castelo Rodrigo, the Portuguese army of the Minho under Pedro Jacques de Magalhães defeats the Duke of Osuna
June 20	The Portuguese army seizes Valença de Alcántara after an eight-day siege

1665

June 17	The Spanish army is thoroughly defeated by the Portuguese at Montes Claros
September 17	Death of Felipe IV of Spain; the government is held by a Council of Regency presided over by the widowed Queen Maria Anna of Austria.

1666

June	Maria Anna of Austria appoints Cardinal Nithard as a member of the Council of Regency and first councillor of the Queen of Spain

1667

May 24	Start of the War of Devolution between France and Spain
Summer	Inconclusive Portuguese campaigns in Galicia
June 2	The French army under Turenne seizes Charleroi
June 6	Bergues surrenders to the French under d'Aumont; six days later the French seize Furnes.
June 16	Ath surrenders to Turenne
June 22	The French besiege Tournai; the Spanish garrison surrenders four days later.
July 7	Douai surrenders to the French
July 18	D'Aumont conquers Courtrai
July 31	Oudenarde surrenders to the French; days later Fort de Scarpe and Armentières also fall.
August 5	Successful Spanish defence at Dendermonde during the five-day French siege
August 6	The Spaniards defeat a French cavalry corps at Jodoigne in Brabant
August 28	Lille is seized by the French after a 10-day siege
August 31	The Spanish relief force for Lille is repulsed near Bruges
Sept. 12–13	Surrender of Alst and Mons in the Spanish Low Countries

1668

February 7	The French seize Besançon in Franche-Comté; Salins surrenders three days later
February 13	Treaty of Lisbon. Spain recognises the independence of Portugal; end of the Restoration War
February 16	The garrison of Dole surrenders to the French army in Franche-Comté. Five days later the fortress of Gray also falls.
March 15	The French besiege Genappe in Flanders but leave three days later
May 2	Treaty of Aix-la-chapelle; end of the Devolution War. France retains Lille, Douai, Tourney, Charleroi, Ath, Armentières and Bergues but returns to Spain Franche-Comté and other conquest in the Low Countries.

1669

January 31	Don Juan of Austria moves from Barcelona to Madrid for a coup against Nithard
February 25	Nithard is removed as head of government; Pedro Fernández del Campo succeeds him.

1671

January 27   English privateer Henry Morgan defeat Spanish regular forces and militiamen at the battle of Panama and seizes the city

December 25   Dutch Stadtholder Johan de Witt and the Spanish governor general of the Low Countriesm the Count of Monterrey, sign an alliance to provide reciprocal military support against France

1672

March–April   Riots in Messina (Sicily)

April 8   France declares war on the Dutch Republic

May 17   The French army invades the United Provinces of the Netherlands

December 15   The Dutch-Spanish army under William III besieges Charleroi, but he is forced to break camp the day after

1673

July 1   Austrian emperor Leopold I signs alliance with Spain and the Dutch Republic against France

August 28   The Spaniards occupy the islands of Las Alhucemas in North Africa

September 13   The Dutch-Spanish army under William III recaptures Naarden

1674

January   Skirmish between Catalan militias and French regular troops in the Ampurdan

February 28   The French under Navailles seize the fortress of Gray in Franche-Comté

March 6   Veseul in Franche-Comté surrenders to the French after a short resistance

April 3   Failure of the conspiracy of Vilafranca to bring Roussillon and French Catalonia back under Spanish rule

May 14   The Spaniards seize the fortress of Bellaguarda in Roussillon; days later Maureillas also surrenders.

May 16   The French army under Condé invades the Spanish Low Countries

May 23   The French fortress of Ceret in the eastern Pyrenees surrenders to the Spaniards

May 25   Besançon surrenders to the French after 29 days of siege

June 6   The French under Condé seize Dole in Franche-Comté

June 19   The Spaniards under the Count of San Germano defeat the French at Maureillas in the Pyrenees

July 7   Anti-Spanish insurrection in Messina

August 11   The battle engaged at Seneffe between Dutch–Spanish–Imperialists and French results in heavy casualties for both sides

September 16   The Dutch–Spanish–Imperial army besieges Oudenarde

September 19   The French under Condé cross the River Scheldt at Tournai; the allied army interrupts the siege of Oudenarde

1675

February 26   The French fleet defeats the Spaniards at the Battle of Lipari Island

May 29   The French conquer Dinant in the Spanish Low Countries

June 6	Huy surrenders to the French
June 10	Condé besieges Limburg, which surrenders on 21 June
July 27	The French retake Bellaguarda after 13 days of siege
August 11	German princes with Imperial and Spanish troops defeat the French at the Battle of Konzer Brücke near Trier
September 6	French garrison of Trier surrenders
November 6	Carlos II of Spain comes of age

1676

January 6	Naval battle of Stromboli between the Dutch-Spanish fleet against the French under Duquesne
April	Don Fernando de Valenzuela takes control of the Spanish government
April 22	Naval battle of Augusta in Sicily
April–July	The French seize Condé-sur-l'Escout, Bouchain, Maubeuge and Bavay in the Spanish Low Countries
May	Talks for a peace agreement open at Nijmegen
June–July	Portuguese recruitment and gathering of troops close to the border causes alarm in Madrid
July 8	The Dutch-Spanish under William III of Orange lay siege to Maastricht, but are forced to retreat on 27 August
July 31	Aire surrenders to the French under Schomberg and d'Humiéres
September 10	French troops supported by Messinese militiamen seize Taormina in Sicily

1677

January 6	Valenzuela is arrested; Don Juan of Austria becomes prime minister supported by the aristocracy.
March 17	The French army of Flanders seizes Valenciennes after 18 days of siege
April 11	Dutch-Spaniards are defeated at Mont Cassel
April 17	The French seize Cambrai; Saint-Omer surrenders on 22 April
June 1	The Spanish garrison of Puigcerdá in Catalonia surrenders to the French after 30 days of siege
July 12	The Spanish are defeated at Espolla in Catalonia
August 10	Dutch-Spanish besiege Charleroi a second time, but are forced again to leave the siege after the Duke of Luxembourg's relief

1678

March 5	Ghent surrenders to the French
March 26	Ypres is conquered by the French army
April	The French leave Messina; the Spaniards enter the city and re-establish the Royal government
May	Conference to negotiate the peace reopens at Nijmegen
June 29	Beginning of the French blockade of Mons
August 14	French and Dutch delegates at Nijmegen sign a peace; the Battle of Saint-Denis is won by the Dutch–Spanish–Germans.
September 17	Spain adheres to the Nijmegen Treaty. France annexes Franche-

Comté, and Saint-Omer, the province of Cassel, Aire, Ypres Cambrai, Valenciennes and Maubeuge in the Low Countries.

1679

September 14   Death of Don Juan of Austria; the Duke of Medinaceli succeeds him as prime minister

1681

April 30   The Moroccans seize the Spanish fortress of La Mámora

September 30   French troops surround the city of Luxembourg and block access to the city

1682

March   Louis XIV orders a halt to the blockade of Luxembourg and withdraws his troops

1683

September 13   New blockade of Luxembourg

October 26   Following the French refusal to leave the blockade of Luxembourg, Spain declares war on France; start of the War of the Reunions.

November 6   Courtrai surrenders to the French under Humiéres and Vauban

November 10   The French seize Dixmude

Dec. 22–26   The French under Marshal de Créqui bombard Luxembourg

1684

April 29   Start of the siege of Luxembourg

May 2   French troops enter Catalonia

May 5–17   French fleet bombards Genoa

May 15   Spanish troops in the Milanese are gathered to succour Genoa

May 20   The French besiege Gerona, but fail to conquer the city

May 22–25   New bombardment of Genoa; the French landing is repulsed by Genoese and Spanish troops

June 3   The Spanish garrison of Luxembourg surrenders to Créqui

June 12   Spanish cavalry defeat the French in the encounter at Thuin in Flanders

August 20   The peace between Spain and France is signed at Regensburg. France returns Courtrai to Spain, but retains Luxembourg and its territory.

1685

March   Count of Oropesa succeeds Medinaceli as Prime Minister

Foreword

It was a very pleasant surprise that Charles Singleton, 'Century of the Soldier' Series Editor, asked me to write a few words about the present work.

It is something very special for me, since I have been an avid reader of this collection since its very beginnings, and I follow it with great interest. It is now the turn of the subject that arouses the most interest in me: the armies of the Hispanic Monarchy during the reign of Charles II.

In 2014 my interest in the armies of the second half of the seventeenth century began, and I quickly discovered how difficult it was to find good information on the subject, and especially on the Spanish army, even in my own language.

Thanks to the '17th Century Wargaming' Facebook group, I had the pleasure of speaking to Bruno Mugnai, among other great people, and I am immensely grateful to them for their informative work on military history in general, and this time on Spanish history in particular, as it is the first time that this subject has been written about in such a precise, reliable and profound way in the English language.

Bruno has managed to give historical justice to a forgotten army, that of Charles II of Habsburg, which although it was not the famous army of tercios which fought through most of the sixteenth century into the middle of the 1600s, was able to maintain and preserve the honour and most territories of the Spanish Monarchy, while fighting alongside the other allied nations against the almost invincible hosts of Louis XIV.

This book completes one of the gaps that remained in the military history of the 'Century of the Soldier', and Bruno has done it again, he presents us an outstanding work both in quality and quantity, exquisitely illustrated with many photographs and drawings never before published.

We are probably looking at the best series of its kind in the world.

Jose María Cagiga, late summer of 2021

Acknowledgements

As author of this book, I am grateful to the scholars and friends who supported me in this work and for the permission to publish here pictures and accounts coming from their personal archives. I thank them for their patience, attention to detail, and trust in me. In this regard, the help provided by Francesco Pellegrini has been invaluable for tracing the chain of command of the Spanish units. The quality of his research and his reflections on this complex topic were a motivation to deepen in detail the many aspects of the Hispanic war machine, thanks to the accessibility of sources in the European archives, which he explores with meticulous zeal. In addition, I also appreciate the generous help of Jose María Cagiga Mata from Cartagena, who supplied a lot of invaluable notes. Ives Martin from Paris also contributed to the search of written sources, a task which he may accomplish being an actual authorities in matter of military history bibliography. I really appreciated the enthusiasm of the audience, which helped me to work toward publication. Among them, Ciro Paoletti served as energetic and incisive discussant to the making of this book.

I also thank Professor Davide Maffi of the University of Pavia, for his kind help concerning the written sources, as well as for the suggests of useful archival documents. His authority in the field of the Hispanic military history was an added value of which this book can thankfully praise.

Finally, it is a pleasure to work with Charles Singleton who patiently waited for the completion of this book, indulging in my slowness for this task: the most difficult to date.

Last but not least, I thank Colin Ashton who reviewed the entire manuscript. His comments helped to improve the overall quality of my work.

BM
Florence, 10 May 2021

Spain and the Sources for Seventeenth-Century Military History

With this book, the fourth, we are approaching the halfway point in the series entitled 'Wars and Soldiers in the Early Reign of Louis XIV'. The first three books dealt with some of the major powers of the century and with this title another important state has added, the largest from the territorial point of view, since Spain extended its rule in central Europe, Italy, America and Asia as well. Consequently, in several respects, the Hispanic armies represent a very complex and intricate subject.

This was not the greatest concern, however: as I was proceeding to write the first three books, the apprehension grew at thinking that, sooner or later, the turn of Spain would come. This concern was motivated by many factors. The Spain of *Los Austrias* is a topic that more than any other have received the attention of the most recent historiography dealing with the birth of the permanent army.[1] The last few decades has provided to readers and scholars with an increasingly accurate and better-documented view on this age. The research has produced a very detailed analysis concerning the evolution of the different territories constituting the 'Spanish Monarchy' and their main political actors, and many of the works deal with the army. Possibly, few other armies in the world can boast a quantity of publications comparable to those dealing with the last Spanish Habsburgs, and this was certainly a great

---

1   In the 1980s Luís António Ribot García with 'El ejército de los Austrias, aportaciones recientes y nuevas Perspectivas', in *Pedralbes: Revista de Historia Moderna*, N. 3, pp.89–126, brought new knowledge on this period of the Spanish history hitherto almost less investigated. The government of *Los Austrias* finally received different attention from that which, until then, had condemned their state to the rank of a power in full political, social, economic and moral decay. Interest has progressively grown with other valuable contributions by Spanish scholars, such as António José Rodríguez Hernández, António Espino López, António Álvarez-Ossorio Alvariño, Jesús Martínez de Merlo, Roberto Quirós Rosado, Luís Sorando Muzás, and many others who continue their research in the field of the Hispanic military history and related issues. For this dissemination, much is due to the Spanish central government and to the regional parliaments, which actively support such publications with special initiatives and funding. Together with the Spaniards, a small but proud handful of non-Spanish researchers has enriched the panorama of Iberian military history. Among these scholars stand out the contributions of Frenchman Pierre Picouet, the Belgian Etienne Rooms, and above all the Italian Davide Maffi, author of invaluable essays not only concerning the 'military' of Spanish Italy, but also the whole Monarchy.

Allegory entitled 'Defeated Spain', by Charles Le Brun, 1679 (Frescoes of the salon de la guerre, Versailles). Considered as an era of irreversible decadence, the age of Felipe IV and Carlos II never enjoyed a great reputation in Spanish and international historiography. After the glories of the sixteenth century and the great conflicts of the first half of the seventeenth century, the retreat of Spain from the position of primacy to a lower rank within the great Continental powers led to a strong disinterest in the long but not particularly fortunate reign of the unhappy last Habsburg kings. Forgotten for decades, only over the past two decades has there been a renewed interest in the activities of the government of the last Austrias.

advantage for those, like me, preparing to write on this topic. It seems very complicated to comprehensively cover the Hispanic military historiography of the last years. It would result in a mere catalogue or enumeration of works that can be consulted in any current online database.[2] Trying to find a common feature of these works, surely there is the highlighting of the importance of the army in the process of conformation of modern monarchies and European states throughout the seventeenth century. The gradual transformation of the old late-feudal military structures would lead to the creation of models of armies controlled and financed by the states. On this last point, in this incipient process of monopolisation of legitimised violence, several scholars have pointed out in a clarifying way the link between the concept of fiscal state and military state in the Old Regime, a period in which significant changes are registered regarding logistics, the capacity to mobilise human and financial resources, as well as the progressive introduction of new techniques of fortification and siege, or the significant technological improvement of portable firearms and artillery. Several of these works accurately deal with

2   A quick examination of the mass of publications on the rule of the last Spanish Habsburgs in any of the web search engines lists more than 600 articles, books and essays published in Spain as well as in Belgium, Italy and in other countries in the last 30 years, many of which dealing with the 'military'. In this regard, the statement of G.C. Boeri, J.L. Mirecki and J. Palau, in *The Spanish Army in the War of the League of Augsburg, 1688–1697* (London: Pike & Shot Society, 2002), appears in strong contrast. In the Introduction, the authors state that: 'As it is well known, there is not very much documentation on the organisation of the Spanish armies of the end of the seventeenth century … Nor has the period received great attention in Spain, Italy or Belgium, as it is considered a period of decadence of power.' The statement is partially reiterated at the end of the introduction: 'Very recently, a few very well documented studies have been published.'

organisation and logistics of the Spanish armies, and address such important aspects as the structure and evolution of the army, the sociology of the military class, the commanders and their professional career, as well as the thorny question of financing the mobilised forces and the enormous fiscal burden that fell on the Castilian population. In the author's opinion, these issues explain the defeat of the Spanish army in the last decades of the seventeenth century, and not so much the stagnation of the army, the ineptitude or the lack of preparation of its officers as commonly stated. The investigation on the economic impact of armies and the sources of war funding was another favourable opportunity, since each scholar dealing with this matter has to focus his research on the military administration. Like a detective, the historian has to investigate the economic balance and the net of channels through which money flowed to the troops, because following the money they could find the 'suspects'. The abundance and quality of the published sources, combined with the possibilities offered by online research, offered a large field of investigation for illuminating even the most hidden aspects.[3] However, any further research could be conducted only through different archives scattered throughout Spain, and abroad, particularly in Belgium and Italy. But this was not the only limit. As the work took shape, I realised that one of the most serious problems was the interpretation of the sources. Although some ideological conditioning was to be expected on a subject like Spain's *Los Austrias*, which was very different from the Bourbon establishment, the persistence of many inaccuracies made writing difficult. In the first place, many modern historians were conditioned by the classical view, deriving from the works of authors such as Quincy,[4] and also most recently like Pascal[5] and Hardÿ de Périni,[6] each pursuing the political objective of glorifying the action of Spain's greatest adversary, namely Louis XIV's France. The succession of military episodes are often described as a triumphal march, in which the Spanish armies are always overwhelmed by the best French organisation and leadership. Whilst any military historian should know that in wartime no source is certain, even leading contemporary authors tend to underestimate the Spanish contribution during the wars of Louis XIV.

This feature happens more or less in every conflict, from the Thirty Years' War (and before) to the present day, as it is known that winners write history. However, this trend is even more pronounced in the conflicts fought by Spain. It often happens to find reports stating the death of a commander and instead he is alive and well.[7] These kind of errors also reverberate in the works of later

---

3   Among the most detailed investigations about the Spanish military history and its historiography, see António Jiménez Estrella, 'La historiografía militar sobra la España moderna en los últimos años', in F. Labrador Arroyo (ed.), *II Encuentro de Jóvenes Investigadores en Historia Moderna. Líneas recientes de investigación en Historia Moderna* (Madrid: Universidad Rey Juan Carlos-Cinca, 2015), pp.13–48.

4   Charles Sevin Quincy, *Histoire militaire du règne de Louis-le-Grand, roi de France* (Paris, 1728).

5   Adrien Pascal, *Histoire de l'armée et de tous les régiments* (Paris, 1860–1864).

6   Édouard Hardÿ de Périni, *Batailles Françaises* (Paris,1894).

7   Among the resurrected, in 1663 the *maestre de campo* Pedro de Fonseca is declared as dead at Ameixial-Estremoz in the Portuguese and French sources, but the following year he is alive, in Valença de Alcantara.

historians and contribute to distort the events.[8] In this context, the reaction of Spanish historiography has recently started, depicting with fewer dark colours the political and military framework of *Los Austrias* after 1659. In their research the scholars come across episodes referred to by one of the factions in a completely different version compared to that of the other side, as if they were two different events. The examples are innumerable. The French sources claim the encounter that took place on 31 August 1667 near Bruges as a significant victory, and subsequent historiography continued to recount this episode in the same terms. The victory was even celebrated on one of the tapestries woven by Gobelins to depict the Sun King's military achievements.[9] On the contrary, the coeval Spanish sources state that the Count of Marchin, commander of the relief force, engaged a stronger French contingent, and after considering the surprise as unsuccessful, he retired to Ghent after inflicting heavy casualties on the enemy. Likewise, it appears less surprising how the clash that took place on 6 August 1667 near Jodoigne, resulting in a Spanish victory, is little mentioned in France, and instead highly celebrated in Spain.[10] This trend does not end, and again Quincy, and after him several modern scholars, debunks the French defeat suffered at Maureillas in 1674.

The reliability of the sources is a problem that has always conditioned the work of historians and even the great novelists have faced the same problem when confronted with texts and chronicles of the seventeenth century.[11] In the Spanish historical context, these difficulties are even greater and oblige scholars to take an even more cautious approach. The reasons are many. Although in historiographical fields such as Anglo-Saxon or French, military history was perfectly integrated into the academic and scientific world, enjoying prestige and specific research centres; in the Spanish case, political circumstances determined that for a long time military history was monopolised by army professionals, anchored in a factual 'history of battle' of a markedly ideological approach. As for Spain, in 1738 the matter became particularly complex after Juan António Samaniego completed his 'Dissertation relating the seniority of the Spanish regiments'.[12] This work

---

8 Even the authoritative John Childs falls into error, writing that Don Juan of Austria died in 1663 after the wounds he received during the battle of Ameixial-Estremoz. See Childs, 'The English Brigade in Portugal', in *Journal of the Society for Army Historical Research*, Vol. 53, N. 215 (Autumn 1975), p.142.

9 French sources claimed the destruction of the Spanish rearguard and the capture of 1,500 prisoners, 18 flags and standards, and five kettledrums, out of an overall strength of 6,000 Spaniards. See Quincy, *Histoire militaire*, vol. I, pp.184–185. The Spanish sources do not confirm such a high number of casualties, but admit that the failure had serious consequences for the morale of the army.

10 According to the Spanish sources, the French lost the whole cavalry corps. The casualties were 200 dead and a further 200 men prisoners, including the commanders La Haye and Baubrun (or Ambrum). The rest of the French cavalry escaped capture during the night. See António José Rodríguez Hernández, *Espana, Flandes y la Guerra de Devolucion (1667–1668). Guerra, reclutamiento y moviliziación para el mantenimiento de los Países Bajos Españoles* (Madrid: Ministerio de Defensa, 2007), p.182.

11 Among them, Friedrich Schiller and his use of the *Theatrum Europaeum* as a source for the Thirty Years' War. On this subject, see Hazel Katherine Clark, *Merian's 'Theatrum Europaeum' as a source for Schiller's 'Thirty years war' to the year 1629* (Berkeley 1912; thesis).

12 *Disertación sobre la antigüedad de los regimientos* (Madrid, 1738).

Illustration from the *Álbum de la Infanteria Española* by the *Conde* de Clonard (1861). Serafín María de Sotto y Abach Langton, third Count of Clonard and fifth Marqués de la Granada (1793–1862), was a Spanish noble, politician, writer and statesman who served as prime minister of Spain for one day in October 1849. He was of Irish patrilineal descent from John Sutton, first Baron Dudley. In Spain, the family name had been Hispanicisd as 'Sotto'. Clonard is especially known for his monumental works relating the history of the Spanish army, but unfortunately, a large part of his information concerning the seventeenth century contains errors and inaccuracies.

provided a 'historical' support for establishing the right of precedence of the Spanish regiments, but several reconstructions and filiations were at least arbitrary. As a result, the actual history of several units was accomodated after the requests imposed from above.

All research relating to the Spanish army calls into question the monumental work of the Count of Clonard, entitled *Historia orgánica de las armas de Infantería y Caballería españolas*, written and published between 1851 and 1859.[13] This title consists of 15 volumes including the history of the army of the Spanish Monarchy from its origins to the nineteenth century. Clonard completed his meritory mission in 1861, with the *Álbum de la Infantería española* and the *Álbum de la Caballería española*, which dealt with the uniforms of the Spanish armies. The Count was among the first to study

---

13 Serafín María de Sotto y Abbach, 3rd Count of Clonard and 5th Marquis of la Granada (1793–1862).

the documents preserved in the archive of Simancas, in Valladolid, which is considered the principal institution where all the documentation relating to the army has been collected. Clonard tried to give a coherent structure to this complex matter, but as for the seventeenth century, the research did not include other archival sources relating to the army, such as those of the kingdoms forming the Spanish Monarchy, as well as the archives outside Spain. Furthermore, the most recent investigations place Clonard's work among the almost unreliable sources, at least with regard to the Spanish military history of the seventeenth century, concerning the formation of the units, their filiation and ultimately their actual origin. Subsequent works, including the authoritative *Historia del Ejército Español* by Francisco Barado,[14] and *El Ejercito y la Armada* by Manuel Giménez González,[15] followed the line established by Clonard. In other words, most of the contributions written in the next 150 years were limited to copying what was traced in Clonard's works with all its discoveries but also its inaccuracies.[16] After Clonard, military historiography has contributed to making this matter incredibly tangled, with further errors and hasty reconstructions.[17] Therefore, the history of many of the units recruited during the seventeenth century is difficult to reconstruct. To trace the historical evolution of the Spanish military corps, establishing their origins and therefore their seniority, is a matter that has received considerable attention in recent years, but this is possible only with many gaps, at least before 1718, for infantry, cavalry and dragoons as well. For the period of about 40 years between 1659 and 1699, there are many data that scholars lack knowledge of when providing the actual number of units existing in this period. Among the greatest difficulties, there is the disparity of geographical places where the units were formed either in Belgium or in Italy, in addition to the ones located in Spain. Another difficultly comes from the organisation of these units and the number of troops, which varied greatly in peace and in wartime, and this caused continuous reforms and dissolution of the *tercios* as well as many of the companies.[18] To these difficulties must

---

14 Francisco Barado, *Historia del Ejército Español. Armas, Uniformes, Sistema de Combate Instituciones, Organización del Mismo* (Barcelona, 1889), vols I–II.

15 Manuel Giménez González, *El Ejercito y la Armada: desde la antiguedad hasta 1862* (Madrid, 1862).

16 Jesús Martínez de Merlo, 'La caballería entre Los Austrias y Los Borbones', in *Revista de Historia Militar* N. 121, 2017, p.141.

17 I am referring to publications such as *Soldados de España: el uniforme militar español desde los Reyes Catolicos hasta Juan Carlos I*, by José María Bueno Carrera (Malaga: Gráficas Summa, 1978), which gives a very inaccurate picture about the armies of Felipe IV and Carlos II.

18 An effective method to reconstruct the chain of command of a regiment or *tercio* is to follow the events of individual companies and their captains. Usually this method works fine, especially when the *tercio* is disbanded and the companies amalgamated into another. There are also cases in which all the captains belonging to a reformed regiment disappear into thin air and then no clue is available. The cases are innumerable, such as the one regarding the German regiment of Count Gerardo d'Arco in Lombardy in 1636, which was licensed notwithstanding the colonel's lively protests against the Marquis of Leganes. Apparently, none of the companies or officers appear in a later muster, and the odds that they were all dead or hadleft military service at the same time are very improbable. However, in some cases the solution comes from unexpected sources. In the Biblioteca Apostolica Vaticana in Rome is preserved a collection of *Avvisi* (in the *Manoscritti Capponi*). In the volume dated 1636, an *Avviso* relates that 'following the

be added those deriving from the large number of units formed during this period both inside and outside the Peninsula.[19]

Finally, it is important to remember how much documentation relating to this age has unfortunately been lost. This includes the *Cancelleria di Stato* preserved in the State Archives of Milan, which was destroyed by the bombs of the Second World War and with it most of the correspondence and government acts concerning the Milanese 'military' have been lost. Equally painful was the loss of the documentation relating to the Portuguese army destroyed in the earthquake of 1755. This loss makes a coherent reconstruction of several facts impossible, and deprives the historian of many interesting details that would have been useful for understanding many of the events that occurred and the decisions that determined these.

In the century of great contradictions, the contradictions of the sources always reveal a view that opens up new perspectives.

---

reform of the Spanish infantry in Lombardy, the regiment of Count Gerardo d'Arco is reformed, amalgamating the companies in the *tercio* of Prince Borso', and that colonel Gerardo 'as an action of protest' returned to Germany. With him, all the captains followed the same route in solidarity with the commander. Thanks to Francesco Pellegrini for noticing this.

19 Many other diligent researchers coming from the ranks of enthusiasts have even delved into the more technical aspects of the Spanish and Portuguese military history of this period. Among them it is a must to mention Juan Luís Sánchez Martin, who was the first who heroically tried to unravel the tangled skein of the Spanish *tercios* and their history in the seventeenth and eighteenth centuries, both through the numerous articles written for specialised magazines and on the web. In January 1996 the publication of the magazine *Researching & Dragona* continued the task begun with the three first issues of the magazine *Dragona*. Both magazines published a series of articles from various eras by renowned authors in their field of research. Juan Luís Sánchez was among the editor of both magazines who was also led the investigation in the Spanish archives and abroad, such as those of Simancas, the Spanish National Library, and the *Archives Générales du Royaume* in Belgium. Much of this data was also collected on the web page www.tercios.org, which today is unfortunately lost. He went as far as they could and scholars really must recognise that since then very few researchers have faced this topic with such perseverance.

Abbreviations

ACA   Archivo General de la Corona de Aragón (Barcelona)
AGMM   Archivo General Militar de Madrid (Madrid)
AGI   Archivo General de Indias (Seville)
AGP   Archivo General de Palacio (Madrid)
AGS   Archivo General de Simancas (Valladolid)
AHMB   Archivo Histórico Municipal de Barcelona
AHN   Archivo Histórico Nacional (Madrid)
AHNOB   Archivo Histórico de la Nobleza (Toledo)
AMT   Archivo Municipal de Toledo
AGR   Archives Générales du Royaume (Brussels)
ASMi   Archivio di Stato di Milano (Milan)
ASNa   Archivio di Stato di Napoli (Naples)
ASS   Archivio Storico Siciliano (Palermo)
ASV   Archivio Segreto Vaticano (Rome)
ASVe   Archivio di Stato di Venezia (Venice)
BNE   Biblioteca Nacional de España (Madrid)
RAH   Real Academia de la Historia (Madrid)

Castilian Currency

Escudo de oro, equal to 30 *reales de vellón* or 1,020 *maravedíes*.
Escudo de plata, equal to 12 *reales de vellón*.
Escudo de vellón, equal to 10 *reales de vellón*.
Doblón de a dos escudos de oro, equal to 60 *reales* or 2,040 *maravedíes*.
Doblón de a cuatro, equal to 4 *escudos de oro*.
Doblón de a ocho, equal to 8 *escudos de oro*.
Ducado, equal to 11 *reales* and 1 *maravedí* or 375 *maravedíes*.
Real de vellón, equal to 34 *maravedíes*.
Cuartillo, equal to ¼ *de real*.
Cuarto, equal to 4 *maravedíes*.

1

The 'Resilience' of Spain

In the seventeenth century, the Spanish domains constituted the largest Empire of the world, larger, as its ideologues rarely tired of stressing, even than Rome itself been. Contemporary commentators stated that territories and people were the most widely distributed and embraced the greatest number of nations and cultures.[1] The emphasis on the role of Spain, and more particularly Castile, in the creation of the empire had a very long pedigree. This imperialist and Eurocentric perspective has dominated traditional history writing, and Castilians were from the first proud of their part in the state, which they usually referred to not as an 'empire' but as a 'monarchy'.

Despite the extension of their domains, the image of the last Spanish Habsburg rulers – *Los Austrias* – is that of a declining dynasty. The efforts of the warlike Felipe IV to maintain Spain as a major global power and the dream of a 'universal Monarchy' broke up in the long and painful war against the United Provinces of the Netherlands and France. Nationalist forces shook the Spanish domains in Italy, and even in the Iberian Peninsula Catalonia and Portugal tried to escape domination, the latter successfully achieving this goal. The bitter twilight of the last Spanish Habsburgs became even gloomier with Felipe IV's successor, Carlos II. Usually, classic historians attributed the collapse of royal authority after 1665 as a result of Carlos II's minority. The physical weakness of the monarch, his lack of direct heirs and the deterioration of his leadership led to the traditional identification of the dynastic crisis coupled with the decline of the complex political framework constituting the Hispanic Monarchy.

When historians of the nineteenth and early twentieth centuries tried to explain the survival of the Monarchy in this period, they tended to emphasise the collapse of Spain's own military and naval institutions. In this regard, they put the emphasis on the importance of foreign aid and the intervention of former enemies – above all the Dutch Republic and England – now determined to defend a weak Spain against Louis XIV. However, this explanation largely

---

1   Anthony Pagden, 'Heeding Heraclides: Empire and its Discontents, 1619–1812' in R.L. Kagan and G. Parker (eds), *Spain, Europe and the Atlantic World. Essays in honour of John H. Elliott* (Cambridge: Cambridge University Press, 1995), p.317.

Below: Carlos II, 1681, by Juan Carreno de Miranda (Museo del Prado, Madrid). Carlos II became king at the age of four under the tutelage of a council of regency presided over by his mother. The last Habsburg king already showed bouts of poor health during his childhood, and the continuous illnesses crippled him mentally and physically, so much so that in the last months of his life he could not even sign government decrees. His suffering gave birth to legends to which he himself gave credit, declaring that he was the victim of a curse, which earned him the nickname *elhechizado* (the bewitched). Faced with the threat of the expansionism of Louis XIV's France, he was forced to fight a continuous war, meanwhile all the European powers waited for his death so they could negotiate the Spanish inheritance. The fate of the Monarchy appears even more closely linked to the suffering in life, and especially in his death, of Carlos II. How much the King's health had become a topic of international politics was already evident in 1668, when the major powers agreed to a partition of his territories. In the age of absolutism, the Spanish Monarchy under Carlos II still appeared far from the application of the methods of government that was characterising the major European powers, making Spain the 'great outdated actor' of the century.

Above: Felipe IV of Spain and III of Portugal (1605–1665), portrayed by Velázquez in the 1650s (Museo del Prado, Madrid). Felipe had inherited a huge empire from his father, spanning the known world, but many of his most difficult challenges as king stemmed from domestic problems in Spain itself. Felipe was idealised by his contemporaries as the model of Baroque kingship. Outwardly he maintained a bearing of rigid solemnity; foreign visitors described him as being so impassive in public that he resembled a statue, and he was said to have been seen to laugh only three times in the entire course of his public life. By the time of his death, the Spanish Monarchy extended across approximately 12.2 million square kilometres, including the overseas colonies, but in other respects this huge empire was facing a serious crisis, a process to which the King contributed with his inability to achieve successful domestic and military reforms.

ignores the fact that Spain deployed large armies and navies, which did not sustain defeats comparable to the ones suffered in the Thirty Years' War. The navy, as well as the army, contributed to the defence of the Spanish domains and often played an important role in containing of Louis XIV's expansion. Historians who damn the entire Habsburg dynasty's reign on the basis of a snapshot in time of its armed forces in 1700, a year of peace in Europe, are committing a superficial error, and underestimate the efforts the Monarchy had made since 1659. Popular literature depicts the Spanish struggle against the territorial and hegemonic ambitions of Louis XIV like a series defeats and the loss of territories in Europe. Effectively, in the last quarter of the seventeenth century, Spain appears like a boxer at the ring's corner. Furthermore, Carlos II did not benefit from propaganda comparable to that celebrating Louis XIV, and certainly, nothing is more difficult to restore than a ruined reputation. After 1700, dynastic change worsened this view, since the new ruler had every interest in describing in the worst terms the government that had preceded him. Finally, on the military level, the Spain of the last Habsburgs had been often described as a power of lesser rank. The Napoleonic wars contributed to increase this negative image of the Spanish armies to the point of becoming the object of the most derogatory comments.

The most recent trend in the findings of historical research shows a less negative situation. In recent decades, historians have investigated the capacity of the Spanish Monarchy to weather the challenges it faced in the last quarter of the seventeenth century, and they argued that the balance between centre and periphery was the secret of the survival of Spain as a great power long after its economic and demographic base had been eroded.[2] Any in-depth analysis of the topic reveals how the Spanish scenario was very complex, since *Los Austrias* reigned over an empire where the financial conjuncture differently affected the domains. The ability to withstand external threats, while maintaining the integrity of the state, has generated the myth of Spanish Resilience.[3] This effort was all the more impressive given that Spain experienced a sustained domestic political crisis. Nonetheless, if it is excessive to describe the reigns of the last Habsburg kings like an age of irreversible decline, it is certainly possible to consider it as a period of loss of power from a military point of view. Carlos II, the last of *Los Austrias*, undoubtedly ruled a weaker empire than his great-grandfather Felipe III, and the decisions that affected its future were taken in Paris, Vienna and London rather than in Madrid.

Although the armies fielded by Felipe IV and Carlos II fought bravely, by 1659 many of France's territorial conquests came at the expense of Spain. Recent research tends to minimise the territorial losses suffered by Spain, but from 1668 to 1684, the Monarchy progressively lost one third of the Low Countries, the Franche-Comté, and Luxembourg. In 1697, the Peace of Rijswijk returned the latter province to Spain, together with Mons and Courtrai, but the balance remained strongly negative. In the periods of

---

2   R.L. Kagan and G. Parker, 'Spain, Europe and the Atlantic World', p.15.

3   Among the scholars who has focused this topic, see Christopher Storrs, *The Resilience of the Spanish Monarchy: 1665–1700* (Oxford: Oxford University Press, 2006).

Portrait of an unknown Spanish general, 1680, by Adrian Backer (Prado Museum, Madrid). Popular myth, supported by some historians, propagandised the poor military knowledge of Spain's commanders. However the development of new and successful battle tactics from Northern Europe did not mean that Spain's generals continued to apply the most obsolete practices, since they had learned many new ideas in the matter of warfare while facing the Dutch from 1568. In this regard, Spanish armies could experiment with modern tactics, formations and siege practices. Though some commanders performed with a more conservative attitude, other officers elaborated on the new model of warfare as it suited the strategic scenario, at least at a theoretical if not practical level.

Facing page: the Spanish Monarchy in the seventeenth century. Though the Spanish Habsburgs ruled on four continents, since the reign of Carlos I, the centre of the 'Monarchy' was Europe, with the Low Countries, Portugal between 1580 and 1640 and above all Italy, 'the garden of the Empire', as Mercurio de Gattinara, echoing Dante, once called it.

greatest mobilisation from the war against Portugal and France in the 1660s, to the Grand Alliance in 1689–97, the Spain was rarely able to muster more than 90,000 men in all.[4] The numbers are based upon evidence, and ultimately the comparison appears even more unfavourable to Los Austrias when observing the growth of the military forces of their major opponent: France. When Felipe II was reigning over his huge empire, Henry IV of France had a small peacetime army of 10–12,000 men. In wartime the number could rise to 70,000 men on paper, just over half of the numbers that Spain was able to field during the crisis due to the succession of Cleves and Juliers in 1610. From 1635, the growth of French military power began to increase steadily. With Richelieu, the army received enough resources to mobilise 150,000 men, both French and foreigners. In 1638, the target increased to 160,000, which however resulted in 70–80,000 soldiers actually being available for the field armies deployed on the borders with the Low Countries, Roussillon, Franche-Comté and Italy. However, alongside the garrisons, the French army is now three times the size it was 20 years before. In 1660, after the return to peace, the army was reduced to 70,000 men on paper: the same number of the wartime strength under Henry IV. For the invasion of the Spanish Low Countries in 1667, Louis XIV assembled 134,000 men, of which 80,000 were available in the field. During the Franco-Dutch War, the French army grew to an unprecedented 250,000 men, before being reduced to 130,000 after the peace of Nijmegen.[5]

According to the most recent research, Carlos II possessed a military force more important and numerous than was traditionally believed, but certainly much reduced compared to the armies of Felipe IV at his greatest

---

4   Davide Maffi, *Los últimos tercios: el ejército de Carlos II* (Madrid: Desperta Ferro, 2020), pp.123–130, and Etienne Rooms, *De organisatie van de troepen van de Spaans-Habsburgse monarchie in de Zuidelijke Nederlanden* (Brussels: Koninklijk Legermuseum, 2003), pp.85–111, 142–153. Other authors move this figure to 112,000 men in 1675–76. See Antonio José Rodríguez Hernández, 'Guerra y alianzas en la lucha por la hegemonía europea durante la segunda mitad del siglo XVII. El papel de España', in L. Ribot and J.M. Iñurritegui (eds), *Europa y los tratados de raparto de la Monarquia de España, 1688–1700* (Madrid: Biblioteva Nueva, 2016), p.251, and Storrs, *The Resilience of the Spanish Monarchy 1665–1700*, pp.31–32.

5   Olivier Chaline, *Les armées du Roy. Le grand chantier. XVIIe–XVIIIe siècle* (Paris: Armand Colin, 2016), pp.209–210.

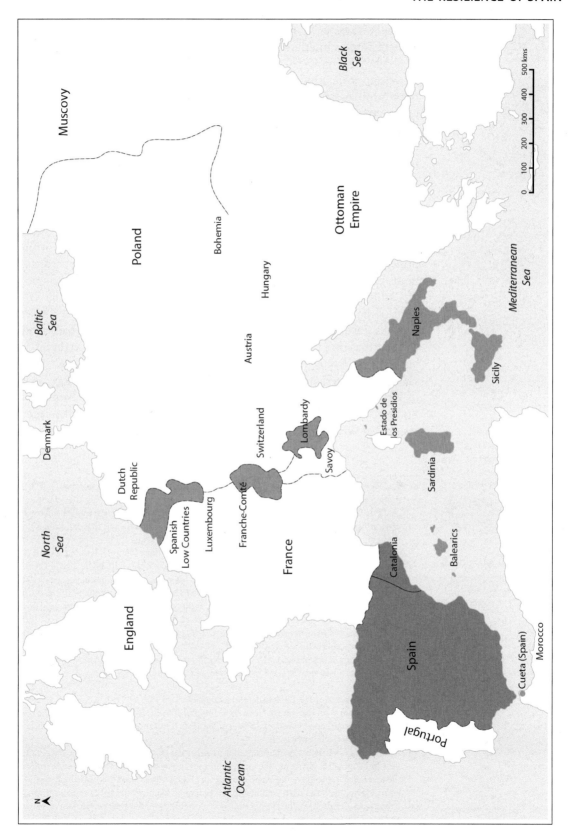

apogee.[6] However, a major problem was that the Spanish troops were scattered over a multitude of territories and garrisons. Moreover, Spain was forced by economic crisis to reduce the army's strength when the major European powers increased their own. Though Spain was able to recover from the financial crisis of the 1660s and 1670s, allowing the government to assemble stronger armies, the gap with France was never filled. The notable reduction of the military force occurring in the last years of Carlos II's reign has always been seen as a sign of the Spanish military decline in the second half of the seventeenth century, an issue much discussed judging by some of the exaggerated descriptions made shortly thereafter by authors such as the Marquis of San Felipe, who affirmed that in 1700 there were not more than 20,000 soldiers available on the arrival of Felipe V.[7]

Historians have stated that 'nobody would dispute that the seventeenth century saw a relative decline in Spanish power when compared with its principal European rivals.'[8] But the paradox of survival amid this decline had been explained by two distinct developments. On the one hand, the experience of Castile (the heart of the empire) differed from the other domains. Other parts of the Iberian Peninsula, especially along the periphery, either suffered less than Castile from the seventeenth-century recession, or even made modest gains, so that, over the course of the century, there was some shift in the internal balance of economic forces, to Castile's detriment.[9] On the other hand, the last Habsburgs' experience proved far from unique. In fact, many other powers in Western Europe experienced severe economic and social problems in the mid seventeenth century, but Spain became the archetype of all the negative features of this age.[10] This condition contributed to obscuring reality with a

---

6   Rodríguez Hernández, 'Guerra y alianzas en la lucha por la hegemonía europea', p.252. This decline appears even more drastic if compared to the overall strength that the Spanish army could deploy at the turn of the century. However, further problems derive from the overstating of some figures. The statement that has had the greatest impact is the one that determines that at the beginning of his reign Felipe IV had an army of 300,000 paid soldiers and another 500,000 militiamen distributed throughout Spain and Europe. These figures, declared by the King himself to the Council of Castile in 1627, are undoubtedly exaggerated. On several occasions the army strength has been corrected downwards by various authors, reducing it to 170,000, 150,000 or even less. New data warn us that in 1633 Felipe IV, facing the political situation in Italy and Central Europe, could dispose of 93,000 men in Flanders and Lombardy as field troops, and another 30,000 in North Africa, Southern Italy, the Franche-Comté, and the Iberian Peninsula. In 1640, the overall force increased, with at least 180,000 men in the different fronts and garrisons, this being surely the year of greatest mobilisation in the history of *Los Austrias*. This last figure is supported by the great recruiting efforts, since only in 1639 at least 25,000 soldiers from Spain went to serve in the armies of Flanders and Italy.

7   *Ibid.*, p.251.

8   Kagan and Parker, *Spain, Europe and the Atlantic World*, p.15.

9   *Ibid.*: 'It would seem that we are faced with a diminution of Castile's capacity to bear the cost of empire, and consequently with the problem, in the first instance, not so much of the decline of Spain as of the decline of Castile.'

10   *Ibid.*, 'Instead of dismissing Spain's decline as either the inevitable result of some deeply rooted flaw in the Spanish character, the consequence of the personal shortcomings of its rulers, or the inexorable outcome of "strategic overstretch", Elliott viewed it as a process that might have been reversed with the right combination of economic, political and social reforms. Instead of irreversible decline, then, the key questions became how could the great empire best be managed and how could its power and reputation best be maintained.'

multitude of myths and fantasies, which, paradoxically, transformed the Spain of the late seventeenth century into a largely unknown historical subject.

The Spanish Monarchy: Centre and Periphery

Habsburg Spain appears very different from the present one. Since the Iberian domains were the result of the progressive annexation of the Muslim caliphates, the crown ruled a variegated mosaic of kingdoms. Spain was a collection of possessions all loosely joined together through the institution of the Castilian Monarchy and the person of the King. In the mid seventeenth century, the Iberian Peninsula comprised the three major kingdoms of Castile and León, Aragón, and Portugal, the latter claimed until 1668. Within these, other royal provinces were included, each with its own identity and administrative autonomy and even currency. The Kingdom of Castile included not only Old and New Castile and León, but also Navarre, Seville, Córdoba, Grenada, Jáen, Murcia and the principality of Asturias. Aragón also comprised the kingdoms of Valencia and Sardinia, the principality of Catalonia and the Balearic islands. Each had different rules for taxation, privileges and military arrangements; in practice, the level of taxation in many of the more peripheral provinces was less than that in Castile, but the privileged position of the Castilian nobility at all senior levels of royal appointment was a contentious issue for the less favoured provinces.

The same pattern was repeated more or less similarly in the domains located outside the Iberian Peninsula. The *Ducado* or *Estado de Milán* included Spanish Lombardy and also controlled the Marquisate of Finale. The Kingdom of Naples comprised the provinces of *Terra di Lavoro*, Abruzzo *Ultra*, Abruzzo *Citra*, *Capitanata*, *Terra di Bari*, Otranto, Basilicata, Calabria *Ultra*, Calabria *Citra*, county of Molise, and the principalities of Ultra and Citra. Naples also controlled the *Estado de los Presidios* and the vassal principality of Piombino in Tuscany. Milan and Naples benefited from a high level of autonomy. Both had their diplomatic representatives in the foreign courts, different currencies, and the latter also possessed its own war fleet. Unlike the continental Italian domains, which had been conquered militarily, Sicily had joined Spain as an independent kingdom under Aragon and enjoyed a status similar to Catalonia. The island comprise of three provinces, each with their administrative structure and their own senate and tribunal. The high degree of autonomy enjoyed by the Sicilians was considerable since Messina considered itself like a 'Republic' under Spanish protection. As ruler of Sicily, the Spanish kings also extended their authority on Malta and the Knights of the Order of the Saint John.

A certain degree of autonomy also existed in the Spanish Low Countries but, by comparison, here there was a less complicated division of land, resulting in eight provinces, which included the duchies of Luxembourg, Brabant and Limburg, the counties of Flanders, Hainaut and Namur, the lordship of Malines and the marquisate of Antwerp. In 1659, Spain still ruled on the memory of a ninth province, the county of Artois, preserving the towns of Saint-Omer and Aire, ceded to France in 1668. Brussels was

The Treaty of the Pyrenees, by Jacques Laumosnier: Felipe IV and Louis XIV meet to sign the Treaty of the Pyrenees on Pheasant Island. After a truce agreed in March 1659, peace talks began and finally, on 7 November, the Peace of the Pyrenees was signed on this island in the river Bidasoa, on the frontier between Spain and France. Artois, Roussillon, and part of Cerdaña were absorbed permanently into France. The most important territorial changes occurred with the Low Countries frontier, where France gained a broad belt of fortresses from the Channel coast to the Moselle, including Gravelines, Landrecies, Le Quesnoy, Avesnes, Philippeville, Marienbourg, Montmedy and Thionville. In return, France gave back some conquests in Flanders. The Peace of the Pyrenees also gave France considerable trading advantages in the Spanish colonies. A key clause of the treaty arranged for the marriage of the *infanta* Maria Teresa, daughter of Felipe IV, to Louis XIV.

the historical capital of the Spanish Low Countries and residence of the viceroy appointed from Madrid. Finally, Franche-Comté comprised the three *bailliages* of d'Amont, d'Aval and Dôle, with this latter the seat of the parliament or *Estados Generales del Franco Contado*.

The strong military presence and the resulting expense for the maintenance of strong contingents in the Italian and Flemish Walloon provinces had consequences that were not at all ideal, but it was all possible thanks to the substantial support not only from the local aristocracy, but also the majority of the common class. In this sense, the vision of a universally-hated Spanish power appears at least open to dispute. The perception growing in favour in Spain today is of a paternalistic power, but one respectful of regional autonomy, and is perhaps a deserving perception of the last Habsburg rulers.

Moving on to the overseas domains in America and Asia, there were two further viceroyalties, each with their *audiencias* or provinces. The *Virreinato de Nueva España*, comprised the *audiencias* of Santo Domingo, Florida, México

(today south-east Mexico and Yucatán) Guadalajara (north-west México with the modern states of Texas, New México, Arizona and California, also extending to Nevada, Utah, Colorado, Idaho, Oregon and Washington), *Los Confines* (Guatemala, Belize, El Salvador, Honduras, Nicaragua, Costa Rica, Chiapas), Manila (Philippines and Micronesia). The other major *virreinato* was that of Peru, with the *audiencias* of Lima (modern Peru with Arica); Panama, Quito (Ecuador), Chile, *Nuevo Reino de Granada* (Colombia), Charcas (Bolivia), and Buenos Aires (Argentina and Paraguay).

Finally, the Monarchy included the North African outposts of La Mamora, Larache, Ceuta, Velez de la Gomera, Melilla, Mazalquivir and Oran, which faced the Muslim state of Morocco and Algiers with their privateer fleets.

Until recently, no reliable data existed to provide an accurate estimate of the Spanish population in the second half of the seventeenth century. Historians are divided on this issue. Some of them argue that for the whole century the King of Spain's subjects on the Iberian Peninsula did not exceed eight million, whilst other scholars stated that between 1601 and the end of the century, the population was reduced to six million.[11] The most recent studies have brought new knowledge to this matter. Thanks to the economic recovery in the last quarter of the century, and despite the great plague of 1648–54, some researchers indicate a progressive increase in the population of the Iberian peninsula that would have already exceeded 8 million in the 1690s. However, the recovery was greater in the coastal regions, while

The Guzmán powder storage arsenal of Orbetello, in the *Estado de los Presidios*, is a perfectly preserved building erected in the Tuscan enclave during the reign of Carlos II. The arsenal provided gunpowder to the local garrison and to Naples and Milan, exploiting the sulphur and saltpetre mines in the area. (Author's photo)

---

11 *The New Cambridge Modern History*, Vol. 5, *The Ascendancy of France, 1648–1688*, ed. F.L. Carsten (Cambridge: Cambridge University Press, 1961), p.479.

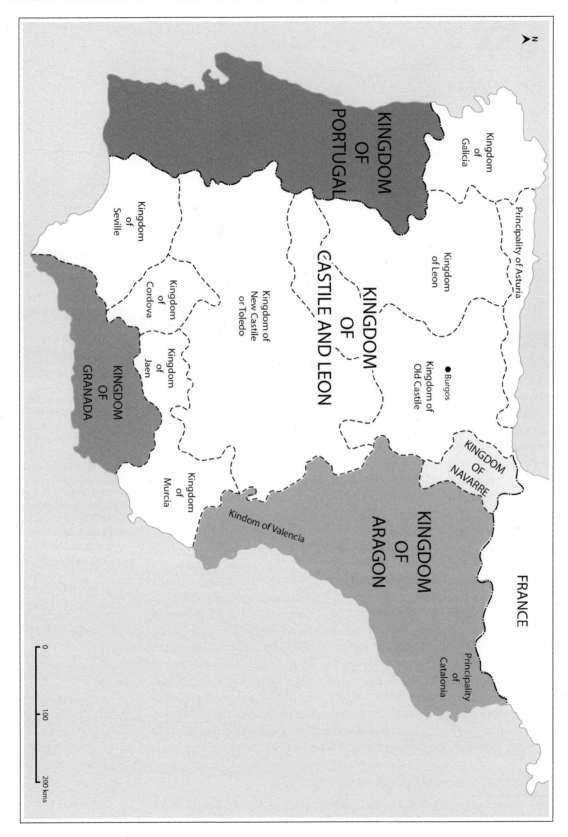

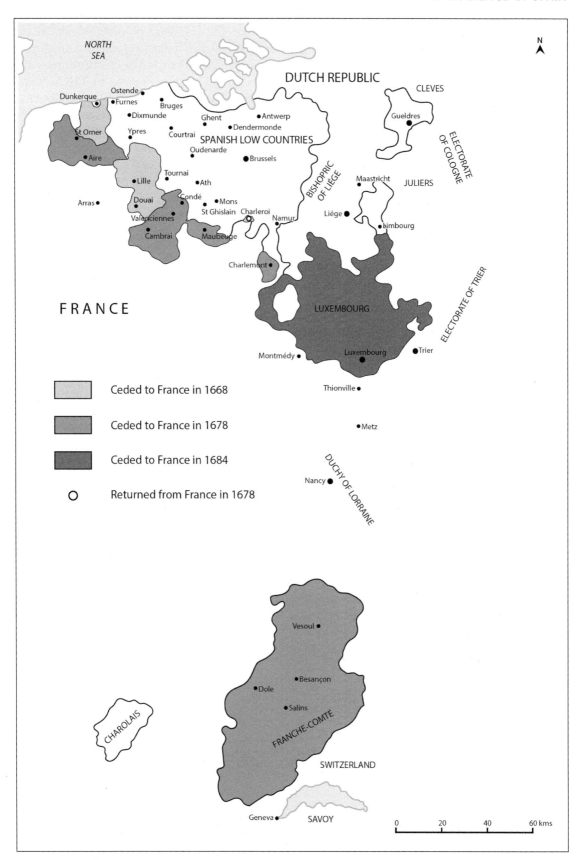

NORTH
SEA

DUTCH REPUBLIC

CLEVES

Dunkerque

Ostende
Furnes
Bruges

Gueldres

ELECTORATE
OF COLOGNE

St Omer

Dixmunde
Ghent
Antwerp

Aire

Ypres

Courtrai

Dendermonde

SPANISH LOW COUNTRIES

Oudenarde

Tournai
Lille

Brussels

Maastricht

JULIERS

Ath
Arras

Douai
Valenciennes

Condé
Mons
St Ghislain
Charleroi
Namur

Liége
Limbourg

Cambrai

Maubeuge

Charlemont

LUXEMBOURG

FRANCE

Montmédy

Luxembourg

Trier

Thionville

Metz

Ceded to France in 1668

Ceded to France in 1678

Ceded to France in 1684

O   Returned from France in 1678

Nancy

CHAROLAIS

Vesoul

Besançon

Dole

Salins

FRANCHE-COMTÉ

SWITZERLAND

Geneva

SAVOY

0   20   40   60 kms

Previous pages: The
Iberian kingdoms; the Low
Countries

inland the population decreased.[12] The Habsburg possessions outside the
Iberian Peninsula contributed with further human resources, estimated at
about 3.7 million in Southern Italy, 2.4 million in the Low Countries and
Luxembourg, 800,000 in Lombardy, and 215,000 in Franche-Comté. As for the
demographic density of the inhabitants, there were considerable differences
between one province and another. While Franche-Comté and Lombardy
had partially recovered the loss of population suffered after the Thirty Years'
War, the kingdom of Naples registered a considerable demographic growth,
with Naples confirming its primacy as the first city of the Spanish empire and
third in Europe for the number of inhabitants after Paris and London.

Alongside their European subjects, the Spanish kings also ruled over the
population of the overseas domains. By the 1660s, Spanish America had
about 10–11 million inhabitants, of which 3.8 million lived in Mexico and
Caribbean, and 2.5 million in Peru. The vast majority of this population,
about 80 percent, were indigenous, and the rest were African slaves, *mestizos*,
persons of mixed race and a minority of Europeans.[13] Finally, the remote
domains in the Philippines and Micronesia possibly numbered 1.5–2 million
native inhabitants and a few Europeans.[14]

Spain's prospects as a European power depended on Castile's capacity for
recovery from the debilitating weakness of the first half of the century. The
immediate need was a long period of good governance, but unfortunately,
the ruling class were unprepared to provide it. This partially explains the
progressive decline of Castile, which finally lost its predominant position
among the Spanish kingdoms.[15] After the age of strong centralisation under
Gaspar de Guzmán y Pimentel, *conde-duque* de Olivares, the peripheral
provinces earned an increasing influence in Spanish policy. It should be noted
that the first *pronunciamento* or coup in modern Spanish history, namely the
one planned by Don Juan of Austria in 1669, started from Catalonia and was
supported by the *cortes* of Aragon. In the following decades, the Monarchy
gradually took on the appearance of a confederation of kingdoms.

As had happened throughout Europe, the transition from the medieval
state to the modern centralised one led to an ever-increasing complexity in
the organisation of power. Since the Spanish kings were never able to unify
the legal and administrative systems of the various kingdoms over which
they ruled, the exercise of power had to be constantly negotiated with local
parliaments. This political mosaic reverberated in the growth of bureaucracy at
central, regional and local levels, where an ever-increasing number of officials
were settled. This institutionalisation articulated the central administration

---

12 John Elliott, *Imperial Spain, 1496–1716* (London: Penguin Books, 2002), p.700: 'The population
    of Burgos, which had been about 13,000 in the 1590s, was down to a mere 3,000 by 1646, and
    Seville lost 60,000 inhabitants – half its population – in the terrible plague of 1649.'

13 About 75,000 Europeans were settled in mid-seventeenth century Peru. See also Colin McEvody
    and Richard Jones, *Atlas of World Population History* (New York: Facts on File, 1979), p.310.

14 *Ibid.*, p.202.

15 *The New Cambridge Modern History*, Vol. 5 – *The Ascendency of France, 1648–1688*, p.477:
    'Between 1680 and 1700, Barcelona's commercial activity increased by almost double, while
    Seville's fell by half. The textile production of Catalonia and Valencia received a considerable
    boost in this period thanks to the clauses of the Peace of the Pyrenees.'

in a network of collegial bodies, the *Consejos* (councils), some inherited from the previous governments or created by the new system. Contrary to what is commonly believed, it was not the king who consulted the councils, but it was the councils that prepared the consultations and submitted them to the king for his decision. In this sense, the composition and nature of the councils was of great importance, because this implied that the action of the government proceeded under the responsibility of the respective council, and it was always applied according to the laws in force in each kingdom and domains. Since the councils were an expression of the king's power, they were the delegated holders of that power, and had to apply the royal decisions.[16] Since the organisation of the council's system in the seventeenth century was the result of compromise and adaptation, each council had its own particular constitution. This led to the maintenance of the late medieval councils of each kingdom, as in the case of those of Castile, Aragon and Navarre. Furthermore, in the previous century, new councils had been created to better manage the states affairs.[17] Basically, the councils were collegiate bodies composed of a president, with a variable number of councillors, secretaries and secretary's staff. Exclusively native Spaniards could compose the executive level. The councils supported the king on matters within their competence and could exercise legislative, administrative and judicial autonomy depending on the case. Generally, the councils could be classified in categories depending on their relationship with the Monarchy in particular and the state in general. The most important councils exercised their jurisdiction over the whole empire and were the ones of State, War and Inquisition.[18] The *Consejo de Estado* (State Council) was the central organ of the Monarchy and occupied the first position in the political organisation of the state. It constitutes the supreme advisory office of the king, who was also its president, and it was composed of high-ranking nobles and prelates. Its competence focused on

---

16 'Most Spanish law writers of the sixteenth and seventeenth centuries praised the system of government through the Councils, which, according to some authors, had been founded on divine law. Likewise, they agreed on how advantageous it was for the king to make his decisions with the support of the authority of the Council; but in the specific case of the resolutions contrary to the consultation of the Council, almost all the doctrine agreed that the decision-making power belonged to the king since the Councils were delegated organs of the royal power. This statement did not imply that the king could rule against the law. Exceptionally, some authors even argued that if the king deviated from the resolution proposed in the consultation, he could be considered a tyrant.' Sánchez Prieto and Ana Belén, 'La Administración Real bajo Los Austrias y la expedición de títulos nobiliarios', in S. Cabezas Fontanilla and M. del Mar Royo Martínez (eds), 'V Jornadas Científicas sobre Documentación de Castilla e Indias en el siglo XVI' (Madrid, 2005), p.380.

17 In this way, the Councils of Portugal and Flanders were established, or other councils to deal autonomously with specific matters in some kingdoms, such as the Council of Chivalry Orders, or concerning the entire Monarchy, namely the Council of State, that of the Inquisition and that of war. Ultimately, there were five categories of councils, established according to their competence: material, in specific matters; or territorial, with attributions only to the geographical framework, in order to facilitate the work of the ancient original councils.

18 The Council of the Inquisition, better known as *Consejo de la Suprema y General Inquisición*, or simply *La Suprema*, was the central organ of government of the Holy Office and represented in the apparatus of the Monarchy the nationalisation of inquisitorial activity in matters of religion. See Prieto and Belén, *La Adninistración Real bajo Los Austrias*, p.382.

Facing page:
The *Estado de Milán*, and Finale.

the most serious matters of state interest, including international politics as well as other matters of an economic nature, appointment of high officials, conflicts between councils, and also book censorship. The *Consejo de Guerra* (War Council) operated in parallel with the previous council, and like this it was chaired by the king. The exclusive relevance of both these councils gave them a special character over all the others, and generally, there were no problems of precedence or rank among them. The war council was divided into two secretariats: army and navy, and like the council of state was composed of high nobles and senior commanders. They were in charge of proposing the commanders of the armies and fleets, building fortifications, manufacturing weapons, launching ships, recruiting troops and sailors, and generally all military affairs of the Monarchy, although the Council of State dealt with the most important issues, such as declaration of war and peace negotiations. Depending on the question examined, both councils could be convened in a single *Consejo pleno de Estado y Guerra*.

The government councils of the various territories constituting the domains of the Monarchy were represented by the councils of Castile, Aragon, Indies (America and Philippines), Italy, Flanders and, until 1668, Portugal. The Council of Castile was the 'Royal Council' par excellence, and in fact occupied the first place in the hierarchical scale of the territorial councils. Although the Royal Council was downsized after the creation of the Council of State, it enjoyed important administrative, judicial – as the supreme court – and legislative functions; moreover, the presidency was always assigned to a central figure of the court. A further particular council was the *Consejo Real de Navarra* (Royal Council of Navarre). Unlike the other territorial councils, which resided in the Madrid court, the seat of this council always remained in Pamplona. All the councillors were natives of Navarre.

With the Councils of Castile and the Indies came the parallel *Consejos de Cámara* (Councils of the Chamber), competent in the proposal of appointments, pardons and justice. The Council of the Chamber of Castile was formed by three secretariats corresponding to the triple activity. Its counterpart for America and the Philippines was the *Consejos de Cámara de Indias*, newly established in 1644 after its suspension in 1606. These offices were substantially detached commissions for their respective territorial councils. However, the volume and extent of the posts and subsidies transformed both, and in particular the one of Castile, into a powerful and influential political instrument also in matters of appointments in the army and navy. The next category included administrative councils, such as the *Consejo de Órdenes*, the one of the *Cruzada*, and the important *Consejo de Hacienda*, which dealt with the usually critical economic scenario, in charge of the management of the *Real Hacienda*, namely the Crown's ministry of the economy.

Alongside the councils, the other pre-eminent office of the Spanish Monarchy was the *Secretario del Rey* (Secretary of the King). Each kingdom had its own State Secretary, and this charge was often associated to the one of *Secretario de Estado* when he served as 'particular councillor' of the king. This office was usually held by a member of the high nobility selected among the *Grandes de España*. He also held the position of main secretary in all councils, and in particular the Council of State. The King usually appointed

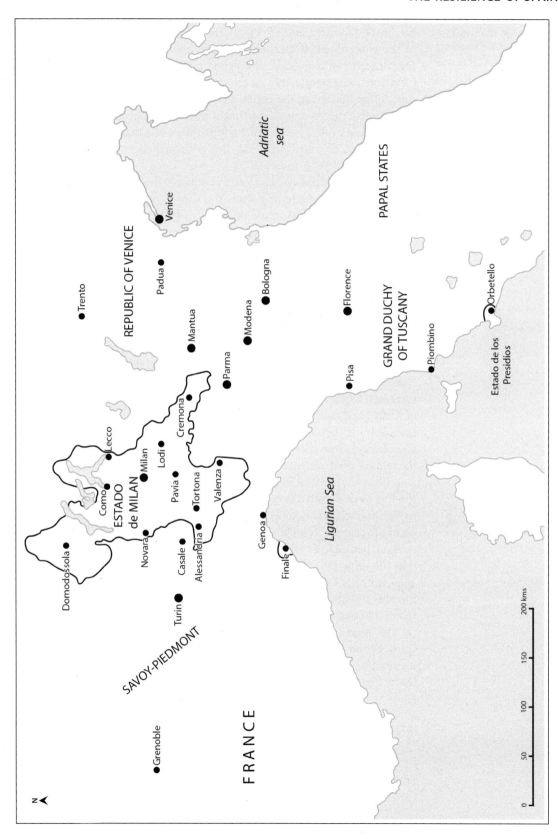

Facing page: The Kingdom of Naples and the *Estado del los Presidios.*

his Prime Minister among them. He was comparable to a modern chief of the government because he was the holder of executive power. In the seventeenth-century Spain, the prime minister, along with the secretaries, played a fundamental role in the central administrative apparatus of the state, often becoming the actual master of the empire, as occurred during the mandate of Olivares. The prime minister managed military matters too, and he could even serve as army commander, like the successor of Olivares, Luis Méndez de Haro, who led, but with indecisive results, the army of Estremadura in 1658 and 1659.

Luis Méndez de Haro belonged to the age of the *validos*, or favourite, who created a proven system of power. The Crown was lavish in its conferment of patents of nobility and even of the title of Grandee of Spain, but after the death of de Haro in 1661, Felipe IV avoided re-establishing the system of the *validos*. In 1665, the death of Felipe IV left the government without a guide. The King's will provided that his widow, Maria Anna of Austria, should rule as regent until their son attained his majority, namely when he reached the age of 14, in November 1675. The queen would have received the support of a five-man regency council, or *Junta de Gobierno*. Maria Anna initially maintained this criterion, avoiding entrusting the leadership of the government and the political dominance to a single person, and relied on people who were not part of the circle of the grandees of Spain and the former titled nobility. However, Maria Anna's difficulties were substantial enough and were increased by the ambition of the late king's adult illegitimate son, Don Juan of Austria. He, who had extensive military experience in Italy, Catalonia, and Portugal, had been excluded from the regency by his father, but sought a government's role. The regent Queen, with little experience on the matter, left the reins of government to her confessor, Cardinal Johann Eberhard Nithard, who became the latest in a succession of favourite ministers.[19] The Cardinal too had to deal with a very complicated situation, but ultimately turned out to be as politically incompetent, and soon Don Juan led a rebellion against Nithard's regime. The Prince, unconditionally supported by the kingdom of Aragon, became the arbiter of the situation, but lacked the determination to take the reins into his own hands.[20] However, the rise of Nithard ended in 1669 with his expulsion from the court. Now, neither Maria Anna nor the members of the council could do more than struggle for survival against internal and external crises.

The regency was oriented to broaden and diversify the support for court, preventing a single courtier from gaining control of the office and the distribution of the royal patronage's prebends. After 1669, the government was led by Pedro Fernández del Campo. Other prominent figures were the Count

---

19 In adherence to the Monarchy's law, Felipe IV's will excluded foreigners from the regency council; therefore in 1666, Maria Anna obtained naturalisation from the Jesuits, and his appointment as inquisitor-general and *ex officio* member of the regency council.

20 Elliot, *Imperial Spain*, p.706: 'Don Juan lacked the political skill to exploit a situation which seemed to have turned decisively in his favour. He duly obtained from the Queen the creation of a *Junta de Alivios* intended to introduce far-reaching reforms, but it succeeded in devising only minor improvements in Castile's fiscal system and left the fundamental abuses untouched.'

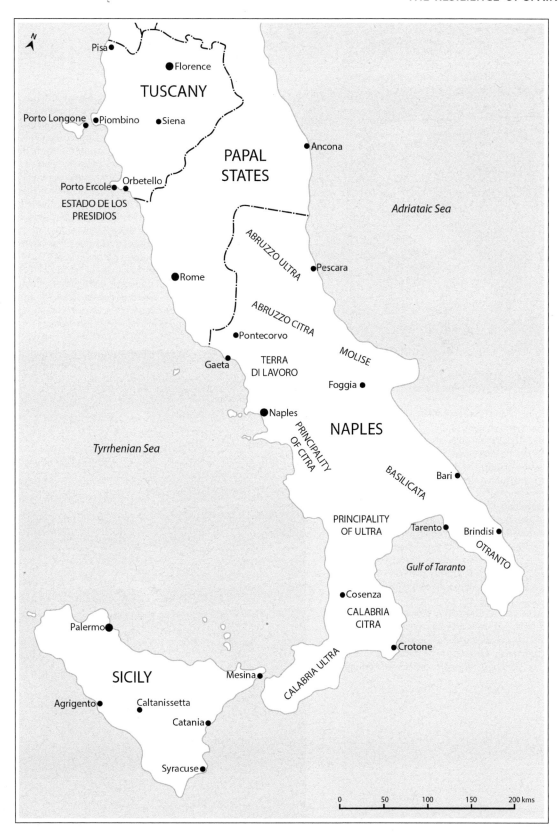

Left: Luis Méndez de Haro y Guzmán, Marquise del Carpio (1598–1661). He made a career at the Spanish court under the protection of his uncle, Gaspar de Guzmán, Count-Duke of Olivares, whom he succeeded as Prime Minister in 1643; he held the office until his death. The last Habsburgs lacked charisma and were unable to exercise the leadership required by a highly personalised system of government, as the absolutist monarchies were becoming. The fate of the country was governed by their few close friends, the *validos* or favourites, so typical in Spain at the end of the seventeenth century, almost all coming from the ranks of the kingdom's grandees. Méndez de Haro's main success was the suppression of the Catalan uprising, and the reconquest of Barcelona in 1652. However, his campaign during the Portuguese Restoration War was a complete failure. He personally led the army of Extremadura at the Battle of the Lines of Elvas in 1659, which ended in a heavy Spanish defeat.

Right: Johann Eberhard Nithard (1607–1681). After the long government of the Conde-Duca de Olivares (1622–1643), the slightly shorter one of Marquis Luis Méndez de Haro (1643–1661) followed; then it was the turn of Austrian Cardinal Jaun Everardo (Johann Eberhard) Nithard (1665–1669) to lead the kingdom as 'prime minister' or *valido* during the years of the War of Devolution. The Austrian prelate had accompanied the Archduchess Maria Anna of Habsburg to Madrid as confessor when she married her maternal uncle King Felipe IV of Spain in 1649. When the King died, Maria Anna became regent for her four-year-old son Carlos. She appointed Nithard as Grand Inquisitor in 1666, which gave him access to the Regency Council, from where he became the most important person of the Spanish Court. From then on he was the de facto *valido* of Spain. In foreign policy Nithard did not succeed in bringing Vienna close to support Spain and ultimately, according to his detractors, in 1668 he accepted an unfavourable peace with Portugal.

of Villaumbrosa, president of the Council of Castile from the same date, as well as some presidents of the councils, such as the Count of Peñaranda, president of the council of Italy since 1671 and Dean of the State Council. From the end of 1674, after the creation of the King's Household and the appointment of the gentlemen of his chamber, new figures emerged with a growing rise in the King's confidence, such as Juan Francisco de la Cerda, Duke of Medinaceli and Manuel Joaquín Álvarez de Toledo, Count of Oropesa. From the beginning of 1675, the king's chamber became the platform of power and influence, as some key positions held by his mother's men had been until then. The person most listened to by the King in those years was the aforementioned Duke of Medinaceli, who held the post of cup-bearer since November 1674. He became the shadow of the monarch, accompanying the young Carlos II from the moment he awoke until he went to sleep. In the midst of this plurality of prominent figures in the government, the gradual rise of Fernando de Valenzuela, supported by the Queen, took also place. Historians have damned Valenzuela, depicting him a 'palace *picaro*' (rogue) and 'an excellent organiser of hunts and picnics'.[21] Valenzuela was able to create a powerful net of relations and clientele holding key positions in the government, and in 1676 he became *de facto* prime minister, notwithstanding the hostility of the grandees. However, on 6 November 1675, Carlos II attained his majority and the situation changed irreversibly.[22] Although Maria Anna had hitherto prevailed in the factional struggle, the King could now begin his own rule. The last Spanish Habsburg reigned for 25 years, during which he was always ailing, several times critically ill, and subject to serious physical and psychological disturbances. The grandees were exasperated by Valenzuela's government, so joined together in December 1676 to demand the recall of Don Juan of Austria. Soon he marched to Madrid at the head of the army which had fought the French in Catalonia. However, the mandate of Don Juan from 1677 until his unexpected death in 1679 was attended by disappointment at home and humiliation abroad. As he failed to tackle even the most obvious abuses, he forfeited in turn the support of the army, the Church, and the populace, and was mercilessly lampooned in the streets of the capital.

This dark situation was finally brightened in the 1680s. It was after the death of Don Juan and the government of his mediocre successor, the Duke of Medinaceli, that the Monarchy arrested its fall.[23] Though all the most important offices in the State and the army went solely to men of rank, the

---

21 *The New Cambridge Modern History*, Vol. 5, *The Ascendancy of France, 1648–88*, p.380.

22 Antonio Álvarez-Ossorio Alvariño, *Precedencia ceremonial y direcciión del gobierno. El ascenso ministerial de Fernando de Valenzuela en la corte de Carlos II*, in B. García and A. Álvarez-Ossorio Alvariño (eds), 'Vísperas de Sucesión, Europa y la Monarquía de Carlos II' (Madrid: Fundación Carlos Amberes, 2015), p.29: 'Since the creation of the King's household in December 1674, a 'King's party' had been formed, led by the Duke of Medinaceli with some gentlemen of the *Cámara del Rey*. They were Aristocrats interested in the opportunities that could open up for them as the King came of age.' Ultimately the same dynamic that had created the *validos* during the reign of his grandfather, father and mother.

23 It is on this period that modern research has focused its attention, overturning many of the existing beliefs about the Monarchy of Carlos II. In the last 20 years, it has been possible to shed light on the structure and the projects of Carlos II's Monarchy, which was marked by several changes in the political-economic-social dynamics.

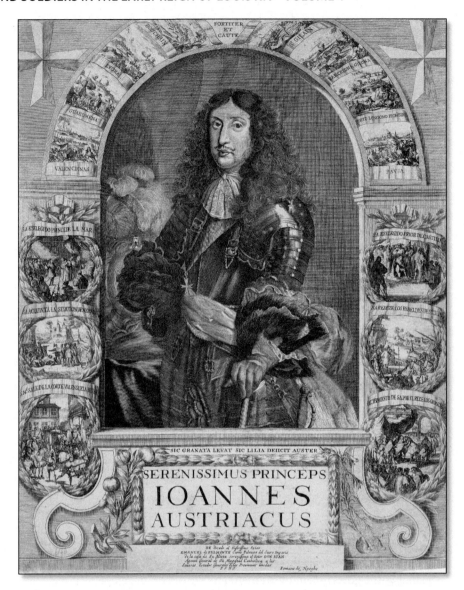

The ambitious and unscrupulous Don Juan of Austria (1629–1679), illegitimate son of King Felipe IV and the actress María Calderón. In 1642, the King recognised him officially as his son, and soon he began his lifetime career as a soldier, participating in the suppression of the uprisings in Naples and Catalonia. In 1656 he was sent to Brussels as governor of the Spanish Low Countries. At the storming of the French camp at the Battle of Valenciennes on 16 July 1656, Don Juan displayed great personal courage leading a brilliantly executed cavalry charge that caught the French totally by surprise. In 1658, he was decisively defeated at the Battle of the Dunes and failed to raise the siege of Dunkirk. He held the command of the Spanish army of Extremadura from 1661 to 1663 against Portugal, but again with poor results until he was finally defeated at Ameixial-Estremoz. After the death of Felipe IV in 1665, Don Juan became the recognised leader of the opposition to the government of the widowed Queen. In 1669 he put himself at the head of an uprising of Aragon and Catalonia, which led to the expulsion of the Queen's prime minister Cardinal Nithard on 25 February. However, Don Juan was forced to content himself with the viceroyalty of Aragon. In 1677 the Queen Mother aroused universal opposition by her shameless favouring of Fernando de Valenzuela. Don Juan was able to drive her from court and establish himself as prime minister. Great hopes were entertained for his administration, but it proved disappointing and short; he died on 17 September 1679. (Print after an engraving by Romeyn de Hooge)

THE 'RESILIENCE' OF SPAIN

Monarchy at last acquired a talented politician in the Count of Oropesa. He served as first minister from 1685 to 1689 and made important attempts to restore order in government affairs and spending, and although he was finally overcome by the opposition of strongly entrenched interests, he had at least achieved several positive results, and marked out a path for others, more fortunate, to follow.

Recent research outlines the efforts to change the organisation of the Monarchy undertaken during the reign of Carlos II. Among the major changes, Carlos II and his ministers tried to control the power of the grandees within the court and introduced new bodies of government such as the *Despacho* universal's secretary, which caused the loss of predominance of the ancient Madrilenian *Consejos*.[24] Another substantial change may be noted in international policy. The new alliances created by Carlos II seem to stand in contrast with the continuity of devotional and cult practices through which the Monarchy confirmed its aspiration to be the guarantor of the Catholic faith. In contrast with the traditional alignments there is, for instance, Carlos II's support to William of Orange after the outbreak of the Glorious Revolution in England.[25]

Despite the commendable effort made by some loyal courtiers, the Spanish ruling class offered few personalities of value. Many of the important posts continued to be held by poorly trained people. On them, as on much of the Spanish nobility of the period, the shadow sharply outweighs the light, and their work was often a source of grave embarrassment for the reputation of the Monarchy. The admission of supernumeraries in several institutional organisations and the acquisition through venality of the provincial offices was aimed at collecting money for the crown and creating a consensus among the provincial nobility in support of the Queen Maria Anna of Austria in her conflict with the grandees. The literature of the period has passed on a very negative image of the Spanish nobility during the reign of Felipe IV and Carlos II. Spanish aristocrats disdained commercial ventures as vulgar and lived off the rents of their large estates. Their hostility to change and devotion to past military glories were stronger than the ones of nobles elsewhere, but largely prevented the rise of a middle class.[26] The aristocracy comprised different levels of nobility: the grandees of Spain were a minority but were a dominant

---

24 Antonio Álvarez-Ossorio, 'The Legacy of Carlos II and the Art of Government of the Spanish Monarchy', in A. Álvarez-Ossorio, C. Cremonini and E. Riva (eds), *The Transition in Europe between XVIIth and XVIIIth Centuries. Perspectives and case studies* (Milan: Franco Angeli, 2016), pp.33–34: 'A major change which took place during the reign of Carlos II was the *mediatizzazione* of the court's government through the ever more important role of the Grandees of Spain (the major institutions, court offices, and *consejos'* presidencies were granted exclusively to the titled aristocracy). The eclipse of the *valimiento* system corresponded to a strengthening of the *Despacho* universal's secretary. Presumably, all these elements had an effect on the governance and management of the whole body of the poli-synodal Monarchy.'

25 *Ibid.*: 'In the Italian context, the issue of Spanish loyalty has raised a certain interest. In organising the discussion, scholars wanted to emphasise that the reason for the provincial élites' loyalty to the Spanish System was also connected with Carlos II's testament, which assigned local governance to the *naturales*.'

26 Merry E. Wiesner-Hanks, *Early Modern Europe, 1450–1789* (Cambridge: Cambridge University Press, 2010), p.335.

A Spanish *hidalgo*, from a treaty about horse riding dated 1660. The *hidalgos* are usually credited to have gained their negative attitudes in the army, however within this 'minor' aristocracy, there were also some positive careers. For instance, in 1667 Gaspar Zorrilla y Arretondo, *caballero* de Santiago, recruited at his own expense one infantry company in exchange for the appointment to the rank of captain in the army of Flanders. In 1673, after his service in the War of Devolution, he was awarded the most prestigious rank of cavalry captain. One year later he passed to the army of Catalonia, where he served positively until 1684, distinguishing himself in the defence of Gerona.

group and they proceeded the *Caballeros*. After them, there were a large number of unemployed and unproductive low-ranking nobles, the *hidalgos*, who represented one of the most negative features in the Spain of *Los Austrias*. Although it is difficult to generalise on the qualities of this component, which was certainly varied and subject to the regional cultural differences of seventeenth-century Spain, the *hidalgos* represented a sort of 'proletariat' of the Spanish nobility, who became a constant source of political instability.[27] Despite the declining economic scenario, the dominant culture among this low rank aristocracy continued to proclaim the incompatibility between manual labour and honour. Their presence grew considerably during the reign of Felipe III and his son Felipe IV because the status of nobility could be purchased through the payment of a tax introduced to feed the royal treasury. It must consider the consequences of the Monarchy's serious financial crisis, which provoked an exceptional rise in the venality of nobility titles, feudalities and offices in all the Spanish domains.[28] The original 55 aristocratic families of the reign of Carlos I became 99 under Felipe II; Felipe III added another 45, Felipe IV a further 92, and Carlos II a massive 292![29] Obviously, a wealthy bourgeois had everything to gain by purchasing a title. Aristocrats of all levels benefited from tax exemption in exchange for military service, but when the crown was forced to limit the already very high number of aristocrats, it granted tax

27 The Duke of Maura, a late-seventeenth century observer, who knew them well, defined the *hidalgos* as 'a weak, impoverished and troublesome oligarchy'. Other commentators have reproached the hidalgos for 'their miserable pride', while others have attributed to them that code of laziness described by their contemporary Spanish theatre's writers. See *The New Cambridge Modern History*, Vol. 5, *The Ascendancy of France, 1648–1688*, p.474.

28 On this topic see also Felices de la Fuente, María del Mar, 'Recompensar servicios con honores. El crecimiento de la nobleza titulada en los reinados de Felipe IV y Carlos II', in *Elpoder del dinero. Dimensiones de la venalidad en los siglos XVII y XVIII* (Ediciones Universidad de Salamanca, 2013), pp.409–435.

29 Various authors, *La Storia*, vol. 8, *Il Seicento. L'età dell'Assolutismo* (Turin: UTET, 2004), p.107.

exemption only for personal taxes, while the general ones became a duty also for the aristocracy. However, the *hidalgos* transmitted their negative attitudes in the army, since the profession of the arms was the only one they could accept.

In this period of the Spanish history, there was also a considerable increase among the clergy. Along with people who chose a religious life by vocation, others did it to obtain privileges or just to survive. Even the cadets of aristocratic families, excluded from the inheritance, submitted to monastic life to find an alternative means of subsistence. Prudent evaluations state that in 1660 there were in Spain over 200,000 men in religious orders. Despite the interference of religious institutions in the social life of the state, Spain experienced a period of religious tolerance in this period, and this was not just because the presence of mercenary contingents recruited in Lutheran Germany was favoured.[30]

Regarding the economic scenario, a strong characteristic of seventeenth-century Spain was the progressive concentration of wealth in a small number of people, namely families belonging to the great landed nobility, who, together with the clergy and the Monarchy, owned 95 percent of the cultivatable land.[31] The economic depression accentuated the polarisation of society into a privileged minority and a large majority of the poor people, further aggravated by the recurrent monetary reforms, which caused periods of inflation alternating with others of deflation, no less harmful for businesses and trade.[32] This caused the decline of the bourgeoisie, which was able to recover again with the economic growth that began in the 1680s. The common classes experienced a very difficult situation: 'the unsuccessful joined the great army of the idle, which was swollen by recruits from above and below. The penurious student and the displaced peasant travelled the same road. Fiscal oppression, poor harvests, bad trade could turn the artisan or the peasant of today into a pauper tomorrow; it was easier, and in the long run no more unprofitable, to live in idleness and trust to native wit and the charity of the church.'[33] Already at the beginning of the reign of Felipe IV, the

---

30 Already in 1639, the commercial treaty with England established that the religious belief of the English residents in Spain had to be respected, as long as they were not a cause for scandal. The same principle was applied in 1641 with Denmark, until Felipe IV allowed Protestants from every country to enter Spain; then after 1648, the Dutch tradesmen too acquired the same right. In 1679, Carlos II issued a decree to encourage the immigration of foreign artisans, without religious restrictions. Moreover, for many years, the presence in the army of Lutheran mercenaries like the Germans had become a custom to which no one paid more attention: the defence of the most embattled territories in the great Catholic Monarchy were therefore left in the hands of heretics. *The New Cambridge Modern History*, vol. 4, *The Decline of Spain and the Thirty Years' War 1609–48/59*, ed. John Phillips Cooper (Cambridge: Cambridge University Press, 1971), p.450.

31 Kagan and Parker, *Spain, Europe and the Atlantic World*, p.17.

32 This trend is demonstrated by the change in the distribution of properties. Observing the data of the kingdom of Valencia, in the period 1620–23, agricultural activity was 85 percent owned by the aristocracy, 13 percent by the clergy and another 13 percent by the bourgeoisie. By the end of the century, the bourgeois held 55 percent of agricultural property, while the clergy remained stable at 12 percent, and the aristocracy had fallen to 14 percent. See James Casey, *The Kingdom of Valencia in the Seventeenth Century* (Cambridge: Cambridge University Press, 1979), p.83.

33 *The New Cambridge Modern History*, vol. 4, *The Decline of Spain and the Thirty Years' War 1609–48/59*, p.452.

Possibly a portrait of a youthful Manuel Joaquín Álvarez de Toledo, Count of Oropesa (1641–1707), wearing the dress of knight of the Order of Calatrava. The Count was prime minister and *valido* of Carlos II on two occasions from 1685 to 1689 and from 1698 to 1699. During his government, Oropesa tried to heal the precarious financial situation by continuing the policy of reducing expenses, already initiated by his predecessor, implemented monetary reforms and tried to make the tax authorities fairer by eliminating some tax exemptions for the benefit of the clergy and the nobility. Almost as a reflection of their financial policy, the political development of Spain also reveals the same general trends. After a policy of centralising power inaugurated by the Count-Duke of Olivares, a phase of decentralisation followed with the return of authority to the *Cortes* under Carlos II. In this respect, the last Spanish Habsburg showed greater attention to legality in relations with different parts of the kingdom than his father did. However, the fate of this unfortunate monarch and the dynastic question constituted a burden that reverberated in the European political arena throughout his life. (Author's collection)

Spanish treasury faced a significant decrease in precious metals. This decrease, combined with the exhaustion of gold and silver reserves in America, represented one of the major causes of the impoverishment of the economy of the empire, while it was heavily engaged in the war against France and the Dutch Republic. Furthermore, the separation of Portugal from Spain in 1640 had seen as one consequence the flight of Portuguese financiers from Spain. They transferred their assets from the peninsula to northern Europe, principally Amsterdam, thus depriving the Spanish crown of their services and resources.[34]

The incongruous Spanish tax system contributed to complicate the situation. Even for contemporaries, the Spanish fiscal arrangements appear extremely complex, as each territory paid to the royal treasury taxes established by tradition or local privileges. For instance, the revenues of Naples, Milan and Flanders were entirely absorbed by the military expenses of these domains, and only a small part reached the royal treasury. In overall, the taxes paid by non-Spanish kingdoms were just over one sixth of what the royal treasury received from the kingdom of Castile. This does not mean that there were inequalities between the domains because local taxes were also paid, however the existence of different tax systems was at the origin of the financial difficulties of the Monarchy and brought to conflicts, which from the 1640s resulted in open rebellion in Portugal, Catalonia, Naples, Sicily and Madrid. In the next decade, the reports sent each year by the council of Castile to the King testify to the financial difficulties of the Monarchy, which was forced to increase the tax burden. In 1654, Felipe IV declared to the *Cortes* that the royal

---

34 Henry Kamen, *Spain's Road to Empire*, pp.398–399: 'There was a reaction against them in New Spain, where they had significant business, and the Inquisition arrested several. In Portugal, to make matters worse, the new regime arrested and in one case executed financiers who were too closely identified with the Habsburg regime. The famous Spanish *asiento* for supplying African slaves to America had been before 1640 in Portuguese hands. It was now suspended for over 20 years, until 1662.'

treasury had received only half of the 18 million *ducados* collected from the treasury, as the other half had already been mortgaged, and that the debt had now reached 120 million *ducados*. During the *cortes* of 1662 in Castile, the resulted was that the taxes paid had increased in just three years from 8.5 million to over 16 million *ducados*.[35]

In this dramatic scenario, the volume of revenue from the American colonies also suffered severe setbacks. The decrease in Potosí silver in Bolivia was accompanied by the growing monopoly of foreigners. The accounts of the 1660s and 1670s describe a real 'drying up' for Spain, noting that foreigners (particularly the Dutch) exploited the best part of the colonies' wealth to their advantage, and now dominated the finances after taking over many offices and privileges.[36] The fiscal burden affected all the production activities, and this was inevitable, because the taxes were more difficult to collect in a declining economic scenario. The ancient *alcabalas* – the indirect taxes – had been the main resource of the first Habsburg kings. In 1621, the indirect taxes had reached an amount of 2.9 million *ducados*, decreasing to 2.584 million in 1665, mainly because part of the original taxes were transformed by the crown – always short of cash – into an extraordinary tax. By the mid seventeenth century, the stagnation of the Spanish economy led to the collapse of customs revenues and the already diminished contributions coming from the colonies were now the only source of money. All hopes then turned to the *miliones*, the new indirect tax introduced at the end of the sixteenth century, established at 2.5 million *ducados* during the peaceful reign of Felipe III, but then increased to 4 million under Felipe IV. But even this source of financing ended up being burdened by an increasing number of mortgages, so much so that already in 1632 it was necessary to introduce a new tax, the *quiebras*, equal to two million *ducados*. The government's tax system had to stop at that point, not so much because of the opposition of the *cortes*, but because of the material unwillingness to extract more

---

35 *Ibid.*

36 *The New Cambridge Modern History*, vol. 5, *The Ascendancy of France, 1648–1688*, p.478. The United Provinces needed the support of the Spanish empire in order to maintain their own economy and protect themselves against the encroaching interests of the English and the French. And the Spanish reciprocated. Spanish humanist and diplomat Antoine Brun, from Franche-Comté, informed the Estates General in 1651 that 'nowhere in the world have your merchants and commerce received better welcome than in the territories of my master'. From the 1650s Dutch commerce with Spain increased, and developed into a profitable trade to the Mediterranean. They brought grain, fish, timber and naval stores from the north; in return they collected from the Peninsula silver and more silver, with some wool, olive oil, wine and occasionally salt. They gained an advantage from Spain's wars against England in 1655–60 and against France in subsequent years, stepping into trade in goods that were forbidden to nationals of these two countries. Dutch vessels carried most Spanish wool exports to northern Europe or to Italy. In subsequent decades the Dutch made available the capital required for financing the slave trade to America. The Spanish Empire, in its turn, benefited from the military protection of what was still the world's biggest maritime power. The appearance in 1657 of 16 Dutch warships at anchor in the bay of Alicante, Spain's largest Mediterranean port, was a sight that soon became familiar in the major ports of southern Spain. Spanish merchants were happy to trade with their former enemies. 'All the English merchants upon the coast', reported an English official visiting Spain in the 1660s, 'complain of the Spanish partiality towards the Dutch.' See also Kamen, *Spain's Road to Empire*, p.405.

money from the disastrous Spanish economy. From this situation derives the assumption that the military policy of the last Habsburgs of Spain was conditioned by the inability to meet new expenses. For other historians, the reality was much more articulated and complex, so much so that – despite the passivity of governments – there was not always that resignation to the decline that certain historians have propagated, but under Charles II, much more than under his father, attempts were promoted to reform the economy and especially the fiscal machine. By the middle of the century, it was estimated that of the nearly 10 million *ducados* collected, about seven million were swallowed up by the mechanism of collection. In 1666, an inquiry estimated that the crown received just 20 percent of the revenues after the expenses due to the procurement of collections and interest to the banks.[37] Despite the financial difficulties and the chronic economic crisis, in 1667 the whole budget recorded an increase in tax revenues which amounted to 12.7 million *ducados*. This increase had also occurred by resorting to forced expropriations and the confiscation of the assets of the feudal lords accused of embezzlement. Other resources flowed thanks to the amnesties. These expedients, however, had the drawback of mortgaging income in the long term, to the advantage of immediate collections. Since foreign creditors – Swabian and above all Genoese bankers – accepted only silver coin, in 1667 the ministers of Carlos II had to pledge 2.7 million copper *ducados* to send one million silver cash to Flanders, which was acquired by obtaining a not negligible discount.[38]

Despite resorting to the most disparate measures, the Crown's difficulty in coping with the debt and liquidity crisis led to the bankruptcies of 1662 and 1666, which followed the ones that had already occurred in 1627, 1647 and 1653 and preceded the crisis of 1677 and 1692. At the end of the reign of Felipe IV the economic and financial situation of Spain was so critical that it is surprising how the government could find bankers willing to negotiate further loans. In this emergency, the government could not further increase the tax burden for fear of the uprisings and the opposition of the *cortes,* and therefore Spanish economic policy essentially consisted of the monetary reforms, started by minting an ever-increasing quantity of copper coins, in substitution for those in precious metal. Already in the 1640s, silver had disappeared from circulation. The Brazilian gold temporarily restored the situation, but with the Portuguese rebellion and the beginning of the Restoration War this too became increasingly rare. Inflation began to alternate with periods of revaluation and deflation with negative consequences in all the domains. Inflationary measures were particularly frequent in the 1650s, when the government introduced a drastic monetary reform.[39] This caused a sudden rise in prices and to a 190 percent increase in the premium of silver,

---

37 Various authors, *La Storia*, vol. 8: *Il Seicento*, pp.108–109.

38 *Ibid.*

39 The *vellón* – copper coin – was minted at respectively twice and three times the nominal value of the coins of four and two *maravedis*. The value of the 12 and eight *maravedis* coins was reduced to two, and the ones of six and four to only one. *The New Cambridge Modern History*, Vol. 5, *The Ascendancy of France, 1648–1688* (Cambridge: Cambridge University Press, 1964–68), p.472.

which was followed by a drastic deflation within a few months.[40] The war expenditures forced the government to take new inflationary measures, which was followed in 1651 by a new deflation. The period between 1652 and 1680 marks the greatest imbalance in the Spanish economic situation. In 1659, after the Peace of the Pyrenees and at the end of a new inflationary phase, the government tried to achieve deflation with new monetary measures. Despite this, inflation did not stop, and the issuing of new currencies resumed on a large scale.[41] Prices too increased considerably in the two-year period 1663–64, coinciding with the decisive campaigns against Portugal. The cycle of inflation and deflation, coupled with monetary chaos, price instability and their disproportion compared to salaries, with the former rising faster than the latter, had disastrous consequences in the final years of the war against Portugal as well as in the War of Devolution of 1667–68. In the 1670s, the economic scenario remained critical and forced the government to introduce in 1680 strong monetary deflation, which caused prices to collapse. However, these severe measures finally brought some order to the monetary chaos and six years later the situation was more or less stabilised thanks the salutary introduction of the *Junta de* Comercio y Moneda.

In 1663, the balance of the Monarchy were estimated at 22,162,917 *escudos*, however, no one expected that this sum would be reached except by reducing the obligations towards creditors. The recourse to private credit always produced new debts. Four years later, the *consejo de hacienda* expected that treasury could collect about 12,769,326 *ducados*, but 71 percent were already committed for covering the interests claimed by the creditors. This data implied an economy in sharp decline. Undoubtedly, the darkest moment for the Monarchy was the period 1677–1685, when the lack of funds became more than evident, but not to the majority of the contemporary commentators, who did not see that the state was on the verge of collapse.[42] The prolonged war involvement gave no respite to the Treasury, and therefore the recovery

---

40 Javier de Santiago Fernández, *Moneda de vellón en el reinado de Carlos II. Asientos para su emisión* (Madrid: Universidad Complutense, 2006), p.189. The *premio de la plata* was a surcharge applied to the official price of the precious metal. This method served to give each coin the value it deserved based on the demand and the esteem received, but it also resulted in the increasing loss of value of some coins, or their abundance and the growing scarcity of precious metal. Therefore, the premium was a meter of the monetary situation: the thermometer that measured the disease of the Spanish monetary system.

41 Prieto and Belén, 'La Administración Real bajo Los Austrias', pp.381–382. In 1660 the government withdrew all the copper coins that circulated below their actual value and replaced them with new coins of 'strong copper'. Meanwhile, the premium on silver increased by another 150 percent and to avoid total collapse the government resorted to halving the value of the coins issued years earlier. In 1664 the premium of silver fell by 50 percent, but between 1665 and 1680 inflation reached exorbitant levels again. Unauthorised coinage and circulation of counterfeit coins again caused the premium of silver to rise to 275 percent and made the drastic deflation of 1680 inevitable.

42 *The New Cambridge Modern History*, Vol. 5, *The Ascendancy of France, 1648–1688*, p.373. On the eve of the financial catastrophe of 1680 the *tratadista* (social theorist) Alfonso Nunez de Castro wrote: 'Let London make the finest cloths; Holland, cambric; Florence, homespun; India, pelts; Milan, brocades; Italy and Flanders, linen … for our capital to enjoy; this proves only that all nations produce craftsmen for Madrid, and that she is the Queen of the Cities, since all serve her, and she serves nobody.'

was difficult and slow. The Monarchy's lack of financial resources, and their inadequate use, worsened the situation when these limitations became increasingly evident in all the European courts. To this dramatic scenario was also added contributions and plunder executed by the French, especially in the Low Countries, and the territorial losses that followed, which undermined the human base and the subsistence of the Spanish armies. In addition, the priority of helping other fronts, such as Sicily, Catalonia and North Africa, did not allow the arrival of more resources from the Crown.

The Spanish Domains in the European Strategic Scenario

In the second half of the seventeenth century, military expenditure registered a strong increase in Europe, because of the raise of the permanent armies, leaving the Spanish treasury to face a dramatic spiral of expense. As a result, after 1659, the Spanish geostrategy moved in a contest where war commitments and lack of resources accompanied every action of the Crown. The financial framework on which the army had based its livelihood for nearly a century was beginning to show its obsolescence and insufficiency. In this regard, the increase in the expenditures for the army of Flanders, the instrument that was to ensure the Spanish Monarchy the possession of the most strategically important theatre due to its proximity to Paris, is the best example. The Spanish Low Countries, as effectively stated by the Count of Peñaranda in 1666, were the principal parade ground and the safest bastion for the defence of the Monarchy, because from its border, Paris was only 60 leagues distant. Despite the strategic importance of the Spanish Low Countries, Spain received less than one fifth of the money necessary to support the army, and it did not even arrive to pay for fodder and foodstuff.

In the last decades of the seventeenth century, the Spanish Low Countries 'became a window in which other European states witnessed the dynamics of the Monarchy's military policy'.[43] Therefore, the study concerning their defence is the better way to understand the Spanish military situation and its evolution. After the peace of Aix-la-Chapelle in 1668, the military endowment was intended to be maintained thanks to the annual appropriation from Spain of 1,200,000 *escudos*, in addition to the tax contributions from the Spanish Low Countries, which would amount to 2,500,000 florins annually, and this expense did not include the cost of bread and fodder.[44] Despite this dismal situation, between 1669 and 1674 the Army of Flanders received enough funds, and in general its maintenance

---

43 Rodríguez Hernández, 'Guerra y alianzas en la lucha por la hegemonía europea', p.260.

44 *Ibid.*, p.262. 'These estimates were not realistic, since the Spanish Low Countries' treasury was too overloaded with debts and arrears, which meant that only 1,668,893 florins annually remained in liquidity, from which another 475,313 had to be subtracted for the payment of salaries, pensions and other minor expenses to the civil administration. The local *hacienda* was too bent on the war, which made it run out of funds. This amount taken from the provinces was insufficient to pay for the army, which – according to the 1669 quotation – would consume 1,269,437 florins monthly in salaries, ammunition, bread, fodder and the salaries for the officers.'

Louis XIV, depicted as Mars by Charles Le Brun, in an allegory of the War of Devolution. In 1667 the Sun King laid claim to the Spanish Low Countries on behalf of his wife and Felipe IV's daughter, Maria Theresa, invoking a principle of Brabant civil law as one of international law. In order to prevent acquisition by France, Maria Theresa renounced her inheritance rights in 1660; in return, Louis was promised a dowry of 500,000 gold *escudos*, a sum that was never paid. When Spain rejected the French claim, Louis XIV invaded the Spanish Low Countries.

was not in great danger. However, without the constant financial support from Madrid, the Spanish Low Countries would be lost. If compared with the past, the proportion was higher, reducing the difference by half, but it never reached the levels of the beginning of the seventeenth century. In 1672, the expenditure for the Army of Flanders totalled 640,124 florins per month, since the reducing of units had reduced the spending.[45] But since 1674 the remittances of funds decreased as the resources moved to other war fronts or to pay for the strong subsidies accorded to Habsburg Austria. In July 1674, the city of Messina rebelled against the Spanish rule. Spain had to form a new army in Sicily to quench the rebellion, which was being supported by France. Spain therefore had to dedicate a considerable amount of its resources to the war in the Mediterranean Sea, Catalonia and Italy. In the following months, the Spanish treasury tried its best to

---

45 Rooms, *De organisatie van de troepen van de Spaans-Habsburgse monarchie in de Zuidelijke Nederlanden*, pp.204–205.

send their consignments on time; however, punctual payment of the promised subsidies proved impossible, resulting in continuous complaints from Vienna and The Hague. By 1675, the Spanish Low Countries were ruined, and little could be expected from their financial assistance, given the destruction and excesses committed by the enemies as well as the allied troops who had fought in the territory. According to the dispatches sent by the Dutch ambassador Van Heemskerck from Madrid, the economic position of Spain was an actual nightmare. In early January 1676, he discovered that there was little to be expected from Spain 'before the arrival of the American galleons, which are said to be delayed by two months more than usual and are awarded with impatience'.[46] In spring, the financial problem began to be serious. It was stated that a large part of the country had been consumed by both the French and the allied armies, while the Spanish officials were unable to obtain the economic contributions from the areas involved in the war.[47] Therefore, half of the country did not give their tributes, or instead paid the French for fear of destruction, rendering the army impossible to sustain. The agreements signed with the Allies represented a further financial burden. In 1678, after the unsuccessful campaigns in Flanders of the previous years, Madrid remitted only a small fraction of the pay due to its own army, but nonetheless contributed to the maintenance of the Imperial troops.[48] However, the strategic importance of Flanders served to ensure the survival of the Spanish army in the country.

A Spanish possession equally close to France was Franche-Comté, but here the military spending followed a completely divergent trajectory compared to Flanders. In several ways, Franche-Comté represented the political paradigm of the Spanish Habsburg domains in central Europe. The province benefited from a special regime with ample fiscal autonomy and few military obligations.[49] Franche-Comté was included within the 'legal

---

46 Van Nimwegen, Olaf, *The Dutch Army and the Military Revolutions, 1588–1688* (Woodbridge: The Boydel Press, 2006, English edition), p.488: 'Only when the Dutch ambassador had threatened that without a substantial military contribution from Spain, the Republic would be compelled to negotiate a separate peace with France, did the Spanish court at last, on 15 February 1676, give the undertaking that the Viceroy of the Spanish Low Countries would be provided with the means to prepare the army for the oncoming campaign. The fiscal crisis continued to afflict the Spanish army, now heavily engaged also in Catalonia and Sicily.'

47 Rodríguez Hernández, 'Guerra y alianzas en la lucha por la hegemonía europea', p.263. 'In this period the situation was almost untenable in Flanders, given the lack of allied support, which caused the losses of the fortresses that occurred between 1676–78, including Condé-sur-l'Escout, Bouchain, Cambray, Valenciennes, Saint-Omer, Saint-Ghislain, Ypres and Gand, before the Dutch Republic – more concerned with its own interests such as recovering Maastricht – intervened to support the Spanish army.'

48 *Ibid.*: the total contribution amounted to 530,000 *Reichsthaler*: 'After the end of the war, the Spanish treasury continued to send money to the Emperor, but in smaller quantities; in spite of their efforts, they managed to deliver only two-thirds of the subsidies they had promised.'

49 In 1581, Felipe II ordered that the parliament of Franche-Comté establish its own tax burden. The States General made a counterproposal and after a long negotiation, it was established that the resources would be used exclusively for the province. The self-managed regime was one of the reasons Franche-Comté remained loyal to Spain. From an economic point of view, the most important contribution was the *dono gratuito* (free gift), which from 15,000 florins in 1507 grew to 120,000 in 1552, to reach 200,000 in 1621, then 448,000 in 1635 and again 200,000 in 1666. Further reading: François Pernot, *La Franche-Comté espagnole. A travers les archives de*

Cavalry encampment in Flanders, 1673. After the reverses of the War of Devolution, in the court of Madrid many members of the government, eager to forge alliances with other states, did not realise the importance of the thin line that separated the preservation of the army from the preservation of the entire Spanish Monarchy. Despite the unfavourable scenario, until the end of the Franco-Dutch War the Crown continued to assemble troops and from 1673 acted as a protective shield for the Dutch Republic and the rest of the allies to allow them to recover from the victorious French offensive of the previous year. However, in the final phase of the war, the Monarchy faced many financial problems that limited its efforts, making it the party that lost the most in the Nijmegen peace treaty. Painting of Johannes Lingelbach (1622–1674). (Collection of the Hermitage, St. Petersburg, Russia)

boundaries' of the Empire and the city of Besançon was itself an Imperial city. On the Spanish side, the King ensured that there were a limited number of foreign troops in the territory, as the defence was borne by the natives. The autonomy enjoyed by Franche-Comté is usually highlighted as the main reason why the Spanish crown was unable to maintain possession of the province. Furthermore, the Spanish Monarchy's behaviour regarding this province seems to allude that Franche-Comté meant financially, politically and militarily little for Spain.[50] In 1568, when the rebellion of the Dutch provinces began, Franche-Comté became one of the areas crossed by the Spanish 'road to Flanders' traced by the Duke of Alba.[51] This certainly increased the strategic value of the region, but the transit of troops heading north created serious difficulties, as the provincial authorities had to provide accommodation and provisions for thousands of men, as well as fodder for the horses that accompanied the troops. All these problems were aggravated when the transit of soldiers coincided with poor harvests, but Franche-Comté fortunately remained for many years untouched by the military operations. The period of peace lasted until 1636, interrupted by the French invasion and the siege of Dole. The war caused serious damage to Franche-Comté, which lost half of its population, fled or perished as a consequence of the war. As its strategic value diminished, Franche-Comté is usually described as a territory of secondary importance to which Spain paid little attention.[52]

The second largest 'parade ground' of the Monarchy was Milan, which consequently absorbed another considerable mass of capital. The Thirty

---

Simancas, une autre histoire des Franc-Comtois et de leurs relations avec l'Espagne, de 1493 à 1678 (Besançon: Presses Universitaires de Franche-Comté, 2003), p.69.

50 Enrique Martínez Ruiz, *Introducción. Los escenarios de procedencia*, in E. Martínez Ruiz (ed.), 'Presencia de flamencos y valones en la milicia española', *International Review of Military History* N. 96 (Madrid: International Commission of Military History, 2016), pp.16–17.

51 Roberto Quirós Rosado, *La fiel nación. Una aproximación al servicio militar borgoñón bajo los últimos Austrias españoles (1674–1714)*, in E. Martínez Ruiz (ed.), 'Presencia de flamencos y valones en la milicia española', *International Review of Military History* N. 96 (Madrid: International Commission of Military History, 2016), p.77: 'Franche-Comté was the 'first estate of the King', and at the same time 'the jewel that everyone wants to take from the Crown' – starting with the influential Baron de Bergeyck – despite its loss seriously could compromise the existence of the Imperial Circle of Burgundy. The Emperor himself feared that in the negotiations that took place in the Dutch town, the possible transfer of ownership of the Golden Fleece order, linked to the House of Burgundy, would be taken into consideration if Franche-Comté were definitively annexed to France. All fears that, on another level and with divergent interests, were shared by the ranks of royal officials, military, aristocrats or private individuals who decided to leave Franche-Comté to continue to exercise their personal or family service to the House of Austria in Madrid.'

52 Franche-Comté has received little consideration from Spanish historians, who have always attributed little strategic value to the region. The definitive loss of the domain following the Peace of Nijmegen was regarded as a marginal and inevitable defeat, due to the impossibility of an effective defence. The fact of the annexation of the province to France seems almost to have been erased, and still today many authoritative Spanish historians evade the topic and argue that despite the fact that the Franco-Dutch war ended unfavourably, the Monarchy did not suffer considerable territorial losses. However, the attempts tried by the Spanish diplomat in the Dutch Republic, Manuel Francisco de Lira, to recover Franche-Comté during the preliminary rounds of the negotiations for peace at Nijmegen, does not confirm this disinterest. The loss of the province, foretold by de Lira and his correspondents Bernardo de Salinas and the Duke of Villahermosa, Viceroy of the Spanish Low Countries, definitively took shape. See Kamen, *Spain's Road to Empire*, p.408, and Quirós Rosado, *La fiel nación*, p.77.

Years' War had dragged the province into war and aggravated discontent. The highest circles of the aristocracy in Lombardy had successfully identified their careers with the Spanish presence, but they did not cease to complain of the cost of the war against the French. Their letters to Madrid in the 1650s, affirm explicitly that the worst enemy of the people was the army, 'which served in theory to protect them, whose departure for the front every year was treated as nothing less than a liberation.'[53] The burden of military expense strongly affected the Milanese economy until the end of the century, despite which Spanish Lombardy remained safe from any direct military involvement between 1659 and 1690. Nonetheless, the *Estado de Milan* always maintained a strong corps of troops and contributed with money and men to fuel the Spanish army on the other fronts. The same occurred in Naples, which contributed substantially to the military effort in the last decades of the seventeenth century, despite the threat of new rebellions. Finally, after Extremadura ceased to be a war front in 1668, Catalonia became another major centre for military spending.

Before the peace of the Pyrenees, Spain had usually faced its enemies on four different fronts in Europe: Flanders with Franche-Comté, Catalonia, Lombardy and the borders with Portugal. A fifth, often eluded to, theatre of war were the North African outposts, which constantly remained under Moroccan and Algerian pressure. The Mediterranean also saw the growing shadow of the Ottoman expansion. Here Spain held the Kingdom of Sicily, which was the first-line outpost to protect access to both the Adriatic and Tyrrhenian Seas.[54] Sicily also supported Malta in the struggle against the Porte with its fleet. The overseas colonies had also become theatres of war, in Jamaica and the Caribbean, where the Spaniards faced mixed fortunes with English as well as the expansionism in the region. However, after the peace of Westphalia, the United Provinces of the Netherlands no longer constituted

---

53 Kamen, *Spain's Road to Empire*, p.399.

54 Spanish historical research, even recently, has often insisted on the poor collaboration of the Sicilians in providing recruits for the Spanish armies, and the obstinate defence of the privileges enjoyed by the kingdom. However, historians do not always take into account the island's role as a barrier against the Ottomans, and for this reason the Crown preferred to keep Sicilian manpower intact. See Salvatore Barbagallo, *La guerra di Messina, 1674–1678* (Naples: Guida Editori, 2017), pp.21–25. Furthermore, after the Peace of Westphalia, Spain remained engaged on the French and Portuguese fronts, but little could financially be hoped for from the Kingdom of Sicily where half of the income and part of the Kingdom's assets had been sold, and what remained was barely enough to cover the internal military and administrative expenditure, without however being able to meet the regular payments of interest. A report dated 1669 records an income of 588,000 *escudos* (excluding direct assignments and uncertain income) and an expenditure of 640,910 *escudos*, of which at least 407,070 were reserved for defence, and almost all of the remainder committed to salaries. In the 20-year period 1650–1670, the contraction in finances brought the percentage of military spending back to a high level (42.6 percent in all: 20 percent infantry, 11 percent navy and 5.7 percent fortifications), which increased further in the decade 1670–1680 marked by the Messina revolt, passing from an average of 474,000 to 738,469 *escudos*. The end of the Messina rebellion and the war against France did not result in a significant reduction in military spending, which in fact in the period 1681–1693 was at the highest level of the entire century in absolute and percentage terms: to the usual disbursements it was added, in fact, the financial commitment for the strengthening of the fortifications and in particular for the construction of the citadel of Messina. See Domenico Ligresti, *Le armi dei Siciliani Cavalleria, guerra e moneta nella Sicilia spagnola (secoli XV–XVII)* (Palermo: Mediterranea ricerche storiche, 2013), pp.119–120.

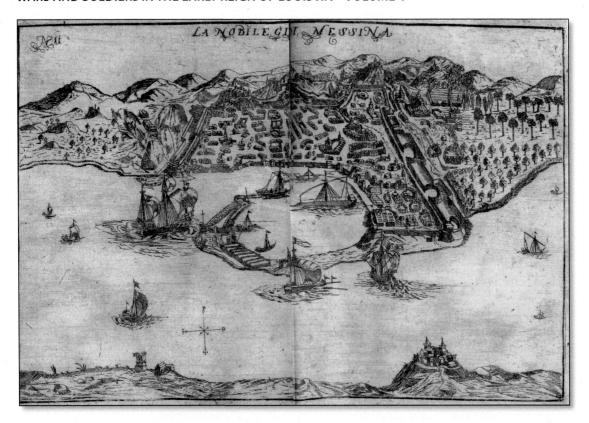

LA NOBILE CHI MESSINA

a threat, and after 1659, Italy was not affected by war until 1674. In 1668, the Portuguese front was neutralised after the recognition of the independence of Portugal, reducing the principal theatres of war to the Spanish Low Countries and Catalonia. For the first time after nearly half a century, Spain could finally concentrate its resources in only two regions, but this state of affairs only lasted for a few years, since in 1667 and 1673, France brought the war back in the Spanish Low Countries, and in 1674 the Franco-Dutch War opened a new front in Sicily with the revolt of Messina. The strategic scenario was clear: France pursued a role of hegemonic power and Spain appeared to be the predestined victim to pay the price.

As for the central European strategic scenario, the inevitable consequence of French expansionism was an alliance between Spain and the United Provinces of the Netherlands. A rapprochement between the two antagonists had been developing already during the negotiations for the Treaty of Westphalia. The Dutch were by no means friends of the Spanish Habsburgs; on the other hand, they never ceased to be aware that ties of language and economy bound them close to the Spanish Low Countries.[55] After the Peace of Westphalia, Dutch built ships were acquired for Spain's *Armada*; during the years before the Peace of the Pyrenees, Dutch

---

55 After the Peace of Westphalia, Dutch-built ships were acquired for Spain's armada, and during the years before the Peace of the Pyrenees, Dutch armaments were sold to the army of Flanders. See Kamen, *Spain's Road to Empire*, p.404.

Facing page: Messina in the seventeenth century, in a contemporary print. Events in the Mediterranean were uniformly disastrous for Spain. In 1674, the city of Messina rose in revolt against Spanish rule and asked for France's protection. Spain sent a fleet of 30 vessels to deal with the rebels, who were able to count on the support of France. A French fleet of 20 ships was sent to attack the Spaniards, who on 11 February 1675 were defeated in an engagement off Lipari Island. French troops with their Sicilian allies assaulted Taormina, Milazzo and other places taking advantage of the weakness of the Spanish military forces on the island. The war turned to a static confrontation without the Spaniards being able to blockade Messina from the sea. The Spaniards entered Messina in 1678, after the French evacuation.

armaments were sold to the army of Flanders.[56] No sooner had the Treaty of Münster been agreed in 1648 between the Dutch and Spain than both sides found they had several interests in common besides the peace. Officials and ministers in Brussels encouraged the rapprochement. A part of the Dutch leadership looked for trade advantages, while the Spaniards counted on help against the Portuguese.[57] The contact between both sides became closer when in the 1650s they found themselves at war against the England of Oliver Cromwell. From 1656, when Don Juan of Austria as governor of the Spanish Low Countries opened negotiations with The Hague, the two former enemies drifted into a working alliance and for the first time a Dutch representative was in Madrid from 1656.[58] The talks, however, were less about commercial accords. The Hispano-Dutch rapprochement also allowed new wide-ranging strategic possibilities for Spain. More or less secured on the northern front, in 1659 there was still unfinished business, principally the war to recover Portugal. Sadly, for Spain, changes in the balance of power in Europe now made that objective almost impossible. The Portuguese had the active help of France by land and England by sea; they also received supplies from the Dutch. The Spanish government recognised that without a strong naval force the conquest of Portugal could not be achieved.[59] Moreover, an alliance between Portugal and England had been made in 1661, by which the English agreed to contribute troops until Portugal achieved its freedom. The Portuguese definitively defeated Spain's field armies in 1665, and in 1668 the government formally recognised its independence with the Treaty of Lisbon.

---

56 Spain valued Dutch naval expertise. Immediately after the signing of peace in 1648, construction began at Amsterdam of 12 frigates for the Spanish navy. See also Jonathan I. Israel, *Conflicts of Empires: Spain, the Low Countries and the Struggle for World Supremacy 1585–1713* (London: The Hambledon Press, 1997), p.209.

57 David Salinas, *La diplomacia española en las relaciones con Holandadurante el reinado de Carlos II (1665–1700)* (Madrid: Dirección General de Relaciones Culturales y Científicas, 1989), pp.56–57. In 1653 the State Councillor Pedro Fernandez de Velasco y Tovar, Marqués del Fresno, also known as Count of Peñaranda de Bracamonte, summarised what in his view were the relative merits of the two Protestant powers: 'if I were to be asked which is the stronger and more solid power I would reply England under its Parliament; but if I were asked which is the better as friend, and offers both benefits and confidence, I would always reply Holland.'

58 No sooner had France and Spain signed the Treaty of the Pyrenees in 1659, the State's General of the United Provinces sent a special diplomatic delegation to talk business with Madrid. One week before Christmas 1660 the Dutch ambassadors paid their respects to the Catholic majesty of Felipe IV at the palace of *Buen Retiro*, addressing him in French while the King replied in Castilian. In that act, nearly 100 years of conflict and mistrust between the two nations was undone. See Jonathan I. Israel, *The Dutch Republic: Its Rise, Greatness and Fall, 1477–1806* (Oxford: Clarendon Press, 1995), pp.740–748.

59 Kamen, *Spain's Road to Empire*, p.77

The defeat in Portugal had very serious consequences, but also opened new possibilities to Spain. The continuing threat from the enemy fleets had for 80 years forced the Spanish reinforcements for the Low Countries to transit along the winding and insecure 'Road to Flanders'.[60] In 1668, the sea routes became free, and some regions were going to lose their strategic value, like Franche-Comté. From a geostrategic point of view, this province had been the weak spot of the Spanish domains in Europe. The border with France, poorly protected by the local militias, was guarded by a net of fortresses manned by mediocre garrisons with a few regular troops. The Treaty of Westphalia restored the full sovereignty of the province to Spain but left open the question of its belonging to the Empire, omitting the Imperial Burgundian *Kreis* in the peace negotiations.[61] Though this condition ceased upon the termination of the Franco-Spanish hostilities in 1659, doubts continued as to whether the vulnerable provinces of the Spanish Low Countries, Luxembourg and Franche-Comté were entitled to assistance under Imperial collective security. Cardinal Mazarin and later Louis XIV knew the Spanish weakness in Franche-Comté, and their diplomats skilfully exploited these ambiguities to isolate the province already by the early 1660s. The precarious control over the region was clearly perceived in Madrid, and for this reason a mighty vision of solidarity and a diplomatic safety net had been prepared. However, Spain initially relied on compliance with the 1522 agreement signed with France and the Swiss cantons to guarantee the neutrality of Franche-Comté, a pact continually confirmed in the following century.[62] However, when in 1663 Louis XIV renewed the alliance with the Swiss, the province's security seemed again to be seriously threatened. In Spain's strategic plans, the defence of the province was entrusted to Milan, but this could be compromised if the cantons denied access to Spanish troops through their territory.[63] The threat could be averted by resurrecting the Imperial bond of Franche-Comté. In 1664, the hitherto non-existent Burgundian *Kreis-contingent* was assembled to support Vienna in the war against the Porte.[64] In the plans of the Spanish Low Countries' governor Francisco de Moura Corterreal, Marquise of Castel Rodrigo, the inclusion

---

60 Martínez Ruiz, *Los escenarios de procedencia*, pp.13–14.

61 See Bruno Mugnai, *Wars and Soldiers in the Early Reign of Louis XIV*, vol. 2, *The Imperial Army (1657–1687)* (Warwick: Helion & Company, 2019), pp.39–40.

62 Davide Maffi, *La cittadella in armi. Esercito, società e finanza nella Lombardia di Carlo II 1660–1700* (Milan: Franco Angeli, 2011), p.21: 'Assigning the protection of Franche-Comté to the State of Milan was nothing new. Already in 1595, the decisive intervention of the constable of Castile at the head of a relief army gathered in Milan, had prevented Henry IV from conquering the region. In 1632, the Duke of Feria had led an army from northern Italy to the Rhine not only to ensure communications between Lombardy and Flanders, but also to face a possible Swedish offensive. Following the French invasion of Franche-Comté in 1636, Milan had sent cash relief for the defence of the province.'

63 In 1666 and 1667, the Parliament of the Franche-Comtè and Paris were involved in secret negotiations. The Parliament offered to pay annually 300,000 *livres tournois* for the neutrality of the province. See Léonce Marie Philpin de Piépape, *Histoire de la réunion de la Franche-Comté à la France: événements diplomatiques et militaires (1279 à 1678) avec notes, pièces justificatives et documents inédits* (Paris-Besançon, 1881), vol. II, pp.219–220.

64 See Mugnai, *Wars and Soldiers in the Early Reign of Louis XIV*, vol. 2, p.114.

of the Spanish domains in the *Kreise* system could guarantee the Empire's defence of the region from France.[65] However, Spanish hopes were dashed in 1668, when the War of Devolution moved from Flanders to Franche-Comté, which was conquered by the French within a few weeks. Though defeated, Spain recovered the province thanks to the diplomatic intervention of the Triple Alliance of England, Sweden and the Dutch Republic. Neither the Swiss nor the Emperor had intervened; furthermore, some German states also began to appreciate the area's value as a buffer zone, since the French threat continued to escalate after 1668, but leaving Franche-Comté in a situation of chronic insecurity.[66] Further attempts were made for securing Franche-Comté in other neighbouring states, such as the Duchy of Lorraine.[67] In 1668, with the Peace of Aix-la-Chapelle, France returned Franche-Comté to Spain, but retained some fortresses in Flanders. However, the Triple Alliance did not support the Spanish plenipotentiary, Count of Peñaranda, who hoped for an exchange for Franche-Comté with Roussillon and other lost territories in the Pyrenees.

After 1668, the policy of rapprochement between Spain and the United Provinces received a decisive boost. In 1670, Spain confirmed its intention of reaching an understanding with the Dutch, who were now the chief guarantors of the integrity of the Spanish Low Countries. In Madrid Peñaranda stuck firmly by the alliance, driving the English ambassador to observe that 'here they all desire extremely to assist the Dutch, and would do it without any hesitation even though the French were yet more powerful than they are'. Unfortunately for the Dutch, their friendship with Spain was soon called upon in 1672, when Louis XIV and his German and English allies opened hostilities against the Republic. The invasion, which had carefully avoided touching the Spanish territory, was decisive to bring the Dutch and Spanish closer together, a policy which had been taken yet further by Spain's ambassador in The Hague from 1671 to 1679, the brilliant diplomat Manuel Francisco de Lira. It should be emphasised that for almost a year, the governor of the Spanish Low Countries, Juan Domingo de Zúñiga y Fonseca, Count of Monterrey, had provided to the Dutch Republic not only supplies, but also troops without having formally declared war between Spain and France.[68] The desperate situation of the Dutch and the evident threat to the

---

65 Martínez Ruiz, *Los escenarios de procedencia*, pp.13–14: 'A change of strategy occurred in 1664, when the Marquis of Castel Rodrigo decided to restore the ancient link with the Empire by participating in the Burgundian circle and to enter the Imperial defensive system, in order to protect the Spanish Low Countries (and Franche-Comté) from a possible French invasion. A policy that largely failed.'

66 Peter Wilson, *German Armies. War and German Politics, 1648–1800* (London: UCL Press, 1998), p.18: 'The Imperial Diet formally acknowledged that the *Kreis* was entitled to help in 1674 and empowered Emperor Leopold I to protect it two years later. By that time, much of the territory had already been lost to France.'

67 Quirós Rosado, *La fiel nación*, pp.73–96. Baron Franz Paul von Lisola, in the service of Emperor Leopold I, and a native Comtois, attested to this approach. In the last years of peace before the region's annexation by Louis XIV, Lisola 'shouted in defence of Spain to avoid the collapse of the border of the State, counting, for this, also on the protection of the Duke Lorraine.'

68 The Spanish–Dutch agreement was signed in The Hague on 17 December 1671 and established a mutual military collaboration between Spain and the Dutch Republic. If the French had attacked

Spanish Low Countries forced The Hague and Madrid–Brussels to come at last to a formal agreement, which took the form of the Treaty of The Hague, signed on 30 August 1673. After this accord, Spain's government instructed its Viceroy in the Spanish Low Countries to declare war on France that same month. The alliance with the former enemy was of undeniable benefit to Spain but could not stop the might of the French military machine, now the biggest in Europe, which completed the conquest of almost one third of the original territory of the Spanish Low Countries.

Not only the Dutch Republic could become an ally of Spain in central Europe since the Austrian Habsburgs had the same need to face French expansionism in this area. Austria could ensure that overland communications with Flanders and the Franche-Comté were secure, and furthermore, the Austrian domains represented a useful source of soldiers for the Spanish armies. The financially weak Austria in turn needed funds and subsidies from Spain. The relationship between Spain and the Emperor experienced a marked shift in the geostrategy of the seventeenth century. Although there were certain constants such as the recruitment of soldiers in Germany, the evolution of events caused considerable changes in the politics of collaboration maintained by the two monarchies.[69] Since the beginning of the seventeenth century, the Spanish army recruited soldiers in the Austrian domains in the form of whole regiments who passed into the service of Spain. In exchange for these military contributions, Vienna received financial compensation. In 1648, the clauses contained in the Treaty of Westphalia forbade Austrian military aid to Spain in Germany and the Low Countries, and from this date, the Emperor now almost completely abandoned his Spanish cousin in the struggle against France. Despite this limitation, Spain continued to recruit German soldiers for the still open theatres of war in Lombardy and Portugal, areas both excluded in the Westphalia agreement. Therefore, in the 1650s, the Spanish kings continued to ask for Imperial troops. Due to the Emperor's financial difficulties, the Spanish ministers thought he would accept the Spanish proposals and approve the departure of the veteran troops that Spain needed so much. Despite the limited collaboration, and the fact that the war against Portugal tied up large amounts of funds, Madrid continued

---

the Low Countries the Dutch would have had to help the Spaniards with 13 infantry regiments, 10,400 men in all, paid and commanded by the Republic, but quartered by Spain. Under the same terms, the Spaniards would have ceded 3,000 horsemen to the Republic, in consideration of the inexperience of the Dutch cavalry. AGS, *Estado*, leg. 2117, *Copia del papel que los diputados extraordinarios de los Estados General dieron a S.E.*, Bruxelles, dated 18 March 1672.

69 Antonio José Rodríguez Hernández, *Financial and Military Cooperation Between the Spanish Crown and the Emperor in the Seventeenth Century*, in Peter Rauscher (ed.) *Die Habsburgermonarchie und das Heilige Römische Reich vom Dreissigjährigen Krieg bis zum Ende des habsburgischen Kaisertums* (Vienna: Aschendorff Verlag, 2010), p.576: 'These changes can be classified as different stages in their bilateral relationship. While these politics are well known for the beginning of the seventeenth century, when Spanish imperialism reached its zenith, the following years have been, as yet, far less documented.' In his essay, the author focuses on the period 1648–1700, and analyses these important changes by including new archival sources and investigating aspects that have not been comprehensively studied until now.

to pay generous amounts to the Emperor.[70] For the front of Portugal, the market of men continued until the last phase of the war, notwithstanding the increasing resistance of Vienna, which unwillingly ceded its best troops.[71] Relations between Vienna and Madrid were not always serene, and ultimately the choice to turn toward their Imperial cousins resulted in a substantial economic burden for Spain. In Austria, the Spanish interests at the Imperial court coagulated into a party, whose efforts were concentrated on inducing the Emperor to focus his attention on the French threat, and to divert him from Hungary and the confrontation with the Porte. In 1663, the movements of the Ottomans and the fear of a new war in Hungary obliged the Emperor to take decisive measures to reinforce his army, and since he needed money, Leopold I requested the subsidies from Spain he had not received on other occasions. The flow of troops from the Imperial domains decreased but it was not interrupted completely, since between 1663 and 1664, Vienna sent 6,000 soldiers to Spain in order to receive money for the Imperial army in Hungary.[72]

In 1667, the War of Devolution was a turning point in the trilateral relationship between France, Spain and the Emperor. One year before, Spain had tried to reach an agreement with the Emperor: if a French attack was staged, the Emperor would have declared war on France joining with the Spaniards in the defence of Flanders and Franche-Comté. Although these negotiations had failed, Spain tried to involve the House of Austria in the war when it began, aiming at a collaboration against the French not only with troops and supplies in Flanders, but also in the opening of a front on the Rhineland and Alsace, in order to alleviate the military pressure on the Spanish Low Countries. In 1666, the Emperor had received economic subsidies for his help in the recruitment of soldiers in Germany for the army of Flanders, but at the beginning of the war, the governor of the

---

70   *Ibid.*, p.586: 'In February 1661, the Council of State approved the dispatch of 100,000 *escudos* to the Emperor, thereby trying to reactivate the negotiations with Vienna for more soldiers. On the Portuguese border, a professional and multinational army was being formed to invade Portugal and end a war that had already lasted for twenty years.'

71   In 1660, the Marquis de la Fuente expressed, in a letter to Madrid, the impressions he had gained from a talk with Johann Ferdinand Count Portia, a minister with great power within the Imperial Court because of his position as mentor of the young Leopold I. In his letter, the Marquis confirmed that the recruited German soldiers requested by Spain for the Portuguese front would be sent, in spite of Viennese fears of another war against the Porte. The reason for this understanding and the concession of troops, according to La Fuente, was that the Emperor urgently needed money. See also Mugnai, *Wars and Soldiers in the Early Reign of Louis XIV*, vol. 2, p.52.

72   Rodríguez Hernández, *Financial and Military Cooperation Between the Spanish Crown and the Emperor in the Seventeenth Century*, p.587. The Emperor's minister, Prince Johann Ferdinand Portia, following a very controversial discussion, finally granted a corps of auxiliary Imperial troops to Spain. In the agreements, according to Portia, these troops would not cost Spain anything. Nevertheless, it was clear that this concession of troops was a purchase. Not only did the Spaniards have to give the soldiers several payments at the beginning of their service, but Portia succeeded in obtaining a commitment from Spain to support the Imperial army with monthly payments of 20,000 *escudos* and a one-time payment of 50,000 *escudos*. The generous contribution would have helped the Imperial army in Hungary. However, fulfilling the agreements with Vienna proved difficult because Spanish finances were exhausted due to the war against Portugal, and thus the specified amounts were not always paid.

Spanish Low Countries wrote to Madrid stating that nothing was to be expected from the Emperor, since it seemed that the French had bribed him to avoid intervention. Furthermore, in this period the first talks between Paris and Vienna regarding the future partition of the Spanish Monarchy began, which further separated the Emperor from his cousin in Madrid. When Spanish suspicions concerning the bribery was confirmed in June, the State Council knew that more money had to be quickly sent to the Emperor if he was to give up his 'neutrality' and levy an army to help Spain against France.[73] The Spanish criticism was especially directed against the princes Lobkovitz and Auersperg, as neither had helped during the negotiations.[74] The Spanish ambassador in Vienna complained about the Emperor's passive reaction and informed Madrid that he had little hopes of obtaining troops, in spite of the continuing negotiations.[75] In fact, in the winter of 1667 the Emperor prevented a number of Spanish colonels, sent from the Low Countries, from recruiting men in his territories. However, at the end of 1668, after the war had ended, Spaniards were again allowed to recruit German contingents in Austrian lands. According to the Spanish ministers, the Emperor deserted Spain during the War of Devolution not because of a lack of will or means, or because of his having broken the traditional alliance between the two houses, but because Leopold I seemed to have been ill advised by his pro-French ministers. The scenario changed in 1672, when Lobkovitz was replaced at the Imperial Court, and the pro-French party lost its influence. This event opened the possibility for a renewed understanding between Vienna, Spain and the Dutch Republic. In addition to the Dutch subsidies, from September 1672, Spain committed itself to pay the Emperor with a monthly subsidy of 30,000 *Reichsthaler*. In August 1673, after the formal declaration of war between Spain and France, the amount rose to 50,000; with these resources, the Emperor raised new troops and assembled an army to support the allies.[76]

In 1667, the War of Devolution had marked an important change in the relationship between Spain, the Emperor and the Holy Roman Empire. Though these latter had not intervened in support of Spain, Madrid had received some help from German states in the defence of the Spanish Low Countries. In early 1668, the Spanish ambassador reached an agreement with the elector of Brandenburg and the dukes of Brunswick-Lüneburg,

---

73 *Ibid.*, p.589: 'Spain did not have enough financial resources to counteract the French diplomatic progress at Vienna, as Flanders needed money with even more urgency. However, in August, the Emperor offered 25,000 men for the defence of the Spanish Low Countries. In return he demanded a million *escudos* in subsidies, which was clearly too much for the Spanish treasury.'

74 According to the Spanish ambassador, they had been bought by the French and he thought they should be punished. But to the Spaniard's surprise, the Emperor did not seem to be willing to take any measures against his ministers. See also in Jean Berenger, 'Une tentative de rapprochement entre la France et l'Empereur: le traite de partage secret de la Succession d'Espagne du 19 janvier 1668', *Revue d'Historie Diplomatique* 1965, pp.291–314.

75 Rodríguez Hernández, 'Financial and Military Cooperation Between the Spanish Crown and the Emperor in the Seventeenth Century', p.590.

76 For further details on this agreement see also Mugnai, *Wars and Soldiers in the Early Reign of Louis XIV*, vol. 2, p.173.

who promised to contribute 20,000 men for the defence of the Spanish Low Countries in exchange for subsidies that were not quite as high as those demanded by the Emperor were.[77] These troops, however, never reached Flanders because the war had already ended before they had arrived. Despite this failure, the agreement favoured the beginning of intense collaboration between Spain and individual German princes like Brandenburg, both the Brunswick-Lüneburg duchies, Osnabrück, Münster, and Württemberg. As happened eight years before, in 1675 Spain demanded collaboration and military support from the German princes for the defence of the Spanish Low Countries against France to compensate for the meagre Austrian support. At the end of 1676, the Spaniards had to send not only the monthly sum to the Emperor, but at least another 105,000 *Reichsthaler* to Brandenburg, Münster, Brunswick-Lüneburg, Osnabrück, Kur-Trier, Kur-Mainz and Denmark for the collaboration of these states in the defence of the Spanish Low Countries and for military operations against Sweden, now an ally of France. These subsidies were also frequently delayed, even more so than those sent to the Emperor. In addition, the rapprochement with Brandenburg was interrupted in 1680, due to the delayed payment of the subsidies agreed during the Franco-Dutch war, which resulted in the capture of Spanish ships in Ostend by the Brandenburg navy. Two years later, the Brandenburg fleet even tried to surprise, but without success, the Spanish squadron while it transported silver from America.[78]

As for the southern European front, Spain held a dominant position thanks to its Italian domains. Italy continued to be the sheet anchor of Spain's power in Europe throughout the seventeenth century. Armaments, ships and men from all over Italy continued to be an essential support for Spanish-led campaigns in the rest of Europe.[79] The 'luxuriant garden of the Monarchy'[80] had the dual effect of strengthening the strategic presence of Spain in the Mediterranean and to maintain its predominance in the Italian states. Naples and Sicily constituted the first line of defence against the Ottomans and their North African vassals. Madrid consolidated their access to the Mediterranean by occupying Finale and the Tuscan *Presidios*. However, the naval routes were not sufficiently secure, and southern Italy remained exposed to external assaults. Already, in the first half of the century, France did not forget the Mediterranean in its efforts to destabilise the Spanish Monarchy. In Naples and in Sicily the French helped, provoked and actively supported two major rebellions against Spanish power, and in 1646, the French fleet supported by Portuguese ships had seized the Spanish harbour of Orbetello in Tuscany, in order to isolate southern Italy from Spain. After 1659, the problems of

---

77 There is extensive documentation relating to the negotiations between Spain and Brandenburg in AHN, *Estado*, 2797, exp.47: *Copia del tratado firmado por el marqués de Castel Rodrigo con el Elector de Brandeburgo ajustado en Brujas el 6 de noviembre de 1667.*

78 Rodríguez Hernández, 'Guerra y alianzas en la lucha por la hegemonía europea', p.267.

79 Antonio Álvarez-Ossorio Alvariño, 'The State of Milan and the Spanish Monarchy', in *Spain in Italy: Politics, Society, and Religion 1500–1700* (Leiden–Boston: Brill, 2007), p.121.

80 A citation from Mercurio da Gattinara echoing Dante Alighieri, in Anthony Pagden, 'Heeding Heraclides: Empire and its Discontents, 1619–1812', in Kagan and Parker, *Spain, Europe and the Atlantic World*, p.316.

southern Italy had always been serious, and Spanish rule had not significantly improved matters.[81]

Naples, with Sicily, represented the most extended Spanish domains in Italy, but as in the first half of the century, the actual centre of gravity for Italy was located in Milan. Though the city was much smaller than today, Milan was the terminal of the Spanish trade in Northern Italy and could be considered as an actual capital. To outline the role of the city as the heart of the state, a contemporary Venetian ambassador commented that 'Milan is the true crucible where all the designs of the Spaniards in Italy are prepared.'[82] In Milan and Naples, through the Council of Italy, the Spanish government succeeded to exploit the large amount of political and administrative information collected in their domains, opening indispensable channels of collaboration with the local dominant elites and co-operation between them and the Spanish crown.[83] The result was better than in other parts of the Monarchy, and at this regard, it should be noted that the *Milanesado* was one of the domains that did not experience any significant rebellions. However, in the 1640s, the strategic scenario worsened considerably. In particular, the increasing costs of war caused a further increase in the burdens imposed on the domains in Italy as well as in the other domains. Madrid feared that the French would take advantage of the discontent of their subjects in Italy and elsewhere, exacerbated by the dramatic economic situation. Madrid could not neglect this danger. Spanish Lombardy had the strategic task of keeping the Alpine passes open and remaining permanently vigilant in respect of its three immediate neighbours: the Swiss Cantons, Savoy-

---

81 Classic historiography depicts the Spanish rule in southern Italy in very negative terms. According to some scholars, the Naples rebellion exposed the weakness of Spanish rule and predicted the beginning of the end of Spain's power in Italy. The Neapolitan revolt was accompanied in the same year of 1647 by a serious revolt in Palermo which confirmed the alienation of the ruling classes in Sicily. Kamen, in *Spain's Road to Empire*, p.399, states: 'The task was not difficult, considering the existing deep separation of interests between a large part of the population and the Monarchy, which was supported almost exclusively by the aristocracy. After nearly two centuries of Spanish predominance, few themes united Italians so much as the desire to rid themselves of their unwanted masters.' Most recently, this topic has been better investigated, focusing on the action of the Spanish government in Italy capable of obtaining a greater consensus than that previously stated. Among the most recent and valuable works on this matter, see Antonio Álvarez-Ossorio Alvariño *La República de las Parentelas. El Estado de Milán en la monarquía de Carlos II* (Mantova: Arcari, 2002); P. Civil, A. Gargano, M. Palumbo, E. Sánchez García (eds), *Fra Italia e Spagna: Napoli crocevia di culture durante il vicereame* (Naples: Liguori, 2011), and Alessandro Buono, 'Guerra, èlite locali e Monarchia nella Lombardia del Seicento. Per un'interpretazione in chiave di compromesso di interessi', in *Società e Storia*, N. 123 (2009), pp.3–30.

82 Giuseppe Galasso, and Luigi Migliorini, *L'Italia moderna e l'unità nazionale* (Turin: UTET, 1998), p.325.

83 As for the State of Milan, the years of the governorship of the Count of Fuentes (1600–1610) were very important. The Count's government, energetic to the point of being perceived as tyrannical by the Milanese elites, was aimed not only at consolidating the fiscal innovations introduced in the previous decade but was characterised by the attempt to make the Lombard defensive system more autonomous and stable. See Maffi, *La cittadella in armi*, p.204.

Piedmont, and Venice.[84] Spain guarded the routes, taking over adjacent fortresses in Novara in order to maintain the link between the Duchy of Milan and southern Italy. In this area, Spain also built an imposing stronghold named Forte de Fuentes after Pedro Henríquez de Acevedo, the talented governor of Milan between 1600 and 1610. The main purpose of this fortress was to control the mountain route through Valtelline which linked Milan with the Tyrol and the Austrian Habsburgs. The Spanish governors had to reckon with the hostility of the major states of the Italian peninsula. Venice and Savoy represented the most direct challenge to the Spanish predominance in the area. Venice especially had been invited by Louis XIV in 1657 to join the alliance with Modena in exchange for his military aid against the Ottomans at Crete. The French attempts to separate Spain from the Italian states did not interrupt in the following decades. In the 1680s, Louis XIV began to elaborate a plan for greater penetration into Italian affairs, which included a military action against Milan.

A more concrete threat of a French invasion came from the direction of the border along the Pyrenees. Here, the war against France had involved the principality until 1659, ending with the French conquest of Catalan speaking Roussillon and some important strategic outposts on the Pyrenees. It was nothing new for the northern regions of Catalonia to be a battlefield as a frontier land. The traditional French–Aragonese rivalry of the medieval period, continued in the foreign policy of France and the Habsburgs. For many centuries, the history of these territories was punctuated by French invasions and sieges of the main cities and fortresses. Furthermore, Catalonia had entered the sights of Paris as a tool to destabilise the Spanish Monarchy in the Iberian Peninsula, financing and supporting the rebellion of the 1640s. The constant French threat transformed Catalonia in a very special strategic area, since the province had lost most of its autonomy as a consequence of the rebellion put down in 1652. As a result, Spain had to face its enemy on very unfavourable ground, badly defended by an obsolete net of fortresses manned by garrisons mainly formed by foreigners, who represented a constant source of danger as they caused riots and protests among the local inhabitants.[85] This scenario, in addition to having serious political–institutional and economic–demographic repercussions, left a significant mark on Catalonia and turned in an active resistance of the local Estates against Castile's interests through the *Generalitat* and the *Consell de Cent*. These were the local governmental institutions respectively for

---

84 Around 1650, according to the Spanish governor of Milan, the King of Spain had to deal with the scheming of the Republic of Venice, the efforts of the Papacy in Rome to ensure 'that Spain's Monarchy does not expand in Italy or any other part of Europe', the enmity of Savoy, and the unreliability of the states of Modena, Tuscany and Mantua; of all the Italian princes 'only the duke of Parma could be trusted'; see G. Signorotto, 'Il Marchese di Caracena al governo di Milano', in *Cheiron*, n. 17–18, 1992, p.149.

85 In the spring of 1640, the burdens for billeting the troops and the excesses committed by the soldiers, who returned from Roussillon, were the immediate causes of the peasant revolt that began in the province of La Selva. The following French occupation was even worse, for being more durable than the presence of the Castilian soldiers.

the Principality and the city of Barcelona, and both held jurisdiction on fiscal matters. After the peace with Portugal in 1668, Catalonia became the strategic terminal of Spanish armies in the Peninsula, as it was necessary to maintain a strong army on the border in case of French aggression.[86] Nonetheless, the economic resources for maintaining the troops remained largely insufficient, since the Principality did not always collaborate with the Monarchy, and until 1674, there were few concrete signs of an understanding between Castile and Catalonia.

---

86 'During the reign of Carlos II, Catalonia became the *main battleground* of all Spain, suffering the continuous offensives of the French armies that occupied the Ampurdan and other northern regions of the Principality for long periods, committing all kinds of excesses against life, honour, religion and natural property.' Antonio Espino López, *Cataluña durante el reinado de Carlos II. Política y guerra en la frontera catalana, 1679–1697* (Barcelona: Bellaterra, 1999), p.10.

2

Soldados del Rey

The Spanish (or more appropriately the Hispanic) military reflected the structure of the Monarchy in several respects, since each kingdom managed its own forces, and the armies operating in the different strategic areas were actually autonomous entities, albeit under the authority of the King.[1] Though Spain raised powerful armies at the beginning of the century, the Crown was always forced to negotiate its military policy with the kingdoms' parliaments. These were the representative institutions of the local estates and generally enjoyed military prerogatives, like the raising of militia, as well as the right to refuse the recruitment of soldiers for the Royal armies without the payment of a 'financial consideration' or 'donation', or a reduction of taxes previously agreed, and this only after a direct request from the Crown. Under this system, the Spanish kings had much in common with their cousins in Vienna, whose government too was as much conditioned by the decisions of the provincial estates.[2] Furthermore, other factors of an organisational nature, and peculiar to Spain, contributed to make the military machine deployed by *Los Austrias* even more complex.

Since Spain mostly faced its enemies outside of the Iberian Peninsula, the army resulted in a distorted pattern. The armies operating outside Spain, the *ejércitos exteriores* (external armies), were composed of troops from a different provenance, organised in *tercios*, *trozos* and regiments; while in the Peninsula there was a mosaic of units that carried out the double task of a military force and police. The existence of these domestic corps was often short or intermittent due to the shortage of recruits and lack of money. They formed a heterogeneous corps that included local militias, urban troops and other units with various different tasks and compositions. Consequently, since each province had different taxation and privileges, military arrangements

---

1   The attempt to create an actual supranational unitary Army had been made with the *Unión de Armas* (Union of Arms) in 1626. It was a political proposal, put forward by Gaspar de Guzmán, Count-Duke of Olivares for greater military co-operation between the constituent parts of the composite Monarchy. The plan aimed to gather a force of 140,000 men but encountered resistance from the *Cortes*.

2   See *Wars and Soldiers in the Early Reign of Louis XIV, Vol. 2: The Imperial Army 1657–1687* (Warwick: Helion & Company, 2019), pp.44–45.

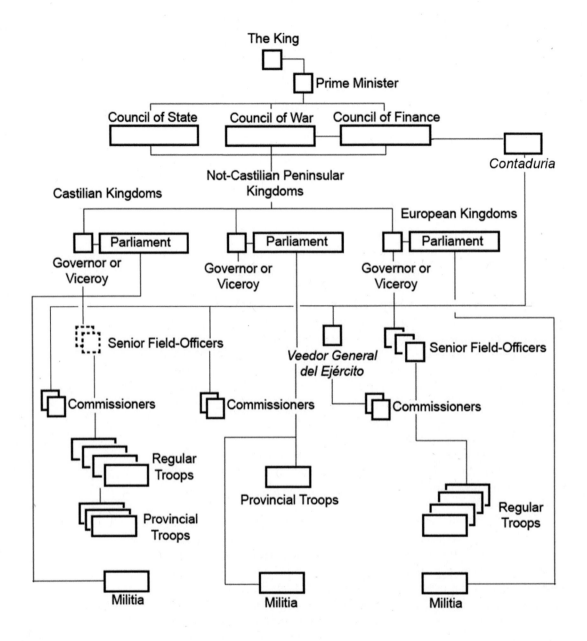

The Hispanic Army's Chain of Command

operated at further levels. The military roles were entrusted to a permanent force composed of veteran professionals quartered and garrisoned in the major towns and fortresses outside of the Iberian Peninsula, which formed a cadre to operate against external enemies as well as bandits, agitators, and insurgents. In wartime, the contingents located in the areas of most strategic relevance increased their strength with the enlistment of recruits gathered from the country or the different kingdoms, in addition to mercenary forces, usually from Germany, in order to form a field force for countering enemy operations, more often than not the French. In the last decades of the seventeenth century, this military mosaic remained unaltered, except for some changes made as a result of the moving strategic situation.

The classification of the different units of the Hispanic army also shows the heterogeneous nature of the troops that composed it. These could be classified by their nationality, and consequently by the administrative organisation in which they were assembled. Therefore, there were units managed by the Crown, and other raised by the kingdoms and provinces, or even private individuals. Further differences existed with regard of the denomination. In the infantry, the denomination *tercio* (or *terzo* in Italy) identified only the Spanish, Italian, Flemish Walloon and Burgundian (Franche-Comtois) units, while German and foreign mercenaries were gathered in the more familiar *regimiento*. In the cavalry, the Spaniards were assembled in *trozos*, while Walloons, Franche-Comtois and Italians formed the cavalry *tercio*. However, this classification was only in the terminology because role and function remained the same, and some differences existed just in the organisation. Finally, the Germans with other foreigners were also assembled in cavalry *regimientos*.

The ethnic classification of the troops followed a simplified terminology, since the Italians could come from three distinct regions of the Peninsula, namely the *Estado* or *Ducado de Milán*, the *Reino de Nápoles*, and the one of Sicily, but each domain held its own rights in terms of enlistment, maintaining *tercios*, and the strategic relevance. In the Spanish Low Countries, instead, there were no differences between Walloon and Flemish soldiers. All these non-Spanish troops were also known as *soldados de naciones*. These ethnic classifications had been introduced in the sixteenth century and was usually always respected, even if there were some exceptions. The Spanish infantry companies should not have had soldiers from any other nation, except for the fifes and drums, and some officers, usually Italians or from French-Comté, who had served for a long time in the Spanish infantry.[3] Similarly, the Italian or Flemish Walloon infantry should have had no Spaniards or soldiers from any other nation, except perhaps for some Spanish NCOs and officers. In the foreign regiments, the nationality of the officers more or less coincided with the one of the soldiers. Usually, the Swiss were led by officers of their country,

---

3   In 1685, more than two thirds of the captains of the Italian infantry *tercios* in the Army of Flanders had Italian names, the same as for the Flemish Walloons. See AHNOB, *Osuna*, ct. 197, d. 83, *Relación del modo en que quedaron los tercios y regimientos de infantería después de la reforma ejecutada por el marqués de Grana* (1st January 1685).

although the German regiments had Spanish, Italian, and Flemish Walloon colonels and captains without any limits.

Other classifications followed the location of the units, and therefore there were troops of Flanders, Extremadura, Catalonia, Lombardy, *Indias* (America and the Philippines), Africa, and so on; or if they were mercenaries recruited in Germany, Switzerland, Grisons, and the British Isles. The foreign infantry should have contained no Spaniards nor Italians, but Spanish, Italian or Flemish Walloon officers could serve within the companies, or even as commander, especially in the German regiments. The latter included soldiers coming from other north European countries and even Flemish Walloons. A further classification was established by the unit's employment, therefore there was a marine infantry regiment of *Armada* if these troops were embarked on the Atlantic fleet or assigned to the galleys in the Mediterranean. Finally, in the second half of the seventeenth century, a further distinction concerned the financing of the units, with the contingents raised by the provinces.

At the eve of the Peace of the Pyrenees, in the Iberian Peninsula the Crown maintained household corps, domestic units, and garrisons located in Spain and in North Africa. These latter troops formed the presidios distributed in the border provinces as well as in the major cities. In 1659, permanent garrisons were located in Catalonia, Navarre, Aragon, and the Pyrenees, while other presidios guarded the seaports and harbours of Barcelona, La Palma de Mallorca, Valencia, Alicante, Cartagena, Malaga, Cadiz, Seville, Gibraltar, Orio, Bilbao, and Santander. Further garrisons secured the Spanish outposts in Morocco and Algeria at Melilla, Oran, Ceuta, Mazalquivir, Larache, La Mámora until 1681, and from 1673 in the islands of las Alhucemas. In Italy, there were strategic outposts with garrisons in Orbetello, Porto Ercole and Talamone in the *Estado de los Presidios*, Porto Longone on Elba and Finale di Spagna on the Ligurian coast. Given their sedentary garrison duties, obviously the bulk of these troops was formed by infantry and artillery. A few Spanish regular forces formed the garrisons in America and Philippines. Before the establishment of a standing *Ejercito de America* in the second half of the eighteenth century, these forces were often inadequate to deal with any serious threat. The government was therefore obliged to send more troops to the *Indias*, particularly following serious incursions there in the 1660s and in the following decades.

Viceroyalties and *Capitanias*

The Spanish metropolitan territory was divided into nine *Capitanías Generales*, which in 1650 were incorporated in the *Virreinatos* (Viceroyalties). These were Canarias, Nueva Castilla, Vieja Castilla, Galicia, Extremadura, Jaen, Costa de Granada, Costa de Andalucía and Guipúzcoa. Four further provinces, the Princedom of Asturias, Kingdom of Seville, Navarre and Murcia, constituted other military partitions, alongside the territories belonging to the Kingdom of Aragon, respectively: the viceroyalty of Aragon,

Mallorca, Valencia, Sardinia and the princedom of Catalonia.[4] Each territory had also a corps of militia according to its law, customs and rules.

In 1659, the majority of Spain's military forces was located outside of the Iberian Peninsula. This force comprised garrisons located in the European as well as in American and Asian domains. The major force in Europe was quartered in the Low Countries, with others in Lombardy, Southern Italy, and Franche-Comté. In turn, some *Capitanías* managed further garrisons located outside their territories. The governor of Milan dealt also with the garrison of Finale on the Ligurian Sea, while Naples sent troops to the *Estado de los Presidios* in Tuscany, which completed the net of useful harbours connecting Spain to Italy. Each *Capitanía General* was governed by a captain-general, who had two distinct roles: one military that gave him the command of regional forces, and one civilian that awarded to him the seat of presidency of the regional assembly when it was present in the capital. The specific powers of these officials changed according to provinces and period and were regulated by the decrees of the captaincy.

The office of captain-general usually coincided with the one of Viceroy, who received the title directly from the king. Therefore, viceroy-governors were the key figures of the Spanish Monarchy and could act as semi-independent rulers. The viceroy exercised power by delegation of the king, but his power was not absolute. Under no circumstances could he start an offensive war or transfer the troops outside the Kingdom without a specific order of the king. Despite these limitations, he enjoyed great autonomy in order to ensure the defence of the territory, but he had to negotiate every act with the kingdoms' parliament, estates, and officials, especially in matters of finance. He also decided on the composition of troops, and the only limitation in the military affairs was to relinquish the rank of *maestre de campo*, namely the *tercio*-regiment's commander. The Captain General was superior to all the ministers, both sea and land, and was assisted by a Council convened in the case of external threat. The council did not have an established number of members, but always comprised the officials in charge of the economic matters.

The autonomy of the governors could extend to foreign policy matters in extreme circumstances. In 1671, the governor of the Spanish Low Countries, Juan Domingo de Zúñiga y Fonseca Count of Monterrey, after he signed a secret agreement with the Dutch Statholder in the face of a French invasion, in 1672 sent on his own initiative troops to support his ally, involving Spain in a new war against Louis XIV, something he seriously desired. Likewise, in 1685, the Viceroy of Naples, Don Gaspar Méndez de Haro, and the governor of Milan, Juan Tomás Enríquez de Cabrera y Melgar, agreed with Venice to the participation of their troops in the war against the Ottomans, after a brief consultation with the king's minister.

As omnipotent as they were, governors too were subject to rivalries and power dynamics. In this regard, even the valiant and highly esteemed

---

4   Alongside the viceroyalties, Portugal was also formally included, but after the 'Acclamation' of December 1640, Madrid lost control of the province.

Below: Juan Domingo de Zúñiga y Fonseca, Count of Monterrey (1640–1716), engraving by Christian Hagen. Monterrey was the son of Don Luis Méndez de Haro, sixth Marquis of Carpio, and Prime Minister to King Philip IV of Spain. Known for his warlike temperament, from 1670 Monterrey devoted much of his government action in the Low Countries to the army, in order to progress the war against France at the first opportunity. However, during the Franco-Dutch war his offensive was hampered by the allies and by the shortage of resources. (Author's collection)

Above: Alexander II Hyppolite, Prince of Bournonville and third Count of Hénin-Liétard (1616–1690). Despite the negative outcome of the campaign of 1674, when he held the command of the Imperial army in Alsace, Bournonville was the most skilled Hispanic commander of his age. In 1684 the Duke of Alba left an extensive account about the Duke, describing him as 'one of the last remaining military talents of the Monarchy'.

JUAN DOMINICO de ZUNIGA en FONSECA, &c.
Grave van Montery, Gouverneur en Opper Velt-heer der Spaenße Neederlanden en Bourgondien.

Alexandre Hippolyte Balthasar *duque* de Bournonville failed a second mandate in Catalonia in 1684. Although he successfully defended Catalonia during the short War of the Reunions, and the Council of Aragon came to decisively support him to renew for another three-year period in the Viceroyalty, the Council of State was not of the same opinion, complaining of its ineffectiveness as he had, in its opinion, sufficient troops to perform more offensively. Privately some leading personalities defended Bournonville, since the enemy's withdrawal had been achieved and, it was presumed, the besieged Gerona should be returned intact. Instead, the Constable of Castile emerged as the leader of the opposition to Bournonville's confirmation. Ultimately, this faction obtained the appointment of the Marquis of Leganés for the Viceroyalty of Catalonia.

Usually, the positions of governors were subject to a continuous turnover, since the office rarely lasted more than five years, three being the most common term. In the last quarter of the seventeenth century, the governorship of Francisco Antonio de Agurto, Marquis de Gastañaga, stands out with an unprecedented eight year's term as Viceroy of the Low Countries from 1685 to1692. There were also some personalities who held offices in two places, like Francesco Tuttavilla Duke of San Germano, who was appointed as Captain General of Catalonia while he was serving in the governorship Sardinia in 1671, or Íñigo Melchor Fernandez de Velasco, who held the roles both of governor in Galicia and Low Countries in 1668.

The Spanish Crown also managed its overseas territories and garrisons under the respective *Capitanias*. These had their locations in Nueva España (Mexico), Perù, Santo Domingo, Puerto Rico, Yucatán, Bogota (*Nuevo Reino de Granada* or Colombia), and the Philippines. In the first half of the seventeenth century further American *Capitanías*, such as Guatemala in the Yucatán, Chile in Perù, and Venezuela in Colombia, were created and separated from their respective viceroyalty to better manage the territories. Although the commanders were subject to the jurisdiction of the local viceroys, in the military tasks they retained a certain degree of autonomy and could manage the matter directly with Madrid through the *Consejo de Indias*. Communications with homeland were constant, but the distance of some provinces represented a serious obstacle for regular communications and control.

To get an idea of how difficult it was to maintain a regular flow of information, it is enough to consider that a royal letter sent from Madrid to Manila in the Philippines could take up to six months before arriving at the destination, and another six months could be necessary to deliver the answer. Obviously, the grade of autonomy depended on more factors, and therefore the viceroy of Philippines could take advantage of his distance from Madrid, but also in Italy or in the Low Countries the governors always acted with a large degree of autonomy. For the external relations with Madrid, each Viceroy was assisted by the *Secretario de Estado y de Guerra* of the Kingdom.

Each viceroyalty had its own major staff, which included a variable number of officers in charge of the management of military affairs. Usually, one lieutenant with the rank of *gobernador general de las armas* flanked the governor in wartime and stood in for him when he moved to the court

Don Pedro Nuno Colon de Portugal, sixth *duque* of Veraguas (1618–1673) here portrayed as a viceroy of Nueva España (Mexico). According to Clonard, in the 1640s before the American appointment Don Pedro was lieutenant colonel of the *Regimiento de la Guardia del Rey*, the old *Coronelia* raised by the *Conde Duque* Olivares, but in 1648 he actually held the rank of *sargento mayor* in the *tercio* of Diego de Portugal, which was quartered in Naples. Don Pedro succeeded to command of the *tercio* in 1655, serving in Lombardy against the French, and in 1658 or 1659 he finally held the rank of lieutenant colonel in the *Coronelia del Rey* until the unit was reformed as a provincial *tercio* in 1663. The Duke ended his career as viceroy of Nueva España. Along with Pedro Nuno Colon, in 1640 a significant proportion of the Portuguese elite, including many of the greater nobility, had gravitated to the royal court in Castile. Some of these people were in Spain when the uprising occurred; others were serving with Habsburg armies in Flanders or Catalonia. Felipe IV, after he had learned of the coup, was therefore able to convene a credible meeting of prominent expatriate Portuguese in Madrid to discuss what should be done. About 80 persons, overwhelmingly nobles, attended this gathering, and most subsequently maintained their loyalty to Spain, despite all of Lisbon's efforts to attract them back to Portugal. (Author's archive)

every six months. After him, the major staff comprised the *maestre de campo general* and the *capitán general de la caballería*. Both the ranks were a stepping stone to the office of captain general or even to a prominent office in the colonies. A further rank completed the major staff, usually without any limitation in number. This was the *general de la artillería*, a rank often awarded on an honorary basis, namely an officer did not need to have specific experience in artillery or sieges matters, for which the rank had been originally created. When more artillery generals were present, one of them held the charge of *capitán general de la artillería*. As with the rank of *general de la artillería*, more *generales de la caballería* were also appointed. The general staff of the army of Extremadura in 1662, comprised the *Generalissimo* Don Juan of Austria, with the *capitán general y gobernador de las armas del ejército*as his lieutenant, plus one *maestre de Campo general*, one *capitán general de la caballería*, one *capitán general de la artillería*, one *teniente general de la caballería* and one *general titular de la artillería*.

This apparently fixed pattern underwent some changes and updates with the introduction of new criteria for the leadership of troops in battle. Some of these began already under the reign of Felipe IV. In 1642, the positions of *comisario general de la infanteria* and the one of *teniente de maestre de campo general* were established.[5] In the 1650s, the same ranks were also created for the cavalry, in order to select field officers for the command of foot or horse.

Another important reform was the establishment of the commission in charge to the appointment for the rank of *maestre de campo*. This opened the way to the army's command to people who did not have a noble birth, or without the support of some grandee. But the most important act concerned the introduction of the rank *sargento mayor de batalla*, initially only for the army of Flanders, in 1648, and later extended also for Milan. This rank was to be used to improve the communication of the orders from the commander in chief to the units on the field. The presence of these officers in the frontier posts became usual

---

5   Serafín María de Sotto y Abach, conde de Clonard, *Historia orgánica de las armas de infantería y caballería española desde la creación del ejército permanente hasta nuestros días* (Madrid, 1851–62), vol. IV, p.415.

as an adjutant of the commander or viceroy. The *sargento mayor de batalla* and the *maestre de campo general* also performed autonomous command tasks in certain sectors of the border, often to exercise a role of control over military expenses. Usually, the *sargento mayor de batalla* was also the officer in charge to supervise the training of the militia, and in the 1660s the organisation in the field of the permanent provincial *tercios* also fell under his oversight.

A typical feature of the Hispanic armies of this period is the presence of a large number of senior officers with positions and designations not always consistent with the size of the armies. For instance, in the army of Lombardy there was the rank of *maestre de campo general de la caballería alemana*, who in practice held the command of the German cavalry companies in the *Estado de Milán*. Milan also established the office of *general de las armas del Estado de Milán*, and further positions dealing with the army, like the *comisario general del ejercito*, the *lugartenente general de la caballería* and others, who exercised the direction of work on the fortifications, recruitment, garrisons and supplies. Some of these were just honorary ranks, often created to satisfy an aristocracy which collected such positions for perpetuating their self-importance. After these major ranks, the military structure of each kingdom also comprised the officials in charge of control and administration. Their number varied accordingly with the strength of the contingent housed in the province, but each major army always included the *Veedor General del Ejército*, who managed the military finance and supervised the work of *Contador del Ejército* (army accountant), *Pagador General* (general paymaster), *Contador de la Artilleria* and *Contador de Viveres* (foodstuff accountant). Alongside them, the administration of the justice within the army was held by the *Superintendente de Justicia Militar*. In the management of finances, there was also an *Audiencier*, who could replace the *Veedor General del Ejercito* in the kingdoms without a large army, and finally a *Proveedor de la Armada* when a fleet was based in the province.

Infantry ensign, by Justus van Egmont (1601–1674), Flanders 1664–68 (Netherlands Institute for Art History). The Spanish Crown supplied resources in men and money for protecting its domains, but in the 1670s the war expenses were close to causing bankruptcy. To a large extent, the crisis accelerated the growing deterioration of the economy in Spain as well as in Flanders, already evident since the end of the sixteenth century, but increasingly dramatic during the next century. The deficit dragged on in the pay of the troops as well as the gap between the actual and paper availability of troops, growing until it reached scandalous figures.

The Officer Class

In early 1600s, the Italian–Albanian general Giorgio Basta attributed half of the effectiveness of a military unit to the commander, and the other half to his subordinates, excluding the soldiers. According to him, these latter were a mere instrument in the hand of the officers, who were the actual backbone of the army. Under this viewpoint, the Spanish army of the last Habsburgs has been often depicted like a military force directed by poorly trained officers. Nepotism, corruption, and lack of knowledge seems to be the most diffused defects of the Spanish officer class. However, the Spanish officers followed an apprenticeship similar to that of their colleagues in the rest of Europe, and nothing suggests that their training was worse than that received in other countries.

In this era there was not an academic military teaching method, therefore it was inevitable that the officer class would be highly inconsistent. Generally, the less prepared individuals were dropped as a result of the internal selection process, and this was probably what was lacking in Hispanic armies. Very often, the candidate officers gained their ranks thanks to the bonds of patronage typical of the Spanish social body in the age of *Los Austrias*.[6] Published research has focused on the fact that many of the senior officers came from the high aristocracy, and consequently it was their status that determined their career and not any knowledge or military talent. Certainly, being a member of the great nobility was a useful requirement, especially for accessing the higher ranks, but this background helped to create a negative image of the Spanish officer corps. Effectively, it appeared as if a world obsessed with hierarchy and noble titles that lengthened the names in a sometimes even comical way, and the negative attitudes of the aristocracy fuelled this picture. However, even in absence of any commander comparable to the greater captains of this age like Turenne, Condé or Montecuccoli, it seems incorrect to assume that background and nepotism were the main regulating factors of officers' careers in the age of *Los Austrias*, as several talented officers completed a first-rate military apprenticeship from the most renowned commanders of the previous generation.

Another recurring negative assumption regarding the army of the last Spanish Habsburgs is the one relating to the progressive disinterest of the nobility in the military profession. This view continues to be believed widely by historians. Nevertheless, a quick investigation is enough to understand that the statement cannot be applied everywhere. In the second half of the seventeenth century, the attractions of military service to the sovereign still exerted a significant influence on Castilian society.

Data and evidence would show that the aristocracy of all ranks did not lose interest in the army. In a multitude of testimonies concerning the military profession in Spain in the second half of the seventeenth century, the vast majority regard it as the most honourable, not only by the high-ranking nobility, but also by the *hidalgos* and bourgeois.[7] Officers of all classes considered the

---

6   On this topic see also Antonio Jiménez Estrella, 'Mérito, calidad y experiencia: criterios volubles en la provisión de cargos militares bajo los Austrias', in J.F. Pardo Molero and M.L. Cortés (eds), *Oficiales reales. Los ministros de la Monarquía Católica (siglos XVI–XVII)* (Valencia: Universitat de València, 2012), pp.241–264.

7   Augustin Moreno Jiménez, 'El estatus social de la profesión militar', in *Desperta Ferro* special issue XIX, June–July 2019, p.30.

profession of arms as the closest to the actual concept of nobility. What was happening, if anything, was the lack of incentives and gratifications, which was of concern to the officer class, including senior commanders.[8]

Obviously, the reality was not straightforward, but although the nobility did not abandon the military profession, on the other hand the misery and the boring conditions of garrisons life made a career in the army less attractive. As a result, there was a progressive reluctance of aristocrats to enter the army: this moved the more enterprising people to other occupations but enlarged the mass of cadets from the less well educated and inept subjects. Further problems arose from internal power relations. It is enough to read the lists of the senior officers of the armies of Flanders, Milan or Catalonia, to see that almost always the titled nobility monopolised the high ranks.

Among these officers there were also skilled commanders, like Juan Thomas Enriquez de Cabrera, Count of Melgar and future Duke of Medina de Rioseco; Carlos Guerra de Aragón, Duke of Villahermosa; Diego Felipe de Guzman y Rojas, Marquis of Leganes and Morata; or Francisco Antonio de Agurto, Marquis of Gastañaga; just to mention some of the most important and renowned. They all belonged to the higher level of the Spanish nobility, as well as holding the rank of senior commanders in the army. Alongside them and following a very representative career, Juan Antonio de Fonseca y Zuñiga Count of Monterrey (1640–1716) was the typical example of the high nobility who achieved important posts in the army after a lightning fast military career. In his youth, he served as a boy and gentleman to Felipe IV. From 1663, he was appointed as a knight of the Order of Santiago, and in 1664 entered the army as captain of cavalry in the Spanish Low Countries. In 1666 he was promoted to *maestre de campo* (colonel) of infantry, and one year later, after his generous financial support to the army of Flanders, he became *gobernador general de las armas*; an office which opened to him the appointment to viceroy of the Spanish Low Countries in 1670. Important positions in the army also went to personalities of the clergy, like that which occurred in 1662 in Galicia, when the bishop of La Coruña held the strategic direction of the defence, and in Sicily in 1674, with the viceroy-cardinal Portocarrero.

Nineteenth-century historiography has often portrayed the Spanish aristocracy as the main reason for the military decay of the Monarchy. However, it is not right to consider it as a whole as a ruling class lacking in talented men. Monterrey himself showed remarkable organisational skills, and in 1673–74 he offered decisive support to the army of the Dutch Republic in the most dramatic moment of its history. Alongside personalities with careers favoured since their birth, there were other aristocrats who

---

8   Among the most significant writings on the military profession in this age, the most interesting are the text of the *maestre de campo general* Francisco Ventura de la Sala y Abarca, entitled *Después de Dios. La primera obligación y glosa de Ordenes Militares* (Naples, 1681), the treaty of the *maestre de campo* Francisco Davila Gastón Orejón, *Excelencia del arte militar y varones ilustres* (Madrid 1683), and the work of the *teniente de maestro de las Armas* of the kingdom of Navarre, Juan Antonio de Arrieta Arandia, *Resumen de la verdadera destreza y modo fácil para saber los caminos verdaderos en la batalla* (Pamplona, 1688).

Francesco Tuttavilla del Tufo, Duke of San Germano (1604–1679). The Italian general was another skilled field commander of the Spanish Monarchy. In 1663, he suffered a bitter defeat at Ameixial-Estremoz as second in command under Don Juan of Austria, while facing the Portuguese and their allies under Friedrich Hermann von Schomberg. After his service in the Iberian Peninsula, in 1664 Tuttavilla was viceroy of Navarre. At the end of 1668 he was the successor of the assassinated viceroy of Sardinia, Manuel de los Cobos, Marquis of Camarasa, a post he held until January 1673. He then became viceroy of Catalonia, holding the command of the newly established field army of the Principality. In 1674 he captured the fortresses of Bellaguarda and Ceret, and achieved a successful campaign culminating in victory at the Battle of Maureillas, over a French army led by his old enemy Schomberg. However, the revolt of Messina against Spanish rule in 1675 deprived him of troops, allowing the French to retake their lost territories. (Author's collection)

dedicated themselves with zeal and seriousness to the military duties. Luis de Guzmán Ponce de Leon (1605–1668), governor of Milan from 1662, began his military career in 1629 already as *maestre de campo*, but he experienced a hard apprenticeship, participating in campaigns in Piedmont, Flanders, Portugal, Lombardy and Alsace. He was a resolute soldier, and with a strong temperament, who did not hesitate to oppose the opinion of great commanders, as happened in Lombardy with the Marquis of Leganes, who had him assigned to another front.

Even at the lower level, there are many members of some of the noblest families who embraced the military profession both because of their birth, they claimed the appointment to military ranks as their own right and, not least, because of their years of service in the army constituted an excellent springboard for a good career at court. Many aristocrats of all ranks followed a similar professional route, marked by joining the army as simple ensigns, or sometimes even as unpaid volunteers, although the less titled subjects had to work harder than the nobles of high rank did. This was the case of Augustin de Guzmán Portocarrero, future Marquis of Algaba, who, in 1666, after several years as simple voluntary cadet, was appointed as a captain of infantry in one company of the *tercios* raised for the Atlantic fleet. In 1674, he took the command of a *tercio* raised in Seville for the same task. Pedro José Guzmán Dávalos, the future Marquis de la Mina, also served in his company, and he was to become one of the most skilled artillery technicians of his time.[9] If there are numerous examples of Spanish aristocrats, who have chosen the profession of arms, the case of the commoners constitutes an equally large group, and this despite the difficulties which they faced in climbing the military hierarchy. The service reports preserved in the Spanish archives show many careers of officers of non-noble origins, who, more often starting from the rank of simple soldier, or sometimes from non-commissioned officer, began their professional and social rise.

Not too differently, the careers of the many cadets of the nobility also followed particular trajectories. This is the case of Antonio López de

---

9   AGI, *Indiferente, Servicios de Augustin de Guzmán Portocarrero.*

Velasco y Cárdenas, from 1667 Count of Fuensalida as successor to his deceased brother. His military career began in 1662, as captain of an infantry company serving in the fleet. In the war against Portugal, López de Velasco fought under the Marquis of Caracena at Montes Claros in 1665. After the years of service in Extremadura, in 1669 the creation of the infantry regiment of the *Guarda del Rey* offered Fuensalida the opportunity to improve his career. The support of a noble in the creation of the regiment who was highly regarded by the queen and regent Maria Anna of Austria, who assigned him the command of a company. This appointment had a high strategic value in Fuensalida's future career, coupled with a wise marriage which related him to the powerful family of the Marquis of Bedmar. In 1671, the Count assumed the rank of *general de las armas* in Milan, then in 1673, the Queen appointed him as captain in the *Guardias de Castilla*, and in 1676, despite the criticisms received during his office in Milan, he obtained the appointment as Viceroy of Navarre. In 1677, the decline in the powers of Maria Anna of Austria did not negatively affect the career of the count, who between 1681 and 1682 held the position of Viceroy in Galicia, then in Sardinia until 1686 and finally a second mandate in Milan in 1686, an appointment that also earned him a seat into the *consejo de estado*.[10]

Naturally the officers of the Royal Guards, due to their proximity to the monarch, were favoured in their military career and in their ascent to the higher ranks. The military career of José de Garro is a typical case in this context. A native of the Basque Country, Garro joined the army in 1646 as *alférez* (ensign) of an infantry company in Yucatan. Three years later, he obtained permission to return to Spain, where he continued to serve as an officer in the army of Flanders until 1655. A year later, with the rank of captain, he was transferred to Catalonia, and then, in 1659, he was appointed *sargento mayor* in the infantry *tercio* of the Count of Aguilar, with whom he served in Galicia until the end of hostilities with Portugal.

In 1668, Garro was one of the many officers dismissed as a result of the end of the war and the demobilisation of the armed force, but in 1669 he was among the lucky ones who obtained a post as an officer in the newly constituted *Guarda del Rey* foot regiment in Madrid. For merits achieved in the new position, he obtained again the rank of titular *sargento mayor*, and in 1671 he was awarded the Order of the Knights of Santiago by the Queen. The positive continuation of his service is confirmed in the record of service, which describes Garro as 'a soldier of such rank and a well-known veteran', but despite these merits, in 1673 Garro was appointed as *maestre de campo* and rewarded with the modest office of military commander at Tucumán (today San Miguel de Tucumán in Argentina). However, in 1678, Garro was transferred to Buenos Aires, as interim military governor of

---

10 Antonio Alvarez-Ossorio Alvariño, 'La Chamberga: el regimiento de la guardiea del rey y la salvaguarda de la majestad (1668–1677)', in *Gobierno de corte y sociedad politica: continuidad y cambio en el gobierno de la Monarquia de España en Europa entorno a la Guerra de Sucesión (1665–1725)* (Madrid, 2012), pp.60–61: 'It seems significant that one of the European strategic bastions of the Monarchy, the State of Milan, was ruled by former captains of the *Chamberga* (the regiment of Foot Guards) continuously between 1678 and 1691.'

Charles Antoine Count of Calonne (1602–1672), a Walloon *maestre de campo*, who like many others remained without employment after the Peace of the Pyrenees and the subsequent reduction of the army's strength. Calonne served for 10 years in Catalonia, and after temporarily returning to Flanders in the 1660s, he was appointed as governor of Cartagena in the Kingdom of Murcia. (Author's collection)

the Rio de la Plata province, and in 1680 he was in command of the troops that occupied the Portuguese colony of Sacramento, during the diplomatic conflict with the Portuguese court. In 1682, Garro's South American career continued in Santiago de Chile as governor, captain general and president of the province's *Audiencia*, a post he held for 10 years. Upon his return to Spain in 1696, Garro received the title of Governor of Gibraltar and finally, in 1701, he returned to the Basque Country as governor of Guipúzcoa, where he died a year later.[11]

The military careers of the Spaniards are not very different from the ones of the subjects coming from the other domains of the Monarchy. Italian nobles as well as commoners served in the Spanish armies since the Middle Ages. In the following centuries, the Crown welcomed the collaboration of local elites in the European wars as well as in America, making the Italians one of the most significant military elite.[12] Germans, Flemish, Walloons, Irish or other nationalities within the army, rarely came to occupy important positions within the ranks of the senior command, which cannot be said for the Italians. Throughout the seventeenth century, the Italians had been always present in the army and many of them occupied high positions within the general staff. Among them, Francesco Tuttavilla, Duke of San Germano (1608–1679), may be considered the archetypal Italian soldiers and captain of his age to serve Spain, and probably one of the most successful. A veteran in the army of Catalonia; he was assigned to Extremadura during the war against Portugal.

In 1657, San Germano distinguished himself during the siege of Olivença, and one year later directed the defence of Badajoz, a task described as heroic by his contemporaries. In 1662, he held the office of *gobernador general de las armas*. After the Spanish defeat suffered at Ameixial-Estremoz in 1663, San Germano left the army of Extremadura, and from April 1664 until February 1668, he was Viceroy of Navarre. At the end of 1668, he was the successor of the assassinated Viceroy of Sardinia, Manuel de los Cobos, Marquis of Camarasa, a post he held until January 1673. In the same year, San Germano was appointed as *capitán general* of Cataluña and then became Viceroy from August 1673 to October 1675. During this office, he gained great reputation

---

11 Enrique de Arillaga, *Un generalespañol del siglo XVII* (Madrid, 1935).

12 Among the many Italians in the service of Spain, there were many who entered the army thanks to high-ranking kinship. This was the case of Filippo Buoncompagni, son of the Duke of Soria and nephew of Pope Gregory XIII, who obtained the appointment as a cavalry captain in Milan, despite his youth and lack of military competence. See Maffi, *Los últimos tercios*, p.280.

as field commander leading successful actions in Roussillon and the Pyrenees. In 1674, he seized the Fort of Bellagarda, held by the French since 1659, and successively won the battle of Maureillas, defeating the French led by the Duke of Schomberg.

Other prominent Italian military commanders were Giovanni Francesco Serra, Marquis of Almendralejo, *gobernador de las armas* in the army of Catalonia under Don Juan of Austria, or Tiberio Brancaccio, *capitán general de la caballería* in Catalonia since 1647, and later governor of Tarragona. Several Italian captains who entered the army under Felipe IV achieved important careers. Among them, Geronimo Carafa Caracciolo, Marquis of Montenegro, a military professional and member of the War Council, who became Viceroy of Aragon, and Francesco Maria Carafa-Castriota e Gonzaga, Duke of Nocera, a veteran of Nördlingen and later *capitán general* in Aragon. The Italian presence in the command staff continued during the reign of Carlos II also with captains from northern Italy, such as the Prince Alessandro Farnese, great-grandson of the *gran general* of Felipe II. The Prince became a renowned cavalry commander during the war against Portugal, and successively *capitán general* in Catalonia, and later in Flanders. With him, the Genoese Paolo Spinola Doria, nephew of the equally

Manuel Díego López de Zuñiga Guzmán Sotomayor y Mendoza (1660–1686), portrayed as a *maestre de campo* in a print dated 1683. Note the pageboy carrying the shield, which marked the rank of commander. Zuñiga valiantly served during the War of the Reunion (1683–84) in Luxembourg, and in 1685 joined the Imperial army in the war against the Porte. In Hungary, he and other Spanish aristocrats managed to raise a whole Spanish regiment for Imperial service, but despite 500 troops being gathered between 1685 and 1686, the project did not succeed. On 13 July 1686 Zuñiga was killed in action during the siege of Buda. (Author's collection)

famous *generalissimo* Ambrogio Spinola, achieved a successful career as captain and a diplomat. The Neapolitan family Pignatelli appears several time among the Spanish captains under Felipe IV and Carlos II. During the war against Portugal, Giovanni Battista Pignatelli was selected for his service as a *maestre de campo* of an infantry Italian regiment,[13] while his son Domenico was appointed governor of Gerona, where he distinguished himself during the French siege of 1684. In 1686, Domenico became *capitán general* of the cavalry of the army of Catalonia, and successively was appointed *maestre de campo general* and viceroy of Navarre. His continued his career, holding the same office in Galicia.

The Italians could make use of their wide network of relationships that extended to the Austrian Habsburgs and often there were great and lesser

---

13 AGS, *Estado*, leg. 2090, *Consulta del Consejo de Estado*, dated 7 January 1670: in the opinion of the Council, it was necessary to maintain only a single Italian *tercio*, namely the one of the *maestre de campo* Giovanni Battista Pignatelli, because the quality of the troops, and because he always performed positively in every action.

Right: Paolo Spinola (1628–1699), third Marquis of the Balbases and third Duke of San Severino and Sesto, here portrayed by Cornelis Meyssens. The Genoese family gave soldiers and officials to Spain for 10 generations from the sixteenth to the twentieth century. Paolo Spinola held the office of governor of Milan between 1668 and 1670 and then served as Spanish ambassador to Vienna and later Paris. He was another Italian serving Spain who managed the affairs of the Spanish Monarchy in the turbulent era of the last Habsburg kings. With new research leading to a reinterpretation of the issues, increasing attention has been paid to the key regions and the personalities involved, such as the *Estado de Milan*, which was the seat of one of the largest armies of the Monarchy. (Author's collection)

Left: Alessandro Farnese, Prince of Parma (1615–1682). A member of the Ducal house, he served as general of cavalry in Extremadura, achieving several successes against the Portuguese in 1663 and 1664. The Prince became Governor of the Spanish Low Countries from 1678 to 1682.

families of the Italian nobility with members who served in the Imperial army.[14] Along with the multi-referenced family Carafa, who had a long series of captains in both the Habsburgs' armies, the Gonzaga followed with another famed officer: Vincenzo (1602–1694), a member of the cadet branch of the family from Guastalla. He entered the Spanish army as an ensign in 1632 and climbed the military hierarchy serving in Flanders and Lombardy. In 1652, Vincenzo was promoted general of cavalry and four years later received the office of *capitán general* in Galicia, which he held until 1658. In 1664, Vincenzo was appointed as Viceroy of Catalonia and later of Sicily in 1678. Here he successfully achieved the conquest of Messina with the surrender of the rebel city. The career continued at court, as counsellor of the state and later of the Indies, an office that Vincenzo held until 1685. He died aged 92, celebrated with the highest honour.[15] During the seventeenth century, Italians also occupied positions of importance in the command of the Spanish forces in the Iberian Peninsula, and several took over the governments and commands of primary importance in the army of Catalonia, like Carlo Giovanni Gandolfo in the 1670s, or Bernardo and Martino Carafa in the 1680s.

Throughout the seventeenth century, the nobility of the Spanish Low Countries was always considered as a highly reputed warrior elite and warlike aristocracy, which had played a decisive role in defending the country since the previous century. From the beginning of Spanish rule, the region continued to provide loyal and trusted soldiers and captains, and whilst relations between Madrid and Brussels intensified over the centuries, the Flemish Walloons soon formed a core component of

Gregorio Carafa della Roccella (1615–1690), after *Il Genio Bellicoso di Napoli* (Naples, 1694). Great Master of the Knights of Malta, Carafa served in the Monarchy's army between 1641 and 1652. From 1660 to 1690, the Neapolitan Carafa family supplied to the Hispanic armies six senior officers, and further members served in the Imperial army in the same years. Between 1660 and 1663, 11,000 Italians arrived in the Iberian Peninsula to serve in Extremadura, a similar number serving during the following decades in Flanders and Catalonia, making the Italians the second nationality in the Monarchy's armies. As proudly stated by contemporary commentators: 'without Spaniards and Italians there would be no army of Flanders'.

14 See Mugnai, *Wars and Soldiers in the Early Reign of Louis XIV*, vol. 2, pp.177–181.

15 Davide Maffi, 'Fieles y leales vasallos del rey. Soldados italianos en los ejércitos de los Austrias hispano senelsiglo XVII', in José María Blanco Núñez (ed.), 'Presencia italiana en la milicia española', *International Review of Military History* N. 94 (Madrid: International Commission of Military History, 2016), p.60.

Spanish armies in central Europe. Despite this, and unlike the Italians, the Flemish Walloons appeared only marginally within the chain of command of the armies that fought on the borders of Catalonia and Portugal, and few held prominent positions in the Spanish military leadership outside the Spanish Low Countries, and in general, members of the most important families showed a certain reluctance to leave their country to serve in the Iberian Peninsula.[16]

However, there were some great Flemish Walloon nobles who achieved leadership positions both within and outside their country. Among them, in the central decades of the century, the Prince Claude Lamoral of Ligne was *capitán general de la caballería* in Flanders, then in 1670 became Viceroy of Sicily and in 1674 moved to Milan as governor. There was also the Count of Isenghien, Knight of the Golden Fleece, who held the rank of Lieutenant General of the Cavalry in Extremadura in the 1660s. Another successful career was the one of Louis de Scey, who served as general commissioner of cavalry. Among the other Flemish Walloon professional soldiers who arrived in Spain, there was the Viscount of Lomberque, cavalry commander in the army of Catalonia, and Jean-François Benjamin de Bournonville, younger brother of the Duke Alexandre de Bournonville who, in 1655, had voluntarily recruited an infantry *tercio* for the army of Catalonia. Other prominent Flemish Walloon captains were the Viscount of Furnes, of the house of the Counts of Hornes, who became Lieutenant General of the Cavalry of Flanders, and then after 1660, in Galicia, or the princes of Brabançon, Octave Ignace de Ligne-Arenberg, and his father Albert, who died in 1674 still serving the Monarchy as governor of Ypres.

The presence of Flemish Walloon officers continued and other military dynasties, like T'Serclaes de Tilly and Croÿ contributed to the defence of the Spanish Low Countries with other loyal officers. From the latter family came the charismatic Ferdinand Gaston, Count of Roeulx, who in 1684, after participating in the defence of Luxembourg, had spent 33 years in the army, and closed his career as governor of Hainault in 1697. However, none of them achieved honours and awards comparable to those gained by the aforementioned Alexandre Hippolyte Balthasar de Bournonville. He was the son and heir of Alexandre de Bournonville, first Duke of Bournonville, Earl of Hennin, Viscount and Baron of Barlin and Houllefort, a famous veteran of the campaigns of Ambrogio Spinola at the turn of the century, and second in command to Bucquoy during the campaigns against the Bohemian Protestants. Following the family's tradition, Alexandre Hippolyte enlisted at a very young age into a company under one of his father's captains, and in his early twenties he was promoted to cavalry captain in the Imperial regiment of Count Ottavio Piccolomini. Back in Flanders, he entered the Spanish army and by the last stages of the Thirty Years' War he had achieved a brilliant career: colonel of a German infantry regiment, and in 1652 *sargento general*

---

16 Davide Maffi, 'Una epopeya olvidada. Los flamencos/valones al servicio de la monarquía española (siglo XVII)', in E. Martínez Ruiz (ed.), 'Presencia de flamencos y valones en la milicia española', *International Review of Military History* N. 96 (Madrid: International Commission of Military History, 2016), pp.68–69.

de batalla, and then *governador de armas* of the corps sent to support the Prince de Condé. With this rank he took part in the siege of Arras (1654) and in the defence of Valenciennes (1656). His loyalty to the Habsburgs was compensated for by the granting him the title of Prince of Bournonville and Buggenhout. It was during the War of Devolution that his reputation as a commander gained further prestige, eventually earning the consideration of Carlos II. Thanks to the support from the 'Spanish party' in Vienna, in 1674 Bournonville received the command of the Imperial army in Alsace.

However, the campaign resulted in a bitter failure, even if in partial defence of the prince, some account must be taken of the fact that he had to face one of the best commanders of the century: the Viscount of Turenne.[17] Despite his failure and resignation from the Imperial army in 1675, Bournonville's prestige remained considerable, since in July 1676, he received the position of commanding general of Spanish troops in Catalonia. Together with the Prince Alessandro Farnese, he directed the invasion of Roussillon and succeeded in the expulsion of the French from Cerdaña. After a period spent in Sicily, where he replaced Francesco Gattinara, Marquis of San Martino, as *governador de armas* and commander in chief of the field army during the Messina rebellion, in 1679, Bournonville returned to Catalonia with the rank of governor and captain general of the Principality, and during his time in this office he was successful in the defence of Gerona.[18] Bournonville continued to serve in Catalonia until 1686, when he was appointed viceroy and captain general of the Kingdom of Navarre to replace the Prince of Chimay, another Walloon, who never took charge. The Prince died in Pamplona on 10 August 1690, while still holding this office.

Alongside the Flemish Walloons, Franche-Comté also provided several notable commanders. One of the most prominent Franche-Comtois military leaders, who maintained his functions in the Spanish army after the loss of the country, was the Baron Jean-Claude de Bressey. His military career began around 1650 with the rank of captain. Over the following decades, the Baron continued in service until he was promoted *maestre de campo* of a Walloon infantry *tercio*. In 1674, his loyalty to the Habsburg cause earned him the seizure of his properties in Franche-Comté and, consequently, the protection of the governors of the Spanish Low Countries. Bressey's desire to 'serve under the gentle rule of Carlos II' was rewarded in 1686 with a rich revenue in the County of Namur and, three years later, with the promotion to *sargento general de batalla*. Such awards were supposed to satisfy his

---

17 The criticisms about his command were bitter and came from authoritative personalities: 'The Elector of Brandenburg spoke, and wrote with more vehemence and contempt against him (Bournonville), because he had prevented the execution of the plans he wisely meditated against Turenne. Generals Caprara and Dunevald (*sic*), who in several campaigns, and individually in this one, had performed with admirable valour, both refused to serve again under him. The King of Spain, of whom he was born a subject, then called him for a command in Spain.' In *Scelta di Azioni egregie operate in guerra da generali e da soldati italiani* (Venezia, 1742), p.180.

18 The Duke of Alba left an extensive account about the campaign of 1684 in Catalonia, describing Bournonville as 'one of the last remaining military talents of the Monarchy'; in Antonio Espino López, *Cataluña durante el reinado de Carlos II. Política y guerra en la frontera catalana, 1679–1697* (Barcelona: Bellaterra – Universitat Autónoma de Barcelona, 1999), pp.108–109.

wishes, but after being taken prisoner by Marshal Boufflers in Mons in 1691, Bressey joined the French army. Immediately, Louis XIV promoted him to *Maréchal de Camp* and, on 6 April 1696, *Lieutenant General* together with a large group of officers of the general staff.[19]

The case of Baron de Bressey remained an exception among the Burgundian captains of Carlos II. The striking betrayal of him differs from the behaviour of numerous aristocrats and soldiers who served both in the Low Countries and in the State of Milan. Among the most renowned officer who served in Flanders, Prosper-Ambrose de Precipiano, Count of Soye, *sargento general de batalla* and, in consideration of his excellent qualities as commander, a *protegé* of the court secretary Manuel Francisco de Lira and by the King himself, who remained in the service of Spain even after the cession of Franche-Comté to France. Likewise, Alexandre-Ignace-Guillaume de Pontamougeard had an equally exemplary career. A native of Salins, on 22 December 1672 he was appointed *maestre de campo* of the infantry *tercio de borgoñones* (EI-43) by the Count of Monterrey, and in the following April became governor of his hometown. Despite the few troops under his command, Pontamougeard offered a stubborn resistance and eventually obtained an honourable surrender for his garrison. Transferred to Flanders, he participated in subsequent campaigns against the French and won the favour of the Duke of Villahermosa, the new governor general of the Spanish Low Countries.

Pontamougeard was chosen to be among the signatories of the cessation of hostilities which took place in Mons on 19 August 1678, thus putting an end to the conflict that ended with the loss of his native province. He died in 1689, after receiving the title of Baron of the Holy Roman Empire from Emperor Leopold I. In the same years, Jean Charles de Watteville de Joux, Marquis de Conflans, a nephew of the gallant general Charles de Watteville, came to the fore. After a prestigious military career in the army of Flanders, in 1697 he held the office of Viceroy of Navarre. The Franche-Comtois military history also includes Pierre Sordet de Nozeroy, a cousin of Watteville, who was colonel of a German regiment in Catalonia between 1677 and 1682. His fame derives from having commanded the oldest of the German regiments in Spanish service. Sordet de Nozeroy spent his career in exile, having chosen to remain loyal to Carlos II. Even the Thirty Years' War veteran Jean-Claude Prost, also known as *Capitán Lacuzon*, who had faced the French troops at a very young age in 1636, chose to remain loyal to Spain and, despite infirmity due to his age, after 1674 he served in Italy as an infantry captain in the Burgundian *tercio Grammont* (EI-45).

A last but significant son of the Franche-Comtois who fought for Carlos II was the legendary *Bras-de-Fer*. A bourgeois from Besançon, he left his native country in 1674 as a consequence of the French occupation and moved to the Spanish Low Countries with the aim of continuing to fight against France. In a campaign of 'partisan warfare' and cross-border raids, this skilled guerrilla leader achieved several successes against the French,

---

19   Quirós Rosado, *La fiel nación.* pp.77–78.

especially in the winter of 1677–1678.[20] According to the notices sent from Brussels, on 14 February 1678, *Bras-de-Fer* penetrated with 30 men into enemy territory and headed for the forest of Soignies where he surprised an enemy column. The French were surprised, and the 'Burgundian' chief killed most of the enemies and captured 24 prisoners, which earned him the promise of the Duke of Villahermosa the appointment to the rank of captain in a vacant infantry company. The presence of exiles from Franche-Comté was not limited only to aristocrats, scholars[21] or irregular militiamen, but also included several professional soldiers who kept alive the ancient Burgundian military tradition in the Spanish army. The sudden annexation of the province by France and the establishment of punitive measures against the pro-Habsburg loyalists, fuelled the departure of subjects openly hostile to the new rulers but, at the same time, favoured the careers of those who remained faithful to *Los Austrias*.

Spain always welcomed a large number of commanders from every corner of Europe and among these the foreigners formed an extremely varied group, so much so as to make the Spanish armies among the most cosmopolitan of the whole century. Along with its already wide ethnic makeup, the Spanish army also numbered officers from Germany, France, Lorraine, England, Ireland, Scotland, Denmark and Portugal.

The Financing of the Armies and the Military Administration

In his *Política Militar de Príncipes*, dedicated to Carlos II, Juan Baños de Velasco insisted that the poor pay of the soldiers was the cause of countless problems. The lack of money was the cause of a spiral of multiple complications that could hardly be stopped, such as poor discipline and harassment of the

---

20 *Ibid.*, p.88. At the beginning of 1678, *La Gazeta Ordinaria de Madrid*, published by François Faivre de Brémondans, informed the readers about the pitiful situation of his homeland, and of the fierce struggle against the enemy. The opposition of the faithful inhabitants of Franche-Comté to the new 'inhuman' French rulers gave hope for a possible reconquest of the country.

21 The same confidence from the Viceroys of the Spanish Low Countries was gained by a specialist in matters of the laws of war law: Claude-Joseph Brulez. A direct descendant of the Imperial secretary Louis Mercy, who had been appointed to the Burgundian nobility by Charles V after the Battle of Pavia. Brulez had travelled to the Low Countries in his youth as secretary of several Spanish and Walloons officials. He distinguished himself for more than 30 years in this post, earning a reputation as a skilled translator of Spanish, Latin and French. Sent to Luxembourg, he became the personal agent of governors Villahermosa, Farnese, Grana and the Prince of Chimay to negotiate with the French ministers the 'usurpations' committed in the Duchy, as well as personally taking up arms during the Reunion war of 1683–84. After the transfer of his last master to the post of viceroy of Navarre, Brulez was appointed head of the provincial court of Pamplona. In that city, he subsequently obtained the honorary, but still prestigious, office of secretary to the king and, finally, that of Spanish plenipotentiary commissioner at the border conferences. Some non-military subjects found protection in Lombardy, such as the secretary of the Besançon Episcopal Council, Jean-Claude Fallot. After tampering with a judicial process due to his political ambiguity during the French invasion, he gained the trust of prominent ministers in Madrid, hoping to obtain a future ecclesiastical position in Italy, instead of a military job in Lombardy. See also Quirós Rosado, *La fiel nación*, pp.79–80.

civilian population, desertion and finally the disbandment of the armies.[22] It appears obvious, but this does not mean that the problem seemed less serious and difficult to solve, especially in the dramatic economic scenario of this age. Spain encountered serious problem defending the borders of its overextended empire in the previous centuries. However, during the reigns of Felipe IV, and later Carlos II, the wars became even more expensive both in terms of number of soldiers and increasing costs of paying them. Faced with these challenges, the most serious limitations were that the Spain had an outdated economy and sparse population, which could not be further diverted from work to reinforce the army. The quality of the troops available and, above all, their quantity, was often inadequate.

The major difficulty was not raising soldiers but maintaining and disciplining them until they became fully trained and veterans. This was a status that seemed more difficult to achieve, not because there were no veteran troops, but because most of them had been hired regiments due to a lack of native personnel. Therefore, from the 1650s, the first problem for Spain was not military, but economic. The military and political efforts of the last Spanish Habsburg kings encountered the same insurmountable obstacle: lack of money. In order to curb the debt, there was no lack of attempts to redress the deficit reforming the most antiquated accounting procedures. Much progress was due to the work of the governors, but the initiatives to improve the administrative and the introduction of more functional accounting procedures started from Madrid. The need not to disturb consolidated procedures and interests that involved the *naturales* and the Spanish ministers, forced Madrid to adopt some compromises.

As for concerns the domains outside the Iberian Peninsula, the Crown was forced to accept these compromises in Italy as well as in the Spanish Low Countries. Since both these domains constituted the most key strategic areas, their military administration was a very sensitive nerve for the Spanish Crown. In the attempt to introduce instruments of control, the Crown aimed to limit the extraordinary power accumulated by the senior officers, who had formed in each domain a *cúpula militar*.[23] Strengthened by this position of power, they had been able to extend their control over the management of military spending in favour of their clientele. In Brussels, as well as in Milan and Naples, attempts were made to control the military spending intensifying controls and extending the authority of the local magistrates. Despite this effort, once again, the Crown was forced to move with caution in this delicate dispute in order not to compromise the fragile balance between the ruling house and its domains.

In homage to the principle that 'the sovereign finance the war', the costs for the sustenance of the army were managed by the *Real hacienda*.[24] The still shaky financial conditions of the Spanish Monarchy, however, made even paying the

---

22 Baños de Velasco y Acevedo, *Política militar de Príncipes* (Madrid, 1680), pp.38–39.
23 Alicia Esteban Estríngana, *Guerra y finanzas en los Países Bajos católicos. De Farnesio a Spinola (1592–1630)* (Madrid: Laberinto, 2001), p.31.
24 Mario Rizzo, *Alloggiamenti militari e riforme fiscali nella Lombardia spagnola tra Cinque e Seicento* (Milan: Unicopli, 2001), p.50.

soldiers' wages a challenge. The most critical problem always remained the regularity of the payment.[25] In this regard, in the last years of the seventeenth century, the Milanese Jesuit Corrado Confalonieri wrote that:

> The army has a stomach, indeed of a quite admirable nature. It will continue fasting for up to six months … costing its Prince little more than bread of ammunition, and some little aid. … This custom of waging war without the due payments is a bad cause of two worst effects. The first is the necessity of the Soldiery to get supplies in the friendly, or enemy, country in the pause, and much more in the march. The second effect forces officers and soldiers to imitate the ants, and to provide for themselves in the winter quarters, in order to subsist on campaign in the summer. The country and the villager must therefore provide the Army for almost the whole year in six months of accommodation.[26]

Since the reign of Felipe IV, the most exposed provinces like Flanders and Spanish Lombardy had consumed the largest part of the Monarchy's expenses. The process accelerated throughout the second half of the seventeenth century, with less and less adequate resources being sent from Madrid and the other territories, due to the emergence of new military fronts. In practice, the principle was that each domain paid for their own troops. This rule also applied when the troops served outside their borders: a condition that in the disastrous economic and financial scenario was a source of innumerable problems.

The analysis of the general expenditures between 1659 and 1688 always shows the huge preponderance on military spending, which was close to 90 percent of the total expenses, while the remainder was used for the maintenance of the royal house, diplomacy, pensions and other minor expenses.[27] In 1663, on the eve of the new campaign against Portugal, the government realised that it did not have sufficient funds to maintain the army. As had happened several times before, the budget turned out to be sufficient for just one third of the expenses, as the resources necessary for the maintenance of troops in the domains, and other funds requested by the embassies in Europe, had been wrongly calculated. Nonetheless, the government prioritised the war with Portugal despite the severe shortage of money.

In 1663, after failing to quickly defeat the Portuguese, the Crown was forced to recover from the expense sustained in the period 1659–1662. The military spending was reduced by 32 percent for the army of Extremadura, 24 percent for Galicia, and 37 percent in Castile. A further reduction interested the royal navy and the troops outside the Iberian Peninsula, with 39 and 47 percent respectively, the costs for recruitment diminished

---

25 Geoffrey Parker, *The Army of Flanders and the Spanish Road, 1567–1659: the logistics of Spanish victory and defeat in the Low Countries' wars* (Cambridge: Cambridge University Press, 1972), p.142. The author states – with some exaggeration – that 'the soldiers received the salary so rarely that they could say that they did not know *que cosa es paga.*'

26 Alessandro Buono, *Esercito, istituzioni, territorio. Alloggiamenti militari e 'case herme' nello Stato di Milano (secoli XVI e XVII)* (Florence: Firenze University Press, 2009), p.25.

27 Antonio José Rodríguez Hernández, 'Asientos y asentistas militares en el siglo XVII: el ejemplo del pan y la pólvora', in *Comercio y Finanzas Internacionales en una España en Transición, 1680–1721* (Universidad de Salamanca, 2013), pp.63–64.

by 62 percent, and only the garrisons in Catalonia and in Africa had no budget cuts. The military spending decreased from 15,802,619 to 10,834,839 *ducados*.[28] This measure aimed to produce savings to allow the decisive effort in the campaigns against Portugal.

During the tumultuous years of the reign of Carlos II, the general cost of the war had increased five times compared to the costs sustained by his great-grandfather Felipe II. The army continued to represent one of the most conspicuous items of expenditure in the budgets of the state, and did not show an inversion of tendency, the Monarchy being involved on multiple fronts. The young king and his court secretaries tried to untangle the accounts, but in addition to the involvement in Portugal, in 1667 the War of Devolution against France caused further concerns. The peace of Aix-la-Chapelle was a good opportunity for planning a reform of military expenditure. In 1669, the reports prepared by the *Consejo de Hacienda* estimated that royal rents amounted to nearly 12 million *ducados*, and although they were 3 million more than the previous year, net of interest and other expenses there remained only 5,778,469 *ducados*, which could cover only 80 percent of military spending.[29]

In the 1670s, the threats of a new bankruptcy alienated many of the Crown's traditional financiers, so much so that it had been necessary to turn to the recent adversaries – the Portuguese – who, through their network of relations in the Dutch Republic, were able to bring the money for the army in Flanders, obtaining as a counterpart the income from the Bolivian silver mines of Potosí.[30] Despite all these difficulties, during the Franco-Dutch War the Spanish treasury collected enough resources for financing the campaigns, at least until 1677, when a new dramatic financial crisis caused serious problems to the Spanish war effort, bringing the debt at 20 million *ducados*.[31]

The short period of peace between 1679 and 1682 brought some relief. Despite this, the scenario had not changed, because in 1680, the urgent needs alone would cost 19,849,148 *escudos*, but only barely half sum was available, namely 9,499,471.[32] To face this emergency, the Spanish treasury resorted to various expedients, trying not to increase the tax burden on the country's economy. The refunds for public debt lenders were further deferred, and in some cases even suspended. The government also turned to private credit and even asked for donations from the provinces, including recruits for the army. Loan titles were issued every year with increasing interests, which, however, the treasury did not regularly pay. The consequences of this policy were the progressive depreciation of the titles. The needs of war forced the government to turn to the clergy. In 1678, Pope Innocent XI authorised Carlos II to apply

---

28 AGS, *Guerra Antigua*, leg. 2026.

29 Juan A. Sánchez Belén, 'La financiaión de la guerra en el reinado de Carlos II', in *Desperta Ferro*, special issue XIX, June–July 2019, p.40: 'Practically, moreover, this money was used to cover the expenses for military supplies of the previous years and therefore the treasury remained only with 503,107 *ducados*, a sum that for the fiscal years 1670 and 1671 would have been further reduced to 201,986 and 309,778 *ducados* respectively.'

30 *The New Cambridge Modern History*, Vol. 5, *The Ascendancy of France, 1648–1688*, p.478.

31 Sánchez Belén, 'La financiaión de la guerra en el reinado de Carlos II', p.41.

32 Rodríguez Hernández, 'Guerra y alianzas en la lucha por la hegemonía europea', p.260.

a tithe to the ecclesiastical income, in order to extract 800,000 *ducados* in four years. The sum was reduced to 490,000 *ducados*, because the opposition of part of the ecclesiastical hierarchy, but this act represented a major novelty in the history of the Spanish–Papal relations.

Obviously, each kingdom and province had to contribute with more and more resources to support the troops in their territories, as the royal treasury was no longer able to finance the wars. Resources for the armies were raised not only from the most threatened provinces, such as the Spanish Low Countries, Catalonia and Milan, but the kingdom of Naples also contributed to the war effort with various forms of funding. The conspicuous presence of Spanish troops in Lombardy as well as in the Low Countries took many forms, which helps to explain the complexity of the process of equalizing military burdens.[33] In the *Milanesado* the most important of the military taxes, and the reference point for the entire tax system, was the so-called *mensuale* (monthly).

This was still the original extraordinary tax introduced in 1536 by Carlos I, suspended in 1537 but restored in 1545 and updated several times up to 1653. However, already in the 1560s, this tax was no longer sufficient to pay the troops because the war expenses were quickly increasing; therefore, before the end of the century, further taxes were introduced. The first of these was the *tasso d'ambo le cavallerie* (the tax for the cavalry), consisting of the obligation to supplement the sums paid from the royal treasury to the cavalry quartered in the state. The tax for the cavalry was followed by the burden of the *quattordici reali* (fourteen *reales*), or the monthly payment for each cavalrymen. This tax was also introduced as an extraordinary subsidy, but within a few years it became a new permanent tax.[34]

To complete the financial burdens there were the so-called *presidi ordinari*, namely the obligation to maintain the ordinary presiding forces in the state. In addition to these financial burdens, there were the military servitudes that included services and supplies to which the communities were obliged, like furniture and utensils for the quarters, wood for heating, oil or candles for lighting, and forage for horses. Some of these burdens, especially food, fodder and billets, could be provided by the communities, but the civil authorities preferred to pay, instead of billeting the soldiers in private homes or in the territory, since the forced hospitality always involved significant costs, and sometimes even considerable economic damage, without considering accidents and problems of public order. The expenses deriving from the military presence affected only the communities where the troops were quartered.

---

33 As for the financing of the troops in Spanish Low Countries, see Rooms, *De organisatie van de troepen van de Spaans-Habsburgse monarchie in de Zuidelijke Nederlanden.*

34 It was up to the communities to choose the so-called *composizione* as an alternative to the actual billeting of the soldiers. Theoretically, the sum of 14 *reales* per month per ration corresponded to the limit that the soldiers could have demanded. However, these agreements between the soldiers and the billeting communities had given rise to abuses because the officers often managed to obtain exorbitant compensation in exchange. Further reading in Davide Maffi, *La cittadella in armi*, pp.180–181.

This inequality generated a heated debate both in Italy and in the Spanish Low Countries, where the southern frontier assumed the major burden of the military presence, as occurred in Lombardy and to a certain extent in the kingdom of Naples. Since the beginning of the seventeenth century, the Spanish governors managed this matter with mixed results. In the *Estado de Milán*, the solution took the form of the so-called *Equalanze* (equalities).[35]

From this period, a new model of administration was introduced, through which the Crown's authorities aimed to delete the secular immunity enjoyed by the cities from the disadvantages of the countryside. The government now addressed the question of the management of the military administration of the domains outside the Iberian Peninsula from a unitarian perspective.[36] In Spanish Lombardy, the governor introduced the general *Equalanza* taxation, by which all the military expenses for billeting the troops were shared with the same proportion throughout the state, as already occurred for the other tax burdens.

This act was a decisive turning point on a political level, which, however, certainly did not put an end to the disputes, both because the application of this measure also required the definition of important fiscal and procedural details, and because of the renewed opposition of the cities. However, this did not mean that the expenses for the defence of the Spanish Lombardy were supplied only by the local subjects. On average, only five to six percent of the Milanese budget consisted of civil administrative costs, while the vast majority of expenses were generated by the needs of military defence and the payment of public debt, which was also largely due to military needs. The deficit, however, became more and more significant every year and it was managed through internal loans or foreign financiers, especially Genoese bankers. Relief from other Spanish domains was also needed for this purpose, especially from Naples and Sicily.[37]

---

35 There were three types of *Equalanze*: the *terrera* (within a specific locality), the *provinciale* (within a province), the *generale*, with which the burdens were distributed throughout the state. See also Alessandro Buono, Matteo Di Tullio and Mario Rizzo, 'Per una storia economica e istituzionale degli alloggiamenti militari in Lombardia tra XV e XVII secolo', in *Storia Economic'* Anno XIX (2016), N. 1, p.198.

36 The years of governorship of the Count of Fuentes (1600–1610) were of capital importance for Milan. The Count's government, energetic to the point of being perceived as tyrannical by the Milanese elites, was aimed not only at consolidating the fiscal innovations introduced in the previous decade, but also attempted to make the Lombard defensive system more autonomous and stable. See Maffi, *La cittadella in armi*, p.204.

37 Buono, *Esercito, istituzioni, territorio*, p.49: 'The average amounts of Neapolitan subsidies for the Spanish Army in Lombardy averaged around 1,200,000 *escudos*, a sum equal to the whole Milanese military budget. The sending of money to Lombardy from the Kingdom of Naples became particularly relevant between 1637 and 1643, when 7,760,000 *ducados* were sent to support the Army. According to other scholars, between 1631 and 1644 Naples contributed almost 12 million *ducados* to the Spanish military needs in Lombardy. Sicily between 1620 and 1650 contributed with no less than 10 million scudi. As for Castile, it would seem that up to 1654, one and a half million scudi reached Milan for the financing of the Army. An additional source to support military spending was the administration of the city of Milan, which had to go into debt with the Banco di S. Ambrogio to the point of forcing it to suspend payments in 1658. In the same year, the accumulation of the bank's loans to the City of Milan went from 6 million to almost 22 million *lire*.'

In the mid seventeenth century, these *asistencias* became equal the amount of Spanish Lombardy's tax revenue. However, the delay with which the resources reached Milan forced the authorities to take out short-term loans with Genoa, triggering a spiral of increasingly unsustainable debt. This forced governors to demand tax advances thus always postponing an end to the debt.[38]

In the 1670s, in order to not resort to further foreign loans, which were increasingly difficult to obtain, and granted after exhausting negotiations, the direct recourse from the provinces increased. The Spanish Low Countries had a similar experience and where wages, provisions and quartering of troops were concerned, Spain never did stop maintaining a strong force, since the strategic location of the territory was of the utmost importance.

This arrangement reverberated across the economy. In 1676, after three years of war that had consumed a huge quantity of resources, the economy of the country was collapsing. The lack of funds did not allow for the complete raising of troops for the army, forcing the governor, the Duke of Villahermosa to drop the aggressive strategy of his predecessor, the Count of Monterrey. In 1680 at least 1.5 million *escudos* were needed for the army, but the administration of Brussels did not have these resources, being able to allocate to the army just one fifth of that sum. In this situation, borrowing from private lenders and other expedients were the only measures that local authorities were able to resort to.[39]

Milan and the Low Countries were home to the major professional armies of the Monarchy, but in addition to these, further military operations were necessary to face enemies in Sicily, in the colonies and in the Iberian Peninsula. In 1674, Catalonia collected the money to raise new units in addition to providing for the accommodation costs of the troops, and offered, with some resistance, the tax revenue of Barcelona.[40] The other Iberian provinces and cities also contributed to finance the army.

In 1674, in the kingdom of Aragon, the city of Saragossa raised the funds to maintain on campaign an infantry *tercio* of 500 men for two years, and in 1676 replaced it with another of lesser strength. Further contributions occurred in 1682 and 1684. In exchange for the extraordinary contributions requested by the Crown, the introduction of local taxes on consumer products was negotiated in some provinces.[41] In addition, the trade from the Americas was subject to extraordinary measures. From 1675, the corporation

---

38 The drain on resources also hit provinces historically reluctant to collaborate in the military efforts of the Monarchy, such as the Kingdom of Sicily. It is estimated that during the Thirty Years' War, Sicily paid out 10 million *escudos* for the maintenance of Spanish soldiers in Lombardy. All this excluded the costs of the *tercio* quartered on the island and the galley squadron. See Pierre Picouet, *The Armies of Philip IV of Spain 1621–1665* (Warwick: Helion & Company, 2019), p.211.

39 Echevarría Bacigalupe and Miguel Angel, 'El ejército de Flandes en la etapa final del régimen españo', in E. García Hernán and D. Maffi (eds), *Guerra y sociedad en la monarquía hispánica: política, estrategia y cultura en la Europa moderna (1500–1700)* (Madrid: Fundación MAPFRE, Laberinto; Consejo Superior de Investigaciones Científicas, CSIC, 2006), vol. I, p.565. The lack of money caused the reduction of all the expenses, among others those of foreign representation, with the consequent discredit brought to the government.

40 Sánchez Belén, *La financiaión de la guerra en el reinado de Carlos II*, p.41.

41 *Ibid.*, p.42. In Seville, for example, the tax was applied to the sugar trade.

A guardroom scene, by François Duchatel, Flanders, 1664–68 (Musée Jeanne d'Aboville, La Fere). Transferring of soldiers was another difficulty for the Monarchy's army. According to the regulations, it was expected that, together with the troops, the commissioners of the army would arrive in their quarters. The instructions to the general commissioner or *corregidor* established that the official, upon the arrival at the locations intended for quartering the troops, should ensure that the local authorities allocated the beds – usually straw mattresses – and other facilities in accordance with the orders and receive from the officer in command the signed list with name, surname and country of origin of each soldier. This procedure happened every time the troops took up quarters. This strict control was to limit desertions and it was continued when the recruits joined their units. During the army's transfer from winter quarters to campaign, commissioners registered the soldiers at every stop. Along with the troops, the officials also recorded the names of the *huidos* (deserters). Finally, the muster's commissioners registered again the soldiers in each company and *tercio*.

of merchants and tradesmen of Seville contributed with donations granted in exchange for exemption from duties on French imports.

Extraordinary measures were of course imposed in the kingdom of Castile. In 1674, by reintroducing a taxation introduced for the first time 40 years before, the Castilian communities had to provide for every 100 residents the sum necessary to maintain two infantry soldiers on campaign. Further extraordinary demands such as this intensified after 1675, when the war extended to Sicily, forcing the government to turn to new source of revenues. Palermo became the hub for collecting the resources collected in Southern Italy. Funds came also from Milan, and other substantial contributions were collected in the Iberian Peninsula. Between 1676 and 1677, with new extraordinary measures, Castile supplied one million of *ducados* for the campaigns in Sicily.[42]

The interesting consequence of the financing system introduced to face the demands of war was that it practically generated and developed a decentralised tax system outside of Crown control. To this extent, the local authorities became also the responsible for the administration and collection of the recruits, whose numbers, as well as their maintenance and the expenses generated by the accommodation and transit of the troops would later be deducted from the contributions transferred to the central treasury. Moreover, the local authorities appropriated the incomes to guarantee the reimbursement of sums already advanced.

Though this transformation led to the partial loss of control on troops by the government, the instruments for controlling the military spending continued to operate, despite many difficulties.

The office in charge of managing and surveying the Crown's administration was the *Contaduría Mayor de Cuentas*, which operated under the *Real Hacienda*, the aforementioned secretary of the royal treasury based in Madrid. The *Contaduría* was the instrument of maximum vigilance regarding the correctness of all the procedures and economic affairs of the royal treasury for every matter, and therefore extended its expertise into military affairs. Its origins are imprecise but the existence of accounting personnel reporting to the king, namely of a permanent staff assigned to the registration and control of expenses, was already in existence at the end of the thirteenth century.[43]

Regarding its composition, there were two, sometimes more, *Contadores Mayores de Cuentas* (Senior Accountants) assisted by their lieutenants. The ordinary work was carried out by the minor accountants, like the *contadores de libros* (register accountants) who managed the provisions and the correspondence, and *contadores de resultas* (result accountants), in charge of ordering and checking the accounts and illustrating the results, if any. In addition, several notaries, a relator, advisers and other subordinate personnel attended the *Contadoría*.

The office expanded its field of action and multiplied its activity due to the enormous expansion of expenditure, especially on military matters. The increasing importance of the army and the financial and logistical difficulties due to the formation of permanent armies that was taking place in the Spanish Low Countries and Lombardy led to the development of similar local organisations. These offices were in charge of the muster, organisation of transport, recruiting, quartermaster services, military engineering, and sanitary matters. The administrative officials of the provinces were in direct contact with the accountants of the *Contadoría* of Madrid and took turns managing military spending while they supervised the work of the aforementioned *veedores generales*, *veedores* (commissioners), *auditores* and other officials who joined the army on campaign or the troops in the garrisons.

---

42 *Ibid.*

43 The first known complete ordinance concerning the *Contadoría Mayor de Cuentas* is the 'Royal Letter', or instructions regulation, promulgated by Juan II in 1437; see *Diccionario panhispánico del español jurídico* (Salamanca: Real Academia Española, 2017).

Since the administrative officials dealt with the most delicate matters: money, they were assisted by *veedores* in charge to control the 'good economy' avoiding frauds and maladministration. They operated under the direction of the *Veedor General* who assigned them the tasks and the garrisons under their control. According to the regulations, and to the instructions they received, the *veedores* registered the arrival of soldiers in their quarters, took note of any changes in the strength of the units, and transmitted the report to their superiors. The *veedores* had also to deal with the billeting of the troops, a task that was very demanding work, as soldiers were often housed in private homes.[44]

Another major task charged by the military administration concerned the supply for the army and the net of *asentistas* (suppliers) who significantly proliferated and increased their activity in the seventeenth century. The *Contadoría* also managed payment and intendancy in the different provinces of the Iberian Peninsula, and although this system acted under the control of the local *veedores*, the results were often far from expectations. At the origin of the problem, there was the obsolete structure, since the Spanish military machine had articulated an extensive administrative system composed of officials resident in the provinces and garrisons, but it had not changed for almost a century.[45] Usually the personnel had been selected from Spanish natives, but there were also officials coming from the Italian domains or from foreign countries.[46] As for the *pagadores*, they held a very sensitive place in the chain of administrative affairs, since they managed the flow of money that reached the troops that came from disparate channels. Their task was a nightmare. From the documents preserved in the archive relating to the financing of the army, it is possible to reconstruct the events of many *pagadores* forced to carry out their task in a troubled financial context like the Spanish one.

The difficulties were not the same everywhere, as the Spanish dominions had different laws regarding military spending, but nevertheless the resources for the army remained scarce in the Iberian Peninsula, as well as in the Low Countries and Italy. In the Milan, the local authorities agreed on the amount of taxes to be collected on a monthly basis. From their point of view, the Milanese magistrates tried to reduce the contributions by sometimes using an obstructive tactic to the detriment of the Crown and his army. With the

---

44 The instructions for the commissioners of the State of Milan required the compilation of the names, surnames and nationalities of each soldier, and the owners of the houses where the soldiers were quartered. The commissioners had to register the day of the soldiers' arrival, making the house-to-house visit every day, annotating the ones who were leaving for other locations, the date of absence and the date of return 'warning well not to follow fraud or deception.' These warnings were aimed at avoiding fraud such as that of *piazzemorte*, consisting in the falsification of bills that allowed officers to receive lodgings, tools, and aid for more soldiers than those actually present. See ASMi, *Militare* cart. 406, *Ordini per l'alloggiamento delle compagnie di fanteria dati dal commissario generale* (1674).

45 Francisco Rodriguez Zamora, *La pupilla dell'occhio della Toscana y la posición hispánica en el Mediterráneo occidental (1677–1717)* (Madrid: Fundación Española de Historia Moderna, 2013), p.161.

46 *Ibid.*, p.61. Between the 1670s and 1680s, the Sienese *pagador* Francesco Ventury held this position in the *Estado de los Presidios*.

funds received, the *pagadores* had to pay the wages of soldiers and officers, as well as their maintenance and, in the specific case of several garrisons in Spanish Lombardy, the entrepreneurs of the *case herme* (quarters). The money was often insufficient, or never collected, and this forced the *pagadores* to contract new debts, or not to pay the troops. This problem had already become very serious by the end of the 1650s, when in Milan the soldiers had assaulted the houses of the *pagadores*.[47]

Despite some attempt to reform the whole administration and its personnel, in the last decades of the seventeenth century, the officials in charge of control remained inadequate, or little interested in carrying out an accurate examination of expenses. Some were even the main actors of the actual embezzlement that took place within the army. Certainly, the level of corruption was diffused in Spain, as in other countries, but due to the dramatic financial crisis, the consequences were felt more than elsewhere.

From the seventeenth century onwards, it became increasingly obvious that Spain lacked the financial capacity to carry out such an ambitious policy. As a result, troops were paid on an irregular basis. Supplies also left a lot to be desired and there was no money left over to provide the soldiers with winter quarters. In order to avoid mutiny and pillage, the local authorities often had to step in and assume responsibility for these matters.

The Recruitment of Manpower

The Spanish army, like most European armies of this age, was formed with mercenary volunteers. Mercenary does not mean that only foreigners were enlisted, since recruits from the Spanish domains were also found in the ranks, but every major army was largely composed of non-Spaniards. As a result, the armies of Felipe IV and Carlos II were remarkably cosmopolitan.

Throughout the seventeenth century conscription spread in all Europe as the armies became increasingly national, increasing in size and becoming more permanent. In this regard, Spain had already developed a centralised system of recruitment that had been in place since the sixteenth century. However, the evolution in the size of the armies complicated the capacity of the Crown to obtain the services of volunteer soldiers, either in their own territory or abroad, so new recruitment systems had to be developed which, by different methods, meant enforced enlistment.[48] In order to gather the men that were needed, the Spanish Crown resorted to all possible means to increase the army. Castile remained the core of the Spanish Monarchy and also the region that traditionally supplied mostly of the commanders and soldiers for the army.

However, during the seventeenth century, the loss of prestige, problems of state finance, and accumulation of public debt enabled Castile to preserve

47 Buono, *Esercito, istituzioni, territorio*, p.257.
48 Antonio José Rodríguez Hernández, 'Los hombres y la guerra. El reclutamiento', in *Historia Militar de España – III Edad Moderna. II Escenario Europeo* (Madrid: Comisión Española de Historia Militar – Real Academia de Historia, 2013), p.188.

this prerogative. Furthermore, on a demographic level, Castile, was not at its best. The kingdom had been affected by a strong decrease in the number of inhabitants, and soon the source of recruits became inadequate. Therefore, many bordering territories, such as Valencia, Extremadura, and Galicia were used as a reserve of recruits for the army, a measure already introduced under Felipe IV in the 1640s. Islands like the Canaries and Mallorca also contributed with a significant quota of recruits.[49]

Usually, the most favourable areas where more volunteers could be enlisted were the major cities in Castile, Andalusia and Murcia. In Castile, especially in Madrid and its environs, were pools that traditionally supplied a good number of recruits. Usually, recruitment campaigns in these areas occurred with the raising of companies under newly appointed captains. This method was also used in other areas, although to a lesser extent.

Ultimately, the recruitment of volunteer was less successful in different areas of Spain, because in most of the peninsular territory the population was unused to it, and when the Crown turned to areas outside Castile or Andalusia for recruiting its soldiers, the results were modest.[50] Furthermore, since each kingdom had its own peculiarities and operated under the executive power with the king, the Crown had to find the most suitable way to recruit as many men as possible, adapting to the circumstances that were experienced in each location. For instance, there were regions that were not permitted to send their recruits outside Spain. In this regard, during the reign of Carlos II, no soldier was recruited into the kingdoms of Aragon or Navarre for service outside the Peninsula, despite various attempts to do so.[51]

This, however, did not exclude recruits from other regions from enlisting in Castile or elsewhere, at least in a personal capacity. Despite the fact that recruitment was mainly carried out in the territories belonging to the kingdom of Castile, this did not imply that there was uniformity on this matter in the other regions composing the kingdom. Moreover, in some territories, like Aragon, there were differences among the provinces that formed the kingdom, and also the recruitment in places as distant and different as Galicia or the

---

49 In the seventeenth century Mallorca sent about 21,000 men to the Army and fleet. See Antonio Espino López, 'El esfuerzo de guerra de la Corona de Aragón durante el reinado de Carlos II, 1665–1700. Los servicios de tropas', in *Revista de Historia Moderna Anales de la Universidad de Alicante*, N. 22 (2004), p 73.

50 Among the many cases, problems occurred Galicia between 1673–74, since after trying to recruit a *tercio* of 1,000 volunteers under the Count of Amarante (EI-204), it could only be completed thanks to the collaboration of the local authorities, which turned to the kingdom's militia due to the lack of volunteers. See Antonio José Rodríguez Hernández, 'El Reclutamiento de españoles para el Ejército de Flandes durante la segunda mitad del siglo XVII', in E. García Hernán and D. Maffi (eds), *Guerra y sociedad en la monarquía hispánica: política, estrategia y cultura en la Europa moderna (1500–1700)* (Madrid: Fundación MAPFRE, Laberinto; Consejo Superior de Investigaciones Científicas, CSIC, 2006), Vol. II, p.417.

51 In 1680 an attempt was made to recruit 500 men in Navarre to be sent to Flanders, but it was not possible due to the opposition of the local *Cortes*, which feared a French invasion. See *Consejo de Guerra*, 23 February and 18 March 1680; AGS,*Guerra Antigua*, leg. 2476. *Memoria de los partidosen que se hande levantar los 6.000 hombres que han de pasar a los dominios de Italia y estados de Flandes.*

Canary Islands did not follow the same pattern. Therefore, each territory had its own laws that were applied for enlisting volunteers.

Within the voluntary formula, two recruitment models coexisted, which in many cases were complementary: the *comisión* (commission) and the *asiento* (supply). Both systems had been established in the previous century, the latter having significantly evolved in the second half of the sixteenth century. Most of the seventeenth-century European states resorted to private contractors for soldiers already before 1648, but unlike Spain, they had not always established a centralised military administration. The Spanish Monarchy was one of the first states that introduced a centralised recruitment system directly controlled by a central administration.

In this sense, it was logical that for Spain the change that occurred in the second half of the century would cause a turnaround, which did not happen in the countries where the systems of recruiting and supplying of soldiers remained in private hands. The enlistment of the troops always represented a significant part of military expenditure; however, even when it passed to a greater extent into private hands, where many contractors benefited from it through speculation, it did not result in a loss of control or sovereignty.[52]

The first method, the *comisión,* was a recruiting system directly planned by the governments, which appointed officials and determined places of recruitment, all being paid by the royal treasury. All recruitment was overseen by the Council of War, whose jurisdiction was restricted to Castile but which effectively co-ordinated the Monarchy's global war effort. Usually, the War Council issued the royal orders stating the number of men to be recruited, the places and the companies to be formed to each province. For this purpose, the whole Iberian Peninsula was divided into 50 *partidas de reclutamiento,* each with a city as a collection centre.[53] The matter was managed by the War Council's executive committees, or *juntas,* and by the *comisarios general de infantería* or the corresponding *comisarios general de cavalleria,* who advised where and how men might be raised. The orders reached the cities where the levy was to be carried out together with the officials involved in the recruitment as established in the royal *cédulas,* both for the council and for the magistrate or highest authority of the city where they were. The recruits were collected by the officials and conducted under escort to fortified sites in order to avoid desertions.

A major change happened in the second quarter of the seventeenth century as a result of the crisis in the system due to the lack of recruits. In the 1670s, the commissioners were gradually replaced by the *corregidores,*[54] who took over a part of the functions performed by the *corregidores,* becoming the intermediaries between the Crown and the local authorities where the

---

52 Rodríguez Hernández, *Asientos y asentistas militares en el siglo XVII,* p.67.
53 Rodríguez Hernández, *Los hombres y la guerra. El reclutamiento,* p.192.
54 The *corregidor* was a local administrative and judicial official in Spain and in its overseas empire. The charge was the representatives of the royal jurisdiction over a town and its district. He was the highest authority of a *corregimiento.*

recruiting was carried out.[55] From this time, the kingdoms' chancelleries became the most important factors in the recruitment of soldiers, replacing in several cases the Crown and the military officials appointed for this task.[56] This type of recruitment was not without its drawbacks, as the Crown had to receive the consent of the local authorities before proceeding to enlist the soldiers. More than once, it recruited without the collaboration or approval of the towns or provinces.

In December 1667, the troops recruited in Madrid by the *Commisario General de la Infanteria* departed 'stealthily', because they were enlisted without the full consent of the town.[57] They were 500 men destined for Flanders. The recruitment continued, but this time with the approval of the town council, which agreed that six companies could be raised in the town, 'in the places established by the council, to fulfil the 1,000 men requested.' In 1675–6 the *comisario general*, the Marquis of Ontiveros, prepared a recruitment 'map' of Spain for a levy of 13,300 soldiers for Flanders, Italy, and Catalonia, which produced a positive result.[58] Despite the restrictions, the *comisión* remained the most diffused method of recruitment in Castile, Murcia and Andalusia until 1694, when enforced enlistment was also introduced.

By comparison, the *asiento* was an intermediary recruitment system, in which a private contractor promised to gather a certain number of men in exchange for money per man recruited. In the 1660s, the recruitment managed by private *asentistas*-contractors was not yet a widely spread method to provide soldiers. After discussing the matter for several years, in the 1667, the Crown issued a large *asiento* in Andalusia to Don Juan de Mendoza, a well-known assemblyman who had worked there since 1648. The War Council were in favour of this because 'if the recruitment was done on behalf of Your Majesty, it would cost much more, mainly having to run for the magistrates and officers'.[59] The council insisted as was stated that 'as well as for speeding up recruitment and transportation, which should be carried out in a few months.' During the reign of Felipe IV there were recruitment drives

---

55 'As a result of the arrival of the captains and the documents that the city council brought with them, the council of the cities met, by order of the *corregidores*, to begin the recruitment and to appoint the commissioners of the companies who had to stay in the city. After finding an appropriate place to house the company's guard corps, the officers and soldiers carried out the act of raising the flag in a public place, ideally in an important and central place of passage of the city, after which the recruitment of volunteers began.' See Rodríguez Hernández, 'El Reclutamiento de españoles para el Ejército de Flandes', p.399.

56 During the seventeenth century, the new circumstances meant that the *Chancillería* of Valladolid had a more active military role. These were to fundamentally contribute to the mobilisation of troops. A great example of these new powers can see it in the work carried out by the president of Chancellery of Valladolid in 1676, the nominated superintendent for the recruitment, who was able to raise more than 2.000 soldiers. See 'Las nuevas funciones militares de la Chancillería de Valladolid durante el siglo XVII: el ejemplo de la superintendencia de la leva de 1676', in *Familia cultural, material y formas de poder en la España moderna – III Encuentro de Jóvenes Investigadores en Historia Moderna* (Valladolid, 2–3 July 2015), p.1133.

57 Rodríguez Hernández, 'El Reclutamiento de españoles para el Ejército de Flandes', p.399.

58 AGS, *Guerra Antigua*, leg. 2916.

59 Antonio José Rodríguez Hernández, *Los tambores de Marte. El Reclutamiento en Castilla durante la segunda mitad del siglo XVII (1648–1710)* (Valladolid: Universidad de Valladolid, 2011), p.340.

carried out through private recruiters, but this system rapidly expanded in the 1670s, when over a quarter of the recruits had been enlisted by *asentistas*, especially for Flanders.

Scholars identify three types of *asiento*, each with some differences because they responded to different needs. However, all three have in common the fact that the private contractors were only in charge of recruiting men and delivering them to a port chosen by the Crown, always managing the transportation of recruits to their units at the cost to the Royal Treasury, which curiously was used many times to employ further *asentistas* for this task. Some of them operated in this kind of market, winning a dominant position in Spain, like Juan de Miranda, who between 1671 and 1672 recruited 1,500 infantrymen in Madrid and environs, paying half of the cost required by other kinds of recruitment.[60] Certainly, private recruitment was not untouched by attempts at fraud, but the need for men was so high that the Crown even came to the aid of the *asentistas* in order not to interrupt their work.

In 1671, after receiving the levies supplied by Juan de Miranda, the *corregidores* reminded him that the recruits admitted to the army had to be at least 16 years of age, since a large number of recruits did not receive their wages because they were too young. This was because among the recruits supplied with the previous *asiento*, there were dozens of children between 11 and 12 years old. However, the same drawbacks occurred also with direct recruitment, since in the company gathered by Captain Fernando Rocafull, there were several children, and another seven men suffering from 'incurable diseases'.[61] Between 1665 and 1685, the Crown agreed 14 large *asientos* in Castile and other provinces, which provided the armies with about 9,300 men out of 10,400 recruited overall.[62]

Infantry ensign, Flanders 1664, by Victor Boucquet (1619–1677). This fine work is very probably the portrait of a junior officer of the Spanish Low Countries' town militia. His magnificent appearance strongly contrasts with contemporary accounts of the Hispanic military of Flanders. In 1664, when the number of effective Spanish troops garrisoned there barely exceeded 6,000, the new governor Francisco de Moura Corterreal, Marquis of Castel Rodrigo, on his arrival was horrified to find that the soldiers were - in his opinion - 'unclothed, unshod, dirty and begging'. Though the Spanish government recognised that its presence in the Low Countries was essential if it were to maintain its status as a European power, it had few resources in troops or money with which to uphold that status. Thanks to the need for collaboration against a common enemy, the United Provinces of the Netherlands managed to secure from Spain a concession it considered absolutely necessary to its own survival. (Collection of the Louvre Museum, Paris)

---

60 Rodríguez Hernández, 'El Reclutamiento de españoles para el Ejército de Flandes', p.407. The *asentista* could obtain savings because he did not supply dress and equipment, which remained the responsibility of the Spanish treasury.

61 *Ibid.*, p.408.

62 Maffi, *Los últimos tercios*, p.204.

A further kind of recruitment was the one directly carried out by the units, which dispatched parties of a dozen or so soldiers to enlist volunteers in provinces or cities assigned by the War Council. The methods for recruiting volunteers were different, but normally the captain or the official centred their activity in the major towns, although sometimes some of them were allowed to temporarily visit other smaller locations to try to attract more volunteers. As a general rule, and on rare occasions, soldiers only received money for daily relief when they officially entered the companies. The difficulties facing voluntary recruitment could be overcome by offering more enlistment money, and when there was some urgency to complete a contingent, higher prizes were usually offered to attract more volunteers. In this events, special bonuses were awarded, but these amounted to no more than a few days of pay. Therefore, in the recruitment carried out by the Count of Grajal in Madrid, more than 900 men were enlisted in just three months from November 1681 to January 1682, thanks to the fact that a double bounty was offered as a payment bonus.[63] However, direct recruitment became less frequent, because it required too much time and was more expensive.[64]

The Spanish recruitment situation, constantly marked by a chronic shortage of manpower, presented a variety of cases, especially after 1648, when service in the provincial militia became generalised. This caused a major change in the army, since the militiamen began to operate alongside the professional troops on campaign, involving them in an equally obligatory but less massive recruitments, which meant the transformation of the militiamen into soldiers of permanent corps, although for short period terms.[65] In the 1660s, as a result of the serious financial crisis, the Crown increasingly looked to the provinces and private landowners for assembling recruits. This system was known as *servicio* and consisted in a formal demand of the King addressed to the estates, either secular or religious, including provinces, cities and nobility.

The *servicios* were anything but a novelty, and in fact dated back to similar medieval practices. Each *servicio* had to raise one or more companies of soldiers or the equivalent in money. In turn the Crown issued patents of officers, or commissions, to subjects interested in serving in the army, and the assurance not to authorise further enlistments in the territories under private jurisdiction. The *servicios* issued by the Crown responded not only to the need for soldiers, but above all to the lack of resources.[66] From this

---

63 AGS, *Guerra Antigua*, leg. 2512, *Consejo de Guerra* dated 5 and 11 November 1681.

64 A final method of recruiting soldiers was enforcement, applied in moments of greatest emergency as in 1691. In practice, each district had to register the population in the lists used to form the militias, which were created specifically to find out how many of the male population were able to bear arms. In 1694 this turned in a compulsory recruitment for completing the Army of Catalonia. See Maffi, *Los últimos tercios*, p.201.

65 Rodríguez Hernández, *Los tambores de Marte*, pp.11–12.

66 In 1662, the War Council proposed to enlist all the homeless and unemployed in the Andalusian cities into the Army of Extremadura, forcing them to enlist in companies destined for the Portuguese front. The idea was rejected due to the belief that after receiving the equipment many of them would desert. See Rodríguez Hernández, 'Guerra y alianzas en la lucha por la hegemonía europea', p.193

point of view, the *servicios* were a perfect solution, as they guaranteed an appreciable number of recruits at a very low cost.[67]

The government first relied heavily on the *servicios* in 1667 to cope with the French invasion of the Low Countries. In Castile-León, Andalusia, Navarre and Galicia this kind of recruitment netted about 4,900 men, after the concession of *servicios* to 16 provinces and cities, as many individual nobles and prelates or religious orders.[68] The results, however, were below expectations, not for the number of men collected, initially estimated at more than 6,000, but especially for the low quality of the recruits coming from cities and provinces, who had mostly been enlisted by force or they were former convicts amnestied in exchange for entering military service. As for the *servicios* required of the nobility and the clergy, the results were less negative.

The idea of resorting to the owners of large fiefdoms was aimed at gathering a 'universal levy', which in the plans of the War Council could ascend to at least 20,000 recruits extending the *servicios* to the whole Iberian Peninsula.[69] With this force, the Crown could stabilise the numbers not only the army of the Spanish Low Countries, but also the ones of Milan and Catalonia.[70] The War Council estimated that each noble could either recruit 100 soldiers or pay a 'contribution' of 4,000 *ducados*. Despite the expectations, supported among others by the Viceroy of Navarre, the skilled veteran Francesco Tuttavilla Duke of San Germano, the responses from the nobility were mostly negative, supporting their refusal with arguments of various kinds, including the fact that the able men were already serving in the Kingdom's militia. In León, the local nobles stated that their subjects had 'poor inclinations' to the arms.[71] Ultimately, in 1667–68, the *servicios* assembled a total of men and resources much lower than expected, however this system gave a decisive impulse to private recruitment to which the Crown resorted until the end of the century. The venality of the military charges deriving from the *servicios* represents another negative feature attributed to the Spanish army, but this same method was also applied more or less in the whole Europe.[72]

---

67 There were several forms of *servicios*, but the most widely used was the *reclutamiento a costa*, to appoint a private individual for collecting recruits, providing to them with dress and equipment, and to present the agreed force by a predetermined date. The King, in exchange, issued the patents of officers. In other words, the recruiter received a special license granted by the king that allowed him to hold the appropriate officer rank without the need to certify the seniority required by the military ordinances. For example, in the case of a captain this was 10 years.

68 Antonio José Rodríguez Hernández, *España, Flandes y la Guerra de Devolución, Guerra, reclutamiento y movilización para el mantenimiento de los Países Bajos Españoles* (Madrid: Ministerio de Defensa, 2007), pp.243–244. Madrid and its environs alone contributed more than 600 recruits.

69 *Ibid.*

70 AGS, *Consejo de Guerra*, Reg. 264, f. 171, dated 25 October 1667.

71 Rodríguez Hernández, *España, Flandes y la Guerra de Devolución*, p.271.

72 The appointment to military ranks after the enlistment of recruits was common also in the 'centralised' French army. In the army of the Austrian Habsburgs, this custom lasted until 1704. According to the most recent studies, an exhaustive analysis of the primary sources reveals that the unprincipled and corrupt awarding of ranks and honours in the Spanish Army, in which the enlistment of men was used as an essential means of payment, was not only an important phenomenon during the second half of the seventeenth century; it was a reality that would begin

Among the territories that significantly experienced the *sevicios* were Galicia and Extremadura. The latter especially was even more interested in recruitment since it was a front-line region during the war against Portugal and became the main source of recruits for the only actual field army operations against the Portuguese. It is calculated that in the period 1660–1668, the province supplied more than 1,500 recruits annually.[73] Both provinces raised *tercios* for serving in their respective region, with the provincial infantry *tercios* introduced around the mid century.

The Principality of Asturias was among the first to introduce the *servicios* already in the first half of the seventeenth century. Between 1648 and 1655, Asturias supplied an average of 240–300 recruits per year.[74] From 1661 the Crown needed more and more funds and men to continue the war against Portugal, but Asturias did not contribute significantly before 1663. From this date, the principality intensified the recruitment for rising one infantry *tercio*.[75] This opened the way to further recruitment. In early 1665, the Governor of the Spanish Low Countries, the Marquis of Castelo Rodrigo, requested 2,000 recruits with 500 from Asturias, another 500 from León and the remaining 1,000 from the Canary Islands.

The plan to transfer the recruits from Spain to Flanders was carefully prepared, but the defeat suffered at Montes Claros, diverted the recruits to Extremadura. During the war against Portugal, the Crown recruited 500 men each year in Asturias. In 1667, the War of Devolution involved the whole Monarchy in the raising troops, and Asturians supplied 100 recruits with one *servicio* as well as further men through the direct enlistment for the infantry *tercio* of Francisco de Agurto (EI–157), who recruited of his own 1,575 men.[76]

In 1668, the War Council turned to the Asturians to raise 400 men to form an infantry *tercio* under the Count of Benavente, with another 200 added from León. The project failed because León did not gather any recruits. Before the end of the war, Asturias provided just 185 recruits between April and August.[77] In the next years, the Principality continued to provide hundreds of recruits, then, in 1675, the Crown required them to find recruits

---

to take shape from the end of the sixteenth century and would become widespread during the 1630s, especially after 1635, when hostilities with France began. See Antonio Jiménez Estrella, 'El reclutamiento en la primera mitad del XVII y sus posibilidades venales', in F. Andújar Castillo and M. del Mar Felices de la Fuente (eds), *El poder del dinero. Ventas de cargos y honores en el Antiguo Régimen* (Madrid: Biblioteca Nueva, 2011), p.172, and Antonio José Rodríguez Hernández, 'La venta de títulos nobiliarios a través de la financiacíon de nuevas unidades militares durante el siglo XVII', in F. Andujár Castillo and M. Felices de la Fuente (eds), *El poder del dinero. Ventas de cargo y honores en el Antiguo Régimen* (Madrid: Biblioteca Nueva, 2011), pp.274–302.

73 Fernando Cortés, *El real ejército de Extremadura en la guerra de la restauración de Portugal, 1640–1668* (Badajoz: Servicio de Publicaciones de la Universidad de Extremadura, 1985), p.76–77.

74 Antonio José Rodríguez Hernández, 'El reclutamiento de asturianos para elejército de Flandes durante el reinado de Carlos II', in E. Martínez-Radio Garrido, *Entemu – Aportaciones a cinco siglos de la Historia Militar de España*, N. 17 (2013), p.14.

75 The *tercio provincial de Asturias* (EI–118).

76 Rodríguez Hernández, *Flandes y la Guerra de Devolución*, p.296.

77 Rodríguez Hernández, *El reclutamiento de asturianos para elejército de Flandes*, pp.18–20.

to form another infantry *tercio* for the Army of Flanders. Further companies had to be raised, this time in Galicia. The recruitment took many months and in the summer 1676 the *tercio* was finally ready to sail for Flanders.

The 10 companies were mustered in Ostend and the report addressed to the Viceroy reported a very poor situation: 'the men arrived from the Asturias are useless to serve in the Military, and most of them are children between 11 and 13 years old, while a large part is too old, and incapable of taking the pike or the musket … It is a shame to see these troops, because more of the half are useless.' The complaints even affected some of the officers, since among the captains, only Alonso Rodríguez Dumont had previously served in Flanders, as a sergeant, as recognised by some veteran officers of the army, although he had returned to Spain without a license. The governor, Carlos de Gurrea Aragón y Borja, Duke of Villahermosa, considered this as an affront, and therefore the captain was arrested as a deserter. The governor also ordered that the company of Rodríguez Dumont 'would be reformed not to offer a bad example.'[78]

The Franco-Dutch War (1672–1678) represented a decisive test for the Monarchy. For six years, the Spanish armies had to fight against the French in Flanders, Catalonia and in Sicily, as well as the Moroccans at Oran. Soon the war consumed an impressive amount of resources. Although at first the Spanish armies were able to endure on all fronts, achieving some minor success in Catalonia, and containing the French in Flanders thanks to allied support, the struggle was going to exhaust the Monarchy. Within this conjuncture, the years of conflict appear to be a very interesting period ascertain the war potential of Castile as well as the whole Spanish Monarchy. Every source of recruitment was exploited, including the licensing of veterans, not only of infantry but also of cavalry. Their recruitment was carried out, therefore, in very specific areas to attract people who had already served during the war against Portugal. Thus, more than half of the men were recruited in Extremadura, Galicia and the border of Ciudad Rodrigo and other villages in those environs, while others who volunteered were recruited in Madrid, Valladolid, Burgos and the Cuatro Villas de Costa. The numbers increased with dismounted and reformed horsemen who joined the recruits quartered in the cavalry barracks in Segovia and Toledo. The campaign gathered a total of 1,100 horsemen.[79]

In 1674–75, the government introduced a change in the planning of recruitment, as a result of the new experiences of war which Catalonia and Sicily were going through. In July 1674, the Crown imposed a general distribution of recruits in a large part of the territory of the two Castiles, Andalusia and Murcia. The campaign produced 5,700 men in the last months of the year.[80] Among the other provinces of Spain which contributed with

---

78 *Ibid.*, p.41.
79 Rodríguez Hernández, 'El Reclutamiento de españoles para el Ejército de Flandes', p.404.
80 Rodríguez Hernández, *Flandes y la Guerra de Devolución*, p.344.

significant quotas of recruits, Galicia supplied about 28,000 men during the reign of Carlos II, most of whom were sent to Flanders.[81]

The other provinces acted in sharp contrast. Between the 1670 and 1690s, Valencia supplied 10,300 recruits, but the actual number of men interested in the recruiting possibly was the 80 percent of this number.[82] This latter region did not support a large army on its own territory, and military recruitment was less demanding compared to other provinces, including the ones belonging to the Kingdom of Aragon, such as Valencia.[83] In 1645, Felipe IV came to the Cortes of Aragon looking for 3,000 Valencian recruits a year, 'paid as long as the war lasts in Catalonia'. He had to accept a final offer of 1,200 conscripts, serving six campaigns of eight months each. The original draft for the 'Union of Arms' of 1639 assigned 6,000 men to Valencia for six years. On this basis, the Crown might have hoped for somewhere between 900 and 1,000 men from the kingdom each year. However, the government reduced its demands very drastically to align with the actual ability of the kingdom to recruit, since economic distress had strongly affected the province in the first half of the century. In this regard, the Crown proposed that 1,666 men would be acceptable, but in the following decades, this figure was never reached.[84] In the 1670s, even the spokesmen of the Kingdom themselves were somewhat apologetic about 'the paltry little tercio' of 500 men which Valencia gave to defend Catalonia against the French.[85]

Within certain clearly defined limits, royal power was perhaps greater in Valencia than in other parts of the Aragon. However, in Aragon itself, and Catalonia and Mallorca, the results in the matter of new recruits were ultimately better than in Valencia. This does not mean that there were no problems in these provinces. On the contrary, in many cases even more exhausting negotiations were necessary, but in the end a compromise was reached in order to maintain the level of recruits needed on a regional basis.

After the agreement to recruit 600 infantrymen in 1667–68, in 1674 Catalonia supplied 1,000 recruits paid by the *Generalitat* and the *Consell de Cent*. All the enlisted soldiers were volunteers, who immediately received the enlistment bounty. Usually, the local authority, as well as the Crown, paid 17 Castilian *reales* – or three Catalan *libras* – and further four Catalan *sueldos* per day as a wage for both the recruits enlisted by the city of Barcelona and in the Principality, but the urgency of the need to send reinforcements to the border,

---

81 Antonio José, Rodríguez Hernández, 'De Galicia a Flandes: reclutamiento y servicio de soldados gallegos en el ejército de Flandes (1648–1700)', in *Obradoiro de Historia Moderna* N, 16 (December 2012), p.215.

82 Espino López, Antonio, *Guerra, fisco y fueros la defensa de la corona de Aragón en tiempos de Carlos II, 1665–1700* (Valencia: Universidad de Valéncia, 2007), p.35.

83 Casey, James, *The Kingdom of Valencia in the Seventeenth Century* (Cambridge: Cambridge University Press, 1979), p.32: 'The official figure put forward by the ambassador of the kingdom at court in 1637 was 12,000 men taken for the Spanish armies over the past decade. However, there must have been around 65,000 young adult males in Valencia in any one of the following years. The loss of approximately 1,000 of every year – say two percent of the active male population – was hardly a very dramatic one.'

84 *Ibid.*, p.252. In the end, after further discussions, the Crown settled for cash – 1,080,000 *libras* – which were reckoned sufficient to pay for 1,000 soldiers for 15 years.

85 *Ibid.*

and difficulties in finding volunteers increased the costs.[86] The satisfactory result achieved in 1674 persuaded the Viceroy to ask for a further 4,000 men to reinforce his army in the hypothetical reconquest of Roussillon planned for the campaign of 1675. However, at the decisive moment, Catalonia only recruited 1,800 men and, worst of all, 500 recruits deserted in just two days.[87] Two years later, Catalonia raised the funds for further 1,600 recruits, which rose to 2,000 in 1689.[88]

In Aragon, in 1667, the city of Saragossa recruited 200 men for the army of Catalonia, and offered the same amount for 1668, while the local authorities continued to raise infantrymen in the Kingdom for completing the quota of 1,600 men. Despite favourable promise, this figure was never reached, and the soldiers deserted in great number after joining their companies.[89] For their transfer to Catalonia it was suggested that an armed escort be formed to be sent to the Principality, so the soldiers did not flee, such was the so-called 'quality' of the recruits. In 1669, the Regency requested from Aragon 400 men, and in 1670 the quota was reduced to just 250, although until the summer of 1671 only 80 recruits had been gathered.

After the insistence of Don Juan of Austria, Viceroy of Aragon since 1669, recruitment reached 532 men at the end of 1672.[90] Until the beginning of the Franco-Dutch War (1673–1678) the request for troops did not increase. In 1674, the newly raised infantry *tercio* quartered in Saragossa, which had to join the army on campaign, maintained its peacetime establishment of 500 men. The war strength could be easily completed with recruits from Aragon, but lack of money impacted on recruitment. In June, the Viceroy, and then one month later the Queen, asked the Pope to grant the delay of the loan received from the Spanish church, while the commander of the *tercio* recruited 70 men on his own. In 1675, the increasing danger on the border forced the *cortes* of Aragon to raise the funds for another 500 recruits, reduced to 450 because the funds were insufficient. Finally, in 1676, Aragon agreed to raise funds for recruiting enough men in order to maintain 1,500 infantrymen in two *tercios*,[91] while another *tercio* had to be recruited by the city of Saragossa. The final agreement was the result of some significant financial acrobatics.

The War Council asked that along with the recruits, 50 reformed officers and other persons of rank were included. Since the wages for these ranks cost the equivalent of 200 private soldiers, this allowed the *cortes* of Aragon to decrease the number of recruits, establishing the final number to 1,350 men

---

86 Espino López, *El esfuerzo de guerra de la Corona de Aragón*, pp.16–17. In 1675, after the bad experience of the 1674 campaign when, due to a lack of troops raised in Catalonia, a possible invasion of Roussillon had to be aborted, the Catalan institutions came to pay between 16 and 33 *libras* as a bounty. In 1678 the *Consell de Cent* was forced to pay 11 *libras* to complete its *tercio*.

87 *Ibid.*, p.22. The 4,000 men had to form nine infantry *tercios*.

88 *Ibid.*, pp.20–21.

89 In the words of the viceroy of Catalonia, Gaspar Téllez-Girón, Duke of Osuna, 'the *tercio* of the Count of Montoro has lost more than 700 infants of the 1,100 originally enlisted'. ACA, *Consejo Aragón*, leg. 68, *consultas* dated 2 March and 3 July 1668.

90 Espino López, *El esfuerzo de guerra de la Corona de Aragón*, p.27.

91 *Ibid.*, p.30.

gathered in two *tercios*. In the following years, new resources were allocated, but this money, despite the favourable reports provided by the Aragonese, does not seem to have flowed out in the most appropriate way. In this regard, in 1678, the Viceroy of Catalonia, Alexandre de Bournonville, complained that the troops of Aragon had been poorly supported on campaign. Meanwhile, a request for more troops to protect the fortresses near Lérida, which were completely defenceless, was denied by Aragon. The fact of having two *tercios* outside the Kingdom and open war on its border, although the operations were centred in Puigcerdà, persuaded the Aragonese *cortes* to impose a limit to the involvement of the kingdom in the war, especially because the difficulties both in jurisdiction and economic issues.[92]

In 1680, in consideration of the growing internal difficulties of Aragon, the crown reduced the quota of recruits decreasing the contribution of the kingdom to the defence of the Catalan border. However, when the threat of a new French invasion materialised in 1683, the Crown asked for more recruits from Aragon. The viceroy ordered a campaign of recruitment for 350 men as reinforcements for the *tercio* in Catalonia. However, several problems and the chronic lack of money delayed the Aragonese effort, and the recruitment resumed only in 1684, just before the French siege of Gerona. In June, the kingdom had recruited about 900 men to serve in the army of Catalonia.

Mallorca also participated in the recruitment for the army, despite the fact that most of the conscription carried out on the Balearic Islands was historically destined for the navy. Furthermore, the defence of the archipelago from a French invasion did not allow them to divert manpower to other fronts. Recruitment campaigns had been carried out in Mallorca already, in 1667 during the War of Devolution. Then, in 1675, the Crown asked for further recruits in order to raise an infantry *tercio* for Sicily. Irregularities and fraud affected the recruitment, since among the soldiers there were several outlaws in receipt of amnesties allowing them to enter the army, while 80 of the recruits were children aged between 10 and 12.[93]

In the 1680s, the difficulties of the Royal Treasury would continue to put all the Spanish kingdoms under heavy pressure, from which Mallorca tried get away as best as it could. In the spring of 1680, a levy of 300 recruits was made in the islands on behalf of the King. In October 1680, 394 men sailed to Finale, followed in 1682 by further 500 to Milan and Sicily. In 1684, after the *cortes* of Aragon had opposed a levy of 400 men, another 100 men left the Islands, this time paid by the Crown. Altogether, Mallorca provided, directly or through the Crown, more than 2,000 recruits for the period 1660–1690. This figure, together with 18,586 from Catalonia and 12,488 from Aragon, and the aforementioned 10,300 from Valencia, placed the Kingdom among the major contributors of recruits for the army of *Los Austrias* after Castile.

As part of the Crown of Aragon, Sardinia contributed to the war effort. The recruits were exclusively destined for the Sardinian *tercio* (EI-206) that

---

92 *Ibid.*, p.33.
93 *Ibid.*, p.76.

sailed to Sicily in 1675 to join the army raised to face the revolt in Messina.[94] Each year until 1678, further recruits and free companies joined the army involved in the blockade of Messina.[95] As happened in other provinces, in Sardinia recruitment turned into an opportunity to free the kingdom of undesirables. This method had been practiced several times following a predetermined system. It provided for the notification of every town and village an order to enlist troublemakers, thieves and other criminals. The dispatches were sealed and had to be read at the same hour and day, so that the news would not spread thus avoiding alarming the ones who feared being captured. The recruits were transferred to Cagliari, with a warning not to take men with families or the sons of widows.[96] This expedient was considered healthy, because it removed the dangerous subjects from the territories, but it filled the army with bad soldiers who had a negative influence even on those who had voluntarily enlisted. Furthermore, in 1674, the governor granted a pardon to the criminals who agreed to enter the army as volunteers.[97] However, this negative effect did not arouse any disapproval, because contemporary society considered the profession of soldier as one used to danger, and therefore the soldiers, for their inclination, were destined for a violent and perhaps fatal existence. Since soldiers were men suited to the danger, violent men were the best suited to bear arms.

Banditry was widespread in Sardinia, as well as in the kingdom of Naples and Spain, and the ramifications of some outlaws were very extensive throughout the higher levels of the society, penetrating even into government's circles.[98] Local authorities were often forced to come to terms with the local bosses, and faced with generalised lawlessness, the ministers of Felipe IV recognised the need for total amnesties, if only because 'the guilty are so numerous that you cannot hang them all without tremendous bloodshed'.[99] However, bandits could become another source of recruits, if

---

94 In 1677 the *tercio* had 15 companies, reduced to 10 before the end of the year. ASS, *Appunti e Documenti*,vol. XXIV, p.500.

95 Raffaele Puddu, 'Organizzazione militare e società della Sardegna spagnola', in *La rivolta di Messina 1674–78 e il mondo mediterraneo nella seconda meta del Seicento*, Acts of the International Conference, 1975 (Cosenza: Luigi Pellegrini, 1979), p.107. After the war, the officers received rewards and prizes for his service in Sicily. The *maestre de campo* Marquis of Villasor was granted a gratuity and shortly afterwards received the coveted appointment as *Caballero de la Cámara del Rey*.

96 Jorge Aleo, *Storia cronologica del Regno di Sardegnadal 1637 al 1672* (Sassari: Francesco Manconi, 1998), pp.110–111.

97 Puddu, 'Organizzazione militare e società della Sardegna spagnola', p.107.

98 Casey, *The Kingdom of Valencia*, p.220: 'The conditions conformed to a general pattern under Felipe IV and Carlos II, whereby the outlaws should enlist in the Army of Milan or Naples. As a short-term expedient, it was probably one of the most successful means ever devised for getting rid of troublemakers. The only problem was that it had no permanence: within a few years, the bandits filtered back and renewed their activities.'

99 *Ibid.*, p.213: 'The sheer size of the gangs, at least in the early seventeenth century, is the first clue which we have to go on. The bands roaming the Jiicar Valley have occasionally numbered over 100 men, most of them on horseback, and so overbearing that they do not shrink from entering big towns to execute their evil designs and exact their revenge. The equipment involved … suggests that these were not petty desperadoes, but the private armies of local potentates. Where the names are given, it is possible to identify many of the bandit leaders as powerful individuals in their community. The Ayz and Gisbert in Alcoy (in the Kingdom of Valencia) belonged to

they agreed to enter the army instead of serving their sentence in prison or on a galley. Furthermore, as far as military competences were concerned, many criminal organisations had small private armies, both in Spain and in Italy. For this reason, the Crown offered amnesties to attract former bandits to the army, usually assigned to the most isolated garrisons or to the islands, as happened with the bandits who had passed into the service of His Excellency the governor, assigned to the garrison of Gaeta in 1687.[100]

It is partially true that the manpower pool of the Spanish armies of the late seventeenth century was of poorer quality, since many entered the ranks against their will, the military career not being their first option, as was also the case in the rest of the European armies. However, if the payment was regular, and the officers took care of their men, the units formed by conscription could become of good quality, as was said of the units recruited in the Iberian Peninsula.[101]

Outside Spain, Naples and Milan also faced the increasing demands of recruits, and after 1667 the Spanish Low Countries too experienced this trend being the most threatened Spanish territory. In these territories, the recruitment of the local menfolk remained mostly entrusted to the governments that issued commissions, or directly to the officers of the units present in the territory. The structure established to manage the recruitment had personnel similar to the one operating in Spain, but in the Spanish Low Countries and Italy, the figure of *comisario* did not disappear, and continued to be the main actor in matter of control for these matters.

Assuming the numerical contribution of recruits from each province, in the 1660s the Kingdom of Naples was the second main supplier of soldiers to the armies of the Monarchy. According to the detailed reconstructions of scholars, between 1660 and 1668 more than 20,000 Italian soldiers arrived in Spain to participate on the campaigns against Portugal: an average of 2,100 men each year were recruited for this front. Most of them came from Southern Italy (8,147 troops), while the *Estado de Milán* contributed a further 7,299.[102] A considerable number came also from Piedmont and Savoy, 1,853, Tuscany 1,093, and a small contribution from Sicily with 240 men.[103]

---

two families which both held the post of royal bailiff in the town; the Linares of Villajoyosa must have been related to the Jaime Linares who was deputy for the town in the Cortes of 1645; the Palacios, who were the scourge of *Alcalali* in the 1680s, were also big tithe-farmers in the area. The famous bandit Monreal of Alcira was pardoned in 1636 when he agreed to enlist in Captain Monreal's company of infantry; the outlawed Vicente Escriva of Carlet was chief justice of the town; his associates, the Talens of Carcagente, were royal bailiffs of that town; and finally, the gangsters of the city of Valencia itself, the Anglesolas, Minuartes, Escales, Adells, Zapatas, Sanz and the rest, were among the most powerful financiers and politicians of Philip IV's reign.'

100 ASV, *Segreteria di Stato*, 1026, *Avvisi, Avvisi di Napoli*, 12 July 1687.

101 Rodríguez Hernández, 'Guerra y alianzas en la lucha por la hegemonía europea', p.257: 'The young Galicians took up arms without problem, and the officers said of them that 'once they were in the military profession they embraced it with pleasure and ease in a few days'.

102 Antonio José Rodríguez Hernández, 'Al servicio del rey. Reclutamiento y transporte de soldados italianos a España para lucharen la guerra contra Portugal (1640–1668)', in Davide Maffi (ed.), *Tra Marte e Astrea: Giustizia e giurisdizione militare nell'Europa della prima età moderna* (Milan: Franco Angeli, 2012), pp.272–273.

103 *Ibid.*, p.273.

The Italian presence remained significant in the next decade, to the point that considering the average numerical strength, the Italians in the service of the Monarchy constituted the largest 'Italian army' of the time.

After 1659, the Flemish Walloons finally lost to the Italians the primacy of second *nación* of the Hispanic armies. The Low Countries had supplied the core of army of Flanders since 1630, but although the Spanish Low Countries are often described as a kind of bottomless pit where the Monarchy raised countless soldiers and money, in the second half of the seventeenth century the prudence of the Flemish Walloons in the army significantly decreased. Between 1660 and 1668, native soldiers still represented the larger component in the army of Flanders, totalling from 17 to 29 percent of the infantry, with an average of 25 percent in 1668–69.[104] However, these figures are more relevant, considering that after 1659, the Spanish Low Countries suffered territorial losses, with a considerable proportion of the population. In addition, the Flemish Walloon aristocracy, who had always contributed to the king's service, was deprived of much of its possessions, now passed into French rule, and during the reign of Carlos II the nobility could not make the same contributions to the war effort as in the first half of the century. After an intense recruitment campaign in 1673–74, the number of Flemish Walloons diminished considerably, and in the 1680s, they had become the third largest component in the army of Flanders after the German mercenaries and Spaniards.[105]

To remedy the shortage of native soldiers from Franche-Comté, French deserters were transferred to the existing *tercio*. French soldiers passing into the Franche-Comtois troops did not occur only in Sicily, because in Milan most of the soldiers enlisted in 1676 for the 'Burgundian' *tercio* quartered in Lombardy were French deserters. The need for new recruits had to be taken into consideration. Among the proposals examined, there was the one of the *teniente coronel* Guillaume Cécile, examined by the Council of State in February 1677. Cécile proposed to join all the Franche-Comtois companies into a single *tercio* to be quartered in Lombardy.

The number of exiles and the existing relationships of the officers with relatives and friends in Franche-Comté should have allowed for the formation of eight or 10 companies. The project left several unanswered questions, as it did not guarantee the recruitment of the required number of soldiers for each company, nor the time and methods for transferring the recruits to Milan. The War Council rejected the proposal, mainly for economic reasons, considering that it was too onerous. Cécile did not lose hope and months later he addressed a new proposal to Madrid, with which he offered to recruit a new tercio of 500 men for the army of Catalonia. This time, the proposal received a positive response from the King. The *tercio* had to deploy eight companies of 30 men, not including the staff, in order to assemble at least 200 soldiers. However, the expectations of Cécile were unfulfilled when, in September 1677, only 80 men had been recruited after three months. In June 1678, with the growing need of soldiers for the defence of Catalonia, these

---

104 Maffi, 'Una epopeya olvidada', p.55.
105 Rooms, *De organisatie van de troepen van de Spaans-Habsburgse monarchie in de Zuidelijke Nederlanden*, pp.158–159.

soldiers marched to Finale and from there sailed to Barcelona, where they were taken into the Spanish infantry.

Parallel to the initiative of the willing *lugarteniente* Cécile, in 1674 another Franche-Comtois officer, the dragoon captain Gilles Faivre, offered to recruit 500 men to raise a regiment of *arcabuceros montado* within five months for the army of Lombardy. As he pointed out, the initiative was due to the need to increase the corps of dragoons in the Sicilian kingdom, where, due to the harshness of the country, they were very necessary. Faivre recruited enough volunteers for a single company, which headed to Sicily in 1675. The Franche-Comté also raised cavalry companies, which formed tactical *batallones* and later were mixed with other horsemen from the companies disbanded in 1673. Two years later, a single cavalry company from Franche-Comté still served in Flanders.[106] Three different reports written in the early 1690s refer to the decline of the unit's strength.[107]

It is undeniable that during the second half of the seventeenth century, the strength of the Spanish army decreased in general figures, but the number of Spaniards increased in proportion as confirmed by comparing the data concerning the armies of Felipe IV and Carlos II. According to authoritative scholars, 40,000 to 45,000 Spaniards constantly served in the armies under the reign of Carlos II, in the Iberian Peninsula as well as elsewhere.[108] The case of Milan is a good example, since the number of Spanish soldiers in Lombardy remained stable until the end of the century, deploying between 3,000 and 7,000 men, depending on the period, and within the infantry on average one soldier in every three was a Spaniard.[109]

The other good example of the number of Spaniards under arms occurred in Flanders, where the numbers remained stable until 1667, where they numbered barely half of the men compared to native-born soldiers. In 1668, this percentage was almost identical; then, in 1672, despite the period of peace, there were 11,500 Spanish infantry in Flanders, a few less than the Flemish Walloons, who numbered 13,533. Excluding the foreign mercenaries, this is a figure higher than the of the previous century, when just one soldier in six came from Spain. Through continuous reinforcements from the Iberian Peninsula, in 1672 one soldier in three was a Spaniard, despite the fact that the road to Flanders had long ceased to be travelled.[110] In the following years, despite the frequent reductions or strengthening of the army, Spaniards definitively represented the main nationality in the army.

---

106 Quirós Rosado, *La fiel nación* p.91. The cavalry served under the captain Mathieu Hoest, succeeded after his death by César Morel. In 1683, Morel, who had enlisted in the Army of the Low Countries eight years earlier, was promoted to *sargento mayor*. He held the command until the definitive disbanding of the company in 1699.

107 In 1690 the company deployed three active officers, 32 reformed officers, and 74 horsemen. AGS, *Estado*, leg. 3883: *Relación de los tercios y compañías que ay en los Estados de Flandes*, Brussels (without day or month), 1690. Bruselas, 1690)

108 Rodríguez Hernández, *Los tambores de Marte*, pp.42–43.

109 Maffi, *La cittadella in armi*, pp.101–102, and Luis Ribot García, 'Milán, Plaza de Armas de la Monarquía', in *Investigaciones Históricas* N. 10 (1990), pp.221–223.

110 Rodríguez Hernández, 'El Reclutamiento de españoles para el Ejército de Flandes', p.416.

Hispanic Armies

Historians state that in the seventeenth century the Monarchy deployed barely a third of the forces necessary for an adequate defence, since the official strength of the troops available was never reached for the shortage of money.[111] Furthermore, some troops did not have the necessary means to perform as a field force. Weapons, ammunition and supplies, artillery trains and wagons were always in short supply. There were good professionals among officers, rank and file, but Spain needed many more. This difficult situation persisted unmodified throughout the last quarter of the seventeenth century, although in 1676 the Spanish armies are known to have reached the considerable figure of 112,000 men – the highest since 1659 – but the Crown did not have enough resources for an adequate defence.[112] This figure, like most of the 'official' strength estimates, must be considered with caution, because according to the recent research findings the actual number of available troops would have decreased by one fifth or even by one quarter.[113]

After the Peace of the Pyrenees, the major Spanish field armies were those of Extremadura, Flanders, Milan and Catalonia. With the exception of Extremadura, in 1660 all the armies underwent an enforced process of reform, namely the reduction of costs through a strong decrease in strength. Between 1659 and 1660 in the Spanish Low Countries, 32 Spanish *tercios* and foreign infantry regiments were disbanded. Before 1661, 10 Spanish cavalry *trozos* were also disbanded and further 21 foreign cavalry regiments followed.[114] The reduction in the force was considerable, because in the Spanish Low Countries there were only about 13,000 men, just over half of the 34,770 foot and horse mustered in 1656.[115] This reduction did not turn into a massive disbanding exercise, because a not inconsiderable number of other troops were transferred to the Iberian Peninsula, now that peace with France allowed Spain to focus on the Portuguese conflict.[116] This forced many officers and NCOs to serve in the existing tercios as semi-volunteers known as *reformados* waiting for a new opportunity, when, and if, new units were raised.

Milan's army had greatly increased in size over the previous decades to curb French ambitions in Italy, but when peace arrived it was necessary to reduce costs. This mainly affected the resources of the duchy, so the army had to be reduced to less than half. In 1660 there was a discussion about the option of sending Italian and German units from Milan to the Portuguese border, to join the army gathered for the offensive that was considered decisive to break the resistance of the rebel Portuguese.[117] The demobilisation of the Milan

---

111 Antonio Espino López, E'l ocaso de la maquinaria bélica hispánica', in 'Los Tercios, 1660–1704', *Desperta Ferro*, special issue XIX, June–July 2019, p.14.

112 Rodríguez Hernández, 'Guerra y alianzas en la lucha por la hegemonía europea', p.256.

113 Espino López, 'El ocaso de la maquinaria bélica hispánica', p.16.

114 These figures did not comprise the French Army of Condé, which is discussed later.

115 Picouet, *The Armies of Philip IV of Spain 1621–1665*, p.131.

116 In 1661, of 13,799 soldiers, only 2,887 were licensed; see AHNOB, *Frias*, Ct. 83, d. 439.

117 AGS, Estado, leg. 3377, f.19: Resumen de la muestra que se tomó a la infantería y caballería, in Milan, 24 February 1660.

army continued during 1661, to the point that the infantry was reduced to only the Spanish units, with the exception of some small contingents of Irish and other foreign soldiers, while the cavalry was reduced by half.[118]

Significant reductions also impacted on the army of Catalonia, with an establishment in 1661 of 3,690 foot and about 500 horse.[119] Between 1657 and 1659, the army of Catalonia had lost many soldiers transferred to the war against Portugal. The reduction in numbers continued until 1665, when Catalonia could muster just 1,218 soldiers in all.[120] An important fortress like Puigcerdá, which could easily quarter 1,500 men, was garrisoned by just 80 soldiers.[121] After the reform of 1660–1661, the overall forces of the Monarchy decreased to 35,000 men in all, and more than half of these troops were deployed at the Portuguese. The great expectations of the army of Extremadura to definitively crush the Portuguese rebellion are easily recognisable in the effort sustained by the Crown for mustering its forces. The original establishment, planned before 1659, had to raise 16,000 men, of which 7,000 were for the garrisons on the border.[122] In 1660, the field force was gradually increased, and for the campaign of 1661, Don Juan of Austria, could count on 9,640 infantry and 3,900 cavalry, including Spaniards, Walloons, Italians and foreign mercenaries.[123]

Unfavourable environmental conditions and difficulties in paying the troops' wages caused a large decrease in the size of the force. In 1662, after the arrival of further troops, the Army of Extremadura totalled just over 18,000 men. In April, the field army began the second campaign under Don Juan with 8,886 infantry and 5,374 horse, but when the army crossed the Caya River in May, the infantry numbered 8,503 men, while the cavalry had decreased to 5,074 horsemen.[124] In subsequent years the army of Extremadura continued to receive troops, gathering regular forces as well as further mercenaries and hastily raised militia units. In early 1663 the infantry totalled 22,490 men, of whom 17,220 were Spaniards, 2,830 Italians, 1,810 Germans and 630 Irish.[125] The disastrous defeat suffered at Ameixial-Estremoz marked a turning point in the war but faced with the fading hope of defeating the Portuguese, the Crown assembled new strong armies in Extremadura. In 1664, the overall force numbered 20,239 men on paper thanks to the arrival of further troops; one year later, the field army engaged at Montes Claros deployed about 22,000 men, a figure that with the garrisons along the border represented the largest effort made by Spain to crush the enemy resistance. At the end of

---

118 Maffi, *La cittadella in armi*, pp.46–47.

119 Espino López, *Catalunya durante el reinado de Carlos II*, p.57.

120 *Ibid.*, p.59.

121 Antonio Espino López, *Las guerras de Cataluña. El Teatro de Marte* (Madrid: EDAF, 2014), p.61.

122 Francisco Barado, *Historia del Ejército Español*, p.527.

123 The overall force in Extremadura totalled 16,713 men. See Espino López, *Las guerras de Cataluña*, p.56.

124 Geronimo Mascarenas, *Campaña de Portugal por la parte de Extremadura. El año 1662* (Madrid 1663), pp.26–27.

125 Picouet, *The Armies of Philip IV of Spain 1621–1665*, p.138.

the war in 1668, the army of Extremadura deployed only 7,082 infantrymen and 2,835 horse.[126]

Along with Extremadura, Galicia also continued to be home to a field army until the end of the war against Portugal. In 1658, the army of Galicia numbered just 1,850 infantrymen and 446 horsemen.[127] In 1660, the regular force was optimistically set at 11,000 foot and horse,[128] which resulted in a strength of about 7,000 men being achieved, mainly coming from the local militia. This army had a defensive role, in order to face Portuguese raids from the Douro and Minho, and it gradually increased to 9,000 men in 1664–65.

In 1660, there was another army on the border with Portugal: the Army of Castile. This was a very small force, which had the task of securing the area around Ciudad Rodrigo and Zamora e Puebla de Sanabria, which comprised at its strongest 3,000 men in all, of which more than half were militiamen. After 1668, both these provinces greatly diminished in their strategic role, and consequently the military force was considerably reduced. Ten years later, after transferring a significant number of troops to Flanders, in Galicia the establishment strength of 1,750 infantrymen was actually 632.[129] In 1670, the military forces in Extremadura decreased to 1,434 men in all, including 890 officers still in service as well as other 'reformed' officers on half pay. The persistent threat on the border with Portugal did not allow for complete demobilisation, and this concern echoed in the words of the War Council of November 1672, which complained that 'the army of Extremadura could hardly gather 1,000 men.'[130] One year later, the musters registered just 483 officers, NCOs and soldiers in a single regular *tercio*, 255 foot militiamen, and four cavalry companies with 276 horsemen.[131] In 1674, forced by the needs of troops for Flanders and Catalonia, the government ordered a further reduction. It transformed the army of Extremadura in a tiny force with 161 foot, officers included, and 246 horse. Obviously, the regular troops were considered insufficient, and therefore the government called the local militia to arms, which raised four more *tercios*.[132]

As for the other peninsular armies, Catalonia garrisoned troops in order to protect the Pyrenees, which after the loss of Roussillon in 1659 had transformed the principality into 'the gate of Spain'. In the following years, the strength of the army increased, but the need for soldiers in Flanders contributed to maintain the strength under the expected number. In 1668, the governor of Catalonia Gaspar Tellez Girón, Duke of Osuna informed Madrid that he commanded a force composed of just 1,000 cavalry and 3,200 infantry in all.

---

126 AGS, Guerra Antigua, leg. 2057: *Junta de Milicias* dated 12 December 1667.

127 AGS, *Guerra Antigua*, leg. 1541, ff.16–17, *Relaciónes de los maestres de campo y teniente general de la cavalleria*, the infantry formed five *tercios*, and the horsemen 10 companies.

128 Barado, *Historia del Ejército Español*, p.527.

129 Rodríguez Hernández, *España, Flandes y la Guerra de Devolución*, p.201.

130 AGS, *Guerra Antigua*, leg. 2270: *Junta de Milicias* dated 8 October and 11 November 1672.

131 *Ibid.*, leg. 2300: *Diferentes muestras pasadas a la infantería, milicias, caballería y artillería*, dated 26 May 1673.

132 Espino López, 'El ocaso de la maquinaria bélica hispánica', p.16. Later, these *tercios* also sent officers and companies to North Africa and Navarre.

Gaspar Tellez Giron y Pacheco Gomez de Sandoval Enriquez de Ribera, Duque de Osuna (1625–1694). He was a prominent Castilian aristocrat who entered the army before inheriting the title after the death of his older brother. In 1657 he contributed financially to raise a 500-man infantry *tercio* to serve for two years in the Army of Extremadura. The command was held by his relative Don Rodrigo Giron (El-70). In the same year, the Duke became *general de la caballería* in the Army of Extremadura and in 1662 *capitan general* in Old Castile. Notwithstanding the poor results achieved during the war against Portugal, in 1667 he was appointed as governor of Catalonia and in 1670 passed to Milan with the same position. (Author's collection)

In January 1669, the War Council proposed gathering an army of 12,000 foot and 3,500 horse, of which 3,000 infantry and 300 cavalry were for the garrison of Barcelona.[133] The government authorised new recruitment, but according to the musters carried out in December 1669, the Army of Catalonia now numbered 4,387 foot divided into 15 *tercios* or foreign regiments. In addition, there were further 2,634 horse.[134] Shortage of resources contributed to an unsatisfactory recruitment campaign, and although many of the units had been raised, they were understrength.[135] This situation did not change in the following years. In November 1671, the effect of recruitment netted just 3,697 infantrymen. Moreover, subtracting officers, sick and other unsuitable soldiers, only 2,707 rank and file were actually available. In 1673, on the eve of the French-Dutch War, the army of Catalonia deployed 7,988 men in all, and this force did not increase significantly in 1677, when the French army crossed the Catalan frontier with 15,000 men. In the following years, the experiences accumulated in the war against the French gave better results, since in 1683 the army of Catalonia could deploy 15,691 men, who succeeded in repulsing the French offensive. However, after the war, the size of the army of Catalonia decreased again, and when the War of the League of Augsburg began, it deployed only 11,843 men in all.[136]

In strategic terms, the army on which the Spanish government placed the greatest expectations was the one of Flanders. The Spanish Low Countries, and to a lesser extent Franche-Comté, was one of the wealthiest regions among those ruled by the kings of Spain, and notwithstanding the heavy tribute paid during the Thirty Years' War, both regions experienced an appreciable growth after the Peace of the Pyrenees. When the treaty was signed in 1659, the army of Flanders numbered 33,756 foot and 19,028 horse.[137] This force occupied about 50 large and small garrisons from the English Channel to

133 Espino López, *Las guerras de Cataluña*, p.72.
134 AGS, *Estado*, leg. 2690, letter of Duke of Osuna to Madrid, dated 8 December 1669.
135 In 1668, Barcelona had a garrison of only 600 soldiers, Puigcerdá 200, Rosas 250, Palamós 110; see Espino López, *Las guerras de Cataluña*, p.68.
136 *Ibid.*, p.155. In 1695 the overall force was 16,072 men.
137 AGS, *Estado*, leg. 2095: *Relación de los officiale y soldados que hay en los tercios y regimientos de infanteria y caballeria*, dated 8 November 1659.

Luxembourg. One year later, after the beginning of the general reduction in strength, these figures had decreased to 32,912 foot and 8,499 horse.[138] In the summer of 1661, after completing the reduction of all the armies – excluding the one in Extremadura – the Spanish Low Countries quartered 25,024 foot and 8,186 horse.[139] In this age, the Flemish Walloons always constituted the majority of the infantry of the army of Flanders,[140] while in the cavalry they generally represented between 25 and 30 percent. This percentage changed slightly after the departure of the cavalry companies to Spain. In December 1661, two years after the signing of the peace, and after having transferred some companies to the Portuguese border and licensed as many units as possible, out of a total of 7,984 horsemen serving in Flanders, 2,822 were Flemish Walloons.[141]

The Spanish Low Countries continued to provide recruits to reinforce the army facing enemies in the Iberian Peninsula. After signing the peace of the Pyrenees, the Crown considered sending a part of the troops who had served in Flanders to the Iberian Peninsula to form a veteran corps to subdue the rebellion in Portugal once and for all. At first, the War Council planned to gather 10,000 Germans and Flemish Walloons to be sent to Spain, something that did not happen due to the need to defend the Spanish Low Countries. The officers and men were very reluctant to leave Flanders, so it was difficult to find suitable commanders who wished to embark, and it was necessary to compensate them with promotions and new positions, since the peninsular conflicts had always been hard, and the payments were made in *vellón* and not in silver.[142]

From 1660, a Flemish Walloon contingent served in Galicia. At the end of the year, the Marquis of Caracena, in response to the requests from Madrid asking for some of the troops of Flanders to be transferred to Spain, sent a list of Flemish Walloon units quartered in the kingdom, and indicated that three *tercios* were ready to embark.[143] In the following years, the request for troops

---

138 Rodríguez Hernández, *España, Flandes y la Guerra de Devolución*, p.78.

139 *Ibid.*

140 According to Geoffrey Parker, between 1607 and 1633 the Flemish Walloons represented 47 percent of the infantry in Flanders: see *The Army of Flanders and the Spanish Road*, p.231.

141 AGS, *Estado*, leg. 2098 (without number): *Muestra de la gente de guerra*, dated 20 September 1661.

142 Rodríguez Hernández, 'La presencia militar alemana en los ejércitos peninsulares españolas durante la guerra de restauracion portuguesa (1659–1668)', in L. Ruiz Molina, J.J. Ruiz Ibañez, B. Vincent (eds), *Yakka. Revista De Histudios Yeclanos*, vol. 10 (2015), p.279.

143 Davide Maffi, 'Una epopeya olvidada', p.62. In detail, Caracena proposed the units of the *maestre de campo* Jacques Fariaux, a soldier of fortune reputed to be an officer of valour and experience; the *tercio* of the son of the Count of Bucquoy – adding that he doubted whether the commander was willing to leave the country – and that of the Prince of Robecq, who has offered to serve in Spain with the rank of *sargento general de batalla*. He was a man of recognised quality, although not a great 'scholar', who had shown much valour serving many years as a cavalry captain, and a further eight as *maestre de campo*. In total, some 5,400 officers and soldiers landed in Galicia in 1662, of whom 1,100 were Walloon infantrymen belonging to the *tercio* of Jacques Fariaux, and a further 1,400 were horsemen of various units, many of whom came from the Low Countries. In addition to these Walloon soldiers, a large part of the German regiments sent to Galicia – another 2,000 men – were actually recruits from the Spanish Low Countries.

did not cease, since the war against Portugal required a major mobilisation of resources in an attempt to finally recover the rebel kingdom.

In February 1662, the first naval expedition left Ostend for Galicia, with 18 ships, both merchant men and men-of-war. At the end of 1662, the army of Flanders had sent 3,877 foot and 1,521 horse to the Peninsula theatre of war. After months of further negotiations, in the summer 1663, the army of Flanders finally sent a further 5,400 foot, horse as well as artillery and supplies, together with the soldiers' wives and children, to Galicia. In 1664, another 2,000 soldiers gathered in two new *tercios* arrived in Spain from the Low Countries, along with 500 Irishmen.[144]

The difficulties encountered in supplying the troops on the border with Portugal and the chronic delay in the payment of wages exacerbated the problems, causing the same excesses that occurred in the previous decades when the Walloon *tercios* served in Catalonia. Without resources and in hostile territory, the contingents declined in strength in a few weeks, and each unit soon resembled no more than one bedraggled company rather than an entire *tercios*. Many of the soldiers deserted and their officers, tired and embittered, left the army to return home at the earliest opportunity. For the campaign in Extremadura of 1666, the Flemish Walloon presence had decreased to only 453 men, representing just over three percent of the infantry and they were merged into the *tercios* of the Marquis of Risbourg and the Viscount of Hornes.[145] Despite the efforts of the government to re-establish a Flemish Walloon contingent, by the end of the war the presence of the Flemish Walloons on the Portuguese border was reduced to a purely symbolic force.

In 1668, the few troops still serving on the Portuguese border were transferred to Catalonia. This theatre of war continued to be the only one where the Flemish Walloon soldiers served outside of their country. In the early years of the Franco-Dutch War, they represented between six and nine percent of the infantry, but from 1677, the Flemish Walloons were reduced to a minimum percentage, just three percent.[146] Their presence in the last decade of the seventeenth did not see them recover their past strength, as is clearly seen from the data preserved in the archives. In the 1690, the last infantry *tercio* still active was disbanded being reduced to only 90 officers and soldiers.[147]

In addition to the troops provided by the Crown or recruited at colonels' and captains' expense, the army of Flanders was completed with locally recruited troops. The first act dealing with this matter had been introduced in 1639 by the *Cardinal Infante* Fernando of Austria.[148] The presence of troops belonging

---

144 Rodríguez Hernández, *España, Flandes y la Guerra de Devolución*, pp.90–91; these were the Walloon tercios *Hornes* (EI–109), and *Risbourg* (EI–110) and the Irish *tercio O'Neill* (EI–125).

145 AGS, *Estado*, leg. 2684 (without number): *Relación del número de oficiales y soldados que se hallaron sirviendo en los tercios y regimientos*, dated 7 June 1666.

146 Maffi, *Los últimos tercios*, p.253.

147 Maffi, 'Una epopeya olvidada', p.65.

148 *Ibid.*, pp.56–57. The Cardinal decreed the levy of 10,000 infantrymen, 'distributing this number in proportion to the cities and villages to increase the tercios of this nation'. In subsequent years, the governors resorted to the same act to obtain the necessary soldiers. Between 1645 and 1658

to the Crown, and the ones administered by the provinces, continued to be a remarkable feature of the Hispanic military of the seventeenth century, and mainly featured the cavalry, which in the 1670s deployed 12 free companies under the direct control of the Provincial *Estados*.

These troops were recruited to serve exclusively in the country and mainly consisted of free companies. Alongside these troops, the Spanish Low Countries also maintained foreign contingents. Already in the 1650s, the provinces also took over the recruitment of mercenaries from Ireland and Germany. The latter source of recruitment was also intended for service in the Iberian Peninsula. Actually, these were not truly German units, and many recruits came from Liège and even from the Spanish Low Countries. This was the origin of several German regiments raised after 1660. In the winter of 1660–61, the 'German' troops sent by the Marquis of Caracena to the Portuguese border had been almost entirely enlisted in the Spanish Low Countries.[149] The recourse to enlistment on a local basis continued also in the following years. In 1661, the *maestre de campo* Jean de Coret offered to raise two 'foreign' regiments with local recruits. In 1674, Colonel Cornelius Varhel asked for permission to recruit soldiers in the Imperial territories as well as in the Spanish Low Countries in order to complete his German regiment (EI–155).[150]

Notwithstanding the strategic importance of the region, the Flemish Walloon presence in the armies of the Monarchy experienced a constant decline starting from the 1670s. In the summer of 1672, the Brussels correspondents of the *London Gazette* echoed the changes the army of Flanders was going through. In the multitude of information available, it is difficult to see any signs of diminishing military strength and during the rest of the year, there were many rumours that showed there was an army in good condition and a government that was trying to organise a solid base for the maintenance of all its troops.[151]

---

sizeable contingents were recruited in the larger cities of the country: 1,500 men in Antwerp, 1,000 in Ghent, Bruges and Alost. The provinces were reimbursed with exemption from the royal taxes. In 1655 the deployed force had risen to 6,000 men between infantry and cavalry; a few months later, in the winter of 1656, the Comte de Fuensaldaña required the enlistment of 3,000 infantry soldiers, joined by 2,800 infantry and cavalry from Franche-Comté. A few months later Don Juan of Austria gathered more than 4,300 men to reinforce the units before the campaign began. In the summer of 1658 the Brabant clergy offered to mobilise some 4,800 men and pay their livelihood for four months. Finally, in the weeks following the defeat at the Battle of the Dunes, a new levy was established in order to gather 12,000 infantrymen to reinforce the army. These contributions were not limited to the internal service, since on several occasions the authorities of Madrid asked troops to be sent to the Peninsula, or to other theatres of war where the Monarchy was engaged. As early as 1635, instructions were sent to the viceroy to gather 2,000 infantry from the Walloon and Irish troops to send them to Brazil against the Dutch. The departure of these veterans was eventually delayed by the chronic lack of resources and the entry of France into the war, forcing the governor to use these troops for the garrisons in southern Flanders. In 1655, the levies for two new infantry *tercios* – 2,000 men – were urgently requested for the Army of Catalonia.

149 *Ibid.* p.61.
150 AGS, *Guerra y Marina*, leg. 2323 (without number), the Duke of San Germano to Madrid, dated 22 December 1674.
151 Rodríguez Hernández, 'Guerra y alianzas en la lucha por la hegemonía europea', p.260.

Jean de Brouchoven, Count of Bergeyck (1644–1725). Known for his authoritarian character, the Count carried out a very ambitious and personal policy following the French model of Colbert. In the military sphere, he wanted the Spanish Low Countries to be able to ensure its own defence, constituting an independent army.

At the beginning of 1673, the army of Flanders deployed the unprecedented strength of 42,000 men.[152] This majority of this force were Flemish Walloons, but almost the same number were Spaniards or German mercenaries, and above all, the overall number was still insufficient to have any prospect of success against the French army preparing for the invasion of the Dutch Republic. After the Franco-Dutch War, the army of Flanders never regained its former glory. In the early 1680s, the governors Alessandro Farnese, Prince of Parma, and after him Ottone Enrico Grana del Carretto, planned a series of reforms of the army in order to prepare for a wartime strength of 35,000 men.[153] Soon, the dire state of the finances led the Madrid government to set aside these unrealistic ideas.

In 1684, further ambitious attempts at reform were planned, to have an army of 39,000 men,[154] and in 1686 yet another plan was prepared by the new Viceroy, Francisco Antonio de Agurto, Marquis of Gastañaga, who, however, had to abandon his project. Between 1680 and 1690, the overall force was reduced to between 25,000 and 28,000 troops,[155] a decrease that became much more marked in the following years, to the point that in 1692 the strength of the army was reduced to barely 18,154 men.[156] The Crown appeared to be experiencing a growing difficulty in maintaining its commitments in the Spanish Low Countries, so much so that the local leadership was considering the idea of providing the provinces with their own autonomous army, as was openly wished for by the Count of Bergeyck.[157]

Since the economic shortfalls affected all the Spanish domains, the army of Milan also was subject to reductions in strength. The Peace of the Pyrenees diminished the army of the *Estado* to 3,450 infantry and 2,065 horsemen in all.[158] This redefinition of the strategic framework transferred to Lombardy the role of rear guard and main logistic centre for the army of Flanders. Despite

---

152 *Ibid.*

153 AGS, *Estado*, leg. 3397, d. 100; the monthly cost for the devised army of 35,000 men was 100,000 *escudos*.

154 *Ibid.*, 3876 (nd). 23 July 1684.

155 Rooms, *De organisatie van de troepen van de Spaans-Habsburgse monarchie in de Zuidelijke Nederlanden*, p.159.

156 Maffi, *Los últimos tercios*, p.123.

157 Jean de Brouchoven, Count of Bergeyck (1644–1725), was a member of the Finance Council and Government Commissioner of the Spanish Low Countries, in charge for the payment of troop subsidies between 1668 and 1688. In 1689, he was appointed as a member of the Council of State.

158 AGS, *Estado*, leg. 3378, d. 245–246.

the subordinate role, Milan was the base for the second most important army of the Monarchy after 1668. The *Estado de Milán* thus became a reserve of men and materials essential for the maintenance of Spanish hegemony in Italy.[159] The emergency caused by the War of Devolution and the invasion of Franche-Comté helped to increase the Milanese army to 11,425 men in October 1668,[160] a strength it largely maintained in the following years.

In July 1672, the troops in Lombardy numbered 11,386 men instead of the expected establishment of 13,392. This force provided the soldiers for the major garrisons of Milan, Pavia, Tortona, Valenza, Mortara, Novara, Arona, Como, Varese and the fortress of Fuentes. Further troops manned Alessandria, Lodi, Lecco, Cremona, Serravalle, Pizzighettone, Domodossola, and Trezzo, all places considered of lesser strategic importance. In addition, Finale, on the Ligurian coast, which was essential to guarantee a safe harbour for the galleys and vessels directed from Spain to Southern Italy or for convoying reinforcements from Naples and Sicily to Milan. In the 1670s, Finale had a garrison of four or six Grison companies, four to six Italian companies and six to 12 infantry companies detached from the Spanish or Italian *tercios* in Lombardy, equal to an overall force of about 1,500 foot.[161]

The beginning of the Franco-Dutch war, and the consequent intervention of Spain, reopened the problem concerning the defence of Spanish Lombardy. Already during the first months of 1672, news concerning the French war preparations circulated in Milan with many rumours about the real objectives of Louis XIV's army. The news of French troop movements in Pinerolo and the concentration of men in the Dauphiné had come to the attention of the governor of Milan Antonio Lopez de Ayala Velasco y Cardenas, Count of Fuensalida, who also observed the moves of the Duke of Savoy. Spanish intelligence raised the alarm regarding the Duke's willingness to grant Louis XIV the control of Vercelli and Asti, fortresses both essential for an assault on Lombardy.

The fears of Milan were considered unfounded in Madrid, where the king's ministers were instead certain that the actual objectives of the French were the Low Countries and Catalonia. In 1673, Spain's entry into the war did not change the strategic position of the previous year, and the government of Milan was invited to intervene by recruiting troops for the eventual relief of the Franche-Comté.[162] The only concession obtained by the viceroy was permission to recruit mercenaries to complete the German regiments in Lombardy. After the partial successes of 1673, the disastrous outcome of the campaigns that followed, culminating in the umpteenth invasion of Franche-Comté, was interpreted in Milan as the prelude to an enemy offensive in Lombardy. Without support from Spain, Governor Fuensalida faced a depressing situation. In 1674, the civil authorities of Spanish Lombardy

---

159 Maffi, *Los últimos tercios*, p.125.
160 *Ibid.*, p.126
161 ASMi, *Dispacci Reali*, c. 117.
162 The Royal order provoked an indignant reaction from the Viceroy, who was convinced that the actual target of Louis XIV was precisely Milan and for this reason he bombarded Madrid with letters. Further reading in Maffi, *La cittadella in armi*, p.23.

Claude Lamora, Prince of Ligne (1618–1679), portrayed in the Gualdo Priorato's *Teatro del Belgio*, published in 1683 at Frankfurt am Main. The Prince belonged to most ancient nobility of the Spanish Low Countries and alongside Bournonville, was one of the few Flemish Walloons who held the position of Viceroy. Between 1649 and 1669, he was Captain General of the cavalry in Flanders. In 1660, he was sent as representative of the Spanish King to the court of Charles II of England as the first foreign recognition of the newly restored English monarchy. The Prince held the position of viceroy of Sicily (1670–1674), and from 1674, he was appointed Governor of the Duchy of Milan. During his service in Italy, the Prince succeeded in countering French attempts to invade Lombardy, and in the summer 1678, he did not hesitate to send troops from Milan to Genoa, in order to protect the Republic against an eventual enemy landing. This action went beyond the orders of Madrid, precisely in the months in which peace was being discussed in Nijmegen.

claimed that the economy had not yet recovered from the last war against the French, and the governor informed Madrid that the whole of Lombardy could maintain just 2,160 horsemen in total.[163]

Meanwhile, Fuensalida had lost the trust of the war council in Madrid, who held him primarily responsible for the loss of Franche-Comté, for not cooperating with Monterrey who commanded in Flanders. It was only after the arrival of the new viceroy, Claude Lamoral Prince of Ligne, that the Crown authorised an increase to the troops in Lombardy. The new governor sent detailed reports concerning the condition of troops in Lombardy, describing a miserable situation and the insufficiency in every respect of the forces intended for the defence of such an important strategic region. The distressing picture described by the Prince convinced Madrid to act by giving orders to the Viceroy of Naples to send cash to Milan to allow for the recruitment of new troops. The revolt of Messina and the landing of the French in support of the rebels changed the strategic context again, and therefore in October 1674, the first orders were sent to transfer most of the troops only just gathered during the previous months to Sicily. Despite the protests of Milan, between 1674 and 1676, the army of Lombardy sent 6,842 infantry to Sicily.[164]

Madrid's relative lack of interest in Lombardy was destined to end in the last two years of the war, when increasingly persistent rumours suggested a probable large-scale French invasion. In November 1677, a series of alarming letters from the Prince of Ligne warned the War Council about the intentions of Louis XIV, who, according to the reports from the confidants in Turin and the spies active in Piedmont, was gathering troops in Pinerolo.[165] The War Council debated the matter in order to avoid a similar aftermath as had occurred twice before in the Franche-Comté. However, it is difficult to establish how realistic these rumours were or how artfully they were spread as misinformation by the French.

---

163 ASMi, *Militare Parte Antica*, c. 312.
164 AGS, *Estado*, leg. 3464, d. 116.
165 Maffi, *La cittadella in armi*, p.27. Further news referred to a probable French assault on Finale.

Soon, it became evident that France's plans did not include an invasion of Lombardy but were aimed at diverting the Spaniards from the key fronts. Therefore, a large part of the funds allocated to Milan were destined for the fleet engaged in Sicily, and many of the troops gathered in Lombardy were transferred to Catalonia much to the great regret of the governor. The fear of a French invasion returned to the fore in the last year of the war. In June 1678, the government decided to increase the number of regular troops in Lombardy to 34,000 men but reduced to 22,000 after the Peace of Nijmegen. However, the new governor, Juan Tomás Enríquez de Cabrera, Count of Melgar, worked to increase the army in order to field at least 30,000 men in wartime.[166] Madrid supported the plan, since previous experiences had convinced the Crown not to decrease the forces in the main strategic theatres such as Flanders and Lombardy, which were rightly considered two areas increasingly difficult to defend.

As had occurred in Flanders, the project failed for lack of resources. In September 1681, the annexation of Strasbourg, and in June 1682, the entry of the French troops in Casale Monferrato finally did sound the alarm in Lombardy, where everyone believed as always of a certain French invasion. The state of apprehension reached even higher levels in May 1683, when the news of the French landing in Genoa reached Milan. The governor ordered the mobilisation of all available forces and then sent troops to Liguria in order to support the Genoese resistance. Although the Monarchy was forced to pursue a policy of economic restraint, all these events, and above all the resumption of hostilities against Spain in Luxembourg and Catalonia persuaded the Crown not to further demilitarise Lombardy. In 1683, the army numbered 19,553 men, increased to 22,392 by December 1684.[167] A significant increase, but still insufficient, because Melgar, stated that at least 30,000 men were needed to adequately defend the Duchy.

In Lombardy as elsewhere, the major problem for Spain remained the costs of maintaining armies on multiple fronts. Between 1684 and 1687, namely in a period of relative peace, the army of Milan numbered 222 infantry and 75 cavalry companies, corresponding to 23,530 men, including 219 artillerymen, in 1684.[168] Over 120 companies had been disbanded and more than 6,000 soldiers disbanded. As in the Spanish Low Countries, this was another drastic reduction in terms of military strength, dictated by dramatic economic shortcomings, but despite these measures, expenditure was still unsustainable. In fact, there were a high number of reformed officers whose number had remained too high who were still receiving their pay, and certainly this was largely due to abuses of the system. This forced the government to further reduce military strength, which decreased to 16,302 men in 1687.[169] The actual field force was even lower, because many soldiers

---

166 Ibid., p.29. The project of Melgar was part of the broader plan which provided for a general reorganisation of the army, starting from Flanders up to the secondary fronts of North Africa.
167 Maffi, Los últimos tercios, p.126.
168 Maffi, 'Fieles y leales vasallos del rey', p.53.
169 Maffi, Los últimos tercios, p.126. According to the Mercurio Histórico y Político (Madrid, June 1687), Milan's governor Antonio Lopez de Ayala Velasco y Cardeñas, Count of Fuensalida, was

were unable to serve adequately as they were sick or infirm. As happened everywhere, the garrisons had become a refuge for aged and sick soldiers, often with a family, but still maintained in service by their officers for humanitarian reasons, who were aware that without their meagre pay, they would have only increased the crowds of beggars.

The percentage of unfit soldiers remained considerable, because in 1688, of the overall force of 13,600 infantrymen and 3,000 cavalrymen of the army of Lombardy, only 11,000 were able to perform their regular duties.[170] However, compared to the other armies not based in Spain, the one in Lombardy continued to deploy a significant force. Several clues testify to the importance of the duchy as a shield to keep the French out of Italy, and the clear political turning point of Spain, which in the last decades of the century chose to preserve Italy with all available means, represents a key piece of evidence on this respect. Despite all the difficulties, the presence of an army that, for better or worse, was still able to represent a sizable deterrent, Lombardy did not suffer attacks and when this did happen in the 1690s, the soldiers of the *Estado* performed better than those in other theatres of war.

The second major Italian military force was deployed in the Kingdom of Naples. In some ways the army of Naples was not an actual army, but rather a useful reserve of military forces and economic resources for the most pressed theatres of war. The uprising of the 1640s, aimed above all against the increasing tax burden, had reduced the contribution of the provinces of southern Italy to half a million *escudos* per year, but the Kingdom of Naples' support was always significant in terms of soldiers. In the 1640s, the troops coming from Italy and gathered in Extremadura for the war against Portugal totalled between 12 and 15 percent of the overall force, and about three fifths came from the southern Italian provinces, representing the most significant percentage after the native Spanish. Further Neapolitan troops arrived in Extremadura in 1643. In May, the infantry *tercios* of Francesco Carafa and Giovanni Battista Pignatelli numbered 1,398 men, and the nine cavalry companies under Marcello Filomarino mustered 380 horsemen.[171] Their debut was not especially impressive. Desertions and other problems of various kinds distressed the troops, but on several occasions the behaviour of the Italian units was quite positive. In 1644, during the Battle of Montijo, the infantrymen of Giovanni Battista Pignatelli performed effectively, contributing to the final Spanish victory.

In the 1660s, when the conflict revived, the arrival of soldiers recruited in Milan and Naples became customary. In 1660, the first three Lombard *tercios* sailed from Finale to the Iberian Peninsula with 2,100 soldiers, followed the next year by two Neapolitan *tercios*, about 1,500 men, extracted from the

---

forced to reduce the army at the insistence of the civil authorities. Along with this reduction, the ranks of *maestre de campo general* of the foreign cavalry and *general de las armas de lo Estado de Milán* were also suspended. The same source states that after disbanding some *tercios* Fuensalida joined the companies to another corps, thus he did not significantly diminish the military strength.

170 Espino López, 'El ocaso de la maquinaria bélica hispánica', p.16.
171 Rodríguez Hernández, 'Al servicio del rey', p.234.

army of the kingdom, together with some cavalry companies that included Neapolitans.[172] Their arrival in Extremadura did not pass unnoticed, since their presence was remarked upon by the magistrates of Barcelona.[173] However, these troops were insufficient for the continuous needs of the army of Extremadura, a theatre of war characterised by harsh weather and terrain which made it more difficult to supply the army, and caused the units to disintegrate due to diseases and desertions. Further troops arrived in Spain in 1662, when the newly raised Neapolitan *tercios* of Camillo Dura (EI–112) and Andrea Coppola (EI–113) landed at Barcelona, as did the Milanese *tercio* under the Marquis of Cassano (EI–111). In 1663, the Milanese infantry *tercio* of Geronimo Serbelloni and some reinforcement companies from Naples marched to the Portuguese border.[174] On campaign, the Italian tercios participated in the conquest of Évora, in the unfortunate battle of Ameixial-Estremoz, and then in the Portuguese reconquest of Évora, whose garrison was under the command of the *maestre de campo* Francesco Gattinara (EI–83). The casualties suffered during the campaign of 1663, forced the Court to reiterate requests to the Italian provinces to send more troops. In particular, four new infantry *tercios* were requested from Naples, Milan, and Sicily, but the request to the latter was eventually revoked.[175] In 1664, further companies landed in Barcelona heading to Extremadura.

The following year, the infantry *tercio* of the Marquis of San Giorgio (EI–134) joined the cavalry in Extremadura, as well as several Neapolitan and Lombard free companies of both infantry and cavalry. These troops participated at the campaigns of 1664, especially the defence of Valencia de Alcántara, whose garrison included the *tercio* of Camillo Dura. The number of Italian soldiers increased considerably in the following years, reaching 25 percent during the campaign of 1665,[176] and the troops coming from Naples were in the majority. This percentage does not consider the cavalry, in which there was a significant presence of units recruited in the Italian Peninsula, as confirmed by archive data relating to the period 1660–1668.[177]

In the decisive campaign of 1665, which culminated in the battle of Montes Claros, the Italian infantry *tercios* were deployed in the front line of the battle formation and suffered heavy casualties. The cavalry also performed in important actions, like the one that occurred in 1666, when the horsemen under Prince Alessandro Farnese succeeded in annihilating an enemy cavalry column. Reinforcement continued to land in Spain practically up until the end of the war. In 1666, the Neapolitan *tercio* of Jacinto Suardo de Mendoza arrived with further Neapolitan and Lombard free companies.

---

172 AGS, *Estado*, leg. 3377, d. 94, 99 and 100.

173 'Also on this occasion, veteran troops under the command of the Marquis of Torrecuso and Carlo del Tufo were sent to the Peninsula', in Rodríguez Hernández, 'Al servicio del rey', p.234.

174 *Ibid.*, pp.274–275.

175 Maffi, 'Fieles y leales vasallos del rey', p.51. Sardinia also, as it belonged to the kingdom of Aragon, received the request to provide one infantry *tercio*, which was later cancelled.

176 *Ibid.,* p.52.

177 Luis Antonio Ribot García, 'Las naciones en el ejército de los Austrias', in A. Álvarez-Ossorio Alvariño and B.J. García (eds), *La monarquía de las naciones. Patria, nación y naturaleza en la Monarquía de España* (Madrid: Fundación Carlos de Amberes, 2004), pp.669–670.

Finally, in 1667 and 1668, new companies were recruited to reinforce the units of the army of Extremadura.[178] Moreover, some troops were also recruited in Tuscany, under the *maestre de campo* Marco Alessandro del Borro, and in Piedmont and Savoy, thanks to the efforts of Guido Aldobrandino, Marquis of Sangiorgio,[179] who between 1665 and 1666 recruited not only one infantry *tercio*, but also a unit of cavalry at his own expense.[180]

Peace was signed in 1668, while Spain was still fighting the French in the War of Devolution, forcing the Crown to request further troops for the war. As in the previous years, the Kingdom of Naples and the Duchy of Milan continued to supply troops, while the Kingdom of Sicily limited their contribution to a few recruits.

In the 1670s, when the army of Catalonia had to be rebuilt, the task was completed by turning again to the Italians armies of Milan and Naples. Already in 1672, measures were taken in Naples for transferring the infantry of the veteran *tercio* of Giovanni Battista Pignatelli to Catalonia. Similar requests were made in the following years. In 1674 another *tercio* with 1,087 soldiers left Naples, while other troops were also mobilised in Lombardy, where the *tercio* of Tommaso Pallavicino (in 1673), and the one of Giovanni Mantegazza (in 1676) were also formed, and both were transferred to Catalonia.[181] In 1674, three *tercios* of Italian infantry participated in the campaign under the Duke of San Germano, which led to the victory of Maureillas. In subsequent years these troops continued to participate in major operations against the French, including the victory achieved by Prince Alessandro Farnese at Espollà in 1677, as well as in the unsuccessful defence of Puigcerdá one year later. In this last action, Giovanni Gandolfo's Milanese *tercio* was mentioned for its valour.[182] The campaigns in the Pyrenees considerably reduced the Italian contingent, and worried the commanders, who forced the government to ask

178 Rodríguez Hernández, 'Al servicio del rey', pp.274–275.
179 On 17 August 1664 Guido Francesco Aldobrandino, Marquis of San Giorgio agreed the raising of 1,000 foot and 500 horse for the Army of Extremadura. The first muster was executed in Milan on 23 March 1665. The infantry (EI–134) had 175 officers and 810 soldiers, the cavalry 60 officers and 402 soldiers (EC–82). Shortly after the recruitment was completed, in June 1665 the contingent sailed to Cadiz on Genoese ships. The infantry *tercio* numbered 1,161 men, and that of cavalry 692 men. The contingent was quartered in groups of 200 men in various towns between Seville and Cordoba, in order not to burden on civilian populations. However, the infantry quickly became known for its violent behaviour. As soon as it arrived in Seville the men engaged in excesses and robberies on the island of Cartuya, including the theft of sacred images from churches. The cities refused to billet the troops, and considering the excesses committed and the poor quality of the soldiers, a third were transferred to Catalonia and finally disbanded in 1668. San Giorgio offered to raise new recruits, but this was rejected. Instead the cavalry, under Lieutenant Colonel Marco Antonio Valperga, did not cause any problems and continued to serve until 1678. Thanks to Francesco Pellegrini for this note.
180 Rodríguez Hernández, 'Al servicio del rey', p.275. In 1665 the 692 troopers of the cavalry regiment of San Giorgio included Piedmontese, Savoyard and Franche-Comtois.
181 Maffi, *La cittadella in armi*, p.115. From Milan between 1674 and 1677 more than 4,000 men were sent to Sicily, four times more than the number sent to Catalonia. According to the author, the opening of a new front in Italy and the Spanish effort to face this threat demonstrates that Catalonia had become a secondary front in the Monarchy's strategy.
182 Antonio Espino López, 'Las tropas italianas en la defensa de Cataluña, 1665–1698', in *Investigaciones Históricas* n. 18 (1998), p.64.

for new units to be raised for the army in Catalonia. As in the past, Naples supplied most of the troops.

In 1674, the Messina rebellion impacted badly on operations along the Catalan border, as a considerable part of the Italian troops were now assigned to the Sicilian front to suppress the revolt. Naples supported most of the costs of the war in Sicily; moreover, the kingdom periodically sent troops to Flanders and Lombardy as well.[183] Only after the surrender of Messina, in April 1678, could the exhausted Spanish finances again mobilise the troops of Naples and Milan and send them to Catalonia, in the shape of further recruits under the Marquis of Grottola and Pompeo Litta.[184]

The Italian contribution was also significant in the Spanish Low Countries, where whole *tercios* or free companies of infantry and cavalry were transferred or were already serving there. In 1673, two Neapolitan infantry *tercios* served in the army of Flanders alongside one of cavalry. The infantry increased to three *tercios* in 1675, when one under Franco Bonamico (EI–224) landed at Ostend. Milan followed with two infantry *tercios* by 1677, with a third after 1678.[185]

The Peace of Nijmegen did not interrupt the sending of Italian recruits overseas, since in 1682 and 1683 a total of 1,300 Neapolitan infantry, along with a *tercio* of cavalry, landed in Spain in 1683. The brief War of Luxembourg, which culminated in Catalonia in the frustrating siege of Gerona, brought 1,000 Lombard infantrymen of the *tercio* commanded by Tommaso Casnedi, which was later distinguished in the operations on the Pyrenean border in 1684.[186] Two Italian *tercios* served in Catalonia until 1688, and finally merged with the new three Italian *tercios* that had arrived in 1689. After this, involvement outside Italy decreased and rarely did the Italian domains field more than 6,000 men.

As for the military establishment in Southern Italy, in 1682 the infantry numbered only 1,000, distributed among 29 large and small garrisons, instead of the paper establishment of 5,600 soldiers.[187] Furthermore, the Neapolitan 'military' had to guard the long series of towers and other observation posts along the coasts in the Tyrrhenian, Ionian, and Adriatic Sea, which were part of the defence of the kingdom from the Ottomans and North African corsairs. At the end of the seventeenth century there were 340 sea towers under the control of 1,200 *torrieri*, providing each with a little garrison of paid personnel. The permanent 'regular' force included 11 artillerymen with the rank of *maestri* who directed the service and training of 150 *scolari* (pupils) each year. They were quartered in Naples alongside 189 *guardi* employed as military police and 30 mounted *espressi*, who acted as messengers.

---

183 Luis Ribot García, *The Spanish Monarchy and the Messina War* (Madrid: Editorial Actas, 2002), pp.200, 202 and 206.

184 Maffi, 'Fieles y leales vasallos del rey', p.54.

185 The first two *tercios* already served in the Low Countries: the first was the *Tercio Viejo de la Infanteria Italiana del Ejercito de Flandes* (EI-9), established in 1587, while the other *tercio* (EI-23) had been raised in 1643.

186 AGS, *Estado*, leg. 3405, d. 108, dated 17 May 1684.

187 Espino López, 'El ocaso de la maquinaria bélica hispánica', p.16. This number increased to 4,689 men in 1688, but eight years later the force was diminished to 1,885 soldiers.

The force, even on paper, was clearly insufficient, considering that the *Estado de los Presidios* in Tuscany, which answered to the *capitania* of Naples, originally had to quarter 4,100 men. In 1678, this force decreased to 2,500, but in 1682, only 1,648 soldiers actually formed the garrison dispatched for the defence of this important strategic outpost. Every six months, the garrison was replaced with soldiers from Naples, but after 1686, no more than 1,200 men were gathered for service in Tuscany.[188]

In other regions, such as in Sicily, the actual strength was barely half of what was expected, which had been optimistically estimated at nearly 8,000 men. The core of the contingent was represented by the ancient *tercio de Sicilia*, which had garrisons spread throughout the whole island.[189] The rebellion of Messina forced the Crown to hastily collect troops to secure the kingdom. In 1674, the force gathered on the island increased to 9,048 infantry and 1,000 cavalry. In the following years, the newly formed army of Sicily did not decrease, and in 1677 stood at 11,012 foot and 1,180 horse, including Sicilians, Neapolitans, Milanese, Spaniards, Franche-Comtois, Germans, and other foreigners.[190]

A further, and often forgotten, force was located in Franche-Comté. Despite the political significance that this domain held during the sixteenth and seventeenth centuries, research has shown that little attention had been shown to the region during the last years of the Habsburgs' rule. Even less attention was paid to the military contribution of Franche-Comté to the Hispanic armies as well as to the process of assimilation of the loss of their sovereignty to the Bourbons, first in 1688 and then once and for all in 1674.

Consensual autonomy and even the defensive nature of the territory itself, assured by the ancient neutrality treaty guaranteed by the Swiss cantons, Franche-Comté remained throughout the seventeenth century an important segment of the Spanish military system and, more specifically, a symbol of the identity of the Spanish Crown in western Europe. As in the other domains, the Crown maintained in Franche-Comté a corps of regular infantry, which comprised the ancient *tercio de borgoñones*, but in 1667 this and all the units quartered in the province had moved to the Spanish Low Countries to face the French offensive.

In 1668, the regular forces in the Franche-Comté numbered only 320 infantrymen.[191] In the strategic plan designed in Madrid, the defence of

---

188 ASV, *Segreteria di Stato*, 1026, *Avvisi, Avvisi di Napoli*, 16 April 1686.

189 In 1676 the *tercio* numbered about 2,500 men, see ASS, *Appunti e Documenti*, vol. XXIV, p.498. According to Domenico Ligresti, *Le armi dei Siciliani Cavalleria, guerra e moneta nella Sicilia spagnola (secoli XV–XVII)* (Palermo: Mediterranea ricerche storiche, 2013), p.83: three companies formed to guard the Viceroy, one guarded Palermo port, and one company each was quartered in Trapani, Marsala, Licata, Syracuse, Augusta and Milazzo. The other companies formed detachments in the interior in winter, and in spring they moved to the coastal areas to face the possibility of Muslim corsair landings. In the years of the Catalan revolt, the war against Portugal and the War of Devolution, both the *tercio* and the Sicilian galley squadron were often transferred to the areas where military operations took place, only to be hastily recalled to Sicily as happened in 1647 and 1674 on the occasion of the Palermo and Messina uprisings, or in the case of further enemy threats.

190 Maffi, *Los últimos tercios*, p.258.

191 AGS, *Estado*, leg. 2384: *Relación de la invasión de Borgoña*, dated 14 March 1668.

Franche-Comté was assured by the army of Milan. In this regard, since 1659 the governors of the Spanish Lombardy had received detailed instructions for ensuring the military defence of the *Franco Contado*. The feeling of living an unsafe existence was perceived by the local estates of Franche-Comté and had given rise to a pro-France party. In the following years, military governors often quarrelled with the local estates for their stubborn refusal to raise resources for quartering a stronger army in the country.[192] Historians have sometime described the poor state of the military in Franche-Comté with some exaggeration, but possibly this time the judgment is not far from the truth. The defence of the country was mainly entrusted to the local militia supported by the scarce regular troops. On paper, the army fielded 6,500 men,[193] officers not included, but actually was far less numerous and above all it was not a very efficient contingent, considering that in February 1668 the province was conquered after a *blitzkrieg* of only 15 days. The commander's military knowledge also received the blame of historians. In Franche-Comté:

> Organisation and tactics were always the same in the age of Charles V. No artillery and cavalry were able to perform in open field. The Parliament required to take care of everything and to regulate every detail relating to the troops, the appointment of officers, the wages, including supply and equipment as well.[194]

After Philippe de La Baume-Saint Amour departed the office of the *lugarteniente*, his successor Charles Eugène de Ligne, Duke of Arenberg, supported by Castel Rodrigo, the governor of Spanish Low Countries, required the suspension of the Parliament of Dole in order to interrupt the negative influence exerted by the local magistrates and their clients. In September 1668, Arenberg, demanded the transfer of the parliament to Besançon, because as Castel Rodrigo wrote:

> it is impossible to force this parliament to understand the reasons and to moderate its pernicious privileges without first dissolving it and then completely recreating it … and now it is time to favour such memorable events.[195]

The 'memorable events' about the confusing Burgundian scenario reached the ears of Madrid's court. Unfortunately, the desire of the governors clashed with the delicate balance that existed between the Crown and its province. The debate continued unresolved until 1671, when Madrid sent as

---

192 In 1668 the governor of the Spanish Low Countries the Marquis of Castel Rodrigo, wrote to Madrid that if it had not been possible to exploit the Franche-Comté for an assault on France, this was only due 'to the ingratitude of the inhabitants of that province, who only care about the safety for them and their goods, and seek only solutions that guarantee the neutrality of the country'; in François Pernot, *La Franche-Comté espagnole. A travers les archives de Simancas, une autre histoire des Franc-Comtois et de leurs relations avec l'Espagne, de 1493 à 1678* (Besançon: Presses universitaires de Franche-Comté, 2003), p.296.

193 Piépape, *Histoire de la réunion de la Franche-Comté à la France*, p.219.

194 *Ibid*. Except for Jacques Nicolas de Courgenon, Marquis of Yenne and Saint-Genis, *gobernador general de las armas del Franco-Condado*, complaints were addressed to all the local officers.

195 Pernot, *La Franche-Comté espagnole*, p.297.

Tapestry illustrating the surrender of Dole in 1674, Gobelins' manufactory (Versailles Museum). Although this kind of work had a celebrative purpose, some particulars are very interesting and may have been drawn from life. The officers who are submitting the surrender wear old-fashioned clothing, while the NCOs holding the halberds have modern blue *justaucorps*, one of blue and the other of tanned brown cloth. On the extreme left, in the background, a group of horsemen are also dressed in tan brown.

new *lugarteniente* Gerónimo de Quiñones, Duke of Benavente, a Castilian aristocrat reputed as an able mediator and moderate politician.[196]

In 1671, a compromise was reached, leaving parliament and the civil power in Dole, but assigned the residence in Besançon to the military governor appointed from Madrid. The Crown was aware of the intrinsic weakness of the province and thought that the only way to ensure an effective defence was to assign the key posts to Spanish or Italian commanders.[197] Although Franche-Comté was now the weak link in the formidable Monarchy's bastion of the previous century, the province continued to ensure a degree of surveillance against French moves. When in 1672, as a result of the news relating to French preparations for the invasion of the Dutch Republic, Quiñones found the resources to improve the fortifications of Dole, requiring the civil magistrates to take note of the need for further works and funds.[198] However, even the able Quiñones failed, and when he left his government in mid 1673, the internal tensions to which the province was subjected undermined any possibility of defence against any hypothetical campaign of conquest by Louis XIV. The uncertainty of the actual ability to defend the region was confirmed in 1674, when the long-feared invasion became a reality. Despite the resistance of some garrisons, like the one of Besançon, in no time Franche-Comté was conquered in a single campaign, putting a definitive end to two centuries of political-dynastic identification with Spain.

Household Troops and Guards

As was the case more or less throughout Europe, in Spain there were armed corps directly reporting to form the king and the court. In Spain, several of these corps dated back to the Middle Ages and gradually were transformed into a bodyguard corps. However, unlike the French *Maison du Roi*, in the seventeenth century, the Spanish Guards rarely performed as a military force. Moreover, in Spain, the coexistence between the late medieval models and the permanent household units was a common feature and lasted longer than in the rest of Europe.[199]

The Spanish lifeguards originally represented the *tresnacionnes* (three nations) of the Monarchy: Burgundians, Spaniards, and Germans, but did not include Italians, and served essentially as a palace corps or mounted

---

196 A veteran of the Thirty Years' War, Gerónimo de Quiñonesy Benavente had fought in Rocroi with the rank of *sargento major* in the *tercio* of Gaspar Bonifaz. In 1657, he was promoted to *maestre de campo* of the *tercio provincial de Burgos*, and then to governor of the Canary Islands from 1661 to 1665. He was part of the Spanish delegation in Paris in 1669, and on his return he was appointed as a member of the War Council of Madrid, well reputed for his wisdom, talent in mediation, and as a conciliator.

197 Pernot, *La Franche-Comté espagnole*, p.299. In addition, senior officers from Madrid and Milan would have received command of the garrisons of Dole, Salins, Gray and the castle of Jou.

198 *Ibid.*, p.307.

199 Juan Carlos Domínguez-Nafría, 'El rey y sus ejércitos. Guardias reales, continos, monteros y tropas de Casa Real del siglo XVII', in Enrique Hernán García and Davide Maffi (eds), *Guerra y Sociedad en la Monarquia Hispanica. Politica, estrategia i cultura e n la Europa moderna, 1500–1700* (Madrid: Labirinto Ediciones, 2006), vol. I, p.707.

escort. They performed for celebrating and extolling the Spanish 'royal soul'.

However, the unit closest to the monarch's person and his family was not Spanish but came from the Low Countries. This was the *Guarda de Archeros de Borgoña*, also known as *Guarda de Archeros de la Cuchilla*. Its origins began in 1502, when the Walloon company escorting Felipe II assumed the name of *Garde du Corps*.[200] Task and organisation were successively established with the new ordinances issued between 1545 and 1652. After this date, the company deployed one *capitán*, selected among the most nobles and loyal noble *caballeros*, one *teniente*, one *alférez* (ensign), one *capellán*, one *secretario*, nine *cabosor deceneros* (corporals), one chaplain, two *trompetas*, one *herrador* (blacksmith), one *sillero* (saddler), and 100 mounted guards with 18 supernumeraries; before the end of the century, a single *sastre* (tailor) was added to the company.

Further ordinances were issued in 1663 and 1695, the latter before the disbanding of the company in 1704. Although originally all the members were Flemish Walloons or Burgundians, during the seventeenth century the company became progressively Spanish. However, a family origin from the Low Countries or Burgundy was a requirement to be admitted into the company, as confirmed by the captains of the unit. After Philippe François de Arenberg, Duke of Aerschot and Prince of Gavre, in 1659 succeeded Diego Antonio de Cröy y Peralta Hurtado de Mendoza, Marquis of Falces and Mondéjar, who held the post until 1682, replaced by the first ethnic Spanish commander, the grandee Francisco de Sarmiento y Toledo, Marquis of Montalvo, who, however, served as *mayordomo*.[201] The *archeros* usually served 10

Halberdier of the *Guarda Amarilla*, after the Count of Clonard's *Memorias para la historia de las tropas de la Casa Real de España* (Madrid, 1824). Yellow doublet, breeches and stockings with red-white checked lace; red jacket and headgear with red-white-yellow plumes. Although this kind of dress is confirmed in some early seventeenth century paintings, other sources show different clothing and lace.

years, but at the captain's discretion, and if their service had been excellent, they could serve in the company even longer. They always escorted the king when he moved from Madrid or joined the army on campaign. In dismounted service, they were armed with the *agujas* (curved blade) and obviously they

200 Gil Gonzaláz Davila, *Teatro de las grandesas de Madrid* (Madrid, 1632), p.335.

201 Enrique Martínez Ruiz, 'La Guardia de Archeros de Corps o Archeros de la Cuchilla', in E. Martínez Ruiz (ed.), 'Presencia de flamencos y valones en la milicia española', *International Review of Military History* N. 96 (Madrid: International Commission of Military History, 2016), p.23–24.

Guarda de Archeros de Borgoña, from the painting of Pedro de Valpuesta, dating 1650–1660 (Municipal Museum of Madrid). Yellow *capotillo* and *casaca* with red-white laces; black jacket and breeches and dark grey stockings. Note the different pattern of the royal red-white livery lace.

were authorised to carry arms at court. The *archeros* formed the mounted escort for Felipe IV during his journey to the Island of Pheasants in 1659, when he met with Louis XIV for signing the Peace of the Pyrenees.

The *Guarda Española* originated from the lifeguards of the Emperor Charles V and included three different units, although commanded by the same officer. The first unit, known as *Garda Amarilla* (Yellow Guards) was formed by halberdiers in charge of the service in the royal residences. They numbered 108 men, with one *capitán*, a *sargente*, a *secretario*, a *furriel* (Fourier), four *cabos* (corporals), 96 privates, four fifes and one drummer. This corps had a reserve, the *Guarda Vieja*, which also formed the escort for the princes and other members of the royal family. Their strength was 30 men, with two *cabos*, one *furriel*, one drummer and 26 guards. This latter corps could enlist further members, who served as volunteers without pay, waiting for a vacancy.

The third unit of Spanish lifeguards was the *Guarda de Lancilla*, also known as *estradiotes*, because they were another mounted corps. To be admitted in this latter unit, each candidate should have served before in the foot guards. The *Guarda de Lancilla* deployed one *teniente*, one *alférez*, one *furriel*, two *cabos*, one trumpeter, one saddler, one armourer, a blacksmith, an *astero* (pole maker) and 44 horsemen. They formed the mounted lifeguards in Madrid, and usually escorted the Queen at every public event. The *Guarda Española* was formed by young and healthy noblemen and *cristianos viejos*, able to speak Castilian, French and Flemish, without any known vices and never banned by the Inquisition or the ordinary justices. Furthermore, they could not marry a girl without means and absolute proven honesty, and they also must not have served under another master, not even a Spaniard, or worked in a job not suited to the status of a noble. They were also quartered in Madrid and their service was essentially to escort the king, or foreign dignitaries received at court, and the observation of the royal residences.

The same task was assigned to the *Guarda Tudesca* (German Guards), which also served in Madrid, except for the escort of foreign dignitaries. This unit was formed by German noble cadets received into the ranks to serve at court as a kind of apprenticeship. They served under a *capitán*, assisted by a *teniente*, and a *sargento*, and deployed 100 foot guards with one fifer and one

The entry of Don Juan of Austria in Brussels in May 1658, escorted by the governor's mounted company of *arquebuceros de la guarda* dressed in red, and the footguard halberdiers in yellow with red piping. (Painting attributed to David Theniers the Younger, the Wallace Collection, London)

drummer. All these units essentially performed three tasks: protection of the monarch and his family; defence and watching of the royal residences; escort for the king in all public events, but they did not perform any military tasks on active service.

The actual Spanish household military troops had been formed relatively late compared to other European power. The first step in this direction was done in 1634, when the Count-Duke Olivares raised an infantry *tercio* in order to increase the appeal of the army to aristocrats and to strengthen the infantry with elite troops. The *tercio*, mentioned in the source as *coronelia del Rey*, or *los Guzmanes* after its first colonel, Gaspar de Guzmán *conde-duque* de Olivares, resulted in a 3,000-man unit with 15 companies, and, according to contemporary illustrations, were dressed and equipped very richly.

The *tercio* presumably followed the scheme introduced in 1632 for the infantry, with the *planamajor* completed by *teniente-coronel*, who usually held the command in place of the colonel, and *sargento mayor*. The *Guzmanes* fought against the French in Catalonia and Roussillon alternating defeats and victories. In 1640, Luis Mèndez de Haro replaced Olivares, now at the beginning of his fall from favour, as colonel, while Fernando de Rivera Duke of Alcalá was appointed Lieutenant Colonel and commander in the field. Two years later, the regiment's strength increased adding by a cavalry company. In 1659, the *coronelia del Rey* accompanied Felipe IV to the Island of Pheasants to meet Louis XIV for signing the Peace of the Pyrenees. In the same year, the government planned the raising of another foot guard *tercio* for providing his own lifeguards to the *Infante* Baltasar Carlos, but the project was frustrated by the sudden death of the prince.[202]

In 1661, the *coronelia del Rey* merged two companies from the *tercio Viejo de la Armada del Mar Oceano* (EI–3) and marched to Portugal under its field commander, Lieutenant Colonel de Veragua.[203] Before the beginning of the campaign, Don Juan of Austria transformed this unit into a provincial *tercio*, which assumed the denomination of *tercio de Madrid* (EI–70). Scholars have focused on Juan of Austria's strong aversion to the Guard units. Although it was not an entirely disinterested opinion, Don Juan argued that the existence of an elite, but privileged unit could be detrimental to the army's morale. His experience as field commander strengthened this belief. Furthermore, the formation of military corps in charge of the defence of royal persons had an evident political meaning in the 1660s' Spain. Therefore, in those turbulent years, it was clear to everyone how the creation of a regiment for

---

202 The new *Coronelia* was raised and received the name of the *Infante* 'as happens in France for the Dauphin'. The Count-Duke of Olivares was appointed lieutenant colonel, the *sargento mayor* was Luis Ponce de Leon, and the captains were all important aristocrats, such as the *Almirante* of Castile, the Marquis of San Roman, Salinas and Almenara, 'because the regiment had to involve the nobility'. The expected strength was 3,000 men in 15 companies, but in 1643 soldiers and officers counted between 1,500 and 1,800. The *coronelia* was a short-lived unit, like the titular colonel who died aged 17, in January 1643. After the fall of Olivares, the war council reformed the regiment. Josè de Saavedra Marquis of Rivas was appointed as lieutenant colonel and held command of the regiment until its dissolution in the summer of 1643. See AGI, *Indiferente*, leg. 223, *Servicios de Josè de Saavedra*.
203 Clonard, *Memoria par las Tropas de la casa Real de España* (Madrid, 1828), vol. I, p.110.

the defence of the Monarchy was a countermeasure to temptations for a coup, namely in response to the designs of the bastard son of Felipe IV.

From 1665, Don Juan tried all means available to him to prevent the formation of a new guard regiment, raised this time for the heir to the throne and his half-brother Carlos II. The main support to raise this unit became from Felipe IV's widow, Maria Anna of Austria, and above all from her confessor and first counsellor Cardinal Johann Eberhard Nithard. The regiment had to provide 'the military education of the king',[204] composed of companies of veterans from Castile, Galicia, Navarre and Vizcaya, under the command of experienced and proved loyal officers selected among the *Grandes* of Spain, and other important families. Furthermore, and this was a major novelty compared to the old *coronelia*, the new unit would receive its own quarters in the capital or in the immediate surroundings. The regiment even included a field artillery company with two cannons and two cavalry companies: an actual combined-arms task force to face any attempts to overthrow the government.[205] The new guard regiment also had to distinguish itself from the rest of the infantry in matter of training, because engineering and fortification lessons would be given to the officers.

The political dispute within the court delayed the formation of the *tercio*, which proceeded through a very troubled path. Initially, the project was examined by the government and the War Council, then the discussion was transferred to the Council of State. For weeks, the Queen repeatedly urged the council to express its opinion regarding the formation of the regiment and its quarters in Madrid. Finally, in October 1668, just when the *Junta de Gobierno* secretly voted for the imprisonment of Don Juan of Austria, the Council of State expressed its opinion. According to practice,

Pikeman of the *tercio coronelia del Rey* (EI-15), from the *Memorias para la historia de las tropas de la Casa Real de España* (Madrid, 1824), by the Count of Clonard. This figure wears a *mantilla-casaca* in yellow laced with the red-white livery and carried the embroidered royal coat of arms on his breast and the red Burgundian crosses on the sleeves. According to a contemporary eyewitness, during the journey to Pheasant Island in 1659, to sign the Peace of the Pyrenees, about 500 soldiers of this *tercio* formed the infantry escort of the King Felipe IV and his ministers, and they wore this uniform.

---

204 Alvarez-Ossorio Alvariño, *La Chamberga.*
205 According to Gabriel Maura y Gamazo, in his *Vida y Reinado de Carlos II* (Madrid: Aguilar, 1990) p.66, 'Cardinal Nithard declared more than once that it was folly to entrust the king's life to a few hundred guards dressed in black or yellow (the *Guarda Española*), or in white (the *Guarda Tudesca*) and as many on horseback (the *Archeros*).'

Margrave Hermann von Baden-Baden (1628–1691). The Margrave was a prominent German military leader and a Prince of the Empire. In 1663 he recruited one infantry and one cavalry regiment for Spain in his state, as a contingent of the Burgundian circle, and later joined both units with the Army of Flanders. As a military entrepreneur in Spanish service, the Margrave retained the double rank of colonel of infantry and cavalry, and meanwhile held the command of the Swabian Circle's troops. In 1681 he succeeded to Raimondo Montecuccoli as president of the Aulic War Council of Vienna. (Author's collection)

the most important courtiers and also members of the War Council attended the meeting. The Council strongly opposed the formation of the regiment, declaring that 'in any way does these guards appear necessary, and quartering them in Madrid could lead to negative consequences, such as growth of disquietude, and the loss of trust of the Your Majesty's good vassals', and proposed to employ some companies from the *tercio* of Madrid for the King's education in military exercises.[206]

The supporters of the project replied that 'there was no king in Europe who did not have his own guard, and it will certainly not be a novelty nor cause of anxiety to imitate the example of other monarchies'[207] The political struggle within the court continued until 27 April 1669, the day on which the royal decree for the formation of the regiment was finally signed. It must be emphasised that it occurred in the face of the growing threat from Don Juan, who the previous month had ignited the uprisings in Catalonia and Aragon. After the fall of Nithard, the project to raise the regiment was continued by the Count of Peñaranda, who favoured the appointment as colonel of Guillén Ramón de Moncada, Marquis of Aytona.[208]

The proportion between 'señores' and veterans in the regiment's officers was carefully examined. At the end, the high aristocracy was widely represented by officers belonging to the most ancient noble families of Spain, like Lopez de Ayala, Enriquez, Alvarez de Toledo, Benavides, Silva, Alencastre, Aragón y Moncada. Other prominent captains and junior officer were the Count of Melgar, the Marquis of Jerandilla, the Duke of Abrantes, the Count of Fuensalida, the Count of Caltanissetta and the Count of Cifuentes.[209] The veterans and other professional officers were represented by the *lugarteniente* Rodrigo de Mujica, the *sargento mayor* José del Garro, and the captains Alejandro Nieto and Francisco Barona.[210] Some officers and most of the NCOs were veterans of the campaigns in Lombardy, Portugal

---

206 Alvarez-Ossorio, *La Chamberga*, p.30.

207 *Ibid.*, p.32.

208 This appointment transformed the Marquis of Aytona into one of the most important persons in Spain; see J.C. Domínguez-Nafría, 'El rey y sus ejércitos', in E. García Hernán and D. Maffi (eds), *Guerra y sociedad en la monarquía hispánica: política, estrategia y cultura en la Europa moderna (1500–1700)* (Madrid, 2006), p.733.

209 Alvarez-Ossorio, *La Chamberga*, p.60.

210 For instance, the career of captain Francisco Barona represents an exemplary essay. He entered the army as a private soldier and for 14 years served in Sicily, Catalonia, and Extremadura. Barona

and in the Spanish Low Countries, or had performed excellent service in Italy or in North Africa.

The regiment was quartered in the *calle de la Paloma*, next to the King's residence, and another two quarters not far from the first.[211] The officers could enter the palace wearing the *capotillo* with the King's coat of arms as the Spanish guards. The regiment's uniform suggested the name for the new guards: *Las Chambergas*, after the French *justaucorps*, which had been introduced in the Iberian Peninsula by the French commander in Portugal, the Duke Friedrich Hermann von Schomberg. The popular title even obscured the official title *regimiento de la guarda del Rey*. The theoretical strength was fixed at 2,400 men, with 8 companies of 150 musketeers and as many pikemen; furthermore, 600 horsemen in two companies had to be added and quartered in the villages close to Madrid. According to a spokesman of the council of Castile, the final strength was smaller, numbering 1,800 men in 12 companies.[212] However, at least further 1,000 men had been enlisted in the regiment waiting for the formation of more companies.[213]

The selection of the soldiers was carried out with great care, and enlistment was extended to other regions, excluding Catalonia, in order not to take recruits away from a border region. The peace with Portugal and France favoured the enlistment of veteran soldiers from disbanded regiments. In Madrid soldiers arrived who claimed a pension or a place in some office, and the Guards regiment offered a profitable opportunity, moving the support of the army to the queen, which had before sided generally with Don Juan. Soon, these *reformados* became 'the armed hand of the regency'.[214] Despite the rigorous selection the rank and file were filled with a number of not always reliable subjects, and this could have caused unpleasant consequence. However, on 19 August 1669, at the end of four months of preparation, the regiment of the King's Guards was finally ready to become operational.[215]

Among the duties assigned to the new guards, there was the guarding of the city gates, but this duty was soon abolished, because the soldiers were involved in several accidents. Historians report that in the period in

---

became a captain having served before as an ensign and adjutant of the *Maestre de Campo* of an infantry regiment. He was among the officers mentioned at the battle of Montes Claros, *Ibid.*, p.52.

211 The buildings assigned to the regiment became the first military quarter of Madrid, later known as *Cuartel de San Francisco*.

212 Alvarez-Ossorio, *La Chamberga*, p.58.

213 *Ibid.*, p.76: 'In 1670, these recruits still received pay without performing service and therefore they were completely unemployed. This matter became one of the arguments submitted to the War Council by Lieutenant Colonel Mójica, who complained about the presence of so many inactive soldiers who, 'without control, commit arbitrators and contribute to exacerbate the population against king's regiment'.

214 *Ibid.*, p.53.

215 The review of the first company, under the captain Count of Fuensalida, *Grande de España*, was described by the Imperial ambassador in Madrid: 'The function was performed with courageous ostentation, in the presence of the King and his mother, and of countless audiences ... and this had the opposite effect of which many had spoken, acted and discussed so infamously and with little decency of this nation ... In the evening, Count of Fuensalida offered a rich dinner to the whole company to celebrate the event'. In M. Nieto Nuño (ed.) *Diario del Conde de Pötting, embajador del Sacro Romano Imperio en Madrid, 1664-1674* (Madrid: Ministerio de Asuntos Exteriores, 1990), vol. II, pp.55–56.

Detail from the painting illustrating the celebration for the proclamation of Carlos IIas Count of Flanders, in the *Vrijdagmark* of Ghent, 1666 by François Duchatel (Ghent City Museum). In the foreground is a heavy cavalry company, probably the *Compañía de coraceros de la guarda del Gobernador General de las Armas*, wearing buff coat and breastplate. On the opposite side, dressed in red and on grey horses, there are the *arquebuceros de la guarda*.

which the *Chamberga* remained in Madrid, numerous episodes of violence occurred in which the guards were the protagonists, or at least accused as being the instigators. A strong rivalry had always existed among the palace corps and the jealousy among them involved the *Chambergas*.

Soon their behaviour become one of the main arguments used by opponents who did not appreciate their presence in the capital.[216] One of the most serious incidents occurred during a *fiesta de toros* celebrated on 30 July 1670 in Madrid. The incident began following a quarrel between the escort of the *Almirante* of Castile and the German Guards. A blow from a halberd wounded a page of the *Almirante* and following this a nobleman was also injured. According to the contemporary chronicle, the episode ignited an explosion of violence, and another quarrel occurred during the feast, this time involving two guardsmen, who killed an agent of the *Alguacil* (the Sheriff of Madrid). From that date, not a day passed without duels, ambushes

---

216 Even the soldiers addressed their complaints to the Queen: 'In the regiment there are many soldiers who dishonour their profession with a scandalous behaviour and incite others to do the same, because there are so many thieves, other mutineers, and another drunk and blasphemous, and so on. They enter the taverns, where they eat and drink, and leave without paying, telling the interested parts that if they protest, they will be killed, so that every day there are quarrels, and these acts only serve to disturb the people.' AGS, *Guerra Moderna*, leg. 2225: *Memorial de los Soldados del regimiento de la guardia dirigido a la reina Mariana*, 12 May 1670.

and skirmishes fought in the streets of Madrid between the *Alguaciles* and soldiers of the regiment.

The disorder lasted four days and forced the government to intervene with all the available forces to suppress the struggle, which had caused several deaths among those involved. Hoping to restore public order, the Regency appointed a new colonel, Pascual de Aragón, Archbishop of Toledo, since after the death through natural causes of the Duke of Aytona in March 1670 the position had been vacant. Harsh disciplinary measures followed,[217] but finally the government decided to remove the regiment from the capital. The order was gradually completed, and in November 1674, the last company marched from Madrid to join the regiment in Catalonia, now a front of war in the new conflict with France. The strength of the regiment was completed with recruits from Salamanca, Toro, Zamora, Ciudad Rodrigo, Río Seco, Burgos and Bañeza.[218]

Once at the front, the problems that Don Juan had foreseen occurred. The presence of the regiment of the Guards did not arouse a spirit of emulation in the field army. On the contrary, conflicts over precedence broke out with the Italian regiments, which forced the War Council to intervene with specific ordinances. To prevent any further incidents, reformed soldiers of the Guards regiment were detached to the garrison of Orán in North Africa. However, the *Chambergas* took part in the campaign participating with some merit at the conquest of the fortresses of Bellaguarda and Ceret, as well as the victory at the Battle of Maureillas. Five companies were part of the garrison of the fortress, until they were besieged by the French, where they were part of the surrender of June 1675.[219]

In the autumn, the whole regiment returned to Madrid to serve again as *Guarda del Rey*. The mutual distrust between the Guards and Don Juan had not yet subsided, and when in December 1676, Carlos II called his half-brother to Madrid, the latter demanded the removal of the regiment from the city, fearing a trap was being set against him. The final departure of the regiment from Madrid took place on 22 January 1677.[220] The muster carried out days before registered a strength of 1,527 officers and soldiers.[221] Under

---

217 The Queen ordered the formation of a special commission to restore discipline inside the regiment. See Rosa Isabel Sánchez Gómez, *Delincuencia y seguridad en la Madrid de Carlos II* (Madrid: Universidad Complutense, 1992), p.150.

218 AGS, *Guerra Moderna*, leg. 2324, the council of war to the Queen, dated 25 June 1675.

219 The five companies totalled 172 men in all, including three captains, five ensigns, four sergeants, six *reformados* captains, six *reformados* ensigns, one *reformados* sergeant, 133 private soldiers and 14 wounded and sick. BNF, GMM/2251, *Satisfacion militar y legal por … Luis de Cañas Silva y Pacheco … en respuesta del papel que se ha dado en defensa de el Maestre de Campo de Infanteria Balona Gerardo Diambercht, Castellano que fue de Bellaguardia en los confines de Cataluña y Ruissellon el año de 1675, manifestando su culpa, y omission en el sitio y expugnacion de esta Plaza …* (Madrid 1678), p.11.

220 Domínguez-Nafría, *El rey y sus ejércitos*, p.736.

221 AGS, GM, leg. 2395, *Relación de los oficiales mayores y de primeras planas, reformados, y soldados que tiene el Regimiento de la Guarda de Su Majestad*. According to this source, the regiment deployed 133 officers and NCOs and 1,137 soldiers, comprising of four artillerymen and 87 *reformados*. In this total were included 101 sick soldiers in the hospital, while 37 soldiers and officers were away, engaged in recruitment activities.

Rodrigo Manuel Manrique de Lara, count of Frigiliana y Aguilar, who held the command since 1674, the *Chambergas* returned to Catalonia, deprived of the prerogative of royal guards and downgraded to rank of an ordinary infantry *tercio*. Moreover, the implacable Don Juan of Austria deprived Aguilar of the command and exiled him to Logroño in Castile. The regiment, still known with the name of its last colonel, was assigned to the army of Sicily and incorporated into the Spanish infantry in 1678. The muster recorded before their departure from Majorca registered a final strength of 10 senior officers, 70 company officers and NCOs and 540 private soldiers.[222]

Halfway between the lifeguards and the elite units, cavalry companies were established in each *capitania general* or kingdom as a permanent corps for captain generals, or viceroys, and other senior commanders. They were essentially a company-strength unit in charge of escorting the senior ranks in every public event as well as on campaign. With some exceptions, each company deployed 100 horsemen, including one *capitán*, one *teniente*, one *alférez*, one *furriel*, two *sargentos*, four *brigadieros* (corporals) and one trumpeter. The appointment were usually offered to local aristocrats, but the places for the rank and file were usually sold by the governments.[223]

In the 1670s, the Viceroy of the Spanish Low Countries and his senior commanders, disposed of the following company of horse guards:

> The *Compañía de lanceros de la guarda del Gobernador General*
> The *Compañía de arquebuceros de la guarda del Gobernador General*
> The *Compañía de coraceros de la guarda del Gobernador General de las Armas*
> The *Compañía de coraceros de la guarda del General de la Caballería*
> The *Compañía de arquebuceros de la guarda del Preboste General del las Armas*
> Two companies of *coraceros de la guarda del Teniente General de la Caballería*

In 1672, the first three companies numbered each 128 men, the one of the Cavalry General had 130, the last two 98 and 90 respectively.[224]

In Milan, the governor and his staff deployed a similar but smaller mounted corps:

> The *Compañía de lanceros de la guarda del Gobernador General*
> The *Compañía de carabineros de la guarda del Gobernador General*
> The *Compañía de coraceros de la guarda del General de la Caballería*
> Two companies of *coraceros de la guarda del Teniente General de la Caballería*

---

222 Luis Antonio Ribot García, *La Monarquía de España y la guerra de Mesina (1674–1678)* (Madrid: Actas Editorial, 2002), pp.164 and 202.

223 This strength was the one registered also in the Army of Extremadura in the 1650s. See Picouet, *The Armies of Philip IV of Spain 1621–1665*, p.161.

224 AGS, Estado, Flanders, leg. 1334, *Muestra pasada en los Países Bajos en 1672.*

In Naples, the lifeguards usually deployed two horse companies, since the ranks remained limited to the permanent positions only:

The *Compañía de lanceros de la guarda del Gobernador General*
The *Compañía de arquebuceros de la guarda del Gobernador General*

A foot guard of 60–70 *alabarderos* was usually added to guard the Viceroy's residence in Brussels, Milan, as well as Naples and other major viceroyalties. In Naples there was a further life corps formed by local nobles, called *continui*, which numbered 50 foot guards.

This strategic provinces always benefited from particular attention and therefore their relevance was reflected by the lifeguards assigned to the viceroy and his major staff. In 1674, in Catalonia there were:

The *Compañía de coraceros de la guarda de la guarda del Capitán General*
The *Compañía de arquebuceros de la guarda del Capitán General*
The *Compañía de coraceros de la guarda del Principado de Cataluña*
The *Compañía de coraceros de la guarda del gobernador general de las armas*
The *Compañía de coraceros de la guarda del General de la Caballería*
Two companies of *coraceros de la guarda del Teniente General de la Caballería*

Furthermore, between 1674 and 1679, and 1688 and 1697, a small cavalry company was raised to provide an escort on campaign to the *Preboste General del las Armas*, bringing the total to eight lifeguard companies in wartime. In 1686, the Crown ordered the dissolution of all the companies of *lanceros*.[225]

Also, in Extremadura during the war against Portugal, the Spanish field army deployed six companies of lifeguards. In 1662 they were:

The *Compañía de coraceros de la guarda del Capitá General del Ejercito*, Don Juan of Austria
The *Compañía de arquebuceros de la guarda del Capitán General*
The *Compañía de coraceros de la guarda del General de la Caballería*, don Diego Caballero
The *Compañía de coraceros de la guarda del Teniente General de la Caballería*, Juan Martín Ruano
Two companies of *coraceros de la guarda del gobernador general de las armas*, the Duke of San Germano[226]

One year later in July, the muster of the cavalry in Extremadura also registered the *Compañía de la guardia de S. E. el gobernador* Don Gonzalo de la Guerra,[227] These units were usually formed with horsemen coming from the cavalry *trozos* of the field army. In June 1663, at the encounter of

---

225 ASV, *Segreteria di Stato* 1026, *Avvisi, Avvisi di Napoli*, 2 April 1686.
226 Estébanez Calderón, *De la conquista y pérdida de Portugal*, vol. I (Madrid, 1885), p.213.
227 *Ibid.*, vol. II, p.371.

Estremoz, the Spanish cavalry deployed two companies of lifeguards, the one belonging to Don Juan of Austria, with 280 horsemen, and the other to the Duke of San Germano, with 244; according to contemporary reports, both companies were composed of 'the flower of our (Spanish) cavalry.'[228] Before 1670, several private units were raised to provide an escort to senior officers and these frequently appear in the reports. In 1665, in the opening phase of the Battle of Montes Claros, reports mention the action performed by the *Guarda* of the Marquis of Caracena, which was a lifeguard with a special livery and ensigns.[229] These units were usually a heavy cavalry company raised for a particular war or campaign, sometimes composed of volunteers personally selected by their commander.

Other special corps, referred to as lifeguards or similar, were raised to escort court dignitaries and s of the royal family. The most famous and undoubtedly the most controversial among these corps was the *Guarda de Don Juan José de Austria*. This unit essentially was an assemblage of horsemen from different corps, but later constituted in its own right as an actual military unit. Their origin began on 31 January 1669, when Don Juan left Barcelona escorted by 300 horsemen who originally formed the lifeguard of the governor, the Duke of Osuna, along with other volunteers. In Saragossa, they were joined by further aristocratic volunteers and a captain, Alberto Arañon, who served as a cavalry officer in the kingdom of Aragon and become the commander of the unit. With these troops, about 400–500 horsemen,[230] Don Juan headed to Madrid to order the dismissal of the Cardinal Nithard.

The history of this corps crosses the tumultuous events that occurred in Madrid in the first months of 1669. The capital had descended into chaos. The military blockade caused a shortage of food in the markets and everywhere in the suburbs were 'soldiers and marauders who flaunt the name of their master and captain to insult villagers and to impose contributions.'[231] After the removal of Nithard, in March, the Queen asked Don Juan to disarm his company, and from Guadalajara sent the general of cavalry Diego Correa to encourage all horsemen to leave the service if they wanted to avoid royal punishment. However, Correa did not apply the royal order and Don Juan's lifeguards were officially disbanded weeks later.

Finally, among the corps in charge of protecting the king's court, there were the *Monteros de Espinoza*, who could be considered alongside the lifeguards. Though they were not an actual household corps, they also provided armed escorts for the king and the royal family. Their legendary origin starts in the Middle Ages and the name *monteros* originated from the hunters of the town of Espinoza, near Burgos. The first 'regular' force was raised in 1451, when 24 *monteros a caballo* (mounted hunters) received the privilege of providing the night watch for the king,

---

228 *Ibid.* pp.41–42 and 303. The company of Don Juan of Austria served under a Spanish captain, the Duke of Espinardo; that of San German was under an Italian captain, *elseñor* de Santa Cristina, who was killed in action, and his troops suffered heavy casualties in the battle.
229 *Ibid.*, p.137.
230 Sources differ on this number, stating between 400 and 1,000 men overall.
231 Letter of the Mantuan ambassador to the Duchess, in Alvarez-Ossorio, 'La Chamberga', p.36.

alternating 12 at a time for six weeks. Only *hidalgos* from Espinoza aged over 25 and qualified as free hunters were admitted. King Felipe III suspended the duty of guarding the sleeping monarch and ordered them to perform the service only for the Queen and the *infantes*. The *monteros* continued to form the night guard in the Royal residence and during the burial service of the Spanish kings until 1931.

Many of these corps enjoyed extensive privileges and served above all to maintain a loyal power base closely linked to the Monarchy. Among them, the *Guardias de Castilla* represented another prestigious and privileged corps. They were the most ancient military corps of Spain, being raised in 1493 by Isabel of Castile and Fernando of Aragon, in order to form the nucleus of a permanent military force composed of veterans under the orders of the most loyal and skilled captains. The first ordinance, or regulation, was issued in 1503, and subsequent ordinances updated the duties of the corps until 1649. In 1659, the *Guardias de Castilla* deployed 1,220 horsemen overall, divided into 24 companies.[232] In 1662, the strength decreased to 20 companies, of which 15 were armoured. Each company had a staff with a *capitán*, assisted by a *teniente*, one

Guarda de Don Juan José de Austria, 1663. Units of Household and lifeguard cavalry possessed their own special rank structures. Usually, they were organised only in troops or companies, commanded by a captain and colonel, assisted by a lieutenant and lieutenant colonel, and a varied number of junior officers; other ranks included brigadiers, sub-brigadiers, and trumpeters. The lifeguards of the Prince are mentioned wearing yellow, most likely referring to the colour of the *mantilla*, with red lining. Probably, laces were also added. Weaponry usually comprised pistols and a carbine. (Author's reconstruction)

alférez (ensign), and one *trompeta*. The corps had a *plana mayor* (major staff) formed by a *teniente general*, a *veedor* and a *contador* as commissioners, two adjutants and a *furriel mayor* (senior fourier).

Each member enjoyed special privileges, including permission not to serve without deduction of pay also in the event of the loss of their horse. Each trooper could be absent from duty for 60 days per year and could keep their horse when their service expired. Officers also benefited from great licenses to live in their own residences, upon notice to return when so ordered. They had to appoint a replacement in their absence, who was obviously the lieutenant of the company.[233] The *Guardias* did not perform actual military tasks, since their service was restricted to the Peninsula and were not required to face external enemies.

---

232 Magdalena de Pazzi Pi Corrales, 'Las Guardias de Castilla: algunos aspectos organicos', in Hernán García, Enrique and Maffi (eds), *Guerra y Sociedad en la Monarquia Hispanica. Politica, estrategia y cultura en la Europa moderna, 1500–1700* (Madrid: Labirinto Ediciones, 2006), vol. I, p.774.

233 *Ibid.*

Their main task was to escort the governors and other major officials as they travelled from one city to another in Spain, and occasionally they performed a security role against bandits and criminals, serving as something between the *Gardes d'Honneur* of the Napoleonic era and the Gendarmes of the *Ancien Régime*. They were normally quartered in Castile and Navarre, in the Kingdom of Granada and in Galicia, moving and joining the army as needed, but this occurred very rarely. In the 1650s, reports indicate that the *Guardias de Castilla* spent little time on exercises and that many officers were absent from their companies for a long periods.[234] However, in 1659, a *trozo* of cavalry was raised with rank and file coming from the *Guardias* to join the army of Extremadura. This was the only field task performed by the *Guardias de Castilla*, because the *trozo* was disbanded nine years later.[235]

Though the *Guardias de Castilla* were reformed six times between 1503 and 1649, all the ordinances confirm the same requisites as regards the choice of candidates. Each horseman had to be rigorously selected by the captains and subsequently by the *veedor* and the *contador* of the corps in order to ascertain the good qualities of the candidate and his positive behaviour as a Spanish subject.

Foreign Troops

A constant feature of the Monarchy's military policy was the heavy use of mercenary troops. In the first half of the seventeenth century, Spaniards were often a minority in the Hispanic armies, and none of the military actions of Habsburg Spain would have been possible without the support of foreign officers and men. This allowed the Monarchy to field its armies but by literally paying a very high price.[236]

Since the previous century, Germans had a strong reputation of being fearsome soldiers and they were usually commanded by skilled and well-trained officers, but they were also aware of the problems linked to their presence in the army. Officers often asked for advance payment, and if the money came late, it was not uncommon for them to refuse to fight. In addition, the German mercenaries behaved brutally towards the population and frequently looted and pillaged, especially when the wages were not paid regularly. Although the government did everything it could to guarantee their pay the German regiments were always the most expensive units of the army, since they contained more officers in the companies and on the staff

---

234 *Ibid.*, p.772.

235 The unit was under the command of Coronel Núñez Bustamante, and in 1662 passed to Sancho Fernández de Angulo y Sandoval, who led the *trozo* until its dissolution in 1668. See *Guardias Viejas de Castilla* (EC-65) in Appendix II.

236 According to Kamen, in *Spain's Road to Empire. The Making of a World Empire, 1492–1763* (London: Penguin Books, 2003), p.182, the large employment of mercenaries was one of the most vulnerable aspects of 'Spanish' power.

than the Spanish and Italian *tercios*: a problem that worried both the War Council and the Treasury.[237]

Most of the Germans in Spanish service had been recruited in the hereditary provinces of House of Austria, mainly in Austria, Silesia, Styria and other German-speaking provinces, but some regiments had also been recruited in Bohemia and Moravia. The troops coming from Flanders were mostly from the German territories close to the Spanish Low Countries, but among them was a large number of natives of the latter country, with many captains with Spanish and Flemish surnames, and even some of Italian and Irish origin. It was in fact common in the Spanish army to appoint officers of other nationalities independently of the origin of their soldiers. Limiting the search exclusively to the colonels, it is possible to observe that the German colonels made up more or less half, including those of Italian origin but long settled in Austria.

The Spaniards distinguished the mercenaries recruited in Southern Germany, Austria, and Silesia (and also Bohemia, Moravia, and Croatia): the *alto Alemanes*, from the ones coming from regions like Westphalia and other northern territories (including Denmark and United Provinces): the *bajo alemanes*. However, there was no distinction regarding their religion and already in the 1650s Lutheran recruits were admitted into the Hispanic armies, but preferably for service outside Spain. Before 1659, German mercenaries served mainly in the Spanish Low Countries and Lombardy. In the army of Flanders, they always represented a significant percentage of the field force.[238]

As these troops were a considerable financial burden, reductions in the army mainly concerned the mercenaries. In 1661, there were just two infantry and two cavalry regiments of Germans still in service in Flanders. In 1658, for the last campaign against France, Milan maintained its own contingent of German infantry and cavalry. In June, there were still two infantry regiments and two cavalry regiments, which had entered the Spanish service 10 years earlier. The force amounted to 1,000 infantry and an equal number of cavalry. In September, with the arrival of 800 new German mercenaries from Naples, the infantry increased to over 1,600 soldiers assigned to garrison duty.[239] This was an unprecedented event, since until then the only permanent foreign troops had been the Spanish and Swiss ones.

Together with the troops recruited in Germany, a contingent of soldiers sent to Italy by Emperor Ferdinand III also served in Milan, in the context of military cooperation between the two houses of the

237 Rodríguez Hernández, 'La presencia militar alemana', p.276. In this regard, many problems occurred with the German regiment Kaiserstein (EI–95) in 1660, during winter quarters in Andalusia: 'The officers claimed full pay and minimum conditions were required for the troops, as it was recognised that each soldier should be paid six *reales* per day, a figure considered essential for the sustenance in a province like Andalusia, where scarcity of bread and lack of resources were bitter eventualities.'
238 According to Picouet (p.131), in the Army of Flanders, out of 63,430 men, the Germans amounted to 16,070 men; in 1647 the overall strength had decreased to 53,720, but there were 14,310 Germans.
239 Rodríguez Hernández, 'La presencia militar alemana', p.272.

Habsburgs but limited to the territories not subject to the clauses of the Treaty of Westphalia. It was an auxiliary army, with its own staff, and with ensigns, weapons and equipment provided by the Emperor, whose task was to support the Spanish troops in Lombardy against the French and their allies. On paper there were 12,000 men divided in six regiments of 9,000 foot, and 3,000 horse in four regiments.[240]

From the point of view of Vienna, this contingent was to serve to restore Imperial prestige in Italy. However, this collaboration had its economic price, as Spain had to pay the Emperor 468,000 florins: a sum roughly equal to the cost of recruiting the same number of soldiers in Germany. Furthermore, their arrival, scheduled for the summer of 1656, was delayed and before the winter, just over half of them arrived in Milan, further reduced following the mutiny of some companies. Eventually, only 3,296 infantry and 2,047 cavalry were actually available by the end of the year. Although in the following months, the Spanish ambassador in Vienna asked the Emperor to respect the commitments, only a few troops reached their destination. In 1657, the death of Ferdinand III and the succession of Leopold I contributed to delaying the arrival of the Imperial troops in Lombardy, so much so that in September 1658 the Imperial contingent was reduced to almost half, and even the infantry was less than half of that which had arrived at the end of 1656.[241]

The need of soldiers for the planned campaign against the Portuguese forced the Spanish government to ask for new troops. Throughout 1659 the Spanish representatives in Vienna made significant efforts to obtain Imperial collaboration, including the permission to quarter the troops in the territories of the House of Austria. In Madrid, there are several King's advisers who thought that the war could continue for a long time, therefore it was agreed to authorise the recruitment for Milan of two new German infantry regiments of 1,000 men each, two more of cavalry with 600 men, plus another 150 men to complete the former Imperial regiment *Losenstein* (EI–89) quartered in Milan.[242] Moreover, Vienna and Innsbruck gave permission for Spain to recruit further soldiers in Austria and Tyrol.

The Peace of the Pyrenees did not halt the Spanish need for German mercenaries, because now their attention moved to Portugal. Adjustments were negotiated for the exchange for regiments between the armies of the two Habsburgs kings, now that Vienna too was turning to a policy of rearmament to face its involvement in Poland, Pomerania and Transylvania. Despite these difficulties two infantry regiments passed to Spanish service. Another infantry regiment, formed with the recruits enlisted in 1659, joined the contingent marching to Finale, where the ships were waiting to embark

240 For further detail see Mugnai, *Wars and Soldiers in the Early Reign of Louis XIV,* Vol. 2, pp.263–283.

241 AGS, *Estado*, leg.2367*Consulta del Consejo de Estado*,2111/1657, muster records dated 26 June 1658 and 12 September 1658.

242 Rodríguez Hernández, 'La presencia militar alemana', p.272.

them for their destination of Extremadura.[243] The Germans who arrived in Spain were mainly veterans from the armies of Milan and Flanders, which were beginning to demobilise, but there were also newly-recruited regiments, like some of those released by the Emperor. Most Germans who arrived in Spain during this period marched through the Italian Peninsula, where they were reorganised before embarking for Spain. Almost half arrived via Milan, although a quarter departed from Naples, where the units had remained for nearly a year before being transferred to Spain.

On 11 September 1660, the first contingent of German infantry sailed from Finale with 1,498 men, along with 2,100 Italian soldiers from Lombardy. The voyage was particularly difficult, as of the almost 3,700 soldiers departed from Finale, only 2,978 were mustered in Cadiz; therefore about 700 men had died during the voyage, and the majority of those present were German soldiers.[244] In order to recover from their sea voyage, the troops were quartered in Andalusia for the whole winter, so that at the beginning of the following campaign year they could march into Extremadura to fight the Portuguese. The next year, further German troops sailed to Spain along with soldiers recruited in Naples.[245]

The Kingdom of Naples had repeatedly contributed in the previous century by financing and recruiting German soldiers both for service in the Kingdom and elsewhere. In August 1659, Viceroy Peñaranda received a request from the Spanish ambassador in Vienna to recruit a contingent of Germany mercenaries for the army of Extremadura, although this was in direct competition with the recruits demanded for Flanders and Lombardy. At the end of the year, the Kingdom of Naples paid for the recruitment of 1,200 German infantrymen, but only 850 arrived via Trieste, due to recruitment issues. This regiment was placed under the veteran and entrepreneur in the field of mercenary recruitment, who in previous years had also provided troops for Milan, Colonel Simon Ludwig Spayer (EI–87).[246]

The regiment arrived in Naples at the end of 1659, when the peace with France had already been signed. Fortunately, the end of the war came in time to spare the Kingdom further expenses for further mercenaries who were enlisting in Tyrol. However, Madrid reduced the request to 2,000 infantrymen. The Viceroy was able to complete the contingent requested enlisting with little expense 80 German infantrymen released by the Grand Duke of Tuscany. With these soldiers, along with troops from disbanded

243 *Ibid.*, p.273. These troops formed the infantry regiments Hercolani, Losenstein and Carondelet. The Spanish ambassador at Vienna informed the Austrian Court that the German infantrymen had a strong aversion to embarking on the ships.

244 *Ibid.*, pp.273–274. One merchantman had a leak and took on water, and the biscuit was insufficient for all the troops. However, the worst happened in the bay of Cadiz when two merchant ships sank due to a severe storm.

245 *Ibid.*: 'They included the German regiments of Carlo Emanuele d'Este, Marquis of Borgomanero (EI–36), and *barón* of San Mauricio (EI–105), along with a company for the regiment Carondelet (EI–96; 257 officers and NCOs, and 781 soldiers), 1,317 horsemen, of which 348 were Germans, 71 *especialistas* of artillery, with several German names, and 407 women and children. Although we do not know the nationality of the families, a total of 4,244 people embarked.'

246 AGS, *Estado*, leg.2369; consultation of the *Consejo de Estado* dated 28 August 1659.

companies, Peñaranda formed another German regiment of 1,000 men entrusted to the charge of Colonel Tobias Elfrid von Kaiserstein (EI-95).[247] The regiments were transferred to Barcelona and later to Cadiz at the end of a troubled series of voyages lasting three months due to the shortage of ships. On arrival the muster at Cadiz reported that the first eight companies fielded 101 officers and 691 NCOs and soldiers; a further two companies with 300 men were sailing from Barcelona, where they were expected within a few days.[248] Finally, the regiment headed to Andalusia where it went into winter quarters in readiness for the next campaign season.

The presence of the German troops caused numerous problems. None of the officers nor the soldiers spoke Castilian; the delay in the payment of wages and the shortage of foodstuffs fuelled the thefts and incidents with the local population. Relations with the high command also became strained, because the officers demanded full pay for each month of service: a very common complaint among mercenary contingents.[249]

From the end of April 1661, the four German regiments quartered in Andalusia were sent to Extremadura and in July joined with the ones that had arrived the previous month. The Spanish command had great expectations of these troops. Don Juan of Austria expressed his satisfaction by judging them very positively, describing them as veterans of excellent quality, especially the regiments that arrived in 1660. The contingent was tactically divided into 15 *squadrones* (battalions) of infantry and made a positive contribution to the capture of Arronches, although the German infantry was also put in charge of guarding the artillery train.

In addition to the losses suffered on campaign, a high rate of desertions contributed to the reduction in strength, especially when in winter quarters due to bitterly cold conditions and unpaid wages. Furthermore, the conditions they found themselves living in contributed to an increase in disease. In some regiments, the losses were particularly high, forcing the colonels to ask the local authorities to return fugitives back into their companies, and also asking for new recruits from Germany in order to avoid having to dismiss any regiments. The muster rolls before going into winter quarters shows a very dismal situation. The regiment Carondolet (EI-96) fielded just 250 men still able to serve on campaign; Losenstein had just 200, and only the regiment Kaiserstein (EI-95) appeared in good condition with 800 able men.[250]

The decrease in strength resulted in the disbandment of several infantry companies in the army, especially in the German regiments, which maintained more expensive staff compared to the *tercios*. Although a reform of the regiments in Extremadura was contemplated, the final reform occurred

---

247 *Ibid.*, leg. 2283; consultation of the *Consejo de Estado*, dated 31 August 1660.
248 AGS, *Guerra Antigua*, leg. 1955, the muster on 11 August 1660. The strength was dramatically reduced in the following months. On 2 November the regiment deployed 10 companies, with 51 officers and 860 soldiers in good health, since there were many sick distributed among the hospitals of Seville. The civilian authorities also had to allocate beds to house the women following the troops. The regiment had 56 sick soldiers in Seville and another 53 in Cadiz, still unwell after the poor conditions experienced during the sea crossing.
249 Rodríguez Hernández, 'La presencia militar alemana', p.276
250 Estébanez Calderón, *De la conquista y pérdida de Portugal*, vol. I, p.339.

in November 1661, which resulted in the disbanding of further companies and reducing all the German regiments to eight companies. The regiment of Count Hercolani (EI–88) was disbanded, and its remaining companies passed to Losenstein.[251]

During the campaign of 1662, the German troops still represented 18 percent of the infantry in the army of Extremadura, which participated to the conquest of Juromenha. The high reputation of the Germans in terms of combat was balanced by their not always exemplary discipline and by the continuous disputes with the Italian regiments regarding being part of the avant-garde, because this position guaranteed better prospects of looting in enemy territory. Both the Italians and the Germans were veterans and could easily rely on their knowledge effective of plundering against the Spaniards, who were mostly inexperienced in war.[252] The campaign continued with the siege of Evora and after the fall of the city, two German regiments – Francisco Franquet (EI-37)[253] and Carondelet, and one company from the Kaiserstein – formed the garrison. Again, winter quarters led to many desertions among the German regiments.

This dramatic decline in strength forced the government to find new recruits in Germany. At the end of 1660 offers had already been received from private individuals, generally veteran officers who had serve Spain, to recruit troops and raise new regiments. This kind of proposal increased in 1662, and even dignitaries such as Prince Alessandro Farnese personally offered to recruit 6,000 men in Germany.

However, all these proposals were ignored, due to the higher costs they would incur compared to recruiting in Spain, Italy or Flanders, or the activities continuing in Austria. But the major opponent to these proposals was the War Council, which expressed a negative opinion towards increasing the number of German regiments. The Council explained that a German colonel cost 500 *escudos* a month, and 200 rations of extra bread: an excessive expense compared to the pay and bread issued to the Spanish, Italian or Flemish Walloon *maestres de campo*. Despite these objections, it was decided to enlist further German mercenaries, ordering the Viceroy of Naples to raise funds for the recruitment of 2,000 soldiers for the army of Extremadura, who would arrive via Milan, while another 2,000 Germans would be sent from Flanders. However, these rather optimistic expectations were not fulfilled, since in 1662, only 27 German and Flemish recruits arrived in Extremadura, who had been personally enlisted by Baron de Carondelet for his regiment (EI-96). The situation did not change even the following year, when no German recruits were sent to the regiments in Extremadura.

In the campaign of 1663, the German regiments were involved in the disastrous defeat of Ameixial-Estremoz. Although the Germans fought valiantly, and one foot regiment withdrew with admirable discipline saving

---

251 Rodríguez Hernández, 'La presencia militar alemana', p.277.
252 Estébanez Calderón, *De la conquista y pérdida de Portugal*, vol. II, p.34.
253 Recruited and paid by the Kingdom of Naples.

all their flags and drums, the rest of the infantry fled in disorder. Taking advantage of the chaos, the fugitives looted their own army's baggage.[254]

Alongside the army of Extremadura, there were German units operating in Galicia. In 1662, some free companies participated in the Spanish offensive under general Baltasar de Rojas, which crossed the Miño River and plundered villages and towns under Portuguese rule. The Germans came mainly from Flanders, and among them were the German regiments under Francisco de Rojas y Cardenás (EI–114), and Guillermo Cascar (EI–115), with 606 officers and 1,232 soldiers, recruited and paid by the provinces of the Spanish Low Countries. Both regiments had many officers and few troops; wages were higher than the ones paid to the troops in Galicia, which aggravated the problem of the lack of money. Misfortune hit the Germans again, when in July the regiment Cascar suffered significant losses while serving in Arronches, when an unfortunate accident caused the arsenal to explode, killing 40 soldiers and wounding 77 others.[255]

The defeats suffered in Portugal in 1663 set in motion the machine of the Monarchy to rebuild the army of Extremadura. It was necessary to carry out significant transfers of recruits to bring thousands of soldiers to the Portuguese border. Several options were considered, and it was decided to recruit more Lutherans and other 'heretics', as all that mattered was to recover Portugal.[256] This decision brought into the army Protestant officers too, who had been a rarity in Spain before, but they brought new knowledge and experience to the army. Although the presence of the Germans in Extremadura caused many concerns, they performed effectively in every encounter, and their officers proved to be an important resource in the development of infantry tactics.

Before the end of 1663, further negotiations to obtain soldiers began all over Germany. Altogether, the Government hoped to enlist 2,000 German infantrymen in order to reinforce the veteran regiments in Extremadura. This contingent could be completed by resorting to an approach to the grandson of the Archbishop of Salzburg, a pensioner of Spain, who could get permission to recruit soldiers in the Bishopric. In addition, the Kingdom of Naples and Milan would each raised a new infantry regiment of at least 1,500 soldiers and 180 officers, as well as 500 horsemen. In addition, with an agreement with the King of Denmark, another 1,000 infantry and 1,500 horse would be recruited for Spain. Finally, two further regiments of 500 cavalrymen could be recruited in Liège and Brandenburg.[257]

However, the most significant source of recruiting was still through Vienna, which agreed with Madrid to transfer more infantry and cavalry to Spain. The first to arrive were the two German infantry regiments from Naples, who landed in Spain in early July, with a total of 190 officers and 2,586 soldiers. In September 1664, now that the Ottoman threat had been

---

254 Estébanez Calderón, *De la conquista y pérdida de Portugal*, vol. II, p.47.

255 Rodríguez Hernández, 'La presencia militar alemana', p.280.

256 *Ibid*.

257 AGS, *Guerra Antigua*, leg. 2051: *Mapa de la infante IÍa y caballería que se ha de componer el ejército para la invasión de Portugal para la primavera de 1664.*

averted at Szentgotthárd, the infantry regiment under Alfonso Portia (nephew of the Imperial Prime Minister) sailed to Cadiz with 153 officers and 1,032 soldiers in 11 companies (EI–136). The cavalry followed some weeks ago.[258] The regiment Portia was involved in a series of unpleasant events. While quartered in Jerez de la Frontera, it had serious quarrels with the local population. The Germans got the worst of it and lost several dozen soldiers and officers, in addition to part of their weapons and baggage, which had been looted by the inhabitants. Disease and desertions caused further losses and by December, the regiment had lost more than 300 men.[259]

The cavalry sent by the Emperor arrived in Andalusia in the last months of 1664. They were the cuirassier regiments of Luigi Carafa (EC–84) and Leonardo Edmondo Fabbri (EC–85).[260] Their presence soon caused problems. For two days, the 1,200 dismounted German soldiers of the Fabbri regiment were quartered in Puebla de Cazalla, committing various abuses on the population. Months later, at the end of their stay in Jaén, the regiment was reduced to 95 officers and 687 horsemen, divided into 11 companies. Early in 1665, the cavalry received the first 100 mounts. The regiment remained in Andalusia until May, and then marched to the Portuguese border.

Meanwhile, the German presence in the army of Extremadura was still decreasing, despite the arrival of the new contingents from Galicia and overseas. This prompted the War Council several times to re-examine the possibility of recruiting replacements through the collaboration of the German colonels. Notwithstanding some existing agreements for new recruits, the lack of troops forced the high command to disband most of the veteran infantry regiments, leaving only four, namely the regiments considered as the best and with the most capable officers.[261] However, only one regiment could field 10 companies, while another two only had eight.[262]

Along with the regiments arrived from Italy and Flanders, these troops participated in the last offensive against Portugal. The campaign ended with the defeat at Montes Claros, where the Germans fought with bravery, especially the former regiment Carafa, now Rabatta, but suffered heavy casualties. Both regiments continued to serve in the following years, but they are registered 'without horses'. In spring 1667, regiment Rabatta, always dismounted, formed the garrison of Castillo de Guarda on the border with Galicia, which successfully held out against a Portuguese siege.[263] In Autumn

258 Rodríguez Hernández, 'La presencia militar alemana', p.282: 'The cavalry boarded unmounted weeks later due to the lack of boats and horsemen's protests by depriving themselves of their mounts as they love their horses more than their own women.'
259 *Ibid.*, p.283. The War Council ordered an investigation on the incident, condemning the township to quarter other troops and to pay for the recruitment of 400 German soldiers to compensate the Crown.
260 Luigi Carafa's *Cuirassieren* was a veteran regiment which served during the war against Sweden in 1657–60. However Fabbri's regiment had poor field experience, having served on the Austrian-Hungarian border only for observation duties.
261 They were the infantry regiments Kaiserstein, Carondelet, Losenstein, and Franquete.
262 Estébanez Calderón, *Dela conquista y pérdida de Portugal*, vol. II, p.304.
263 Jonathan Riley, *The Last Ironsides. The Portuguese Expedition to Portugal, 1662–1668* (Solihull: Helion & Company, 2014), p.163.

1668, the German infantry still serving in Extremadura was sent to Catalonia via Cadiz. On 8 October, there were only three infantry regiments with very few soldiers, numbering 364 officers and 634 soldiers, as well as 194 women and 104 children,[264] who would continue their service in Catalonia. As for the cavalry, according to the seniority of the officers, a single regiment was formed and served in Catalonia until the end of Habsburg dynasty.

The War of Devolution again called for the recruitment of more German mercenaries. The army of Flanders was again the one that filled the need for soldiers. Four German infantry regiments were already recruited in 1666, including three from the disbanded army gathered by the Prince-Bishop of Münster for the war against East Friesland and the Dutch Republic. The same source was exploited to enlist four cuirassier regiments, which joined the regiment Metternich (EC–86), already enlisted in 1665 in Austria and Bohemia. Between 1667 and 1668, five infantry and six cavalry regiments entered the army of Flanders, and another German infantry regiment came from Naples.[265]

A further German infantry regiment was recruited by Milan, by turning to the Imperial army, who transferred the former *Strassoldo zu Fuss* (EI–174).[266] The supply routes for German mercenaries had been well established, however the transfer of hundreds of men did not always take place without problems and delays of various kinds. In 1667 the 1,000 Germans recruited in Hamburg by Prince Friedrich of Holstein were detained in Germany by the Dutch authorities, who did not allow them to pass through the territory of the Republic, forcing the whole contingent to transfer by sea to Ostend.[267]

The recruitment of German soldiers also had ups and downs before and during the Franco-Dutch War. Over time, Spain faced problems enlisting German soldiers for Italy and Flanders, because the distance, financial issues as ever, and the Austrian Emperor's resistance as the Spanish conscription activities competed with recruitment for his own army, which prevented the increase in the number of the Germans in the Hispanic armies. Thus, the practise of enlisting German soldiers in non-Habsburg countries had already become common, and as a result, few of the soldiers serving in the Spanish Low Countries were subjects of the Emperor. In 1672 and 1674, only three infantry regiments, a small fraction of the total number of Germans soldiers enlisted for Flanders, had been recruited in the Emperor's domains.[268]

In the 1670s, Spain encountered considerable problems in maintaining its armies because of the lack of German soldiers. However, in the winter 1671–1672, to cope with the international situation that was rapidly deteriorating, the governor of the Spanish Low Countries, Count of Monterrey, ordered the recruitment of 2,000 German infantrymen turning to the Westphalian,

---

264 AGS, *Guerra Antigua*, leg. 3506. *Junta de Armadas, Relación de la gente que se transporta a Cataluña*, dated 8 October 1668.

265 Former Imperial *Regiment zu Fuss* Starhemberg (EI–145).

266 Alphons von Wrede, *Geschichte der K. und K. Wehrmacht* (Vienna, 1898–1901), vol. II, p.165.

267 Rodríguez Hernández, *España, Flandes y la Guerra de Devolución*, p.351.

268 Maffi, *Los últimos tercios*, p.227.

Rheinish and Swabian states. In 1674, Monterrey authorised the recruitment of further 8,000 mercenaries for the last great enlistment push in Germany.[269]

The research of further mercenaries moved to other German states. In January 1678, the Council of State even tried to negotiate with the Duke of Hanover (Brunswick-Lüneburg) to hire troops. The search for German soldiers did not leave out any source of supply. In 1678, two former 'German' regiments of the Dutch Republic joined the Spanish army of the Flanders,[270] while other 'German' soldiers came from Lorraine and Liège.

The last great recruitment of troops in Imperial territories took place in 1675, when one German regiment was sent to Sicily. A further 2,700 Germans recruits were enlisted to serve against Messina, and in addition, a small number of soldiers were also enlisted for Milan. Here, since 1668, a German infantry regiment were garrisoned in the state. In this decade, the percentage of Germans infantry and cavalry in Lombardy represented on average about 20 per cent, increasing to 30 per cent in 1668 and 1670.[271] In the Kingdom of Naples too, the German mercenaries served as a permanent garrison joined by free companies of infantry and cavalry.[272]

In Catalonia, the German presence was smaller but no less significant, numbering between eight and 10 percent of the infantry and rising to 20 percent at the end of the 1680s. In 1674, the Viceroy of Catalonia, the Duke of San Germano, asked for the permission to enlist four German regiments. The Viceroy supported his demand stating that German officers and soldiers were usually of good quality, and 'they served with punctuality and with them the army can hope of some successes.'[273]

No less reputed than the Germans, a small number of Swiss mercenaries came to Spain. The Crown signed a series of agreements with the Catholic cantons starting from 1533, in order to recruit infantrymen, and from 1639 extended the same rights to the Protestant cantons and the League of Grisons. Usually, the agreement was managed by the Milanese ambassador, who signed the recruitment of companies or whole regiments with the Cantons' authorities.

The Swiss and the Grisons usually supplied units already organised with their own senior staff, NCOs and private soldiers, who served for a

269 *Ibid.*, p.229.
270 Regiments Danhanrè (EI–245) and Arenberg (EI–246), in *Gazeta Ordinaria de Madrid, 1678*; p.218.
271 Maffi, *Los últimos tercios*, p.229.
272 Regarding the history of German regiments in Spanish service, there are some recent publications that have made the matter even more confusing due to errors and misinterpretations. In G.C. Boeri, J.L. Mirecki and J. Palau, *The Spanish Army in the War of the League of Augsburg, 1688-1697* (London: Pike & Shot Society, 2002), the regiment Rheyngraf (EI–263) is registered among the units still in service in 1689, but the regiment had been disbanded in 1684. The regiment of Fabian von Wrangel (EI–213) in 1690 is attributed to Diego Suarez Ponce de León, who died in 1688. Further errors concern the regiment of the non-existent Viscount of Ahere, which is possibly confused with the regiment of Octave Ignace de Ligne-Arenberg, who was also Viscount of Davre, and colonel of a German regiment between 1678 and 1680 (EI–246). Several inaccuracies concern the German cavalry regiments also. See Juan Luis Sánchez Martin, 'Recensiones', in *Researching & Dragona* vol. VIII, n. 23 (November 2003), pp.127–131.
273 Maffi, *Los últimos tercios*, p.229.

predetermined number of years, ensuring the maintenance of the agreed contingent. Weapons, dress and equipment, had to be provided by the Crown or the Kingdoms. Compared to the Germans, both Swiss and Grisons costed almost twice as much, although they usually were better disciplined and caused fewer incidents. However, during the Thirty Years' War, Spain relied little on the Swiss, demonstrating a certain distrust towards them, fearing that they would refuse to fight against their compatriots in the French army.[274] The Swiss infantry remained therefore confined to Lombardy, where they formed the garrisons in the north of the state.

The Spain's lack of confidence in the Swiss, and to a lesser extent in the Grisons, did not diminish even after 1659, aggravated as it was by the clauses inserted by the cantons in the contracts, which demanded that their soldiers would not serve outside Milan, this being the state which had enlisted them. However, all these setbacks did not prevent in 1663 the Crown resorting to making approaches to the Swiss and the Grisons for strengthening the army of Extremadura. A first agreement was signed with the canton of Uri for a regiment of 10 companies under *coronel* Johann Josef von Beroldingen, which followed another contract with Lucerne for 2,000 more infantrymen.[275] The Grisons contributed with further five companies. The Helvetic contingent performed poorly on campaign. The harsh environmental conditions and the delay in the payment of their wages caused the officers to complain, and the strength of the contingent dropped to half in less than one year. Furthermore, the non-compliance with the provisions relating to the payment of wages was exploited by the cantonal authorities as they did not provide new recruits to make up losses to the agreed establishment. After their participation in the battle of Montes Claros, the Swiss and Grisons headed to Castile for garrison duties. The regiment of Lucerne was disbanded in 1668, while the one from Uri continued to serve in Lombardy until 1685.[276] With them, 500–600 Grisons in nine companies of foot served in Milan from 1659 to 1690, when a whole regiment was finally raised. Apart from Milan, in the following years the Monarchy did not turn to the Swiss when in search of mercenaries to enlist, notwithstanding the need of manpower for their overstretched commitments in Flanders, Catalonia and Sicily.[277]

The search for mercenaries therefore turned to other territories, such as Corsica. The enlistment of recruits on the island could be exploited thanks to excellent relations with Genoa, and the relative proximity of Corsica to Spain and Italy made their transfer easier. In 1641, a first attempt to raise a regiment had been unsuccessful, but at the beginning of 1675, the Corsican *coronel* Vincentello Gentile personally committed himself for recruiting a

---

274 *Ibid.*, p.233.

275 Acta Helvetica, 26/76 –106, *Abrechnung der Sieben Katholischen Orte und Abtei Sankt Gallen mit König von Spanien.*

276 ASV, *Segreteria di Stato, Avvisi, Avvisi di Napoli*, 15 August 1685.

277 The Dutch representatives in Madrid and Brussels suggested the Spanish government consider more carefully the possibility of relying on the Swiss mercenaries, because the Crown could have reduced the number available to France, which had used them very profitably in the first years of the Franco-Dutch war. See Maffi, *Los últimos tercios*, p.234.

tercio to be sent to Sicily.[278] In October the enlistment had already begun, and in November the first companies sailed to Naples.

In 1675, in Sicily the regiment deployed seven companies of 208 men in all, but without the colonel, who returned to Corsica to raise further recruits. The events relating the raising of this unit were very troubled, however it shows that the Crown and its War Council paid close attention to the quality of the recruits, especially when dealing with expensive mercenaries. After the agreement signed to form a *tercio* of 1,000 men with 10 companies, in April 1676 the War Council intervened for the first time to ascertain the origin of the recruits, in order to know if the Corsican colonel was recruiting King's subjects or even deserters from the Spanish army. Weeks later, the War Council required to Gentile to explain the protests of some recruits who had declared to the Spanish commissioners that they had been enlisted by deception.[279]

Subsequent investigations revealed that while serving the Republic of Genoa, Gentile had been involved in irregularities relating to recruitment, and this persuaded the War Council to ask for a further investigation. Their suspicions were probably justified, considering that after less than two years of service, the regiment still had only 110 soldiers.[280] Regarding the fate of Vincentello Gentile's regiment, the Duke of Bournonville, commander of the army of Sicily, suggested disbanding it and to assigning the soldiers to some border garrison in Spain.[281] Together with the Corsicans, Bournonville also mentioned three companies of 'Albanians'. They were 196 infantrymen who had joined the Army of Sicily in 1675 under a Neapolitan Knight of Malta, with the promise of being enlisted into a Neapolitan *tercio*. Bournonville considered it impossible to merge them into the Italian or Spanish infantry as they only spoke Albanian or Greek. The only person who could understand them was one of their officers, brother of the Orthodox Bishop of Durres, who claimed to have served in Candia under the Venetians in 1669. The Duke recognised that they had served well and therefore proposed assigning their leader the rank of *sargento mayor* and forming the 118 soldiers still present in an autonomous infantry company to serve in Sicily.[282]

Unlike the Germans and the Swiss, who, if they survived, returned to their homes, the Greek-Albanians had severed all ties with their countries becoming exiled mercenaries. Like them, the Irishmen also belonged to this category. The first Irish soldiers in Spanish service arrived in 1587, then in the following century the Irish immigration reached considerable figures, encouraged by the local leaders who opposed the English rule. According to some authoritative historians, in 1635, 7,000 Irish mercenary served in the army of Flanders, and between 1648 and 1668, 22,000 Irishmen crossed the

---

278 AGS, *Estado*, leg. 3614, d 82, *Carta de Antonio Domingo de Mendoza Caamaño, marqués de Villagarcía, embajadoren Génova, a Carlos II, rey de España, sobreel tercio de corsos para el servicio español que ofrece levantar el coronel Vincentello Gentile*, 21 March 1676.

279 *Ibid.*, d 87, 29 April 1676.

280 Ribot García, *La Monarquía de España y la guerra de Mesina*, p.202.

281 ASS, *Appunti e Documenti*, vol. XXIV, p.502.

282 *Ibid.*

sea to enter the Spanish armies,[283] of which 12,000 all together in 1653–54.[284] By the middle of the century, the Irish mercenaries represented the fifth *nación* of the Hispanic army. However, while thousands of resolute warriors were among those who arrived in Spain at the turn of the century, after 1641 most of the new arrivals were of lesser quality, and later exiled or encouraged by the Cromwellian government to leave their country to prevent them from becoming a public order problem. Their service was not positive, as stated by the senior commanders, who described the Irish infantry as 'less disciplined, unwilling to fight and untrustworthy'.[285]

When new infantry regiments were recruited in the 1650s, private Irish colonels were expected to select the soldiers in advance. For his regiment raised in 1650, Colonel Richard White agreed to gather 600 men in six companies, followed in 1652 by Christopher Mayo with 1,500, and Thomas Plunket, the latter committing to raise three infantry regiments of 3,000 men overall.[286] In 1659, there were 12 Irish regiments, all deployed in Galicia, Catalonia and Flanders, one of which was the veteran *Tercio viejo de Irlandeses* (EI–13), raised in Galicia in 1605. High wastage and reductions involved the Irish units in 1660 and 1661, but they did not disappear. In 1663, two regiments still served in Flanders, two in Extremadura and, although with a strength reduced to a few hundred, one in Galicia.

The presence of the Irish in several theatres of war made it difficult to maintain an acceptable combat strength. Some units were regiments just in name: in 1658, the regiment Dungan (EI–20), quartered in Badajoz, had only 41 men, little better than the regiment O'Maloney (EI–90), which in the same year had only 16 soldiers.[287] Both regiments waited for recruits coming from Flanders, where the situation was better. In November 1659, the regiment O'Meagher (EI–51), just arrived in Ostend, numbered 143 officers and NCOs, with 792 private soldiers, while the regiment of George Cussack (EI–51) had 15 companies with 153 Officers and NCOS, with 521 private soldiers.[288]

In 1667 new attempts were made to recruit further Irish mercenaries directly in their country, after an agreement with the King of England for a levy of 4,000 infantrymen to be allocated to Flanders. After six months, just

283 Óscar Recio Morales, 'When merit alone is not enough. Money as a "parallel route" for Irish military advancement in Spain', in *Society for Irish-Latin American Studies* (Burtigny, Switzerland), p.122.

284 Eduardo De Mesa Gallego, *The Irish in the Spanish Armies in the Seventeenth Century* (Rochester, NY: Boydell Press, 2014), pp.111–114.

285 Maffi, *Los últimos tercios*, p.238. In 1658, the Irish commander of the Forte de San Miguel in Extremadura, William Dungan, brother of the colonel Michael Walter (EI-20), surrendered and joined the Portuguese service in the English Brigade. See Meneses, conde de Ericeira Luís de, *Historia de Portugal Restaurado* (Lisbon, 1679), vol. II, p.110.

286 Recio Morales, *When merit alone is not enough*, p.122.

287 *Copia de párrafos de relacion de la gente que había en este ejercito (Portugal), la que ha entrado y va entrando de differentes partes, y del estado en que se halla lo perteneciente á la artillería y víveres*; in Estébanez Calderón, Serafín, *De la conquista y pérdida de Portugal*, vol. I (Madrid, 1885); pp.325–328.

288 Sánchez Martin, Juan Luis, *Tropas Británicas de la Casa de Austria*, in 'Researching & Dragona', vol. IV, n. 8 (May 1999); pp.17–18.

half of this force had been recruited, and many of them deserted because it was not possible to pay their wages.[289]

During the Franco-Dutch War, the Irish regiments were assigned to second-line garrisons and did not take part in any major military actions. Nevertheless, their strength diminished considerably. In the last year of war, the size of the regiments were reduced to a fraction of their establishment: the regiment of Thomas Taaffe (EI–31) had just two companies, while Dennis O'Byrne's (EI–28) had only one.[290] In 1678, the two regiments in Flanders were reformed into one, but the strength diminished again, since in 1681 there were just two companies in all.[291] In May 1681, Colonel O'Byrne obtained permission to recruit '500 dressed and armed men to be presented in Ostend within three months'.[292]

Further attempts were made in the following months, when the governor Prince Alessandro Farnese received permission to recruit 2,000 men in Ireland and Scotland. Once again, economic troubles thwarted the project, and when the recruits arrived in Ostend in 1682, there were a total of 600 men, who were sent to reinforce the garrisons in Flanders.[293] This temporary reinforcement did not solve the problem, because the companies continued to appear strongly understrength. In 1684, the Irish regiment numbered just 340 men, including 25 reformed officers who served as private soldiers.[294]

In the 1680s, the Spanish Low Countries and Catalonia still maintained the largest Irish force, with the last regimental-size units formed by Irishmen, while Lombardy retained one free company until 1678, when it was finally disbanded.[295] The rapprochement between London and Madrid did not encourage the enlistment of the Irish in the army of *Los Austrias*. After 1677, the *Wild Geese* resolutely sided with Louis XIV, and after the Glorious Revolution of 1688, their presence in Spain further withered away.[296]

Belonging to a political party hostile to the London government was also the basis of the English presence in the Hispanic armies. An English mercenary regiment of infantry already existed from 1631, raised by Edward Parham (EI–14) for the army of Flanders. Further English soldiers and

---

289 Maffi, *Los últimos tercios*, p.238.

290 Sánchez Martin, *Tropas Británicas de la Casa de Austria*, pp.17–18.

291 *Ibid.*; these were the company of the colonel Dennis O'Byrne and that of the *maestre de campo reformado* Thomas Taaffe. A bitter dispute began between the two colonels over which of the two was to take command of the regiment. O'Byrne had the support of the War Council, but Taaffe was determined to assert his rights. In 1684, Governor Ottone Enrico del Carretto, Marquis del Grana, warned Madrid that the quarrel would not subside, 'because both officers have their reasons'. In January 1685, the Governor proposed that Taaffe joined his company into the Scottish regiment Gage (EI–180), with the prospect of becoming commander at the first opportunity but he refused, not wanting to serve with Scots. Taaffe probably resigned his commission in the Irish regiment, as before the end of the year the command passed to another officer.

292 *Ibid.*, p.17

293 Maffi, *Los últimos tercios*, p.238.

294 Sánchez Martin, *Tropas Británicas de la Casa de Austria*, p.17.

295 Maffi, *Los últimos tercios*, p.255. In 1676, the Irish company in Lombardy deployed 46 men, 53 in 1677 and 44 in 1678.

296 In the 1690s there was only one Irish regiment in Spanish service. See Sánchez Martin, *Tropas Británicas de la Casa de Austria*, p.19.

officers arrived when Felipe IV offered refuge to the aristocracy who had fought for Charles I against Parliament.[297]

In 1655, Cromwell's England declared war on Spain, and the treaty of alliance with France led to the expulsion of Charles Stuart and all the Royalist leaders from Paris. This act offered the exiled King and his followers the opportunity to gather further troops in the Low Countries, since Madrid hoped to create a diversion against Republican England in order to seize Dunkirk. In 1656, Spain promised to support the refugees with enough funds to raise 6,000 men, after a full agreement signed in April between the Charles Stuart and Felipe IV. Recruitment started, but in the spring of 1657 the King's army numbered just 2,500–3,000 men in all.[298] With this manpower, six infantry regiments were formed, and in 1658 four of these joined the Army of Flanders, followed by a fifth regiment one year later.[299]

Difficulties in finding more volunteers forced the refugees to turn to Irish and Scots recruits, and with typical English tenacity, Charles succeeded in gathering 4,380 men in 1659.[300] The Royal English army in exile was under the command of the King's brother, James Stuart, Duke of York, who joined the staff of Don Juan of Austria. Less trained and probably also less motivated compared to the English soldiers who sided with France, on 14 June 1658, the Royal army again faced its old enemies of the Civil War at the Battle of the Dunes.

After 1659, the army of Flanders underwent a drastic reduction that included the English troops. The War Council was even less inclined to trust the English and the Scots than they did the Irish. The religious question and the support that England had always offered to the United Provinces of the Netherlands also influenced their judgment. However, the English troops were often directed by skilled officers and many soldiers could claim several years of experience accumulated in the Civil War. All the English officers who served Spain were veterans of the Royalist army, and as far as troops are concerned, in 1659 the Marquis of Caracena declared that the English *tercios* were among the best of the Army of Flanders.[301]

In 1662, the English presence in the armies of Spain was represented by a single infantry regiment with some free companies in Flanders, and a few officers serving in Spain. These latter proved to be a useful link for new recruitment in case of need, as occurred in 1667. The governor of the Spanish Low Countries opened negotiations with London to get English troops to be sent to Flanders, but the most immediate help came from a

---

297 Despite the commitments on multiple war fronts, the English refugees tried by any means to extend the conflict to England itself. The archive of the Dukes of Frias preserves the plan devised by George Digby, Duke of Bristol, for an invasion of England to bring Charles II to the throne. The project dates to 1657 or 1658 and was also discussed with the Marquis of Caracena and the Count of March; see AHNOB, *Frias*, leg. 132, ct. 12. Thanks to Francesco Pellegrini for this note.

298 Picouet, *The Armies of Philip IV of Spain 1621–1665*, p.159.

299 These were the King's Own regiment, Livingston's regiment (Scots), Ormonde's regiment, the Duke of York's regiment, the Duke of Gloucester's regiment, and Bristol's regiment. See C.H. Firth, 'Royalist and Cromwellian Armies in Flanders, 1657–1662', in *Transactions of the Royal Historical Society*, New Series, Vol. 17 (1903), pp.93–94.

300 Davide Maffi, *En defensa del Imperio, Los ejércitos de Felipe IV y la guerra por la hegemonía europea* (Madrid: Editorial Actas, 2014), p.402.

301 Maffi, *Los últimos tercios*, p.241.

veteran of the Royal Army who had fought for Spain in the 1650s, James Tuchet, Count of Castlehaven.[302] In early 1667, the Count agreed to raise a regiment of foot, but stressed by financial difficulties, the recruitment proceeded slowly, and the result was far from the one expected. Furthermore, the transfer to Flanders was very complicated, and the recruits, mustered at Ostend in April, were found to be of poor quality. Delay in the payment of wages caused the desertion of many soldiers, who fled at the first occasion, and even the officers refused to continue to serve if they did not receive their money.[303] Another contract was signed in May 1667 with the former Royalist Lieutenant Colonel John Morgan to recruit 500–600 men in order to complete the existing English regiment. Morgan had pledged to present the recruits in 30 days, but after three months he had collected just 136 men, mostly from Wales. Better luck was encountered in the second enlistment campaign managed by the Earl of Castlehaven, who in June 1668 had gathered 950 men.[304]

In 1668, one Scottish regiment was also raised by Colonel Francis Scott (EI–181), which in the muster of June numbered 200 men.[305] The Peace of Aix-la-Chapelle interrupted recruitment, and the English soldiers were gathered in two regiments with 28 companies in all including the Scots.[306] One year later, both the English regiments were reformed into one. In the 1670s, the English and Scottish presence was reduced to a few hundred men quartered in the Spanish Low Netherlands.[307] In 1680, James II agreed to recruit volunteers in England and Scotland for Spain, and thanks to these levies it was possible to bring the English and Scottish regiments to a strength of 600 men each. This was the last Spanish recruiting campaign in the British Isles. In 1685, the Scottish regiment had 11 companies with 175 men in all.[308] The existence of both regiments ended between 1689 and 1692, when the last 159 English soldiers still in service were released or assigned to the foreign units in the army of Flanders.

Along with the English contingent of Charles Stuart, another private army had joined Spain in Flanders in 1653. This was the army of the Louis II de Bourbon, Prince of Condé. During his service for Spain, the Prince had gathered a considerably military force of cavalry and infantry recruited in France with the support of the Fronde's nobility. In 1655 this army numbered about 5,000 cavalry and 3,400 infantry, including Frenchmen but also foreign

---

302 James Tuchet, third Earl of Castlehaven, Baron Audley of Hely (1617?–1684) was the son of Mervyn Tuchet, second Earl of Castlehaven and his first wife, Elizabeth Barnham. The younger Tuchet succeeded to the Irish earldom of Castlehaven and the barony of Audley of Orier (Hely) on 14 May 1631, when his father was attainted and beheaded. Castlehaven was a Catholic Englishman and played a prominent role in the Civil War, especially in Ireland.

303 Rodríguez Hernández, *Flandes y la Guerra de Devolución*, p.230.

304 *Ibid*. According to Rodríguez Hernández, this figure also included the English regiment already serving in Flanders.

305 Sánchez Martin, *Tropas Británicas de la Casa de Austria*, p.21.

306 Rodríguez Hernández, *España, Flandes y la Guerra de Devolución*, p.383.

307 Sánchez Martin, *Tropas Británicas de la Casa de Austria*, p.20. In 1678 the veteran regiment of Castlehaven (EI–14), the only English regiment still in service, had just two companies

308 AHNOB, *Osuna, Relación del modo en que quedaron los tercios y regimientos de infantería después de la reforma ejecutada por el marqués de Grana*, ct. 197, d. 83 (1st January 1685).

Hispanic ensign (and officers?) on the front cover of Johan Georg Pascha's fencing treatise published in 1673. (Author's archive)

mercenaries. Only 3,500 cavalry and 2,000 infantry were paid directly by Condé, since the other troops were supplied by the armies of Flanders.[309] Inevitably, after 1659, the reduction in military spending could not ignore the dismissal of foreign contingents, especially the personal ones, such the Condé's army. The Prince had obtained a pardon from Paris for himself and for those who wanted to return to France, but a number of unyielding *Frondists* asked to continue serving Spain.

Though they were generally considered warlike officers and soldiers, the authorities of the Spanish Low Countries had often complained of the poor attitude of the French towards the local population. However, in 1659 the War Council proposed to raise one infantry regiment and a couple of cavalry companies from the disbanded army of Condé. At the command of the infantry regiment was Louis de Bourbon Orléans de Charny (1640–1692), illegitimate son of the Prince Gaston of Orléans, and cousin of Louis XIV. The regiment (EI–92) was assigned to the army of Extremadura, but soon its existence was threatened by the shortage of recruits. In 1662, the eight companies numbered about 200 men in all.[310] In June 1665, at the Battle of Montes Claros, the surviving companies of the French regiment in Spanish service faced the French soldiers who sided with Portugal. This was the last action performed by the regiment, which was disbanded before the end of 1665. In 1662, a company of French cavalry is recorded in the army of Extremadura with 84 men in all.[311] Spain became a useful refuge for other French nobles who entered military service. Among them, Adrien Blaise de Talleyrand-Perigord de Chalais (1638?–1670), became colonel of a German regiment in Extremadura (E–16) in 1663, and later served in Catalonia. He held the post until May 1670, when he left Spanish service after negotiating his return to France, but he never made it home, dying of fever in Venice a few months later.[312]

---

309 This figure is particularly relevant considering that in 1655 the Army of Flanders numbered 3,000 Cavalry and 5,000 infantry in all; see Fernando González de León, *The Road to Rocroi. Class, Culture and Command in the Spanish Army of Flanders, 1567–1659* (Leiden–Boston: Brill, 2009), p.356.

310 *Plan del ejército de Castilla que con don Jian de Austria entró en campaña contra Portugal en 1662*; in Estébanez Calderón, *De la conquista y pérdida de Portugal*, vol. I; pp.336–340.

311 *Ibid.*

312 In 1662 Chalais took part in a duel in Paris, which ended with the death of the Duke of Beauvilliers. Chalais did not trust in royal forgiveness and fled to Spain in 1663, where he entered the service of Felipe IV.

Left: Jean Gaspard Ferdinand de Marchin (or Marsin) (1601–1673). A native of Huy, in the Bishopric of Liège, in 1635 he entered military service as a captain of an infantry regiment in French service. As a follower of Condé, Marchin was arrested in 1650 and released after 13 months of enforced residence at Perpignan. Marchin joined Condé in Spanish service and in 1657 was appointed commander of the English army in exile by Charles II. In 1659, after receiving his pardon from Louis XIV, and a negotiation to return to French service, he decided to remain in Spain. In 1662 he passed to the command of Don Juan of Austria in Extremadura, but in 1664 refused to serve under Caracena. In 1667, Marchin served with the Army of Flanders, and in August led the attempt to relieve Lille under French siege, but was defeated at the Channel of Bruges.

Right: Louis de Bourbon, Duke of Enghien and Prince of Condé (1621–1686) portrayed as a Spanish commander in the late 1650s. The Prince assembled a private army of considerable strength in Flanders, which sided with Spain until 1659. After the Peace of the Pyrenees Condé and his followers were pardoned, but some irreconcilable Frondists continued to serve Spain. Until 1664 one French infantry regiment served in Extremadura under Louis de Bourbon-Orléans de Charny, along with one cavalry company. (Author's collection)

The Portuguese, the other arch-enemy of Spain, increased the large variety of mercenaries who served in the army. Along with some leading aristocrats who sided with Felipe IV after 1640, Portuguese soldiers continued to serve in the Hispanic army. Until 1668, entire Portuguese companies formed the *tercio* of Francisco de Alarcon de Torres Vedras (EI-92), the same one that became a Provincial *tercio* in 1664 with the denomination *Valladolid*. In August, all the ethnic Portuguese were discharged, and the unit became wholly Castilian.[313] Further Portuguese infantrymen served in Extremadura against their compatriots. They were 200 former prisoners-of-war who formed a *tercio* under the *maestre de campo* Rui Pérez de Vega (EI–116). The Portuguese *tercio* was one of the few that performed positively at the battle of Ameixial-Estremoz in 1663, but the fear of anti-Spanish plots persuaded the War Council to disband the *tercio* in 1664.[314]

Between 1659 and 1688, Hispanic armies included further foreigners, such as the 2,500 foot and horse from Lorraine in the 1650s, of which about 600 formed one infantry regiment in Lombardy from 1659 to 1660 (EI-44). The variety of foreign mercenaries increased in the 1680s, when 1,700 Swedish and Courland infantry joined the army in Flanders.[315]

Infantry Organisation

For centuries Spanish infantry represented the most important component of the army and were always regarded as elite troops, formed by experienced veterans, usually well trained and equipped. Some *tercios* could boast over a century of existence, with battle honours dating back to the Italian Wars of the sixteenth century. In 1659, there were 12 old *tercios* still operating, raised between 1531 and 1596.[316] The oldest *tercios* retained the name of the province where they originally had the quarter. Some *tercios* also carried an appellation that would seem to indicate a foreign origin, like *Napoles*, *Sicilia* or *Flandes*, but in reality, they were composed of ethnic Spanish soldiers. It should be noted that in Spain it was usual for the *tercios* to get a designation, while in Flanders and Italy they were normally identified by the name of the commanders.

Along with these veteran infantry units, further *tercios* had been raised for the service with the fleet, which were also considered as elite. In the 1660s, there were four marine infantry *tercios*, increased to seven in the 1680s.[317]

---

313 See AGS, *Servicios de Pedro de Villacis*, dated 3 September 1677. Concerning the provincial *tercio* of Valladolid, the Count of Clonard has eluded 10 years of history.

314 BNE, *Sucesos del Año 1663*, p.345.

315 Maffi, *Los últimos tercios*, p.241. The first contingent arrived in Flanders in 1683, followed by a second one in 1684, both amalgamated with the German regiments.

316 Juan Antonio Samaniego, *Disertación sobre l'antiguedad de los Regimentos de Infanteria, Cavalleria y Dragones de España* (Madrid, 1738).

317 In 1662 there were the *tercio l'Armada del Mar Oceano* (EI–3), formed in 1562, the *tercio Napolitano viejo de l'Armada* (EI–49), formed in 1655, the *Infanteria de la Armada* (EI–70), 1657, and the *tercio* of Bernardo de Lizarazu (EI–180), raised in 1662. One year later, the *tercio provincial de Jaén* (EI–63) was assigned to the fleet, while in 1664 the *Infanteria de la Armada* became the provincial *tercio de Madrid*. After the disbanding of the former *tercio provincial de Jaén* in 1664. Between 1682 and 1688 three further marine *tercios* were formed.

Although some of these units had been previously formed as temporary corps, joining free companies in *tercios* already established in Spain and southern Italy, in the last quarter of the century, they became regular formations. However, on several occasion the marine *tercios* served in a land campaign like the ordinary ones.

In 1659, the ancient Spanish veteran *tercios* still formed the permanent garrisons in the European domains. These were four in Flanders, three in Lombardy, two in Southern Italy, and three in the Iberian Peninsula. Along with these latter, *tercios de naciones* formed from recruits coming from the domains outside Spain were also raised. In 1659, there were three Italian *tercios* and two of Flemish Walloons with more than 15 years of service. Finally, the Hispanic army also contained large numbers of foreign infantry, probably the most varied and cosmopolitan of this age. Among the foreigners, in 1659 there were seven German regiments raised between 1632 and 1659, a further nine regiments came from Ireland, enlisted between 1605 and 1658, and finally two English regiments raised in 1623 and 1645. Moreover, in 1659 there were a large number of *compañías sueltas* (free companies) of all the nationalities employed in garrison duty in all the domains, including a single company of Grisons raised for the army of Milan. Apart from the latter, most of these companies were composed of aged soldiers and officers unfit for active service in the field.

In addition to the ancient permanent units, there was also a very long list of *tercios* recruited in Spain as well as outside the Iberian Peninsula during the Thirty Years' War or immediately after, in response to the strategic contingencies of the time. As already discussed, to follow the history, organisation and evolution of these units is a very difficult and complex task. In addition to the errors committed by nineteenth-century historiography and by the scholars who followed, there are several significant obstacles that – perhaps – could be resolved only after a thorough search in the *mare magnum* of the archive sources.

With the exception of a minority these *tercios*, whose tradition continued until the next century, most had a very short existence, or were subjected to reforms and reductions of strength, as well as being amalgamated into other units, which makes it increasingly difficult to be sure of their identification, history and succession of commanders.[318] This list is actually huge, and continues right until the end of the century, with a peak in the early 1660s.[319]

---

318 Many authors argue that as far as patents and commissions are concerned, each of these corresponded to an operational unit. The reality was, however, very different. The documentation relating to patents offers a multiplicity of examples of officers who have received a commission to form a *tercio*, but then the affair ends in nothing. Hundreds of cases are documented relating to patents of *maestre de campo* granted to form *tercios* to be sent to the Americas that never materialised. However, there are opposite cases, with officers acting on a temporary basis without a regular appointment. To overcome these drawbacks, some governors had blank patents ready to use any fill out in case of need. In some archives, such as that of the *Generalidad de Cataluña*, there are dozens of patents ready to use, in which only the name of the commander is missing.

319 For instance, it is not clear whether the *tercio* of Pedro de Viedma (EI–63), recruited in 1657, and indicated by Clonard as *tercio nuevo*, is instead the one already existing in 1653 in Jáen, which has no continuity under further *maestres de campo*. The *tercio* of 1657 was recruited in

In this period, in fact, many temporary *tercios* were recruited, and immediately reformed or disbanded at the end of the campaign. For instance, the *tercios* raised in Extremadura, which joined the field army from 1659 to 1665, changed their commanders almost every year. The same *maestres de campo* were subjected to a high turnover. An example is the case of Gabriel Laso de la Vega y Córdoba (1623–1697), Count of Puerto Llano. In 1658, he was appointed *maestre de campo* of a *tercio* recruited in Malaga (EI-73) to relieve the siege of Badajoz. Then, in 1662, the same officer held the command of another *tercio* formed in Malaga (EI-106), with which he participated to the siege of Juromenha, but after only 55 days he and his unit were disbanded.[320] Likewise, there were also several *tercios* assembled in wartime that had a very short life. This is the case of the *tercio* assigned to the *maestre de campo* Iulian Davila, formed in Extremadura with six *compañías sueltas* and sent to Badajoz in June 1665, but it was soon disbanded, in May 1666.[321]

The scenario becomes even more complex with the *tercios* that replaced their commanders at the beginning of the campaign, like the *tercio Casco de Granada* (EI-46), which had seven *maestres de campo* from 1653 to 1659.[322] Several units were recruited at their own expense by private individuals, usually high ranking aristocrats, which usually joined the army for just a couple of years.[323] This composite situation is echoed in the composition of the units, which present a large variety of strengths and organisation. To make matters even more variable, there were the foreign regiments, which were organised differently, and the same occurred with the Italian or Flemish Walloon *tercios* when they served outside their country.

Originally, the strength of the *tercios* varied according to the strategic contingencies, increasing or decreasing the number of soldiers and companies. This always resulted in considerable freedom regarding the number of companies within the *tercio*, and the matter remained unresolved for several years. The reforms introduced in 1632 dealt with the administrative and tactical organisation of the infantry, and established the number of officers, non-commissioned officers and soldiers in each company but only for the army of Flanders.

The reforms tried to re-establish the power of the old *tercio* and to eliminate all the negative features that had decreased the efficiency of the infantry, such as the excessive number of officers and other personnel in the senior and company staff and established a fixed number of companies. The new organisation had to be extended to all the infantry *tercios* throughout the army, but some differences concerning the foreign units continued for

---

Extremadura, but three companies from Jáen were also included. See Clonard, *Historia orgánica*, vol. IV, p.154, and AGI, *Indiferente*, leg. 123, N. 57. Thanks to Francesco Pellegrini for this note.

320 AGI, *Indiferente*, leg. 124, N. 19.

321 *Ibid.*, leg. 123, N. 98, Servicios *del maestre de campo Iulian Davila*.

322 *Ibid.*, leg. 128, N. 3, *Servicios del maestre de campo Joseph de Novoa y Butron*.

323 Among these short-lived *tercios*, the one recruited by Pedro Macedo Leyte in April 1658 (EI–74), was disbanded in January 1659, and the *tercio* of Pedro de Ponte Franca Llerena (EI–184), recruited in Canarias in 1672, was reformed after eight months of service. Also, the Flemish Walloon *tercios* raised in 1668 had a short existence. After the emergency of the War of Devolution, 13 out of 14 *tercios* were disbanded after less than one year of service.

a long time. However, this reform represented the basis of every future arrangement of the Spanish infantry until the end of the century, and the changes introduced after 1636 by *Cardinal Infante* Fernando of Austria and his successors were only updates of the original reform. The 1636 reform introduced the *tercio* formed by 13 companies of pikemen and musketeers and further two companies of arquebusiers. In the Walloon and Italian *tercios* the ordinary company had a strength of 200 men, and 250 in *tercios* raised in Spain. As a result, each Spanish *tercio* would have had an overall strength of 3,650 men, against 3,000 in the Italian and Walloon ones. This pattern remained unchanged until the 1640s. According to contemporary sources,[324] each *tercio* had a *plana mayor* (major staff) composed as follows:

1 *maestre de campo* with two servants
1 *sargento mayor* (major) with two adjutants
1 *auditor* with two *alguaciles* (sheriffs)
1 *escribano* (clerk)
1 *capitán de campaña* (prevost), with four guards
1 *tambor mayor* (drum major)
1 *furriel mayor* (chief quartermaster)
1 *cirujano mayor* (senior surgeon)
1 *capellán mayor* (senior chaplain)

The *plana mayor* could comprise a variable number of *reformados*, namely unassigned officers and private volunteers.

A characteristic feature of the Spanish *tercios* remained in the prerogatives of the senior officers, which differed from those in use in most of the European armies. Indeed, though the *maestre de campo* was also the commander of the first company, the *sargento mayor* did not hold the command of a company. Although some particularities occurred in the last decades of the seventeenth century, the *maestre de campo* was not the proprietor of the *tercio*, but he held the charge after the *patente* of appointment issued by the King, who remained the actual proprietor of all the troops.

The *maestre de campo* usually did not exercise any right regarding the choice of officers, but he could propose them, and held only the judicial authority for disciplinary offenses over the men in his company, as well as acting as a judge of the whole *tercio*. Only the king could appoint the *maestres de campo*, or at least confirm the candidates proposed by the viceroys or by the provinces, and by the War Council of course. The requirements for this rank were generally the ones deemed innate and natural in quality people. This suggests that military knowledge was less important, and in fact it was only in 1632 that the War Council established that the candidates must have served for at least eight years as an infantry or cavalry captain, before they could accede to the rank of *maestre de campo*. However, until the end of the century, the membership of the high aristocracy or providing the funding

324 *Noticias y documentos relativos a la organización del Ejército de Flandes, entre 1535 y 1661* (manuscript without date, Biblioteca Nacional de España), pp.24–28.

for recruiting campaigns could free the way to an appointment to the rank without having served a single year in the army.

These careers were not a novelty in the armies of the *Ancien Régime*, and in some case the sale of ranks was harshly criticised in Spain too. The protests did not go unnoticed, and the War Council periodically returned to the subject trying to introduce a somewhat stricter selection process. This matter was also supported by the intellectuals, such as Francisco Ventura de la Sala y Abarca, who in 1681 still complained the presence of *maestres de campo* who had not performed any military duties before entering the army.[325] Although the presence of such types of officers in command of *tercios* or regiments gradually diminished, the sale of ranks remained a practice that the Crown always resorted to, due to the lack of resources to support its deadly wars with its enemies.[326]

The lack of specific skills could, however, be compensated for by a skilled *sargento mayor*. In fact, he was the officer who most often dealt with the troops on campaign, controlled internal discipline, and managed relations with the captains and their staffs. The *sargento mayor* also dealt with the tactical deployment of the companies on the battlefield. On the subject of the command staff, the company of a Flemish Walloon *tercio* comprised a *primera plana* including:

1 *capitán* (with his page-boy)
1 *alférez* (ensign)
1 *abanderado* (colour bearer)
1 *sargento*
1 *furriel* (fourier)
1 *barbero* (barber-surgeon)
1 *capellán* (chaplain)
3 musicians (2 drums and 1 fife)

The company was completed by:

10 *cabos* (corporals)
180 *plazas* (privates)

An ordinary company comprised 90 musketeers and 90 pikemen. The arquebusier company deployed the same *primera plana*, 10 corporals, 149 arquebusiers and 30 musketeers. The *Cardinal Infante* adjusted this proportion, and the Spanish units they fielded a force on campaign of 200

---

325 Francisco Ventura de la Sala y Abarca, *Después de Dios la primera obligación y glosa de Ordenes Militares* (Naples, 1681), p.33

326 Among the many cases of buying a commission, in 1688 the wealthy Aragonese *asientista* Francisco Villalonga agreed to recruit a third of 600 men at his expense in exchange for the appointment as captain of a cavalry company in Mallorca. The following year his brother Jorge contributed 500 men in Jáen for the marine infantry, obtaining seven blank patents for the appointment of captains, and asking for a noble title like the one granted to his brother.Both Villalongas served as *maestre de campo* in Catalonia and Lombardy. See AHNOB, *Frias* Ct.87, d.45, and Antonio José Rodríguez Hernández, *La venta de títulos nobiliarios*, pp.294–295.

men for the ordinary companies, now with 10 corporals, 69 pikemen and 120 musketeers, and the arquebusiers companies were left unaltered. In 1642 a major reduction impacted on the Spanish *tercios* of the field armies, which reduced the number of men in each company to 100.[327] The number of pikeman, musketeers and arquebusiers was established according to the new field strength. The *primera plana* remained unchanged, except for the introduction of one *lugarteniente* in the commander's company.

The Spaniards had been among the first to successfully combine pike and firearms in their infantry formations. The use of firearms progressively increased at the expense of pikes more or less as in the rest of Europe, however a characteristic of the Spanish infantry was the maintenance of two different types of firearms: arquebus and musket. The presence of three different classes of foot soldier remained a constant feature of the Spanish infantry until the 1690s. The distribution of the weapons within the infantry reflected the theatre of operations. In the 1650s, in Extremadura, the proportion of arquebuses was 41.4 percent, compared with 30.6 of muskets and 28 of pikes. In 1665, in Flanders, the proportion was a third of each, with the arquebusiers numbering 34 percent, and musketeers and pikemen each with 33 percent.[328] Gradually, the percentage of muskets increased following the technical improvement of gunpowder and weapons, but the lighter arquebus did not disappear from the Spanish infantry arsenal until the last years of the century.[329]

The Spanish and Italian or Walloon tercios were structured differently depending on whether they were outside the metropolitan territory or not. Thus, a Spanish *tercio* in Flanders deployed 15 companies of 100 men, while in the Iberian Peninsula it consisted of 12 companies of 150 men including musketeers, arquebusiers and pikemen. According to Francisco Barado,[330] in 1652, the Italian and Walloon *tercios* underwent a reorganisation, which especially concerned the strength of each company. When they served in their respective country, the *tercios* fielded 12 or 13 companies of 100 men. The same organisation was extended to the Burgundian (Franche-Comtois) infantry. The strengths had to double when the *tercios* served outside their own territory, with 186 private soldiers and 14 officers and NCOs, on the paper at least.[331] This scheme continued until 1659 and even after this date, for the formation of new infantry *tercios* the patent still referred to the Spanish, Italian or Walloon strength.

German regiments had a different organisation and strength, which usually comprised 10 companies of 200 men. In the 1650s, the regimental staff could include from 20 to 40 officers and adjutants depending on the prestige of the colonel, or the privileges accorded to him.[332] This was the primary cause of the higher cost of these units, to which could be add one

327 Clonard, *Historia orgánica*, vol. IV, p 415.
328 Picouet, *The Armies of Philip IV of Spain 1621–1665*, p.170.
329 In 1691, the *tercios* of the Army of Flanders had a theoretical strength of 436 men, of which 144 pikemen, 144 musketeers and 148 arquebusiers. See Antonio José Rodríguez Hernández, *Breve historia de los ejércitos. Los tercios de Flandes* (Madrid: Notillas, 2014), p.69.
330 Barado, *Historia del Ejército Español*. vol. III, pp.532–533.
331 *Noticias y documentos relativos a la organización del Ejército de Flande*, p.30.
332 Maffi, *Los últimos tercios*, p.228.

or two commissioners in order to survey the regularity of payments and supplies. The *plana mayor* of the German regiments included ranks which were not seen in the Spanish, Italian or Flemish Walloon *tercios*:

1 *coronel*
1 *teniente coronel*
1 *sargento mayor*
1 *quarrel maestre* (quartermaster)
1 *auditore*
1 *capitán de justicia*
1 *lugarteniente de justicia* with 2–4 *albarderos*
1 *escribano*
1 *capellán mayor*
1 *secretario* with 2 adjutants
1 *municionero*
1 *médico* (physician)
1 *barbero* (barber and surgeon)
1 *intérprete*
1 *cocinero* (cook)
1 *verdugo* (executioner)
1 *portero* (guardian)
1 *maestro de los carros* (waggon master) with three *lugartenientes*

The German *plana mayor* also included a variable number of colonel's servants, and volunteers who served as supernumeraries.[333] The regiments acquired from Austria comprised 18 or 19 persons on the senior staff, and nine in each company's *prima plana*.[334] In the other cases, the company comprised the same ranks as for the Spanish one, but with one *teniente* in all the companies and one *capitán teniente* in the colonel's company. The high number of officers remained a constant feature of the regiments recruited in Germany with few exceptions, but if the major and company staff were always complete, the strengths varied considerably from a unit to another.[335] In terms of the provenance of the officers, the German regiments usually included captains of various nationalities. For instance, among the four captains of the regiment Varhel (EI–155) wounded at Espolla in 1677, there was the clearly non-German Francisco de Sales; while in the regiment Hesse (EI-95) just half of the officers died or wounded had German names.[336] The *primera plana* of the German companies consisted of nine officers and NCOs:

333 *Ibid.*, p.264. In 1658 the regimental staff also included one sergeant who dealt with the prostitutes accredited by the regiment.
334 See Mugnai, *Wars and Soldiers in the Early Reign of Louis XIV,* vol. 2, p.82.
335 In 1659 the German regiments in the Army of Flanders deployed on average 848 men divided in 15 companies. See Picouet, *The Armies of Philip IV of Spain 1621–1665*, p.149.
336 *Gobierno del Duque de Villahermosa* (manuscript, Biblioteca Nacional de España), vol. VI, p.149. National identification remains difficult, considering the custom of the time to Hispanicise the names, therefore Captain Jorge Henrique of the regiment Varhel could not necessarily be the supposed Georg Heinrich.

1 captain
1 lieutenant
1 ensign
1 sergeant major
2 sergeants
1 secretary
1 quartermaster
1 surgeon

German regiments were usually formed by two only specialties, namely musketeers and pikeman. Each company had 8–10 *Gefreiter* (supernumeraries) and the same number of corporals.

According to Clonard, in 1659, the 'regular' number of companies in the Spanish *tercios* was established to 20, but an examination of the musters executed in this period, shows a very different scenario, with *tercios* formed of 20 or 10–12 companies and even less. In this regard, there are innumerable examples. In April 1662, the *tercio* recruited in Malaga for the army of Extremadura deployed just 200 men in six companies.[337] In the 1670s, this disparity persisted, since in 1674 the Spanish infantry in Flanders deployed 12 or 20 companies, and with a strength which varied from 300 to 1,200 men.[338] Although the companies could be detached from the *tercios* for specific contingencies, the survival of autonomous company strength's appears largely unregulated until the 1680s. In Spain the establishment strengths of companies were almost never reached even when forming new units. As a result, the overall strength of the *tercios* constantly fluctuated.

Obviously, all the regulations bore very little similarity with the reality, and the number of officers was also subject to some variations. As established in the reform of 1636, the *tercios* included reformed NCOs and officers from disbanded corps, originally established as two *sargentos* and two *alférez* in each company.[339] Despite this, exceptions were usual because the number of reformed officers remained variable throughout this period, and often the number of *attaché* increased with the admission of volunteers. In some case, the reformed officers even exceeded the number of captains! In February 1685, the Neapolitan *tercio* of Reitano Cantelmo (EI-9) had 11 companies with 21 *reformados*, including one *maestre de campo* and one *sargento* mayor, while in the *tercio* commanded by the Marquis of Torrecuso, again from Naples (EI-252), there were 13 companies with 6 reformed captains. The same number were serving in the Neapolitan *tercio* of Fabio Bonamico (EI-224), while the Spanish *tercio* of Joseph Moncada de Aragón had 24 reformed officers.[340] Figueres, however, noted that they were subject to significant

337 AGI, *Indiferente*, leg. 124, n. 19.

338 AHNOB, Osuna; ct.197, d.84–85: *Listado de los tercios y regimientos de infantería y caballería españoles, italianos, irlandeses, escoceses, ingleses, borgoñeses, valones y alemanes* (March–April 1685) and ct.197, d.82.

339 *Noticias y documentos relativos a la organización del Ejército de Flandes, entre 1535 y 1661* (manuscript without date), Biblioteca Nacional de España, p.28.

340 AHNOB, c. 197, d. 80; *Estado de la fuerza de los oficiales reformados y de los soldados de los diferentes tercios y regimientos españoles de infantería, caballería y dragones, destacados en*

reductions, considering that five years later, the *tercio de la Armada* (EI-49) had just four reformed officers.[341]

All the data show that it is very difficult to establish what was the theoretical strength of the infantry *tercios* and companies in the Hispanic armies between the 1660s and 1680s. There are so many exceptions that each unit represents a specific case. Furthermore, it should be considered that in the mid seventeenth century the *tercio*, like the regiment in other European armies, represented a compromise between administrative corps and tactical unit. For this reason, also, the expected number of companies and men remained a random concept for a long time.

According to the Duke of Albuquerque, in 1673 the infantry company could number up to 120 men, a size reputed the best for effective manoeuvring on the battlefield.[342] As always, the reality did not correspond to the expectations, because the muster rolls seem to confirm how the regulations represented just a general idea, since the strength of the *tercios* swung by many hundreds of men between one *tercio* and another. This happened due to the distances from their place of origin, with the consequent difficulty in finding adequate numbers of replacements.

Drawbacks hit more or less every army of this age, but gradually some commanders imposed some uniformity in the organisation of corps and a homogeneous distribution of forces, while the Spanish Crown seems to have been hampered in this process by various factors, such as regional differences, as well as the resistance of *maestres de campo* and captains, who were unwilling to assign their men to other units.[343] Until the end of the seventeenth century, despite the ordinances issued, campaigns casualties, and other ups and downs of circumstances produced changes in the structure of units.[344]

The difference in the number of companies among the *tercios* was not the only thing characteristic of the Spanish army in these years, as even the numbers of soldiers were often at a minimum. In the 1650s and 1660s the musters often refer the presence of companies with a mere 25 men or less. Several examples are astonishing. For instance, in 1661, the *tercio* of the *maestre de campo* Pedro de Viedma (EI-63) was sent to Extremadura with

---

Flandes en conformidad a la última revista que se les pasó en el mes de febrero de 1685.

341 Jacinto Narvaez Pacheco, *El sitio de San Antonio de Alarache en 1689* (Madrid, 1893), p.70.

342 Maffi, *Los últimos tercios*, p.164.

343 Often the transfer of soldiers from one unit to another took place after negotiations and compromises. From the servicios of Joseph de Garro, it clearly appears that in 1655 he was captain of one of the six Walloon infantry companies raised by Captain Jacques Gour. He landed in San Sebastian and from there transferred to Catalonia, where he joined the *tercio* of Pedro Ernesto de Francia (EI–42). After a long negotiation Garro was appointed *sargento mayor* in exchange for the transfer of his company to another captain. He maintained the rank even when the *tercio* was disbanded and incorporated into the Walloon *tercio* of Diamberg (EI–201). All this was between May 1655 and January 1664, when Garro obtained a discharge to return to Madrid, where he received a command in Galicia AGI, *Indiferente*, 122, n. 137, *Relación de Servicios del Maestre de Campo D. Ioseph de Garro, cavallero de l'orden de Santiago*.

344 For instance, in 1663 at the battle of Ameixial-Estremoz, the five Italian *tercios* deployed respectively 16, 14, 14, seven, and seven companies. See Estébanez Calderón, *De la conquista y pérdida de Portugal*, vol. II, pp.302–305.

only 98 troops in all.[345] In 1659, the old Spanish *tercios* were the only ones to deploy 20 companies, but with just 627 men on average, resulting in 31 men for each company.[346]

In the army assembled in Extremadura in 1663, the 26 Spanish infantry *tercios* numbered on average 250 men with companies of 30 men or less.[347] The weak strength of each company remained a constant of the Hispanic armies and involved the infantry of every nationality.[348] In 1663, the seven Italian and Walloon *tercios* in Extremadura numbered on average 404 men with 81 companies composed of 35 men on average.[349] Throughout the period from 1659 to the late 1660s, the total strength of a *tercio* often corresponded to what a single company was originally supposed to field. As for the foreign units, in the 1660, all the German regiments in Extremadura were below the established 10 companies, and the average strength varied from 44 officers and soldiers per company in 1661, to 32 in 1666.[350]

The scenario becomes even more confusing during the following years, when the pressure of war on several fronts affected the structure of the units. Among the many cases recorded in contemporary documents, the *tercio Viejo de la Armada* (EI-32) in October 1677 deployed in 45 companies; the *tercio de Sicilia* (EI-6) had 28, and *Mallorca* (EI-221) 10. These *tercios* composed the infantry besieging Messina, which included infantry of several nationalities, each with its organisation, like the eight companies in the Milanese *tercio* of Francesco Arese (EI-229), or the 17 companies in the German regiment Cicinelli (EI-216).[351] Obviously the losses caused by the fighting produced gaps in the companies, but the difference in strength between one *tercio* and another was often considerable already at the beginning of a campaign, or even in peacetime. In early 1685, just after the reform of the army of Flanders in 1684, the Spanish *tercios* deployed 21 or 20 companies,[352] but this homogeneity was only apparent, since was not reflected in the overall strength. The *tercio viejo de Flandes* (EI-1) deployed 1,100 men, while the *tercio* Castillo (EI-273) had 460 men, and Moncada (EI-8) only 400, despite all three having the same number of companies.

345 'opia de párrafos de relacion de la gente que había en este ejercito (Portugal), la que ha entrado y vaentrando de differentes partes, y del estadoen que se halla lo perteneciente á la artillería y víveres', in Estébanez Calderón, *De la conquista y pérdida de Portugal*, vol. I, pp.325–328.

346 Picouet, *The Armies of Philip IV of Spain 1621–1665*, p.146.

347 *Copia de Carta venida de Badajoz, que avisa la salida del Exercito de su Alteza del señor Don Juan of Austria en campña, Lunes siete de Mayo de 1663* (Madrid, 1663), pp.153–155.

348 The Neapolitan tercio of Fabrizio Rossi (EI–49) just arrived in Extremadura in 1660, had only 45 men in all. Rodríguez Hernández, 'Al servicio del rey', p.232.

349 Picouet, *The Armies of Philip IV of Spain 1621–1665*, p.149.

350 Rodríguez Hernández, Antonio José, *Financial and Military Cooperation between the Spanish Crown and the Emperor in the Seventeenth Century*, in Rauscher, Peter (ed.) 'Die Habsburger monarchie und das Heilige Römische Reich vom Dreissigjährigen Krieg bis zum Ende des habsburgischen Kaisertums (Vienna: Aschendorff Verlag, 2010), p.284.

351 ASS, *Appunti e Documenti*, vol. XXIV, pp.499–500; relation of the Duke of Bournonville dated 21 October 1677.

352 AHNOB, *Osuna, Relación del modo en que quedaron los tercios y regimientos de infantería después de la reforma ejecutada por el marqués de Grana*, ct. 197, d. 83 (1st January 1685).

The Italian *tercios* were just as unequal since they consisted of 13 or 14 companies but with a strength between 300 and 800. Finally, the Flemish Walloon *tercios* comprised 12 to 14 companies and a strength of between 1,200 and 300 men.[353] The German regiment varied from 10 to 12 companies.[354] Three years later, the army of Flanders deployed 10 Spanish *tercios* with 153 companies of 43 soldiers on average. As for the Italians, they now deployed four *tercios* with 48 companies of 29–30 men each. The Burgundian *tercio* (EI-43), the only in the army of Flanders, deployed 14 companies but with only 252 men in all. Finally, the Flemish Walloons, with 11 *tercios*, deployed 131 companies of 28 men on average. As for the German regiments, their companies now numbered from 25 to 50 men. The list was completed by further 10 Spanish free companies with 1,131 men in all.[355]

It was only towards the end of the 1680s that more regularity began to be observed, albeit with several exceptions. In 1688 all the *tercios* of the army of Catalonia comprised between 13 and 19 companies and more than half of the *tercios* had a strength above 600 men.[356] This trend continued throughout the next years with the notable exceptions of the older corps. In 1689, the Neapolitan *tercio de la Armada* (EI-49) still deployed 10 companies but with only 200 men in all, while the veteran *tercio del mar Oceano* (EI-3) numbered 1,200 men with 20 companies.[357] In 1685 the Italian *tercios* had still not achieved any homogeneity. The *tercio* of Tommaso Casnedi (EI-231) numbered 459 men divided between 12 companies; the same number of companies as registered in the *tercio* of Martino Carafa (EI-236), which had 400 men.[358]

The difference in field strength between one unit and another was a problem that the army had already faced for some time. Usually, the *tercios* were joined to form tactical corps – or *esquadrones* – with a similar overall strength. In the 1650s the Spanish commanders considered as acceptable a 'regular' strength of 600 men. In the next decade the desired strength decreased to 500 or most often to just 400 men. In 1677, Sebastián Fernández de Medrano considered the ideal strength of a *tercio* to be at least 1,000 men, in order to deploy two field battalions of 468 soldiers.[359] A general reform was introduced on 1 May 1685, after the experiences gained in the wars against France. It was again the army of Flanders that introduced these changes thanks to the initiative of the *maestre de campo general* (and later Viceroy) Francisco Antonio de Agurto y Salcedo. The *tercio* was now identified with the tactical *esquadron*-batallion,

353 *Ibid.*

354 AHNOB, *Osuna*;ct.197, d.82: *Estado de la fuerza de los ejércitos de caballería e infantería españoles destacados en Flandes (Bélgica), con expresión del número de compañías que posee cada tercio o regimiento*, dated 3 March 1685.

355 Eduardo De Mesa Gallego, 'Los tercios en combate (III). Organización y tácticas de los ejércitos de la Monarquia Hispánica (1660–1700)', in *Desperta Ferro* Special Issue XIX, June–July 2019, p.37.

356 Antonio Espino López, 'Las tropas italianas e la defensa de Cataluña, 1665–1698', p.55.

357 Narvaez Pacheco, *El sitio de San Antonio de Alarache*, p.70.

358 Espino López, *Las tropas italianas e la defensa de Cataluña*, p.55. The *tercio* Casnedi had been distributed among the garrisons of Bagá, Palamós, Barcelona, Gerona, Olot and Vic; Carafa manned the garrisons of Olot, Ripoll, Barcelona and Rosas.

359 De Mesa Gallego, *Los tercios en combate*, p.36.

established on a regular force of 436 soldiers divided into eight companies. The company staff numbered 12 officers, NCOs and drummers, at the head of eight corporals, 124 pikemen, 268 musketeers, and 36 arquebusiers.[360] However, it should always be remembered that the strength recorded on paper did not consider the sick or even the 'fictitious' soldiers. In some cases, the difference could see a decrease in the total by a third.

However, the major problem that made it difficult to maintain the established strength was the loss of territories and the consequent impossibility to find recruits, as happened in the case of the Franche-Comté. The loss of this province in 1678 did not mean the end of the Franche-Comtois presence in the army. Despite the low number of recruits available, after 1674, two infantry *tercios* survived in the Low Countries and another in Lombardy and later in Sicily, all three avoiding permanent disbandment which could be expected with the loss of the home recruiting grounds. The need to maintain the ancient 'Burgundian' presence had an obvious political value, since the actions performed by the local partisans against the French could encouraged the Crown to retain the 'loyal Franche-Comtois nation' in the army.[361]

In 1678, one of the *tercios* in Flanders, under Alexandre-Ignace-Guillaume de Pontamougeard, was disbanded leaving the veteran *Tercio de Borgoñones* (EI–43) as the only Franche-Comtois infantry unit in the army of Flanders. Under the command of the *maestre de campo* Henri Richard, and *sargentomayor* Baron Philippe-Emmanuel de Monfort,[362] the Franche-Comtois *tercio* continued to serve in the Spanish Low Countries, although reduced to only 262 men.[363] Faced with the lack of recruits, in the spring 1684 the end of the last Burgundian *tercio* was inevitable.

---

360 Francisco de Agurto, *Tratado y reglas militares* (Madrid, 1689), pp.47–50.

361 Quirós Rosado, *La fiel nación* p.88.

362 AGS, *Estado*, leg. 4057. *Memorial* of Barón de Montfort to Carlos II; letter of the Duke of Villahermosa to the king, dated 18 May 1679) and *consulta* of the State Council, 6 July 1679. Montfort, who had served since 1660 in the armies of Milan and Franche-Comté, received the membership of the Knights of Santiago in 1671 from Queen Maria Anna of Austria. In 1673, during 'the last revolution in the county of Burgundy' Montfort obtained the permission to serve in the staff of the Duke Charles IV of Lorraine. After 1674, he lost all his possessions 'as a faithful and good vassal of Your Majesty', for which he had asked Brussels, where he enjoyed the protection of Governor General Villahermosa, for help in obtaining a higher appointment in the Order of Santiago.

363 Quirós Rosado, *La fiel nación* pp.89–90: 'In 1682, the senior officers asked the king to change ensigns and sergeants every three years, since the *tercio* could benefit from the same prerogative reserved for the Spaniards. The governor, Ottone del Carretto, *Marchese* del Grana, warned the monarch that the only reason why the Franche-Comtois *tercio* had not been disbanded was due to the need to maintain its officers, all of whom were excellent and valuable, in service. Most of the soldiers had been in Spanish service for decades and it was agreed that the *tercio* was not disbanded due to the impossibility of finding new recruits. The maintenance of the Burgundian infantry was, therefore, a personal desire of the Marquis: 'I did not want to reform this *tercio*, as reason and good economics would require, in order not to disconsolate and lose so many worthy soldiers who, with great goodness, have always served Your Majesty, and in the spirit of thanking the officers for the dedication they are offering, and therefore I believe that they cannot be granted the grace they require.' Grana was stalling a critical situation, since the number of soldiers was decreasing inexorably. Furthermore, cohesion among staff and company officers was also poor, and internal discipline left something to be desired. The new *sargento mayor*,

Eight years after the loss of Franche-Comté, the *maestre de campo* and *sargento de batalla* Alexandre-Ignace-Guillaumede, Pontamougeard received orders from the Viceroy to disband his unit and turn it into a single infantry company. The reasons given by the governor Ottone del Carretto were simple: and to the point 'the difficulties of the Royal Treasury in financing the Army of Flanders, the increasingly small number of men and the difficulty to find recruits with whom to complete the force, considering that the *Franco Contado* was now under French rule'. The other destination of the Franche-Comtois veterans in the service of Carlos II was Milan. In Lombardy, exactly as in the Low Countries, after 1676 rank and file opted for Italian exile.[364] The infantry *tercio*, under the *maestre de campo* Claude-François de Grammont-Chaunois (EI-43), deployed a larger strength compared to the ones in Flanders, and after its reorganisation in Milan, in 1674 was transferred to the newly-opened theatre of war in Sicily as a result of the revolt in Messina.

The *tercio* passed to the command of *maestre de campo* Charles Emmanuel de Watteville, Marquis de Usier, and was considered to be one of the veteran units of the army in Sicily. The destination of the Franche-Comtois was the outpost of Milazzo, where conflicts of precedence soon broke out with the Spaniards. Viceroy-Cardinal Luis Manuel Fernández Portocarrero, decided to avoid confrontation by choosing a Spanish captain with longer service than the corresponding Franche-Comtois commander, until eventually Carlos II ordered that all troops be placed under the direct command of Spanish officers.

At the end of 1677, the Duke of Bournonville proposed to reduce the number of companies of the Burgundian *tercio* from 11 to six and to place five of the captains on the rolls as 'reformados'. These measures were the direct consequence of the decrease in the Franche-Comtois soldiers in Sicily. Between April 1677, the year in which the first reviews of the unit are known, and April of the following year, the strength fluctuated from 205 men, with a slight increase to 264 soldiers in June, until there were just over 100 at the end of the year.[365] The *tercio* survived thanks to the arrival of recruits from Milan, including the 81 volunteers, mostly exiled from Franche-Comté, who were taken into the existing companies after surviving a shipwreck on the beaches of Formica.[366] In 1687, the last

---

Marignac, regarded as one of the best and bravest officers in the Army of Flanders, was the opposite of his *maestre de campo*. The governor removed Marignac from the *tercio* and promised him employment when a future vacancy arose.'

364 *Ibid*. This was also the decision of the artilleryman Claude Lambert, a native of Besançon, who served in the Milanese army as early as November 1674, and after him, his son, Jean-Baptiste followed the military career as an engineer.

365 Luis Antonio Ribot, García, *La monarquía de España y la guerra de Mesina (1674–1678)* (Madrid: Actas Editorial, 2002), p.200.

366 Quirós Rosado, *La fiel nación*, p.91. Among the Burgundian soldiers sent to Sicily was the veteran Jean-Baptiste Castron who, having served between 1661 and 1676 in Extremadura and Catalonia, obtained the rank of reformed *alférez* and the protection of the viceroy Alessandro Farnese. The Council of State appreciated his services, but despite the petitioner's request for a salary in the *Tercio de Napoles* or in the Castle of Milan, he was transferred to Sicily as a reformed officer.

two 'Burgundian' infantry companies of the Spanish army were finally disbanded and their residual strength merged into the Spanish *tercios* in Flanders and Lombardy.[367]

The experiences of the war against France and the Dutch Republic had shown that the old skeleton of the Monarchy's army needed at the very least an organisational restructure, especially because the war had moved to the Iberian Peninsula and threatened the core of the Crown's domains. Since the old veteran *tercios* were no longer able to ensure the defence of the frontier, already in 1632 and 1634, the government had asked the aristocracy to form temporary *regimientos* of infantry. Several aristocrats received the *patente* of *maestre de campo* and assumed the office motivated by the idea of serving in the army even at their own expense. This ideal was common to many of the nobility and coincided with the King's will. The wealth of the nobility was also justified for their inclusion in military obligations, since those who had the means to serve the Monarchy were required to do their duty, especially in war.

In the 1650s and 1660s, the nobility anticipated the money for the recruitment of *tercios* with a paper strength of 1,375 men. The government in this way to raise new 'feudal' regiments for Catalonia and Portugal, to be progressively licensed over the next 10 years. There is a long list of *tercios* recruited on private initiatives in Castile as in the other Spanish provinces or even outside the Peninsula, all with a variable strength depending by the agreement between the commander and the Crown. One of the most significant financial contributions was the one of the Count of Monterrey, who in 1672 personally contributed to the recruitment of five infantry *tercios* for the Army of Flanders.[368]

In the following years other grandees recruited complete *tercios* or companies at their own expense, often for the duration of the war.[369] Sometimes the Crown supported these initiative, and the reasons for raising of units were very practical, as occurred in 1663 in Catalonia with the *hidalgo* Josep de Pinos. On his own initiative he recruited 600 men for the Army of Extremadura and agreed to serve for at least one year with the rank of *maestre de campo*: a simple method of keeping unwanted subjects out of the principality.[370]

---

367 The Viennese *Gazette* authored by the Flemish Johann van Ghelen claims that in 1707 there was still a Franche-Comtois company in the State of Milan. It could perhaps be the company under Captain Guignoire still active in 1687, and which was attached to the Spanish infantry that entered the service of Carlos III. Other Franche-Comtois officers joined the army of the Habsburg pretender on their own initiative. See Quirós Rosado, *La fiel nación*, p.88.

368 Maffi, *Los últimos tercios*, p.175.

369 *Ibid.*, p.271. Among the major contributors in the 1660s, the Count of Amarante and the Marquis of Tenorio y de los Arcos financed the recruitment of troops for the war against Portugal, while in 1680, the Count of Grayal recruited a whole *tercio* for the Army of Flanders (EI-259). Also, subordinate officers contributed to the recruitment, like the *sargento mayor* Juan Antonio de Villena of the *tercio de Nápoles* (EI-2), who personally paid the recruitment of 110 men for the same *tercio*.

370 Espino López, *Las guerras de Cataluña*, p.59: 'Without making him (Pinos) suspicious (the governor could) organise his departure because everywhere he goes, it will be better than in Catalonia, above all because he is a subject who has never been inclined to the royal service ...

When a license to raise a new *tercio* was issued, the Crown and the War Council had often to negotiate the number of companies with the *maestre de campo*, especially if he advanced the money for the recruitment of soldiers. These 'private *tercios*' are a characteristic feature of the *Los Austrias'* military, which had already been introduced in the first half of the seventeenth century. The demand for new troops, and the lack of resources, favoured the proliferation of this kind of unit. The officers offered, in most cases, to collaborate with the recruitment of their units. Between 1666 and 1668, three new *tercios* were raised in Castile with volunteers enlisted by the *maestres de campo* Count of Monterrey (EI–143), Francisco Antonio de Agurto (EI–157), and Francisco Fernandez de Velasco (EI–156). They were personally in control of whether the expected number of recruits was achieved. However, each *tercio* joined the Army of Flanders each with a different strength, and the companies varied from strengths of between 50 and 100 men.[371]

Some *maestres de campo* even advanced money to recruit troops for the existing tercios momentarily under their command. This was the case of the *Tercio Napolitano viejo de l'Armada* (EI–49), which in 1656 was under the command of the *maestre de campo* Fabrizio Rossi. The Italian officer obtained this rank after offering to recruit at his expense 400 volunteers to bring the unit up to strength. In 1659, Rossi and his *tercio* joined the Army of Extremadura, and after the campaign the *maestre de campo* returned to Naples to recruit further volunteers.[372]

Provincial Tercios

Further initiatives were devised to increase the strength of the infantry, particularly on the fronts considered to be secondary. The idea was to form infantry contingents to support the regular troops only for the duration of a campaign. In this way, the strength of the armies could be increased at a lower cost. In 1635, 16 temporary *tercios* of 10 companies were raised, each with a field strength of 1,000 men excluding the *primera plana*. The raising of this infantry took place unevenly from one province to another. The military participation of kingdoms and provinces of the Crown was managed through the *Cortes* and the result was the creation of 'provincial troops', which were based on the recruitment of soldiers by the kingdoms, councils or cities. These *Regnicola Tercios*[373] were military contingents formed through the contributions of the non-Castilian kingdoms as well, which were in charge of the recruitment of the men and the expenses needed to maintain the companies. This formula generated the armed contributions of Valencia,

---

For this reason it could also be said that it is currently necessary to observe every move of him, observing that his actions can in time become remedies.'

371 Rodríguez Hernández, 'El Reclutamiento de españoles para el Ejército de Flandes', p.400.

372 Rodríguez Hernández, 'Al servicio del rey', pp.236–237. Rossi spent one year in southern Italy because the plague epidemic had slowed recruitment. Consequently the *tercio* did not reach the established number of men required.

373 Rodríguez Hernández, *Los tambores de Marte*, p.12.

Catalonia, Aragon, Mallorca, Navarre and other kingdoms, which generally have been little investigated.

In 1640 Catalonia had raised five temporary *tercios* by resorting to the local militia; in Aragon, on the other hand, only two *tercios* and 500 cavalrymen were deployed, later associated with 4,800 foot militiamen.[374] Further *tercios* were raised in Extremadura and Galicia, but the final result was below the expectations. Furthermore, the formation of the first units caused inconveniences of all kinds: financial speculation by the officers who owned the companies; the high number of *passa volantes* (fake soldiers); the enlistment of unsuitable recruits or even children, recruited for the purpose of profiting from the wages and foodstuffs, without counting 'the bad subjects ready to escape at the first opportunity, or took advantage of their status to engage in extortion and actual looting.'[375]

The overall benefit provided by these troops was so poor that after a few years a new kind of infantry corps was ordered. This new infantry formed the *tercios provinciales*, recruited on a regional basis, but destined for specifically military tasks, even outside the kingdom of their provenance, despite most of the recruits coming from local militias.[376] With this reform, the government hoped to dispose of troops always at an affordable expense, but avoiding the continued call to arm temporary units and hastily raised militia. Furthermore, these new *tercios* could benefit from the turnover that had characterised the history of the Spanish army, turning to the mass of discharged veterans which it was not possible to maintain in arms, but by assigning them to regular service of six or seven month each year. Contemporary evidence suggests that the debate about this project began in 1647, with the proposal to raise the Seville *tercios* in a pattern similar to the one established 10 years later.[377]

The Peace of the Pyrenees and the royal decision to turn the military effort against Portugal served as an accelerator for the formation of a new category of infantry *tercios*. Further *tercios* raised on provincial basis entered the service in 1653, like the ones of Alcántara, Jáen, and Catalonia but the decisive step occurred on 28 January 1658, when Francesco Tuttavilla, Duke of San Germano and Spanish commander in Extremadura, received the permission to assemble 21,500 licensed infantry veterans to distribute among the provinces of Castile, Mancha, Extremadura, Granada, Jaén, Seville, and Galicia. With this force, the government planned the formation of 22 *tercios provinciales* to be maintained only for a single campaign, after which the soldiers returned to their homes to resume service in case of need in the next year. These infantry corps had to consist of 12 companies of 100 men, with a

374 Clonard, *Historia orgánica*, vol. IV, pp.428–429.

375 *Ibid.*

376 Historiography, due to the lack of research, continues to confuse the theoretical framework of these units and to affirm that the *tercios provinciales* were formed with militiamen; a statement that is not correct. See José Contreras Gay, 'La reorganización militar en la época de la decadencia española (1640–1700)', in *Millars. Espaii Història*, XXVI (2003), pp.131–154.

377 AGI, *Indiferente*, leg. 113, N. 62: *Meritos de Jerónimo Pueyo Araciel*; report, on the advisability of appointing *maestres de campo* and captains. Thanks to Francesco Pellegrini for this note.

primera plana of 11 officers. These latter with the *plana mayor* were the only personnel who remained in active service throughout the year.[378]

Though it was a measure dictated by the lack of economic resources, it heralded the creation of a 'national guard' in a contemporary meaning, halfway between regular infantry and the militia. The soldiers received their wages from their province and the food stuff when they joined the field army on campaign. The formation of these units constituted the basis from which the *tercio fijo provincial* originated between 1663 and 1664.

Nineteenth-century historians say that it was Felipe IV himself who ordered the formation of four permanent provincial *tercios*, each of 16 – later 20 – companies, for a total of about 1,000 men each, which took the names *Córdoba* (EI–32), *Madrid* (EI–70), and *Toledo* (EI–97), although the first had half the troops of the other *tercios*, while the *tercio fijo de Sevilla* (EI–15) was established from the reformed *coronelia del Rey*. In 1664, *Burgos* (EI–53) and *Valladolid* (EI–98) joined this group. The Crown classified these *tercios* as *provinciales*, since they had to be equipped and maintained directly by the regional administration from whence they came but retained the right to

---

378 Clonard, *Historia orgánica*, vol. IV, p.418–419. The Count of Clonard lists the following *tercios* for each province: in Galicia *tercios Valladares, Orbieto,* and *Martinez*; in Extremadura *tercios Castañizas, Zúñiga, de Luna, Viedma, Sánchez Pardo*; from Granada *tercio Alarcón*; from Seville *tercios Tello, Guzmán, Henestrosa, Arenales, Córdoba*. A further nine *tercios* had been formed in other provinces; they were *Mugica, Torrejon, Giron, Macedo, Escalante, Alvarez de Toledo, Chacón, Escovedo, Varillas*. Again, there are many doubts about the accuracy of the Count's data because these officers are not confirmed by examining the *servicios* preserved in the archive of Simancas. Some of the *maestres de campo* held the command of other *tercios* in the previous years, and their replacement is uncertain, suggesting that some of these could be the same *tercio*. In 1647 the General of Artillery Simon de Castañizas was in command of the *tercio de elpartido de Alcántara*; in 1656 he was still *maestre de campo*, but in 1656 Castañizas appears with the same rank in another unit quartered in Badajoz. Juan de Zúñiga was already *maestre de campo* of a *tercio* in Extremadura from September 1654. As for Álvaro de Luna, son of the Count of Montijo, and Pedro de Viedma, who at the end of the 1640s was *maestre de campo* of the provincial *tercio* of Jáen, there is no information after 1659. The *tercio* of Francisco de Alarcón was recruited in 1658–59, already raised by Juan Antonio Rodriguez de las Varillas in the Old Castile from the *partidos* of Salamanca, Valladolid, Segovia, Avila and surrounding areas. Juan de las Varillas died at Linhas de Elvas in 1659, and was replaced by Francisco de Alarcón, the elder son of the Count of Torres Vedras. Concerning the *tercio* of Francisco Tello, the *Anales de Sevilla* records that it came from Seville and other *partidos* of Andalusia as contribution for the war effort against Portugal of 1661. The *tercio* of Rodrigo de Mugica (former *maestre de campo* of the *tercio de Lombardia*) was raised in 1657 by Jeronimo de Quiniones y Benavente from the Madrid region; in 1664 it became the *tercio provincial de Burgos*. The *tercio* of the Count of Escalante was also raised in 1657 by Pedro Alvarez de Toledo, who died while he was recruiting soldiers in the *partido* of Toledo, and was replaced by Escalante. The most evident inaccuracy is that relating to the five *tercios* of Seville, which were actually four since Juan Fernandez de Henestrosa and the *Conde* de Arenales are the same *maestre de campo*. See *Anales eclesiasticos y Seculares de … Sevilla* (1677), vol. V, p.757: *Fue este el de Mil Seiscientos y Cinquenta y Siete, en que la guerra contra Portugal algunos anos entretenida, holvio a encenderse, siendo Governador de las Armas Castellanas, en Badajoz, D. Francisco Totavila, duque de San German, que a 30 de mayo ganó, entregandosele a partido la importante placa de Olivenca, para cuya campaña en Sevilla se levantaron quatro tercios de Infanteria, debidos al zelo, y cuidado de su Asistente el Conde de Villa-Umbrosa, de que fueron Maestros de campo, D. Francisco Tello de Portugal, … juntamente de las Milicias, D. Francisco de Guzmán, hijo y hermano de los Marqueses de Algava, D. Juan Fernandéz de Hinestrosa Conde de Arenales, y D. Nicolas Fernandéz de Córdoba y Moscoso, de la Orden de Santiago, con los quales fueron Capitánes de Infanteria muchos nobles sevillanos …* Thanks to Francesco Pellegrini for this note.

confirm the appointment of field officers and captains. Moreover, the *tercios fijos* had to be regularly trained on a monthly basis when rank and file were not serving on campaign, and the companies exercised every Sunday. The war council of 1663 established the following *plana mayor* (major staff):

1 *maestre de campo*
1 *sargento mayor*
2 *ayudantes*
1 *capellán mayor*
1 *furriel mayor*
1 *tambur mayor*

Each company had to be formed with a *primera plana* comprising:

1 *capitán*
1 *alférez*
1 *abanderado*
1 *sargento*
2 *tambores*
62 *soldados*

The first company belonged to the *maestre de campo*, who appointed one *lugarteniente* for standing in for him when the *tercio* was on campaign. The ordinance established that at least 150 soldiers had to be enlisted among the veteran *reformados* of each province.[379] However, 10 years later the expected 20 companies had not been formed, since the *Privilegios* of 1673 record that all the new provincial *tercios* always had 16 captains including the *maestro de campo*.[380] The troops entered the field service in the spring of 1663, reinforcing the infantry of Don Juan of Austria's army for the campaign in Portugal, which ended on 8 June with the Spanish defeat at Ameixial-Estremoz.

The actual strength of these units fluctuated considerably during the years. In 1663, the average number of companies of each provincial *tercio* was 13, with 518 men in all; in 1667 the companies had increased to 18, and the average strength was now 592.[381] In the same year, the five *tercios fijos* of Toledo, Madrid, Burgos, Valladolid and Córdoba numbered 2,122 men in all with, respectively 21, 21, 17, 17, and 16 companies; the strength varied from 525 men for Burgos to 223 for Valladolid.[382] The next year, the five provincial *tercios* in Extremadura numbered 4,405 men in all, equal to an average of 880 men each.[383] Despite their unfavourable debut, these *tercios* became the backbone of the peninsular defence forces in the following

379 AGS, *Guerra Antigua*, leg. 2046.
380 BNE, *Privilegios y policia de Madrid en los reinados del Felipe III, Felipe IV y Carlos II* (manuscript), MSS 18205, p.182.
381 Picouet, *The Armies of Philip IV of Spain 1621–1665*, p.146.
382 Clonard, *Historia orgánica*, vol. V, p.6.
383 AGS, *Guerra y Marina*, leg. 1958.

Infantrymen of the provincial *tercios* of Seville, Madrid and Burgos, after Clonard's *Historia orgánica de las armas de infantería y caballería española*, published in 1851–1862. The establishment of the provincial *tercios* was a political decision that led to great changes in the army: after this infantry structure was created, professional units formed by veterans would later bear the name of their provinces of provenance. This formula transformed these units into a model similar to the one introduced in Portugal with the *terços auxiliares*, to complement a reserve for the permanent and elite forces for border defence. Although the provincial *tercios* have traditionally been considered as an evolution of the militia system, based on military service with Castilian authorities in charge of filling the militia quotas, the truth is that its components were not militiamen, nor did its recruitment procedures, its financing system, nor its way of operating in campaigns correspond to those of a territorial militia.

years, forming a reasonably large permanent core of troops, not subject to the ups and downs of the militia.[384]

Classic Spanish military research excludes the creation of further infantry *tercios* from other kingdoms, or rarely mentions them. Immediately after the creation of the first units in 1663, another order was sent to the viceroys of Naples, Milan and Aragon to prepare the cadres for the formation of permanent corps in imitation of the permanent provincial *tercios*.[385] Further orders involved other kingdoms. In January 1663, Felipe IV ordered the

---

384 Maffi, *Los últimos tercios*, p.140.

385 Clonard, *Historia orgánica*, vol. IV, p.427: 'Felipe IV abounded with ideas during the War Council. Having heard the report of Don Juan of Austria, he ordered that four permanent *tercios* of 1,000 men each be formed, and named *Madrid, Toledo, Sevilla* and *Andalucía*, being in his designs paid for directly by the aforementioned provinces. Likewise, the King ordered the viceroys in Italy and Aragon to take action to raise infantry corps in the kingdoms too, so that each domain would maintain its *tercio*.' Despite the Royal order, no *tercios provinciales* were raised in Italy.

principality of the Asturias to raise one infantry *tercio* organised the same as the provincial units established in the same year.

In February 1664, the Asturian representatives had to provide 500 men in six companies.[386] The first contingent sailed to Galicia on 22 March 1664 with 253 men, followed by three further transports that sailed from Gijón between April and June. On 22 January 1664, the principality and the Crown signed for the continuation of the service of these contingents on campaign, which originally had been agreed for one year. However, after just six months of operating in Galicia, the *tercio* had lost four-fifths of its strength, with just 53 officers and NCOs, and 49 soldiers still able to serve.[387] The subsequent events are known until 2 April 1664, the day on which the governor, Pedro de Gamara y Urquiçu issued an order to recruit the missing 451 soldiers, dividing them within the principality. Despite the authorities raising funds for the recruitment, the *tercio* disappears from the musters relating to the Army of Galicia after 1664.[388]

The participation of the different kingdoms in the formation of the provincial contingents remained subject to the decisions of the local authorities and these *tercios* did not always become permanent units, as happened in the case of Asturias. In other cases, the introduction of the provincial *tercios* enabled some provinces

Thomas de la Cerda Manrique de Lara, Count of Paredes and Marquis of La Laguna. The Marquis was *maestre de campo* of the *tercio de Sevilla* (E-15) approximately between 1664 and 1671. In another instance of the inaccurate statements in Clonard's *Historia orgánica de las armas de infantería y caballería española*, about eight years of history concerning this *tercio* have been overlooked. (Author's collection)

to organise alternative models, as for instance was the case of Granada. In 1657, the *Cortes* authorised the formation of two infantry *tercios* of 2,000 men each, named *Casco de Granada* (EI–46) and *Costade Granada* (EI–47). The latter provided the soldiers for the garrisons of the coast, while the other *tercio* would be destined to join the King's field armies where necessary. As a condition, the Kingdom of Granada demanded that its population be exempted from royal recruitment, except for who those entered military service as a volunteer.[389]

386 José Luis Calvo Pérez, 'El tercio fijo del principato de Asturias, 1663', in *Researching & Dragona*, N. 20, 2003; p.31.

387 *Ibid.*, p.37; muster executed on 11 January 1664.

388 *Ibid.*, p.38. The author records that at present it is impossible to reconstruct the history of this *tercio* after 1664, since the archives for the years from 1665 onwards do not contain information concerning this unit; therefore, even the date of its disbanding remains unknown.

389 Maffi, *Los últimos tercios*, p.203.

With Asturias and Granada, in the 1660s Extremadura, Galicia, Catalonia and Valencia also raised their own provincial *tercios*, all destined for the Portuguese border. In 1664, the Kingdom of Valencia authorised the recruitment of 400 men to raise a *tercio* to be sent to Extremadura. The unit was ready to march in early 1665, and in March received the financing to serve on campaign for seven months. The experiences of this *tercio* are an example of the period of serious economic and organisational difficulties of the Monarchy.

In the summer, the Valencian authorities pledged to recruit more soldiers to fill the voids caused by desertions, sickness and non-combat losses, and to extend their service by a further two months. However, as stated by Viceroy Astorga, the funds were insufficient and only 40 men 'of very poor quality' had been recruited.[390] The government answered urging that the troops were sent to serve as soon as possible, since the Valencians should have marched to Extremadura in August, to avoid any surprises that could occur during the winter.

The affair did not end there, because in September 1665 the viceroy was asked to assemble further 2,000 men in Valencia in case the viceroy of Catalonia, Vincenzo Gonzaga, urgently needed claim them to face local unrest. In October 1666, the Kingdom again authorised the raising of one infantry *tercio* for the war against Portugal, establishing its strength at 400 men in all. Madrid's request to increase the units with a further 200 men was not accepted, since the Council of Aragon declared it as 'an impossible goal' for the exhausted Valencian economy.

The negotiations between the government and the province continued for months, reinvigorated by the new war against France of 1667–68. The Marquis of Aytona, one of the counsellors of the regent Maria Anna dof Austria, insisted on bringing the strength of the Valencian *tercio* to 1,000 men, and meanwhile required the raising of further recruits for Catalonia.[391] The Council of Aragon finally agreed to form one infantry *tercio* of 500 men for the new war, but the results were just one third of the expected total. The negotiations became even more complex, with the submission of proposals from Valencian aristocrats. Among them, Don Manuel Ponce de León y Cardenas, now Marquis of Elche in the Valencian kingdom after his wedding with the Duchess of Aveiro y Maqueda, asked for the command of a *tercio* in exchange for his contribution for financing the enlistment of recruits.

The truce signed with Portugal and the peace of Aix-la-Chapelle meant that the issue was no longer in the forefront of everyone's minds, but now also Valencia had its provincial *tercio*, with a field strength of 400 men in all.[392] Valencia maintained the unit until 1699. As for its strength, the *tercio* fielded 200 men in 1674 and 500 in 1689, alternating its service between Valencia and Aragon or Catalonia. In the same period, further provincial tercios were raised in Aragon, Sardinia and Mallorca.

---

390 Antonio Espino López, *Guerra, fisco y fueros la defensa de la corona de Aragón entiempos de Carlos II, 1665–1700* (Valencia: Universidad de Valéncia, 2007), p.35.

391 *Ibid.*, p.36.

392 AGCA, *Consejo Aragón*, leg. 563, *Gente y tercios para la guerra*.

In Catalonia, following the troops assembled in 1653 by the city of Barcelona's *Consell de Cent*, and the *Generalitat*, six companies were raised in 1667 with funds gathered by the same institutions for serving as permanent corps in the principality. From 1667 to 1673, their strength did not number more than 400–500 men,[393] but in 1673 these companies formed two *tercios*, *Ciudad de Barcelona* (EI–191) and *Deputación de Cataluña* (EI–192), with 500 and 400 men respectively.[394] Before the end of the year, five further *tercios* were raised on a regional basis for the defence of the border with France, to which a sixth joined the Army of Catalonia in 1674.[395] The Catalan *tercios* actively participated in the campaigns against France and some of these performed well at the Battle of Maureillas on 19 May 1674.

Grenadiers

The Spaniards introduced the grenadier relatively late compared to other European armies. However, the absence of companies or soldiers specifically trained in the use of portable explosives devices does not mean that the grenades were not used by their infantry. The presence of this kind of weapon in the Spanish arsenal dates back to the first half of the century, and the presence of a company of *granaderos*, under the Captain Don Pedro Ramos, is already recorded in Galicia in 1662.[396] This unit served alongside the artillery as a free company raised for siege tasks. However, it was only between 1684 and 1685 that the first permanent companies of Spanish grenadiers appeared on the battlefield. The initiative is attributed to the Marquis of Cabezudo, the author of a 'memorial' addressed to Carlos II, who asked the King to be appointed captain of the first grenadier company. The King sent the request to the Duke of Bournonville, Viceroy of Catalonia, who confirmed the request to raise companies of grenadiers.[397] Furthermore, in order to improve their equipment, the Spanish grenadiers would have been the first to receive the new flintlock musket. In April 1685, this issue was confirmed by the State Council, which established the distribution of the new musket and bayonet to the 12 companies of *granaderos* raised in Milan, Flanders and Catalonia, each with a strength of 50 rank and file.[398]

393 Espino López, *Las guerras de Cataluña*, pp.187–188. The *tercio* of Barcelona.
394 *Ibid.* In 1678 the *tercios* of Barcelona numbered 700 men, decreasing to 651 in 1684; the *tercio* *Deputación de Cataluña* in 1675 deployed 500 men, decreasing to 400 in 1676–78, and numbered 500 again in 1684.
395 Narcíso Feliu de la Peña i Farell, *Anales de Cataluña*, vol. III (Barcelona: Editorial Base, 1999), p.357.
396 Rodríguez Hernández, *Flandes y la Guerra de Devolución*, p.88.
397 Espino López, 'El ocaso de la maquinaria bélica hispánica', p.20.
398 AGS, *Estado*, Leg. 3911, d. 1334 (12 April 1685).

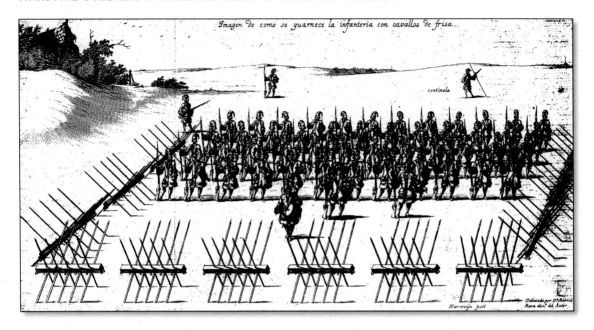

Imagen de como se guarnece la infanteria con cavallos de frisa.

centinela

Above: Grenadiers depicted in the *El perfecto bombardero y pratico artificial*, by Sebastián Fernández de Medrano, published in 1691.

Right: Grenadier, late 1680s, after the Treaty of Sebastián Fernández de Medrano. In 1685, 12 grenadier independent companies were raised in Flanders, Milan and Catalonia. According to this source, the Spanish grenadiers wore a mitre cap similar to the Dutch model. Equipment included a bayonet and flintlock musket. As for coat colours, the Spanish grenadiers in Milan were probably uniformed in red, while in Catalonia and Flanders they wore grey coats. (Author's reconstruction)

Garrison and Free Companies

A characteristic feature of Hispanic infantry, and even to an extent the cavalry, is the existence of a significant number of *companias sueltas* (free companies). These companies were the consequence of the organisational reforms of the armies and were considered as a useful compromise to keep in service a core of veteran soldiers to be employed again in case of a need to increase unit strengths. After the Peace of Aix-la-Chapelle of 1668, in the Army of Flanders there were 118 *companias sueltas* of Spanish, Flemish Walloon, Italian and German infantry. In 1672 in Flanders, free companies formed the standing garrisons of the fortresses along with the *tercios*. In 1685, after the reform of the army established by Ottone del Carretto, Marquis del Grana, there were 7 free companies in the Spanish Low Countries distributed among Leeuwe, Halle and Damme.[399] Free companies were also still in service in the Iberian Peninsula and Italy.

It was normal that the number of people registered in the garrisons included sick, reformed and even wives and children of soldiers. There are numerous examples of this. In 1676, among the 947 infantry that the Kingdom of Aragon was to deploy to defend the border of the Pyrenees, only 219 were actually available, and of these many were ill or too old to serve in the field army.[400] In 1685, in the Balearic garrison of Ibiza, there were only 105 soldiers, of which just 26 were capable of carrying weapons, instead of the expected 500. This lack of soldiers affected not only the garrisons, but also the field forces. Other strategically important places such as Cadiz had just 281 infantry soldiers in 1673 instead of the 1,409 expected. As for Gibraltar, in the 1680s, instead of a planned garrison of 1,500 infantry, there were only 70–80 soldiers present.[401]

Further data shows that infantry, as well as the cavalry, rarely deployed anything like their establishment strengths, and when this did happen it was only in the first months of a unit's existence. The difference between effective and real strength was also due to contingency needs. All the Southern Spain garrisons were understrength because usually they had to feed men into the outposts in North Africa, which were constantly threatened by the Moroccans.

In 1677, it was calculated that the garrisons of Spain and Africa together totalled 10,323 men, and in the early 1690s there were said to be 4,000 men in garrison in Ceuta alone.[402] This military border is often ignored but encounters and skirmishes were numerous and prolonged. Between 1684 and 1689 the Spaniards lost the fortresses of La Mámora and Larache, while Ceuta, Melilla and Oran remained under almost constant threat. However, over the course of the century, the Oran garrison rarely achieved the planned

399 AHNOB, 197, d. 82, Estado de la fuerza de los ejércitos de caballería e infantería españoles desta cados en Flandes (Bélgica), con expresión del número de compañías que poseecada tercio o regimiento (March 1685).
400 Espino López, 'El ocaso de la maquinaria bélica hispánica', p.14.
401 *Ibid.*
402 Storrs, *The Resilience of the Spanish Monarchy 1665–1700*, p.24.

strength of 1,700 men.[403] In Melilla, in 1692, the garrison numbered only 600 infantrymen, 'poor equipped and even worse supplied, and many of them constantly exposed to the elements.'[404] The growing enemy pressure in this region can be noted by observing the forces deployed in the important outpost of Ceuta, which, in the 1690s, increased from a garrison of 953 to 4,500 infantrymen.

Companias sueltas also formed the core of the regular forces in the overseas garrisons. From the point of view of efficiency, very often the companies quartered overseas comprised the worst troops. The service in the *Indias* was often as a result of some punishment or even actual exile for subjects deemed beyond help. Enemy activity required more soldiers, and in 1671, the Council of State urged that 3,000 men be sent to the Americas following the loss of Panama. The need for troops became quite segmented. In 1676, 100 infantrymen were recruited in Andalusia for Florida, 200 for *Nueva Granada* (Colombia), and further 200 for Chile. In 1677, 1,000 men were sent to the Caribbean, and in 1680, the War Council issued the King's order to the Captain-General of the Canaries to levy 1,000 men for America. Soldiers and ammunition continued to be dispatched from Spain, including 400 men in 1683, and at least a further 500 to Colombia in the early 1690s.[405] Overall, between 1660 and 1700, the Crown maintained an average of 5,000–6,000 men in the *Indias*, mainly infantry: a figure which was rarely adequate to deal unassisted with any serious threats.

Cavalry Organisation

The cavalry had played a secondary role in Hispanic armies since the infantry *tercios* had always been the most important and prestigious component. However, during the Thirty Years' War, the Spanish cavalry had already increased its presence in the field army and acquired a relevant tactical role, especially in Flanders and Portugal. Some scholars state that in the 1640s, Spain deployed more than 60 *trozos* and *tercios* of cavalry and dragoons, and as a percentage the cavalry represented almost 50 percent of the troops in the Army of Flanders, including horsemen from Spain, the Low Countries, Italy, Franche-Comté, Germany and other foreign mercenaries.[406] In Italy, where the terrain was less favourable for use of a massive cavalry arm, the mounted force was still significant and in the 1670s represented 20 percent in the army of Lombardy.

Throughout the period between the 1650s and the 1660s, the cavalry comprised two main specialties, *corazas* and *jinetes*, namely the armoured heavy cavalry, similar to the German cuirassiers, and those resulting from the fusion of the Spanish light horse with the Italian *cavallileggeri* of the previous century. In the following decades this differentiation

---

403 Espino López, 'El ocaso de la maquinaria bélica hispánica', p.15.
404 *Ibid.*
405 Storrs, *The Resilience of the Spanish Monarchy*, p.25.
406 Maffi, *Los últimos tercios*, p.171.

gradually disappears, and more frequently the contemporary documents use the generic term *caballos* or even *caballos-corazas* to indicate the horsemen in Flanders, Spain and elsewhere. However, the Spanish *trozos* of *coraceros* retained this appellative, especially the veteran ones raised during the Thirty Years' War.

As with the infantry, cavalry and dragoons had a different organisation depending on their nationality. Moreover, the theatre of operations contributed to increase these differences. On 7 March 1649, the cavalry of Flanders was organised in 24 *trozos* and *tercios* of six companies.[407] This date is conventionally considered the birth of a permanent organisation for the cavalry. According to some historians, the creation of larger units was as a consequence of the defeat suffered by the Spaniards at Lens in 1648, when it was evident that the direction of large numbers of cavalry on the battlefield was becoming a problem without an adequate chain of command above the companies. This organisation was later introduced in Spain by the King's order issued on 2 February 1659.[408]

This seems to indicate that the reform introduced three years earlier was not applied particularly urgently, and it was the coming campaigns against Portugal that determined the acceleration of the process of assembling the companies into larger units. It would therefore be the date of February 1659 that officially started the creation of permanent cavalry units of regiment size.[409] These first *trozos* later assumed the

German cavalryman, 1662–65. In total, during the 1660s, almost 11,500 Germans arrived on the Iberian Peninsula to join the army of Extremadura. The figure is quite revealing, both for the numbers and because these men arrived over just five years. According to contemporary accounts, the heavy cavalry serving in Extremadura was dressed in buff coats. German cavalry usually carried black polished breastplates and lobster helmets, which could be replaced in ordinary service by a broad-brimmed hat, while breastplates were worn in action. The red scarf around the waist distinguished the Hispanic cavalry from the Portuguese, who wore similar dress and equipment. (Author's reconstruction)

---

407 Clonard, *Historia orgánica*, vol. IV, p.462.

408 Jesús Martínez de Merlo, 'La caballería entre Los Austrias y Los Borbones', in *Revista de Historia Militar* N. 121, 2017, p.178.

409 Clonard, *Historia orgánica*, vol. IV, p.459. The Count of Clonard lists 14 *trozos* raised in Spain in 1659. However, the list seems to have been compiled later, since the *trozo* of Antonio Novales de Rojas, coming from Milan, is already mentioned, yet it did not arrive in Spain until 1661. Moreover, there is no mention of the *trozo* of Juan de Isasi created in 1659 and sent to Extremadura. Juan Jacobo Mazacán also appears in the list as *maestre de campo* of cavalry, but he took the command of his *trozo* in 1661, replacing Giovanni Vincenzo Filomarino. Finally, the list also includes the *trozo* of José Daza who was commissioner of the *trozo de los Ordenes* from 1654 to 1658, and then he ceased to be *maestre*

denomination *Osuna, Rosellón, Milán* and others, associated to territories and considered as veteran units like the infantry counterpart of the *viejos tercios*. Among the Spanish veteran cavalry *trozos* there was also a foreign unit. It was the *tercio de Alemanes*, originating from an Imperial cuirassier regiment ceded to Spain in 1662. Six years later, after its conversion into a *trozo*, the unit also included Italians and other foreign recruits. In the last decade of the seventeenth century, this *tercio* was finally formed by Spaniards only. Moreover, there was the German and Croatian cavalry in Spanish service which had operated as regular regimental units since the 1640s.

The *trozo* of the Spanish cavalry and dragoons, as well as the *tercio* formed by Italian, Flemish Walloon or Franche-Comtois horsemen, were entrusted to the orders of a *plana mayor* composed as follows:

> 1 *maestre de campo* with servants
> 1 *sargento mayor*
> 2 *ayudantes*
> 1 *cirujano* mayor (senior surgeon)
> 1 *capellán mayor*

Mestre de campo and *sargento mayor* held the command of the first two companies. In 1649 the cavalry *trozos* and *tercios* had been established at six companies, but exceptions were frequent. In the following years, some changes occurred in the composition of the company, which lost their surgeon and chaplain, whose duties passed to the senior ranks in the regimental staff, but each company received one *escrivano*. Other modifications were introduced in the *plana mayor*, which acquired a *proveedor*, a *secretarios* and, only for the cavalry, a *timballeros* (kettle drummer). Furthermore, since the *maestre de campo* did not always serve with his unit, the ranks of *comisario* and *teniente coronel* were also introduced.[410] The *plana mayor* could also include one or even two kettledrums, but they were paid for directly by the *maestre de campo* and were not registered as regular personnel.

According to the organisation established in 1659, the company had a staff – or *primera plana* – composed of:

> 1 *capitán*
> 1 *teniente*
> 1 *alférez*
> 1 *sargento*
> 2 *trompetas*
> 1 *cirujano* (surgeon)
> 1 *furriel*
> 1 *herrador* (blacksmith)

---

de campo, leaving the office to Antonio Montenegro, who in turn also appears in Clonard's list when he later took command of the *trozo*.

410 Antonio José Rodríguez Hernández, 'La caballería hispánica. Un arma si alza', in *Desperta Ferro* Special Issue XIX, June–July 2019, p.48.

The officers usually had each one servant. The dragoons had the same regimental and company staff, but with two *sargentos* in each company.[411] In 1659, there were two *tercios-trozos* of mounted *arquebuceros*, both serving in the Spanish Low Countries, formed by Spanish and Franche-Comtois recruits. Both units underwent reforms in 1661 and reduced to single companies. In 1668, a new dragoon *trozo* was raised in Flanders, which survived until 1718, but overall, from 1660 to 1690, there were relatively few dragoons compared to the cavalry, at least as regimental-size units.

According to classical Spanish military history, in 1649 the first *tercios* of cavalry began to be formed, in imitation of the infantry *tercios*. However, the archive's documents testify to the existence of one Spanish cavalry *trozos* in 1637, and a further five *trozos-tercios* were raised between 1640 and 1648, of which one was of Flemish Walloons.[412] On 15 September 1656, the King ordered viceroys and governors general in Spain, Italy and the Low Countries to reorganise the cavalry into *trozos-tercios* of 12 companies of 50 men each. However, this measure was not applied in Flanders, where the cavalry had already been organised in units formed by two or more companies. In 1659, the definitive structure of the regimental staff had been introduced, but the presence of independent companies of cavalry and dragoons lasted until the 1690s.

As for each company's strength, this depended upon the nationality of the troops involved. According to the regulations introduced from 1633 and 1649, the Spanish *trozo*, had company of 88 *caballos-corazas* (troopers) and five *cabos*; the Italian, Flemish Walloon and Franche-Comtois companies numbered 48 horsemen with three *cabos*.[413]

As always, the strength on paper did not tally with the actual numbers, and since the 1650s there were a large number of such instances even within the same army or country. In 1659–60, the Spanish cavalry company was established at 40–60 horseman with two or three *cabos*. In the same period the cavalry of Milan had company of 57 horsemen, while in Naples there were 62 troopers. German cavalry companies numbered 86 troopers with 10 officers and NCOs.

Further reorganisation was established when the cavalry served on campaign. According to some authors, in 1656, the Spanish cavalry in Flanders deployed companies with no more than 70 horsemen, while in the Iberian Peninsula and Italy the strength was established at 50 troopers.[414] In the same period, in Extremadura, the strength seemed to be lower, from 20 to 40 horsemen. In 1662, the average company in the Peninsula had 48 men including officers, and one year later the 10 Spanish *trozos* deployed from five to 13 companies with an average strength of 53 horsemen, excluding the *primera plana*.

411 Jean-R. Cayron, 'La véritable histoire de Jacques Pastur dit Jaco', in *La Fourragère* N. 3, December 1951, p.553.
412 Martínez de Merlo, *La caballería entre Los Austrias y Los Borbones*, p.141.
413 Picouet, *The Armies of Philip IV of Spain 1621–1665*, p.160.
414 Barado, *Historia del Ejército Español*, p.532.

When considering the expense necessary for the maintenance of large, mounted units, the cavalry was affected by a large number of reforms, increasing, and soon after reducing their strength. In Flanders, the existence of several veteran cavalry *tercios* and *trozos* was ended in March 1660. Following the royal order of 31 December 1659, between 1660 and 1661 the Marquis of Caracena disbanded at least 46 *trozos-tercios* and regiments of foreign cavalry, with the exception of four German regiments. The cavalry was reduced to single companies, which numbered 111 in all, decreased to 103 in 1662. These were 39 Flemish Walloon, 32 Spanish, 14 Burgundian, 14 German (including the regiments) and four Italian companies. The overall force also included the four companies of the Horse Guards.[415]

Since a horseman cost three times more than a footsoldier, cavalry and dragoons were obviously the most affected by reductions in strength. Nevertheless, the Crown sought to maintain a core of veteran horsemen and tried not to disperse the experience of its mounted force. Moreover, the need for horsemen for the other fronts of war helped to keep the cavalry at a significant strength.[416] Therefore, between 1660 and 1661, hundreds of horsemen from the disbanded units serving in Flanders and Lombardy were transferred to Spain and organised into 16 free companies, including four from the disbanded German regiments.[417] In 1662, a new order from Madrid ask to raise three *trozos-tercios* with troopers from the cavalry companies in Flanders: one of Spaniards and two of Flemish Walloons.[418]

In terms of strength, each territory continued to manage organisation differently. In the 1660s, the cavalry serving in the Iberian Peninsula were assembled in *trozos* of six or 10 companies of 80 men. However, this arrangement was short-lived, as the number of men was reduced to 50 over the next decade due the lack of money. Moreover, in peacetime the disbanding of the cavalry units or their reduction to one or at most two companies continued, but some of them, especially the veteran ones, retained a larger strength.

In 1669 it was decided that the cavalry companies in Spain would deploy a force of 80 horsemen. This reduced the size of the units, but the average number of companies was increased. However, this did not occur everywhere, because in Flanders, during the War of Devolution, *tercios* and *trozos* numbered 400 men.[419] Between 1667 and 1668, the Army of Flanders considerably increased the number of mounted troops. In less than a year, 26 new *trozos-tercios*, and nine German regiments were raised to counter

---

415 Martínez de Merlo, *La caballería entre Los Austrias y Los Borbones*, p.148.

416 On the complex history of the reforms of cavalry, see AGS, *Estado*, leg. 3378; AGS, *Estado*, leg. 3378: *Relación del número de los soldados en que dan las infrascritas compañías de caballos que pasan a España ...* dated Milan, 12 July 1660; AGS, *Secretarías Provinciales*, leg. 1862: *Relación de las compañías de caballos que han de pasar a España ...*

417 Rodríguez Hernández, 'La presencia militar alemana', p.274.

418 These were the *tercios* of Diego Azcona (EC–72), Eugéne Hornes de Fournes (EC–78), and Maximilian de Hornes de Baucigny (EC–79). See also Appendix II.

419 AHNOB, *Frias*, ct. 85, d. 73, and Villahermosa, *Correspondencia*, MS 2412, vol. II, pp.211–212.

the French assault. In peacetime the cavalry strength was again considerably reduced, disbanding nine regiments between 1669 and 1671, and decreasing the strength of each company in the field, since the muster conducted on 21 November 1672, namely on the eve of the Spanish involvement in the Franco-Dutch war, the *trozos-tercios* and regiments registered on average a strength of 200–250 rank and file.[420]

However, the experience achieved in the War of Devolution favoured the development of the cavalry and its reputation did not suffer despite the negative outcome of the conflict. At the end of the War of Devolution, the Army of Flanders deployed 13,553 cavalrymen. The overall mounted force comprised 43 *trozos-tercios* and regiments, equal to 203 companies in all.[421] This force decreased to 10,000 on average during the Franco-Dutch war. In October 1668, the Flemish Walloon cavalry in Flanders deployed 19 *tercios*, a further six *trozos* were formed by Spaniards, two Italian *tercios*, two Franche-Comtois, 14 German regiments, and the single Croatian light cavalry regiment, now reduced to fewer than 200 men. In addition, there were 22 *companias sueltas* of all the nationalities, including the companies of the lifeguards.[422] Cavalry and dragoons still represented 25 percent of the army, a decrease that in percentage terms does not differ greatly from the one deployed years before, which was 26 percent. Subsequent data show that the percentage of mounted troops increased again in the following years, reaching 43 percent of the field army: an indirect confirmation of the growing reputation of the Spanish cavalry in the Army of Flanders.[423] As for the cavalry strength in Catalonia, in the 1670s, horsemen and dragoons numbered between 3,500 and 4,000 men, equal to 25 percent of the field army.

From 1670, Spanish Governor Monterrey, and later from 1675, Villahermosa, paid attention to the organisation of the cavalry of the Low Countries. In general, the Spanish governors sought to assemble regiments from 200 to 350 horsemen, organised into a variable number of companies, usually between six and 10.[424] After the reduction of the army after the Franco-Dutch War, in 1682 the strength of the cavalry companies in Flanders diminished to 30 horseman, and 40 in the dragoons.[425] This measure guaranteed a minimum of men, considering that in the 1680s, the recruitment contracts established a minimum of between 25 and 40 men. In general, in the following decades, the strength of the companies gradually

420 Martínez de Merlo, *La caballería entre Los Austrias y Los Borbones*, pp.158–170. Only three regiments deployed more then 300 horsemen. See Cavalry of the Army of Flanders, November 1672, in Appendix I.

421 Juan Luis Sánchez Martín, 'Apuntes para una reconstrucción histórica de los tercios del siglo XVII' in *Researching & Dragona*, vol. I (1996), n. 2, p.40. This force comprised six Spanish *trozos* with 27 companies, two Italian *tercios* with six companies, 21 Flemish Walloon and Franche-Comtois *tercios* with 81 companies, 14 German regiments with 93 companies.

422 Rodríguez Hernández, *España, Flandes y la Guerra de Devolución*, pp.379–383.

423 Rodríguez Hernández, *La caballería hispánica*, p.48.

424 *Correspondencia de Carlos de Gurrea y Aragón, Duque de Villahermosa, relativa a su gobierno en Flandes* (BNE, MS 2412), vol. III, pp.389–393.

425 Grana del Carretto, *Despachos para Su Majestad del Gobierno de Flandes* (BNE, MS 9988, 1696), p.29.

diminished to deploy just 20 or 30 men, as occurred in the 1685, after the reform established by the governor of the Spanish Low Countries, Ottone del Carretto Marquis del Grana, which affected the cavalry of all nationalities.[426]

The dragoons also underwent several reforms and adaptations. It seems that the dragons were subject to the combining of an indefinite number of companies, as reported in 1674, when the *tercio* Verlóo (ED-3) comprised 22 companies of 30 men.[427] According to the Walloon *maestre de campo* Jacques Pastur, between the 1670s and 1680s the companies of dragoon *tercios* in Flanders varied from seven to 10.[428]

Regarding the history of this first unit of dragoon there persist several inaccuracies. On 29 March 1674, the *tercio* of dragoons of the Baron de Verlóo was raised, and this is considered by traditional historiography as the first dragoons of regimental size of the Army of Flanders. However, and curiously, in the muster on 3 April 1675, no *tercio* is registered, but it reports 35 free companies identified by the names of their captains and garrison where the unit were quartered. Of these companies, two belong to the *maestres de campo* Verlóo and Harnoncourt and four to *sargentos mayores*, Hartmand, Valenzart, Rouland and Gomar de Ville.[429] It would seem that two *tercios* had been already organised, since Dupuys (ED-3) was already registered as *tercio de arquebuceros a caballo* in 1668, while Harnoncourt (ED-4) did the same in 1674.

In 1676 there were three *tercios* organised into nine companies, with 139 officers and 799 soldiers.[430] Governor Monterrey and later Villahermosa sought to increase the number of dragoons in the army of Flanders. In the musters dating 1678, there were five *tercios* of dragoons under the command of Verlóo, Nicolás Hartmand (ED-7), Gomar de Ville (ED-4), Matías Pérez (ED-6) and Antonio Salcedo (ED-5), which added 43 companies plus the independent one under captain Lefevure.[431] The number of men in a company was from 30 to 40 in 1678, decreased to 25 in January 1681, and then increased to 35 in the last months of the same year, of which the half dismounted, and finally between 28 and 35 in 1688.[432] Two further dragoons regiment-size units were raised in Lombardy in 1684, for the initiative of the governor Juan Tomás Enríquez de Cabrera, Count of Melgar.

Except for some details, the differences in the organisation of the cavalry in Flanders, Spain or elsewhere remained minimal, while in Lombardy and Naples no permanent cavalry *tercios* was assembled before the 1690s, and only then, when the troops were sent outside Italy the companies were joined to form a larger corps. In Lombardy, the cavalry remained organised

---

426 AHNOB, *Osuna*, ct. 197, d. 41.

427 Martínez de Merlo, *La caballería entre Los Austrias y Los Borbones*, p.171.

428 Cayron, 'La véritable histoire de Jacques Pastur dit Jaco', p.550.

429 Gomar de Ville (ED–6), Hartmand (ED–7) are registered as *trozo de dragones* in 1675, see *Correspondencia de Carlos de Gurrea y Aragón, Duque de Villahermosa, relativa a su gobierno en Flandes* (BNE, MS 2412), vol. III, pp.306–310.

430 Juan Luis Sánchez Martin, 'El último ejército de Flandes', in *Researching & Dragona*, vol. II (1997), n. 3, pp.24–26.

431 Martínez de Merlo, 'La caballería entre Los Austrias y Los Borbones', p.155.

432 Cayron, 'La véritable histoire de Jacques Pastur dit Jaco', p.552.

Hispanic Infantry, 1660s

1. Officer, unknown unit, Flanders 1665–1668; 2. Musketeer, *tercio fijo provincial de Toledo*, 1665; 3. Arquebusier, unknown Spanish or Flemish Walloon unit, Flanders mid 1660s.

(Illustration by Bruno Mugnai © Helion & Company)

See Colour Plate Commentaries for further information.

Hispanic Infantry, 1670s

1. Musketeer, unknown Spanish tercio, Flanders 1672–73; 2. Arquebusier, *tercio de Zaragoza* (EI-242), Catalonia 1678; 3. Artilleryman, 1680–90

(Illustration by Bruno Mugnai © Helion & Company)

See Colour Plate Commentaries for further information.

Plate C

Hispanic Infantry, 1680s
1. Officer, unknown Spanish unit, Madrid 1683; 2. NCO, unknown Flemish Walloon unit, Flanders early 1680s; 3. Drummer, unknown Neapolitan unit, 1684-88

(Illustration by Bruno Mugnai © Helion & Company)

See Colour Plate Commentaries for further information.

Hispanic Cavalry, 1660s

1. *Coracero*, lifeguard company of the Kingdom of Naples' viceroy, mid 1660s; **2.** Officer, unknown
Spanish unit. **3.** Trooper, unknown Spanish or Flemish Walloon unit, Flanders late 1660s

(Illustration by Bruno Mugnai © Helion & Company)

See Colour Plate Commentaries for further information.

Alférez **– standard-bearer, Spanish *tercio De Puy* (EC-57), Flanders 1684–89**

(Illustration by Bruno Mugnai © Helion & Company)

See Colour Plate Commentaries for further information.

Spanish Cavalry and Dragoons, 1680s

1. Trooper, unknown Spanish unit, Lombardy, 1684–1688; 2. Dragoon private, Spanish *tercio de dragones del Estado de Milán* (ED-8), Greece 1686

(Illustration by Bruno Mugnai © Helion & Company)

See Colour Plate Commentaries for further information.

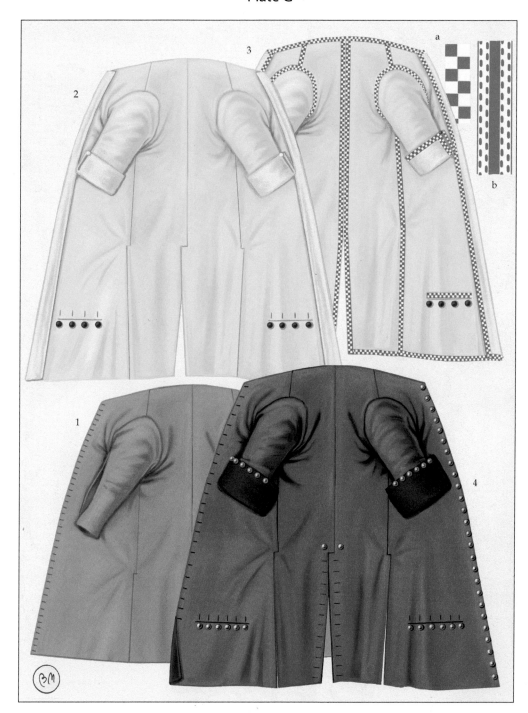

Spanish Coats, 1650–1670

1. Infantry *casaca*, late 1650s; 2. Chamberga coat for private soldier, infantry *tercio Guardias del Rey* (EI-181), 1669–78; 3. Chamberga coat for musician, infantry *tercio Guardias del Rey*; 4. Coat for private soldiers, infantry *tercio provincial de Sevilla* (EI-15),1670s

(Illustration by Bruno Mugnai © Helion & Company)

See Colour Plate Commentaries for further information.

Foreign Soldiers in Spanish Service

1. Guardia *Alemanna* of the Naples' Viceroy, 1650–60; 2. Pikeman, Irish *tercio O'Byrne* (EI-31),
Flanders, 1678; 3. English Musketeer, Regiment Porter (EI-14), Flanders 1680–1685

(Illustration by Bruno Mugnai © Helion & Company)

See Colour Plate Commentaries for further information.

Plate I

Spanish Infantry Ensigns
1. Infantry company ensign, 1670–1680; 2. Infantry company ensign, 1660–70

(Illustration by Bruno Mugnai © Helion & Company)

See Colour Plate Commentaries for further information.

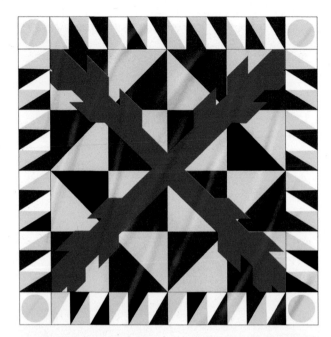

1

2

Spanish Infantry Ensigns
1. Infantry company ensign, 1683, unknown Spanish unit; 2. Infantry company ensign, last quarter of the seventeenth century, Navarre regular infantry or militia

(Illustration by Bruno Mugnai © Helion & Company)

See Colour Plate Commentaries for further information.

1

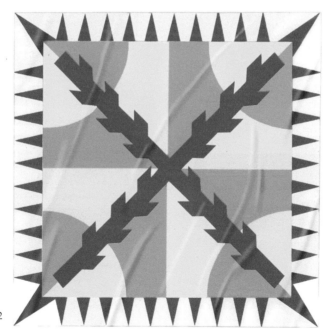

2

Spanish Infantry Ensigns
1. Infantry company ensign, 1663, *tercio provincial de Asturias*; 2. Infantry company ensign (1693), unknown Spanish unit

(Illustration by Bruno Mugnai © Helion & Company)

See Colour Plate Commentaries for further information.

Plate L

Spanish Infantry Ensigns, Early 1690s
1. Infantry colonel ensign of an unknown Milanese *tercio*; 2. Infantry company colour; 3 and 4.
Infantry ensigns belonging to unknown German regiments in Spanish service; 5. Cavalry standard
of an unknown Milanese unit; 6. Cavalry standard of the German regiment *Lorrena* (EC-113)

(after *Les Triomphes de Louis XIV*, Bibliothèque Nationale de France, Paris)

See Colour Plate Commentaries for further information.

Spanish Infantry Ensigns Belonging to Unknown Units, Early 1690s
(after *Les Triomphes de Louis XIV*, Bibliothèque Nationale de France, Paris)
See Colour Plate Commentaries for further information.

Spanish Infantry Ensigns Belonging to Unknown Units, Early 1690s
(after *Les Triomphes de Louis XIV*, Bibliothèque Nationale de France, Paris)
See Colour Plate Commentaries for further information.

Plate O

Guardroom by Gillis van Tilborgh, Flanders, 1664–68 (Hermitage Museum, St Petersburg)

See Colour Plate Commentaries for further information.

Carlo IV Borromeo
See Colour Plate Commentaries for further information.

on a company basis until the end of the century, including Milanese and Spanish cavalry. These troops formed the *Caballería de lo Estado de Milán* with an overall strength of 18–21 companies in the 1660s, traditionally divided in *Gendarmi* or *Hombres de Armas* (Gendarmes), and *Cavalleggeri* light horse. Further cavalry companies could be raised as an additional force. Alongside these, from four to 13 companies of German cavalry also served in Lombardy.[433]

In 1666, the *Gendarmi* had their permanent quarters in the towns outside Milan.[434] The command of the cavalry was held by the *general de la caballería* who resided in the capital. Along with him, one *comisario general* served as commander of the Neapolitan cavalry in Lombardy, and one *general de la caballería alemana* did the same with the German cavalry. In the 1670s, the overall strength of the cavalry in Lombardy fluctuated between 2,500 and 3,000 cavalrymen and dragoons. In 1684, these latter formed a Spanish *tercio* of eight companies (ED–8), which joined the contingent sent to Greece against the Ottomans; before the end of the year, another *tercio* was formed joining the Italian dragoon companies under the *maestre de campo* Bernabò Visconti (ED-09).

The Army of Flanders continued to be the main laboratory in the matter of cavalry organisation. In 1667–68, the governor Marquis of Castel Rodrigo, joined all the cavalry in units composed from six to eight companies divided in six *naciones*.[435] In a letter sent to Madrid in March 1668, Castel Rodrigo submitted the project to raise actual cavalry regiments following the 'German' model. The reform had to create six Spanish *trozos* with 26 companies, two Italian *tercios* with six companies, two Burgundian with seven companies, 19 Walloon with 74 companies and 14 German with 93 companies. In addition, there were the lifeguards and other free companies.[436] The proposal encountered resistance from the government, which was supported by the conservative attitude of several high officials. The Constable of Castile gave his opinion to the Queen, calling into question: 'the reluctance of soldiers and officers to follow the new form, and because in this way the emulation that was positively experienced under the great captains-general would fail. It is therefore appropriate for the service of Your Majesty that the cavalry remained organised in *trozos* as has always been in this army.'[437]

After the peace of Aix-la-Chapelle, most of the cavalry raised in 1667–68 were disbanded or reformed, but the organisation of the cavalry did not change the establishment introduced in the 1650s. The only substantial

433 Maffi, *Los últimos tercios*, p.174. In 1666 Galeazzo Gualdo Priorato, in *Relatione della città e stato di Milano sotto il governo dell'eccellentissimo sig. Don Luigi de Guzman Ponze de Leone* (Milan, 1666), p.180, reports 11 companies of *Gendarmi*, 10 companies of *cavalleggeri*, four companies of German cavalry, and further eight 'extraordinary' cavalry companies.
434 *Ibid.*, p.146. In 1666 two companies of *gendarmi* had their quarters in Cremona, while Lodi, Voghera, Tortona, Abbiategrasso, Marignano, Landriano, Vidigulfo, Treviglio and Como each quartered one company.
435 Rodríguez Hernández, 'La caballería hispánica', p.48.
436 Martínez de Merlo, *La caballería entre Los Austrias y Los Borbones*, p.149, after Juan Luis Sánchez Martín.
437 Clonard, *Historia orgánica*, vol. IV, p.478.

novelty was that this time the *trozos-tercios* were not reformed into single companies, but they maintained a 'regimental' structure, notwithstanding that autonomous companies continued to exist both in Flanders and in the other Spanish domains.[438]

Between 1667 and 1678 at least 35 new cavalry *trozos, tercios* and regiments were raised in the Low Countries, turning not only to local recruits, who formed at least 20 tercios, but also from the German territories, which supplied a further seven regiments. There is not much data on the actual strength of cavalry in Flanders before 1672, when the muster recorded on 21 November registered in detail 10 Spanish *trozos*, 14 Flemish Walloon, one Franche-Comtois, and one Italian *tercios*, then seven German regiments, one of Croats, and one *tercio* of Flemish Walloon dragoons.[439] Most of these *tercios, trozos* and regiments deployed fewer than five companies; some of the Spanish *tercios* had just two companies, which usually were the ones of the *maestre de campo, teniente coronel* and *sargento mayor*. Five years later, the cavalry in the Low Countries consisted of eight Spanish *trozos* with 1,182 men, 15 Walloon *tercios* numbering 1,976 men, and nine German regiments with a total of 1,524 men.[440]

From the 1670s, in peacetime the cavalry regiments of all the nationalities were usually reduced to 100–125 men under the command of a *plana mayor* with six officers and adjutants. This was a compromise between containing the expense and maintaining a reasonable number of veterans. In 1675, after the bloody campaign of the previous year, the Army of Flanders deployed 24 *trozos-tercios* from different nations, and further 10 regiments of German cavalry.

As with the infantry, problems persisted to reliably identify a line of command for establishing the history of several units. The succession of acts which dealt with the organisation of the Spanish cavalry are even more

---

438 Martínez de Merlo, *La caballería entre Los Austrias y Los Borbones*, p.150: 'In this way, in December 1668, the units were again denominated *tercios* and *trozos*. At this point we must ask if these regiment-size units retained the same organisation already existing before 1668. Obviously, most of the companies forming the *trozos* as well as the *tercios* were the same, as the one that had not been reformed continued to exist and some of them with the same captains, including the officers who had been appointed to *maestre de campo*. Also, among the new units there were reformed officers who returned to serve in the corps. However, doubts remain whether these *trozos* and *tercios* maintained the existing organisation, but despite the discontinuity of over 15 years, everything suggests that the structure has remained the same.'

439 *Ibid.*, 'Clonard moves the muster to a date close to the end of 1673, since he lists the Count de la Romrée among the *maestres de campo* and mentions the *tercio* of the Count de la Motterie created in 1673. It should be emphasised that Clonard inserts three Walloon *tercios* that are omitted in the original document, most likely because these *tercios* were paid for by the local Estates and therefore were not registered in the army's payroll. However, one of these *tercios* could not be ignored, since in subsequent years it became the celebrated *Farnesio* regiment, while the other two remained active for several years. In any case, the list of 1672 is the best source from which to follow the events and successions of the commanders, namely the most useful for tracing the continuity of the unit until the beginning of the eighteenth century. Even so, unfortunately it is not always easy to identify the succession of the *maestres de campo* and the fate of several units remains uncertain.'

440 Maffi, 'Una epopeya olvidada', p.65.

complex than those concerning the infantry.[441] In the muster conduced three years later, the cavalry of the army of Flanders deployed 20 *trozos-tercios* and nine German regiments. The major reduction impacted on the Flemish Walloons, now decreased to 11 *tercios*.[442] It is difficult to establish whether some units had been merged into others and consequently new *maestres de campo* had succeeded to the command. Only the Walloon and Italian *tercios* retained the commanders of three years earlier. However, 10 months later, the ordinance of 6 August 1681, established the strength of each company at 30 horsemen and the tercios now totalled 16 in all.[443] Further changes occurred in 1684, after the illusory 20-year period of peace with France signed in the Regensburg truce. In July 1684, there were in the Spanish Low Countries seven Spanish *trozos*, but some of the original Walloon *tercios* had become Spanish, two were formed by Italian and Franche-Comtois, four were of Flemish Walloons and five were German regiments. The following year three Spanish *trozos*, one Flemish Walloon *tercio* and one German regiment were disbanded.

Again, like the infantry, after 1678 the Spaniards constituted the majority of cavalry in the Army of Flanders. Between 1671 and 1672 two whole dismounted *trozos* landed in Ostend. The original idea was to assemble a strong Spanish cavalry corps in Flanders with the units arrived a few years earlier from Galicia, and with the others that had been present from even earlier. To form this corps, it was necessary to recruit a considerable number of soldiers, but above all the attention of the War Council turned the reformed veteran horsemen who had fought in Extremadura. Along with these, other cavalry companies dismounted and quartered in Castile would be formed into *tercios*, a very helpful expedient considering that their presence was generating serious problems with the locals due to their large numbers. Through this plan, some 1,000 cavalrymen, many of them veterans, could be sent to Flanders.[444] In this way 16 companies of 68 horsemen each were assembled.

For the Iberian fronts, the need for cavalry increased considerably in the 1640s, especially on the Portuguese border. The availability of mounted

---

441 The Spanish *trozos* and the Italian *tercio* are identified, while concerning the 15 Walloon *tercios* a problem still persists. In the muster of 1673, there is a *tercio* registered under (Lieutenant Colonel?) Diego Freire. This *tercio* cannot be the one previously identified as *Feux* (EC–100), because both *tercios* appear at the same time, therefore it could be the *tercio Mirecourt/Romrée* (EC–105), or *Merode* (EC–151), which are the only two that do not appear in the muster of 1675. The other case concerns the unidentified *tercio* of the Viscount d' Audrigny, who was certainly in command of a different *tercio* than that belonging to the Baron of Quincy (EC–103, later *Farnesio*), considering that in 1675 both *tercios* operated on two different locations, as is recorded in the same document. Like the previous one, this *tercio* can only be either *Merode* or *Mirecourt/Romrée*. The same problem repeats itself months later with the *tercios Audrigny* and *Bethencourt* (EC–127). Sánchez Martin supposes that the former replaced *Bethencourt* in 1680, but the musters show that the *tercios* were two different units. Martínez de Merlo gives a quote that perhaps provides a solution to the problem: he states that in 1675 Quincy was replaced by the Viscount d'Audrigny and one year later he was succeeded by Bethencourt.

442 Martínez de Merlo, *La caballería entre Los Austrias y Los Borbones*, p.141.

443 Four units were most likely disbanded in early 1681, while the German regiments had been reduced to eight.

444 Rodríguez Hernández, 'El Reclutamiento de españoles para el Ejército de Flandes', p.404.

troops became urgent with the increase of Portuguese raids that skilfully exploited the mobility of their cavalry for incursions into Spanish territory.

To build a cavalry force able to protect the borders, the Crown turned to every source of supply for mounted soldiers. Among the horsemen immediately available there were the aforementioned *Guardias de Castilla*, and the knights of the cavalry orders. Since 1492 the ancient *órdenes militares* – Orden de Santiago; Orden de Calatrava; Orden de Alcántara; Orden de Montesa; Orden de San Juan – represented a military force directly controlled by the Crown.

During the reigns of Felipe II and Felipe III, the cavalry orders were never called upon to support the war effort of the Monarchy, but the situation changed in the middle of the 1640s. After the Portuguese and Catalan uprisings Felipe IV and Olivares applied exceptional measures, one of which was the attempt to recover the original spirit of the military orders, in this case not to fight infidels, but Catholics rebelling against their king. The idea of involving the aristocracy who served in the Orders pursued the plan n already drawn up to exploit the nobles in support of the war effort. As for infantry, the nobility could gather volunteers and horses for the army. A special *junta de caballería* (cavalry council) was appointed by the Crown in order to manage the project.[445]

The *junta* had to discuss a matter that turned out to be very delicate and resulted in a disappointing outcome for the expectations of Felipe IV himself. The council had to consider all the cases of exemption, especially for knights assigned to service positions at court, in the government and for the knights aged under 17 or over 65 years. Therefore, the appointment of substitutes, or the payment of 120 silver *ducados* necessary for the equipment of a horseman was agreed. A sanction of 200 ducats and even imprisonment would have been applied to people who did not present themselves or did not pay for the replacement. Furthermore, the substitutes were to be *hidalgos* who were rewarded with the appointment of knights of a Holy Order after two years of service in the army.

The difficulties in the formation of this cavalry, which would have been the first entirely formed by aristocrats, continued to delay the project. The council reported the difficulties encountered by the knights at court and commanders in finding substitutes to Felipe IV, because since only a single

445 Francisco Fernández Izquierdo, 'Los caballeros cruzados enelejército de la Monarquía Hispánica durante los siglos XVI y XVII: ¿anhelo o realidad?', in *Revista de Historia Moderna – Anales de la Universidad de Alicante*, n. 22 (2004), p.39: 'In this regard there were antecedents to the idea of integrating the knights of the orders into the regular Army. In 1635, the first year of war against France, the project of mobilising the aristocracy, and the orders in particular, took shape first with the invitation to the nobility in 1637 to join the Army, and later in the establishment of the *Junta de Caballería* in late 1639 in order to form armoured horse 'battalions' with members of the orders. The revolts of Catalonia and Portugal modified the original project. Under the supervision of Olivares, who had strongly advocated the proposal, in the early months of 1640 the council included the Count of Monterrey, the Marquis of Castrofuerte, Jerónimo de Villanueva, and the 'council lawyers' representing each of the orders: Melchor de Cistiernes (Montesa), Antonio de Luna (Santiago), Diego de Ceballos (Calatrava) and Juan Chacón (Alcántara) who was replaced in March 1640 by Claudio Pimentel.'

squadron of *hidalgos* had also been recruited there were not enough.[446] The *Junta* proposed that the substitutes should not be nobles, and that the obligated knights pay them 150 ducats to replace them in the army. The king radically opposed the proposal, and also the possibility that foreign mercenaries could serve as substitutes, Felipe IV replied 'by no means do they have to be but Spaniards.'[447]

Further negotiations were necessary to reach an agreement with the knights of the Orders, who were reluctant to join the army as simple troopers. The training also caused much concern, especially in anticipation of the general muster that would be carried out before the King himself and that he would be observed by ambassadors and foreigners who were at court. This concern about the outward appearance of the cavalry in a military parade confirms that the theatrical image of the unit was more important than preparing a corps of professional horsemen. In February 1642, the parade gathered a not negligible strength of 1,543 horsemen, but just 16.5 percent were *caballeros de hábito*, and 5.5 percent were already serving in the army. All the others were substitutes.[448]

After having served in Catalonia, in 1657 the *trozo de los Órdenes* (EC-5) headed to Extremadura. In 1658, they numbered 950 rank and file, placing the *trozo* as the major cavalry unit of the army, but it was considered apart from the army, because of its composition. Furthermore, the knights did not perform the same tasks requested of the regular cavalry, and their employment on campaign had to be agreed by the commander, who usually held the charge of *teniente general de la caballería* and did not allow other senior officers to tactically dispose of his *trozo*.

Artillery Organisation

As with most armies of this era, artillerymen rarely appear in orders of battle and musters, and only the number of guns is recorded without specifying whether it is field or siege artillery. In Spain the artillery was divided in the classical mobile and static categories. The first comprised the field artillery gathered in batteries of six to 12 guns under the direction of captains and lieutenants who were supervised by the *capitán general* appointed in every province. Above them, on campaign there were one or more *generales de la artillería* in each major army, who held the responsibility for the tactical direction of the field and siege artillery, with a staff comprising a *lugarteniente*.

---

446 *Ibid.*, pp.51–52. The *junta* explained to Felipe IV that only 45 knights had answered the last call, since many were already in the service of the King, together with the knights who served as infantry officers or general commanders, and the others who were outside Madrid and could not be included in the cavalry corps. However, it was estimated that about 1,000 horsemen could be assembled, who would have to serve with the payment of 120 silver *ducados*. This sum would have constituted a fund of 120,000 *ducados* needed to maintain a *trozo* of 1,000 men.

447 *Ibid*, p.42. Even Martín de Arana, an elderly noble, was reprimanded by the monarch himself because he had proposed to pay at his expense the recruitment of 50 or 100 sailors and artillerymen who would be more useful in the navy than a single *hidalgo* sent in his place in the cavalry.

448 *Ibid.*, p.49.

Late seventeenth century Spanish artillery. From left to right: 8 lb *sacre*, 16 lb *medio cañon*, 12 lb *tercio de cañon*, 26 lb *cañon*, and 16 lb *colubrina bastarda*, after the *Historia del Ejército Español. Armas, Uniformes, Sistema de Combate, Instituciones, Organización del mismo, desde los tiempos másremotos hasta nuestros días* (Barcelona, 1889) by Francisco Barado.

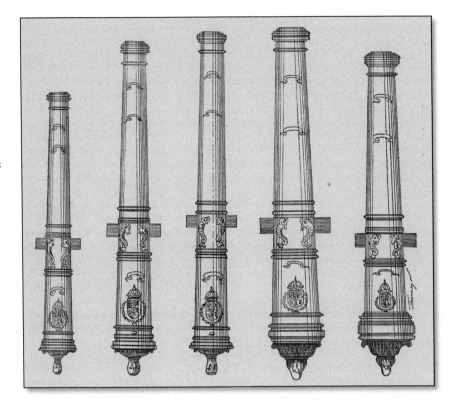

The siege artillery also comprised a part of the static component, which was usually assigned to the fortresses.

Under the senior and field ranks, there were the *gente de artillería*, who included private artillerymen with *sargentos* and *cabos* according to the number of personnel and guns in the army or garrisons. Usually, each NCO served as gun master and could be also identified by the rank of *condestable* or *gentil-hombre*. As happened in other contemporary armies, the artillerymen of the Hispanic armies belonged to a class of professional soldiers specialised in tasks coinciding with the professional background, which assigned them a privileged position, albeit with little prospect of promotion. After 1650, another rank known as *entretenido de artillería* (artillery companion) frequently appears in the roster of the army of Flanders and Lombardy. They were usually aged veterans, reformed NCOs or ensigns who received a place in the artillery and usually formed the lifeguard for captains or artillery generals.[449] On campaign, the train could include technicians, such as a smith, caster, carpenter and master of fireworks, plus auxiliary personnel such as surgeons and chaplains. Finally, in the major garrisons there was a *mayordomo*, who had the job of managing the arsenal with a guard formed by four to six soldiers, and a few sentries for the munitions and equipment.

---

449 It is worth mentioning the dramatist Pedro Calderón de la Barca (1600–1681) who served as *entretenido de artillería* in the Army of Catalonia.

In the 1660s, there were 19 companies of artillery in the Spanish Low Countries quartered in the major garrisons, formed of a captain and a variable number of constables and artillerymen, depending on the importance of the place. Among the 15 most important places was the castle of Antwerp with five *cabos* and 49 artillerymen, while the smallest, Stevensweert, had just two and nine respectively. The other fortresses with artillery companies were Cambrai, Courtray, Malines, Dendermunde, Ghent, Oudenarde, Damme, Ostende, Nieuport, Mons, Ath, Namur, Charleroi, Armentieres, Bruges, Gueldres and Luxembourg.[450] In 1678, their number decreased to 14 after the French conquests in the region. Franche-Comté had three small companies, one in each of the major garrisons in Dole, Salins and Besançon.

In Lombardy artillerymen were distributed in 16 locations, Milan being the most important. In the 1660s, artillerymen also served in the garrison of Pavia, Lodi, Tortona, Serravalle, Pizzighettone, Trezzo, Lecco, Domodossola, Como, Arona, Cremona, Novara, Alessandria, Valenza, and Fort Fuentes.[451] In Catalonia the main garrisons with artillerymen were in Barcelona, Gerona, Tortosa, Cardona and Rosas with other minor ones in Mallorca and Sardinia. Small companies of artillerymen were located in North Africa, as well as in the *Estado de los Presidios*, Finale di Spagna, Naples and Sicily. In these latter provinces, two or more often a single gunner manned the long chain of watchtowers spread all along the coast, together with small detachments of infantrymen, where small calibre weapons or rampart muskets sometime constituted the only artillery of the location.[452]

According to the estimation made by authoritative scholars, in the 1670s the artillerymen in the army of Flanders did not exceed 400 men in all.[453] A similar figure was gathered in Lombardy in the following decade, but more often the overall force was only 200. The general low strength depended on several factors; above all because the artillerymen were the ones who dealt with the guns in a fight, while transport and placement of pieces on the battlefield or in the sieges was performed by infantrymen or civilian labour directed by NCOs. On campaign, the artillery train was usually supplied by *asientistas* who operated under the supervision of the *general de la artillería* or his lieutenant, while the field direction was entrusted to the *conductores*, who served as junior officers.

---

450 Galeazzo Gualdo Priorato, *Teatro del Belgio ò sia Descritione delle Diciassette Provincie del Medesimo* (Frankfurt am Main, 1683), p.19–20.

451 Gualdo Priorato, *Relatione della città e stato di Milano*, p.166.

452 The garrisons of these towers, and guard posts were limited to three or four men: a corporal, a gunner if there were cannons, and one or two soldiers. In the 1680s, in Sicily a contingent of 208 regular soldiers was assigned to this service throughout the year, to which another 665 were added between April and November but, as always, the number of soldiers was often fewer than needed. There were also, according to the importance and the size of the arsenals, a variable number of artillery pieces of various types, registered under the name of *colombrina*, *sagro*, *falconetto* and other heavy firearms. Overall, the Sicilian towers had 93 cannons, of which 11 were useless, 184 arquebuses, 99 muskets, 37 rampart muskets and 147 halberds. See Ligresti, *Le armi dei Siciliani*, pp.80–81.

453 Maffi, *Los últimos tercios*, pp.175–176.

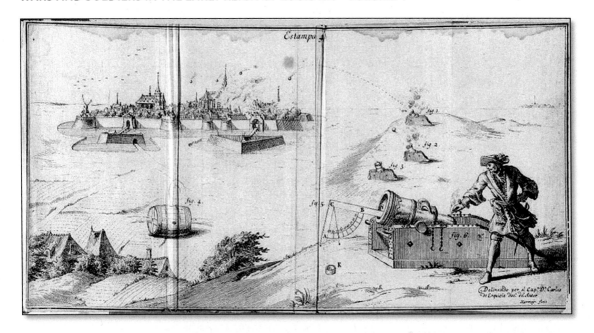

Illustration from *El Perfecto artificial, bombardero y artillero*, by Sebastián Fernández de Medrano. The work is divided into two books. The first is in two treatises with 18 and 14 chapters respectively: the first dedicated to saltpetre, gunpowder and rockets, while the second deals with grenades, bombs, mortars, mines and many other explosive weapons. The second, 18-chapter book is intended for the training of the artillerymen, describing the tools as well as the different type of guns and their characteristics. The last chapter is devoted to a series of warnings about metals, horses, and wagons. The prints were made by the Van Harrewij family of Dutch engravers.

The availability of guns in relation to the size of an army was a key subject of seventeenth-century warfare. In Flanders the initial ratio was one gun for every 1,000 men, but in the course of the Thirty Years' War it doubled, reaching four and even five guns for every 1,000 soldiers in the following decades, due to the high number of sieges that marked the war until the end of the century.[454]

Among the numerous clichés about the *Los Austrias*, the one relating to technological backwardness and the inability to modernise especially involved the artillery. However, although there was some delay, the Monarchy had already established artillery with modern criteria. In 1609, a royal decree officially standardised the artillery in four classes according to the calibre, from eight to 40 lb.[455] The overall availability of guns was also far from scarce. A report dated 1674, reports that in the Iberian Peninsula there were more than 1,200 guns and mortars, and Catalonia was not included in this figure.[456] In the same year, 400 guns formed the artillery of the Army of Milan.[457] Iron and bronze guns were cast in Spain as well as in Flanders and Italy, and the production satisfied the needs of the army.

454 *Ibid.*, p.179.
455 One Spanish pound was equal to 320.758 grammes.
456 Maffi, *Los últimos tercios*, p.182.
457 Picouet, *The Armies of Philip IV of Spain 1621–1665*, p.166

Despite the attempt to reduce the variety of field guns, most of the older weapons were still in use and foundries continued to cast different calibres. Moreover, following the innovations from outside, lighter field guns were introduced, such as the four-pounder pieces cast in Lombardy in the 1630s.[458] In 1638, the Spanish foundries produced another light field gun called *Mansfelte*, which fired projectiles of five to six pounds. Further calibres were introduced in the heavy category, such as the 20 lb weapons produced in Seville from 1620. The result was that in the second half of the century Hispanic artillery featured a remarkable variety of calibres. Carlos II inherited this mass of heterogeneous armaments comprising old and new weapons which coexisted for a long time.

To support its armies on campaign, from the previous century the Crown had established a network of military arsenals that guaranteed self-sufficiency, and production was also destined to be exported. The quality of the Hispanic production was not inferior to the ones from other powers, and the defects were no different from the ones found in the French or Dutch artillery. However, it should be emphasised that the initiatives to update the tactical employment of the artillery to the new era of warfare were mostly due to the personal initiatives of officers and governors, who acted without central coordination. Since his appointment in Flanders, the Count of Monterrey paid close attention to any proposals for improving the artillery. In 1671, 130 field guns of small calibres were produced, and another 30 were cast the following year, in line with the war preparations strongly advocated by Monterrey. During the Franco-Dutch war, the artillery, especially the static ones in garrisons, suffered considerable losses due to the French conquests, and the field train also had to be downsized due to lack of funds. As a result, in 1679, the artillery of the army of Flanders had just 44 field guns of various calibres.[459]

In Lombardy, some innovations were introduced by the Count of Melgar, who in the beginning of the 1680s, ordered the production of modern mortars. He also strengthened the artillery of the *Estado* reorganising the arsenals and replacing the older weapons and the obsolete equipment.[460] In the same period, resources were allocated to improve the field artillery with new guns and portable mortars, and with selective examinations of artillery personnel in the major garrisons.

However, for many years cannon production was characterised by considerable variation. Cannons were cast without the royal mark according to the rules established by the governors or even by the foundries, and this diversity caused continuing confusion in the field of artillery. The problem of the rationalisation of calibres and the standardisation of the different types of weapons was a matter that many asked to be solved. This debate involved not only military and technicians, but also mathematicians and engineers, who left a large number of studies and proposals for reform in the artillery.

---

458 Davide Maffi, *En defensa del Imperio*, p.321.
459 AGS, *Estado*, leg. 3682, *relación* dated 10 April 1679.
460 Maffi, *Los últimos tercios*, p.180.

In 1671, the theoretician Sebastián Fernández de Gamboa proposed 13 different gun classifications, according to weight, calibre and projectile:[461]

Falconete		450 kg	1 to 30–32	1–3 lb
Medio Sacre		450 kg	1 to 30–32	4–5 lb
Sacre		400 kg	1 to 30–32	6–8 lb
Media Colubrina bastarda	300 kg	1 to 26	9–15 lb	
Media Colubrina legitima	350 kg	1 to 30–31	" "	" "
Colubrina bastarda	300 kg	1 to 26	16–30 lb	
Colubrina legitima	350kg	1 to 30–31	" "	
Quarto de Cañon	200 kg	1 to 20–24	7–9 lb	
Tercio de Cañon	200 kg	1 to 18–24	10–15 lb	
Medio Cañon		200 kg	1 to 18–21	16–25 lb
Cañon		150 kg	1 to 18	26–60 lb
Quarto Cañon Pedrero:	150 kg	1 to 12–14	4–9 lb	
Tercio Cañon Pedrero	150 kg	1 to 12–13	10–15 lb	
Medio Cañon Pedrero	150 kg	1 to 12–13	16–25 lb	
Cañon Pedrero	150 kg	1 to 12–13	26–40 lb	

This and other proposals of reform were the compromise between the need for rationalisation and financial resources. From theorists to gunners, as well as cannon casters, everyone was aware of the need to adapt the armaments to the innovations introduced in this field. Each year the War Council examined the proposals submitted from the governors and senior commanders, but once again it was the individual initiative that prevailed, although, as happened in Flanders, it managed to achieve significant benefits. In 1666, the *teniente de maestre de campo general* Juan Bayarte conducted experiments employing different classes of guns and demonstrating, after verified tests, the defects suffered by the heavy artillery. The result opened the way to the modern light field guns, concentrating the production on four to eight pounders firing projectiles of iron, with barrel length 16 or 17 times the calibre.[462]

As for mortars and howitzers, Spain was also lagging behind the major European powers. Mortars had undergone major changes starting mid century. The introduction of modern mortars came on the initiative of the engineer Antonio González, who modified the Dutch model which was capable of firing fused explosive devices. It was for this invention that in Spain the weapons of modern conception were called *morteros a lo González*.[463]

For a long time, the Hispanic artillery was conditioned not only its diversity, but also by a lack of updated scientific studies. Although in 1646

---

461 Sebastian Fernández de Gamboa, *Memorias Militares* (Madrid, 1671).
462 Dolores Herrero Fernández-Quesada, 'La artillería, entre la tradición y la innovación', in *Los Tercios, 1660–1704*, in *Desperta Ferro* special issue XIX (June–July 2019), p.68.
463 *Ibid.*, p.68.

the *Catedra de Matemáticas y Artilleria* was reorganised in Madrid, having been first established in 1600, this institution did not produce significant results and in 1697 it was closed. The problem of the shortage of trained personnel had been discussed by the War Council in 1663. The causes were attributed to the lack of reform in the artillery 'schools' of Burgos and Seville, which caused great damage in this matter. Between 1676 and 1677, the shortage of trained artillery officers was highlighted as one of the most urgent problems to be solved, especially after the alarms signalling unrest coming from Catalonia and Sicily.[464]

The same shortage concerned the technical personnel for the fortifications. The War Council and the Captain General of the Artillery, the Marquis de Carralbo, addressed a proposal to the King for the creation of new schools of artillery, mathematics and engineering in Cadiz, Malaga, San Sebastian, La Coruña, Catalonia, and Mallorca. Once again, the lack of finances hindered the project, and little or nothing was achieved. Thanks to the insistence of the governor of Catalonia, the Duke of Bournonville, in the 1690s the *Real Academia Militar* of Barcelona began to train specialised technicians for the army, following the one established in Brussels in 1685. The schools instructed the pupils in the study of mathematics and geometry, followed by teaching on fortifications and artillery.

Lack of resources does not mean that Spain lacked skilled artillerymen and technicians. The foundries of Seville and Valencia were a fertile ground for experimentation and able artillerymen produced interesting studies on the employment of the artillery in siege warfare as well as in the field. Among the most qualified, there was José Chafrión, author of the treaty *Escuela de palas o sea curso matemático*, printed in 1693, and the renowned Sebastián Fernández de Medrano, who held the office of Director of the *Academia Militar* of Brussels. He was the author of the innovative manual *El perfecto artillero y elarquitecto perfecto enelarte miltar*. In his work, Medrano dealt not only with technical topics, but mainly focused on the industrial aspect including the production of guns and in the preparation of most effective gunpowder. In Spain, the production of guns benefited greatly from the innovations of Medrano and at the end of the century, some of these weapons were also copied outside of the Peninsula. In France, some weapons received a characteristic denomination, like the concave chamber mortars, called in France mortars with *chambre à l'espagnole*, or the *demi-canon d'Espagne* and the *quart canon d'Espagne*, which copied the *cañones* of 12 and 24 lb.

Supply and Logistics

The supply of the armies was the Achilles' heel of the Monarchy, since in the 1650s, the organisation was on the verge of collapse. Procurement based on direct control of royal *administración* had gone through a severe crisis, which led to the development of the system relying on services contracted-out to

---

464 Espino López, 'El ocaso de la maquinaria bélica hispánica', p.20.

supply the army and navy, known in Spain as *asiento*. A close public–private partnership thus increased, thanks to which several private entrepreneurs flourished throughout the century.[465]

The failure of direct management in a range of services was evident everywhere. In particular, the supply of bread, but also gunpowder, artillery and army train with wagons, horses and ammunition, languished not only in the Iberian Peninsula, but also in Flanders and Milan, where the organisation responsible for supplying them collapsed under the weight of an ever growing demand.[466] Not only was this demand growing, but it was spread across multiple fronts, because in the strategic situation during those years. Although in a state of constant evolution, Spain was the first to face the problem of supplying and maintaining armies in operational theatres very distant from each other, and this at a level previously unknown. Army commanders received money for their war chest, but when this was sufficient, it was used to pay for the supply of all kinds of goods and ammunition, such as bread, fodder and horses, artillery, fortifications, hospitals and finally – and if there were still funds – for paying wages to the troops. The most common occurrence was that troops received payments at the beginning and end of the campaign, but not always during the operational period.

In the last years of the reign of Felipe IV, the finances of the army already appeared severely depressed. At the beginning of 1658, the Army of Extremadura was in a miserable state, as the troops had received just three payments in 16 months and had been fed only with bread.[467] In regions like Galicia, it was even considered normal that the army could be maintained with only six annual payments, in addition to bread and the aid from the local authorities. This happened because in Galicia the troops were mostly semi-professionals and militiamen.[468] On the other hand, when professional soldiers were quartered close to the communities, the consequences could be very unpleasant for the local economy.

Although in principle the civil authorities were reimbursed by the royal treasury, the inconvenience could be catastrophic. There are innumerable examples. In 1653, in Catalonia, the representatives of the village of Sant Vicenç de Llavaneres declared that after the transit of the troops heading to Roussillon, eight families had abandoned their homes to avoid further aggravation. The village had housed an infantry company and every day the *alférez* asked for two hens for the officers and a *lliura* (pound) of meat for each soldier. The company halted three weeks and finally the inhabitants offered

---

465 Spain had already introduced this system in a non-marginal way. It is enough to mention Manuel Cortizos, founder of the house of Portuguese financiers, who for three generations was active in Castile. Between 1648 and 1650, the year of Manuel Cortizos' death, the contractor stipulated *asientos* to enlist soldiers, to provide money for the troops of Flanders and to supply horses, saddles, boots for the Spanish troops. Carmen Sanz-Ayán, 'Los Cortizos. Un clan financiero de origen judeo converso', in *Estado, monarquía y finanzas: Estudio de historia financiera en tiempos de los Austrias* (Madrid: Centro de estudios políticos y constitucionales, 2004), pp.189–190.

466 Davide Maffi, 'L'Amministrazione della Finanza Militare nella Lombardia Spagnola: I Veedores e i Contadori dell'Esercito (1536–1700)', in *Storia Economica* V (2002), n. 1, pp.54–106.

467 Antonio José Rodríguez Hernández, *Asientos y asentistas militares en el siglo XVII*, p.66.

468 *Ibid.*

double rations as long as the soldiers moved to another location. In 1656, the village of Cabrera was less fortunate. According to a declaration of the inhabitants to the authorities of Catalonia, the passage of a cavalry *trozo* of 500 horsemen reduced all the inhabitants to ruin in a single day.[469]

The quarters could then be classified as ordinary, for stationary contingents, and extraordinary, concerning troops in transit. These classifications then provided for further subdivisions, the administrative and financial significance of which could be considerable. The ordinances on the matter specified everything that the military could legitimately expect from civilians, but also stipulated that they had to pay the maintenance costs on the spot out of their own pockets.

For this purpose, they had to use the money paid to them from their monthly income. Nevertheless, since the army administration often did not pay the soldiers on time, who in turn found it hard to support themselves while being housed, the communities were forced to bear burdens not within their ability to do so, to which was added a vast array of abuses. Consequently, the provincial administrations claimed the right to compensate those expenses on taxes paid to the Monarchy. In the difficult economic situation of the second half of the seventeenth century, compensation intervened on the wages of the military, reducing them to an extent equivalent to the sums unduly extorted from the communities.[470]

Towns and villages were a profitable resources when the troops were far from the theatre of operations, but when they were out on campaign, the food was acquired entirely from the army's finances. The 'ammunition bread' alone was not enough to sustain the soldiers, so massive numbers of desertions occurred when there were delays in payments which were accompanied by a lack of bread, an event that the commanders always tried to avoid. Nonetheless, not only the soldiers began to desert, but veteran officers as well.[471]

The problem was not isolated to the field armies. Even the permanent garrisons, where the expenses could be estimated more easily, suffered the lack of economic resources. In 1661 the situation had reached such a point that the governor of the garrisons in Guipúzcoa in the western Pyrenees claimed that during the seven years he had been in office, the soldiers had received their wages only nine times. The problem was far from being quickly solved. In 1677, things had not changed, and the military quarters were

---

469 Antonio Espino López, *Cataluña durante el reinado de Carlos II*, p.46.

470 Buono, *Esercito, istituzioni, territorio*, p.29.

471 Rodríguez Hernández, 'Guerra y alianzas en la lucha por la hegemonía europea', p.257: 'In 1678 a report from Flanders referred that the bad practices and the fraud of the officers – in addition to the delay of wages – had reduced the Army, since the best soldiers pass to the to the French side … these troops being the ones that were doing the most damage to the economy of the region, because of the destruction they generated, and their looting and contributions'. The problem continued in subsequent years: 'As early as 1680 the Catalan authorities recognised that Louis XIV maintained an entire regiment of Spaniards, most of them deserters who were financially rewarded for abandoning their units and joining the French Army … In June 1691, the fortress of Seo de Urgel fell into French hands, and its garrison became prisoners of war. After eight months of captivity in France, an officer reported that more than 40 men of his company had sided with the enemy.'

almost defenceless, because the soldiers had 'died of starvation', receiving only bread. This situation continued, because in 1687, deprived even of bread, the soldiers were forced to beg in the churches.[472]

Throughout Europe, the growth in the size of armies and their formation as a permanent force in the second half of the seventeenth century caused an increase in problems for maintaining them. Logistics had become an important component of strategy and needed an advanced and well-resourced organisation to be governed properly. In Spain, the government turned to private entrepreneurs, who through *asientos* (contracts) provided supplies for the soldiers, with the intention of obtaining some flexibility and above all savings.

This decision avoided the creation of a permanent military administration, the introduction of which took place in the following century, and which would take many more years to develop fully and satisfactorily. Given its administrative and financial weakness, Spain was in many cases forced to extend *asientos* that guaranteed further essential services to the troops, which however resulted in a delay or even a total lack of pay for the troops. Historians have outlined how the Spanish Habsburgs were forced by lack of liquidity, embezzlement and lack of integrity of some ministers, to turn to systems of private provisioning, which were even better controlled than the ones administered directly.[473] Every commander knew that by providing the troops with basic stuff, it avoided or at least reduced desertions, since the payments did not always arrive on time, nor did the local farmers or traders have sufficient goods at acceptable prices. The government's direct supply of troops increased expenses but ensured the survival of the troops. Therefore, to face this problem, the Spanish army resorted to the *asentistas*, who at an adequate and convenient price promised to provide all the necessary for at least a year on a specific war front.

Among the *asientos* the most indispensable were obviously the ones covering foodstuffs,[474] and certainly the most expensive and complex was that for the supply of bread, which was also the one that allowed for unparalleled

---

472 Rodríguez Hernández, *Asientos y asentistas militares en el siglo XVII*, p.69. Contemporary documents and reports are full of similar grievances. In April 1679, the commander of the garrison of La Coruña declared that his soldiers had received their last cash aid 23 months before: 'Many soldiers were aged and disabled, now unable to serve, and they had to beg to eat, so they queued in the convents to receive soup, considering that previously they had been forced to sell weapons, and many were trying to earn something improvising as tailors or shoemakers.' Not surprisingly, months later some soldiers looted two boats loaded with grain in the harbour, as they had not received pay for 30 months. AGS, GA, leg. 2.472: letter of the Marqués de Villafiel, Governor of Galicia, dated 28 April 1679.

473 See Maffi, *L'Amministrazione della Finanza Militare nella Lombardia Spagnola*, pp.54–106.

474 Rodríguez Hernández, *Asientos y asentistas militares en el siglo XVII*, p.64: 'The analysis of the expenditures of the field armies, in particular the ones in Extremadura, Galicia and on the border with Castile, indicates that although the cash payments represented between 46 percent and more than 50 percent of the total funds, these were mainly used to meet to the payments of officers and troops, but also for a whole series of minor expenses. This last item of expenditure was the first to be cut when it was not sufficient to meet other needs, equivalent to between 20 and 30 percent of actual expenditure. On the other hand, other expenses did not tend to suffer excessive cuts as it was recognised that they were essential for conducting a campaign. Therefore, the funds for the supply of bread and fodder represented more than one third of the expenditure

margins of profit compared to all other services for the army.[475] During the 1670s and 1680s, just the cost for the *pan de munición* (ammunition bread) delivered to the troops deployed in Catalonia amounted around 3,000,000 *reales* per year, with a peak of over 4,000,000 *reales* in 1685, equivalent to nearly 50 percent of all military spending.[476]

Though this service involved the contractors in a not negligible series of obligations, in Flanders the *asiento* brought to actual factions in the financial world, in order to meet the commitments undertaken with the *proveeduría general*. The fierce competition developed between the various *hombres de negocios*, not only local, but also Genoese and Portuguese, all interested in obtaining the lucrative contracts. In Flanders the situation was different from other regions, as in Lombardy and Catalonia, where the *asientos* were managed as a form of monopoly for several consecutive decades by the same contractor.[477]

Several factors attracted so many entrepreneurs in the *asientos* for the army. First of all, there was the protection granted by the *fuero militar*, a right granted to all suppliers of the army, which allowed them to avoid ordinary justice in the case of lawsuits brought by other merchants or for contractual breaches. The importance of the protection offered by military justice was such that often the contractors themselves made an express request to be judged only by the military *auditores*.[478] Moreover, thanks to the opportunity offered them to travel to other regions, the *asentistas* could circumvent duties by exporting or importing other goods obtaining additional income.

In January 1658, an investigation was carried out on a supplier of bread to the garrisons in Galicia. The investigation was decided because the *asentista* owed 10,000 rations of bread per day, but several times he had not been able to supply the quantity agreed. In addition, there had been many complaints about the poor quality of the bread provided. Then, eight loaves were delivered to Madrid. The examination revealed that some of these were even empty inside, and mostly made with poor quality or rotten flour. Subsequent investigations by the Treasury Council had an impact on the abuses of *asentistas* and the methods devised to enrich themselves at the expense of the army. The most common irregularities were the use of poor-quality flours and the difference in weight of the rations provided; moreover,

---

of the Army, followed by the horses – between 5 and 10 percent – weapons and ammunition – about 5 percent – and carriages – about 15 percent.'

475 Maffi, *Asentistas del rey*, p.142.

476 *Ibid.*, p.143.

477 *Ibid.*, p.144. Catalonia housed the third most important army of the Monarchy. Here, starting from 1666 until 1688 practically without interruption, Francisco Monserrat y Vives from Barcelona monopolised the supply of food for the army, obtaining, in exchange for the services rendered to the Crown, the title of Marquis of Tamarit.

478 An example is the case involving Francisco Monserrat y Vives, a Catalan *asentista*, who for a long time insisted on obtaining this privilege, probably to evade the numerous accusations of wrongdoing addressed to him, not least an investigation for embezzlement initiated by the *Contaduría Mayor de Cuentas* in 1682, which referred to events that occurred at the beginning of the previous decade. Privilege that was granted to him in 1683, so that he could continue without any impediment to supply the army. See Carmen Sanz Ayán, *Los Banqueros de Carlos II* (Valladolid: Ediciones Universidad de Valladolid, 1989), p.358.

as supplementary profit, the *asentistas* did not pay for the wood provided for their ovens by the suppliers in the province.[479]

The *asiento* system allowed the government to save resources but did not prevent misappropriation and fraud. Although the privatisation of the bread supply had averted the risk of famine for the army, mismanagement continued to be the weaknesses of the Spanish military administration. *Proveeditors* and accountants could check that the suppliers sent the requested rations, and that these were delivered and correctly accounted for, but they could hardly notice the irregularities that occurred within the regiments and companies. *Provveditors* (*veedores* or commissioners) were unable to control this process, as there were not enough of them. Before the ordinance of 1656, rations were delivered to captains or their lieutenants who distributed them to soldiers. But sometimes they kept some portions, appropriating rations from those who had deserted or discharged, creating countless abuses.

After this date, to avoid fraud, it was established that the rations of bread and barley had to be delivered to each soldier by the *veedores*. This method could be applied easily in the garrisons, but on campaign it encountered many problems. In many cases, the *asentistas* delivered the rations to an officer appointed to perform the function of commissioner. Moreover, due the absence of updated information regarding the strength of the companies, the bread was delivered to each company according to the latest muster carried out, which often did not correspond to reality. This led to the delivery of more rations than needed, as losses and desertions had not been subtracted.

In 1663, it is estimated that 63,119 extra bread rations had been delivered: a considerable economic loss difficult to recover.[480] Now, the problem had not to do with the privatisation of the supply, but with the officers of the regiments, who in many cases were the main actors in the fraud, alongside the *veedores* as accomplices.[481] The countermeasures introduced did not stop the fraud, which continued to consume more rations than indicated by the musters, although in some cases the authorities acted against the people involved, who were expelled from the army.

After 1663, the contractors fulfilled their contractual obligations and allowances with sufficient punctuality, but in 1665 the complaints about the supplies increased. Soldiers protested about the shortage of bread, and in the opinion of some officers this influenced the disastrous outcome of the campaign. Although it was decided to increase the bread rations from 13,000 to 18,000 per day in anticipation of the operations, problems began to arise in the spring. The financial allowances did not arrive and there was no reserve of provisions. Moreover, the contractors had neither flour nor credit to continue. All summer supplies for the army remained paralysed, as the *asentistas* had no money. Therefore, the military authorities had to intervene and requisitioned the grain in order to provide bread to the troops, having to discharge the militiamen because the army could not give them the bread. The army commander, Luis Francisco de Benavides Carrillo de

---

479 *Ibid.*, p.402.
480 Rodríguez Hernández, *Asientos y asentistas militares en el siglo XVII*, p.84.
481 Maffi, *L'Amministrazione della Finanza Militare nella Lombardia Spagnola*, p.87.

Toledo, Marquis of Caracena, stated that 'the suppliers do not obey, nor do they have a way to do so', asking for an explanation of what was happening to the Madrid government.[482]

Investigations conducted by the Council found that the contractors did not honour the supply of bread and that the ovens were closed for lack of flour. As for the money to be paid, of the theoretical 310,000 *escudos* requested for the campaign of 1663, only 67,483 had been sent to the army. Another 33,300 had been received as letters of credit, but a further 31,800 *escudos* remained to be paid to the *asentistas*. The campaign's reports indicate that the supply system in Galicia was a disaster, considering that the suppliers had no means to advance the money and the government had no other short-term income. The organisation of supplies worked better in Extremadura, where the *asiento* was assigned to a single supplier.[483]

However, the criticism of contemporary commentators concerning this system was very harsh, and generally describes the *asientos* as very negative: 'the way in which this method of providing food through businessmen was introduced is the major cause of the desertion of the soldiers'.[484] Some officers confirmed that the problem was with the contractors themselves, since 'when they were less dishonest and more conscientious, and there was money to pay them, they were useful, but today (1660) they have become absolutely vicious, they increase the incomes, they buy poor grain and they make the pestilential bread that infects our armies … and when the treasure delays the payment they justify the omissions for lack of funds'.[485]

The problem was partially contained by trying to imitate the allies. During the Franco-Dutch War of 1672–1679, the Army of Flanders introduced the Dutch system, which consisted in distributing to the soldiers the equivalent in money of the rations of bread for the infantry, and bread and barley for the cavalry and artillery. Unfortunately, the expected result was negative, because the soldiers used the money to gamble and other activities that nothing had to do with the rations, and 'making the soldiers even worse assisted'.[486] In the following decade, in Flanders bread and barley was again to be supplied by private contractors, who also met the request of the allied armies, also maintaining this system in Catalonia and Lombardy.[487]

---

482 Estébanez Calderón, *De la conquista y pérdida de Portugal*, vol. II, p.392.

483 This was the commercial house of Sebastían Silíceo. By fulfilling his *asientos* more or less regularly, Silíceo became an essential figure for the Spanish army and the court too. In subsequent years he considerably enlarged the volume of his business, which included the loan of coin for Flanders and the court and, together with other partners, even the slave trade with America; see Rodríguez Hernández, *Asientos y asentistas militares en el siglo XVII*, p.77.

484 *Ibid.*, p.85.

485 *Ibid.*

486 AGS, Estado, leg. 3866: *Consulta del Consejo de Estado*, dated 25 February 1681.

487 Nevertheless, the problem persisted. In 1681 a report from Flanders recommended that 'the most important is to supply bread to the soldiers at the rate of two portions a day, and the officers according to the number of mouths they have for servants. The soldiers had to be paid every week so that they can buy anything else to eat, even if it is a soup, because when the payment came late, the Army goes to ruin.' AGS, *Estado*, leg. 3867, *Memoria y traducción de la forma en que se debe distribuir el caudal de su majestad en Flandes*.

Along with food, the other fundamental requirement of any army was the production of armaments and ammunition. In this matter, Spain already had a well-established tradition, but the absence of a permanent army in the Peninsula before 1635, did not favour the development of the local industry. The return of the war on the Pyrenean borders and the subsequent revolts in Catalonia and Portugal forced the Crown to make an unprecedented effort to be able to supply its armies. However, Spanish industry was not able to adequately respond to the growing demands of the army; consequently, the strong demand for weapons and ammunition could only be satisfied by resorting to massive imports. Already before 1648, the Crown made provision for purchasing firearms in Milan.[488]

Since the fifteenth century, gunpowder was produced exclusively under royal license and managed exclusively by the government. Throughout the following century, the Crown established new factories, banned the export of gunpowder, and purchased sulphur mines to ensure production. At first the production was mainly concentrated in the cities of Malaga, Burgos, Pamplona and Cartagena and they were able to meet the demand, but at the end of the 16th century the need for gunpowder doubled. Therefore, the government had to resort again to the *asiento* in order to satisfy the growing needs. Gradually the situation changed, and in 1632 the War Council decided to sell the factories in Malaga and Pamplona to private individuals and to convert both in *asientos*. Three years later, most of the production of gunpowder in Spain was managed by private contractors. By the middle of the century, the major suppliers of gunpowder to the Spanish armies had become the Genoese Antonio Graffion, who was succeeded by the widow Ana Ducque de Estrada after his death,[489] and the Italian-born Dutchman Guglielmo Bartolotti.[490]

---

488 It is astonishing enough to follow the extensive merchant networks, which linked to the Genoese bankers but also to the ones in Portugal. They undoubtedly benefited the most from this arms race. In particular, both the groups were able to adequately exploit the solid friendships with the houses of Dutch business to activate a thriving smuggling of 'prohibited' products from Amsterdam, the main market of the international trade of weapons and strategic weapons throughout the seventeenth century. See Maffi, *Asentistas del rey*, p.154.

489 Rodríguez Hernández, *Asientos y asentistas militares en el siglo XVII*, p.88. In 1649, the widow signed a contract for the supply of 50,000 quintals of gunpowder in 10 years, at the price of 13 *escudos* per quintal. The agreement provides the chivalry in one of the military orders of Castile for the one who would marry Ana and Antonio's daughter, Catalina Graffion.

490 Maffi, *Asentistas del rey*, p.155: 'In Amsterdam the entrepreneurial group linked to Elias Trip, with his colleagues Louis de Geer and Guglielmo Bartolotti, became practically the undisputed leader on the European scene as regards arms trade. Here Bartolotti was the trusted man of the Balbi family in the Dutch city and managed numerous supplies of arms and ammunition for the Spanish forces in Spain and Italy. But besides him, other Italian merchant entrepreneurs, well rooted in the Dutch Republic, offered their services to the Catholic king. Not least Giovanni Battista Benzi, born in Milan, where his family and his brother still resided, who enjoyed great credit with the burgomasters of Amsterdam and who took on a series of orders for the Army of Flanders. But in addition to the Italians also the Portuguese, mostly of Jewish origin, managed the arms market in collaboration. The link between the great Sephardic financial elite of Amsterdam and the Spanish Crown strengthened in the second half of the seventeenth century, starting from the Dutch war, when Spain and the United Provinces allied to face Louis XIV. Among the Jewish suppliers, the case of Antonio Lopes Suasso, a new Christian of Antwerp emigrated to Amsterdam in 1652, who supplied, in concert with the Machado and Pereira houses, also of

Asentistas enjoyed apparently incongruous privileges, but the authorities did not object if the agreement was fulfilled. In order to respect the conditions agreed in the contracts, the *asentistas* had the right to export 500 quintals of gunpowder to allied countries without paying duties. Despite all these concessions, the method proved to be ineffective, and in the first years only a third of the agreed gunpowder had been produced. The *asentistas* justified themselves due to the lack of funds and for the problems deriving from the plague of 1648 and the floods of 1651, which in Murcia had destroyed mills and other key elements of the local infrastructure.

From 1652, the government intervened in the matter due to delays, appointing *veedores* and their personnel to verify the regularity of the production of gunpowder, ensure delivery and guarantee payments. However, in the following decade this method continued to show some inefficiency, forcing the government to buy gunpowder in the Dutch Republic and in Italy, and even in the Spanish Low Countries. In 1660, to provide the army raised for the campaign against Portugal, 4,280 quintals of gunpowder were imported into Spain from Naples and Sicily. Two years later, when the inadequacy of domestic production had been verified, gunpowder from the Kingdom of Naples was imported again, since without that it would have been impossible to supply the field army in Extremadura.[491] The situation improved slightly in the 1670s, and the *asentistas* continued to benefit from the monopoly they had acquired (or created).

In Flanders the cities of Mons, Tournai, Namur, and naturally Antwerp, became among the main European centres in the manufacture of weapons, but also nearby Liège where a large arms production manufacturing process developed and flourished, destined to prosper in the following century. The artisan shops were transformed into small industries and spread widely over the Spanish Low Countries and also in Lombardy, where, alongside the Milanese artisans, new production centres emerged in Pavia, Alessandria and Novara. In the second half of the seventeenth century, over 80 musket manufacturers were operating in the Milan area.[492]

Militia

In Spain as well as in the external domains, the primary role of the militiamen was the replacing of the regular troops in their ordinary duties, like the guarding access to the towns, escorting personalities, and other tasks when the regular force was engaged in field operations. In general, each province and major town had its corps of militia. Big Castilian and Andalusian cities, such as Madrid, Valladolid, Seville and Córdoba, deployed more companies of militiamen, usually grouped by the residence or even professional categories. Border provinces also organised their militia in response to the

---

Portuguese origin, substantial quantities of weapons and ammunition, as well as several *asientos* with the Brussels' authorities in advance of large sums of money.'

491 Rodríguez Hernández, *Asientos y asentistas militares en el siglo XVII*, p.93.
492 Maffi, *Asentistas del rey*, p.152.

rowing external threat. The size could vary considerably, and, in many cases, there were excess officers in order to gratify the most important families, attracting other aspirants to serve in the ranks.

Though each province had its own militia, the effectiveness of the companies was obviously different from one case to another. However, militiamen represented the first reliable force for the maintenance of public order in the towns as well as in the countryside. The companies had their own officers with an undetermined number of drummers and NCOs. The troops comprised musketeers and pikemen in proportion probably not much different compared to the regular infantry. Sources do not always confirm the presence of pikes and probably the musketeers were equipped with the older weapons. However, pikes were registered in the town's arsenals, since in the 1660s, the governors of Extremadura and Galicia ordered to provide muskets, swords and pikes inside the arsenals, in order to distribute these weapons to the provincial militia.[493]

In times of war, city councillors ensured that the soldiers of the militia companies were trustworthy citizens since they constituted their first line of defence.[494] Another very important requirement was that the soldiers be neighbours or permanent residents of the city or town they were guarding, because the War Council thought, not wrongly, that the residents were the ones who more than others had the most to lose in terms of the security of the country.

The Spanish militia had a tradition that dated back to the Middle Ages, but only in the 1640s, had the obligation to serve for the defence of the country been extended throughout the Iberian Peninsula. After 1659, and after some notorious failures, the Crown reconsidered its defensive policy and the need to initiate a reform program that sought to replace the complicated mosaic of the old formulas for local defence and mobilisation of the citizens, with a model of territorial militia directed and controlled from the centre of the Monarchy.

In Castile the goal was, as on previous occasions, to raise 60,000 men between the ages of 18 and 50. Thirteen royal commissioners, who would be assigned a specific district, were appointed to direct the registering of the recruits, in collaboration with the magistrates and local authorities, in order to enlist one tenth of the adult male population.

The projects responded to a coordinated territorial defence plan whose final results were not as expected. The system revealed the transformation of the politics and its new projection over the territory, as the militia aspired to further sustain the process of centralisation legitimised by the Monarchy, with the competition of the municipal oligarchies as intermediaries between the former and the people.[495] However, in accordance with the increasingly

---

493 Fernando Cortés, *El real ejército de Extremadura en la guerra de la restauración de Portugal, 1640–1668*, p.14.

494 Lorraine White, 'Los Tercios en España: el combate', in *Studios Historica*, Ediciones Universidad de Salamanca, 2009, p.143.

495 Antonio Jiménez Estrella, 'Las milicias en Castilla: evolución y proyección social de un modelo de defensa alternative al ejército de los Austrias', in J. Javier Ruiz Ibáñez (ed.), *Las milicias del rey*

growing military needs of the Monarchy, in the seventeenth century the militiamen, with few exceptions, represented a formula for military participation inappropriate to the new political situation and incapable of mobilising intervention forces in areas far from their radius of action, namely the municipal area or the province at most.

The defects and limitations of the local militias made it necessary to articulate an alternative to territorial defence that implied the transition from a model of defence of a citizen base under local control to a general militia capable of embodying the power of the Monarchy in the territory. However, the local elites often hampered this process. The Count of Clonard stated that the main reason for this failure was the opposition of the nobility to a project that could be used by the Crown to counteract their power.[496] It is convenient, however, to consider other factors, such as the problems generated by the militiamen, or the contrary reaction of the citizen oligarchies, for which it was unfeasible for the municipalities to have to face the financing of the militia with modern and expensive weapons and equipment.

The reality of the local militias was somewhat different in other Castilian border territories. For instance, the Kingdom of Murcia, a border and coastal area, marked by the constant threat of privateering and Ottoman–Berber corsairs, had a different experience. The division of the kingdom into seven defensive *partidos* – districts established under the direction of the local *capitanía* – allowed the articulation of a staggered assistance system that in the event of major attacks was called to arms to assist the professional troops, mobilising (according to data provided in a recent study), some 16,000 available militiamen.[497]

The same scheme was applied in Extremadura and Galicia. In this latter kingdom, the notable increase in military activity had important consequences for the local militia. Whole *tercios* of militia foot were raised to reinforce the regular force on the border with Portugal. However, the increasing presence of soldiers and officers generated a positive effect on the economy,[498] since cities like La Coruña benefited from the business generated by the troops quartered in the province: a fairly rare case for Spain at that time. Extremadura was a much poorer territory compared to Galicia, therefore the communities were not burdened by billeting strong regular contingents, at least until 1659. In the 1650s, Extremadura raised five *tercios* of militia to aid securing the border, and especially around Badajoz. In the following decade, the local militia reduced its military tasks to only winter months, but with a great burden on the region, so much so that the regular troops had to be transferred to other provinces during the winter quarters.

---

de España. Política, sociedad e identidad en las Monarquías Ibéricas (Madrid: Fondo de Cultura Económica, 2009), p.72.

496 Clonard, *Historia orgánica*, vol. IV, p.318.

497 Antonio José Rodríguez Hernández, 'La contribución militar del reino de Granada durante la segunda mitad del siglo XVII: la formación de los Tercios de Granada', in A. Jiménez Estrella and F. Andújar Castillo (eds), *Los nervios de la guerra. Estudios sociales sobre el Ejército de la Monarquía Hispánica (siglos XVI–XVIII): nuevas perspectivas* (Granada: Editorial Comares, 2007), pp.149–189.

498 Jiménez Estrella, *Las milicias en Castilla*, p.75.

Alongside Galicia and Extremadura, citizen-based defence corps enjoyed greater development and effectiveness in territories such as Navarre or Guipúzcoa, where a long tradition of town militia existed. Since the sixteenth century, the Crown carried out an important military deployment and a policy of building and restoring fortresses aimed at avoiding any surprise invasion from France. Navarre contributed with resources and men for the border defence tasks, construction of fortifications, accommodation for the troops and provision of food.

However, mandatory militia quotas were too heavy a burden for many other municipalities. At the beginning of the seventeenth century, demographic depletion made the procedure of enlistment increasingly difficult, expensive and unpopular, and this difficulty had to be translated, inevitably, into a profound change of orientation of the primitive plans to establish the general militia. Instead of consolidating itself as a stable defence project directed from above and called to replace the traditional local companies, the militia was replaced by other formulas that advocated more for the creation of a professional army financed by the municipalities than by a model purely composed of militiamen. Therefore, the institution of the militia became of secondary importance in Castile and elsewhere, after the introduction of the Provincial *tercios* and their expansion in the 1660s.

In general, the militia incorporated all the negative features of Spanish society in the seventeenth century. In Málaga, the organisation of the territorial militia was a faithful reflection of the social hierarchy, since the *regidores* distributed the command positions for themselves, showing from a very early date an clear coincidence between the highest military positions and the main families of old Christian origin that ruled the city from 1492.[499] In 1612, in Granada, the definitive establishment of the *Batallón de Milicias* was only achieved after a long negotiation and after transferring the control of the militia to the local authorities. The command fell to a *sargento mayor* chosen by the council among a shortlist of candidates, and eight captains also came from a closed group of influential families. In the surrounding villages, the captains were chosen among candidates exclusively belonging to the local oligarchy, thus achieving certain privileges to perpetuate themselves and their descendants in office until the eighteenth century.[500]

In the non-Castilian kingdoms, the militia followed different practices. In Aragon and Valencia, the service in the militia remained on a voluntary basis, but the *Cortes* authorised the deployment of militiamen outside the provinces in the defence of Catalonia. In the 1660, the Viceroy raised officers and NCOs to gather the infantry *batallón* of the Valencian militia. The strength on paper, 6,000 man, was enough to form eight *tercios* with companies of 75 militiamen each.[501] Expectations were dashed, since most of the companies met for training without officers.[502] In Aragon, the militia was

---

499 *Ibid.*, p.97.

500 *Ibid.*, p.98.

501 Espino López, Antonio, *Guerra, fisco y fueros la defensa de la corona de Aragón en tiempos de Carlos II, 1665–1700* (Valencia: Universidad de Valéncia, 2007), p.36.

502 ACA, *Consejo Aragón*, leg. 563, *consulta*dated 6 October 1665.

organised on the same pattern starting from 1665. In 1674, the rights of the Aragon council over the kingdom's militia were resolutely reaffirmed when the governor Marquis de Astorga demanded to enlist militiamen to serve in the regular infantry. The Council of Aragon insisted he was 'to use his good office to try, give the urgency, but respecting voluntariness, since the Valencian and Aragonese militiamen could help the defence of Catalonia in case of need and if it were the case.'[503]

Though the whole Iberian Peninsula organised its own militia, only the border province actually relied on this force for facing the enemy threat. After Galicia and Extremadura during the war against Portugal, Catalonia also raised a significant number of militiamen and employed them in the defence of the borders. The most important and numerically relevant was the militia of Barcelona. Since this corps was administered by the city council, the command was held by the first councillor, who served as *maestre de campo* but without payment. In 1631, Barcelona had enlisted 26 companies of militiamen, which in 1636 were gathered in a *tercio*.

As always, the paper strength did not correspond to the actual strength, since of the 4,000 men expected there were only 2,888 militiamen who regularly met for training and just 763 had complete equipment.[504]Other inconveniences occurred due to the fact that the councillor and mistress of the field did not always give their service for free, considering that in 1679 a memorandum denounced the accumulation of wages by the commander of the militia *tercio*.[505] As was the case in many other parts of Spain, in the following decades the Catalan militia developed into a pool of recruits for the provincial *tercios*. Consequently, a decrease was seen in the number of staff.

In 1667, Tarragona had 600 militiamen, 400 fewer than in 1640; Gerona had 1,000 gathered in eight companies and Vic the same number, while Seo de Urgel had only 300 militiamen. A further 3,000 militiamen were in arms in other locations of the Principality, such as Puigcerdá, Lérida, Belaguer and Berga. This force replaced the regular infantry in 1674, when the Duke of San Germano began the campaign against the French in Roussillon. Together with the militia of the Principality, the Crown resorted in Catalonia to other militia, formed by Pyrenean mountaineers and known as *miqueletes*. According to the authoritative statement of the French *Maréchal* de Noailles, the *miqueletes* fought better than the regular infantry. Taking advantage of their knowledge of the terrain, these daring mountaineers operated in small groups and ambushed the enemy troops as they ventured along the mountain trails. In 1695, more than 4,000 *miqueletes* were registered in Catalonia, divided into 114 *esquadras*.[506]

The militia of the other European domains generally preserved the original structure based on the local tradition and social composition. The Flemish Walloon 'military' retained many aspects of the medieval heritage

---

503 Espino López, *Guerra, fisco y fueros la defensa de la corona de Aragón*, p.69.
504 Espino López, *Las guerras de Cataluña*, p.204.
505 *Ibid.*, p.206.
506 *Ibid.*, p.236.

Detail from the painting of Nicolaas van Eyck (1617–1679), illustrating the City Militia of Antwerp in 1673. Despite the superb appearance of the companies gathered in the main square of the city, the militia of the Spanish Low Countries performed very poorly with few exceptions. Note the transitional style of the officers' dress in foreground, wearing old-fashioned doublets and Rhinegrave breeches and others with Dutch-French style *justaucorps*.

and one of the most iconic feature was the burgher militia, which shared the same origin as the Dutch one. The local militia usually formed an infantry reserve force, descended from the town's ancient bands instituted in the fifteenth century, named *Eslues* (elects). Service in the militia was originally on voluntary basis, but the provincial estates could call to arms civilians in case of imminent danger, paying them as a regular force. Usually, enlistment into the militia granted special permission and tax exemption, and generally only the wealthy citizens could rise up the ranks to the position of officer.

Brussels, Antwerp and Ostende each had more than 12 companies, and usually each town deployed at least one or two companies of infantry. Unlike the Dutch *Schutterij*, the Flemish Walloon militia did not acquire a political role in the seventeenth century. Their participation in the defence of the country was never decisive, and they often performed poorly. In 1667, during the siege of Tournai, 450 *eslues* supported the regular troops, but after a few days, the citizens voted against the request of the commander to continue in the defence of the city.[507] However, at least on a couple of occasions, in 1668 at Dendermonde, and in 1684 at Luxembourg, the militiamen effectively supported the regular force during the French sieges.

In Franche-Comté, the militia constituted the major force dealing with the defence of the province, and always depended on the local Parliament. The local force of *Esleuz* consisted of three infantry regiments, which had the name of the respective *bailliage* of Amont, Aval and Dole. The regiments did not have the same strength: the militia of Amont and Aval formed 10 companies, while Dole had five. The strength of each company varied depending on where it came from. For instance, the first company of the regiment of Aumont had 250 rank and file, while the second and third numbered 255; the other companies varied from 208 to 257.[508] Differences also existed between the companies of the other two regiments. In overall, the regiment of Aumont numbered 2,395 men; Aval had 2,294 and Dole 1,093. Furthermore, each bailliage raised a cavalry company of 97, 103 and 50 troopers respectively.

In theory the local Estates had to bring together 6,032 Franche-Comtois militiamen, officers not included, but in reality, the force was less than this, as the Spanish governors complained about several times. In 1667, the three regiments numbered together 25 companies equal to a theoretical strength of 5,112 men, supported by an *arriere ban* of 300–400 *maîtres* or cavalrymen 'from the good nobility.' In 1668, 20 of the 25 companies gathered between Dole, Gray, Salins, Saint Anne and some villages had just 50–60 men each.[509]

Contemporary comments about Franche-Comtois militia are generally poor. On 5 October 1666, a Spanish official reported that 'three thieves … had gathered a band of militiamen who in the

Portrait of an unknown ensign of the Franche-Comtois militia, dated 1656. Note the flag with red-white background carrying the coat of arms of ancient Burgundy and the image of the Virgin Mary. (Private collection). The Franche-Comté parliament strongly opposed the financing of a strong army, relying on local forces to face any enemy threat, or trusting in Swiss intervention to grant the agreement of neutrality signed in 1522: an event that did not happen. In 1673 France took advantage of Franche-Comté's weakness, and after some minor offensive actions performed by the Spaniards in Bourgogne, the French army launched a series of cavalry raids that involved the local militia. In 1674, a new stronger French offensive conquered the country in just a few weeks. With only the significant exception of Besançon, which resisted for 29 days, the major fortresses surrendered one after the other, but in the countryside some bands of pro-Habsburg Franche-Comtois, known as *les loups des bois* (forest wolves), offered a fierce resistance. The French reaction was brutal: reprisals and summary death sentences were ordered against the communities suspected of helping the 'bandits'. In July 1673 some armed peasants of Arcey died in the firing of the building where they had found refuge, and days later a whole French infantry company was ambushed and slaughtered near Salins. The struggle continued until 1678 and fuelled strong anti-French sentiments in the country. Historians relate that the most fanatical partisans demanded to be buried with their faces turned down, in opposition to the sun of Louis XIV.

---

507 Rodríguez Hernández, *España, Flandes y la Guerra de Devolucióni*, p.161.

508 Bibliothèque Municipale de Besançon, *Collection Chifflet*, MS 23, *Première conquête de la Franche-Comté*, vol. II, pp.322–327.

509 Piépape, *Histoire de la réunion de la Franche-Comté à la France*, vol. II, p.219.

inspection has showed all the wicked state of defence and the incompetence of parliament in matters of war.' According to a local historian, the officers had no knowledge of the updated tactics and trained their men in with the same exercises of the previous century. Another commenter stated: 'A large number of militiamen had considered it as appropriate not to participate in the review. Others had come with equipment defective and with old wheel-lock harquebuses, instead of the matchlock in use everywhere.' In the ranks, there were children from 13 to 16, and many elderly; some were foreigners and even Frenchmen.[510]

Similar negative opinions were directed at the Sicilian militia. Even on the island, the militia service was regulated by the laws established at the beginning of the Spanish rule, without updating the most anachronistic features. The oldest Sicilian military corps was represented by the baronial militia on horseback. The obligation of military service, consisting of fielding a force of 1,800 horsemen in case of invasion.[511] The funds for maintaining this corps was divided on the basis of the income of the feudal properties and therefore concerned the great families of landowners. This mounted militia was a permanent corps and originally the service was provided by the nobles, but already at the end of the sixteenth century, most of the officers were substitutes hired and paid by the barons. The service could last for a maximum of three months, after which the horsemen were entitled to a wage for the remaining time they served.

Contemporary comments about this ancient military body were generally unflattering. Already in the previous century, the Duke of Medinaceli considered the baronial militia to be ineffective and with obsolete armament.[512] Instead, other commentators found the baronial cavalry 'expert' and 'considerably useful militia' who could be more effective if properly equipped and trained. In 1674, in the opening phase of the Messina uprising, the Viceroy Francesco Bazan y Benavides, did not wish to mobilise the mounted militia and in their place he requested only the cash contribution for the service. The Viceroy's decision deeply mortified the barons that they felt deprived of their military prerogative, provoking the angry protest from the Kingdom's *Deputación*, whose members belonged to the feudal nobility. Benavides was forced to modify the order calling the barons to raise their militia in the customary tradition. Another cavalry militia corps, known as *cavallileggeri*, had been raised in Sicily in the previous century to support the baronial horsemen in case of major emergence. In the seventeenth century the established number of 300 light cavalrymen was uncertain, but sources tell that they were still raised among the wealthy residents aged 18–50. With them, infantry militiamen were also raised and organised in *sargenzie* under a Spanish-born *sargento mayor*, with a variable number of companies under Sicilian captains.

---

510 *Ibid.*
511 Ligresti, Le armidei Siciliani, p.57.
512 *Ibid.* Medinaceli declared that 'their old armour is ridiculous, and they look like the knights of King Arthur'.

The inhabitants of Palermo, Messina, Catania, Syracuse, Trapani, Licata, Augusta and Milazzo were not required to serve in the militia. Each company had a captain, a standard-bearer, a sergeant and a corporal for every 25 militiamen. The mounted soldiers could be replaced by a trained substitute, but in 1636 the cavalry was disbanded, leaving the baronial horsemen the only mounted militia in Sicily. As for the infantry, in the 1660s, there were on paper 10 *sargenzie* with 57 companies of foot with a theoretical strength of 10,000 militia gathered in three *terzi*. Although the efficiency of the service offered by the militia was poor, nevertheless the cost to be incurred for the defence of the island would have been exorbitant if the militiamen were discharged and regulars used instead.

In the opinion of contemporaries, the cavalry was able to counter the threat of the Ottoman corsairs, but otherwise their discipline and training were very poor. The Viceroys highlighted inefficiency and embezzlement that weakened their regular service, while others judged the Sicilians as 'warlike and fit to the fatigues of war'.[513] Ultimately, the opinion expressed by the governor Bournonville in 1676, confirm that the Sicilian militia mobilised after the uprising of Messina performed very badly. The Sicilian militia numbered 17 companies, and just the *terzo* under the Prince of Roccafiorita were considered as 'passable', while the ones under Luis de Moncada and Carlo Valdina were composed of undisciplined and cowardly subjects.[514]

In the nearby Kingdom of Naples, the militia had been reorganised after the revolt of 1647. As was the case in Sicily, for the larger cities Naples was also exempted from forming a city militia. As in Sicily, service in the militia in the Kingdom of Naples included some privileges, such as the right to bear arms, the suspension of imprisonment for crimes that did not require being downgraded; the deferral of debts; exemption from any personal harassment due to the nobility. In the seventeenth century, the officers of the militia exercised a limited influence in the society of southern Italy, nevertheless they took advantage of their office exploiting the militiamen for free services. With regard to these abuses, which were reported several times, the Viceroy ordered that no officer could summon the militiamen without express orders, or without request from the towns or villages threatened by hostile force. The Viceroy also obliged officers not to grant any exemption from service against payment. In general, the establishment of the militia in southern Italy had greatly decayed in the second half of the seventeenth century and was limited to a little more than formal presence. In the 1680s the militia still included a 'feudal cavalry' of *uomini d'arme* with 15 companies of cuirassiers and four of light cavalrymen, each with 120 horsemen, on paper, but in reality only half this number.

Unlike Sicily and Naples, Spanish Lombardy had organised its militia at an enviable level of efficiency. In 1666, the city of Milan had six *terzi* of *milizia urbana a piedi* (city militia on foot), each under veteran *maestri di campo* and company officers coming from the regular army. Each *terzo*

---

513 *Ibid.*, p.85.
514 ASS, *Appunti e Documenti*,vol. XXIV, p.501. Bournonville reported that the regular Sicilian *tercio* too had performed poorly, since the rank and file seemed more like peasants than soldiers.

Lamellar breastplate and morion manufactured in the Philippines with carabao horn plates, mid seventeenth century. (Private collection)

deployed seven companies with approximately 1,000 militiamen. The gates of the city gave the name to the *terzi*: Porta Orientale, Porta Romana, Porta Ticinese, Porta Vercellina, Porta Comasina, Porta Nova.[515] These troops were administered by the *Giunta sopra la Militia Urbana*, with the *Vicario di Provisione* as president. Other militia corps were raised enlisting males aged 18 to 50 in all the major towns of the state, which were regularly trained on Sunday and mustered every month.

Since the 1630s Milan had also deployed the *milizia forese*, formed from the rural populace when ordered by the governor. This militia underwent several attempted reforms, but after 1659 its importance had decreased significantly. However, in 1667 the governor called for 5,000 infantry ready to march to the border, and a similar number was requested in 1672, to face the feared French invasion. Milan usually contributed a larger number but after 1647 the city reduced its contribution, at the expense of the other provinces.[516]

Regular training was one of the most sensitive requirement of the militia. Normally this took place every Sunday and in the religious festivities, usually after the morning Holy Mass, which of course all the militiamen took part in. This was an appointment that occurred more or less regularly in all the domains of the Monarchy. Even in Manila, in the far Philippines, the local militia were gathered for training every seven days in the main square of the city.[517] In overseas colonies, training was probably considered with greater attention, since in the Philippines, as in America, the militia was the main force in charge of the defence of the inhabitants. The enlistment was even wider compared to the European domains, since all the males aged from 16 to 60 were registered in the militia.[518] There are little information about the Spanish-American militia in the seventeenth century, except for the one of Puerto Rico.

According to local historians, the first militia was raised in 1511 to defend the Spanish settlement in the island against the Caribe natives, and the

---

515 Gualdo Priorato, *Relatione della città e stato di Milano*, pp.182–184.

516 Enrico Dalla Rosa, *Le Milizie del Seicento nello Stato di Milano* (Milan: Vita e Pensiero, 1991), pp.81–85. In 1667, Milan's *milizia forese* had to gather 1,741 footmen, Lodi 555, Cremona 400, Novara 420, Pavia 453. In 1672, a little variation affected Milan, now with 1,776 militiamen, and Lodi with 555.

517 Pedro Murillo Velarde, *Historia de la Provincia de Philipinas* (1749), vol. II, p.174.

518 Carlos Fernando Chardon, *Reseña historica del origen y des arrollo de las Milicias Puertorriqueñas bajo el regime español* (Puerto Rico: Puerto Rico National Guard, 1978), p.4.

European corsairs and privateers in the following century. In 1625, Puerto Rico had its permanent militia, which in 1637 repulsed a French attempt to establish an outpost in the island of Vieques. In the 1670s, three companies of *milicia urbana* were raised in San Juan, each with a staff comprising captain, lieutenant, NCOs, drums and fourier In 1673, this force successfully faced the French privateer D'Orgeron who had landed with his men to plunder the settlements on the coast. The Spanish-American militia remained organised in irregular companies coinciding with the *capitanías*, and only from the 1690s did the first urban corps begin to be formed in each province. As for Puerto Rico, in 1691 each company numbered 225 men; and one of these was raised enlisting *pardos libres* (persons of mixed race), while a fourth company of 20 horsemen was also raised.[519]

---

519 *Ibid.*, p.8.

3

Spanish Warfare

Since the previous century, Hispanic armies had been a test bed of battle tactics. The presence of officers from every corner of the Monarchy and foreign mercenaries led to the creation of the 'Spanish school', which for many years represented a model in Europe. However, in this age of Montecuccoli, Turenne, Condé and other great captains, no Spanish commander has left his name among such elevated company in the history books. This absence could be explained in several ways, but the main reason may be found in the strategy chosen by the Monarchy. After 1665, with few exceptions the Hispanic armies conducted a defensive warfare. The commanders had no other task except for defending the fortresses and avoiding pitched battle. Moreover, after the defeat suffered in Portugal, the Monarchy was rarely able to gather enough forces to face their enemies without the support of its allies. It is significant to note that after Montes Claros in 1665, Hispanic armies fought just five field major battles until 1688, and only twice, at Maureillas in 1674 and Espolla in 1677, did they face the French without the support of allied troops. At Seneffe, in 1674, Spanish involvement was limited to mainly cavalry with a few infantry and artillery, while at Mont Cassel in 1677, and Saint-Denis in 1678, just cavalry and dragoons joined the army under William III. The same is also true of Konzer Brücke in 1675.

This defensive strategy required a large number of troops, but if soldiers could be hastily recruited, they were of poor quality. The officers could not gain experience, and this resulted in the armies' progressive worsening of combat effectiveness in the field. However, the development of new successful battle tactics from Northern Europe did not mean that commanders continued to apply the most obsolete theories, since they had learned many new ideas through fighting the Dutch from 1568. The war against the Dutch Republic had been a battle for infantry and engineers, and the Spanish armies could experiment with modern tactics, formations and new siege engineering practices. Though some commanders still performed more conservatively, other officers extended the new models of warfare suited to the new strategic scenario, at least at a theoretical level.

In the later phase of the pike and shot period, the development of tactics reflected an effort to determine the best way to integrate the two weapons systems after the improvement of infantry firearms. One of the main debates centred on how to protect the vulnerable musketeers on the battlefield. Experience demonstrated that, in order to be truly effective, foot soldiers needed to be employed en mass, but the slow loading time of the matchlock muskets and harquebus, and later the faster flintlock musket, made them vulnerable to charges by heavy cavalry. Spanish commanders were clearly influenced by the Dutch and Swedish reformer of the first half of the century. However, although all of these developments foreshadowed later tactics, there were a number of changes in the second half of the seventeenth century that would be crucial in Spain as elsewhere.

Some of these changes were technological, though slow to take effect rather than a revolutionary overnight sensation. One of the lessons that commanders learned was the devastating effect of firepower on the battlefield. Therefore, the most significant improvement centred on the emphasis on firepower as an instrument of offence as well as defence. After 1648, the *tercio* had improved its structure, turning into a more mobile and flexible *squadron*, or battalion. A further improvement was in the firepower of arquebusiers' *mangas* at the wing of the battle formation: a trademark of the Spanish infantry in this period. On the battlefield, battalions were grouped together in brigades. The Spanish brigade normally numbered three or four *squadrones*. These corps deployed in two mutually supporting lines, as clearly shown in the print of the Battle of Montes Claros in 1665.

Attached to the centre of the formation were many light field guns, which could be dragged forwards and added to the infantry firepower. Though the Spanish tactics emphasized firepower, the standard formation for the infantry in the 1660s was six ranks deep, with the pikemen formed in the centre of each battalion. In this formation, the best trained infantry could employ musketeers and arquebusiers in firing by salvo, introduced by the Swedes during the Thirty Years' War. It was a relatively easy drill to conduct, recommended in the contemporary tactical documents,[1] and applied when the enemy was approaching. On command,

Gaspar de Haro y Guzmán, Marques del Carpio y Eliche (1629–1687). In 1662 he was accused of wanting to attempt to take the life of King Philip IV, and sentenced to 10 years of exile or serve in the army of Extremadura. According to Clonard, the Marquis was in command of the tercio of the late Gonzalo Fernández de Córdoba, the former *Regimiento de la Guardia del rey*, or *Coronelia del Conde Duque* (El-15). Captured by the Portuguese at the Battle of Ameixial-Estremoz on 8 June 1663, he was locked up with other distinguished prisoners in the Castillo de San Jorge in Lisbon, where he remained until 1668. During his captivity, he was appointed *maestre de campo* of a newly raised *tercio* from Seville. In the painting, executed during his imprisonment in Lisbon, he still wears all the attributes of his rank as a Spanish officer. The red-gold brocade scarf is carried on the chest over a Spanish-style tailored pale-yellow (leather?) coat with short open sleeves, and a rich baldric with gilded fittings. Under the coat he wears a fashionable shirt and breeches with ribbons in a style usual in Spain and elsewhere in the 1660s. Note the ribbons and the red plumed headgear both edged with a narrow gold piping. (Author's collection)

---

1   Guglielmo Di Rampone, *Esercitio Militare generale della fanteria e cavallaria* (manuscript dated 1662, Biblioteca Nacional de España).

the musketeers were ordered to 'double their files'. The three rearmost ranks of musketeers and arquebusiers moved into the interval between their file and the one next to them, thus changing in a single movement from a six- to a three-rank formation. While in this formation the front rank would kneel, the second would crouch and the third would stand. At the command, all would fire at once.

Spanish commanders also relied on firepower from their infantry in support of the cavalry. While the cavalry undertook offensive actions through the charge (rather than using the caracole tactic relying on pistols), they were often deployed with units of infantry in between the cavalry units. The musketeers provided the defensive support to keep enemy forces at bay until the cavalry were ready to launch the charge. This kind of deployment survived in the next decades and in 1674, at Seneffe, the cavalry was supported by two large infantry *squadrones* placed in the intervals.[2] In the 1670s, shortage of troops resulted in a reduction in the number of ranks, forcing the commanders to deploy five or even four ranks, in order to maintain the frontage of the formation to cover more terrain. However, before 1690, the Hispanic infantry was rarely engaged in battles in the open, being destined to garrison and defend the border fortresses.

By the last quarter of the seventeenth century, the ratio of musket to pike had shifted dramatically in Western European armies. The infantry of most nations of the period had seen the number of pikemen reduced to around one fifth of the unit, while in Spain this ratio was about one third or even less.In this regard, Hispanic armies relied on the defensive role of the pikes and not everyone agreed that the future lay in gunpowder weapons. This attitude did not change over the following years, and when Francisco Antonio de Agurto, Marquise of Gastañaga, printed his *Tratado y reglas militares* the most significant change occurred in the decrease in the number of the ranks, from six to four. Although the proportion pikes to firearms remained the same, Gastañaga introduced a more modern looking approach in the matter of battlefield tactics. He experienced these changes during his service as *maestre de campo* and field commander in the Army of Flanders between 1673 and 1685, when he finally became governor of the Spanish Low Countries. Newly appointed to this office, the Marquise introduced a new tactical discipline in order to improve infantry performance on the battlefield, which included manoeuvres and formations derived from the French and Dutch models. Musketeers and arquebusiers had to be trained in the rank-fire system. Officers and NCOs were distributed at the wings, behind and before each *squadron* in order to maintain good order of the formation during manoeuvres on the battlefield. Ensigns, drummers and fifers occupied the centre of the battalion between the second and the third line, escorted by a guard of one arquebusier for each ensign.

Significant progress also came in the field of siege warfare, in which the engineers of the Army of Flanders developed successful tactics. The essay

---

2   *Beschreibung der Schlact so den i. ii. Augusti 1674 zwischen den Kayerlichen Spaniern und Hollanddern bey Seness mid den Frantzosen gehalten worden* (Frankfurt, 1674).

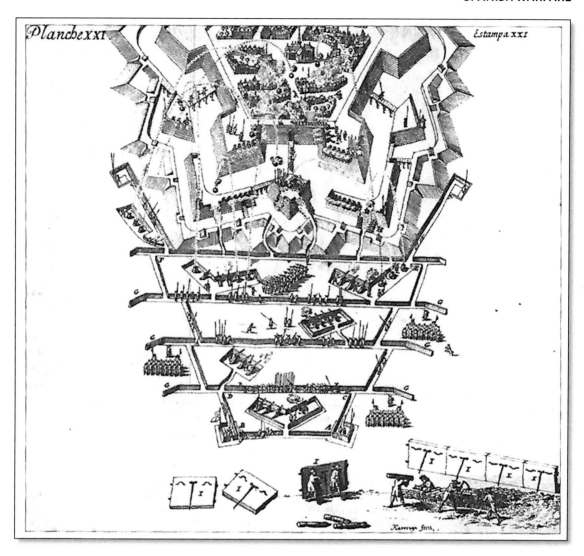

Above: Approach trenches against a bastion from *El arquitecto perfecto e nel arte militar*, by Sebastián Fernández de Medrano (Author's archive). The prevalence of sieges as a consequence of the Monarchy's defensive strategy favoured the development of siege warfare techniques, of which Medrano's work is one of the most complete.

Overleaf: Print illustrating the siege of the Portuguese town of Elvas in January 1659 (*Vestigum sive effigies urbis Helviae quam a Castellanis obsessam Emanuel Praefectus Castrorum defendit: Anto Ludovicus menesius, Cantaniedii Comes, execritus Lusitani Ductor obsidione liberavis 14. Januar die an. MDCLIX*). The war against Portugal was another unsuccessful event in the history of the last *Austrias*. Tax collectors, recruiting officers, billeted soldiers, and depredations by Spanish and foreign troops were loathed and feared by the population of Extremadura and Castile as much as raids by the enemy. Local militias bore the brunt of the fighting, and the absence of these part-time soldiers was extremely harmful to agriculture and local finances. Since there was often no money to pay or support the troops or reward their commanders, the Crown turned a blind eye to the smuggling, contraband, profiteering, disorder and destruction that became rampant on the frontier. Similar conditions existed on the Portuguese side.

of the aforementioned Sebastián Fernández de Medrano represents an interesting development of Vauban's techniques. On the other hand, the improvement of the fortifications in Flanders and Lombardy had intensified the exchange for experience on this matter since the 1660s. At the end of the century, the Monarchy's fortified places 'had become the best laboratory of Europe', as proudly stated in some texts.[3]

After years relegated to secondary duties, Hispanic cavalry gained a considerably good reputation, especially on the battlefields of Flanders. Organisational reforms, selection of officers, and the preservation of a core of skilled veterans, certainly contributed to its efficiency on the battlefield. The only significant victory of the Army of Flanders during the War of Devolution

---

3   Maffi, *Los últimos tercios*, p.101.

was achieved by the cavalry at Jodoigne. The troops in action were commanded by the Prince Claude Lamoral de Ligne with 1,000 horsemen from the Spanish, Walloon and German cavalry quartered in Brussels. On 6 August 1667, the Prince intercepted and destroyed a French cavalry column that was imposing forced contributions on the rural population.[4]

During the Franco-Dutch war, the valour and skill of the Spanish horsemen was repeatedly testified to by the allies, especially the Dutch, who expressly asked in the agreement establishing the alliance, signed in 1672, that the main military support should be represented by the cavalry, established at 3,000 horsemen. In June 1672, a corps of 2,000 horse joined the Dutch field army under Prince William III at Utrecht, then for the campaign of 1673, a further 1,000 cavalrymen marched alongside the Dutch to besiege Naarden. One year later, the Spanish cavalry which fought at Seneffe numbered about 3,500 men.[5] Their role was critical, especially in the opening phase of the battle, when the rear guard, under Charles Thomas de Lorraine-Vaudemont, sustained the first French assault, and notwithstanding his numerical inferiority, repulsed the enemy, buying time for William III to deploy the allied army.

Military manuals for the cavalry of this period are full of complex techniques for performing tactical manoeuvres to bring maximum firepower to bear on various enemy formations and arms. The most favoured system was the caracole, a tactic that became standard in the Iberian Peninsula and also in Flanders. Although cumbersome and slow moving, seldom being performed faster than the trot, the major problem with the caracole was that although it delivered shot it could never deliver enough to do much harm. Cavalry battles were slow and noisy affairs and although they could disrupt an enemy formation, they apparently did not cause many casualties, unless the cavalry commander was able to bring overwhelming numbers of units into action. Close combats were enough rare in this age, since the Portuguese and the French cavalry operated in similar ways. The campaign in Flanders saw significant developments in the tactical role of the cavalry, and in the 1670s, in order to perform with large corps, the cavalry squadrons were combined into brigades led by a *sargento general de batalla*.

As in encounters on the field of battle, Hispanic cavalry also earned a great reputation in marauding actions. Taking advantage of mobility and flexibility to employ often greater numbers than the French, the Hispanic cavalry performed very well on several occasions. In Flanders, the allied commanders often resorted to the use of cavalry to relieve besieged cities, and especially in the so-called 'partisan warfare' that had great developed throughout the Flanders theatre of war.[6] This kind of warfare was not a novelty, since it had been learned in Portugal, during the War of Restoration. In Extremadura, like in Flanders, the

---

4   Rodríguez Hernández, *España, Flandes y la Guerra de Devolución (1667–1668)*, pp.181–184.

5   Mugnai, *Wars and Soldiers in the Early Reign of Louis XIV*, vol. 1, *The Army of the United Provinces of the Netherlands* (Warwick: Helion & Company, 2019), pp.114–116.

6   Although now associated with guerrilla fighters, the term *partisan* in the seventeenth century literally meant a leader or adherent to a party. In terms of war, this meant a *parti de guerre*, and partisan warfare involved those actions of war conducted by special parties or detachments from the regular army. In a general sense, partisan warfare consisted of almost every military action besides those of armies when deployed for siege or battle. See George Satterfield, *Princes, Posts and Partisans. The*

Marzio Origlia (or Oreglia) di Arigliano, portrayed in *Il Genio Bellicoso di Napoli*, written by friar Raffaele Maria Filamondo, and printed in Naples in 1694, containing the biographies of the major Italian captains in Spanish service since the sixteenth century. Origlia was another prominent Italian officer with a long military service in Spain and Flanders. He held the command of the Spanish infantry in Maastricht during the French siege of 1673; the Dutch–Hispanic garrison fought valiantly, and after the surrender of the city Origlia was honoured by Louis XIV, who invited the Italian officer to dinner with him and his senior staff. Released after an exchange of prisoners, Origlia resumed service in the army of Flanders in 1674. According to Filamondo, on 11 April 1677, he opposed the Prince of Orange when he unwisely decided to engage the French at Mont Cassel.

cavalry stationed in the advanced garrisons carried out functions of protecting the surrounding towns and villages, countering the enemy who demanded financial and materiel contributions inside Spanish territory, or devastated the countryside to deprive the other side from food and fodder.

With the stalemate on the battlefield, this kind of action took on a role of primary importance in the attritional siege warfare that ensued in Flanders. After the initial experiences of the War of Devolution, hardly a day went by in the Franco-Dutch War without some kind of raid or small expedition sent out to forage, take prisoners, or enforce payment of contributions in the enemy territory. While field armies disappeared into winter quarters, Dutch-Spanish and French war parties unceasingly carried death and destruction to the enemy: burning stores of forage in towns, storming strongholds and castles, disrupting the flow of supplies and engaging enemy parties conducting their own *petite guerre*. According to authoritative scholars, it has been estimated that during the Franco-Dutch War, the cavalry quartered in Namur launched 200 raids into enemy territory from October 1673 to September 1678.[7] The ambush of convoys, and a hard-fought struggle waged against enemy foragers, had near disastrous consequences in the summer of 1674 for the Prince of Condé, who commanded the French field army in Flanders. Dutch-Spaniards put their strategy into action, and patiently waited from May to the middle of July for the impact of the limits of the French supply system, time, and nature to do its worst to Condé's army, before attempting to undertake a major operation. Condé's campaign of 1674, and his supply difficulties, underlines the intensity of the partisan warfare and its impact on the course of the campaign.

Official French sources confirmed the effectiveness of enemy raids, and despite the biased interpretation in the chronicles, the dramatic events, for the most part, did occur. According to one of these sources, in January 1676, the Marquis of Conflans organized a raid

---

Army of Louis XIV and Partisan Warfare in the Netherlands (1673–1678) (Leiden–Boston: Brill, 2003), p.3.

7   *Ibid.*, p.219.

from Namur directed against a French garrison in the town of Châtelet. The party marched there with a mixed force of approximately 400 infantry and 200 cavalry to overrun the enemy garrison. On the night between 1st and 2 January, Conflans led his troops over the walls of the town by ladders. They pushed aside the militia watch and were soon marching through the streets.

The startled French garrison of about 100 troops might have been slaughtered, had they not requested quarter. The town inhabitants paid a high price. Of particular importance to Conflans, and his reason for the raid, was the fact that the inhabitants of Châtelet, instead of paying contributions to Spain, had welcomed a French garrison.[8] The raid was conducted with great efficiency, speed and discipline. The raiding party was composed for the most part of natural-born Spaniards.[9] A few days later, another Spanish party from Namur seized a boat that plied the route between Maastricht and Liège on the Meuse River. Possibly informed by a spy, the Spanish party took hostage an abbot, disguised as a well-dressed merchant, who had forbidden his abbey to pay contributions to the Spaniards. The same party, now advancing down an open road, later encountered and defeated some French horsemen who were escorting a real merchant. From the defeated French, the Spanish party took several horses and captured the merchant who was kept as a hostage at Namur until his ransom was paid. In February, a Spanish party encountered several French supply wagons and three merchants on their way to Charleroi. The Spaniards gave chase to the small escort, which it routed, and then set about to pillage the untended wagons. The Spanish party scattered and destroyed what they could not carry and unlimbered the draught horses, returning into Spanish territory with the horses and eight French prisoners. In the following month of March, a Spanish party ambushed another French supply column. The party returned to Namur with a small herd of cattle that had been destined for the French troops at Charleroi.[10]

Spanish Wars of Attrition

The positive performance of the cavalry in partisan warfare could only delay the enemy progress. The major problem was, as already discussed, the lack of money. The poor financial situation of the 1660s dramatically affected the last campaigns against Portugal. The Crown assembled a large number of troops to achieve the victory over the rebel kingdom, but all attempts failed, more for shortage of resources than for the performance of the Portuguese in the field. The attempts led by Don Juan of Austria failed in 1663, followed by the even more disastrous campaign of 1665. After the bitter defeat at Montes Claros, the War Council received a detailed analysis of the defeat from the commanders

---

8   *Ibid.*, p.217: 'In the hours that followed the assault, the Spanish plundered the small burg; the inhabitants were terrorised as shops and homes were violated and fires started. The Spanish sent a message to towns throughout the Sambre and Meuse region not to place their destiny in the hands of the French, who, as the readers learned, slept during a surprise attack.'
9   *Ibid.*
10   *Mercure Hollandois*, March 1676.

Portrait of Francesco Arboreo Gattirana di Sartirana, *maestre de campo* of an Italian *tercio* in Portugal between 1660 and 1663, after *Il Genio Bellicoso di Napoli* (Naples, 1694). The presence of different nationalities in the armies of the Monarchy generated healthy competition, but also rivalry. In 1662, the dispute between Italians and Spaniards for the assignment of places of honour in the order of battle reached Madrid and forced Felipe IV to intervene to settle the quarrel. Similar disputes had occurred in the past, but in 1662 the disagreement seemed irreconcilable and risked jeopardising the continuation of the campaign. The Italians claimed the right of precedence as a tradition that recognised the privilege when they fought far from their country. The Spaniards opposed this, claiming the privilege for themselves, it being in their country. On 12 September 1662, the King confirmed this right for the Italians, recognising the granting of a fixed place in the battle order, namely the left flank and in the rearguard.

involved in the last campaigns. According to the statements of the commanders in Extremadura and Galicia, Luis Francisco de Benavides, Carrillo de Toledo Marquis of Caracena, and Gaspar Téllez-Girón Duke of Osuna, it was obvious that the delay in the payment of wages had a very negative results in the strategic contest, because the soldiers deserted and often joined the other side.[11] Already,at the beginning of the war, the 400 Neapolitans who defended Valverde in 1643 not only gave up the fortress to the Portuguese without a fight, but many of them even entered the enemy army.[12]

In 1663, Don Juan of Austria also complained about the poor state of the troops as the main reason of the defeat suffered at Ameixial-Estremoz. In September 1667 desertions were so high that the army of Extremadura was reduced to a few thousand men due to the fatal conjunction of these two factors. In some units, the situation was so serious that the newly arrived soldiers deserted after seeing the misery suffered by their comrades.[13] Caracena commented on the quality of the troops, complaining about the presence of too many inexperienced officers and soldiers. Since they were not used to the privations of campaign, morale and effectiveness had considerably worsened, while, Caracena felt assured, with more veteran *tercios* the aftermath should have been different. If these troops could not be transferred from Flanders or Italy, the Crown had to enlist further 5,000 German mercenaries.[14] The negative outcome of the operations in Portugal did not seem to prompt the court to remedy the drawbacks occurred during the campaigns, as many of the members of the War

---

11 The Duke of Osuna faced a trial after the disastrous campaign in Entre-Douro e Minho of 1664, but he was finally discharged. See Estébanez Calderón, *De la conquista y pérdida de Portugal*, vol. II, pp.93–111.

12 Fernando Dores Costa, *A guerra da Restauração 1641–1668* (Lisboa: 2004), p.54. The surrender of Valverde occurred in September 1643. In the following decades, the desertion of Italian and German soldiers permitted the formation of a whole terço.

13 AGS, *Guerra Antigua*, leg. 2136: letters of the Marquis of Caracena from Badajoz, dated 10, 11, 12 and 14 September 1667.

14 Estébanez Calderón, *De la conquista y pérdida de Portugal*, vol. II, p.392.

Council had hoped. Unfortunately, the passive and fatalistic climate of resignation conditioned Spanish military policy, aggravating the state of unpreparedness of the military in all Spain's domains.

Traditionally, classical historiography states that the War of Devolution was an unexpected event for Spain. Nonetheless, clear signals had long been received in the Spanish Low Countries about French war preparations, yet no one was able to determine when France would initiate the assault. Suspicions about an enemy invasion had increased starting in 1665, when Spanish agents across the border had informed Brussels about the increase in enlistments and the creation of new units in France, and in the following months further preparative announced the offensive as imminent. In Madrid however, these signals were misinterpreted, and the only countermeasure adopted was to increase the strength of the garrisons with some 100 soldiers from Spain and Italy. Meanwhile, Spanish diplomacy and men of law had intervened to repulse the Sun King's requests as compensation for the French renunciation to the 'right of devolution'.

However, by the end of 1666, fears in Brussels had reached their peak, forcing the governor, Francisco de Moura Corterreal, Marquis of Castel Rodrigo, to ask the Spanish ambassador in London to negotiate military aid at any cost to face the incoming French invasion with a stronger army. In Madrid, the Crown did not endorse Castel Rodrigo's request and therefore the enlistment of 6,000 English soldiers planned as necessary to guarantee the defence of the Spanish Low Countries was not actioned.[15] The signs of a new war became more concrete every day, so much so that the French side had been ordered to intercept all the couriers and even Spanish tradesman returning to the Low Countries or Spain.[16] However,

Luis de Benavides, Marquis of Caracena (1608–1668). After he managed the reduction of the Army of Flanders in the early 1660s, Caracena was appointed captain-general in Extremadura, with the goal of crushing the Portuguese resistance and to restore Habsburg rule. In 1664 and 1665, the Monarchy performed the last offensive campaigns of the war, trusting in its veteran commander. Caracena was proceeded by the fame of 'Spanish Mars', but after a promising beginning, he did not achieve the decisive success, and at Montes Claros, on 17 June 1665, his army suffered a serious defeat, ending Spanish hopes for a final victory. (Author's collection)

---

15   Rodríguez Hernández, *España, Flandes y la Guerra de Devolución*, p.148. See also Chapter 2 of this work.

16   Rooms, *De organisatie van de troepen van de Spaans-Habsburgse monarchie in de Zuidelijke Nederlanden*, pp.116–118. This was the case of the Marquis de Monroy, one of the most prominent ministers and commanders in Brussels, whose papers and correspondence containing vital information for Madrid were confiscated.

Map of the fortification of Dendermonde, from the *Atlas van Loon* (author's archive). During the War of Devolution, Dendermonde was the only fortress of the Spanish Low Countries that offered resistance and repulsed the French in August 1667.

even if the news had arrived in Madrid in time, the outcome of the French invasion would hardly have been different.

On 24 May, the French army numbering 60,000 to 70,000 men crossed the border with the Spanish Low Countries in three large columns. According to the most recent investigations, Castel Rodrigo disposed of 515 foot and 132 horse companies, equal to a strength estimated at between 27,000 and 35,500 men.[17] This force was not enough to repulse the French, who in a single campaign conquered 13 major fortresses in an unprecedented run of success. Only Dendermonde offered any resistance and the French failure in seizing the city was the only strategic success achieved by the Spanish in 1667. This and other minor successes spread an exaggerated feeling of optimism among the Spanish. Reports claimed that at the end of the 1667 campaign,

17 According to Rooms (*De organisatie van de troepen van de Spaans-Habsburgse monarchie*), the army of Flanders totalled 27,000 infantry and 8,500 cavalry. The author reconstructs this total assuming an average strength of 53 men per foot company, and 65 per horse company. These figures are produced from the data preserved in the Belgian *Archives Générales du Royaume*, collected in the *Contadurieet Pagadorie des Gens de Guerre* dating 1667. This strength is not agreed with by Rodríguez Hernández, *España, Flandes y la Guerra de Devolución*, pp.153–154, who instead lowers the average number of men in companies to 30 for the infantry and 40 for the cavalry. This overall strength results in 20,000 foot and 7,000 horse.

the French had lost 6,000 soldiers, and there were so many prisoners that the governor did not know where to send them.[18] After the Peace of Aix-la-Chapelle, Castelo Rodrigo was blamed for his excessive prudence, since he surrendered territory to the enemy while waiting for a favourable moment to arise, but this never came. Though he saved the small force at his disposal, the war resulted in a French victory, and only the intervention of the Triple Alliance avoided the complete loss of the Spanish Low Countries.

The Franco-Dutch War was welcomed as the long-awaited act of revenge by the successor of Castelo Rodrigo. The Count of Monterrey had patiently gathered troops and resources to join the allies for an offensive war against France. In 1672, Spain saved the Dutch Republic from complete destruction, sending 10,000 men to sustain the defence led by Prince William III. The campaign of 1673 saw the cavalry of the Army of Flanders engaged in the seizure of Naarden, but the Spanish–Dutch collaboration did not produce the hoped for results, nor did the Imperial intervention in 1673 bring significant gains for the Spanish. French diplomacy thwarted the net the alliance patiently set by Madrid in previous years, since England did not break their alliance with France, and Brandenburg agreed a separate peace with Louis XIV.

In the following campaigns it emerged how the allies each followed a different goal. Misunderstandings and errors contributed to the failure of the campaigns.[19] Furthermore, William III and Monterrey maintained deep differences about the conduct of the war, until the latter was replaced by Villahermosa in March 1675. In the following campaign, the Spain sent small contingents of troops to the allied army. Cavalry and infantry from Luxembourg participated at the victorious battle of Konzer Brücke, fought on 11 August by an army including German and Imperial troops, and in the siege of Trier, where the small corps of infantry from the Army of Flanders performed very well. However, for the campaign of 1675, the Crown issued clear instructions to its governor, which explicitly ordered him not to engage the army in risky operations that could result in the loss of a fortress or key locations in the theatre of war. In this regard, the Council of State addressed a letter to William III reiterating their refusal to Villahermosa to allow him to conduct an offensive campaign.[20]

This substantial stalemate in Flanders led to the second conquest of the Franche-Comté in 1674. Historians recognised that during the first conquest of Franche-Comté in 1668, resistance had been purely to preserve some honour. Many Franche-Comtois, headed by their leaders, seemed to consider the French invasion as inevitable, and from February to June 1668, the local

---

18 Maffi, *Los últimos tercios*, p.8.
19 See Mugnai, *Wars and Soldiers in the Early Reign of Louis XIV*, vol. I, *The Army of the United Provinces of the Netherlands* (Warwick: Helion & Company, 2019), pp.111–142.
20 Maffi, *Los últimos tercios*, p.103. The Duke of Albuquerque, a member of the War Council, justified the strategy with these words: 'Engaging the enemy in battle is the one and main purpose of the war, and with luck it works better, and the experiences of weapons … make the Duke (of Villahermosa) wish the best, but he believes that the worst will come, and the security of Flanders should not be seriously risked in the battle, because if we preserve the Low Countries, the rest of the Monarchy will be safe.'

Youthful portrait of Carlo Emanuele d'Este, Marquise of Borgomanero and Count of Porlezza (1622–1695), by Anthony Van Dyck (Kunsthistorisches Museum, Vienna). He became *maestre de campo* in 1647, when the Este family allied to the French, and therefore Borso d'Este renounced the rank of commander of a German infantry regiment which passed to the more faithful Carlo d'Este. In 1661 the regiment – more or less 500 men – headed to Spain to join the Army of Extremadura, but without the colonel: Carlo refused to go with it because in Spain the rank of *sargento general de batalla* which he carried in Lombardy would not be honoured. In 1674 he held the command of Dole during the French siege, and on 6 June negotiated the surrender that concluded more than a century of Spanish rule in Franche-Comté.

authorities had even collaborated with France. But in June, the French had left the country after dismantling the fortified towns, razing the castles, and emptying the arsenals and state coffers. When the Franco-Dutch war began, Franche-Comté remained untouched, apart for some skirmishing on the border.

In 1674, the French campaign of conquest encountered stronger resistance compared to that of 1668, but the final aftermath was the same as six years before. In the first months of the French occupation, there were no incidents and probably most of the inhabitants thought that the country would be returned to Spain with a new peace agreement. The only serious events occurred at the end of the autumn of 1674 when as a consequence of the French presence in Alsace, the news of the probable march of an Imperial army into Franche-Comté alarmed the Dole Parliament and the common people. The pro-Spanish leaders went to meet the Imperial emissaries in Montbéliard, and 200 remount horses intended for Turenne's army were kidnapped in Omans, in the heart of Franche-Comté. French soldiers were taken in their sleep and delivered to the enemy by peasants, and others were ambushed. Without the prompt victories of Turenne in the Vosges, with which drove the Imperialists from Alsace, the contacts made at Montbéliard would perhaps have resulted in an uprising in Franche-Comté.[21] However, these actions were the prelude for the bitter struggle of the following years, which was ,

21 Up to the Treaty of Nijmegen, three factions emerged into Franche-Comté. The most important comprised the mass of people deciding to 'wait-and-see', who did not want to compromise themselves before the end of the war. It was framed by two antagonistic minorities. On the one hand, the Francophiles who compromised with the French, demanded or accepted charges, and managed links in France. On the other side there were the declared Francophobes, who were recruited above all within the Church and within the popular class in the towns as well as in the countryside. Among them, those whom the French qualify as *voleurs* (thieves) or *loups des bois* (forest wolves) and who considered themselves as 'resistant', if this anachronism is allowed. See Maurice Gresset, 'Les complots antifrançais en Franche-Comté dans la guerre de succession d'Espagne', in *Complots et conjurations dans l'Europe moderne, Actes du colloque international organisé à Rome, 30 septembre–2 octobre 1993* (Rome: École Française de Rome, 1996), pp.373–392.

Above: Detail from an Austrian print illustrating the final phase of the Battle of Seneffe, fought on 11 August 1674. The army of Flanders contributed 6,000 cavalry and 3,000 infantry. Note on the left, marked with 'm' (circled for clarity), the Hispanic troops alternating infantry and cavalry. (*Beschreibung der Schlact so den i. ii. Augusti 1674 zwischen den Kayerlichen Spaniern und Hollanddern bey Seness mid den Frantzosen gehalten worden*, Frankfurt 1674)

Below: 'Soldiers' watch', by David Theniers (1610–1690) (Rijksmuseum, Amsterdam). The Monarchy tried to face French pressure in Flanders, Catalonia and Italy hastily gathering troops assigned to the garrisons in the key areas. Despite some attempt at offensive strategy, since the 1660s, the Crown turned to a resolute static defence, which proved to be a monumental error because it left the strategic initiative to its mightiest enemy: Louis XIV of France.

Infantry ensign lost at Seneffe: a white background with a red Burgundian cross, after *Les Triomphes de Louis XIV* (Bibliothèque nationale de France, Paris). According to some scholars, this ensign with just two colours belonged to a veteran infantry unit. At Seneffe, companies from the *tercios Viejo de Hollanda* (EI-8) also participated in the battle.

marked by a string of reciprocal atrocities. Franche-Comté did not receive support from Spain, since the troops from Milan could not march to the relief of the insurgents, because the Duke of Savoy and the Swiss cantons did not agree to them crossing their territories.

The loss of Franche-Comté was a serious defeat for the Monarchy's global strategy, whether on the field of battle or in diplomacy, since Madrid was not able to persuade the Swiss cantons to intervene to protect the neutrality of the province.[22] However, the events of 1674 show the substantial inefficiency of the Spanish military for acting in the common defence of the region. Milan's governor Antonio Lopez de Ayala Velasco y Cardeñas, Count of Fuensalida, was too worried about the weaknesses of the Army of Milan to deprive himself of troops at such a delicate moment. The Crown's support did not go beyond generic and vague promises of help, but the interests at stake were more important than the conservation of Franche-Comté, as the war was extending dangerously into Sicily and in the Iberian Peninsula. The war was going to involve the Monarchy on multiple fronts as occurred in the 1640s: a commitment that the exhausted Spanish finances would not be able sustain.

Since the French strategy aimed to reduce the Spanish presence in the Low Countries, Catalonia was little affected by the War of Devolution in 1667, other than when the French tried to invade the country in the summer, but were repulsed by the Duke of Osuna, who was able to contain the threat with only a very few regular troops, totalling 2,300 infantry and 200 cavalry. In the following January, the Spaniards crossed the border with a stronger force of 1,000 horse and 3,200 foot.[23] Osuna destroyed enemy facilities in Roussillon but failed to seize the fortress of Bellaguarda. In 1673, hostilities resumed and after months of inactivity on both sides, in the spring 1674, the Duke of San Germano invaded Roussillon by crossing the Pyrenees through the Col de Portell. The Spanish army was heavily supported by the *Angelets de la Terra*, the pro-Spanish *miqueletes* from Roussillon. French troops, commanded by Monsieur Le Bret, were unable to stop the stronger Spanish army, and after being defeated in some minor encounters when trying to block the passage of the Spanish on the Tech River, all available troops were concentrated around Perpignan. The Spaniards easily seized in succession the castle of Maureillas and the town of Ceret.

22 It was Berne that opposed the intervention in Franche-Comté, in contrast to the Catholic cantons, which were oriented to impose the respect of the 1522 treaty. See Maffi, *La cittadella in armi*, p.23.

23 Maffi, *Los últimos tercios*, p.9.

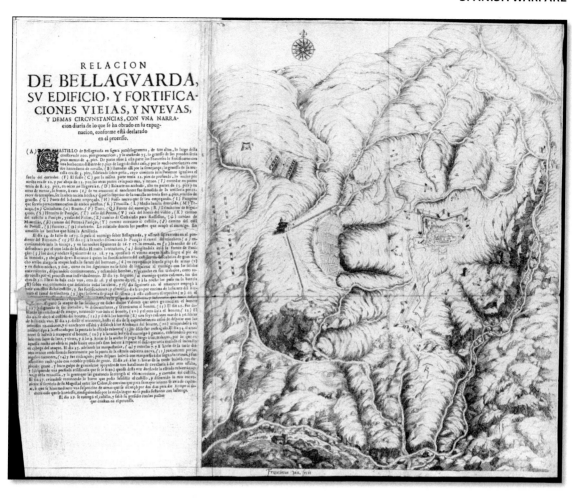

Print of the French siege of Bellaguarda in 1675, after Luis de Valencia (Biblioteca Nacional de España 2/18552). After Bellaguarda's surrender the Flemish commander Gerard Diamberg van Remen was tried by the Military Court to establish his responsibility in the loss of the strategic fortress conquered just one year before. The outcome of the trial was published in a book entitled *Gerardo Dienbercht Vanrremen, Maestro de campo de Infanteria Valona, y Gouernador que fue del castillo de Bellaguardia, en los confines de Cataluña, y Rossellon en elaño de 1675. Defendido, iustificando eniuridico, y militar Discurso, que defendiò el Castillo, de la expugnacion de las armas Francesas, y capitulò con ellas, observando envno, y otroel rigor de las leyes Militares.*

The greatest success came on 4 July, when the fortress of Bellaguarda, which allowed the French to freely enter Catalonia surrendered without resistance. After these failures, Le Bret was replaced by the talented Friedrich Hermann von Schomberg. He scored a small success over his adversary San Germano by forcing him to abandon the siege of Banyuls. Meanwhile, Schomberg was reinforced with further troops, and now he could muster 12,000 infantry, 3,000 horse and an auxiliary militia of 10,000 men. The harsh terrain and heat, and the need to disperse troops in different garrisons had left San Germano with only 4,300 infantry and 700 horse. The Italian general, seeing his troops outnumbered, retreated to the southern bank of the Tech River, and entrenched in a fortified encampment. From this position, Catalan *miqueletes* did not stop harassing French positions and convoys, even killing

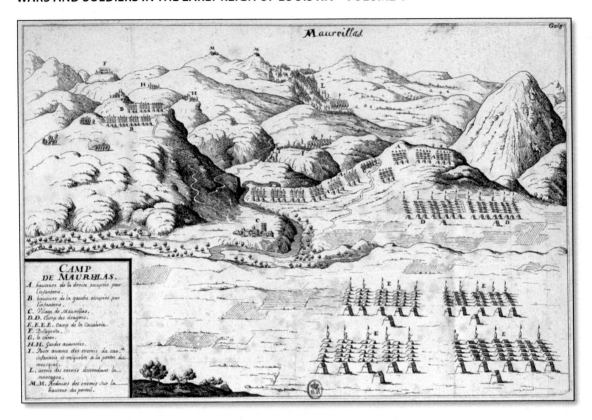

Print illustrating the opening phase of the Battle of Maureillas, fought on 18 June 1674. In foreground, the French columns are crossing the mountains. (Author's collection).

in an ambush Josep d'Ardena, one of the main leaders of the anti-Spanish revolt of 1640. Schomberg decided to deal with the main threat: the army of San German, and then finish off the guerrillas. He ordered a surprise attack on the Spanish camp. However, the *miqueletes* thwarted the plan, first discovering the French troops and then helping to repel the enemy assaults Finally, the Spanish cavalry expelled the French beyond the Tech River.

In this action, a French Swiss regiment was almost completely annihilated. The Duke of San Germano, in order to prevent a crisis, deployed his troops in order of battle and first of all ordered the baggage train to march. However, the French resumed the assault, and they attacked the Spanish army on both flanks. On the right wing, the French onslaught was repelled by the *tercios* of Barcelona (EI–191) and Vic (EI–193), then, reinforced by the cavalry wing of the Count of Lumiares, which defeated the French squadrons, both *tercios* forced the French infantry to retreat. On the left flank the French regiments were held back by the *tercios* of Marquis of Aytona (EI–97) and the *Chambergas* (EI–181). The French cavalry was also defeated on this flank, and the infantry finally fled, crossing in disorder to the northern bank of the Tech River. The French casualties were about 1,000 dead, and some 1,500 or 1,600 were taken prisoner, including Schomberg's eldest son, who was a cavalry colonel. The French also lost all their artillery, 600 draft animals, and most of their baggage. In addition, the Spaniards spiked the captured cannons that could not be dragged away. On the Spanish side, there were also many casualties. The cavalry *trozo* of Milan (EC–69) lost nearly its whole strength. Maureillas was the last Spanish battlefield victory of the century.

Unfortunately, the enemy pressure in the other fronts caused a decrease in the force based in Catalonia, and within a few months, the success achieved by San Germano was lost. The siege of Messina and the emergency in Flanders absorbed what residual resources the Monarchy possessed.

In 1675, the gradual French retreat from the United Provinces transformed the Spanish Low Countries into the main battlefield, resulting in a new round of looting and forced war contributions for the local population. The allied strategy was constrained by the weakness of Spain, which was going through one of the worst periods of its history under the government of the scandalous Fernando de Valenzuela. In April 1675, the Army of Flanders numbered approximately 48,000 men, of which the larger part manned the garrisons from Furnes to Luxembourg, leaving only the cavalry and a small percentage of infantry for the field operations.

On 12 June, Villahermosa joined the allied army with 6,000 horse, but the French anticipated the move, and on 29 May seized Dinant after a short siege. Then, the French turned to Huy and Limburg, which surrendered on 6 and 21 June. Villahermosa and his generals strongly complained about the behaviour of William III, who did not try to save Limburg and avoided any field engagement with the besieging army. The French offensive continued with the conquest of the fortress of Tienen, and they then stood on the defence waiting for winter quarters. Meanwhile the relations between the allies worsened, since Villahermosa opposed the Dutch plan against Liège, whose master sided with France, and insisted in not moving the army away from Flanders: 'because the Monarchy does not make war against a Catholic Bishop.'[24] This reverberated across the field of diplomacy, requiring the ambassadors to resolve the quarrel and agree to a common strategy, but this met with little success. Villahermosa followed the order from Madrid and concentrated his effort in the defence of the country: a very difficult task given his army had decreased to less than 30,000 men. Once again, the delay in the payment of the wages for the troops caused desertions, which were double the losses suffered in battle.[25] The overall allied field army numbered approximately 41,000 men: too few to fight the French. Therefore, the campaign of 1676 saw the French again take the initiative. After a feint against Ypres, the French seized Condé-sur-l'Escout on 26 April, and without opposition headed towards Bouchain, which surrendered on 9 May. Villahermosa's attempts to reinforce both the garrisons with a few troops were in vain.

The loss of Bouchain caused great concern because it exposed Cambrai and Valenciennes to a French assault. Villahermosa and William III accused each other of being at fault for the negative outcome of the campaign. Fortunately, after the conquest of Bouchain, the French did not continue their offensive, but before the end of the July, Maubeuge and Bavay also fell.

---

24 Bacigalupe Echevarria, Miguel Ángel, 'El ejército de Flandes en la etapa final del régimen español (1659–1713)', in E. García Hernán and D. Maffi (eds), *Guerra y sociedad en la monarquía hispánica: política, estrategia y cultura en la Europa moderna (1500–1700)* (Madrid: Fundación MAPFRE, Laberinto; Consejo Superior de Investigaciones Científicas, CSIC, 2006), vol. I, p.564.

25 AHNOB, *Osuna*, ct.91, d.1 *Carta de Valeriano Servent a Manuel Diego López de Zúñiga Mendoza Sotomayor, Duque de Béjar*, 1685.

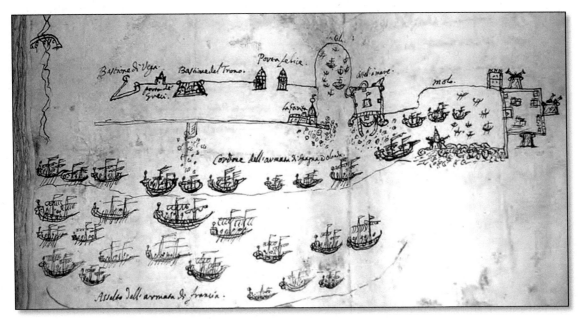

Sketch representing the battle fought between the French fleet against Spaniards and Dutch on 2 June 1676 before Palermo. As was the case on the land, at sea Spain's principal naval force was entrusted to the supreme command of a Dutch admiral. It was perhaps the most astonishing development in the entire saga of the Monarchy, which was now underpinned by the resources of nations that in former times had been its most bitter enemies. Dutch Protestant generals now commanded Spanish troops, and Dutch Protestant admirals directed the Spanish navy. (Drawing in pen, in *Memorie varie di Sicilia nel tempo dellar i bellione di Messina dell'anno 1674*, collected by Vincenzo Auria. Municipal Library of Palermo)

The campaign was marked by skirmishes between the opposite armies in attempts to resupply the besieged cities. In one of these, on 10 June, Spanish cavalry defeated the French near Cambrai. This success enabled Villahermosa to send troops to reinforce the garrisons of Cambrai, Valenciennes and Saint-Omer which were almost cut off. Again, the difference between the Dutch and Spanish plans caused friction at a strategic level.

Battered by the exhausting arguments, in July William III moved his own army against Maastricht; however, Villahermosa gathered 5,000 horse and 1,000 foot under Vaudemont and Louvigny to support the Dutch on campaign along with 20,000 men under Waldeck, and at the same time watch over Spanish Brabant and Flanders. According to Spanish reports, the Prince performed badly at Maastricht, and the Dutch engineers demonstrated little knowledge in siege warfare. The siege lasted until 27 August and was a complete failure that cost heavy casualties. Meanwhile, on 22 July, the French under Schomberg and d'Humières took advantage of the situation to besiege Aire. Villahermosa tried to save the city, sending a relief force of 5,000 Spaniards and 4,000 Dutch, but Aire surrendered after just one day of siege, since the local authorities refused to continue the defence. The French achieved these successes because they demanded the surrender in return for saving the city from looting if they did not resist.

In January 1677, news from Madrid announced that the unpopular Valenzuela had been arrested, but this event would bring no immediate changes. Though the new Prime Minister Don Juan of Austria, a champion of a plucky war policy, promised that Spain would deploy 25,000 men for the

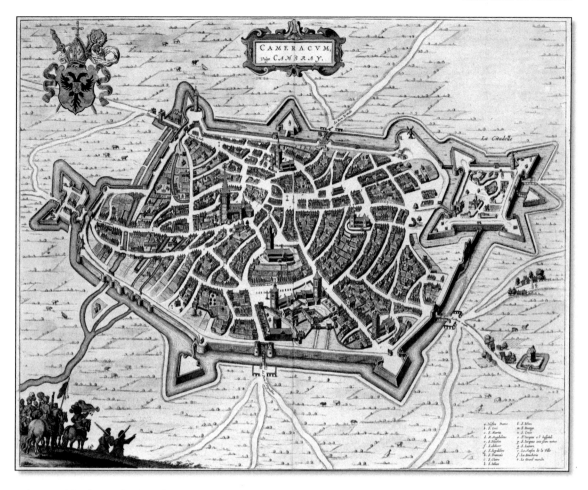

The city of Cambrai in the Spanish Low Countries, in a seventeenth-century print (*Atlas van Loon*, 1663). Cambrai was the most powerful fortress in Flanders and key to the Spanish defensive network since the War of Devolution. The French campaigns of 1675 and 1676 proved that the Spanish hopes to face their enemies with a static defence strategy were a mere illusion. After conquering Valenciennes, the French moved to Cambrai, which they reached on 20 March 1677. Two days later Louis XIV arrived in person to see the progress of the campaign. On 2 April the regular siege began, and three days later the city surrendered after the offer of the benefits already granted to Lille, but the Hispanic garrison managed to take refuge in the citadel and the siege continued until 17 April. After 29 days of siege, the King made his triumphal entry into the city on 19 April, Easter Monday.

coming campaign in Flanders, these good intentions did not correspond with reality. The strenuous resistance offered by the Army of Flanders consumed the residual resources in material and soldiers. In just three months the surrender of Valenciennes, Cambrai, and Saint-Omer caused the loss of 13,000 men, who were taken prisoner by the French.[26] The allied attempt to divert the French from their objectives was frustrated at Charleroi and Mont-Cassel. Villahermosa contributed with 3,400 horse to the field army, but before the end of the campaign, the French had also seized Saint-Ghislain.

The next year, Ypres and Ghent also surrendered, and in August the French laid siege to Mons. Finally, on 17 September, after months of negotiations, the

---

26 Storrs, *The Resilience of the Spanish Monarchy 1665–1700*, p.27.

Debello Superbos.

Anthonio Agurto Marchioni Gastanage Regi Hispan.s à consiliis prafecto Belgii. atq Exercitus Hispani. Supremo. D.D.D.Petrus Schenck.

Den Groten kastilyaan, vorst karelnam behage,
In 't opperste gezag van 's koninkx nederlant,
Te stellen, wie 's Rykxroem den Edlen Gastanage;
Daar Brussel en Madrid geen klein vermaak in vint;
Warom? den hele zoekt 't best van Oostenryk en Spanje.
Van Bateos Vryestaat, van Vlaänderen, en Briianje.

Francisco Antonio de Agurto, Marquis of Gastañaga (1640–1720), governor of the Spanish Low Countries between 1685 and 1692. He was a skilled politician and military theorist who introduced new infantry tactics to the army of Flanders. Gastañaga led the Hispanic troops at Fleurus (1690) and unsuccessfully defended Mons against the French, for which failure he was recalled to Madrid. In 1694 he became Viceroy of Catalonia where he was confronted with a French invasion during the War of the Grand Alliance.

Spanish delegation at Nijmegen signed a peace treaty with France. By this time, Villahermosa held only Furnes, Dixmude, Bruges, Namur, Nieuport, Malines, Courtrai, Guelders, Brussels, Ostend, Antwerp, Luxembourg, and Mons, which had resolutely resisted the recent siege. The war resulted in complete failure for Madrid, since the Monarchy paid the major cost with the loss of further territories in the Spanish Low Countries, comprising Saint-Omer, Aire, Cambrai, Valenciennes, Maubeuge and Charlemont.

The peace agreement reached at Nijmegen did not guarantee the Crown against further French conquest.[27] A few months after the peace treaty was signed, French patrols crossed the border and imposed contributions in the south of the Spanish Low Countries and Luxembourg. In September 1681, the French entered the Duchy of Luxembourg and assaulted supply convoys heading towards the city.

This blockade at a distance did not turn into all-out war, but skirmishes continued until March 1682, when finally, the French retreated from the Duchy fearing a Dutch-English intervention. However, in September 1683, Louis XIV ordered a new blockade of Luxembourg, while another French corps under d'Humiéres besieged Courtrai and Dixmude, which both fell before December. The short War of the Reunions of 1683–84 was another dark page in the tormented history of *Los Austrias*.

Isolated and exposed to invasion from every side, the Crown declared war on France in December 1683,albeit without a hope of success, since the Austrian Habsburgs were involved in the war against the Ottomans, England had reconciled with France, and the States Generals of the United Provinces refused to send their troops to relieve the unfortunate Duchy. Despite this unfavourable scenario, the French plan to easily seize Luxembourg was thwarted by Ottone Enrico del Carretto, Marquis del Grana, appointed as governor of the Spanish Low Countries in 1682. The Italian governor resorted to every resource for mustering a garrison and placed it under the command of the brave Charles-Louis-Antoine d'Henin, Prince of Chimay, who faced the enemy blockade heroically.

---

27 The Peace of Nijmegen granted Louis XIV the right to claim the right of annexation of the provinces that in the past were united to territories incorporated by France. The Sun King established for this task the *Chambres de Rèunion* in 1681.

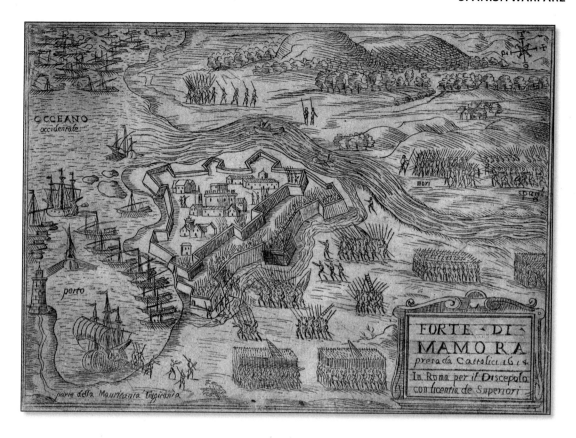

Above; The Spanish fortress of La Mamora, in Morocco, in a seventeenth-century print. Like the other Spanish outposts in Africa, La Mamora faced many enemy sieges. The first Moroccan attempt to seize the fortress occurred in 1629, followed by further sieges in 1625, 1628, 1647, 1655, 1668, 1671, 1675, and 1678. Finally, on 26 April 1681, the weak garrison of just 160 regular soldiers surrendered having lost any hope of relief.

Overleaf: Spanish dragoons, *tercio Estado de Milán* (ED-8), in yellow coat with red facings, siege of Methoni (Greece) 1686, portrayed in the manuscript of the *codice* Rossi-Cassigoli (Biblioteca Nazionale Centrale, Florence). In April 1685 the governor of Milan, Juan Tomás Enríquez de Cabrera, Count of Melgar, agreed to raise an infantry and dragoon contingent to join the Venetians in their war against the Ottomans. The infantry comprised eight companies of 100 rank and file each, while the dragoons numbered 200 men. Months later, one German infantry regiment was added in order to increase the contingent to 2,400 men. The infantry *tercios* were formed by Italians, and the dragoons were the only actual Spaniards, belonging to the *tercio Estado de Milán*. The infantry companies still included pikemen, although the Venetian infantry had replaced the pikes with muskets. This contingent marched to Venice in May 1686 to embark on vessels bound for the Peloponnese. The 'Milanese' contingent participated in the glorious campaign which began with the capture of Nauplia and later earned distinction at New and Old Navarino and Methoni. Engagements caused friction between the allies after the Milanese claimed to be the first to enter into the cities and chose the best part of the booty. During the campaign the Milanese authorities complained that their contingent lost many men, especially from disease. These casualties included the colonel of the German regiment, Antonio Visconti, who died shortly thereafter. The following year three 'Milanese battalions' fought at Patras and in the subsequent conquest of Athens on 29 September 1687. Afterwards, the contingent joined the garrisons in Attica and awaited reinforcements. The recruits did not arrive until the following spring. Unfortunately the Genoese vessel *Santa Maria*, hired by the governor to transport the recruits to Greece, accidentally exploded in the Gulf of Corinth and sank with all on board, including the *maestre de campo* Antonio Caratino, who had replaced Pietro Francesco Visconti the previous year. Losses from epidemics considerably reduced the contingent during the siege of Negroponte, and each unit formed only a single battalion. Since the campaign's catastrophic outcome affected the Spanish–Milanese troops, their participation in the conflict ended in 1688.

During the winter, Spanish troops made a commendable defence, forcing the besiegers into a bloody struggle that began in April 1684 with a regular siege. The French covered the siege with a strong corps of observation, but the Spanish could not deploy enough troops to engage the enemy in open battle. Grana launched cavalry incursions from Charleroi, Mons and Namur against the enemy depots and facilities. Some groups penetrated as far as Mézières and Sedan, while the garrison of Luxembourg performed some successful sorties against the enemy approaches. Parties on both sides exhorted contributions from the provinces across the border. In April 1684, despite the desperate situation, Chimay informed the governor that his cavalry had defeated a large enemy force capturing a convoy containing useful resources, since the city did not receive supply for several months. The heroic resistance claimed a heavy price amounting to 2,900 casualties from 27 April to 7 June, when the garrison, without ammunition, food or other supplies and with no hope of relief, finally surrendered.

4

Uniforms, Equipment and Flags

As it is well known, information relating to armies between 1660 and 1690 usually includes little and imprecise information on soldiers' clothing. Though this period may be considered 'pre-uniform', this does not mean that the need to dress soldiers uniformly was any less important. In fact, on this matter, Spain dealt with regulating soldiers' dress much earlier than other powers. In the seventeenth century, soldiers were normally supposed to pay the officers for their clothing, and uniformity depend on several factors, such the availability of cloth and the available budget. Except for some exceptions, in the major European armies it was the colonels who assumed the task of equipping the troops that they assembled and dressing them to their liking. On the contrary, in Spain the cost of clothing used to be borne by the government, or the provinces and kingdoms that contributed to a uniform dress for soldiers. In fact, already by the end of the reign of Felipe III, the Royal Treasury began to pay the clothing allowances to the soldiers, deducing the price from their wages. This meant that, at least at the beginning of a campaign, the Spanish armies were dressed uniformly, and therefore the soldiers of the Monarchy could be easily recognised by those of other nations. The foreign mercenary contingents were the only ones who maintained an obligation to be dressed and equipped by their colonels until eighteenth century.

It is difficult to establish how actually 'uniform' these items were since the quality of the fabrics mattered more than the uniformity of the style and colour of the clothing. However, several clues confirm that in the 1650s, *casaca* (jacket) or *hungarina* (coat) distributed to the troops in Italy, Spain and Low Countries, had been usually manufactured in *pardo* (tanned brown) cloth.[1] This kind of undyed fabric was common in Spain and survived in the production of Spanish military uniforms until the Napoleonic period. A similar colour was also used in the French army for the Italian infantry

---

1   The infantry of the army of Extremadura were mostly dressed in *pardo*, see *Relación de la frontera de Portugal*, 1664; BN, MS 9394, f. 427. See also Picouet, *The Armies of Philip IV of Spain 1621–1665* (Warwick: Helion & Company, 2019), pp.191–192.

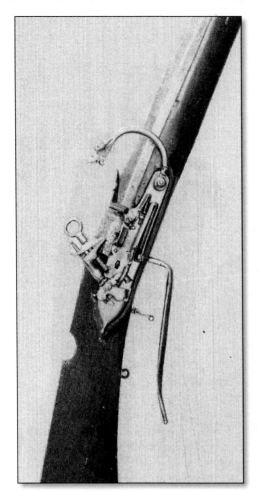 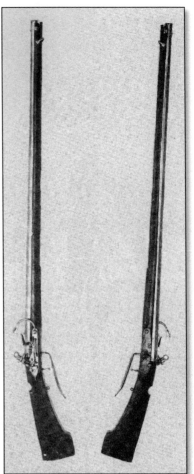

Above: Spanish musket with double mechanism dating 1680–90 (private collection, Milan). Many of the problems related to the procurement of weapons came in the decades after 1670, when the growth of the manufacturing centres in Spain allowed the Crown complete self-sufficiency in the production of firearms, but also to allocate an increasing share of production for export. The Spanish soldiers, who previously arrived at their destination without weapons, were now armed with locally made muskets, and large quantities of weapons were sent to Naples, as well as Brussels, to equip the troops. The decline of Milanese manufacturing began after 1659, and the same occurred in the Spanish Low Countries, due to losses of territory and important centres of production. In 1671, the Crown authorised the sending of 1,000 arquebuses and muskets to Milan to equip the troops. Between the 1670s and 1680s the infantry muskets manufactured in Spain became lighter, making the musket rest unnecessary.

Below: Infantry sword for a private soldier; Spanish manufacture dating 1670–80. (Collection of the *Musée de l'Armée*, Paris)

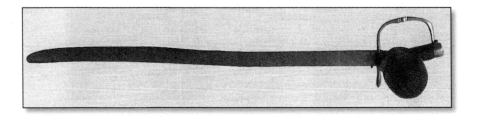

regiments until the following century, and in the army of the Prince-Bishop of Münster since the early 1660s.

There is extensive documentation regarding the distribution of garments as early as 1639. The clothing distributed to a soldier equipped with firearms included a coat, headgear, shirt, breeches, stockings and shoes. According to Clonard, who quotes two sources, in 1652 the infantry in Spain received shirt, jupon, *hungarina* of tanned brown cloth, breeches of the same cloth, stockings, a pair of shoes (of Córdoba leather), and headgear (usually white); the basic equipment for musketeer and harquebusier also comprised bandolier, baldric and Walloon sword, while pikeman received a three-quarter corselet and helmet.[2] The Count of Clonard returns more than once to the early Spanish uniforms in his works, and not always accurately. However, he indirectly confirms that the distribution of clothing and equipment for the soldiers was entirely managed by the state.

This represented important advantages as it favoured the standardisation of uniform clothing. This process would not have happened if the uniforms had been provided by private individuals. In fact, the role of the authorities on this matter frequently appears in the documentation relating to recruitment, mentioning the dress for soldiers. In Spain, the most important evolution in this sense took place in the 1660s, when the *vestidos de minición* turn into uniforms. It went from a minimal dress provided by the central administration, which was cheap, crude and often of unknown colours, to an actual uniform with a characteristic shape and distinctive colour, which served to differentiate the soldiers from civilians, and also identify a specific unit. By the 1660s, the recruits of the Hispanic armies were already hoping to obtain complete military dress or, if they did not need it, some financial assistance to procure it. This meant that the soldiers were usually dressed and equipped in a short time and, above all, that 'the men leave their homes with greater *lucimiento* (brilliance).'[3] Already in the 1660s, the orders given in this regard implied that the soldiers had to move from their province 'well equipped for the march, and wearing the military dress'.[4] This is evidence that providing clothing to the recruits was already becoming a common practice.[5] Furthermore, it was considered another incentive to join the military life, since the cost of dress could amount to three or four month's pay.

The manufacture of the *vestidos de minición* issued to the soldiers represented one of the greatest expenses for the army. However, everyone agreed that it was money well spent, because in addition to attracting those who aspired to be dressed in brand new, sometimes brightly coloured coats, the uniform served to shelter the soldier from inclement weather, and also to differentiate a unit from another. The state's management

---

2   Clonard, *Historia orgánica,* vol. IV, pp.416–417.

3   Antonio José Rodríguez Hernández, 'La evolución del vestuario militar y la aparición de los primeros uniformes en el ejército de la Monarquía Hispánica, 1660–1680', in *Obradoiro de Historia Moderna,* N. 26 (2017), p.182.

4   *Ibid.*

5   AGS, Guerra Antigua, libro 304, f. 71: Instrucción al Corregidor de Córdoba, dated 26 November 1668.

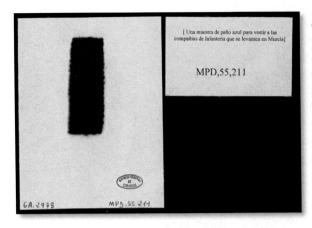

[Una muestra de paño azul para vestir a las
compañias de Infanteria que se levanten en Murcia]

MPD,55,211

GA.2978   MPD.55.211

The archive of Simancas in Valladolid preserves a collection of cloth samples for the manufacture of military uniforms. The series starts in the 1690s, but the fact that there are no samples relating to previous years does not mean that these never existed, but that most likely preservation did not begin as soon as the practice was introduced in the previous decades. Uniform manufacture documents of the 1660s and 1670s often refer to fabric samples that suppliers had to guarantee quality and colour.

of clothing expenditure for the army has produced an extensive administrative body of documentation,which today is preserved in the archives. Unfortunately, it is rare to find specific mention of clothing colours before the 1690s, when the fabrics for manufacturing the uniforms were registered and preserved alongside the samples. This lack of information relating to the uniforms before 1690 does not mean that the issue was less important, but in all probability its introduction after that year was only the natural continuation of a process already begun, but not yet regularised.

Scholars have paid a lot of attention to the first Spanish uniforms. The leading twentieth-century Spanish military historian and illustrator, José María Bueno, also dealt with the Spanish soldiers of *Los Austrias*. Like others after him, the reference sources were the works of the aforementioned Clonard and Manuel Giménez, with a few exceptions.[6] Both these authors have left extensive documentation about the uniform of this period. According to them, from the mid 1660s, the Spanish soldiers, both infantry and cavalry, would have worn the same style of clothing, a regimen which lasted uninterrupted until the end of the century. This consisted of a coat substantially similar to the French *justaucorps*, provided with sleeves cuffed above the elbow, lined with a different colour, and with a pair of lapels extending along the length of the coat's front opening. Breeches of natural canvass, stockings with ribbons, and light grey broad-brimmed hat completed the uniform. This clothing is attributed to every kind of infantry unit, including the provincial *tercios* and also dragoons. Authoritative illustrators have also followed this representation in recent publications.[7] However, an easy check carried out on the contemporary pictorial sources show little coherence with the reconstructions produced by these authors.

Some details of the soldiers' clothing in the Clonard and Gimenez illustrations are consistent with the *carlino* style, such as the lapels down the front of the coat, which appear in the dress of the nobility as early as the late 1650s. However, some 'romantic' interpretations seem far less convincing. Among these, the shape of the cuffs raise many doubts. The high position, above the elbow, is typical of the coats in the 1660s and early 1670s, but this type of pattern does not appear in any contemporary illustrations and looks like a coarse reconstruction from inaccurate drawings. Similar cuffs appear in some portraits of the Flemish Walloon school in that same period, but without the side cut, replaced by a central one along the sleeves of the coat.

6   Manuel Giménez González, *El Ejército y la Armada* (Madrid, 1862).
7   See Ignacio and Iván Notario López, *The Spanish Tercios 1536–1704*, illustrated by Gerry and Sam Embleton, Osprey Man-at-Arms, MAA 481 (Oxford: Osprey Publishing, 2012), plate G.

A pageboy carrying a *justaucorps* in a guardhouse with flags and weapons, by David Theniers the Younger, dated to the late 1660s (Art Institute of Chicago). Less renowned than the contemporary Dutch painters of the 'golden age', the Flemish Walloon artists supply an accurate picture of Hispanic military clothing for the years 1660–1690. Breastplates and other armour seem to be conventional, but the saddle and the pistol holster are reproduced very accurately.

The absence of buttons or other fasteners also adds to the unreliability of the nineteenth-century sources, considering that the cuff would tend to fall along the arm without something holding it in position.

Nineteenth-century scholars, like those of the following century and indeed almost up to the present day, base the reconstructions of the 1660s Spanish uniforms after a print included in Clonard's book entitled *Memorias para la historia de las tropas de la Casa Real de España*. In this work, published in 1824, a musketeer is depicted of the newly raised regiment of the King, also known as *las Chambergas*. The name of the unit originates from the French-German born Marshall Friedrich Hermann von Schomberg, who, in 1660, introduced a new style of clothing in the Iberian Peninsula. This style coincided with the influential French fashion popularised by the generals of Louis XIV during the war against Portugal. Since this was the clothing worn by the enemy, Madrid strongly opposed this fashion, which was spreading everywhere, including

Gentleman's portrait, Flemish Walloon school, mid 1660s (private collection, England). This young man wears a *carlino*-style coat over a single-breasted doublet and *rabat* collar. Note the tailed flap cuffs and buttons for securing them to the sleeves. This pattern is probably the one misinterpreted in nineteenth century sources illustrating early Spanish uniforms.

in Spain and in their domains in Italy and the Low Countries. The hostility to the French style was so strong that the War Council asked that royal audiences be denied to people wearing the new fashion.[8]

The severe Spanish *etiqueta* remained the style of the Monarchy, at least until the death of Felipe IV in 1665, when the situation changed. The heir, Carlos II, *el rey infante*, would reign once he reached the age of majority. This did not go unnoticed at court, and many predicted a destiny for the young monarch, that from a prince under tutelage would rise a warrior king, just as had happened with his cousin Louis in Paris. The new age would bring a new style that could also be an adaptation of the French one. This change was also favoured by Don Juan of Austria, who adopted the new fashion coming from Northern Europe. In the 1670s, the court's chronicle registered the phase of the change from the old to the new style. On 21 February 1677, a diary reports that the King and Don Juan had gone hunting, and the night before the King had worn a *chamberga* and did not want to have dinner in bed because he had been dressed longer. In another passage of the chronicle, the King's taste in this matter is again confirmed:

Today the King got dressed at five in the morning, and because he liked the new fashion, His Majesty's and His Highness's entourage was also dressed without the golilla (high collar), wearing chamberga and cravat, and the King is said to have liked this so much this dress, which is supposed to ban collars, and the new fashion is called by Her Highness: Carlina, and it is more pleasant, while with the high collar results less attractive.[9]

The King and his stepbrother introduced the *justaucorps* at court following the influential French fashion, after Don Juan tried to introduce the new style to avoid calling to mind the regiment he had recently disbanded. The term *chamberga* has remained in the use of the Castilian language for generations, since the regiment of the King's Guard wearing the coat tailored in the French style had been associated with the regency of the Queen. These testimonies would indicate that the uniform worn by the soldiers of the King's Guard was substantially tailored in a similar pattern, and that it would become the pattern after 1669, when the regiment was raised. Several portraits actually show Don Juan and other grandees already dressed in the new style by the

---

8   Alvarez-Ossorio Alvariño, *La Chamberga*, p.93.
9   Diario de todo sucedido en madrid desde el sabad 23 de enero de 1677, in Alvarez-Ossorio Alvariño, *La Chamberga*, p.93.

Above: The Duke of Pastrana, portrayed by Juan Carreno de Miranda in 1660–65 (Museum of Art, São Paulo) wearing Spanish court dress. Note the *golillo*-collar and the open sleeves of the coat in brocade fabric. (Author's archive)

Top left: Musketeer of *Las Chambergas* in 1669, after the Clonard's *Memorias para la historia de las tropas de la Casa Real de España*.

Left: Angel, School of Cuzco, Peru 1675–80. Native Peruvian painters depicted the Bible's angels dressed like the Spanish ruling class (a hidden metaphor of the Spanish conquest?) Their sophisticated clothing follows the pattern of the *carlino* style introduced in the 1670s to replace the severe style of the previous decades.

early 1660s, while other aristocrats still wear in the same period dress of the style codified in the Spanish court. Both Clonard and Gimenez also assigned the *carlino*-style coat to the provincial *tercios* established in 1664, which were already wearing their brightly coloured uniforms. This course of events would seem to go against the possibility that these units had already adopted this kind of coat in 1664, unless we take as gospel the report about the clothing distributed to the *tercios provinciales*. In fact, it would have been Don Juan of Austria himself, in 1663, to impose uniforms of different colours, excluding the provincial units to wear the *vestido de munición* identical to the one distributed to the infantry in Extremadura.

The Prince examined the 500 coats manufactured for the recruits coming from Córdoba and according to the chronicle, he pronounced that the appearance of the soldiers dressed in the rough tanned brown clothes 'would have disgusted the most miserable of shepherds'.[10] For this reason, he gave orders covering the shape, style, accessories and colours that each of the new *tercios* should have worn, and to prepare samples for the manufacturers. This tale seems to have all the characteristics of a legend, since this kind of information belongs to the regimental histories transmitted orally, but the use of the extensive range coloured clothes for the uniforms distributed to the provincial *tercios* confirms this order.[11] According to the research of some intrepid scholars, the price paid for the uniforms manufactured for these soldiers had the drawback of being significantly high. Although the *tercios* made use of *asientos* who sought supplies at the best price, especially in Madrid, the model established by Don Juan led to an increase in costs equal to one and a half times that of the old *vestidos de munición*. Despite this, the Prince's wishes prevailed, and in the following years these *tercios* tried to follow the established guidelines, organising in advance the replacement of their clothes, in anticipation of distributing a new uniform every year.[12] In the eyes of Don Juan of Austria, some *reales* were not worth saving, as such savings would have an impact on the recruits, as it made them feel like a 'lackey serving the most miserable masters.'[13]

True or not, this story proved that military clothing was becoming an element of prestige that encouraged the enlistment of recruits, who 'seeing the soldiers well dressed' would have been attracted by the desire to emulate them.[14] The issue of new clothing was not much delayed as it was one of the extra measures with which it was intended to help restore the honour, respect and esteem that the armies of the Monarchy had once enjoyed. Although the styles of military clothing developed in France and in the United Provinces of the Netherlands were also imposed on the Hispanic army, it should be emphasised that, at least in the Peninsula, there was a mixing of styles, and the result was

---

10 Rodríguez Hernández, *La evolución del vestuario militar*, p.186.
11 *Ibid.*, pp.188–189 and 203–204.
12 *Ibid.*, p.186. It was also established that interned prisoners in Portugal had the right to receive clothes and other garments while in captivity, which would substantially improve their living conditions.
13 *Ibid.*
14 *Ibid.*

Detail from 'Guardroom' by Gillis van Tilborgh, Flanders, 1664–68 (Hermitage Museum, St. Petersburg). Note on the right, the officer wearing an overcoat with 'Brandenburg' button laces (see Plate O in the colour section).

the creation of autonomous and distinctive military clothing, emphasised by the use of broad-brimmed headdresses of light colours, and by fabrics and accessories even more elaborate than the ones introduced in France.

A much more elegant model of military clothing thus began to assert itself, made with clothes of higher quality and more lasting. However, it remained to be established whether the cut of these new clothes was exactly the one shown in the nineteenth-century illustrations. It is hard to believe these uniforms were really in such bright colours. In the seventeenth century, the palette was actually very limited as only six or seven shades of dyes could be produced at a reasonable cost: red, azure-blue, green, orange, yellow, grey and brown. Natural colours like linen, straw, or ochre yellow and butternut were also available, and white was essentially from cotton or silk, while the wool clothes could become actually fade to white after several washings, and until the early eighteenth century, all the most colourful wool textiles were very expensive.

According to tradition, the provincial *tercios* received the new uniform of *morado* (purple-violet) with red lining for *Seville* (EI–15), while *Córdoba* (EI–32) had azure blue coats lined red, *Burgos* (EI–55) yellow lined white, *Madrid* (EI–73) vermillion red lined azure blue, *Toledo* (EI–100) blue

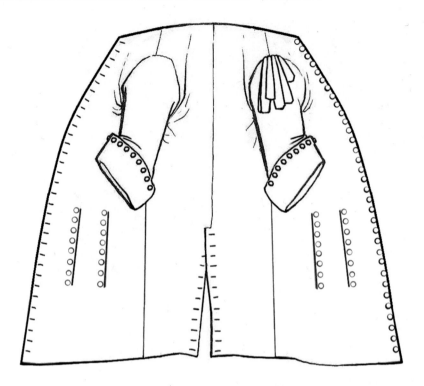

Above: Officer's coat pattern, 1664–68, after Gillis van Tilborgh.
Below: Private soldier's coat, early pattern, after Gillis van Tilborgh.
(Author's reconstructions)

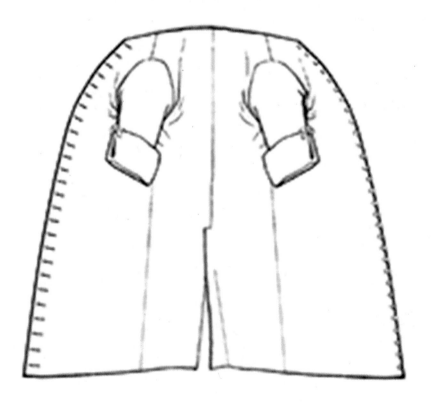

lined white,[15] and *Valladolid* (EI–101) medium green lined white. These colours would not have changed in the following decades, and when 10 new provincial *tercios* were raised in 1694 receiving uniforms similar to the ones of the existing units, the old corps continued to be recognised by their colour, adding the qualifying of *viejos* (old). The assignment of uniforms with distinctive colours to the provincial *tercios* does not seem to be extended to all the units of this type, since in 1663, the provincial *tercio* of Asturias wore in *pardo* with red lining.[16] Although the rough *pardo* cloth continued to be used, some details registered in the contract suggest that even the clothing of the Asturian provincial infantry was provided with better accessories than the one issued to the regular troops. Among these, there are specified buttons of red wire, headgear with ribbon, and a Bilbao-manufactured sword.[17]

The colours established for the provincial *tercios* should have identified the units until the early eighteenth century, as stated in the classic works on the Spanish army.[18] However, there are some doubts as to how these colours were actually retained throughout the years. This puzzle is supported by a document relating to the provincial *tercio* of Burgos, which in 1678 may have changed its uniform, as suggested by the attempt of the local *corregidor* to purchase *morado* clothes in Madrid to dress the recruits.[19]

In some respect, the decision to assign a specific uniform represented a novelty twice over. The first one concerned the troops directly, as the soldiers received a complete dress the same for all, sometimes of a characteristic colour, or of simple undyed fabric, but more resistant and more suited to their status. The other major novelty concerned the whole corps, as the members of the units were now marked by a distinctive dress and colour, in order to rise an *esprit de corps* within the unit, enforce its cohesion and increase the dignity of the soldiers. This process was nothing new, since a similar change was taking place all over Europe, but as a consequence of the involvement of the state, the Spanish case continued to be rather different from what happened in the other armies.

On the other hand, some recent studies relating to the first uniforms of the Hispanic armies, seem to ignore this background. In some of these

---

15　The Municipal Archive of Toledo preserves an interesting document relating to the manufacture of clothing distributed to the provincial *tercio*. This is a certificate of delivery, which refers to further details that form a different picture to the one reconstructed by Clonard and Giménez. See Archivo Municipal de Toledo, C.M. 28, 1665. Thanks to África García Fernández for this note. For further details, see the commentaries to colour plate A in this volume.

16　In 1663, for the provincial *tercio* of Asturias, the local authorities established a *vestido* – uniform consisting of a wool coat lined with coloured (red) cloth; wool breeches lined with canvas; a linen doublet lined with red; a brimmed hat with its coloured wool band or lanyard of Cologne; English wool stockings; a pair of square-toed shoes with calfskin soles; two shirts; a bandolier from Rouen; a baldric of sheepskin and a sword from Bilbao with its hilt. AGS, *Guerra Antigua*, leg. 2047; *Cartas del gobernador de Asturias*, in Oviedo, dated 10 February 1663, and *Cuentas de la leva realizada en Antequera*, in Madrid, dated 9 July 1663. See also in Pérez Calvo, José Luis, *El tercio fijo del principato de Asturias, 1663*, in *Researching & Dragona* n. 20 (2003), pp.35–36.

17　*Actas de las Junta & Diputaciones del Principado de Asturias*, vol. III. 1657–1672, *contrato por los vestidos de municion del tercio de Asturias*, 1663.

18　Pierre Picouet, on his website *Los Tercios y el Ejército Español, 1525–1704*, states that in the late 1680s, Burgos' coat became yellow and azure, while Toledo's was changed to azure and red.

19　Rodríguez Hernández, *La evolución del vestuario militar*, p.199.

'Soldiers' rest', Flemish Walloon school, early 1680s (Arts Collection of the Castello Sforzesco, Milan). Private soldiers are dressed in grey, while NCOs and officers wear red or blue.

works, it is stated rather dogmatically that actual military uniform did not exist before the 1690s.[20] In this regard, much more accurate and illuminating investigations reveal something completely different. On 5 September 1677, the nobles of the *Cortes* of Aragon addressed a proposal put before the assembly relating to soldiers' dress. The text reveals interesting details on the importance assumed by military clothing and the introduction of the first modern concepts of uniform. They wrote that since the soldiers must dress at the expense of the King (of Aragon), it was appropriate for the infantry *tercios* to dress in blue, which was the colour of the dress worn by the horse and foot guards of the Aragonese kingdom. With their blue uniforms the Kingdom's *tercios* were easily identified by the others in the army. The identification of the troops on the basis of a distinctive colour for the manufacture of clothing with defined characteristics is, without any doubt, a fact.

A month later, the veteran Leonardo Vicente de Alhambra sent an equally interesting letter to the nobles of the *Cortes* in which, proposing other possible colours for the uniforms, he provides invaluable information concerning the clothing of the infantry in the 1670s. Vicente de Alhambra praised 'the fine appearance and discipline of the provincial *tercios* to whom the funds that each Kingdom has granted them are punctually paid, while the Royal *tercios* (the regular ones), which are paid less regularly, always have

---

20 Pierre Lierneux, 'El uniforme militar en los Países Bajos españoles: mecanismos de un nacimiento esperado', in *Revista de Historia Militar* N. 121 (2007), pp.91–136. The author traces a historical profile of the military clothing in the Spanish Low Countries, without however finding anything new regarding types and colours used by the local troops. Curiously, he never quotes one of the major sources concerning on this subject, namely the memoirs of Jacques Pastur. See Cayron, 'La véritable histoire de Jacques Pastur dit Jaco', in *La Fourragère* N. 3 (December 1951), pp.533–592.

a multitude of sick and desertions.'[21] Vicente de Alhambra closed his letter by referring to several interesting details, namely the uniforms of the *tercios*. He agreed with the Aragonese nobles that 'the colour of the cloth for the uniforms must be in accordance with the Kingdom's livery' and that 'blue is a very suitable colour' but it caused some drawbacks, since in Catalonia there was already another *tercio* wearing blue uniforms, and he considered other possible colours, such as yellow and red, both included in the coat of arms of the kingdom of Aragon. Even in this case, however, there was a risk of similarities, 'since the *tercio* of the Duke of Monteleón (EI–53), which belonged to the Marquis Leganés, was dressed in yellow, the one of the Diputación de Catalunya was in red (EI–192), Medina Sidonia (EI–97) was in blue and another was dressed in green (EI–98)' and having to differentiate the Aragonese units with a specific colour, he proposed to use clothes with the heraldic colours of the Kingdom, namely red and yellow. However, Vicente de Alhambra concluded by writing that the true colour of Aragon was the blue 'and the soldiers will recognise each other and will not sell their coats to other soldiers, since they will wear that colour, no one will want to buy these.' As a further remark, he proposed to line the coats in yellow, in order to be different from Medina Sidonia, which instead was completely in blue. The decision of the nobles was finally approved on 10 December 1677 and entered into force on the following 20 January 1678. An important date for the birth of the Spanish uniforms and their history.

Since the 1670s, the instructions regarding the colour of the clothes and other items became more detailed, with samples of the uniforms or equipment being sent to the factories. Drummers also had to be differentiated from the rest of the soldiers. To this end, the order indicated the use of different clothes, but it seems that this was not always possible, since availability depended on the territory in which the drummers were recruited.[22] The archives keep a vast amount of documentation in which all the items of clothing are recorded, which is now moving towards a definitive degree of standardisation. Among the many examples, the papers relating to the administration of the clothing of the Aragonese troops in 1678 list the expenses for the manufacture of the uniforms, which comprised headgear with coloured headband, cravat, coat, shirt, breeches, stockings, and shoes.[23]

Although these preconditions contributed towards the introduction of 'uniformed clothing', direct feedback is unfortunately rare. Despite the large number of excellent painters active in Spain during this period, few of them have left evidence relating to the Spanish soldiers in the years 1660–1690. The

---

21 Luis Sorando Muzas and Antonio Manzano Lahoz, 'El tercio de Aragón: notas sobra su Evolución, indumentaria y emblematica (1678–1698)', in *Emblanata* n. 1 (1995), p.156. Furthermore, the Aragonese veteran advocated the opportunity to pay an extra monthly *escudo* to each musketeer 'because they are elite soldiers who must carry muskets, which weigh 25 to 30 pounds, and this requires sustenance, and if they are not paid this sum, which it is customary to give to everyone it is very likely that no soldier will be found who wants to carry a musket, and if imposed it by force, they will go away and we lose weapons and soldiers, as has often happened in recent years.'
22 *Ibid.*, p.200.
23 ACA, Consejo de Aragón, Consejo, leg. 72, Planta de los soldados, Pagam. to y Vestidos, ff.222–224, 1678.

Detail from the painting of an 'auto da fé' by Francisco Rizzi, 1683. This is one of the rare sources showing the Spanish military dress in the 1680s. Although these officers cannot be attributed to a specific *tercio*, the painting suggests that ranking personnel dressed in colours unrelated to the unit's uniform.

prints are rare, or depict senior officers wearing conventional armour. Only palace guards appear more frequently in the paintings, but only once the aforementioned regiment of the King's Guard is portrayed. *Las Chambergas* are depicted in the view of the Alcazar of Madrid, a painting by an unknown Spanish artist dating between 1675 and 1677, where a picket of the regiment wears a straw-yellow coat with white facings, straw-yellow stockings and grey-white broad-brimmed hat with red ribbons around the top. The *alférez* bears a white flag with the red Burgundian cross. Some images of Hispanic infantry and cavalry appear in the Portuguese *azulejos* (painted tin-glazed ceramic tile work) illustrating the battles of the War of Restoration, but the style in which they have been reproduced allows us only to know some of the more conventional details, such as the use of the waist scarf by most of the cavalrymen, or the use of armour and helmets by officers, such as in the representations of the Battle of Ameixial-Estremoz in 1663, and the Battle of Montes Claros in 1665.[24]

One of the best-known pictorial sources relating to Spanish soldiers in the second half of the seventeenth century is the painting by Francisco Rizzi representing an *auto-da-fé* which occurred in Madrid in 1683. The artist depicts a group of officers and NCOs wearing *justaucorps* very similar to the style then introduced throughout Western Europe, and quite different to the coat that Gimenez, Clonard and others that they describe for the soldiers of the Monarchy. Only the *alférez*, who carries a flashy yellow and black checked ensign, wears a shorter coat. All the officers are dressed in very elaborate clothing manufactured in brocade or with very elaborate single or double piping.[25] The officers are dressed in carmine red, yellow, green or medium brown; to left, a servant boy with armour, morion helmet, shield and sword appear close to the ensign, while on the other side a drummer wearing a dark green coat with broad golden yellow lace is beating his instrument.

The dress of the musicians, like the ones of the servants, followed the code of this age, which provided an extensive use of livery. As for the infantry and

---

24 Both preserved in the collection of Palácio Fronteira, Lisbon.

25 Some scholars would have identified this officer as belonging to the *tercio* provincial of Burgos (EI–55), but more probably they are officers of some professional *tercio* quartered in Madrid or even the provincial *tercio* of the city, also known as *los Colorados* (EI–73).

cavalry, Clonard and Gimenez give musicians the same clothing as the private soldiers, but with the royal livery in white and red lace on the coat. This kind of dress may be appropriate for the units belonging to the Crown, like all the old *tercios* and *trozos* of the professional army, while some reports point to a much more varied scenario. A chronicle of 1659 describes the use of customised liveries by some pages and musicians who attended the arrival of the English ambassador to Barcelona.[26] They wore clothing of crimson velvet edged with silk of *colores*, and large twisted lanyards in the 'gold of Milan'. The four Catalan cavalry companies forming the picket of honour wore coat tailored from Segovia cloth of *salmorado oscuro* (dark vermillion red), green scarf with silver fringes, green and silver lanyards, boots of natural leather, and plumed headgear.[27]

The lack of contemporary illustrations is partially replaced by these archival sources and especially by eyewitness' reports. Among these testimonies, a little known but very interesting sources are the *Relazione* and *Diari* written in 1668–69 by the companions of the Prince of Tuscany, later Grand Duke, Cosimo III de' Medici, during his European tour.[28] Among the members of the expedition,

Morion helmet, Spanish manufacture, 1650–1660. (Private collection)

26 Juan Gomez De Blas, *Relacion del viage, que desde la villa de Madrid ha hecho a la de Yrun, el excelentissimo señor Don Luys Mendez de Haro y Sotomayor … hasta el dia primero de agosto deste año de 1659* (Madrid, 1659).
27 *Ibid.*
28 From the autumn of 1668 to the autumn of 1669, the Grand Prince Cosimo, son of the Grand Duke of Tuscany Ferdinand II, made an educational journey through Europe visiting Spain, Portugal, the British Isles, the Dutch Republic and the Spanish Low Countries, and returning home travelling through France. An official travel report, without any indication of the author's name, is preserved in two Florentine manuscripts: one at the Biblioteca Mediceo Laurenziana, and the other at the Biblioteca Nazionale Centrale. The first manuscript includes a detailed series of drawings showing the places visited by the Prince. In addition to the report, the diaries of some of Cosimo's companions, who were high-ranking members of Tuscan court, are preserved in the State Archives in Florence. They were Lorenzo Magalotti, Filippo Corsini, the prince's physician, the housemaster, and the travel expenses administrator. Thanks to their diaries, it is possible to follow the journey day by day and to read the descriptions of the regions, cities, populations and other things that aroused the interest of the participants in the expedition, including information relating to the Spanish and Portuguese armies. The Prince and his entourage left Florence on 18 September destined for Leghorn where he would set sail. On 30 September, Cosimo reached Barcelona where he stayed until 5 October. After leaving there, he reached Madrid on 24 October. He remained in Madrid and the surrounding area until 25 November. He then carried on his voyage, travelling to Córdoba and Seville, followed by Talavera la Real, and Badajoz. On 9 January 1669, after almost five months pilgrimage through the southern and central regions of Spain, and after several social-political contacts, the Tuscan expedition left Badajoz for the Kingdom of Portugal, taking the route to Campo Maior and Elvas

Buff coat after Lambert de Hondt. (Author's reconstruction)

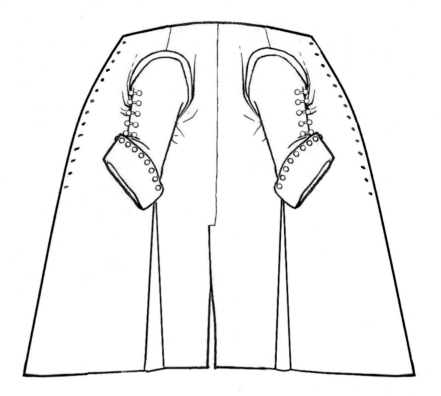

the Prince's secretary Lorenzo Magalotti left some detailed accounts concerning the troops in Spain and Portugal. As for the former, he noted in Barcelona that the officers wore clothes in the French style, but with some local features, and broad-brimmed hats in white felt with red plumes, while the foot soldiers were dressed in *cinabro* (madder red). In Seville, he reports that the soldiers wore coats of *nocciola* cloth (hazelnut, namely tanned brown *pardo*).

Magalotti also noted some cavalrymen near Talavera, perhaps belonging to the *Guardias de Castilla*, who were in three quarter armour over leather buff coats. The diary describes the dress of more cavalrymen at Badajoz, who wore buff coats and plumed hats, but they had very poor horses.[29] Unfortunately, the information is limited to these summary notes, and there are no further indications of what units they were. Moreover, although the *Relazione* also contains many detailed illustrations of the places visited, no soldier appears in the drawings. Further details about the Hispanic uniform were recorded by their enemies, like the *maréchal* Friedrich von Schomberg, or Luís de Meneses, Third Count of Ericeira, who left some descriptions of the Spanish cavalry in Extremadura.[30]

---

where, as stated by Magalotti 'there is no other mark of a border than that of a large stone placed beside the main road.'

29 ASFi, *Mediceo del Principato, Diario di Lorenzo Magalotti* (s.n.) 1668, pp.98–99 and 102–103.

30 Charles François Dumoriez, *Campagnes du Maréchal de Schomberg en Portugal depuis l'année 1662 jusqu'en 1668* (London, 1807), and Luís de Meneses, Conde de Ericeyra, *Historia do Portugal Restaurado* (Lisbon, 1679), vols I–II.

Cavalry or infantry officer wearing a laced buff coat, unknown Flemish Walloon artist, 1665–70 (National Galleries Scotland). The painting offers a very good example of officers' dress in the Spanish Low Countries, which was substantially similar to that of Dutch and German officers.

Though the contemporary pictorial sources relating to Peninsular military clothing from the 1660s–1680s are not as numerous, the ones depicting military life in the Spanish Low Countries or Italy are more diffused. The artistic level of these works is not comparable to the ones of the contemporary Dutch painters; however, thanks to these artists, it is possible to form a more accurate picture of Hispanic military clothing in these years. The Flemish Walloon painters, in particular, offer a wide range of military subjects of infantry as well as of cavalry. The paintings of Gillis van Tilborgh (1625–1678) and Jan van der Stoffe (1611–1682), who were active in Flanders until the years of their death, almost make a visual chronicle of the military clothing in the Low Countries. In the paintings depicting military subjects from the early–1660s, infantry officers and soldiers wear doublets, or coats tailored like the contemporary styles introduced in France, in the neighbouring Dutch Republic and in England, but shorter: a feature coming from the aforementioned *hungarinas*. The officers are usually dressed in light grey or natural leather, while the private soldiers are in dark grey or in brown.

Accessories and other details are substantially the same as tailored in the neighbouring countries, and comprised some old-fashioned items, like half boots and shirts with large collars. In the paintings dating between 1665

Cavalry officer and trooper, detail, after a painting attributed to Lambert de Hondt the Younger dating 1665–70 (private collection). The officer wears a red coat with a fully embroidered baldric and black broad-brimmed hat with white plumes, while the trooper in background is dressed in *pardo* – tanned brown. Military clothing was a matter that expanded its relevance in the 1660s. Before this decade, supplies in money and clothing from Spain remedied the most urgent shortages of the Spanish units located in the Low Countries, but in the 1660s, both these resources became smaller. Flemish Walloon *tercios* paid by the provinces of the Spanish Low Countries often looked abroad to provide clothing, but this became impossible during the War of Devolution (1667–1668). In subsequent years, the deplorable condition of the troops of the Army of Flanders is testified by numerous eyewitnesses.

Facing page, top: Officers and infantrymen, by Gillis van Tilborgh. This provides another example of a buff coat for officers dating 1665–70, in this case without sleeves, worn over a shirt and Rhinegrave breeches.

Facing page, bottom: Soldiers' Guardroom, by Lambert de Hondt the Younger (1642–1709), dating to the early 1680s.

and 1668, Tilborgh portrays the soldiers with more evolved clothing. The infantrymen now wear coats more similar to the ones introduced in France or in the Netherlands, and the accessories are more fashionable, like the cravats, which have replaced the large collars, and only the officers maintain a more conservative appearance. It is interesting to note that in the most recent paintings the officers' coats have the flap cuffs above the elbow as was usual in these years, and in one case they show the colour of the lining, pre-dating the facings introduced in the following decades. Therefore, these paintings show subjects that have nothings similar to the usual representations of nineteenth-century illustrators and the improbable standardisation of the clothing of Spanish soldiers.

It is difficult to establish whether the subjects portrayed are actually soldiers of the professional army or militiamen; however, certain details suggest the first hypothesis. In this regard, it is worth noting the presence of a cavalry trumpeter and a non-commissioned officer wearing sleeveless buff coats: a very common dress for ranking personnel in the professional armies of this period. This kind of dress also appears in some contemporary paintings of artists active in the Spanish Low Countries like Lambert de Hondt the Older (1620–1664), Michiel Sweerts (1618–1664), Gonzales Coque (1618–1684), and others, and usually it is worn by ensigns or senior officers.[31] All these paintings show that Hispanic military clothing, at least that relating to the Low Countries, was in a full phase of transition. Similar dress appears in the paintings of some Italian artists, especially the Neapolitan Carlo Coppola (active between 1653 and 1665), and his school, or Carlo Ceresa (1609–1679), but with more conservative features.

Almost five years older than Tilborgh, David Theniers (1610–1690) shows with equally accurate detail the clothing of the soldiers of the Spanish Low Countries in the following decades. His works relating to military life belong to the period of the artist's period of full maturity and mainly portray

31 This kind of coat appears in the stunning portrait of an ensign painted by Victor Bouquet, and in the scene of Gillis van Tilborgh, which is worn by the officer in foreground. Both paintings date to 1660–65.

Soldiers playing dice, 1672–73, by David Theniers. (*Neue Pinakothek*, Munich)

infantry soldiers, as well as the wardrobes of some high-ranking officers, including the equipment of the horse. In a painting preserved in the *Neue Pinakothek* of Munich, datable between 1672 and 1673, a private soldier is playing dice together with a non-commissioned officer, while two other soldiers, smoking tobacco, are watching the game.

The former wears a grey coat, with flap cuffs showing the lining, and red stockings. The pattern of the coat is modern, and only the absence of pockets suggests that the clothing of ordinary soldiers is still being improved. The breeches are also of dark grey fabric. This item is clearly visible since the coat is shorter compared to the contemporary *justaucorps*. This is probably not artistic license by the painter because, to save money, some inches of cloth were usually spared from the coats destined for the private soldiers.[32] On the opposite side of the table, a standing soldier wears a dark green coat, also without pockets, while the seated soldier is dressed in grey. The NCO centre stage is wearing a leather coat, this time with sleeves. The figures in background, possibly infantrymen, wear grey and red coats – or *hungarinas* – that in one case shows a livery of broad silver lace. This item could belong to a drummer or even to a soldier who formed the personnel under the *capitán de campaña*, the officer in charge of managing the military police within the unit.

---

32 This expedient, also applied in the army of the Imperial cousins in Vienna, was also harshly criticised by Raimondo Montecuccoli in the 1660s, who complained about the too-short coats distributed to the soldiers. See Mugnai, *Wars and Soldiers in the Early Reign of Louis XIV* (Warwick: Helion & Company, 2019), vol. 2, p.208.

A Spanish or Flemish Walloon musketeer, Flanders, 1650s (unknown artist, Bibliothèque nationale de France, Paris). The Spanish crown had dealt with military dress since the 1630s, a few years later than Sweden. The first ordinance concerning military dress dates to 1639, and it was issued to the Army of Flanders, in order to distribute standard clothing and equipment – *vestido de munición* – to the infantry. *Casaca* and *Hungarinas* were generally manufactured with undyed cloth, *pardo* and grey being the more usual colours.

The broad-brimmed hats are either of black, dark grey, brown and even straw-yellow or light grey material. The grey coat of the infantry in Flanders is also confirmed by news published in the *London Gazette* of May–June 1671. The journal reported that the governor of the Spanish Low Countries, Count of Monterrey, had ordered all the Spanish infantry in Flanders to be dressed in grey with red facings, and he wanted to extend this uniform to all the infantry in the country, Flemish Walloons and Italians included, probably with different facings.[33]

This decision represents an almost unique case, since in the Iberian Peninsula the infantry wore multi-coloured uniforms, while in the Low Countries the governor extended almost complete uniformity to the troops under his command. He also insisted on dressing the soldiers regularly, and

---

33 *London Gazette*, May–June 1671: 'His Excellence (Count of Monterrey) hath since his arrival caused the Grey coats he had ordered to be here made, to be distributed to among the Spanish Regiments, and the like are preparing for the rest of the army … His Excellence has given directions for the making of four thousand grey Coats, lined with Red, for the clothing of the Spanish Regiments.' Thanks to Edwin Groot for this note.

therefore a new coat with breeches, stockings and headgear had to be issued to the soldier at the beginning of the campaign. In the 1680s, governors and Crown learned that this factor had a significant influence on recruits, since these uniforms were also an important hook for soldiers, especially for the younger ones.[34] Furthermore, the distribution of distinctive clothing served to limit the desertions, or at least facilitate the capture of fugitives. Proof of this is that one time the provision came into force, in 1665, the local authorities managed to capture 11 deserters from the provincial *tercio* of Madrid, since knowing the distinctive colour of the unit, the authorities were able to quickly find the fugitives.[35]

A similar event occurred in 1687 in Naples, when a soldier who had deserted from a garrison in Abruzzo had been identified because he still wore the *turchino* (azure-blue) coat of the Italian infantry.[36] As early as the second half of the 1670s, the sources refer that the different nations of the army each received their own distinctive colour. In Naples and Lombardy, the Spanish infantry wore red, while the Italians were dressed in blue, and the German usually were in grey. In the Low Countries and Spain, the colours followed a different pattern, since the German infantrymen usually distinguished themselves by the blue coats.[37] In the Iberian Peninsula there was a much greater variety, however the soldiers of the British Isles were distinguished by a specific colour: red for the Irish, blue for the English, and yellow for the Scots. In the same period, the Catalans wore red, while the infantry from Valencia were in blue.[38] This tradition continued to be respected, albeit with some exceptions, considering that the availability of fabrics in large quantities did not always exist. The shades of the clothes to be manufactured were therefore subject to some variation, and even to an outright change of colour, as seems to have happened in Naples in 1687. The local intendancy requested the supply of 2,000 infantry uniforms, of which 1,000 were red, 800 in English cloth (probably grey kersey) and another 200 in *violetto* (purple-violet).[39] According to the contemporary *Avvisi* of Naples, the redcoats were destined for the Spaniards, while the violet was to be issued to the Italians.

The involvement of the government authorities in the field of uniforms for soldiers became an increasingly onerous and difficult task to manage as the army increased its strength, such as occurred between 1673 and 1674,

---

34 AGS, *Guerra Antigua*, leg. 2509. War Council dated 14 May 1681: 'As for this item (the uniform), it is of the utmost necessity, since the nudity of the soldiers is often great, and the main goal is to give them the dress and with it the daily relief which prevents many inconveniences.'

35 Rodríguez Hernández, *La evolución del vestuario militar*, pp.186–187.

36 ASV, *Segreteria* 1026, *Avvisi, Avvisi di Napoli*, 13 September 1687.

37 AGS, *Estado*, leg. 3428, *Regimiento Aleman Ulbin*,1682 (EI–214) 'the Colonel is obliged to dress the Regiment every two years, giving each soldier a *marsina* (coat) of good blue cloth with good red lining, red cloth breeches, stockings, shoes, hat, shirt, tie, bandolier with ammunitions, and baldric.'

38 On 5 September 1677 the *Cortes* of Aragon approved that 'since the soldiers have to dress at the expense of the Kingdom (of Aragon), both the *tercios* have to be dressed in blue, which is the colour that this Kingdom has used for the Horse Guards and infantry, and for this colour they are better known in the King's army'; in Sorando Muzas and Manzano Lahoz, *El tercio de Aragón*, p.156.

39 *Ibid.*

A firing squad scene with cavalry and infantry, Neapolitan school (possibly a follower of Carlo Coppola) 1675–80 (private collection). The painting is very realistic and offers many interesting details on the Hispanic soldiers' dress of this age. The cavalry on the left in the foreground wears the classic heavy cavalry buff coat with breastplate and helmet. The horseman with the plumed helmet (red and white), probably a corporal, carries the same equipment as the private trooper, carbine included. Iron headdresses are closer to a morion rather than a lobster helmet. It is difficult to establish if this is artistic license or an actual feature. All the horsemen wear red scarves around their waists. With them, a trumpeter wears a fashionable dark blue coat laced in white-red. In the centre, on the opposite side, another cavalry troop observes the scene with an officer wearing breastplate, pauldrons and oversized red plume on the helmet. Further to the left, in the background, another armoured officer stands before a group of infantrymen all wearing grey coats. Private soldiers and NCOs are mainly uniformed in grey, but some musketeers wear red coats. There are also a couple of drummers in azure-blue. Note on the right in the foreground, the two convicted soldiers throwing dice to save one of them from the death sentence: a cruel practice often offered in this age as a disciplinary measure. They are facing this dramatic trial before the *capitán de campaña* wearing a yellow coat (a buff coat?), while two of his men, of which one wearing a blue-grey short coat, medium brown breeches and red stockings, are surveying the convicted soldiers. All the infantry coats have cuffs, but of a small size, while the cavalry buff coats have plain sleeves. On the extreme right, a red-yellow striped ensign with red *aspa de Borgoña* confirms these troops are the Monarchy's soldiers..

Particular from *Le Nozze Festive*, printed in Naples and illustrating the celebration for the royal wedding of 1680. Note the lifeguard company (left) with breastplates and iron helmets. (Author's archive)

and again in 1688. This period dates the introduction of a codified uniform regulations within the Spanish infantry and cavalry.[40] The government faced this considerable effort by turning to *asientistas* and private contractors. Once the orders were received, everything had to be organised according to the instructions attached to the samples. The commission sought to obtain robust hard-wearing clothes in order to improve the quality and longevity of the uniforms. In the 1670s, not only the uniform, but also the equipment began to be more and more homogeneous, and the cavalry and dragoons also expanded their clothing with increasingly standardised accessories. In this decade, the distinction between *coraceros* and *jinetes* begins to disappear and the cavalry usually wore their clothes with coats like the infantry.

Only the officers retained the armour as a distinction for their rank, usually a classic corselet with front and back plates. With them, the heavy lifeguard cavalry companies continued to carry breastplate and iron protection for the head until the 1690s, usually a lobster helm. In this regard, in the painting of Françoise Duchatel (1625–1694) depicting the celebration for Carlos II in the *Vrijdagmarkt* of Ghent in 1666, there is a company of heavy horsemen wearing yellow, natural leather buff coats and white metal armour; some have lobster helms and others just pale-coloured broad-brimmed hats with white plumes. They also have dark pink waist scarves, and their officer is wearing a similar armour but with pauldrons and half-arm iron protection. On the opposite side, another cavalry company is dressed in red coats and cloaks. In all likelihood, these horsemen belong to the Governor's lifeguard, the former troops could be the *compañía de coraceros de la guarda del Gobernador General*, and the latter the corresponding *compañía de arquebuceros*. There are some direct or written testimonies about the clothing of lifeguards from different kingdoms. Heavy cavalry units were to be similar to the

---

40   Rodríguez Hernández, 'Guerra y alianzas en la lucha por la hegemonía europea', p.260.

horsemen depicted by Duchatel in the *Vrijdagmarkt* of Ghent, while others are mentioned wearing *mantillas*, or *capotillos*, of blue cloth in Aragon, red in Catalonia, or yellow with red facings, like Don Juan of Austria's *Guardias* in 1663.[41]

A dress similar to the heavy cavalrymen in the Duchatel's painting is depicted in a Neapolitan print dating 1666.[42] The Governor's lifeguards wear corselets with pauldrons and gauntlets, and their appearance is very similar to that depicted by the Neapolitan artist Carlo Coppola in some of his paintings, except for the headdress, which was a plumed broad-brimmed hat. Dress for this kind of units seems to undergo little change throughout the years. In January 1680, in another Neapolitan print representing the celebrations for the royal wedding, the heavy cavalrymen escorting the Viceroy are wearing the same dress of the *coraceros* depicted 17 years before by Duchatel.[43] Some companies were distinguished by their horse, such as the *coraceros* of the governor of the Spanish Low Countries who rode bay horses, while the *arquebuceros* had grey mounts.

Unlike infantry, who were moving towards differentiating the nationality of units by a specific colour in the 1680s, cavalry appears wearing grey almost everywhere, at least on the basis of the information we have today. In just a few cases, there are records indicating Spanish *trozos* wearing blue, or in red as did the aforementioned Catalan horsemen in 1659. The use of grey uniforms is confirmed in at least a few cases, both from the army of

---

41 Luis de Meneses, Conde de Ericeyra, *Historia de Portugal Restaurado* (Lisbon, 1679), vol. II, p.531.

42 The print celebrates the arrival of the Spanish Viceroy Pedro Antonio de Aragón, Duke of Segorbe and Cardona, preserved in a private collection in Florence.

43 Print of the *Cavalcata Reale*, by Domenico Antonio Parrino, in Anne Brown Collection, Brown University Library, Providence (RI).

An Exact LIST of the Royal Confederate Army in Flanders, Commanded by the King of Great-Britain. In Four Lines ; As it was Drawn up at Gerpines-Camp, July 27. 1691.
With the different Colours of Cloathing, by which each Regiment is distinguished.

Horse and Foot Regiments, of the Left Wing of the First Line.

Names of their Country.	Names and Commanders of the Regiments.	Colours of the Soldiers Cloaths.
Dutch Horse	Tilly	White lined red
Dutch Horse	Flodont	White lined red
Dutch Foot	Frisome	White lined white
German Horse	Charnet	White lined red
Lunenburgh Horse	Darmstadt	White lined red
Lunenburgh Foot	Deduin	Blew lined red
German Horse	Dampset	White lined blew
German Horse	Lippe-Zell	White lined red
Brandenburg Foot	Pr. of Brandenburg	Blew lined red
Dutch Horse	Stein	White lined red
Dutch Horse	Count Nassau	White lined red
Sarbrug		
Dutch Horse	Prince of Frize	Blew lined red
Dutch Horse	Huybert	White lined red
Brandenburg Foot	Deffinges	White lined red
Dutch Horse	Huybert	White lined red
German Horse	Wirtemberg	White lined blew
German Horse	Saxen Aedelburg	White lined Green
Hess Foot	Swerine	Blew lined red
German Horse	Heydelburg	White lined Green
Brandenburg Horse	Spaen	White lined blew
Dutch Horse	Tilly	White lined red
Hess Foot	Swerine	White lined red
Dutch Foot	Rhingrave	White lined white
Dutch Foot	L' Ecluse	White lined red
Lunenburg Foot	Sibirg	Red lined green
Dutch Foot	Schmelpenning	White lined white
Lunenburgh Foot	Bemar	Red lined green
Lunenburgh Foot	Holl	Blew lined red
Brandenburgh Foot	Bois David	White lined red
Dutch Foot	Count Horne	White lined red
Dutch Foot	Prince Waldeck.	Red lined red.

Horse and Foot Regiments, of the Right Wing of the First Line.

Names of their Country	Names and Commanders of the Regiment.	Colours of the Soldiers Cloaths.
Horse Granadiers		
Troop of English Guards } Duke of Ormond		} Red lined white.
Troop of Dutch Guards }		
Spanish Horse	Castinaga's Guard	Red lined white.
Spanish Horse	Pr. Vaudemont's Guard	Red lined red.
Spanish Horse	Marquess de Grigny's	Red lined red.
Spanish Dragoons	Wodimont	White lined white.
Brandenburg Foot	Guards of Brandenburg	Blue lined red.
Spanish Horse	Betancour	White lined red.
Spanish Horse	Maskay	White lined red.
Brandenburg Foot	Prince Philips	Blue lined red.
Spanish Horse	Hartman	White lined red.
Spanish Horse	Prince Lorraine	White lined red.
Spanish Horse	Vaissine	White lined red.
Brandenburg Foot	Prince of Brandenburg	Blue lined red.
Spanish Horse	Statenberg	White lined red.
Spanish Horse	Cordova	White linen red.
Hess Foot	Skenck	Blue lined red.
Brandenburg Horse	Lutwitch	White lined green.
Hess Foot	Kelder	Blue lined red.
Hess Horse	Spinola	White lined red.
Brandenburg Horse	Dorfinger	White lined red.
Hess Foot	Rottendorf	Blue lined red.
Hess Horse	Kersendorf	White lined red.
Brandenburg Horse	Prince of Brandenburg	Blue lined white.
Brandenburg Horse	Grand Musqueteers	
English Foot	1. Regiment of Guards	Red lined blue.
English Foot	2. Regiment of Guards	Red lined yellow.
Dutch Foot	1st. Battalia of Guards	Blue
English Fusileers	Marlborough	Red lined yellow.
English Foot	Bath	Blue lined red.
English Foot	Hodges	Red lined white.
English Foot	Fitz-Patrick	Red lined green.
Dutch Foot	Delwick	Red lined blue.
Dutch Foot	Sable	White lined green.
Dutch Foot	Wynbergen	White lined green.

Left Wing of the Second Line.

Names of their Country	Names and Commanders of the Regiments.	Colours of the Soldiers Cloaths.
Dutch Horse	Count Nassau	White lined red
Wellburg Horse		White lined red
Dutch Horse	Reytreich	White lined green
German Horse	Saxen Gotham	White lined red
German Horse	Brenneck	White lined blue
Dutch Horse	Warfort	White lined red
Dutch Horse	Count Nassau	White lined white
Sarbrug		White lined red
Dutch Horse	Friez	White lined white
Dutch Horse	Lippe	White lined red
Dutch Horse	Teeburg	White
Dutch Horse	Ittesum	White lined blue
Dutch Foot	Pr. of Birkenfelt	White lined red
Dutch Foot	Pr. of Frietland	
Dutch Horse	Opdam	White lined red
Lunenburgh Horse	Briquemault	White lined red
Lunenburgh Horse	Neylburg	White lined green
Lunenburgh Horse.	Walfenbuttle.	White lined blue.

Right Wing of the Second Line.

Names of their Country.	Names and Commanders of the Regiments.	Colours of the Soldiers Cloaths.
Spanish Horse	du Puy	White lined red
Spanish Horse	Brancaccio	White lined blue
Spanish Horse	Don Augustine	White lined red
Spanish Horse	Sinocle	White lined white
Spanish Horse	Spinosa	White lined red
Spanish Horse	Pignatelli	White lined green
Hess Horse	Spiegle	White lined red
Brandenburg Dragoons	Hamal	Blue lined red
Brandenburg Horse	Guards of Brandenburg	White lined blue
Scots Foot	Scots Guards	Red lined white
Scots Foot	Douglass	Red lined white
Scots Foot	Mackey	Red lined red
Scots Foot	Ramsey	Red lined white
Scots Foot	Offarrel Fusileers	Red lined red
Scots Foot	Angus	Red lined white
Dutch Foot	Slangenburg	Red lined red
Dutch Foot	Tway	Red lined blue
Dutch Foot	Noyelle	White lined red
Dutch Foot	Salis	White lined red
Lunenburg Foot	Dalberg	Red lined green
Sweeds Foot	Louvenshop	Blue lined yellow
Dutch Foot	Fagel	Red lined yellow
Dutch Foot	Du Tell	White lined blue.

Horse and Dragoons, 184 Squadrons, each Squadron consisting of 120 Men ——— In all 22080
Foot, 83 Battallions, each Battallion consisting of 800 Men ——————— In all 66400

Total of Horse, Foot, and Dragoons   88480

Printed at London, and Re-Printed at Edinburgh, by the Heir of Andrew Anderson, Printer to Their most Excellent Majesties, 1691.

Page from the *Exact List of the Royal Confederate Army in Flanders, Commanded by the King of Great Britain. In Four Lines; As it was Drawn up at Gerpines Camp, 27 July 1691*. This and the *List of Our Army as it was drawn up at Tillroy Camp* of 1689, contains the description of the uniform of the allied army in Flanders, including some details concerning the Hispanic cavalry.

Flanders in late 1689 and 1691.[44] This dress was similar to that introduced by the Dutch cavalry during the same period.[45]

In Italy, the cavalry of Naples is recorded wearing coats of *pavonazzo* (turquoise?) in 1685, when all the troops quartered in the capital received new clothing on the occasion of the King's birthday.[46] It is very likely that the distribution of uniforms of distinctive colours was the continuation of a process that had already commenced in the previous decade. Unlike the cavalry, since the 1670s dragoons retained more colourful uniforms. In the next decade, the *tercio* of the Spanish dragoons of Milan (ED–8) is well documented in the drawing of an eyewitness who accompanied the Venetian army in Greece, which included Hispanic contingents from Milan and Naples.[47] Some dragoons are depicted wearing their yellow coat with red facings, the same distinctive colours of these units until the early eighteenth century. In the drawing, the dragoons wear pale-coloured broad-brimmed hats, instead of the bonnet or cap issued in Flanders. In several respects, cavalry followed the infantry in the matter of uniforms, which varied according to the territory they were from. In 1677, the administrative records of the Army of Catalonia refer to the distribution of coats manufactured with *pardo* cloth lined and faced in red.[48] In the next decade, the *trozos* of Milan, Osuna and Ordenes had grey coats, while Extremadura's wore azure blue.[49]

In the 1680s, more detailed regulations began to be introduced, and even the equipment was improved with new items. Proof of this is in the documentation preserved in the archives. In this regard, the *Archives Général du Royaume* in Brussels has a lot of well documented information going back as early as in the 1670s. The information is the accounting records relating the purchase of fabrics and accessories for the manufacture of the military uniforms, and therefore they are extremely reliable and accurate. In 1676, the dragoon *tercio* of Mathias Pérez (ED–6) received *justaucorps* of red cloth, with cuffs and lining of blue grey, white metal buttons, and blue bonnet, probably similar to the style worn by French dragoons.[50]

In 1683, the information becomes even more detailed. The coat remained of the same colour, but now it is specified that there are 72 white metal buttons, which suggests that each side could be closed with two rows of buttons when the dragoon served dismounted. As headgear, the dragoon retained the cap of blue-grey piped with 'fake silver', like the lanyards on the right shoulder of

---

44 *List of Our Army as it was drawn up at Tillroy Camp* (1689), in *A Journal of the late motions and actions of the Confederate Forces against the French, written by an English Officer who was there during the last campaign* (London, 1690); and *An Exact List of the Royal Confederate Army in Flanders Commanded by the K. of Great Britain in Four Lines as it was drawn up at Gerpines-Camp,* July 27. 1691.

45 Mugnai, *Wars and Soldiers in the Early Reign of Louis XIV* (Warwick: Helion & Company, 2019), vol. I, pp.187–198.

46 ASV, *Segreteria* 1026, *Avvisi, Avvisi di Napoli,* 6 November 1685. Note that in archaic Italian, the term *pavonazzo* means also lilac grey.

47 Biblioteca Nazionale Centrale di Firenze, *Codice Rossi-Cassigoli,* BNC 199, fol. 245.

48 Antonio José Rodríguez Hernández, 'La caballería hispánica, Un arma al alza', in 'Los Tercios, 1660–1704', *Desperta Ferro,* special issue XIX (June–July 2019), p.45.

49 AGS, *Estado,* leg. 1332, d. 55.

50 Cayron, *La véritable histoire de Jacques Pastur dit Jaco,* p.552.

Right: Equestrian portrait of Marquis Carlo IV Borromeo (1657–1734), unknown artist, Milan, 1678–1680 (private collection). Borromeo was one of the richest and most powerful patricians of Milan, as testified by the consistency of its feudal heritage, which included Arona, Vergante, Cannobio, Lesa, Vogogno, Val Vigezzo, Laveno, Omegna, Intra, Degagna di San Pietro, Angera, and again titles from Camairago, Borgo Ticino, Palestro, Cressa, Formigara, and Cesano Maderno. In 1678 he became captain of the Milanese cuirassiers, starting a career that always switched between politics, diplomacy and military engagement. In 1686 he was chosen by Carlos II of Spain as ambassador to Rome. Subsequently he was made governor of Novara and *maestro di campo* of the Milanese infantry.

Left: Private musketeer, German regiment Visconti (El-271), Greece, 1688. Ash-grey coat, dark blue breeches and stockings. The documents preserved in the Venice State Archive record details of the 'Spanish' infantry that in 1686 joined the Venetians in Greece and wore coats of grey cloth with different facing colours. In 1692, before returning to their state, Milanese troops were dressed by the Venetian government. The correspondence of the *Provveditori sopra le Camere* extensively deals with the problems encountered supplying the ash-coloured cloth 'not used by other parties', but the contract signed with the governor of Milan in 1685 forced the 'Most Serene Republic' to return the contingent fully dressed and equipped. (Author's reconstruction)

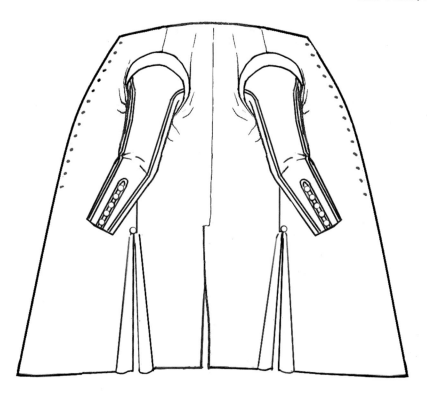

Left: Buff coat pattern after the portrait of Carlo IV Borromeo. The buff coat probably belonged to Borromeo's clothing as an officer of the Milanese heavy cavalry.

Right: Another portrait of Carlo IV Borromeo, dating 1680–82, wearing an elaborate blue coat lined and faced red with floral embroidery in silver and gold and red-white lace. Ribbons and bow are also in red and white. This is a good example of the late Spanish 'carlino style' in the version introduced in Italy in the last decades of the seventeenth century (see Plate P in the colour section).

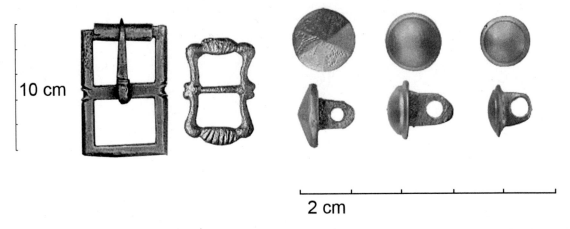

10 cm

2 cm

Brass buckles and buttons, Spain, 1660–1680. Fragments of armour, weapons, and military equipment such as small buckles, clothing, straps, accoutrements, harnesses and saddles have been recovered from settlements utilised by the explorers and early colonists in Spanish America. It is important to note that buttons and buckles were worn by soldiers and civilians alike. Often, particularly in the colonies, civilians and soldiers were one and the same. The above items were recovered from the cargo of two Spanish ships sunk off Saint Augustine in Florida, and probably were part of the military clothing and equipment destined for the local garrisons. Unlike buttons, which evolved through a series of stylistic changes relatively rapidly through time, buckles of the period remained largely unchanged in overall appearance and configuration in the seventeenth century. (Private collection, USA).

the coat. Musket and sword were carried on a bandolier and baldric of buff leather, a not insignificant detail, and the armament was completed with a bayonet. A red cloak lined blue completed the uniform of the dragoon.[51] The clothing and the equipment for the cavalry represented a considerable cost, because more items were provided compared to those issued to infantry. In 1692 a detailed list of these items distributed to the cavalry in Catalonia reports *casaca*, breeches, headgear, cravat, two shirts, stockings, boots and *mantilla* (cloak). The equipment included sword, two pistols, carbine as well as horse furniture.[52] The expense was clearly much greater than that necessary to dress and equip an infantryman, and this despite the absence of the waistcoat, and the disappearance of all armour such as a cuirass and helmet.

With regard to the armour, its use decreased considerably starting from the 1670s, although in some cases it was kept by a few units for a longer period. In the 1660s existing illustrations show that the cavalry in Flanders usually wore coats, especially of *pardo* cloth, or, more rarely, a natural leather coat devoid of metal protections. Apart from the companies of the governor's lifeguard already mentioned, several paintings, especially the ones of Italian provenance, show horsemen still equipped with the traditional leather kollet and metal breastplate in the 1670s. Some further clues suggest that a breastplate continued to be worn under the coat, however this was preferably only worn in action, or when combat was expected.

Although financial conditions were often volatile, the central government as well as the Kingdom's governors always tried to ensure good clothing and

---

51 AGR, Secreterie d'Etatt e de Guerre, n. 97: Compte du rehabillement fait au terce de dragons du M.re du Camp Mathias Perez, au mois de février mil six cent quatre vingt et trois dand la ville d'Ath.

52 ACA, Consejo, Memoira del gasto que se ofrece para vestir un soldado de caballeria, April 1692.

equipment for their soldiers. The Crown assumed its obligation to dress its troops, sending clothing from other places for this purpose, or arranging for the preparation of clothing and equipment in the garrisons or ports. This affected Castile as well as the other Spanish provinces. For instance, in 1667, for the production of 1,000 uniforms in Malaga, the Royal Treasury paid to dress the recruits gathered by the *asentista* Juan de Mendoza for Catalonia. In other cases, to save resources, the manufacturing was carried out in Madrid.[53] It was in this way that the 1,500 men that Juan de Miranda tried to recruit in Castile between 1670 and 1671 were dressed and equipped in a short time before being sent to Flanders.[54]

Recruits also received clothing when the nobility, the Church or some provinces committed themselves to finance the recruitment of troops, as frequently happened from 1667. Moreover, even when the kingdoms mobilised their troops, as was the case of the two *tercios* of Granada, the recruits received the necessary equipment and dress after they entered military service. The only exceptions to this rule were the *asientos* arranged in the Peninsula between 1660 and 1670, since the contracts usually provided that the Crown should take charge of dressing the recruits.[55] Only when the distance between the places of recruitment and the garrisons or boarding was considerable, the *asentistas* were obliged to issue stockings and shoes, so that the recruits could reach their destinations with adequate items.

In the 1670s the maximum expense for the clothing of each recruit was assessed in advance, and after that, the official in charge had to submit detailed accounts to the War Council, which could later be approved or not. The increase in costs was closely related to the need to improve the quality of the soldiers' clothing. Further increases in costs came after the decisions taken at the end of 1677, coinciding with the ministry of Don Juan of Austria, who, more than 10 years after the first changes with which he managed to improve the manufacturing of uniforms, he was now proceeding to introduce further plans.

Despite the commendable effort of dressing the soldiers, the quality – and durability – of the uniforms was often poor, especially if they were manufactured at the expense of the provinces, and for this reason, it needed to be replaced more frequently. The manufacture of uniforms also confronted the authorities with new kinds of problems. In 1664, two years after a first production of clothing for one infantry company recruited in Malaga, the excess cloth could not be used, because it was so moth-eaten that no one would pay a *real*, but when it was originally purchased, it cost 100 times more. However, clothing and equipment always had a basic intrinsic value, to the point that in the capitulations of garrisons and fortresses in Flanders

---

53 Rodríguez Hernández, 'La evolución del vestuario militar', p.184.

54 *Ibid.*, 'Although it does not seem that, in this case, this system managed to reduce costs, given that the expense for making and transporting this stuff amounted to 36,036 escudos, equal to 240 reales for each vestido, more than the treasury had paid for this kind of items on previous occasions.'

55 AGS, Guerra Antigua, leg. 2323, Consulta del Consejo de Guerra dated 18 May 1665: Conditions proposed by Juan de Miranda and AGS, Guerra Antigua, leg. 2084; Consulta del Consejo de Guerra dated 3 May 1675.

in the 1660s and 1670s it was customary to specify that life, clothing and weapons of the soldiers would be respected, when what usually occurred was that the winners kept everything they could lay their hands on of value. While military equipment and clothing were regarded as legitimate loot among soldiers of opposite sides, they could even be stolen by the troops of the same army. For example, in 1661, in Extremadura, a company of newly recruited soldiers from Madrid was unclothed by some cavalrymen, since they had not been paid for several months.[56] It is therefore not surprising that the reports sent by the officers serving in Extremadura warned that the new arrivals had joined the army practically naked.

On 25 July 1668, a regulation was published in Spain establishing the subsistence payments to soldiers. The principle that officers were responsible for clothing and equipping their men was maintained. Therefore, they had to ensure that everything was in good condition 'as honour and good manners require' and to ensure that soldiers were equipped and provided with weapons and horses, as well as military clothing, including boots, shoes and other necessities. Samples of these items were established, and officers kept alert to the most serious violations. In cases of negligence, soldiers were held accountable and had to repay any damage or loss to the officer of the company in which they served.[57]

These directions were reiterated in the same terms 10 years later. This implied, on one hand, some consistency in the system but also that there were some difficulties in its application. The result was far from complete uniformity, because, for obvious reasons, certain differences could still be found between units, above all, between those from the different domains of the Monarchy. A further step was taken when the Royal treasury, aware that the Spanish provinces were unable to dress their recruits or pay for their equipment, it intervened by subsidising these costs. This measure was similar to the system introduced in the Dutch Republic after the mid seventeenth century. This aid became most evident from 1679, although the quantities delivered varied greatly from one province to another. The Crown's initiative was aimed at standardising the clothing of troops, and this has most in common with similar policies carried out five years earlier in France. However, the imposition of a standardised uniform and equipment in every one of the Spanish domains actually began in the 1680s.[58]

The advances in funding the issue of military clothing had a positive impact on rationalising spending and on streamlining logistics, as it allowed uniforms to be made in advance, through an orderly and more convenient system. This was very important to ensure the smooth functioning of the army, above all because it limited the diffusion of resources and discouraged fraud. The first procedures introduced were very simple. The items to be supplied were summarily described and accompanied by samples, although in most cases leather work, cloth and lining were given more detailed specifications. Then, the contracts were entrusted to the factories that had

---

56 Rodríguez Hernández, 'La evolución del vestuario militar', p.184.
57 Lierneux, 'El uniforme militar en los Países Bajos españoles', p.113.
58 *Ibid.*, p.135.

presented the most appropriate offers. The technical characteristics proposed for the soldiers' clothing were basic, and the sizes and qualities of the first uniforms were not always specified down to the smallest detail, which gave the tailors a certain amount of freedom in the production process.

At this point, the *corregidores*, or commissioners depending on the location, in charge of supervising the movement of the recruits, had to certify whether the men had received equipment and clothing that conformed to what was contracted for, sometimes reusing surplus material from previous orders. When the suppliers failed and the troops did not receive adequate clothing, the state's official in charge of this had to explain the reasons to the War Council and also try to remedy the fault. Thus, in 1668, the president of the Royal Chancellery of Valladolid had to justify why the first group of recruits he had sent to Galicia for embarkation to Flanders went, according to the reports sent from La Coruña 'only with a shirt ... and the *hungarinas* were not lined as established in the contract.'[59] In his defence, the president sent to Madrid the copy of the certified muster of the company, specifying that the recruits had left Valladolid dressed from head to toe; although, he recognised, 'instead of cravat they wore only a handkerchief around the neck.' He also added that the losses of clothing had occurred during the transfer, as many soldiers had either sold their clothes, or had not taken proper care, so they were irreparably damaged. He also indicated that the textile used was the same as always, cloth of Brihuega, bought at a good price, despite the general increase in production costs.[60] The president concluded his letter by promising that the next company departing from Valladolid would be dressed in fully lined coats and breeches of the best quality cotton and wool, along with two shirts and two cravats, as stipulated in the contracts.

The magistrates also had to check the quality of the fabrics used for manufacturing the uniforms and this is another aspect that reveals the complexity of their work, given the continuous development of clothing distributed to the recruits. In these circumstances, it was not uncommon to find some *corregidores* who indicated in their correspondence with the military authorities the results obtained in this regard, particularly if the coats were made with better fabrics and at a reasonable price. For example, in 1674, the *corregidor* of the city of Toledo warned that he had been able to obtain good quality clothing by paying 210 *reales* in cash for each uniform, sword, shoes and headgear, 'and all the soldiers were happy.'[61] The cloth was certainly better, because as the magistrate wrote in his letter, 'it was what the lackeys wore, a *catorceno* that, although not excellent, was of more than acceptable quality for the manufacture of soldier's uniforms.'

The manufacture of uniforms was concentrated in some places on the Peninsula, such as Madrid, Valladolid, Santiago de Compostela and other towns in Galicia, where there was a high concentration of woollen mills

59 AGS, *Guerra Antigua*, leg. 2190, *Cartas de Luis de Varona*, President of the Chancellery of Valladolid.
60 *Ibid*. Each uniform cost about 170 *reales*, and for that price, as the president wrote, 'it was impossible to buy higher quality fabrics, like the one produced in Segovia.'
61 Rodríguez Hernández, 'La evolución del vestuario militar', p.188.

Above: Detail of the hilt of an officer's sword; Spain, second half of the seventeenth century. (Collection of the *Musée de l'Armée*, Paris)

as well as hat manufacturers. Further production centres were located in central regions, although the quality was not always as good. In the 1670s, Madrid and Galicia entered into competition in the management of military clothing and equipment. From the middle of the 1670s, Madrid also began to meet the demands across the whole Iberian Peninsula, due to the fact that in some territories there was a lack of goods, or they were priced too highly. In Italy, both Milan and Naples produced clothing to satisfy the demand of uniforms in their respective domains, and Brussels, with Antwerp to the same extent,[62] did likewise in the Spanish Low Countries. The growing demand for military clothing also encouraged the birth of private companies owned by foreign tradesman for manufacturing uniforms. In La Coruña, in the 1680s, there were entrepreneurs from Hamburg, Ireland and the United Provinces who were in charge of providing fine cloths like damask, *cariseas*, *bombaz*, gauzes and canvas, from England, Flanders and France, as well as the rough and strong cloths required for military uniforms. Although able to supply themselves from overseas, foreign entrepreneurs were not always able to meet the demands, and in some case they provided poor quality items.

In 1673, clothing and equipment destined for the recruits sent to Flanders proved to be very bad. The broad-brimmed hats had been manufactured in Galicia, while the coats were of bad fabric lined with grey from Palencia or England; swords came from Castile and Vizcaya, 'stockings were from English frison and cravats from French canvas of Morles', but the result was so poor that the recruits had to be newly dressed at Ostend.[63] Six years later, Galicia offered the recruitment of a *tercio* for the Army of Flanders, paid for and dressed by the province, although in the end, the dress of the 1,235 soldiers was paid for by the Crown. As had occurred before, the difficulties concerning the provision of military clothing remained unresolved and continued in subsequent years.

In 1680, out of 340 soldiers recruited in Galicia, almost half of them left Spain without uniforms and equipment. The solution was to send money for each soldier, so that they would be uniformed in the Low Countries. In some peripheral regions or in the islands there were also difficulties in supplying military clothing to the recruits. In Mallorca, for example, due to the difficulty in the appointment of *asientos*, the solution was to give seven silver *escudos* to each recruit to equip themselves. In the Canary Islands it was also difficult to provide the recruits with regular clothing as the items, generally of English origin, had to be imported.

62 Lierneux, 'El uniforme militar en los Países Bajos españoles', p.100.
63 Rodríguez Hernández, 'La evolución del vestuario militar', p.192.

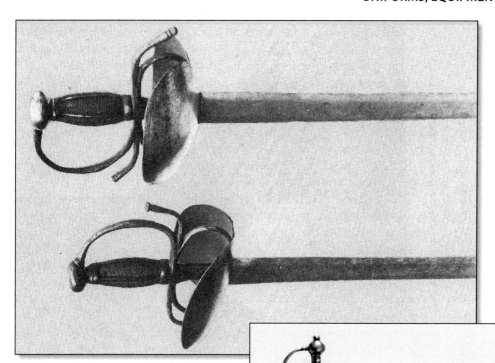

Above: Walloon-style swords for private cavalrymen, Flanders 1680s. (Private collection, Milan)

Right: Officer's sword, Spain, last quarter of the seventeenth century (private collection, Milan). A fine example of sword with a double-edged blade manufactured in Toledo. Riveted bell with a pronounced edge, cut iron knuckle-bow hilt with fish scales-covered grip and slightly compressed and riveted ball knob. Length 102 cm.

Not surprisingly, the uniforms continued to be a problem and irregularities did not disappear until the end of the century, notwithstanding the effort of the Crown and local authorities. To reduce the problem the instructions given to *corregidores*, chancellery presidents, and other officials became ever clearer. In the early 1670s, the provinces had to ensure that the necessary clothing, and complete equipment, were distributed to the recruits, specifying every single item supplied. Likewise, they also had to account for the deliveries made to the men once they arrived at their destinations, indicating that each recruit had been controlled and supervised following an administrative system that was very advanced for the time.

The main difficulty in this complex process was the lack of money, which locally had a direct impact on clothing requirements. The government in Madrid tried to remedy this situation by sending funds, so that the soldiers were properly dressed and equipped. Thanks to these efforts, the troops departed from the recruitment areas dressed more or less regularly and retained the full issue of equipment and clothing even when they were sent out of the peninsula. Several times economic shortages led to the opposite outcome. Such an episode occurred in 1666, when an infantry company destined for Flanders was recruited in Castile under the direct supervision of the local *corregidor*. The first troops that left the city were regularly dressed, but then, when the funds were exhausted, the next recruits arrived in San Sebastián without clothing, which had to be purchased in the town.[64] All these reforms aimed to introduce significant improvement in the equipment and clothing of the soldiers, while causing an increase in expenditure, which would then be controlled by the *Comisaría* and *Contadoría General*. In order to establish a standard level, complete uniform samples were made in Madrid, specifying the colours of each, and sent to the local authorities so they could take note. The Royal Treasury also set a guide price.[65] In the following years this policy was maintained, which meant that the Crown considered that uniforms were an important matter. Military clothing held a fascination that could be exploited to encourage voluntary enlistment. Hence, by 1666, when the Viceroy of Naples needed soldiers for the garrisons in Southern Italy, but he had no royal authority to recruit, he sent a captain to Spain with some *vestidos*, and taking advantage of the galley's journey, he tried to enlist men irregularly in the Mediterranean ports en route.[66] The results seemed to outweigh the costs, even if in order not to excessively increase the expense, the uniforms had to be manufactured where good fabric and an acceptable price could be obtained.[67]

However, despite having received all the necessary clothing and equipped according to the regulations, the troops that departed from Spain and arrived

64 *Ibid.*, p.190.
65 AGS, *Guerra Antigua*, leg. 2395; *Carta de Melchor Portocarrero, Comisario General*, Madrid, 12 January 1678; the established price was 345 *reales*.
66 Rodríguez Hernández, 'La evolución del vestuario military', p.182.
67 *Ibid.*, p.192. 'In 1677 it was estimated that recruiting a company of 100 men would cost about 7,000 *escudos*, and nearly 60 percent was spent on the soldiers' clothing and equipment. This amount that contrasts with the fact that, between 1670 and 1676, raising an infantry company cost no more than 4,000 *escudos*.'

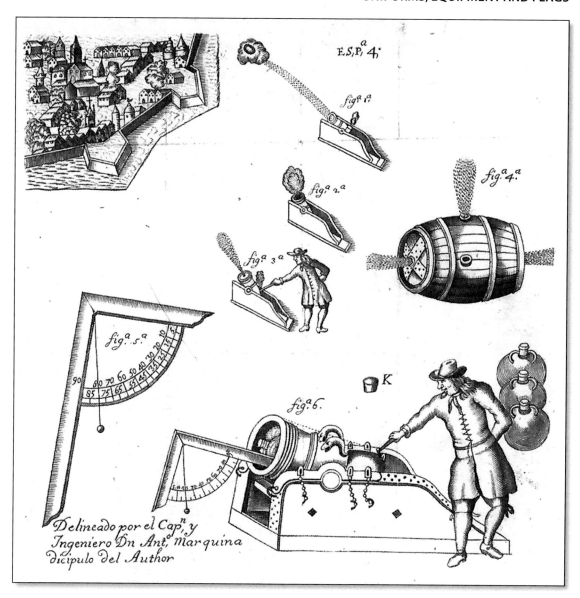

Print after *El perfecto bombardero y pratico artificial*, by Sebastián Fernández de Medrano, published in 1691, illustrating the mortars and explosive weapons devised by the author. This is one of the few sources illustrating Spanish artillerymen of the last quarter of the seventeenth century. While the figure in the centre wears a coat with plain sleeves (a waistcoat?), the artilleryman to the right seems to be dressed in a buff coat, as suggested by the zig-zag pattern on the breast. Little is known about the artillery uniform of the Hispanic armies in this age, but probably the Spanish private gunners wore the same colour of the infantry – grey in Flanders and red in Italy – while the Italian artillerymen possibly had blue coats in Milan and Naples.

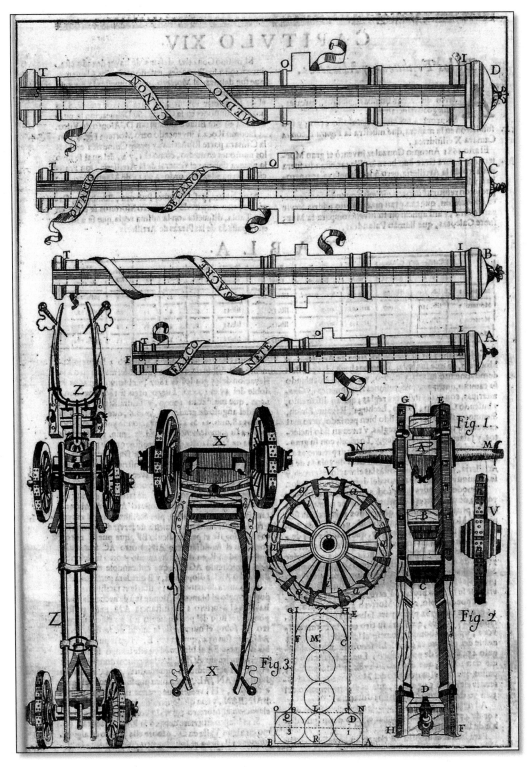

Guns and artillery carriages, after Medrano's *El perfecto bombardero y pratico artificial*. Contemporary images show the Spanish artillery limbers and carriages unpainted.

in Flanders or Italy often had to be reissued new uniforms and equipment, which generated new administrative expenses. According to the report of the *veedores* of the Army of Flanders, written in the autumn of 1677, the clothing distributed to the Spanish troops from Galicia and Asturias was so bad that it aroused the laughter of civilians.[68] The same critical issue often happened with all the troops coming from afar, such as the Italians. This drawback also distressed the soldiers of isolated garrisons, such as those of the *Estado de los Presidios* who, in 1689, 'had been found naked'.[69]

All these factors forced the Madrid government to issue new instructions so that this situation would never happen again. The authorities of the Low Countries were reluctant to anticipate money for the soldiers' clothing, but in Madrid the War Council were urged that recruits must not march without proper equipment and clothing, as well as deciding what the soldiers had to wear while it was being made. For some time, this policy was not interrupted, which meant that the authorities of the Spanish Low Countries accepted the idea that clothing was an incentive for voluntary enlistment and also reduced desertion.

A problem that was becoming a major evil for the Hispanic armies, in the Iberian Peninsula, where the temptation to flee was encouraged by the continuous arrears in the payment of wages and, obviously, for the proximity to their homes. Don Juan of Austria said of the deserters that they were 'people whose profession is to go around Spain selling clothes and provisions to the places where they were recruited'.[70] In Spain they were called *tornilleros*, individuals who supported themselves with the war without ever having taken part and who, in many cases, enlisted up to two times a year to receive the bounty offered, together with the clothing. They then fled as soon as was prudent with the intention of reselling their uniforms and equipment to obtain a profit. This was a practice that the Crown tried to eliminate, but which could in practice it could not be stamped out. The sufferings of the soldiers were certainly recognised, and they often deserted out of necessity, but the activities of the *tornilleros* generated enormous additional expense and caused great damage to the reputation of the armies of the Monarchy.[71]

In 1677, a new role given to the *corregidores,* and other officials was to prevent the recruits from deserting, especially after they had received their bounty, clothing and equipment. Severe sentences were given to captured deserters, and many were hanged while others were sentenced to North African jails or to the oars of the galleys. Likewise, whoever hid them was also charged. However,despite these measures, the best remedy to avoid desertion was found to be to provide the soldiers with decent clothing and regular pay. Even so, this solution was not easy to implement, as evidenced

---

68 AGS, *Guerra Antigua*, leg. 2393, letter of Pedro de Oreytia, in Brussels, September 1677. The recruits were in such a bad state that when they disembarked many of them were almost naked due to the poor quality of their clothes. According to the report, the civilians welcomed them as *la risa de las naciones* (the laughter of the nations).

69 ASNa, *Scrivania di Razione e Ruota dei Conti*, f. 9, 4 March 1689.

70 Rodríguez Hernández, 'La evolución del vestuario military', p.194.

71 Clonard, *Historia orgánica*, vol. IV, p.421.

by the difficulties in eliminating the desertion of the recruits once they had received their uniforms after enlisting. Even though the uniform incentive was the best way to recruit volunteers and re-enlist veterans, the government was always forced to weigh the outcome between costs and benefits. Therefore, every winter soldiers who had deserted the previous year arrived in Castile, with the intention of obtaining new engagement bounties and clothing. Sometimes these recruits were recognised and arrested by local authorities for the simple fact of wearing suspicious or uniform-like clothing. However, instead of being sent to punitive destinations, such as North Africa, or sentenced to the galleys, they were still re-enlisted to save the costs of imprisonment and transfer. Moreover, it was too difficult to identify the people who actually resorted to this stratagem in the absence of a reliable registration system of the population, and therefore these frauds continued into the following century.

The process of establishing a uniform in the modern sense came to a halt in the following decade due to the government's policy of enforced reductions in spending. Economic hardship also affected soldiers' clothing. The Count of Mérode-Westerloo wrote in his *Memoires* that 'at the end of the century there were in the (Low) Country eighteen miserable infantry regiments and 14 of cavalry and dragoons: six thousand beggars and thieves overall, for which there was no money to pay them three times a year, and that they were never properly dressed.'[72]

Ensigns and Standards

The traditional Spanish symbol, the red *Aspa de Borgoña* (Burgundy cross) on white background, has been adopted in Spanish flags since 1506, when it was introduced in opposition to the Armagnac white cross used by the French army in Italy. Under Felipe II, the infantry flags began to change the colour of the background. Usually, the *aspa* appears on a red or yellow background, and, in fact, alongside the white background, these three colours predominated. During the reign of Felipe II, the term *bandera* (flag) began to be synonymous of company and, around 1560, the flag with the Cross of Burgundy was already used by all the Royal *tercios* becoming the distinctive emblem of the infantry of all Hispanic armies.

Today, the red Burgundian cross appears in the coat of arms of the Spanish ruling house as well as in various military ensigns. Though the first ensign were very simple, during the sixteenth and seventeenth centuries, colours and design of the ensign varied considerably, but the red Burgundy cross remained with few exceptions, the main symbol on the military ensigns of infantry as well as cavalry. In the seventeenth century, the backgrounds became more varied and colourful. Examples of these designs are preserved thanks to the images painted by the artists when portraying battles in their

---

72 Jean-Philippe Eugène Mérode-Westerloo, *Mémoires du feld-maréchal comte de Mérode-Westerloo* (Brussels, 1840), vol. 1, p.193.

Left: Reconstruction of the standard belonging to the *Los Órdenes* cavalry *trozo* (EC-5) in the 1660s, after *La heráldica y la orgánica de los Reales Ejércitos*, by Jesús Martínez de Merlo and Juan Álvarez Abeilhé. Scarlet red background with crimson red *aspa de Borgoña*; silver fringes and embroidery. Crosses of the Orders, clockwise: Santiago (crimson-red), Alcantara (light-green), Montesa (black and red) Calatrava (crimson-red). According to further modern reconstructions, the *Guardias Viejas de Castilla* (EC-65) had green standards with a black double-headed eagle carrying the King's coat of arms on the breast.

Right: Cavalry standard lost at Neerwinden in 1693, probably belonging to the Flemish Walloon *tercio Du Puy* (EC-57): red background with red Burgundian cross; gold fringes, crowns, monograms and golden fleece. (*Les Triomphes de Louis XIV*, Bibliothèque nationale de France, Paris)

Ensign of an unknown infantry company from Aragon, 1680–90. The original was preserved in the *Armería Real* of Madrid, but it was unfortunately lost in the fire that occurred on 9 July 1884. Drawing and pattern is known thanks to a sketch preserved in the collection of the *Servicio Histórico Militar*. The red cross is without the usual nodes, and the colour of the field are white,-yellow-dark blue: the centre is the coat of arms of Aragon. Similar ensigns were captured by the French at the Battle of Ter in 1693, of which one is represented in colour plate O in this work. (Author's drawing)

paintings. An example can be seen in Vicente Carducho's paintings 'Victory of Fleurs' of 1634, or in one of the most famous Velázquez's painting 'The Surrender of Breda' dated between 1634 and 1635 where the flags with the Cross of Burgundy are clearly visible. In the second half of the seventeenth century, Felipe IV ordered that the flags of *tercios* and companies were to be the same: red with an image of the Virgin Mary, but the older traditional patterns did not disappear, and these older-style infantry ensigns continued to be used: red, white, striped and chequered, but always with the *aspa de Borgoña*, as can be seen in many contemporary illustrations.

Most of the current knowledge on Spanish insignia in the last quarter of the seventeenth century comes from sources preserved in France, like the famous *Triomphes de Louis XIV*. It is difficult to establish a match between the numerous flags reproduced in this catalogue of trophies with a specific *tercio*. Among the ensigns, only one captured before the 1690s is reproduced: a classic white flag with red cross, which belonged to one of the infantry *tercios* involved in the bloody battle of Seneffe fought on 11 August 1674. The simpler ensigns are believed to correspond to the ones belonging to the old veteran *tercios*, but this white flag could also be a colonel's colour. For some details only, it is possible to attribute an ensign to a specific unit, such as the pomegranates that appears in one of the colours lost in 1694 at the Battle of Ter, in Catalonia, almost certainly belonging to a company of the *tercio Casco de Granada* (EI–46).

Regarding the colours employed in infantry ensigns, the rules of heraldry were often strained, and the patterns do not seem to follow the established rules. Sometimes, the colours allude to the kingdom's coat of arms, or to the one of the commanding officer. In the period between the 1660s and 1690s, the most common element of the company flags are the borders, which show an equally variable design, while the flags without an border probably are colonel's colours. The background was, in most cases, divided into squares, triangles or circles of various colours, sometimes with a border also consisting of geometric design or flames. After 1660, the dimensions also appear more standardised, however they still measured up to two meters per side, as can be seen in some original ensigns that have survived until today. Pictorial evidence suggests that companies within the same *tercio* could have flags with common colours, but with considerably varied designs for the field and the borders. However, it is difficult to establish how widespread this criterion was found in all the armies, given that individual companies were often disbanded and their complement transferred en masse to other *tercios*.

In cavalry and dragoon colours, the *aspa* appears to be employed less. Most of the cavalry standards of this period had a red background, with much less variation in the design and disposition of the decorative elements or insignia compared to the infantry ensigns. During the reign of Felipe IV, the red background field was established as the norm for all the Hispanic cavalry. This colour remained, with a few exceptions, the most common in the cavalry ensigns until the end of the century.

Appendix I

Tabular Data and Orders of Battle

Economic Balance for 1663

Currency: *Escudos de vellón*

	Expected	After the Reduction	Reduction Percentage
Provisions destined for outside Spain	3,743,740	1,999,088	47%
Army of Extremadura	8,401,772	5,742,304	32%
Army of Galicia	1,867,368	1,411,768	24%
Troops on the border of Castile	428,000	268,000	37%
Garrisons	1,339,575	1,339,575	–
Recruitment	221,164	84,104	62%
Armada Real (War Fleet)	2,056,434	1,256,434	39%
Royal House	1,008,200	1,008,200	–
Court's provisions	500,000	500,000	–
Embassies	327,854	104,096	68%
Debt Interest	2,014,810	1,395,757	31%
Other Expenditures	290,000	290,000	–
Total	22,162,917	15,353,326	31%

Source: Antonio José Rodríguez Hernández, 'Asientos y asentistas militares en el siglo XVII: el ejemplo del pan y la pólvora', in *Comercio y Finanzas Internacionales en una España en Transición, 1680–1721* (Universidad de Salamanca, 2013), pp.63–64.

Army Expenditure in 1663

Army of Extremadura	Expected	After the Reduction	Reduction Percentage
Salaries	3,874,358	1,701,000	65%
Bread and Fodder	2,267,510	1,999,510	8%
Artillery, Weapons and Ammunition	335,778	335,778	–
Train and Carriages	920,000	677,740	26%
Horses for Cavalry	312,000	312,000	–
Dress	83,400	30,000	64%
Beds, Saddles and Blankets	47,330	14,880	69%
Enlistment and payment to Militia	661,416	661,416	–
Total	8,401,772	5,732,304	32%

Army of Galicia	Expected	After the Reduction	Reduction Percentage
Salaries	855,600	400,000	53%
Bread and Fodder	540,000	540,000	–
Artillery, weapons and ammunitions	65,744	65,744	–
Train and Carriages	250,000	250,000	–
Horses for Cavalry	120,000	120,000	–
Beds	12,000	12,000	–
Other	24,024	24,024	–
Total	1,867,368	1,411,768	24%

Troops on the Border of Castile	Expected	After the Reduction	Reduction Percentage
Salaries	240,000	80,000	67%
Bread and Fodder	140,000	140,000	–
Horses	48,000	48,000	–
Total	428,000	268,000	37%

Source: Antonio José Rodríguez Hernández, 'Asientos y asentistas militares en el siglo XVII: el ejemplo del pan y la pólvora', in *Comercio y Finanzas Internacionales en una España en Transición, 1680–1721* (Universidad de Salamanca, 2013), p.65.

Governors (Viceroys) of the Spanish Low Countries

Gobernador general de los Países Bajos y de Borgoña:
Juan José de Austria (1656–1659)
Luis de Benavides Carrillo, Marquis of Caracena (1659–1664)
Francisco de Moura Corterreal, Marquis of Castel Rodrigo (1664–1668)
Íñigo Melchor Fernández de Velasco, Duke of Frías (1668–1670)
Juan Domingo de Zúñiga y Fonseca, Count of Monterrey (1670–1675)
Carlos de Gurrea Aragón y Borja, Duke of Villahermosa (1675–1678)
Alessandro Farnese, Prince of Parma (1678–1682)
Ottone Enrico del Carretto, Marquis del Grana (1682–1685)
Francisco Antonio de Agurto, Marquis of Gastañaga (1685–1692)

Lugartenientes del gobernador en el condado de Borgoña (Franche-Comté):
Claude de Bauffremont, Baron de Scey (1642–1660)
Philippe de La Baume-Saint Amour, Marquis of Yennes (1661–1668)
Charles Eugène de Ligne, Duke of Arenberg (1668–1671)
Gerónimo de Quiñones, Duke of Benavente (1671–1673)
Francisco Gonzales d'Avelda (1673–1674)

Governors (Viceroy) of Catalonia

Francisco de Orozco, marchese di Mortara (1656–1663)
Francisco de Moura y Corterreal, Marquis of Castel Rodrigo (1663–1664)
Vincenzo Gonzaga-Doria (1664–1667)
Gaspar Téllez-Girón, Duke of Osuna (1667–1669)
Francisco Fernández de Córdoba, Duke of Sessa (1669–1673)
Francesco Tuttavilla del Rufo, Duke of San Germano (1673–1675)
Juan Antonio Pacheco Osorio Toledo, Marquis of Cerralbo (1675–1676)
Alessandro Farnese, Prince of Parma (1676–1677)
Juan Domingo de Haro (1677–1678)
Diego Dávila Mesía y Guzmán, Marquis of Leganés (1678)
Alexander de Bournonville (1678–1685)
Diego Dávila Mesía y Guzmán, Marquis of Leganés (1685–1688)
Juan Tomás Enríquez de Cabrera, Count of Melgar (1688)
Carlos de Gurrea Aragón y Borja, Duke of Villahermosa (1688–1690)

Governors of the *Estado de Milán*

Alfonso Perez de Vivero, Count of Fuensaldaña (1656–1660)
Inigo Velez de Guevara, Count of Onate (1657–1658), died before to assume the office
Francesco Caetani, Duke of Sermoneta(1660–1662)
Luis de Guzmán Ponce de Leon   (1662–1668)
Paolo Spinola Doria, Marquis of Los Balbases (1668)

Francisco de Orozco, Marquis of Olias(1668)

Paolo Spinola, Marquis of Los Balbases (1669)

Gaspar Tellez Girón, Duke of Osuna (1669–1671)

Antonio Lopez de Ayala Velasco y Cardeñas, Count of Fuensalida (1671–1674)

Claude Lamoral, Prince of Ligne (1674–1678)

Juan Tomás Enríquez de Cabrera, Count of Melgar (1678–1686)

Antonio Lopez de Ayala Velasco y Cardeñas, Count of Fuensalida (1686–1691)

Governors (Viceroy) of the Kingdom of Naples

García de Avellana Y Haro, Count of Castrillo (1653–1659)

Gaspar de Bracamonte y Guzmán Pacheco de Mendoza, Count of Peñaranda (1659–1664)

Cardinal Pascual de Aragón (1664–1666)

Pedro Antonio de Aragón, Duke of Segorbe and Cardona (1666–1671)

Fadrique Álvarez de Toledo y Ponce de León, Marquis of Villafranca (1671–1672)

Antonio Pedro Sancho Dávila y Osori, Marquis of Astorga (1672–1675)

Fernando Joaquín Fajardo-Zúñiga-Requeses y Álvarez de Toledo (1675–1683)

Gaspar Méndez de Haro, Marquis del Carpio (1683–1687)

Lorenzo Onofrio I Colonna, Prince of Paliano (1687–1688)

Francisco de Benavides, Count of Santisteban (1688–1696)

Army of Extremadura (Winter 1660–1661)

Cavalry	No. Horse
Trozo de Diego Zúñiga (EC–64)	1,400
From Catalonia	1,400
del partido de Fregenal (Kingdom of Sevilla)	100
De remonta han llegado, hasta ahora	1,343
Not included are the cavalry assigned to the garrisons of Alcántara, Albuquerque, Badajoz, Valencia (de Alcántara), Olivenza, Barcarota and Jerez (600 horse)	
Total	3,643

Infantry (assembling in Badajoz and Olivença)

Tercio	No. Soldiers
Tercio of the *general de la artilleria* Simon de Castañizas (EI–62)	457, & 36 reformed officers
Tercio de Juan de Zúñiga (EI–39)	434
Tercio de Alvaro de Luna (EI–64)	258
Tercio de Pedro de Viedma (EI–63)	98
Tercio de Rodrigo de Mugica (EI–53)	13
Tercio del Conde de Escalante (EI–58)	7
Tercio de Francisco de Alarcón (EI–71)	34
Tercio de Juan Enríquez (EI–101)	71
Tercio de Baltasar de Urbina (EI–100)	4
Tercio de Francisco Tello (EI–54)	9
Tercio de Francisco de Araujo (EI–59)	19
Tercio de Alonso Feijóo (EI–76)	13
Tercio de Antonio Paniagua (EI–70)	46
Tercio de Francisco de Guzmán (EI–55)	54
Tercio de Miguel Dungan (Irish) (EI–20)	41
Tercio de Dionisio Omahun (Irish) (EI–90)	16

(Note: the document does not include officers and soldiers who are in winter quarters outside Extremadura)

Recruits coming from Extremadura	800
Troops coming from different provinces	
Regimiento de la Guarda del Rey (EI–15)	900
Regimiento de Carondelet (Germans) (EI–96)	250
Regimiento de Carserstain (Germans) (EI–95)	800
Regimiento de Ercolaum (Germans) (EI–88)	140
Tercio de Sartirana (Italians) (EI–83)	550
Tercio de José Fossán (Italians) (EI–82)	500
Tercio de Antonio Troto (Italians) (EI–84)	350
Tercio de Manuel Carafa (Italians) (EI–80)	500
Recruits from Grenada	1,000
Total	7,600
Regimiento de Losenstein (Germans) (EI–89)	?

Source: 'Copia de párrafos de relacion de la gente que había en este ejercito (Portugal), la que ha entrado y va entrando de differentes partes, y del estado en que se halla lo perteneciente á la artillería y víveres', in Serafín Estébanez Calderón, *De la conquista y pérdida de Portugal*, vol. I (Madrid, 1885) pp.325–328.

Army of Extremadura (Est. Strength 18 April 1661)

Infantry	No. Foot
Regimiento de la Guarda (EI–15):	2,000
Four *tercios* from Extremadura	6,000
Tercios of *Naciones*	4,000
Casco de Granada (EI–46) and *Costa de Granada* (EI–47)	2,000
Militia of Seville	2,000
Militia of Madrid	800
Total	16,300

'Considering 4,000 infantrymen for the garrison of the fortresses (which cannot be large), 12,800 men remain for the field army. In addition to this infantry, that is considered to be raised in Madrid and Castile for the *tercios* coming from Catalonia and Estremadura, there shall be further 54 companies. And the infantry coming from the *Capitania general de la costa de Andalucia* are not considered either.'

Cavalry	No. Horse
From Extremadura	1,500
Trozos coming from Catalonia	1,300
Companies from Guipuzcoa	500
Trozo de don Carlos (?) de Cuñiga (EC–64)	300
To which are added 900 horse coming with the remounts	900
Total	4,500

'In this month 1,100 horses have arrived, and a further 2,000 from the factory of don Sebastian Corticos. With this number there will be actually 5,000 horsemen, because most of them are now without horses.'

Source: AGS, *Secretaria de Guerra*, leg. 1958, d. 1028.

Army of Extremadura (April 1662)

Generalissimo Don Juan José of Austria, *Gran Prior de Castilla*

Capitán General y Gobernador de las armas del ejército, Don Francesco Tuttavilla, *ducque de San Germán*

Mestre de Campo general, Don Francisco Podesico, *caballero de la orden de Calatrava*

Capitán General de la caballería, Don Diego de Illescas, *de la orden de Santiago*

Capitán General de la artillería, Don Gaspar de la Cueva Enríquez, *gentilhombre de la cámara de S.M.*

Teniente General de la caballería, Don Diego Correa, *de la orden de Santiago*.

General Titular de la artillería, Don Nicolás Langres (French)

Infantry	
Tercio de Gonzalo Fernández de Córdoba (EI–15) with the *tercio de Juan Salamanqués* (EI–102	640
Tercio de Lope de Agreu (EI–07) with the *tercio de Álvaro de Luna* (EI–64)	443
Tercio de Francisco Tello de Portugal (EI–54) with the *tercio de Francisco de Araujo* (EI–59)	554
Tercio de Rodrigo Mogica (EI–53)	596
Tercio de Francisco de Alarcón (EI–71)	567
Tercio de Baltasar de Urbina (EI–100) with the *tercio de Dionisio Omahun* (Irish) (EI–90)	593
Tercio de Fernando de Escovedo (EI–66) with the *tercio de Juan Enríquez* (EI–101)	491
Tercio de Ignacio de Altarriva (Tercio de Aragón) (EI–77) with the *tercio de Felipe Vicentelo de Castillana* (EI–103)	503
Tercio de Francisco de Guzmán (EI–55) with the *tercio de Francisco Paniagua* (EI–70)	517
Tercio de Juan de Zúñiga (EI–39)	705
Tercio de Escalante (EI–58) with the *tercio de Juan Barbosa* (EI–32)	484
Tercio de Torrecusa (Italians) (EI–81)	548
Tercio de José de Fossán (Italians) (EI–82) with the *tercio de Sartirana* (Italians) (EI–83)	383
Tercio de Manuel Carafa (Italians) (EI–80)	592
Regimiento de Kaserstein (Germans) (EI–95)	520
Regimiento de Francisco Franquete (Germans) (EI–37)	270
Regimiento de Charní (French) (EI–92) with the *tercio de Losenstain* (Germans) (EI–89)	480
Total	8,886

Cavalry	No. Horse
Las Guardias de S.A. (commanded by Melchor Portocarrero)	280
Las Guardias del duque de San Germán (commanded by Santa Cristina)	244
Las Guardias del General de la caballería	216
Trozo de Alejandro Morera (EC–73)	516
Trozo de Luís de Ley (EC–74)	429
Trozo de Juan Cortés (EC–49)	214
Trozo de Juan Ángel Balador (EC–3)	321
Trozo de Juan Jácome Mazacán (EC–76)	404
Trozo de Juan de Rivera (EC–50)	464
Trozo de Miguel Ramoni (EC–53)	362
Trozo de Antonio Guíndaro (EC–75)	600
Trozo de José de Larreategui (EC–51):	399
Trozo de Antonio de Montenegro (EC–5)	315
Trozo de Juan de Novales (EC–69)	526
(company) *de M. De Corral* (French)	84
Total	5,374

Source: 'Plan del ejército de Castilla que con don Jian de Austria entró en campaña contra Portugal en 1662', in Serafín Estébanez Calderón, *De la conquista y pérdida de Portugal* (Madrid, 1885), vol. I; pp.336–340.

Army of Flanders: Strength 1661–1689

Date	Infantry	Cavalry	Total
August 1661	25,024	8,186	33,210
June 1662	–	–	16,000
(Spring) 1664	–	–	11,000
October 1668	–	–	62,498
July 1670	–	–	39,602
May 1672	–	–	33,704
August 1672	32,949	10,538	43,487
April 1675	–	–	48,143*
November 1676	23,074	6,915	29,989
April 1678	–	–	33,897
March 1684	16,931	5,147	22,078
November 1689	14,923	9,757	24,680

*This figure includes only the field troops; a further 4,486 soldiers were in various garrisons.

Source: Davide Maffi, *Los Ultimos Tercio. El ejercito de Carlos II* (Madrid: Desperta Ferro, 2020), p.126; Antonio José Rodríguez Hernández, 'Guerra y alianzas en la lucha por la hegemonía europea durante la segunda mitad del siglo XVII. El papel de España', in L. Ribot and J.M. Iñurritegui (eds), *Europa y los tratados de raparto de la Monarquia de España, 1688–1700* (Madrid: Biblioteva Nueva, 2016), p.262.

Army of Flanders: Composition

October 1668

Infantry	Companies
15 Flemish Walloon *tercios*	196
Flemish Walloon free companies	72
Garrisons in Ghent, Antwerp and Cambrai	7
8 Spanish *tercios*	173
Spanish free companies	12
2 Italian *tercios*	32
Italian free companies	12
1 Franche-Comtois *tercio*	15
19 German regiments	213
German free companies	22
1 Irish *tercio*	8
Total: 8,815 officers and NCOs, 40,150 privates	

Cavalry	Companies
19 Flemish Walloon *tercios*	74
Flemish Walloon free companies	9
6 Spanish *trozos*	27
Spanish free companies (including the lifeguards)	7
2 Italian *tercios*	6
Italian free companies	1
2 Franche-Comtois *tercios*	7
Franche-Comois free companies	4
14 German regiments	93
German free companies	1
Total: 13,553 horsemen	

November 1669

Infantry	Officers and NCOs	Privates
13 Flemish Walloon *tercios*	1,221	6,418

Garrisons in Ghent, Antwerp and Cambrai	137	503
9 Spanish *tercios*	1,487	8,804
4 Italian *tercios*	776	1,168
4 Irish,English and Scottish *tercios*	205	662
1 Franche-Comtois *tercios*	131	302
10 German regiments	1,864	7,700
111 free companies	969	5,217
Total	6,690	31,214

Cavalry	Officers and NCOs	Troopers
3 lifeguard companies	32	379
12 lifeguard companies of the *Sargentos Generales*	106	1,090
15 free companies	155	999
24 cavalry *tercios* of various nations (66 companies)	593	3,806
11 German regiments (22 companies)	776	3,884
2 Spanish *tercios* arrived from Spain (22 companies)	170	1,050
Total	1,832	11,208

Artillery	Officers and NCOs	Gunners
2 companies	8	85

Source: Antonio José Rodríguez Hernández, *España, Flandes y la Guerra de Devolución (1667–1668). Guerra, reclutamiento y movilización para el mantenimiento de los Países Bajos Españoles* (Madrid: Ministerio de Defensa, 2007), pp.379–383.

Army of Lombardy: Strength 1661–1689

Date	Infantry	Cavalry	Garrisons	Total
April 1661	3,450	2,065	–	5,515
June 1661	3,022	2,019	–	5,241
February 1666	5,424	1,382	961	7,767
October 1668	8,098	3,327	–	11,425
March 1669	7,625	2,509	1,149[1]	11,273
March 1670	6,553	2,443	1,885	10,881
December 1671	6,979	2,486	1,890	11,355[2]
March 1673	7,074	2,363	1,908	11,345

June 1674	6,243	1,908	1,060	9,211
December 1674	6,930	2,400	2,052	11,382
May 1676	7,714	2,969	3,316	13,999
May 1677	8,838	2,387	1,636	12,861
March 1678	12,404[3]	3,359	–	15,763[4]
November 1678	9,158	2.933	1,728	13,819
March 1679	9,693	2,977	1,674	14,344
October 1680	12,340	3,405	1,627	17,012
September 1681	10,730	2,232	1,708	14,670
June 1682	13,554	3,604	1,674	18,862
December 1683	15,077	4,476	–	19,553
August 1684	15,240	4,437	1,781	21,458
May 1686	12,056	4,187	1,801	18,044
September 1687	10,871	3,642	1,789	16,302
March 1689	11,310	3,222	1,790	16,399

Notes:
1) Does not include the garrison of Finale
2) Includes 180 artillerymen
3) Includes the garrison of Finale (450 men)
4) Does not include the garrisons in Lombardy, except Finale

Source: Davide Maffi, *Los Ultimos Tercio. El ejercito de Carlos II* (Madrid: Desperta Ferro, 2020), p.126.

Army of Catalonia: Strength 1661–1689

Date	Infantry	Cavalry	Total
November 1661	3,960	500	4,460
June 1663	1,500	–	1,500
September 1665	1,218	–	1,218
April 1667	1,150	–	1,150
May 1668	5,952	4,077	10,029
December 1669	4,387	2,734	6,481
November 1671	3,697	2,400	6,097
December 1673	5,467	2,684	8,151
January 1675	6,476	3,343	9,819
July 1676	9,287	3,333	12,620
December 1677	5,898	3,774	9,672
November 1678	9,481	4,301	13,782
September 1683	6,319	2,481	8,800

| December 1684 | 6,591 | 1,490 | 8,081 |
| July 1689 | 8,150 | 2,778 | 10,928 |

Flemish Walloon Infantry in the Army of Catalonia (1673–1688)

Year	Total Infantry	Flemish Walloons	*Tercios*
December 1673	5,467	451	2: Diamberg, Sucres
January 1675	6,476	392	
September 1676	7,397	206	1: Diamberg
December 1677	5,898	175	" "
July 1678	6,062	123	" "
November 1681	5,093	159	" "
December 1682	5,202	169	" "
September 1683	6,319	317	" "
December 1684	6,591	331	1: Caron
September 1689	8,027	99	" "

Source: Davide Maffi, 'Una epopeya olvidada. Los flamencos/valones al servicio de la monarquía española (siglo XVII)', in E. Martínez Ruiz (ed.), 'Presencia de flamencos y valones en la milicia española', *International Review of Military History*, N. 96 (Madrid: International Commission of Military History, 2016), p.65.

Italian Infantry in the Army of Extremadura (1661–1666)

Year	Total Infantry	Italians	No. *Tercios*	*Tercios*
1661	7,600	1,900	4	Sartirana,Fossani, Trotti, Carafa
1662	8,886	1,523	6	Sartirana,Fossani, Trotti, Carafa, Oreglia, Guindazzo,
1663	10,257	1,588	8	Sartirana, Fossani, Trotti, Carafa, Oreglia, Dura, Coppola, Cansano.
1665	9,576	2,398	6	Oreglia, Belgioioso, Sangiorgio, Serbelloni, Cansano, Domenico Pignatelli
1666	13,451	1,737	4	Oreglia, Belgioioso, Cansano, Sangiorgio

Sources: Serafín Estébanez Calderón, *De la conquista y pérdida de Portugal*

(Madrid, 1885), vol. I; pp.325–328 and 336–340; Luis Antonio Ribot García, , 'Las naciones en el ejército de los Austrias', in A. Álvarez-Ossorio Alvariño and B.J. García (eds), *La monarquía de las naciones. Patria, nación y naturaleza en la Monarquía de España*, Madrid, 2004, pp.653–677; AGS, *Estado*, leg. 2684, *Relación del número de oficiales y soldados*, dated 7 June 1666.

Italian Infantry in the Army of Catalonia (1673–1689)

Year	Total Infantry	Italians	*Tercios*	*Maestres de Campo*
December 1673	5,467	1,128	3	Giovanni Battista Pignatelli, Domenico Pignatelli, Parravicino
January 1675	6,476	1,063	3	" "
September 1676	7,397	677	3	Domenico Pignatelli, Gandolfo, Mantegazza
December 1677	5,898	373	2	Casnedi, Gandolfo
July 1678	6,062	924	3	Casnedi, Gandolfo, Litta
November 1681	5,093	690	2	Casnedi, Carafa
December 1682	5,202	549	2	" "
September 1683	6,319	937	2	" "
December 1684	6,591	786	2	" "
September 1689	8,027	1,130	3	Serra, Pignatelli, Secchi

Sources: Davide Maffi, 'Fieles y leales vasallos del rey. Soldados italianos en los ejércitos de los Austrias hispanos en el siglo XVII', in José María Blanco Núñez (ed.), 'Presencia italiana en la milicia española', *International Review of Military History* N. 94 (Madrid: International Commission of Military History, 2016), pp.54–55; Antonio Espino López, *Las tropas italianas e la defensa de Cataluña, 1665–1698*, in *Investigaciones Históricas*, N. 18 (1998), pp.53–54.

Italian Cavalry in the Army of Catalonia (1684–1690)

Year	Total Cavalry	Italians
September 1684	3,770	595
November 1690	2,925	294

Source: Antonio Espino López, 'Las tropas italianas e la defensa de Cataluña, 1665–1698', in *Investigaciones Históricas*, N. 18 (1998), pp.53–54.

German Infantry in the Army of Galicia (1662–1663)

Date	Total Infantry			German Infantry				
	Officers	Sold.	Total	Regts	Coys	Officers	Sold.	Total
Jul 1662	1,533	7,402	8,953	2	43	680	1,034	1,714
Aug 1662	1,552	9,161	10,713	2	43	505	1,054	1,559
Dec 1662	1,317	5,466	6,783	2	43	507	892	1,399

Source: Antonio José Rodríguez Hernández, *Financial and Military Cooperation between the Spanish Crown and the Emperor in the Seventeenth Century,* in Peter Rauscher (ed.), *Die Habsburgermonarchie und das Heilige Römische Reich vom Dreissigjährigen Krieg bis zum Ende des habsburgischen Kaisertums* (Vienna: Aschendorff Verlag, 2010), p.280.

German Infantry in the Army of Extremadura (1661–1668)

Date	Total Infantry			German Infantry				
	Officers	Sold.	Total	Regts	Coys	Officers	Sold.	Total
May 1661	2,601	11,898	14,499	4	37	429	1,215	1,644
Jul 1661	2,066	10,366	12,432	4	?	416	1,357	1,773
Oct 1662	3,158	12,863	16,021	5	46	579	1,351	2,303
Apr 1663	3,745	18,738	22,483	5	44	560	1,249	1,809
Dec 1663	4,598	8,436	13,034	6	?	889	1,385	2,274
Jul 1664	2,129	7,137	9,266	4	?	508	936	1,444
Sep 1665	2,908	9,929	12,837	7	56	604	1,532	2,136
May 1666	2,446	10,005	12,451	6	52	625	1,118	1,743
Jun 1666	2,516	11,711	14,277	6	51	612	1,046	1,658

Source: Antonio José Rodríguez Hernández, 'Financial and Military Cooperation between the Spanish Crown and the Emperor in the Seventeenth Century', in Peter Rauscher (ed.), *Die Habsburgermonarchie und das Heilige Römische Reich vom Dreissigjährigen Krieg bis zum Ende des habsburgischen Kaisertums* (Vienna: Aschendorff Verlag, 2010), p.284.

Nationalities in the Infantry of the Army of Extremadura, 1657–1663

Year	Spanish	Italians	Germans	Irish	Total
1657	12,830	–	–	260	13,090
1659	6,100	830	1,390	60	8,380
1663	17,720	2,830	1,810	630	22,990

Source: Pierre Picouet, *The Armies of Philip IV of Spain 1621–1665* (Warwick: Helion & Company, 2019), p.138.

Nationalities in the Infantry of the Army of Flanders, 1661–1689

Year	Span.	Ital.	Fr.-Comté	British & Irish	Germans	Flemish Walloons	Total
1661	4,660	1,179	449	2,317	7,470	8,025	24,100
1673	11,071	3,046	551	618	12,716	13,553	41,553
1676	7,484	1,617	512[1]	–	6,484	2,922	23,074[2]
1678	7,719	1,426	252	618	10,149	3,686	23,853
1684	5,468	2,047	–	1,401	4,873	3,542	16,931
1689	6,190	1,451	109	153	1,184	5,166	14,923

Notes:
1) Figure includes English, Scottish and Irish infantrymen.
2) The total includes 2,955 infantrymen without specification of nationalities, but very probably recruited in the Spanish Low Countries.

Source: Davide Maffi, *Los Ultimos Tercio. El ejercito de Carlos II*, p.253.

Cavalry of the Army of Flanders, November 1672

ID #	*Trozo*	Nat'y	Coy	Officers* & NCOs	Troopers mount.	Troopers dism.	Total
EC–93	Javier	Spanish	5	76		73	149
EC–94	Pimentel	"	1	9		74	83
EC–95	Ugarte	"	3	32	135	12	189
EC–96	Rada	"	4	55		180	236
EC–97	Ulloa	"	4	40	180	19	239
EC–98	Cardona	"	1	12		83	95
EC–99	Del Valle	"	5	73		225	298
EC–115	Sarmiento	"	5	51	225	19	295
EC–122	Audemont	"	4	43		186	229

?	Salinas	"	3	44		135	179
EC–22	Lietberghe	Walloon	4	53	180		223
EC–87	Fiennes	"	4	37	225	23	285
EC–100	Feux	"	5	68	225		293
EC–103	Quincy	"	4	51	180		223
EC–105	Mirecourt	"	4	41	180	19	240
EC–106	Mérode-Monfort	"	4	41	180	14	235
EC–107	Courrières	"	4	56		180	236
EC–117	Boulers	"	3	42		135	177
EC–118	Vessmael	"	4	41	180	19	240
EC–120	Roeulx	"	2	42		135	177
EC–123	Gravelens	"	5	49	225	15	289
EC–126	Saint Jean-Steen	"	5	51	225	26	302
?	D'Ennetieres	"	4	61		180	241
?	Lumbres	"	4	60		225	285
ED–3	Dupuis	"	15	172		748	920
EC–113	Saint Jean	Franche-Comtois	5	77		225	302
EC–116	Carafa	Italian	7	72	315	24	411
EC–83	Baden	German	6	109		270	379
EC–86	Holstein	"	7	129		315	454
EC–109	Salm	"	5	94		225	319
EC–111	Waldenburg	"	4	53		180	223
EC–112	Vaudemont	"	6	100	270	41	411
EC–124	Egmont	"	3	30	135	6	171
?	Holsbrecke	"	5	89		225	304
EC–6	Hajder	Croats	4	64		180	244
Total			158	2,117		7,459	9,576

* Includes *reformados*

Source: Jesús Martínez de Merlo, 'La caballería entre Los Austrias y Los Borbones', in *Revista de Historia Militar*, N. 121 (2017), pp.158–170.

Dragoons of the Army of Flanders, September 1678

ID #	*Tercio*	Nat'y	Coy	Officers & NCOs:	Troopers		Total
					mount.	dism.	
ED–4	Gomar de Ville	Walloon	9	97	223	108	428

| ED–5 | Salcedo | Spanish | 7 | 81 | 201 | 45 | 327 |
| ED–6 | Perez | Walloon | 9 | 98 | 207 | 50 | 355 |

Source: Jesús Martínez de Merlo, 'La caballería entre Los Austrias y Los Borbones', in *Revista de Historia Militar*, N. 121 (2017), pp.171–173.

Infantry in the Army of Flanders (March–April 1685)

Spanish Infantry

ID #	*Tercio*	Companies	Strength
EI–1	Mariño	20	1,100
EI–8	Moncada	20	400
EI–11	Bejar	21	630
EI–17	Grajal	20	550
EI–21	Castillo Fajardo*	20	460
EI–129	Los Rios	20	700

* On 3 March there were 23 companies.

Italian Infantry

EI–9	Cantelmo	14	400
EI–23	Buonamico	13	300
EI–252	Torrecusa	14	800

Scottish Infantry

| EI–180 | Gage | 11 | 175 |

Irish Infantry

| – | – | 2 | 180 |

English Infantry

| – | – | 1 | 100 |

Burgundian Infantry

| – | – | 1 | 100 |

Flemish Walloon Infantry

| EI–12 | Vanderpiet | 13 | 1,200 |
| EI–152 | Tilly | 12 | 1,200 |

EI–153	Aurech	12	500
EI–257	Bressey	14	400
EI–260	Thian	12	300
EI–265	Audrigny	12	1,200
–	Free companies	8	720

German Infantry

EI–179	Baden	10	200
EI–188	Lorrena	12	300
EI–212	Jonge	10	300
EI–217	Auteil	10	200
EI–238	van der Straten	10	300
EI–261	Braunsfeld	11	550

Source: AHNOB, *Osuna*; ct.197, d.84–85, *Listado de los tercios y regimientos de infantería y caballería españoles, italianos, irlandeses, escoceses, ingleses, borgoñeses, valones y alemanes* (March–April 1685) and ct.197, d.82, *Estado de la fuerza de los ejércitos de caballería e infantería españoles destacados en Flandes (Bélgica), con expresión del número de compañías que posee cada tercio o regimiento*, dated 3 March 1685.

Siege of Olivença (1657)

Commander-in-chief: Francesco Tuttavilla Duke of San Germano
Maestre de campo general: Rodrigo de Mogica
Capitán general de la caballeria: Duke of Osuna y Giron
Capitán general de la artillería: Gaspar de la Cueva Enríquez

Infantry *Tercios*: de la Cueva (EI–3), *Zúñiga* (EI–70), *Mugica* (EI–60), Tello (EI–54), Guzmán (EI–55), Hinestrosa (EI–56), Fernandez de Córdoba (EI–15), Alvarez de Toledo (EI–58), Viedma (EI–63), Luna (EI–64), Torrejon (EI–67), Giron (EI–68), Lanzarote (EI–70), Dungan (Irish) (EI–20), O'Callaghan (Irish) (EI–28)

Cavalry: Filomarino (EC–4), Guerrero (EC–42), Daza de Guzmán (EC–5), Larreategui (EC–51), Ramona (EC–52), Linan (EC–49), Alvarez (EC–52)

Sources: Agustín Moreto y Cabana, *El Defensor de su Agravio* (Madrid, 1670), *Parte* 35, pp.318–320; Serafín Estébanez Calderón, *De la conquista y pérdida de Portugal*, vol. I (Madrid, 1885); pp.153–161.

Spanish Order of Battle at Ameixial-Estremoz (8 June 1663)

Commanders: Don Juan of Austria; *Capitán General y Gobernador de las armas del ejército*, Don Francesco Tuttavila, Duke of San Germano

Infantry, First Line
1st battalion: Guzmán (EI–70) 14 comp.; Frias (EI–66) 20 comp.
2nd battalion Fernández de Córdoba (EI–15) 14 comp.; Escalante (EI–58) 15 comp.
3rd battalion: Mujica (EI–53) 14 comp.
4th battalion: Enríquez (EI–101) 21 comp.; Gómez de Abreu (EI–7) 9 comp.
5th battalion (French-Germans): Kaiserstein (EI–95) 8 comp.; Chargny (EI–92) 8 comp.
6th battalion (Italians): Cansano (EI–111) 16 comp.
7th battalion (Italians): Guindazzo (EI–104) 14 comp.; Dura (EI–112) 7 comp.

Infantry, Second Line
8th–11th battalion formed by: Bracamonte (EI–107) 11 comp.; Pérez de Vega (EI–116) 6 comp.; Tello (EI–54) 15 comp.; Urbina (EI–100) 26 comp.; Vera (EI–97) 5 comp.; Araujo (EI–59) 15 comp.; Villalva (EI–46) 12 comp.; Gomin (unidentified) 5 comp.
12th battalion (Italians): Origlia (EI–81) 14 comp.; Coppola (EI–113) 7 comp.
13th battalion (Germans): Kaiserstein (EI–95) 10 comp.

Total: 2,154 officers and NCOS, 8,968 private soldiers (11,122 men; source: muster dated 25 May 1663)

Cavalry (right and left wing)
Borgoña (EC–62) 11 comp.; *Guardias viejas de Castilla* (EC–65) 13 comp.; Fregenal (EC–49) 5 comp.; Milan (EC–) 10 comp.; Órdenes (EC–5) 7 comp.; Flandes (EC–73) 10 comp.; Cataluña (EC–71) 11 comp.; Feria (EC–69) 11 comp.; Extremadura (EC–60) 13 comp.; Italian (Milan) 7 comp.; *Guardias de Don Juan of Austria*, 2 comp.; *Guardias del ducque de San German*, 2 comp.; *Guardias del General de la caballería*, 1 comp.; *Guardias del Teniente* General D. Diego Correa, 1 comp.: *Guardias del Teniente General* Juan Mazacan, 1 comp.; *Guardias del Teniente General* Alejandro Moreda, 1 comp; *Guardias del Teniente General* Melchor Portocarrero, 1 comp.; *Guardias del Preboste general del ejército*, 1 comp.; *Guías* 1 comp.

Total: 598 officers and NCOS, 5,556 troopers (6,154 men with 5,935 horses; source: muster dated 25 May 1663).

Sources: Serafín Estébanez Calderón, *De la conquista y pérdida de Portugal*, vol. II (Madrid, 1885); pp.302–305.

Spanish Order of Battle at Montes Claros (17 June 1665)

Commanders: Luis Francisco de Benavides Carrillo de Toledo, third Marquis of Caracena
Capitán General de la caballería Don Diego Correa

Cavalry right wing, first and second line (*trozos* and regiments)
Lifeguard companies, Correa (EC–55), plus unidentified cavalry units.

Infantry, first line (*tercios* and regiments)
Torres Vedras (EI–78); Rodrigo Moxica (EI–53); Anielo Guzmán (EI–70); Diego de Vera (EI–97); Franquet (EI–36); Porcia (EI–136); Leyde (unidentified); Francisco Roxas (unidentified); Konrad Beroldingen (EI–126); Carlos Cloos (EI–127); Furnes (EI–109); Risbourg (EI–110); Cansano (EI–111); Origlia (EI–81)

Infantry; second line (*tercios* and regiments)
Guzmán del Carpio (EI–15); Juan Barbosa (EI–32); Casco de Granada (EI–46); Juan de la Carrera (EI–47); Bernardo O'Neill (EI–125); Gumin (unidentified); Alfonso Porcia (EI–137); Natermann (EI–86); Belgioioso (EI–122); Chalais (EI–16), Grisons (5 companies)

Cavalry left wing, first and second line (*trozos* and regiments)
Fabbri (EC–85); Rabatta (EC–84); Fuéntes (EC–81); San Giorgio (EC–82), plus unidentified cavalry units.

Approximate strength: 15,000 infantry and 7,600 cavalry.

Spanish Order of Battle at Maureillas (19 May 1674)

Commander: Francesco Tuttavilla Duca di San Germano

Infantry
Tercio de la Reina or *de la chamberga* (EI–181); *Tercio de Diego Antonio de Viana* (EI–46); 2 *tercios de napolitanos* of Juan Bautista and Domingo Pignatelli (EI–24 and EI–133); *Tercio de Barcelona* (EI–191); *Tercio de la Deputacion* (EI–192); *Tercio de Pedro Rubí* (EI–195); *Tercio de Luis de Cardona* (unidentified); *Tercio del conde de Puño en rostro* (EI–15); *Tercio de Vic* (EI–193); *Tercio de Valencia* (EI–202); *Tercio de Montijo* (EI–53); *Tercio de Santa Eulalia o nuevo de Barcelona* (EI–198); *Tercio de Valladolid* (EI–98)

Cavalry
Trozo de Medina (EC–69)
1 German cavalry regiment (unidentified)
8 Cavalry *batallones* under Count of Lumiares
Cavalry Companies of Gerona

Cavalry Companies of Mallorca
Compañia de caballos de Lorenzo Puig

Approximate strength: 8,000 infantry and 2,500 cavalry.

Source: Narcíso Feliu de la Penya, *Annales de Cataluña*, vol. III (Barcelona, 1709), pp.364–365.

Spanish officers and NCO Casualties at Espolla (4 July 1677)

Infantry	Dead	Wounded
Tercio de Monteleón (EI–53)	3	11
Tercio de Medina Sidonia (EI–97)	15	16
Tercio del conde de Palma (EI–98)	5	8
Tercio de Thomás Arias (EI–15)	–	4
Tercio de Fuentes (EI–218)	1	4
Tercio de Ramon Caldes (EI–235)	1	1
Tercio de Gabriel Carrillo (EI–234)	1	2
Tercio de Diego de Vrana (EI–46)	1	3
Tercio de Pedro Enriquez (EI–47)	–	8
Tercio de Pedro Figuerola (EI–202)	1	4
Tercio de Joseph Agulo (EI–192)	1	10
Tercio de Marí (EI–191)	1	3
Tercio de Raphael Capri (EI–207)	–	3
Tercio de Lorenzo Ripalda (EI–239)	–	2
Regimiento de Varhel (EI–155)	9	7
Regimiento de Hesse (EI–95)	3	12

Source: Biblioteca Nacional de España, *Gobierno del Duque de Villahermosa*, vol. VI, pp.147–149.

Infantry Besieging Messina (October 1677)

Tercio de Sicilia (EI–6)	2,500 men, 28 companies, could be reduced to 20
Tercio de Baraona (EI–4)	500 men, 5 companies
Tercio de Napoles (EI–2)	10 companies
Tercio Viejo de la Armada (EI–32)	45 companies, could be reduced to 20
Tercio de Lisboa (EI–7)	Could be reduced to 12 companies

Tercio de Cerdeña (EI–206)	15 companies, could be reduced to 10
Tercio de Mallorca (EI–221)	10 companies, could increase to 12 with those disbanded by Cerdeña.
Tercio de Borgoñones (EI–43)	11 companies, could be reduced to 6
Tercio de Ares (EI–229)	8 companies.
Tercio de Palavesino (EI–231)	16 companies.
Tercio de Don Blas de Aflitto (EI–228)	11 companies
Tercio de Juan Bautista de Palma (EI–230)	7 companies
Tercio de Marino Carafa (EI–236)	12 companies
Tercio de Oracio Mastro Nuncio (EI–227)	9 companies, could increase to 12
Tercio de Sicilianos (EI–208)	5 companies
Regimiento Alemano de Ulbin (EI–214)	12 companies, could be reformed to 10
Regimiento Alemano de Andrea Cicinelli (EI–216)	17 companies, could be reformed to 10
Regimiento Alemano de Salcedo (EI–215)	Could be reformed to 10 companies
Tercio de Corsos (EI–232)	7 companies

Approximate strength: 12,000 infantry including local militia (and 1,200 cavalry).

Source: ASS, *Appunti e Documenti*, vol. XXIV, pp.498–502; relation of the Duke of Bournonville dated 21 October 1677.

Order of Battle at Saint-Denis (14 July 1678)

Commander in Chief: Prince William III of Orange
Spanish Commander: Carlos de Gurrea Aragón y Borja, Duke of Villahermosa

Cavalry right wing, first line
Guardas del Virrey, 1 sqn.
Guardas del Comisario General de la Caballeria, 1 sqn.
D'Audrigny (EC–103), Leiva (EC–95), Mastaing (EC–126), 2 sqn.
Dupuys (EC–57), Haute-Pont (EC–102), 2 sqn.
Ulloa (EC–97), Pimentel (EC–95), 2 sqn.
Chauvries (EC–109), Havré (EC–119), 2 sqn.
Lucart (EC–125), Holstein (EC–86), 2 sqn.
Egmont (EC–124), Holstein (EC–86), 2 sqn.
Hartman (ED–3), 2 sqn.

Cavalry right wing, second line
Torsy (EC–89), Betancourt (EC–127), Dongelberghe (unidentified), 2 sqn.

Pérez (ED–6), 2 sqn.
Arnoncourt (EC–106), Buendia (EC–130), 2 sqn.
Salcedo (ED–5), 2 sqn.
Mervaux (EC–121), Amenzaga (EC–100), 2 sqn.

Centre (cavalry reserve)
Boulers (EC–117), 2 sqn.
Freyre (EC–105), 2 sqn.
Theis (EC–83), 2 sqn.

Approximate strength: 4,200 cavalry and dragoons.

Sources: BNE, *Correspondencia de Carlos de Gurrea y Aragón, Duque de Villahermosa, relativa a su gobierno en Flandes*, MS 2415 (1678), and Alex Claramunt Soto, 'Saint-Denis y Casteau. Los dragones españoles en acción, in Los Tercios, 1660–1704', *Desperta Ferro*' special issue XIX (June–July 2019), p.52.

Siege of Gerona, Spanish Garrison (May 1684)

Commander: *General de la artillería* Domenico Pignatelli
Gobernador de la plaza: sargento de batalla Carlos de Sucre
Teniente general de la caballería Agustin de Medina

Infantry
Tercio de Sevilla (EI–15)
Dos regimientos alemanes: Baron Christian de Beck (EI–16) and Cristóbal Arias (unidentified)
Tercio de Barcelona(EI–191)
Tercio de la Diputación (EI–192)
Tercio de Antonio Serrano (Gasco de Granada) (EI–46)
Tercio de la Costa de Granada (EI–47)
Tercio Azules Viejos (Toledo) (EI–98)
Tercio italiano di Tommaso Casnedi (EI–231)
Tercio de Valencia (EI–202)

Cavalry
Trozo de Julian Lezcano (EC–135)
Trozo de Pedro Pacheco (EC–136)
Guardias del Virrey
300 dragoons under the *sargento general de batalla* Jose de Agulló.
Tercio de la ciudad (Gerona) militiamen, *coroneldotor* Juan Vilar. The citizen militia included companies formed by monks and priests.

Source: Enrique Claudio Girbal, *El sitio de Gerona en 1684* (Gerona, 1882), p.8.

Tercios, Trozos and Regiments, 1659–1688

Infantry *Tercios* and Regiments

ID #	Year	Commander / *Maestre de Campo*	Name / Notes	Nat'y	Garrison / Engagements	Regt History	Uniforms
EI–1	1531	(1659) Francisco Deza de Velasco y Colmenar, 1662 Juan de Toledo y Portugal, 1668 Fernando Luis de Moncada–Montalto, 1676 Diego de Covarrubias, 1684, Antonio Mariño de Andrade	*Departamental de Flandes* or *Viejo de Flandes*	Spanish	Flanders (1659); Furnes (1667); Ostende (1668); Maastricht (1673); Anvers (1679–1684); Ghent (1685)[1]	*Galicia* in 1715	(1671)[2] Private, dark grey coat with red facings. (1680s)[3] Private: grey-white coat with red facings.
EI–162	1548	(1649) Francisco Carnero de Santa Cruz, 1670 Lesmes Merino de Porres y Ruiz, 1682 Luis Espluga y Juste	*Nápoles* or *Viejo de Nápoles*	Spanish	Naples; Messina (1674–1678)	Disbanded in 1707 as *Nápoles*	(1676)[4] Private: red coat. (1685)[5] Private: red coat with yellow facings.
EI–3	1562	1658 Isidro Melchor de la Cueva, 1662 Francisco Pereyra Freire de Andrade(?), 1673? Bernabé Alonso de Aguilar, 1686 Geronimo Marin	*Tercio de l'Armada del Mar Oceano* (marine infantry)	Spanish	Extremadura (1657); Olivença (1657), Tagus River (1660); Barcelona (1675); Naples (1680); *Estado de los Presidios* (1685–1687); Melilla (1688)	*Nápoles* in 1734	(1685)[6] Private: red coat with yellow facings. (1688)[7] Private: blue coat with red facings & lining.
EI–4	1566	(1657) Agustín Sañudo, 1665 Miguel Fernández de Córdoba, 1677? Baraona, 1684 Francisco Fernández de Córdoba	*la Mar de Napoles* or *Nuevo de Nápoles* (marine infantry)	Spanish	Catalonia (1649); Messina (1674–1678); Lombardy (1685)	*La Corona* in 1718	(1676)[8] Private: red coat. (1685)[9] Private: red coat with yellow facings.
EI–5	1568	(1659) Pedro de Cunha-Asentar, 1665 Gaspar de Tevés y Córdoba, 1672 Rodrigo Manuel Fernandez Manrique de Lara conde de Aguilar y Frigiliana, 1688 *Marqués* de Solera	*Estado de Milán* or *Viejo deLombardia*	Spanish	In Lombardy in Lodi (1659) In Catalonia (1678) In Lombardy (1680) Genoa (1684)	*Príncipe* in 1777	(1675)[10] Private: red coat

ID #	Year	Commander / *Maestre de Campo*	Name / Notes	Nat'y	Garrison / Engagements	Regt History	Uniforms
EI-6	1568	1657 Fernando Fernandéz Mazuelo y Nalda, 1662 Vasco Colmonero de Andrade y Morais, 1674 *príncipe de Belvedere*, 1680? Diego Enríquez de Castañeda	*Sicilia* or *Viejo de Sicilia*	Spanish	Sicily (Palermo); Messina (1674–1678)	Disbanded in 1715, and merged into *Africa*	
EI-7	1579	(1654?) Jose Funes de Villalpando, 1659 Lope Gomez de Abreu, 1663 Francisco Pereyra Freyre de Andrade,[11] 1670 Cristobal de Villaroel, Alonso Torrejon de Penalosa, 1674? Feliciano Aponte, 1680?	*Lisboa* or *Departamental de Portugal*	Spanish	Catalonia (1659); Extremadura (1661); Borba, Juromenha, Malpica, Beira, Monforte, Ocrato, Onghela (1662); Évora, Estremoz (1663); Lisboa (1666); on the fleet (1667–1672); Messina (1674–1676); Palermo (1676); Lombardy (1685)	*Zaragoza* in 1791	
EI-8	1580	(1654?) Juan Pacheco Osorio de Cerralvo, 1660 Pedro de Zavala y Laezeta, 1663 Luis Zúñiga y Carrillo, 1666 Juan Domingo Méndez de Haro y Sotomayor (de Zúñiga y Fonseca) de Monterrey 1672 Diego Gómez de Espinosa, 1672 Rodrigo Tello, 1677 Ordonez de Lara, 1679? Juan Caro, 1682, Joseph de Moncada y Aragón	*Departamental de Holanda* or *Viejo de Hollanda*	Spanish	Flanders; Dendermonde (1667); Brussels (1668); Naarden (1673); Seneffe, Oudenarde (1674); Bouchain (1676); Cassel (1677); Ypres (1678); Brussels (1685)[12]	*Zamora* in 1715	(1671)[13] Private: grey coat with red facings. (1680s)[14] Private: grey-white coat with red facings.

ID #	Year	Commander / Maestre de Campo	Name / Notes	Nat'y	Garrison / Engagements	Regt History	Uniforms
EI-9	1587	(1652) Bernardo Carafa, 1672 Paolo Bustanci, 1681 Ludovico Secchi d'Aragona, 1682 Reitano Cantelmo di Popoli e Pettorano	Tercio Viejo de la Infantería Italiana del Ejército de Flandes	Italian (Milan)	Flanders; Charleroi (1685)[15]	Disbanded in 1715	(1671)[16] Private: grey coat. (1690)[17] Private: grey-white coat with blue cuffs & lining, blue waistcoat, breeches & stockings, white buttons. Drummer: blue coat with grey facings.
EI-10	1591	(1655) Diego de Aragón, 1665 Pedro de Cunha-Asentar(?) (1681) Carlos Brizeño de la Cueva-Villanueva de las Torres		Spanish	Lombardy	Saboya in 1707	
EI-11	1591	1663 Antonio Hurtado de Mendoza, 1669 Luis de Costa Quiroga, 1673 Francisco Antonio de Agurto y Salcedo, 1682 Manuel de Zúñiga Sotomayor-Bejar, 1686 Gaspar de Zúñiga y Salinas	Brabante or Viejo de Brabante	Spanish	Flanders; Dunes (1658); Alost (1667); Mons (1668); Charleroi (1677); Saint Denis (1678); Oudenarde (1685)[18]	Soria in 1715	(1671)[19] Private: grey coat with red facings.
EI-12	1596	(1641) Claude Eustache de Croy (1659?), 1682? Ferdinand Jacques, Lindeman de Nevelstein, 1685 Vandewin Van der Pit, 1689 Lannoy	Flandes	Walloon	Flanders	Disbanded in 1792 as Flandes	
EI-13	1605	(1641) Hugh Eagan O'Neill de Tyrone, 1660 Arthur O'Neill, 1664 Hugh O'Neill de Tyrone, 1673 Brian O'Neill de Tyrone	Tercio viejo de Irlandeses	Irish	Galicia (1642–1668); Guarda (1667); Catalonia (1681)	Disbanded in 1681	(1678)[20] Private: red coat with dark blue facings, breeches & stockings, brass buttons.

ID #	Year	Commander / Maestre de Campo	Name / Notes	Nat'y	Garrison / Engagements	Regt History	Uniforms
EI–14	1631	(1653) Thomas Nelson, 1673? Mervin Tuchet of Castlehaven-Audley, 1683 George Jouavet, 1680 James Thomas Porter (Diego Porter)	*Tercio de Ingleses*	English	Flanders; Ghent (1668)	Disbanded in 1692	(1678–1692)[21] Private: blue coat with red facings, red breeches & stockings; brass buttons.
EI–15	1634	(1640) Luis de Haro 1662 Gonzalo Fernández de Córdoba, 1663 Gaspar de Haro y Guzmán, 1664? Thomas de la Cerda Manrique de Lara (*Marques de la Laguna*), 1671 Juan Arias Dávila y Bobadilla de Puñoenrostro, 1676 (?) Thomás Arias, 1685 Thomás de los Cobos	(1634) *Coronelia del Rey*, 1660 *Castilla*, 1666 *tercio fijo provincial de Sevilla* or *Los Morados*	Spanish	Olivença (1657); Irun (1660); Extremadura (1661); Borba, Malpica, Juromenha, Veiros, Monforte, Évora (1662); Évora, Estremoz (1663); Vila Viçosa, Montes Claros (1665); Ayamonte (1666); Gibraltar, Ceuta (1668–1670); Catalonia (1671–1672); Ceret, Maureillas, El Pertús (1674); El Pertús, Bellaguarda (1675); Espolla (1677); Gerona (1684)	*Inmemorial del Rey* in 1766	(1664)[22] Private: *morado* (violet) coat with red facings & lining, natural linen breeches, red stockings, brass buttons. (1680s)[23] Private: *morado* coat with red cuffs & lining, red breeches & stockings, brass buttons.
EI–16	1632	(1659) Lamb, 1663? Adrien Blaise de Talleyrand-Perigord de Chalais, 1670 Guido Francesco Aldobrandino di San Giorgio, 1677 Pierre Sordet de Nozeroy, 1683 Christian von Beck		German	Extremadura (1660); Juromenha (1662)?; Montes Claros (1665); Catalonia (1668); Bellaguarda (1675); Espolla (1677); Gerona (1684)	Disbanded in 1698?	(1680s)[24] Private: grey coat with dark blue facings & lining.

ID #	Year	Commander / *Maestre de Campo*	Name / Notes	Nat'y	Garrison / Engagements	Regt History	Uniforms
EI–17	1637	(1653) Gaspar Bonifaz de Escobedo, 1661 José Manrique de Luyando, 1669 Fernando del Valle, 1681? Nuño Salido de Rivera, 1683 Pedro Alvarez de Vega-Grajal de Campos, 1689 Gaspar de Rocaful y Rocaverti	*Auxiliario des Flandes*	Spanish	Flanders (1665); Cambrai (1668); Mons (1685)[25]	*Jaén* in 1707	(1671)[26] Private: grey coat with red facings. (1680), Private: dark grey coat, yellow facings & stockings.[27]
EI–18	1638	(1656) Francisco de Meneses		Spanish	Flanders	Disbanded in 1660	
EI–19	1639	(1649) Antonio Pimentel de Prado		Spanish	Flanders	Disbanded in 1660	
EI–20	1640	(1657) Michael Walter Dungan, 1658?		Irish	Extremadura (1657); Olivença (1657); Forte de San Miguel (1658); Badajoz (1659)	Disbanded in 1661	
EI–21	1643	(1643) Fernando de Valladares[28] 1671 Pedro de Aldao Barbeito,[29] 1675 Melchor de la Cueva-Benavides y Bedmar, 1682 Francisco Arias del Castillo Fajardo-Villadarias, 1686 Luis de Aguiar (or Aguiar)	(Provincial *tercio*; becomes regular in 1665)	Spanish (Galicia)	Galicia; Salvatierra (1659); Valença de Alcantara (1661); Monterrey (1664); Flanders (1668); Seneffe (1684); Dendermonde & Antwerp (1685)[30]	Disbanded in 1749 as *Portugal*	(1671)[31] Private: grey coat with red facings.
EI–22	1643	1665 Sebastian de Parada, 1668? Luis Venegas Osorio,		Spanish	Albuquerque (1650–1668)	Disbanded in 1677, merged with (EI–77)	
EI–23	1643	(1644) Carlo Campi, 1669 Geronimo Silva, 1682 Fabio Buonamico, 1689 Domenico di Francia		Italian (Milan)	Flanders; Valenciennes (1668)	Disbanded in 1733	(1671)[32] Private: grey coat.

ID #	Year	Commander / *Maestre de Campo*	Name / Notes	Nat'y	Garrison / Engagements	Regt History	Uniforms
EI-24	1643	(1643) Giovanni Battista Pignatelli, 1676 Carlo Giovanni Gandolfo		Italian (Naples)	Extremadura (1643); Catalonia (1658); Naples (1670); Catalonia (1673); Bellaguarda, Maureillas (1674); Puigcerdá (1678)	Disbanded in 1678	(1687)[33] Private: Blue coat
EI-25	1643	(1650) Hennin, 1660 Barlin, 1668 Capres, 1672? Bournouville, Sotta, Macuca, 1679 Nicolas Jacot de Seranville de Bellerose, 1680 Nicolas Ignace de Fariaux-Troisville		German	Flanders	Disbanded in 1682	
EI-26	1646	(1656) Mauricque, 1658 Jean de Berlo		German	Flanders	Disbanded in 1659	
EI-27	1646	(1649) Nassau 1665 Jean de Berlo		German	Flanders	Disbanded in 1665?	
EI-28	1647	(1650) Bernard O'Calahan (Bernardo Oncale), 1667 Dennis O'Byrne		Irish	Catalonia (1655); Extremadura: Olivença, Mourau (1657); Badajoz (1658), Arronches (1661); Juromenha (1662); Flanders (1666); Cambray, Oudenarde (1667); Nieuport (1668)	Disbanded in 1678 and merged into Taaffe (EI-31)	
EI-29	1648	Pleuren, 1666 Tello		German	Lombardy	Disbanded in 1666?	
EI-30	1649	Reichling, 1658 Joachim Alexandre Marmie du Gye (Gie)		German, then Walloon	Flanders	Disbanded in 1660?	
EI-31	1649	1669 Sean Murphy, 1672? Niall Taaffe, 1675? Thomas Taaffe,1678 Dennis O'Byrne, 1685 Owen O'Neill de Tyrone, 1690? Bernard Fitzpatrick		Irish	Flanders; Tournay (1667)	Disbanded in 1699 as free company	(1678)[34] Private: red coat with blue cuffs & lining, blue breeches & stockings.

ID #	Year	Commander / *Maestre de Campo*	Name / Notes	Nat'y	Garrison / Engagements	Regt History	Uniforms
EI–32	1650	(1650) Isidro Melchor de la Cueva, 1658? 1662 Juan de Barbosa, 1668?, 1682 Carlos de Eguia, 1686 Bernabé Alonso de Aguilar	*tercio viejo de la Armada del Mar Océano* (marine infantry) 1664: *tercio fijo provincial de Córdoba*, 1674: *tercio viejo de la Armada*	Spanish	Extremadura, Olivença (1657), Arronches (1658); Borba, Juromenha (1662); Vila Viçosa, Montes Claros (1665); Córdoba (1672–1673); Messina (1674–1678); Catalonia (1681); Llinars del Vallés (1689)	*España* in 1718	(1664)[35] Private: blue coat with red lining & facings. (1690s)[36] Private: blue coat with red facings.
EI–33	1650	Barlin, 1660 Barros		German	Lombardy	Disbanded in 1660	
EI–34	1652	Francisco Gorraiz y Beaumont, 1659 Esteban de Angulo y Velasco		Spanish (Navarre)	Badajoz (1659); Líneas de Elvas (1659); Catalona (1660)	Disbanded in 1660	
EI–35	1652	Robecq		Walloon	Flanders; Galicia (1660); Catalonia (1669)	Disbanded in 1669?	
EI–36	1652?	Carlo Emanuele d'Este-Borgomanero, 1662 Francisco Franquete, 1668 Pierre Sordet[37]		German	Extremadura(1661); Arronches (1661); Vila Viçosa, Montes Claros (1665)	Disbanded in 1669?	
EI–37	1652	Orinelli, 1660 D'Avalos		German	Flanders	Disbanded in 1660	
EI–38	1652	Bühren, 1659 Gyldenlöve		German	Flanders	Disbanded in 1659	
EI–39	1654	Juan de Zúñiga		Spanish (Extrem.)	Extremadura (1657); Olivença (1657); Borba, Juromenha (1662)	Disbanded in 1663?	
EI–40	1654	Richard Burke		Irish	Catalonia	Disbanded in 1663?	
EI–41	1655	Pedro Arnesto de Francia		Walloon	Catalonia	Disbanded in 1664	

ID #	Year	Commander / Maestre de Campo	Name / Notes	Nat'y	Garrison / Engagements	Regt History	Uniforms
EI-42	1655	(1655) Charles Joseph de Torsy, 1674? 1688 Charles Hubert de Grobendonck		Walloon	Flanders (1659); Dendermonde (1667); Linquen (1668); Ghent (1685)[38]	Transferred to Naples in 1734 as *Hainaut*	(1671)[39] Private: grey coat (with blue facings?) (1690s)[40] Private: grey coat with red facings, red waistcoat & breeches, red stockings, tin buttons.
EI-43	1655	*Conde* de Saint Amour, 1668 Henry Richard, 1680 Alexandre-Ignace-Guillaume de Pontamougeard	*Tercio de borgoñones*	Franche-Comté	Besançon (1668); Trier (1674)	Disbanded in 1684 and reduced to a company	
EI-44	1655	La Batterie		Lorraine	Lombardy	Disbanded in 1660	
EI-45	1656?	Claude-François de Grammont-Chaunois, 1674 Charles-Emmanuel de Watteville-Usier		Franche-Comté	Dole (1668); Sicily (1674); Lombardy (1678)	Disbanded in 1678	
EI-46	1653	(1657) Sebastián Graneros de Alarcón, 1663 Gill de Villalva, 1664 Francisco Osorio de Astorga,[41] 1674 Diego Antonio de Viana y Hinojosa, 1685, Fernan de Arias de Saavedra	1664 *Casco de la Ciudad de Granada* (Provincial *tercio*)	Spanish (Granada)	Extremadura (1657); Valencia de Alcántara (1657); Olivença (1658); Juromenha, Crato (1662); Évora, Estremoz (1663); Montes Claros (1665); Catalonia (1673); Ceret, Maureillas (1674); Espolla (1677); Gerona (1684); Melilla (1689)	*Granada* in 1708	(1680s)[42] Private: green coat.

ID #	Year	Commander / Maestre de Campo	Name / Notes	Nat'y	Garrison / Engagements	Regt History	Uniforms
EI–47	1653	(1658) Quinones, 1661 Pedro Enríquez, 1664 Juan de la Carrera, 1668 Martin Gomez Serrano, 1674 Juan de la Carrera, 1677 Pedro Enríquez, 1685, Diego Hurtado de Mendoza	1664 *Costa del Reyno de Granada* (Provincial *tercio*)	Spanish (Granada)	Extremadura (1658); Lineas de Elvas (1659) Arronches (1661); Borba, Juromenha, Estremoz, Évora (1662); Évora, Estremoz (1663); Valencia de Alcántara (1664); Vila Viçosa, Montes Claros (1665); Catalonia (1674); Espolla (1677); Gerona (1684)	*Vitoria* in 1718	(1690s)[43] Private: grey coat, cuffs and lining.
EI–48	1655	José Temprado, 1659 Andres Pérez Trigueros, 1662 Ignacio de Zayas Bazan, 1669 Andres de Robles, 1672, Antonio del Castillo Portocarrero, 1676 José Moreno de Zuniga, 1677 Alonso de Salazar Cantareno, 1681 Rodrigo Godinez Brochero, 1684 Gabriel Arevalo de Zuazo, 1689 Juan de Ovando y Flores	(Provincial *tercio*)[44]	Spanish (Extrem.)	In Alcanizas and Carvajales (1657) In Badajoz (1668)	Disbanded in 1698	
EI–49	1655	(1656) Fabrizio Rossi, 1664 Giovanni Antonio Simonetta di Santa Cristina, 1676 Domenico di Costanzo,[45] 1685 Antonio Domenico di Dura, 1695 Giovanni Battista Visconti	*Tercio Napolitano viejo de l'Armada*	Italian (Naples)	In Extremadura (1659) Valencia de Alcántara (1664) Melilla (1687)	Disbanded in 1698	(1670s) Private: blue coat?
EI–50	1656	George Cussack		Irish	In Flanders	Disbanded in 1662	
EI–51	1656	Philip McHugh O'Reilly, 1660? Theodore O'Meagher		Irish	In Flanders	Disbanded in 1660	

ID #	Year	Commander / Maestre de Campo	Name / Notes	Nat'y	Garrison / Engagements	Regt History	Uniforms
EI–52	1657	José Martínez de Salazar, 1659 Gabriel Sarmiento de Sotomayor		Spanish (Galicia)	In Galicia (1658)	Disbanded in 1671	
EI–53	1657	Geronimo de Quiñones y Benavente, 1660 Rodrigo Mujica, 1668 Diego de Alvarado Bracamonte, 1674 Diego Dávila Mesía y Guzmán de Leganes, 1676 Ettore Pignatelli de Monteleón, 1677 Antonio Serrano, 1689 Pedro Tolesano	1663 tercio fijoprovincial de Burgos or Los Amarillos	Spanish (Burgos)	Galicia then Extremadura (1657); Badajoz, Mayas (1658); Lineas de Elvas (1659); Arronches (1661); Juromenha, Estremoz, Vila Viçosa, Veiros, Monforte, Ocrato (1662); Évora, Estremoz (1663); Vila Viçosa, Montes Claros (1665); Catalonia (1672); Bellaguarda, Maureillas (1674); Espolla (1677); Puigcerdá (1678); Genoa (1684)	Guadalajara in 1707	(1664)[46] Private: yellow coat with white (light grey) facings & lining, natural linen breeches, red stockings. (1680s)[47] Private: yellow coat with white cuffs & lining, white breeches & stockings.
EI–54	1657	Juan Tello de Portugal, 1658 Francisco Tello de Portugal	(Provincial tercio)	Spanish (Seville)	Extremadura (1657);[48] Olivença (1657); Arronches (1661); Borba, Juromenha (1662)	Reformed in 1663?	
EI–55	1657	Francisco de Guzmán, 1659?	(Provincial tercio)	Spanish (Seville)	Extremadura (1657); Olivença (1657); Borba, Juromenha (1662)	Reformed in 1663?	
EI–56	1657	Juan Fernandez de Hinestrosa de Arenales, 1661 Juan Enríquez	(Provincial tercio)	Spanish (Seville)	Extremadura (1657); Olivença (1657)	Reformed in 1664?	
EI–57	1657	Nicolas Fernandez de Córdoba y Moscoso	(Provincial tercio)	Spanish (Seville)	Extremadura (1657); Olivença, Elvas (1657)	Reformed in 1659	
EI–58	1657	Pedro Alvarez de Toledo, 1658 conde de Escalante	(Provincial tercio)	Spanish (Castile)	Extremadura (1657); Olivença, Elvas (1657); Arronches (1661); Borba, Juromenha(1662)	Reformed in 1663?	

319

ID #	Year	Commander / *Maestre de Campo*	Name / Notes	Nat'y	Garrison / Engagements	Regt History	Uniforms
EI–59	1657?	Francisco de Araujo		Spanish	Extremadura (1661) Arronches (1661); Borba, Juromenha (1662); Estremoz (1663)	Disbanded in 1663?	
EI–60	1657	Agustin de Bustos y Mujica (1658?)		Spanish	Extremadura; Badajoz, Olivenz, Elvas (1657)	Disbanded in 1659?	
EI–61	1658	Francisco de Arbieto	(Provincial tercio)	Spanish (Galicia)	Galicia (1658)	Disbanded in 1668?	
EI–62	1657	Simon de Castañizas	(Provincial tercio)	Spanish (Extrem.)	Extremadura (1649)	Disbanded in 1661?	
EI–63	1657?	Pedro de Viedma (or Biedma)	*Tercio provincial de Jaén,* 1663 *Tercio de Armada*	Spanish (Extrem.)	Extremadura (1657); Olivença (1657)	Reformed in 1664?	
EI–64	1657	Álvaro de Luna y Montijo	(Provincial tercio)	Spanish (Extrem.)	Extremadura (1657),[49] Olivença (1657); Juromenha (1662)	Reformed in 1663	
EI–65	1657	Martin Sanchez Pardo	*Tercio provincial de Alcántara*	Spanish (Extrem.)	Extremadura (1657)	Reformed in 1660?	
EI–66	1657	Francisco Fernando de Escobedo, 1663 Luis Frias		Spanish	Castile (1658); Extremadura, Juromenha (1662)	Disbanded in 1663?	
EI–67	1657	Alonso Torrejon de Penalosa		Spanish	Extremadura (1657); Olivença (1657)	Disbanded in 1660?	
EI–68	1657	Rodrigo Giron		Spanish (Andalusia)	Extremadura (1657); Olivença (1657)	Disbanded in 1659	
EI–69	1657	Gonzalo Chacón		Spanish		Disbanded in 1660?	

ID #	Year	Commander / *Maestre de Campo*	Name / Notes	Nat'y	Garrison / Engagements	Regt History	Uniforms
EI-70	1657	Francisco Pedro Paniagua y Zúñiga de Lanzarote, 1658 Antonio Paniagua de Lanzarote, 1663 Anielo de Guzmán y Cárdenas (1665?) Felix Nieto de Silva (1670?) Domingo Alvarez de Otero, 1680 Martin de Guzmán y Cárdenas, 1684 Joseph Orel de la Hoz	*Infanteria de la Armada, 1664: tercio fijo provincial de Madrid or Colorados*	Spanish (Castile)	Extremadura (1657); Olivença (1657); Badajoz, Lineas de Elvas (1659), Arronches (1661); Borba, Estremoz, Juromenha, Veiros, Monforte, Cabeza de Vide, Alter de Chau, Alter de Pedroso, Crato, Fronteira, Azumás, Onguelha (1662); Évora, Estremoz (1663); Badajoz (1664); Vila Viçosa, Montes Claros (1665); in Navarre and Catalonia (1672–1673); Gerona (1674)	*Sevilla in 1707*	(1664)[50] Private: red coat with blue facings & lining, natural linen breeches, red stockings; white cravat. (1670)[51] Private: white broad-brimmed hat, red coat with blue cuffs & lining, red breeches, yellow stockings. (1680s)[52] Private: red coat with blue cuffs & lining, red breeches & stockings, white cravat.
EI-71	1657	Juan Antonio Rodriguez de las Varillas, 1659 Francisco de Alarcón		Spanish	Extremadura (1660)	Disbanded in 1668	
EI-72	1658	Pedro Garces	(Provincial *tercio*)	Spanish (Toledo)	Extremadura (1658)	Disbanded in 1659	
EI-73	1658	Gabriel Laso de la Vega y Córdoba de Puerto Llano	(Provincial *tercio*)	Spanish (Malaga)	Extremadura (1659); Badajoz, Lineas de Elvas (1659)	Disbanded in 1659	(1658) Private: medium brown coat.[53]
EI-74	1658	Pedro Macedo Leyte		Spanish	Extremadura (1658); Lineas de Elvas (1659)	Disbanded in 1659	
EI-75	1659	Juan de Zúñiga, 1668? Sebastian de Parada, 1677 Luis Venegas Osorio, 1678 Martin de Guzmán y Cárdenas, 1680 Antonio de la Vega Acevedo	*Viejo de Extremadura* (Provincial *tercio*)	Spanish (Extrem.)	Badajoz (1659)	Disbanded in 1738 as *Badajoz*	
EI-76	1659	Alonso Feijóo[54]		Spanish	Extremadura (1661)	Disbanded in 1664	

321

ID #	Year	Commander / *Maestre de Campo*	Name / Notes	Nat'y	Garrison / Engagements	Regt History	Uniforms
EI–77	1658	(1662) Ignacio de Altarriva	*Tercioprovincial de Aragón*	Spanish (Aragón)	Extremadura (1662); Juromenha, Monforte (1662)	Reformed in 1667	
EI–78	1658	Antonio Rodríguez de las Varillas,[55] 1660 Francisco de Alarcón y Torresvedras		Spanish	Extremadura (1659); Lineas de Elvas (1659); Vila Viçosa, Montes Claros (1665)	Disbanded in 1668	
EI–79	1658	George Digby (2nd earl of Bristol), 1659 Lewis Farrell		Irish		Disbanded in 1660	
EI–80	1659	Emanuele Carafa, 1669 Paolo Gualtieri		Italian (Naples)	Extremadura (1661); Juromenha (1662); Vila Viçosa, Montes Claros (1665); Flanders (1668); Cambrai (1668)	Disbanded in 1669, and merged into *del Mar Oceano*	(1671)[56] Private: grey coat.
EI–81	1659	Gerolamo Maria Caracciolo di Torrecuso, 1662 Marzio Origlia d'Arigliano, 1679 Filippo d'Auria		Italian (Naples)	Extremadura (1662); Estremoz (1663); Vila Viçosa, Montes Claros (1665); Sardinia (1667); Flanders (1668); Namur (1672); Maastricht (1673); Mont Cassel (1677); Kingdom of Naples (1680)	Disbanded in 1682	(1671)[57] Private: grey coat. (1685)[58] Private: azure-blue coat with red facings.
EI–82	1659	Giuseppe Fossani (Fossan)		Italian (Milan)	Extremadura (1662); Juromenha? (1662)	Disbanded in1663?	
EI–83	1659?	Francesco Arboreo Gattinara di Sartirana		Italian (Milan)	Extremadura (1662); Juromenha (1662); Estremoz? (1663)	Disbanded in1663?	
EI–84	1659?	Antonio Trotti		Italian (Naples)	Extremadura (1661)	Disbanded in 1663?	
EI–85	1659	Jacques Fariaux-Troisville		Walloon	Galicia (1662); Extremadura (1666)	Disbanded in 1668	

ID #	Year	Commander / *Maestre de Campo*	Name / Notes	Nat'y	Garrison / Engagements	Regt History	Uniforms
EI-86	1659	Francisco Franquet, 1665? Victor de Notermann		German	Extremadura (1660); Arronches, Alconchel (1661); Juromenha, Évora (1662); Vila Viçosa, Montes Claros (1665)	Disbanded in 1665?	
EI-87	1659	Simon Ludwig Spayer[59]		German	Extremadura (1660)	Disbanded in 1660?	
EI-88	1659	Alfonso Filippo Hercolani	(Former Habsburg Austria)	German	Extremadura (1661); Arronches (1661)	Disbanded in 1661	
EI-89	1659	Ferdinand Wenzel von Losenstein	(Former Habsburg Austria)	German	Milan (1659); Extremadura (1661); Arronches (1661); Juromenha, Évora (1662); Estremoz (1663)	Disbanded in 1663?	
EI-90	1659	Dennis O'Maloney(Dionisio Omalum or O'Mahoney)		Irish	Bajadoz (1658); Arronches (1661); Juromenha, Monforte (1662)	Disbanded in 1662?	
EI-91	1659	James Dempsey		Irish	Galicia (1659)	Disbanded in 1662?	
EI-92	1659	Louis de Bourbon-Orléans de Charny		French	Extremadura (1662); Juromenha, Évora (1662); Vila Viçosa, Montes Claros (1665)	Disbanded in 1665	
EI-93	1660	Diego de Alvarado y Bracamonte		Spanish (Canaries)	Galicia (1660)	Disbanded in 1668?	
EI-94	1660?	Pedro de Aldao Barbeito	(Provincial *tercio*)	Spanish (Galicia)	Galicia (1660); Flanders (1668)	Disbanded in 1668	

323

ID #	Year	Commander / Maestre de Campo	Name / Notes	Nat'y	Garrison / Engagements	Regt History	Uniforms
EI–95	1660	Tobias Elfrid von Kaiserstein,[60] 1672? Adam Christobal Hesse		German	Extremadura (1660); Arronches (1661); Juromenha, Évora (1662); Estermoz (1663); Catalonia (1668) Bellaguarda (1675); Espolla (1677)	Disbanded in 1678 and merged into Sordet (EI–16)	
EI–96	1660	Carondelet[61]		German	Extremadura (1660); Alconchel (1661); Juromenha, Évora (1662)	Disbanded in 1644?	
EI–97	1661	Diego Fernandez de Vera, 1665 Rodrigo Manuel Fernandez Manrique de Lara (conde de Aguilar y Frigiliana),1672 Gaspar Francisco Manrique de Lara, 1676 Juan Carlos Alonso Pérez de Guzman duque de Medina Sidonia, 1678 Diego de Mitafuentes, 1683 Manrique de Noroña	1664 tercio fijo provincial de Toledo or Los Azules	Spanish (Castile)	Galicia, then Extremadura; Arronches (1661); Évora, Estermoz (1663); Vila Viçosa, Montes Claros (1665); Madrid (1669); Catalonia (1672–1673) Bellaguarda, Maureillas (1674); Banyoles, Espolla (1677); Gerona (1684)	Toledo in 1707	(1664)[62] Private: dark blue coat with white facings & lining, dark blue breeches & stockings, (1678)[63] Private: blue coat & facings (1690s)[64] Private: black headgear with white piping, dark blue coat with red cuffs & lining, red breeches & stockings.
EI–98	1661	(1665), Francisco de Alarcon de Torresvedras, 1668 Pedro de Villacis, 1674 Luis Antonio Tomas Fernandez Portocarrero, Conde de Palma, 1680 Juan Batista Moreno	1664 tercio fijo provincial de Valladolid or Los Verdes	Spanish (Valladolid)	Extremadura (1663); Castel Rodrigo (1663); Albuquerque (1667); Catalonia (1672); Maureillas, Ceret (1674); Puigcerdá (1676); Espolla (1677); Pamplona (1684)	Córdoba in 1707	(1664)[65] Private: green coat with white facings & lining, natural linen breeches, green stockings. (1670s)[66] Private: green coat.
EI–99	1661	Vegas (Juan Flores?)		Spanish	Extremadura (1662);[67] Castel Rodrigo (1663)	Disbanded in 1665?	
EI–100	1661	Baltasar de Urbina	(Provincial tercio)	Spanish (Seville)	Extremadura (1661); Arronches (1661); Borba, Juromenha (1662); Estremoz (1663)	Reformed in 1663?	

ID #	Year	Commander / Maestre de Campo	Name / Notes	Nat'y	Garrison / Engagements	Regt History	Uniforms
EI-101	1661	Juan Henríquez	(Provincial tercio)	Spanish (Seville)	Extremadura (1661); Estremoz (1663)	Reformed in 1663?	
EI-102	1661	Juan Gonzalez Salamanqués, 1663 Pedro de Fonseca		Spanish	Extremadura (1662); Valencia de Alcántara (1664)	Disbanded in 1665 and merged into Frigiliana (EI–101)[68]	
EI-103	1661?	Felipe Vicentelo de Castillana		Spanish	Extremadura (1662)	Disbanded in 1664?	
EI-104	1661?	1662 Antonio Guindazzo		Italian (Naples)	Extremadura (1662); Estremoz (1663)	Disbanded in 1663	
EI-105	1661	Fernando di San Maurizio,[69] 1661 Louis de Bourbon-Orléans de Charny		German	Extremadura (1661); Arronches (1661)	Disbanded in 1664	
EI-106	1662	Gabriel Laso de la Vega y Córdoba de Puerto Llano	Tercio provincial de Malaga	Spanish (Malaga)	Juromenha (1662)	Reformed in 1662	
EI-107	1662	Diego Alvarado Grimon y Bracamonte, 1663 Diego de Ledesma?		Spanish	Extremadura (1663);[70] Estremoz (1663)	Disbanded in 1655?	
EI-108	1662	Bernardo de Lizarazu, 1678? Pedro Fernandez Navarrete	Tercio de Armada (marine infantry)	Spanish	Catalonia	Disbanded in 1689	
EI-109	1662	Philippe-Eugène de Hornes		Walloon	Galicia (1664), then in Extremadura, Vila Viçosa, Montes Claros (1665); Flanders (1670); Zandvliet (1685)[71]	Disbanded in 1715 as *Limburgo*	(1671)[72] Private: grey coat (with blue facings?)
EI-110	1662	Risbourg		Walloon	Galicia (1664), then in Extremadura, Vila Viçosa, Montes Claros (1665)	Disbanded in 1668	
EI-111	1662	Cansano (*Marchese di Cansin*)		Italian (Milan)	Extremadura (1663); Estremoz (1663); Vila Viçosa, Montes Claros (1665)	Disbanded in 1666?	

ID #	Year	Commander / *Maestre de Campo*	Name / Notes	Nat'y	Garrison / Engagements	Regt History	Uniforms
EI-112	1662?	Camillo Dura		Italian (Naples)	Extremadura (1663); Évora, Estremoz (1663); Galicia (1664)	Disbanded in 1668?	
EI-113	1662	Andrea Coppola		Italian (Naples)	Extremadura (1663); Estremoz (1663)	Disbanded in 1663?	
EI-114	1662	Francisco de Rojas y Cardenás[73]		German	Galicia (1662); Extremadura (1663); Vila Viçosa, Montes Claros (1665)	Disbanded in 1665?	
EI-115	1662	Guillermo Cascar[74]		German	Galicia (1662); Extremadura (1663); Vila Viçosa, Montes Claros (1665)	Disbanded in 1665?	
EI-116	1662	Rui Pérez de Vega		Portuguese (former POWs)	Estremoz (1663)	Disbanded in 1664	
EI-117	1662?	John Morgan? 1668 William Trisham (Trezzani)		English	Flanders	Disbanded in 1669	
EI-118	1663	Sancho de Miranda Ponce de León	*Tercio provincialde Asturias*	Spanish (Asturias)	Galicia (1664)	Reformed in 1664?	(1663)[75] Private: red lanyard on the headgear, tanned brown coat lined red, red wire buttons, tanned brown breeches, red stockings.
EI-119	1663	Pedro de (Fonseca) y Fuentes, 1667 Juan de Barbosa, 1668 Francisco Manuel Portocarrero y Luna	*Tercioprovincial de Extremadura*	Spanish	Extremadura (1663)[76]	Reformed in 1668	
EI-120	1663	Josep de Piños		Spanish (Catalonia)	Extremadura (1663)	Disbanded in 1664?	
EI-121	1663	Geronimo Serbelloni		Italian (Milan)	Catalonia (1663)	Disbanded in 1664?	

ID #	Year	Commander / Maestre de Campo	Name / Notes	Nat'y	Garrison / Engagements	Regt History	Uniforms
EI–122	1663	Giovanni Barbiano di Belgioioso-Trivulzio, 1678 Fabio Bonamico, 1688 Domenico di Francia		Italian (Naples)	Extremadura (1663); Vila Viçosa, Montes Claros (1665); Flanders (1668); Charleroi (1685)77	Disbanded in 1689	(1676)[78] Private: blue coat. (1687)[79] Private: grey coat with red cuffs, red breeches & stockings. Drummer: Red coat with blue cuffs, red breeches & stockings.
EI–123	1663	Georg Carl von Schöneich, 1664 Carl Ferdinand von Balenstein	(Habsburg-Austria)	German	Naples (1663); Extremadura(1664)	Disbanded in 1668	
EI–124	1663	Abraham Bernhard Steiner von Zwilling	(Habsburg-Austria)	German	Naples (1663); Extremadura(1664)	Disbanded in 1668	
EI–125	1663	Brian O'Neill de Tyrone, 1668 Hugh O'Neill de Tyrone		Irish	Flanders (1663); Extremadura (1664); Vila Viçosa, Montes Claros (1665)	Disbanded in 1668 or 1673	
EI–126	1663	Johann Josef von Beroldingen[80]		Swiss (Uri)	Galicia (1663), then Extremadura, Vila Viçosa, Montes Claros (1665); Milan (1685)[81]	Disbanded in 1687	
EI–127	1663	Karl Hyeronimus Cloos,[82] 1665?		Swiss (Lucerne)	Galicia (1663), then Extremadura, Vila Viçosa, Montes Claros (1665)	Disbanded in 1668 and merged with Beroldingen.	
EI–128	1664	Gaspar de Haro y Guzmán, Marques del Carpio y Eliche (in captivity)		Spanish	Extremadura (1664); Vila Viçosa, Montes Claros (1665)	Disbanded in 1665?	

ID #	Year	Commander / *Maestre de Campo*	Name / Notes	Nat'y	Garrison / Engagements	Regt History	Uniforms
EI–129	1664	José García de Salcedo, 1669 Lazaro de Aguirre, 1675 Diego de Rada y Alvarado, 1682 Martin de los Rios 1686 Juan Francisco Manrique de Arana y Iraola	*Marina* (naval infantry)	Spanish	Estremoz (1663); Galicia (1666–1668); Flanders (1668); Ostende (1685)[83]	*Cuenca* in 1710	
EI–130	1664	*Ducque de Montoro*[84]	(Provincial *tercio*)	Spanish (Aragon)	Extremadura (1664); Catalonia (1667)	Disbanded in 1668	
EI–131	1664	Manuel de Leon		Spanish (Galicia)	Galicia; Flanders(1667)	Disbanded in 1668	
EI–132	1664	Jorge de Madeira de Aguilar,		Spanish (Galicia)	Galicia; Flanders (1667)	Disbanded in 1668	
EI–133	1664	Domenico Pignatelli[85]		Italian (Naples)	Extremadura (1665); Galicia (1666); Flanders (1668); Catalonia (1673); Bellaguarda, Maureillas (1674)	Disbanded in 1678	(1671)[86] Private: grey coat.
EI–134	1664	Guido Aldobrandino di San Giorgio		Italian (Piedmont)	Extremadura (1666); Catalonia (1668)	Disbanded in 1668	
EI–135	1664	Hermann von Baden		German	Valenciennes (1668)	Disbanded in 1673 and merged in Kriechingen (EI–179)	
EI–136	1664	Alfonso Portia (Porcia)	(Habsburg-Austria)	German	Vila Viçosa, Montes Claros (1665); Catalonia (1669); Lombardy (1671)	Ceded to Austria in 1675	
EI–137	1664	Rambaldo Portia (Porcia)		German	Vila Viçosa, Montes Claros (1665)	Disbanded in 1668?	
EI–138	1664?	Ponce de León		German	Galicia (1664–1666)	Disbanded in 1669?	
EI–139	1664	Bernsau		German	Flanders	Disbanded in 1669	

ID #	Year	Commander / Maestre de Campo	Name / Notes	Nat'y	Garrison / Engagements	Regt History	Uniforms
EI-140	1665	Iulian Davila		Spanish	Extremadura (1665)	Disbanded in 1666	
EI-141	1665	Franz von Jonghen	(Habsburg-Austria)	German	Mons (1668)	Disbanded in 1672	
EI-142	1665	Anton Montfort zu Tettnag-Argen	(Habsburg-Austria)	German	Flanders; Dendermonde (1667); Ypres (1668)	Disbanded in 1669	
EI-143	1666	Jacinto Suardo de Mendoza		Italian (Naples)	Extremadura (1666); Flanders (1668); Valenciennes (1668)	Disbanded in 1669?	
EI-144	1666	Ernst Rüdiger von Starhemberg	(Habsburg-Austria)	German	Naples (1666); Flanders (1668); Namur (1668)	Disbanded in 1669	(1664) Private: pearl grey coat?
EI-145	1666?	Udekem		German	Namur (1668)	Disbanded in 1669?	
EI-146	1666	Friedrich Rheingraf von Wildt (Reyngraf)	Former Münster regiment	German	Armentieres (1667); Valenciennes (1668)	Disbanded in 1673	
EI-147	1666	Daurer	Former Münster regiment	German	Flanders; Dixmude (1668)	Disbanded in 1668	
EI-148	1666	Walpott	Former Münster regiment	German	Namur (1668)	Disbanded in 1668	
EI-149	1667	Juan Domingo Méndez de Haro y Sotomayor (de Zúñiga y Fonseca) de Monterrey		Spanish	Flanders	Disbanded in 1668	
EI-150	1667	Ignacio de Altarriba[87]	(Provincial tercio)	Spanish (Aragón)	Catalonia	Disbanded in 1668	(1668)[88] Private: red madder coat?
EI-151	1667	Pau d'Arenys y de Armengol[89]		Spanish (Catalonia)	Gerona	Disbanded in 1669	

ID #	Year	Commander / *Maestre de Campo*	Name / Notes	Nat'y	Garrison / Engagements	Regt History	Uniforms
EI–152	1667	Maximilien de Merode-Westerloo, 1675 T'Sercleas de Tilly, 1685 Mouscron, 1689 Jean-François-Hippolyte d'Ennetiéres		Walloon	Condé (1668); Seneffe (1674); Oudenarde (1685)[90]	*Namur* in 1718	(1671)[91] Private: grey coat (with (blue facings?) (1690s)[92] Private: red coat with red cuffs & lining, blue breeches & stockings.
EI–153	1667	? Utreck, 1684 Aurech, 1688 Mornas or *Principe de Hornes*		Walloon	Brabant (1685)[93]	Disbanded in 1734 as *Limburgo*	(1671)[94] Private: grey coat (with blue facings?) (1687)[95] Private: light grey coat with blue cuffs & lining.
EI–154	1667	Santa Cristina		Italian	Flanders(1668)	Disbanded in 1669?	
EI–155	1667?	Erasmus Corwarem, 1667 Cornelius Varhel		German	Extremadura (1667); Catalonia (1673)	Disbanded in 1678	
EI–156	1668	Francisco Fernandez de Velasco y Tovar, 1673 Luis de Velasco de Balveder y Salazar		Spanish	Low Countries	Disbanded in 1681	
EI–157	1668	Francisco Antonio de Agurto y Salcedo, 1673 Juan Antonio Sarmiento y Zamudio		Spanish	Brussels (1668); Seneffe (1674)	Disbanded in 1682	
EI–158	1668	Juan de Mesa y Ayala		Spanish (Canaries)	Flanders (1668)	Disbanded in 1669?	
EI–159	1668	Alessandro dal Borro		Italian (Tuscany)	Catalonia	Disbanded in1669?	
EI–160	1668	Jacques Fariaux-Troisville		Walloon	Cambrai (1668)	Disbanded in 1672?	
EI–161	1668	Fay		Walloon	Saint-Omer (1668)	Disbanded in 1672?	

ID #	Year	Commander / Maestre de Campo	Name / Notes	Nat'y	Garrison / Engagements	Regt History	Uniforms
EI–162	1668	Marle		Walloon	Aire (1668)	Disbanded in 1669?	
EI–163	1668	Herentals (Herenbakt?)		Walloon	Aire (1668)	Disbanded in 1669?	
EI–164	1668	Bossu		Walloon	Condé (1668)	Disbanded in 1669?	
EI–165	1668	Solre		Walloon	Condé (1668)	Disbanded in 1669	
EI–166	1668	Havre		Walloon	Nieuport (1668)	Disbanded in 1669	
EI–167	1668	Paul Bustancy		Walloon	Mons (1668)	Disbanded in 1669	
EI–168	1668	Marquenbourg		Walloon	Condé (1668)	Disbanded in 1669?	
EI–169	1668	Cruykenbourg		Walloon	Ypres (1668)	Disbanded in 1669?	
EI–170	1668	Sharemberg		Walloon	Saint Ghislain (1668)	Disbanded in 1669?	
EI–171	1668?	Ostiche		Walloon	Cambrai (1669)	Disbanded in 1669?	
EI–172	1668?	Rache		Walloon	Ostende (1668)	Disbanded in 1669?	
EI–173	1668?	Vainmini		Walloon?	Saint-Omer (1668)	Disbanded in 1669?	
EI–174	1668	Nicola Strassoldo, 1668 Salcedo	(Habsburg-Austria)	German	Lombardy	Disbanded in 1669	
EI–175	1668	Walter (Balthazar) Mias		German	Charlemont (1668)	Disbanded in 1669	
EI–176	1668	Prince Friedrich of Holstein		German	Tournay (1667); Ghent (1668)	Disbanded in 1670	

331

ID #	Year	Commander / Maestre de Campo	Name / Notes	Nat'y	Garrison / Engagements	Regt History	Uniforms
EI–177	1668	Isenghien (St. Ouain)		German	Dendermonde (1668)	Disbanded in 1669	
EI–178	1668	Knobelsdorf		German	Flanders	Disbanded in 1669?	
EI–179	1668	Kriechingen, 1673 Hermann von Baden		German	Flanders; Leuven (1685)[96]	Disbanded in 1732 as *Creange*	
EI–180	1668	Francis Scott, 1680? Henrique (Henry) Gage		Scottish	Bruges (1668); Mons (1685)[97]	Disbanded in 1689?	
EI–181	1669	Guillem Ramón de Montcalda-Aytona, 1670 Pasqual de Aragón, 1672 vacant, 1674 Rodrigo Manuel Manrique de Lar (conde de Frigiliana y Aguilar)	*Guardias del Rey (Las Chambergas)*	Spanish	Catalonia (1673); Bellaguarda, Maureillas (1674); Bellaguarda (1675); Messina (1677–1678)	Disbanded in 1678	(1670s)[98] Private: light grey broad-brimmed hat with red ribbon, white cravat, yellow coat lined & faced white, yellow breeches, red stockings, red buttons.
EI–182	1670	Bernardo Carafa		Italian (Naples)	Catalonia (1674)	Disbanded in 1678?	
EI–183	1670	Beaumont, 1674 Ousbeck		German		Disbanded in 1674	
EI–184	1672	Pedro de Ponte Franca Llerena		Spanish (Canaries)		Disbanded in 1673	
EI–185	1672	Alexandre-Ignace-Guillaume de Pontamougeard		Franche-Comté	Salins (1674)	Disbanded in 1678	
EI–186	1672	Tommaso Parravicino, 1676 Giovanni Mantegazza		Italian (Milan)	Catalonia (1673)	Disbanded in 1677	
EI–187	1672	Cleves		Walloon		Disbanded in 1674	(1672)[99] Private: grey coat (with blue facings?)

ID #	Year	Commander / Maestre de Campo	Name / Notes	Nat'y	Garrison / Engagements	Regt History	Uniforms
EI-188	1672	Charles Thomas de Lorraine-Vaudemont	Lorrena	German	Leuven (1685)[100]	Disbanded in 1694 as Davalos	(1688)[101] Private: grey-white coat.
EI-189	1673?	Ettore Pignatelli de Monteleón, 1676 Gabriel Carrillo de Sotomayor		Spanish	Catalonia (1675)	Disbanded in 1677 and merged into Sevilla (EI-15)[102]	
EI-190	1673	Alexandro de Boxadós[103]		Spanish (Catalonia)	Cerdaña (1674)	Disbanded in 1677	
EI-191	1673	Francisco de Marí 1684, Joaquin de Grimau y Monserrat	Ciudad de Barcelona[104]	Spanish (Catalonia)	Bellaguarda, Maureillas (1674); Gerona (1675); Espolla (1677); Puigcerdá (1678); Gerona (1684)	Disbanded in 1698	(1680s)[105] Private: red coat with blue facings & lining.
EI-192	1673	Miguel Francisco de Aytona, 1674 José Agullo y Pinos, 1684 Juan de Marimón	Deputación de Cataluña[106]	Spanish (Catalonia)	Bellaguarda,Maureillas (1674); Espolla (1677); Gerona (1684)	Disbanded in 1698	(1680s)[107] Private: red coat with yellow facings & lining.
EI-193	1673	Manuel de Sentmenat	Tercio de Vic (Provincial tercio)[108]	Spanish (Catalonia)	Bellaguarda,Maureillas (1674)	Disbanded in 1679	
EI-194	1673	Joaquin de Grimau y Monserrat	(Provincial tercio)[109]	Spanish (Catalonia)	Cerdaña (1674)	Disbanded in 1678	
EI-195	1673	Pedro Rubí	(Provincial tercio)[110]	Spanish (Catalonia)	Puigcerdá (1674)	Disbanded in 1678	
EI-196	1673	Joseph d'Arenys y de Armengol	(Provincial tercio)[111]	Spanish (Catalonia)	Catalonia (1673)	Disbanded in 1678	
EI-198	1673	Juan de Lanuza	(Provincial tercio)[112]	Spanish (Catalonia)	Barcelona (1674); Maureillas (1674)	Disbanded in 1678	
EI-199	1673	Carlos de Sucre		Walloon	Catalonia (1673); Bellaguarda (1675)	Disbanded in 1676	
EI-200	1673	Gerard Diamberg van Remen, 1684 Florence Caron		Walloon	Catalonia (1673); Bellaguarda (1675)	Disbanded in 1690	

ID #	Year	Commander / Maestre de Campo	Name / Notes	Nat'y	Garrison / Engagements	Regt History	Uniforms
EI-201	1673	Miernich		German		Disbanded in 1677	
EI-202	1674	1677 Pedro Figuerola, 1685 Centellas	*Reyno de Valencia (Provincial tercio)*	Spanish (Valencia)	Maureillas (1674); Espolla 1677); Gerona (1684)	Reformed in 1698	(1680s)[114] Private: blue coat(?).
EI-203	1674	Juan Antonio Fernández de Melo de Ferreira Conde de Fuentes, 1676 Pedro Figuerola,[113]	*(Provincial tercio)*	Spanish (Aragón)	Catalonia (1674); Espolla (1677)	Reformed in 1676	(1674)[114] Private: blue coat.
EI-204	1674	García de Ozores de Amarante		Spanish (Galicia)		Disbanded in 1681	
EI-205	1674?	Diego de Covarrubias, 1677?		Spanish	Namur (1685);[115] 1676 (Seneffe)	Disbanded in 1685?	
EI-206	1674	Villasor		Spanish (Sardinia)	Sicily; Messina (1675–1678)	Disbanded in 1678	
EI-207	1674	Raphael Capsir y Sanz (Capri)	*Tercio provincial de Cataluña*[116]	Spanish (Catalonia)	Espolla (1677)	Disbanded in 1678	(1670s)[117] Private: red coat
EI-208	1674	Bonanno di Roccafiorita	*Tercio de Sicilianos*	Italian (Sicily)	Messina (1674–1678)	Disbanded in 1678	
EI-209	1674	Francisco Migueldel Pueyo,	*(Provincial tercio)*	Spanish (Aragon)	Catalonia (1675)	Disbanded in 1677	
EI-210	1674	Daun, 1677 Braida		German	Flanders	Disbanded in 1678?	
EI-211	1674?	Roeulx		German	Flanders	Disbanded in 1684	
EI-212	1674?	Gilles de Jonghen		German	Flanders	Disbanded in 1684	

ID #	Year	Commander / Maestre de Campo	Name / Notes	Nat'y	Garrison / Engagements	Regt History	Uniforms
EI-213	1674	Reuss, 1682 Diego Suárez Ponce de León, 1685 Jonge, 1688 Fabian von Wrangel		German	Seneffe (1674); Mons (1685)[118]	Disbanded in 1690	(1685)[119] Private: dark blue coat with red cuffs & lining, red breeches & stockings. NCOs: (sleeveless) natural leather coat.
EI-214	1674	Tobias Elfrid von Kaiserstein, 1677 Miguel (Michael) Ulbin		German	Sicily (1677); Messina (1677–1678); Catalonia (1682); Lombardy (1689)	Disbanded in 1706 as *Louvigny valones*	(1676)[120] Private: grey coat. (1682)[121] Private: blue coat with red cuffs & lining, red breeches.
EI-215	1674	Soye, 1678, Luis de Salcedo		German	Sicily (1675); Messina (1676–1678)	Disbanded in 1679?	(1676)[122] Private: grey coat.
EI-216	1674	Maximilian Ernst von Starhemberg, 1677 Andrea Cicinelli		German	Sicily (1675); Messina (1676–1678)	Disbanded in 1679?	(1676)[123] Private: grey coat.
EI-217	1674	Elteren (1685) Jean-Louis d'Auteil, 1686 Hendrik Theyst (Enrique Theiste) von Braunsfeld	*D'Auteil*	German	Leuven (1685)[124]	Disbanded in 1693 as *Mendoza*	
EI-218	1674	Kielmannsegg		German	Flanders	Disbanded in 1677?	
EI-219	1675	Wied		German	Flanders	Disbanded in 1677?	
EI-220	1674?	Lede, Chales 1677 San Jorge (Fuentes)		German	Catalonia (1674); Espolla (1677)	Disbanded in 1677	
EI-221	1675	De los Arcos y Tenorios		Spanish	Flanders	Disbanded in 1676	
EI-222	1675	Nicolás de Santacilia	(Provincial *tercio*)	Spanish (Mallorca)	Messina (1675–1678)	Disbanded in 1678	
EI-223	1675	Fernando Yáñez Álvarez de Sotomayor y Arcos Tenorio		Spanish (Asturias & Galicia)	Flanders (1676)	Disbanded in 1678	

ID #	Year	Commander / Maestre de Campo	Name / Notes	Nat'y	Garrison / Engagements	Regt History	Uniforms
EI-224	1675	Jean-Claude de Bressey, 1681 Philippe Charles Baptiste Spinola-Brouay, 1684 (or 1685) Mouscron		Walloon	Flanders (1675); Leeuw (1685)[125]	Disbanded in 1685	
EI-225	1675	Giulio Sanchez di Grottola		Italian (Naples)	Sicily (1676); Catalonia (1678)	Disbanded in 1685	(1676)[126] Private: blue coat.
EI-226	1675	Pompeo Litta		Italian (Naples)	Sicily (1676); Catalonia (1678)	Disbanded in 1678?	(1676)[127] Private: blue coat.
EI-227	1675	Orazio Mastronunzio		Italian (Naples)	Sicily (1676); Messina (1676–1678)	Disbanded in 1678?	(1676)[128] Private: blue coat.
EI-228	1675	Biagio d'Afflitto		Italian (Milan)	Sicily (1676); Messina (1676–1678)	Disbanded in 1680?	
EI-229	1675	Francesco Arese		Italian (Milan)	Sicily (1676); Messina (1676–1678)	Disbanded in 1687?	
EI-230	1675	Giovanni Battista di Palma		Italian (Milan)	Sicily (1676); Messina (1676–1678)	Disbanded in 1679?	
EI-231	1675	Pallavicino, 1677 Tommaso Casnedi		Italian (Milan)	Sicily (1676); Messina (1676–1678); Catalonia (1679); Gerona (1684)	Disbanded in 1691	
EI-232	1675	Vincentello Gentile		Corsican	Sicily (1675)	Disbanded in 1677	(1677)[129] Private: blue coat.
EI-233	1676	Tomas Casaña	(Provincial tercio)	Spanish (Aragon)	Catalonia (1675)	Disbanded in 1678	(1674)[130] Private: blue coat.
EI-234	1676?	Gabriel Carrillo		Spanish	Espolla (1677)	Disbanded in 1678?	
EI-235	1676	Ramon Caldes		Spanish (Catalonia)	Espolla (1677)	Disbanded in 1678?	
EI-236	1676	Martino Carafa, 1685 Fernando Pignatelli		Italian (Naples)	From 1677, on the Fleet and in Sicily; Messina (1677–1678); Catalonia (1681)	Disbanded in 1704 as *Castell Ayrolo*	(1676)[131] Private: blue coat. (1680s)[132] Private: blue coat with white facings.

ID #	Year	Commander / *Maestre de Campo*	Name / Notes	Nat'y	Garrison / Engagements	Regt History	Uniforms
EI–237	1676	Manger		German		Disbanded in 1676	
EI–238	1676	Gottfried van der Straten		German	Flanders; Namur (1685)[133]	Disbanded in 1701 as *Spinolavalones*	(1687)[134] Private: grey coat with red cuffs, grey breeches & stockings.
EI–239	1677	Lorenzo Ripalda y Ayanz	*Tercio provincial de Navarra*	Spanish (Navarre)	Espolla (1677)	Disbanded in 1678	
EI–240	1677	Four, 1679 Roeux		German		Disbanded in 1681	
EI–241	1677	Dennis O'Byrne		Irish	Flanders	Disbanded in 1685	
EI–242	1678	Artal de Azlor de la Guara	*Tercio de Zaragoza*	Spanish (Aragon)		Disbanded in 1698	(1678)[135] Private: blue coat with yellow facings.
EI–243	1678	Antonio de la Cabra y Córdoba	*Tercio provincial de Aragón*	Spanish (Aragon)	Catalonia	Disbanded in 1680	(1678)[136] Private: blue coat.
EI–244	1678	Alessandro Visconti		Italian (Milan)	Flanders	Disbanded in 1684	
EI–245	1678	Colins, 1678, Danhanrè	Former Dutch regiment	German	Flanders	Disbanded in 1681	
EI–246	1678	Octave Ignace de Ligne-Arenberg, Prince de Brabançon,[137] 1681 Mornaux,	Former Dutch regiment	German	Flanders	Disbanded in 1684?	
EI–247	1678	Paul Anton von Houchin	(Habsburg-Austria)	German	Sicily (1678)	Disbanded in 1680?	(1675)[138] Private: dark grey coat, red stockings.
EI–248	1679	Monderscheid		German	Flanders	Disbanded in 1682	
EI–249	1680	Fernández de Córdoba		Spanish	Naples	Disbanded in 1700	

ID #	Year	Commander / *Maestre de Campo*	Name / Notes	Nat'y	Garrison / Engagements	Regt History	Uniforms
EI–250	1680	Gaspar de Vega y Benavides de Grajal		Spanish	Flanders	Disbanded in 1684?	
EI–251	1680	Diego de Rada y Alvarado		Spanish	Flanders	Disbanded in 1682 and merged into I–1	
EI–252	1680	Carlo Andrea Caracciolo di Torrecuso		Italian (Naples)	Flanders; Ath (1685)[139]	*Parma* in 1718	(1687)[140] Private: blue coat with red facings.
EI–253	1680	Giovanni Battista Caracciolo		Italian (Naples)	Naples	Disbanded in 1687	(1687)[141] Private: blue coat.
EI–254	1681	Antonio de Sota Cevallos		Spanish	Flanders	Disbanded in 1681	
EI–255	1681	Nicolò Moscoso		Spanish	Naples	Disbanded in 1685	(1685)[142] Private: red coat.
EI–256	1681	Pedro Alvarez de Vega-Grajal de Campos		Spanish	Flanders	Disbanded in 1683	
EI–257	1681?	Jean Claude de Bressey		Spanish	Charleroi (1685)[143]	Disbanded in 1689?	
EI–258	1681	Erard du Châstelet-Trichâteau		German	Venloo (1681)	Disbanded in 1684	(1681)[144] Private: light brown coat with red facings.
EI–259	1682	Pedro Fernández de Navarrete, 1688 Martin de Aranguren y Zavala, 1685 Carlos San Gil y la Justicia	*Tercio nuevo de Armada*	Spanish (Mallorca)	Oran and Gibraltar (1688)	*Mallorca* in 1808	(1690s)[145] Private: yellow coat with azure cuffs & lining.
EI–260	1682?	Thian de Lede		Walloon	Mons (1685)[146]	Disbanded in 1698?	
EI–261	1682	Wagenseil, 1684 Hendrik Theyst (Theiste) von Braunsfeld, 1687 AntoineLenoir Du Ménil		German	Mons (1685)[147]	Disbanded in 1698 as *Lannoyvalones*	(1676)[148] Private: blue coat with grey (?) facings.
EI–262	1682	Juan Bautista de la Ringada		German	Flanders	Disbanded in 1684	(1676)[149] Private: blue coat.

ID #	Year	Commander / *Maestre de Campo*	Name / Notes	Nat'y	Garrison / Engagements	Regt History	Uniforms
EI–263	1682	Friedrich Carl Rheingraf von Wildt (Reyngraf)		German	Flanders	Disbanded in 1684	
EI–264	1684	Diego de Salinas	*Reyno de Navarra* (Provincial *tercio*)	Spanish (Navarre)	Pamplona (1684–1698)	Disbanded in 1698?	
EI–265	1684?	Audrigny		Walloon	Nieuport (1685)[150]	Disbanded in 1698?	
EI–266	1685?	?	*Nuevo de Extremadura* (Provincial *tercio*)	Spanish (Extrem.)		Disbanded in 1698?	
EI–267	1685?	Francesco Maria Spinola di San Pietro		Spanish	Lombardy	Disbanded in 1700 and merged into *Mar de Nápoles*	(1685)[151] Private: red coat.
EI–268	1685	Antonio de Heredia Biyar (Haurels)		Spanish	Namur (1685)[152]	Disbanded in 1689?	(1685)[153] Private: grey coat with azure facings.
EI–269	1685	Pietro Francesco Visconti, 1687 Antonio Caratino, 1688 Benedetto Ali		Italian (Milan)	Greece (1686–1688); Nauplia, Navarino, Methony (1686); Patras, Athens (1687); Lombardy (1689)	Disbanded in 1698	(1685)[154] Private: grey coat with red (?) facings
EI–270	1685	Annibale Moles		Italian (Milan)	Greece (1686–1688); Nauplia, Navarino, Methony (1686); Patras, Athens (1687)	Disbanded in 1698?	(1685)[155] Private: grey coat with blue (?) facings

ID #	Year	Commander / *Maestre de Campo*	Name / Notes	Nat'y	Garrison / Engagements	Regt History	Uniforms
EI–271	1685	Antonio Visconti, 1686 Fadrique Enríquez de Cabrera		German	In Greece (1685–1688) Nauplia, Navarino, Methony (1686) Patras, Athens (1687)	Disbanded in 1701	(1686)156 Private: grey coat and cuffs, red lining, red breeches and stockings. NCOs: red coat and cuffs, red breeches and stockings. (1688)157 Private: black headgear, ash grey coat and cuffs, blue breeches and stockings.
EI–272	1686	Juan Simón Enríquez de Cabrera		German	In Lombardy (1686) In Catalonia (1688)	Disbanded in 1698?	(1686)158 Private: black headgear, grey coat with blue cuffs and lining.
EI–273	1687	1684 Fernando del Castillo Cabeza de Vaca y Carrasco		Spanish (Canarias)	In Flanders in 1687	Disbanded in 1688	
EI–274	1687	Francisco Villalonga de la Cueva159		Spanish (Aragon)	In Lombardy (1688)	Disbanded in 1690	(1680s)160 Private: blue coat
EI–275	1687	1687 Gonzalo Davila Pacheco de Casassola		Spanish	In Flanders(1689)	Disbanded in 1693	
EI–276	1687	Jorge de Villalonga	*Tercio de Armada*	Spanish (Jáen)	In Catalonia	Disbanded in 1690?	
EI–277	1688	*Marqués de Deynse*		Walloon	In Flanders	*Utreckt* in 1718	(1688)161 Private: light brown coat, breeches and stockings. (1690s)162 Private: grey-whitecoat with yellow cuffs, yellow waistcoat, grey-white breeches and stockings, brass buttons

ID #	Year	Commander / *Maestre de Campo*	Name / Notes	Nat'y	Garrison / Engagements	Regt History	Uniforms
EI–278	1688	Francisco González de Albelda		Walloon	Flanders	Disbanded in 1693	
EI–279	1688	Giovanni Battista Spinola		German	Flanders	Disbanded in 1693	
EI–280	1688	Winterfeldt		Walloon	Flanders	Disbanded in 1718	(1690s)[163] Private: grey-whitecoat with yellow cuffs, yellow waistcoat, breeches & stockings. Drummer: yellow coat.
EI–281	1688	Hugues de Noyelles-Falais (Fallay)		Walloon	Flanders	Disbanded in 1706	(1690s)[164] Private: grey coat with grey cuffs, waistcoat & breeches.
EI–282	1688	Jacinto Sarmiento		Spanish	Flanders(1689)	Disbanded in 1693	
EI–283	1688	*Conde* de Falaix		Walloon	Flanders (1689)	Disbanded in 1690?	
EI–284	1688	Antonio Joaquin Canales	*Tercio de Armada*	Spanish (Jaen)	Catalonia	Disbanded in 1699	

Cavalry *Trozos, Tercios,* and Regiments

ID #	Year	Commander	Name / Notes	Nat'y	Garrison / Engagements	Regt History	Uniforms
EC-1	1636	Louis de Savary	*(coraceros)*	German	Flanders	Disbanded in 1661	
EC-2	1636	Peter Brouck	*(coraceros)*	German	Flanders	Disbanded in 1661	–
EC-3	1637	(1662) Gianangelo Ballatore	*Nápoles*	Spanish	Extremadura (1662); Lombardy (1668)	Disbanded in 1668 and merged with *Milan* (EC–71)	–
EC-4	1640	(1657) Giovanni Battista (Giovanni Vincenzo) Filomarino, 1661 Giovanni Giacomo Mazzacani-Mazza, 1664 Carlo Tasso, 1676 Juan Manuel de Pueyo Garcés de Marcilla, 1684 Fernando de Toledo y Portugal	*Trozo de Rosellón*	Spanish	Extremadura (1657); Olivença (1657); Juromenha, Veyros, Monforte, Crato (1662); Évora, Estremoz (1663); Cabeza-da-Vide, Arronches (1664); Albuquerque (1667); Catalonia (1668–1673); Bellaguarda, Maureillas (1674); Puigcerdá (1678) Gerona (1684)	*Borbón* in 1718	(1680)[165] Trooper: blue coat with red facings.
EC-5	1642	(1654) José Daza de Guzmán y Neira, 1659 Juan Antonio de Montenegro 1668 García Sarmiento de Sotomayor, 1682 Salvador de Monforte Salgado de Araujo, 1689 José Martínez de Salazar	*Los Órdenes*	Spanish	Extremadura (1657); Olivença (1657); Borba, Elvas, Jurumenha (1662); Évora, Estremoz (1663); Catalonia (1670–1674); Le Perthus (1675); Puigcerdá (1676); Espolla (1677); Puigcerdá (1678)	*Infante* in 1794	(1690s)[166] Trooper: grey-white coat with red facings.
EC-6	1642	1663 Gersin,1668 Pavinowich, Hejder	(light cavalry)	Croatian	Jodoigne (1667)	Disbanded in 1670	
EC-7	1644	? 1685 Dionisio Obregón, 1689 Marco Antonio Valperga	*Valones*	Spanish	Flanders	Disbanded in 1698	

ID #	Year	Commander	Name / Notes	Nat'y	Garrison / Engagements	Regt History	Uniforms
EC-8	1646	1661 Louis Scey de Chevroz d'Emagny d'Epenoy, 1673 Jean-Claude de Scey de Chevroz de Buthiers de Pin de Beaumotte	*Borgoña*	Spanish	Franche-Comté (1667) Saint Ghislain (1668); Mons (1685)[167]	Disbanded in 1686?	
EC-09	1647	Wardt, 1659 Yorck		German	Flanders	Disbanded in 1660	
EC-10	1649	Friedrich von Hessen-Homburg, 1653 Jean-Charles de Wateville Conflans-Vries	*(coraceros)*	Walloon	Flanders	Reduced to a single company in 1661; in 1667 merged into Trauttmannsdorf (EC-104)	
EC-11	1649	Aleve		Spanish	Flanders	Disbanded in 1661	
EC-12	1649	(1653) Wezemaal		Spanish	Flanders	Disbanded in 1661	
EC-13	1649	(1656) Gregorio Gutiérrez de Castro-Melon		Spanish	Flanders	Disbanded in 1661	
EC-14	1649	Luis Cayro		Spanish	Flanders	Disbanded in 1660	
EC-15	1649	(1653) Silverio de Benavente y Quiñones		Spanish	Flanders	Disbanded in 1661	
EC-16	1649	Villanueva, 1668 Gaspar Francisco Manrique de Lara (conde de Frigiliana)		Spanish	Flanders; Jodoigne (1667)	Disbanded in 1669	
EC-17	1649	Zurimendi		Spanish	Flanders	Disbanded in 1661	
EC-18	1649	1654 Antoine La Hott (La Hoult or La Hoz) de Conflans		Walloon	Flanders	Disbanded in 1660	

ID #	Year	Commander	Name / Notes	Nat'y	Garrison / Engagements	Regt History	Uniforms
EC-19	1649	René Albert de Boulers[168]	(coraceros)	Walloon	Flanders	Disbanded in 1661	
EC-20	1649	Jacques Drouhot		Walloon	Flanders	Disbanded in 1660	
EC-21	1649	Longueval		Walloon	Flanders	Disbanded in 1661	
EC-22	1649	(1657) Lietberghe		Walloon	Flanders; Jodoigne (1667)	Reduced in 1661; newly raised in 1667; disbanded in 1672.	
EC-23	1649	Württemberg, 1658 Hüneken		German		Disbanded in 1660	
EC-24	1649	(1661) Arenberg-Aerschot	(coraceros)	German	Flanders	Disbanded in 1667	
EC-25	1649	Clinchamps	(coraceros)	German	Flanders	Disbanded in 1661	
EC-26	1649	Custine	(coraceros)	German	Flanders	Disbanded in 1661	
EC-27	1649	Principe de Hessen-Darmstadt	(coraceros)	German	Flanders	Disbanded in 1661	
EC-28	1649	Donckel	(coraceros)	German	Flanders	Disbanded in 1661	
EC-29	1649	Egmont	(coraceros)	German	Flanders	Disbanded in 1661	
EC-30	1649	Feurs	(coraceros)	German	Flanders	Disbanded in 1661	
EC-31	1649	Henri Garnier	(coraceros)	German	Flanders	Disbanded in 1661	
EC-32	1649	Holsbeecke	(coraceros)	German	Flanders	Disbanded in 1661	
EC-33	1649	Holstein	(coraceros)	German	Flanders	Disbanded in 1661	

ID #	Year	Commander	Name / Notes	Nat'y	Garrison / Engagements	Regt History	Uniforms
EC-34	1649	Claude-François de Lannan	(coraceros)	German	Flanders	Disbanded in 1661	
EC-35	1649	Magni	(coraceros)	German	Flanders	Disbanded in 1661	
EC-36	1649	Neunburg	(coraceros)	German	Flanders	Disbanded in 1661	
EC-37	1649	Hans Otto	(coraceros)	German	Flanders	Disbanded in 1661	
EC-38	1649	Selles	(coraceros)	German	Flanders	Disbanded in 1661	
EC-39	1649	Michael van der Werden	(coraceros)	German	Flanders	Disbanded in 1661	
EC-40	1649	Vizconde de Woestijne	(coraceros)	German	Flanders	Disbanded in 1661	
EC-41	1649	Mathias Haider	(coraceros)	German	Flanders	Disbanded in 1674?	
EC-42	1651	Pedro Ardila Guerrero, 1662 Antonio Cañizares		Spanish	Extremadura (1657); Olivença (1657)	Disbanded in 1668	
EC-43	1652	Robecq		Walloon	Flanders (1652); Galicia (1660); Catalonia (1669)	Disbanded in 1669?	
EC-44	1653	Jerónimo de Noroña-Castelmendo		Spanish	Flanders	Disbanded in 1660	
EC-45	1653	Claude Henry de Rocca-Aymeries		German	Catalonia (1653)	Disbanded in 1667	
EC-46	1655	Waldenburg		German	Catalonia (1653)?	Disbanded in 1659	
EC-47	1655	Jeger		German	Catalonia (1653)?	Disbanded in 1659	
EC-48	1655	Chimay		German	Catalonia (1653)?	Disbanded in 1660	

ID #	Year	Commander	Name / Notes	Nat'y	Garrison / Engagements	Regt History	Uniforms
EC-49	1656	Juan Cortés de Linan	*Fregenal*	Spanish	Extremadura (1657); Olivença (1657); Elvas, Juromenha (1662)	Disbanded in 1668	
EC-50	1656	Juan de Rivera	*Feria*	Spanish	Extremadura (1657); Elvas, Juromenha (1662)	Disbanded in 1668	
EC-51	1656	José de Larreategui, 1665 García Sarmiento de Sotomayor		Spanish	Extremadura (1662); Elvas, Juromenha (1662)	Disbanded in 1668	
EC-52	1656	Diego Alvarez		Spanish	Extremadura (1657); Elvas, Juromenha (1662)	Disbanded in 1663?	
EC-53	1656	Miguel Ramona (Ramoni)		Spanish	Extremadura (1657); Olivença (1657); Elvas, Juromenha (1662)	Disbanded in 1663?	
EC-54	1656	Diego Cavallero		Spanish	Catalonia (1656) Extremadura (1661)	Disbanded in 1662?	
EC-55	1656?	Diego Correa		Spanish	Catalonia (1656); Extremadura (1661); Montes Claros (1665)	Disbanded in 1665?	
EC-56	1656?	Joseph Daza		Spanish	Catalonia (1656); Extremadura (1661)	Disbanded in 1662?	
EC-57	1656	Jean François D'Ennetières (Nestien), 1675 Nicolas Richard de Puy (Dupuis or du Puys)		Walloon	Lille (1667); Naarden (1673); Seneffe, Oudenarde (1674); Valenciennes (1676); Saint-Omer, Charleroi (1677); Naarden, Saint-Denis (1678); Nivelles and Wavre (1685)[169]	*Alcántara* in 1718	(1691)[170] Trooper: grey-white coat lined grey-white.
EC-58	1658	Bucquoy		Walloon	Galicia (1660)	Disbanded in 1664?	
EC-59	1659	Antoine Octave (?) T'Serclaes de Tilly		Spanish	Flanders	Disbanded in 1763 as *Brabante*	

ID #	Year	Commander	Name / Notes	Nat'y	Garrison / Engagements	Regt History	Uniforms
EC-60	1659	Antonio de Isassi, Juan de Rivera, 1669 Antonio Cañizares, 1678? 1689 Nicolas Rodriguez de Sotomayor	*Trozo de Extremadura*	Spanish	Elvas (1659); Ongelha, Veyros, Alconchel (1661); Elvas, Juromenha, Crato, Ongelha (1662); Évora, Estremoz (1663); Alcántara, Cabeza-da-Vide, Arronches (1664); Nodar, Veyras (1665); Paymogo, San Lucar de Guadania (1666); Albuquerque (1667); Navarre (1676–1679); Extremadura (1680–1688)	*España* in 1762	(1690s)[171] Trooper: blue coat with yellow cuffs & lining.
EC-61	1659	Pedro Diaz de Quintanal		Spanish		Disbanded in 1660	
EC-62	1659	Daza, 1662 Juan Ángel Balador (Valador)	*Trozo de Borgoña*	Spanish	Extremadura (1662); Elvas, Juromenha(1662)	Disbanded in 1665?	
EC-63	1659	Francisco Aguilar, 1662 Moreda		Spanish	Galicia	Disbanded in 1663?	
EC-64	1659	Diego Zúñiga, 1662 Andres de Robles		Spanish	Extremadura (1660); Arronches (1661)	Disbanded in 166?	
EC-65	1659	Núñez Bustamante, 1662 Felipe de Angulo y Sandoval	*Guardias Viejas de Castilla*	Spanish	Extremadura (1665); Catalonia (1666)	Disbanded in 1668	
EC-66	1659	De Rocca		Walloon	Flanders	Disbanded in 1661	
EC-67	1660	Guillermo Regimont, 1675 Marco Antonio Valperga, 1679 Antonio Hidalgo de Cisneros, 1685 Juan Colón Larreategui	*Trozo de Alemanes* (until 1679)	German, after 1679 Spanish	Catalonia (1668); Madrid (1677)	Disbanded in 1699 as *Guardias de Carlos II*	(1685)[172] Trooper: grey-white coat
EC-68	1660	Yennes, 1661 Grisperre		German		Disbanded in 1662?	

ID #	Year	Commander	Name / Notes	Nat'y	Garrison / Engagements	Regt History	Uniforms
EC–69	1660	Jaun Antonio Novales de Rojas, 1671 *Conde de la Palma y Medina*, 1677 Julian de Lazcano, 1689 Francisco de Santa Cruz	*Trozo de Milán*	Spanish	Galicia (1660); Extremadura (1661); Alconchel (1661); Elvas, Juromenha (1662); Évora, Estremoz (1663); Albuquerque (1667); Catalonia (1673); Maureillas (1674); Espolla (1677); Puigcerdà (1678); Gerona (1684)	*Rey* in 1762	(1690s)[173] Trooper: grey-white coat with red cuffs & lining.
EC–70	1661	Josep Ruguera, 1680 Manuel de Arcos	*Trozo de Cataluña*	Spanish (Catalonia)	Extremadura and Galicia (1662) Flanders (1680)	Disbanded in 1681?	
EC–71	1661	Gaspar Tellez Girón de Osuna, 1674 Manuel Corada Olivera, 1688 Juan Jerónimo Abarca	*Trozo de Osuna*	Spanish	Catalonia (1675)	Disbanded in 1695	(1685)[174] Trooper: grey-white coat.
EC–72	1661	Diego de Azcona, 1664 Juan de Villegas, 1667 Antonio Hidalgo de Cisneros	(Cuirassiers) *Trozo viejo de Flandes*	Spanish	Galicia	Disbanded in 1668	
EC–73	1661?	Alejandro Morera		Spanish	Extremadura (1662); Elvas, Juromenha (1662)	Disbanded in 1663?	
EC–74	1661?	Luis de Ley		Spanish	Extremadura (1662); Elvas, Juromenha (1662)	Disbanded in 1663?	
EC–75	1661?	Antonio Guíndaro		Spanish	Extremadura (1662); Elvas, Juromenha (1662)	Disbanded in 1663?	
EC–76	1661?	Juan Jácome Mazacán		Spanish	Extremadura (1662); Elvas, Juromenha(1662)	Disbanded in 1663?	
EC–77	1661	Domingo Olea		Spanish	Extremadura (1663)[175]	Disbanded in 1665?	
EC–78	1661	Eugène Hornes de Fournes			Galicia (1662); Extremadura (1664)	Disbanded in 1664?	

ID #	Year	Commander	Name / Notes	Nat'y	Garrison / Engagements	Regt History	Uniforms
EC–79	1661	Eugène Maximilien de Hornes-Baucignies,[176] 1663 Philippe Eugène de Hornes	Bausigny	Walloon	Galicia (1662); Extremadura (1664); Flanders (1668)	Limburgo in 1711	(1680s)[177] Trooper: grey-white coat.
EC–80	1661	Rougemont		German	Naples (1661); Extremadura (1666)	Disbanded in 1668	
EC–81	1662	Pedro de (Fonseca) Fuéntes		Italian	Extremadura (1663);[178] Montes Claros (1665)	Disbanded in 1665?	
EC–82	1664	Guido Aldobrandino di San Giorgio, 1670 Marco Antonio Valperga, 1674?		Italian	Extremadura (1665); Montes Claros (1665); Flanders (1668)	Disbanded in 1678	(1670s)[179] Trooper: grey coat
EC–83	1664	Hermann von Baden, 1673 Moerbeck, 1677 Hendrik Theyst (Theiste) von Braunsfeld		German	Flanders; Bruges, Jodoigne (1667); Seneffe (1674); Mont Cassel (1677); Saint-Denis (1678)	Disbanded in 1682	
EC–84	1664	Luigi Carafa, 1665 Rodolfo Rabatta	Habsburg Austria	German	Extremadura (1664); Montes Claros (1665) Guarda (1667)	Disbanded in 1665	(1664) Trooper: lobster helm, buff coat & black polished breast armour
EC–85	1664	Leonardo Edmondo Fabbri	Habsburg Austria	German	Extremadura (1664); Montes Claros (1665); Galicia (1666)	Disbanded in 1668	(1664) Trooper: lobster helm, buff coat & black polished breast armour
EC–86	1665	Metternich, 1666 Holstein, 1682 Hendrik Theyst (Theiste) von Braunsfeld		German	Bruges (1667); Seneffe (1674); Mont Cassel (1677); Saint-Denis (1678)	Disbanded in 1684	
EC–87	1666	Massiete, 1672 Charles de Fiennes (Thiennes)	Former Münster regiment	German then Walloon	Flanders; Jodoigne (1667)	Disbanded in 1673?	(1666)[180] Trooper: buff coat & black polished breast armour.

ID #	Year	Commander	Name / Notes	Nat'y	Garrison / Engagements	Regt History	Uniforms
EC-88	1666	Efferen	Former Münster regiment	German	Flanders	Disbanded in 1667	(1666)[181] Trooper: buff coat & black polished breast armour.
EC-89	1666	Erbaix, 1674 Jean de Noyelles–Torsy, 1689 Nicolò Pignatelli	Former Münster regiment	German	Flanders; Jodoigne (1667); Mont Cassel (1677); Saint-Denis (1678); Diest (1685)[182]	Disbanded in 1698 as *Gaetano* or *Aragona*	(1666)[183] Trooper: buff coat & black polished breast armour. (1691)[184] Trooper: grey-white coat with green facings.
EC-90	1666	Post	Former Münster regiment	German	Jodoigne (1667)	Disbanded in 1669	(1666)[185] Trooper: buff coat & black polished breast armour.
EC-91	1666	Stein		German		Disbanded in 1668?	
EC-92	1667	Felipe de Maella		Walloon	Jodoigne (1667)	Disbanded in 1669	
EC-93	1667	Juan Batista Wacant , 1670? Antonio Francisco Javier, 1674 Antonio de Jauregui, 1676? Juan Lasarte		Spanish	Flanders; Seneffe (1674); Mont Cassel (1677)	Disbanded in 1678?	
EC-94	1667	Geronimo Pimentel de Prado[186]		Spanish	Flanders; Mont Cassel (1677); Saint-Denis (1678)	Disbanded in 1685	
EC-95	1667	Bernardo Salinas Román y Ugarte, 1673Antonio Leiva, 1682 Gabriel del Bau (or Boé)		Spanish	Sicily (1674); Flanders (1677); Saint-Denis (1678)	Disbanded in 1685	
EC-96	1667	Diego de Rada, 1673 Bassecourt de Huby		Spanish	Flanders	Disbanded in 1668?	

ID #	Year	Commander	Name / Notes	Nat'y	Garrison / Engagements	Regt History	Uniforms
EC–97	1667	Eugenio López de Ulloa		Spanish	Flanders; Saint-Denis (1678)	Disbanded in 1685	
EC–98	1667?	Antonio Francisco Javier, 1672 Francisco de Cardona		Spanish	Flanders	Disbanded in 1681	
EC–99	1667	Wragnies, 1671 Antonio Luis Del Valle, 1684 Antonio de Zúñiga, 1686 Joseph Encio de San Vicente		Walloon then Spanish (1671)	Jodoigne (1667); Seneffe (1674); Oudenarde (1685)[187]	Disbanded in 1706 as *Peñalosa*	–
EC–100	1667	Feux, 1676 Amenzaga		Walloon then Spanish (1673)	Jodoigne (1667); Saint Denis (1678)	Disbanded in 1678?	
EC–101	1667	*Baron* de Wezemaal, 1672 Charles-Louis-Antoine d'Henin de Chimay-Beaumont, 1676 León de Rocca-Feurs		Walloon	Jodoigne (1667); Seneffe (1674)	Disbanded in 1678	
EC–102	1667	Gravelens, 1676 Haute-Pont (?)		Walloon	Flanders; Saint Denis (1678)	Disbanded in 1678?	
EC–103	1667	1667 Trauttmansdorff, 1669 Quincy, 1675 d'Audrigny, 1684 Severin de Bethencourt (or Betancourt)		Walloon	Furnes (1667); Maastricht (1673); Seneffe, Oudenarde (1674); Saint-Omer (1675); Condé, Bouchain (1676); Mont Cassel, Charleroi (1677), Mons, Saint Denis (1678); Ghent (1685)[188]	*Farnesio* in 1718	(1691)[189] Trooper: grey-white coat with red facings.
EC–104	1667	François Louis Baltazar d'Ognies de Courrières		Walloon	Flanders	Disbanded in 1668?	
EC–105	1667	François Florimond des ArmoisesMirecourt, 1673 Freyre		Walloon	Flanders	Disbanded in 1675?	

351

ID #	Year	Commander	Name / Notes	Nat'y	Garrison / Engagements	Regt History	Uniforms
EC–106	1667	Ferdinand de Mérode-Monfort, 1677 Jean de la Fontaine de Harnoncourt		Walloon	Flanders; Saint-Denis (1678)	Disbanded in 1679?	
EC–107	1667	François-Joseph de Courriers		Walloon	Flanders	Disbanded in 1673?	
EC–108	1667	Salm		German	Flanders	Disbanded in1673?	
EC–109	1667	Hünecken, 1672 Orsbeck, 1677 Chauvirey		German	Jodoigne (1667); Seneffe (1674); Saint-Denis (1678)	Disbanded in 1684?	
EC–110	1667	Rheingraf (Reyngraf)		German	Bruges (1667)	Disbanded in 1669	
EC–111	1667	Waldenburg, 1676 Schewen		German	Seneffe (1674)	Disbanded in 1676	
EC–112	1667	Vaudemont, 1674 Charles Henry de Lorraine-Vaudemont	Lorrena	German	Seneffe (1674); Aalst (1685)[190]	Disbanded in 1698 as *Avez*	(1691)[191] Trooper: grey-white coat lined red.
EC–113	1668	Saint Jean (San Juan), 1677?	Franche-Comté	Spanish	Saint-Denis (1678)	Disbanded in 1678?	
EC–114	1668	Leiba? Alfonso de Norsalise		Spanish		Disbanded in 1671	
EC–115	1668	Gregorio de Castro, 1672 Bernardo Sarmiento de Sotomayor, 1677 Domingo de Isassi	*Coraceros de Galicia*	Spanish	Flanders(1668); Seneffe (1674) Mont Cassel (1677); Ghent (1678); Messina (1680) (dismounted)	Disbanded in 1685	
EC–116	1668	Mario Carafa, 1684 Scipione Brancaccio		Italian (Naples)	Mons (1685)[192]	Disbanded in 1706 as *Fraula*	(1691)[193] Trooper: grey-white coat lined blue.
EC–117	1668	Boulers		Walloon	Saint-Denis (1678)	Disbanded in 1678?	

ID #	Year	Commander	Name / Notes	Nat'y	Garrison / Engagements	Regt History	Uniforms
EC-118	1668	Anton Ignace Schetz de Wessmael		Walloon		Disbanded in 1675?	
EC-119	1668	La Motterie		Walloon	Seneffe (1674)	Disbanded in 1674?	
EC-120	1668	Roeulx, 1669 Lieberg		Walloon, then German	Flanders	Disbanded in 1672?	
EC-121	1668	Chimay, 1677 Marraux (Mervaux)?		Walloon	Mont Cassel (1677); Saint-Denis (1678)	Disbanded in 1678?	
EC-122	1668	Philippe de Gulpen-Audemont	(coraceros)	Walloon	Ath (1685)[194]	Disbanded in 1715 as Drouhot	(1689)[195] Trooper: grey-white coat lined blue.
EC-123	1668	Enmanuel Kesselde Gravelens		Walloon	Flanders	Disbanded in 1678?	
EC-124	1668	Luis de Grave-Egmont		German	Saint-Denis (1678); Lier (1685)[196]	Disbanded in 1710 as Caetani	(1691)[197] Trooper: grey-white coat lined red.
EC-125	1668	Wilhelm von Lucart, 1680 Nicolás (Nikolaus) Hartmand, 1685 Louis Ernest d'Egmont-Gavre		German	Saint-Denis (1678)	Disbanded in 1706 as Landas-Louvigny	
EC-126	1670	Adrien-Honoré de Saint Jean-Steen, 1676 Mastaing		Walloon	Saint-Denis (1678); Dendermonde (1685)[198]	Disbanded in 1763 as Barcelona	(1691)[199] Private: grey-white coat lined red.
EC-127	1674?	Severin de Bethencourt (or Betancourt)		Walloon	Saint Denis (1678)	Disbanded in 1684	
EC-128	1674?	Dongelberghe		Walloon	Saint Denis (1678)	Disbanded in 1678?	
EC-129	1674?	Charles de Croy-Havré		German	Flanders; Saint-Denis (1678)	Disbanded in 1703?	(1680s)[200] Trooper: grey-white coat.

ID #	Year	Commander	Name / Notes	Nat'y	Garrison / Engagements	Regt History	Uniforms
EC–130	1675?	Gabriel de Buendia		Spanish	Saint-Denis (1678)	Disbanded in 1678?	
EC–131	1676	Philippe Charles d'Arenberg-De Aerschot (Aerschoff)	*Trozo borgoñón*	Franche-Comté, then Walloon	Leuven (1685);[201] Seneffe (1674); Mont Cassel (1676)	Disbanded in 1706 as *Toulengeon*	(1691)[202] Private: grey-white coat lined red.
EC–132	1679	1688, Alexandro de Bay (d'Huby)		Spanish	Flanders; Malines (1685)[203]	Disbanded in 1698	(1691)[204] Private: grey-white coat lined red.
EC–133	1680?	1685? Nicolás Hartmand		German	Lier and Herentals (1685)[205]	Disbanded in 1701?	(1691)[206] Private: grey-white coat lined red.
EC–134	1682	Gabriel de Buendia, 1688 Cardona		Spanish	Mons (1685)[207]	Disbanded in 1698 as *Zúñiga*	(1691)[208] Private: grey-white coat lined blue.
EC–135	1682	Lietberghe		Walloon	Flanders	Disbanded in 1684	
EC–136	1683	Julian Lezcano		Spanish	Catalonia; Gerona (1684)	Disbanded in 1684	(1677)[209] Trooper: *pardo* coat with red facing & lining.
EC–137	1684	Pedro Pacheco		Spanish	Catalonia; Gerona (1684)	Disbanded in 1684	(1677)[210] Trooper: *pardo* coat with red facing & lining.
EC–138	1688	Juan Augustin Hurtado de Mendoza		Spanish	Flanders (1689)	Disbanded in 1698	(1691)[211] Private: grey-white coat lined red.
EC–139	1688	Antonio Jacinto de Landbaum y Zumarraga		Spanish	Flanders (1689)	Disbanded in 1691	

ID #	Year	Commander	Name / Notes	Nat'y	Garrison / Engagements	Regt History	Uniforms
EC-140	1688	François Dumont-Dielsen		German	Flanders (1689)	Disbanded in 1691 and merged into Pignatelli (EC-91)	
EC-141	1688	Martin Fernández de Córdoba, 1689 Joaquim de Fuenmayor y Dávila		German	Flanders (1689)	Disbanded in 1698	(1689)[212] Trooper: grey-white coat lined red.
EC-142	1688	Charles-Louis-Antoine d'Henin de Chimay-Beaumont		German	Flanders	Disbanded in 1710 as *Lacatoire*	
EC-143	1688?	Anthon Ulrich d'Arberg-Fresin		German	Flanders	Disbanded in 1690	
EC-144	1689	Gaspar Gómez de Espinosa- Ribaucourt		Spanish	Flanders	Disbanded in 1763 as *Malta*	(1691)[213] Private: grey-white coat lined red.
EC-145	1689	François Hugues Ferdinand de Nassau		German	Flanders	Disbanded in 1691	

Dragoons

ID #	Year	Commanders	Name / Notes	Nat'y	Garrison / Engagements	Regt History	Uniforms
ED-1	1649	Mormal		Franche-Comté	Flanders	Disbanded in 1661	
ED-2	1649	D'Andermont		Spanish	Flanders	Disbanded in 1661	
ED-3	1668	(1672?) Nicolas Richard de Puys (Dupuis), 1674 Jean de Verlóo (or Berlóo), 1678 Nicolás Hartmand, 1680 François Sigismond de la Tour y Taxis, conde de la Tour Valsassine, 1683 Montifaux, 1684 Juan Vazquez de Acuña, 1685 François d'Ognies de Courrières-Ourges	Viejo de dragones	Spanish	Flanders; Seneffe, Oudenarde (1674); Konzer Brücke (1675); Charleroi (1677); Saint-Denis (1678)	Dragones de Belgica in 1718	(1675)[214] Private: red coat & facings
ED-4	1674?	Jean de la Fontaine de Harnoncourt, 1676 Gomar de Ville-Maugremont		Walloon	Flanders; Saint-Denis (1678); In Brussels (1685)215	Disbanded in 1698?	
ED-5	1675	Antonio Salcedo, 1688 Fedrique de Castro	Nuevo de dragones	Spanish	Saint-Denis (1678)	Disbanded in 1689	(1676)[216] Private: red cap and coat
ED-6	1675	Gomar de Ville-Maugremont, 1676 Mathias Pérez		Walloon	Flanders; Charleroi (1677); Saint-Denis (1678); Thuin (1684)	Disbanded in 1691	(1676)[217] Private; blue cap; red coat, blue cuffs & lining; natural linen breeches; white metal buttons. (1683)[218] Private: blue cap piped white; red coat, blue cuffs, lapels & lining; natural linen breeches; blue stockings; white metal buttons; red cloak lined blue.

ID #	Year	Commanders	Name / Notes	Nat'y	Garrison / Engagements	Regt History	Uniforms
ED-7	1675	Nicolás Hartmand, 1678 Vandewin Van der Pit, 1684 Theodore Valensart, 1685 François Sigismond de la Tour y Taxis, conde de la Tour-Valsassina		Walloon	Flanders; Bouchain (1676); Cassel, Charleroi (1677); Luxembourg (1683–1684); Ghent (1685)[219]	*Batavia* in 1718, then *Almansa* in 1765	(1676)[220] Private: green coat & facings.
ED-8	1684	Giovanni Battista Calderani(Scheldon), 1689 Prospero Crivelli	*Estado de Milán*	Spanish	Lombardy (1684); Greece (1686–1688); Nauplia, Navarino, Methony (1686)	*Pavia* in 1718	(1686)[221] Private: yellow coat with red cuffs & lining.
ED-09	1684	Bernabò Visconti, 1686 Ussief		Italian	Lombardy (1685)	Disbanded in 1698	(1688)[222] Private: red coat with yellow cuffs & lining.
ED-10	1688	Claude Richardot de Steenhuyssen		Walloon	Flanders	*Vila Viçosa* in 1765	
ED-11	1689	Nicolás de Agüero y Zarate		Walloon	Flanders	Disbanded in 1693	
ED-12	1689	Ernst de Bossu d'Alsace		Walloon	Flanders	Disbanded in 1690	(1689)[223] Private: red coat
ED-13	1689	Jacques Pastur Cousiers		Walloon	Flanders	Disbanded in 1693	(1690s)[224] Private: blue cap trimmed with fur, blue coat & cuffs, blue waistcoat, natural leather breeches, blue cloak.

Footnotes

1   Archivo Histórico de la Nobleza (hereafter AHNOB), Osuna, Estado 45168, Estado de la fuerza, Ct.197, d.82, ES.

2   *London Gazette* (May–June 1671).

3   Archivo General de Simancas (hereafter AGS), Estado-Flandes, leg. 1374, d. 26.

4   Archivio Segreto Vaticano (hereafter ASV), Segreteria di Stato 1026, Avvisi, Avvisi di Napoli, 24 May 1676.

5   ASV, Segreteria 1026, Avvisi, Avvisi di Bologna, 6 November 1685.

6   *Ibid.*

7   AGS, Guerra Antigua, leg. 2533. Consejo de Guerra, 18 June 1688.

8   ASV, Segreteria di Stato 1026, *Avvisi, Avvisi, Avvisi di Napoli*, 24 May 1676.

9) ASV, Segreteria 1026, *Avvisi, Avvisi, Avvisi di Bologna*, 6 November 1685.

10 *Ibid.*

11 Servicios of Francisco Pereyra Freire de Andrade.

12 AHNOB, *Osuna*, Ct.197, d.82.

13 *London Gazette* (May–June 1671).

14 Enrico Ottone Grana del Carretto, Marchese del, *Despachos para Su Majestad del Gobierno de Flandes, en tiempo del Excmo. Sr. Marqués de Grana, desde primero de abril 1682* (manuscript 9888, Biblioteca Nacional de España)

15 AHNOB, *Osuna*, Ct.197, d.82.

16 *London Gazette* (May–June 1671).

17 AGS, *Guerra Antigua*, leg. 2541. *Consejo de Guerra*, 13 December 1690.

18 AHNOB, *Osuna*, Ct.197, d.82.

19 *London Gazette* (May–June 1671).

20 Juan Luis Sánchez-Martín, 'Las tropas británicas de la casa de Austria', in *Researching & Dragona*, n. 8, 1999; pp.4–21.

21 *Ibid.*

22 Manuel Giménez González, *El Ejército y la Armada* (Madrid, 1862).

23 *Ibid*

24 AGS, *Estado-Flandes*, leg. 1374, d. 22.

25 AHNOB, *Osuna*, Ct.197, d.82.

26 *London Gazette* (May–June 1671).

27 AGS, *Estado-Flandes*, leg. 1374, d. 26.

28 José De Santiago y Gómez, *Historia de Vigo y su Comarca* (Madrid, 1896). pp.398–401.

29 According to Sánchez-Martín, there possibly existed a second Pedro de Aldao y Taboada, *maestre de campo* of a *tercio* serving in Flanders until May 1693.

30 AHNOB, *Osuna*, Ct.197, d.82.

31 *London Gazette* (May–June 1671).

32 *Ibid.*

33 ASV, Segreteria 1026, *Avvisi, Avvisi, Avvisi di Napoli*, 16 November 1687.

34 Sanchez Martin, *Las tropas británicas de la casa de Austria*, pp.4–21

35 Giménez González, *El Ejército y la Armada*.

36 *Ibid.*

37 Raised by the Kingdom of Naples.

38 AHNOB, *Osuna*, Ct.197, d.82.

39 *London Gazette* (May–June 1671).

40 Archives Générales du Royaume (hereafter AGR), *Contadurie et Pagadorie des Gens de Guerre* (1697) N.879.

41 Archivo General de Indias (hereafter AGI), Indiferente, leg. 122, N. 50: Servicios del maestre de campo Francisco Osorio de Astorga

42 Giménez González, *El Ejército y la Armada*.

43 *Ibid.*

44 AHNOB, Luque, Ct.626, d.26, and Cesareo Duro Fernandez, *Memoria Historicas de la Ciudad de Zamora su provincia y Obispado*, vol. II–IV.

45 Filamondo, fra' Raffaele Maria, *Il Genio Bellicoso di Napoli, Domenico di Costanzo Maestro di campo del Terzo napoletano su l'Armata dell'Oceano* (Napoli, 1694).

46 Giménez González, *El Ejército y la Armada*.

47 *Ibid.*

48 Serafín Estébanez Calderón, *De la conquista y pérdida de Portugal* (Madrid, 1885); vol. I, p.245.

49 *Ibid.*, vol. I, p.246.

50 Giménez González, *El Ejército y la Armada*.

51 José Maria Bueno, *La infanteria y la artilleria de marina, 1537–1931* (Madrid: Graficas Summa, 1985)

52 Giménez González, *El Ejército y la Armada*.

53 AGI, *Indiferente*, leg. 124, N. 19.

54 *Ibid.* N. 4.

55 Biblioteca Nacional de España (hereafter BNE), *Sucesos del año 1659–1660*, pp.10–12.

56 *London Gazette* (May–June 1671).

57 *Ibid.*

58 ASV, Segreteria 1026, *Avvisi, Avvisi di Napoli*, 6 November 1685.

59 Paid by the Kingdom of Naples.

60 *Ibid.*

61 Paid by the State of Milan. Antonio José Rodríguez Hernández, *La presencia militar alemana en los ejércitos peninsulares españoles durante la guerra de restauracion portuguesa (1659–1668)*, in L. Ruiz Molina, J.J. Ruiz Ibañez, B. Vincent (eds), *Yakka. Revista De Histudios Yeclanos*, vol. 10 (2015), p.272.

62 Giménez González, *El Ejército y la Armada*.

63 Luis Sorando Muzas and Antonio Manzano Lahoz, 'El tercio de Aragón: notas sobra su Evolución, indumentaria y emblematica (1678–1698)', in *Emblanata – Revista Aragonesa de Emblemática*, N. 1 (1995), p.161.

64 África García Fernández, *Toledo entre Austrias y Borbones: su aportación al inicio del la Guerra deSucesión (1690–1706)* (Departamento de Historia Moderna – Facultad de Geografía e Historia, Universidad Complutense de Madrid, 2012), p.887.

65 Giménez González, Manuel, *El Ejército y la Armada* (Madrid, 1862).

66 Sorando Muzas and Manzano Lahoz, 'El tercio de Aragón', p.161.

67 Estébanez Calderón, *De la conquista y pérdida de Portugal*, vol. II, p.92.

68 AGI, Indipendiente, leg. 125, n. 45: Relación de Servicios del capitán de Cavallos coraças Don Diego Hidalgo de Cisneros.

69 Paid by the Kingdom of Naples.

70 Estébanez Calderón, *De la conquista y pérdida de Portugal*, vol. II (Madrid, 1885), p.96.

71 AHNOB, *Osuna*, Ct.197, d.82. (Regiment reduced to a single company?)

72 *London Gazette* (May–June 1671).

73 Paid by the Spanish Low Countries.
74 Ibid.
75 Actas de las Junta & Diputaciones del Principado de Asturias, vol. III. 1657–1672, contrato por los vestidos de municion del tercio de Asturias, 1663.
76 Estébanez Calderón, De la conquista y pérdida de Portugal, vol. II, p.68.
77 Ibid.
78 BNE, Despachos para Su Majestad del Gobierno de Flandes, en tiempo del Excmo. Sr. Marqués de Grana, MS 9888.
79 ASV, Nunziature, Nunziatura di Napoli, 21 May 1687.
80 Acta Helvetica, 26/76–106, Abrechnung der Sieben Katholischen Orte und Abtei Sankt Gallen mit König von Spanien.
81 ASV, Segreteria di Stato 1026, Avvisi, Avvisi di Napoli, 13 June 1685.
82 Acta Helvetica, 26/76 –106, Abrechnung der Sieben Katholischen Orte und Abtei Sankt Gallen mit König von Spanien.
83 AHNOB, Osuna, Estado de la fuerza de los ejércitos de caballería e infantería españoles destacados en Flandes (dated 3 March 1685).
84 Anales de Aragón desde al año MDXXV (Saragossa, 1697), p.39.
85 Antonio José Rodríguez Hernández, España, Flandes y la Guerra de Devolución (1667–1668): guerra, reclutamiento y movilización para el mantenimiento de los Países Bajos españoles (Madrid: Ministerio de Defensa, 2007), p.367, and AGS, Guerra Antigua, Leg. 2.193, Consejo de Guerra (dated 9 September 1668).
86 London Gazette (May–June 1671).
87 Anales de Aragón desde al año MDXXV, p.39.
88 Biblioteca Mediceo Laurenziana, Florence, Diari di Lorenzo Magalotti.
89 Tercio raised by the Consell de Cent of Barcelona; Antonio Espino López, 'El esfuerzo de guerra de la Corona de Aragón durante el reinado de Carlos II, 1665–1700. Los servicios de tropas', in Revista de Historia Moderna Anales de la Universidad de Alicante, N. 22 (2004), pp.9–11.
90 AHNOB, Osuna, Estado de la fuerza, Ct.197, d.82.
91 London Gazette (May–June 1671).
92 AGR, Contadurie et Pagadorie des Gens de Guerre (1686) N. 718.
93 AHNOB, Osuna, Estado de la fuerza, Ct.197, d.82. Regiment reduced to a single company.
94 London Gazette (May–June 1671).
95 AGR, Contadurie et Pagadorie des Gens de Guerre (1686) N. 718.
96 AHNOB, Osuna, Estado de la fuerza, Ct.197, d.82.
97 Ibid.
98 Clonard, Memorias para la Historia de las tropas de la Casa Real de España (Madrid, 1848), p.132.
99 London Gazette (May–June 1671).
100 AHNOB, Osuna, Estado de la fuerza, Ct.197, d.82.
101 AGR, Contadurie et Pagadorie des Gens de Guerre (1686) N.718.
102 AGS, S.P. leg. 2096, f. 627: Relación de Servicios del Maestro de Campo Don Gonçalo Cegri.
103 Narcís Feliu de la Peña i Farell, Anales de Cataluña, vol. III, p.357.
104 Tercio raised by the Consell de Cent of Barcelona.

105 AHMB, *Consell, Deliberacions*, vol. 191.
106 *Tercio* raised by the *Generalitat* of Catalonia.
107 AHMB, *Consell, Deliberacions*, vol. 191.
108 La Peña, *Anales de Cataluña*, vol. III, p.357.
109 *Ibid.*
110 *Ibid.*
111 *Ibid.*
112 *Ibid.*
113 La Peña, *Anales de Cataluña*, vol. III, p.357.
114 Sorando Muzas and Manzano Lahoz, 'El Tercio de Aragón', pp.61–65.
115 AHNOB, Osuna, *Estado de la fuerza*, Ct.197, d.82.
116 La Peña, *Anales de Cataluña*, vol. III, p.357.
117 Archivo General de la Corona de Aragón (hereafter ACA), Consejo de Aragón, Consejo, leg. 72, Planta de los soldados, Pagam.to y Vestidos, ff. 222–224, April 1678.
118 AHNOB, *Osuna, Estado de la fuerza*, Ct.197, d.82.
119 BNE, Correspondencia de Carlos de Gurrea y Aragón, Duque de Villahermosa, relativa a su gobierno en Flandes, MS 2412 (1676), p.117–118.
120 ASV, *Nunziature, Nunziatura di Napoli*, 11 May 1676.
121 AGS, *Estado*, leg. 3428.
122 ASV, *Nunziature, Nunziatura di Napoli*, 11 May 1676.
123 *Ibid.*
124 AHNOB, *Osuna, Estado de la fuerza*, Ct.197, d.82.
125 *Ibid.*, regiment reduced to a single company. In Leeuw there are two further *companias suelats: Duque de Hauve* and *Conde de Boucquoy.*
126 ASV, *Nunziature, Nunziatura di Napoli*, 11 May 1676.
127 *Ibid.*
128 *Ibid.*
129 Archivio Storico Siciliano (hereafter ASS), *Appunti e Documenti*, vol. XXIV (1677), p.209.
130 Sorando Muzas and Manzano Lahoz, 'El tercio de Aragón', p.161.
131 ASV, *Nunziature, Nunziatura di Napoli*, 11 May 1676.
132 ASV, *Segreteria* 1026, *Avvisi, Avvisi di Napoli*, 13 September 1687.
133 AHNOB, *Osuna, Estado de la fuerza*, Ct.197, d.82.
134 AGR, Contadurie et Pagadorie des Gens de Guerre (1686), N. 718.
135 Sorando Muzas and Manzano Lahoz, 'El tercio de Aragón', p.161.
136 *Ibid.*
137 *Tercios* Arenberg and Danhanrè: in *Gazeta Ordinaria de Madrid*, 1678, p.218.
138 Archivio di Stato di Napoli (hereafter ASNa), *Museo*, vol. 994146 (Antonio Carafà di Stigliano).
139 AHNOB, *Osuna, Estado de la fuerza*, Ct.197, d.82

140 ASV, *Segreteria* 1026, *Avvisi, Avvisi di Napoli*, 13 September 1687.
141 *Ibid.*
142 ASV, Segreteria 1026, *Avvisi, Avvisi di Napoli*, 6 November 1685.
143 AHNOB, *Osuna, Estado de la fuerza*, Ct.197, d.82
144 Sánchez-Martín, in 'Researching & Dragona', N. 24 – November 2003, p.129.
145 AGS, *Guerra Antigua*, leg. 2541. *Consejo de Guerra*, 13 December 1690.
146 AHNOB, *Osuna, Estado de la fuerza*, Ct.197, d.82
147 Sánchez-Martín, in *Researching & Dragona*, N. 24 – November 2003, p.129.
148 BNE, Correspondencia de Carlos de Gurrea y Aragón, MS. 2412 (1676), p.117–118.
149 *Ibid.*
150 AHNOB, *Osuna, Estado de la fuerza*, Ct.197, d.82
151 ASV, Segreteria 1026, *Avvisi, Avvisi di Bologna*, 6 November 1685.
152 AHNOB, Osuna, Estado de la fuerza, Ct.197, d.82
153 AHNOB, *Osuna* ct.107, d.18; Carta de Antonio de Heredia Biyar.
154 Archivio di Stato di Venezia (hereafter ASVe), *Stato da Mar, Provveditori sopra le Camere*, c. 341.
155 *Ibid.*
156 Biblioteca Nazionale Centrale di Firenze (hereafter BNC), *Codice Rossi-Cassigoli*, BNC 199, fol. 245.
157 ASVe, *Stato da Mar, Provveditori sopra le Camere*, c. 341.
158 ASV, Segreteria di Stato 1026, *Avvisi, Avvisi di Bologna*, 23 Aprile 1686.
159 Antonio José, Rodríguez Hernández, 'La venta de títulos nobiliarios a través de la financiación de nuevas unidades militares durante el siglo XVII', in F Andújar Castillo and M. Felices de la Fuente (eds), *El poder del dinero. Ventas de cargo y honores en el Antiguo Régimen* (Madrid: Biblioteca Nueva, 2011), pp.294–295. When the *tercio* was disbanded, the document refers to it as *tercio de los Mallorquines* (Mallorcans); see AHNOB, *Frias* ct.87, d.45.
160 ACA, Archivo de la Diputación de Zaragoza, ct. 772, d. 61 (1685).
161 AGR, Contadurie et Pagadorie des Gens de Guerre N. 761 (1688).
162 *Ibid.*, N. 879 (1697).
163 *Ibid.*
164 *Ibid.*
165 AGS, *Guerra Antigua*, leg. 2511. *Consejo de Guerra*, 1 June 1682.
166 *Ibid.*
167 AHNOB, *Osuna, Estado de la fuerza*, Ct.197, d.82. *Trozo* reduced to a single company.
168 The company of the *maestre de campo* survived the disbanding of the regiment, and in 1677 become the core of the future cavalry regiment *Farnesio*.
169 AHNOB, *Osuna, Estado de la fuerza*, Ct.197, d.82, one company in 1685.
170 *Exact List of the Royal Confederate Army in Flanders, Commanded by the King of Great–Britain. In Four Lines; As it was Drawn up at Gerpines Camp, July 27, 1691.*

171 AGS, *Guerra Antigua*, leg. 2685, d. 12.
172 AGS, *Estado*, leg. 1332, d. 55.
173 AGS, *Guerra Antigua*, leg. 2685, d. 12.
174 AGS, *Estado*, leg. 1332, d. 55.
175 Estébanez Calderón, *De la conquista y pérdida de Portugal*, vol. II, p.68.
176 *Comte de Hornes et de Houtkercke, Seigneur de Gaeskek el Houikercke, Hondschoot, de Stavele, de Crombreek, de Herlies; Vicomte de Furnes et de Bergues-Saint-Winoc; Grand-veneur héréditaire de l'Empire.*
177 AGR, Contadurie et Pagadorie des Gens de Guerre (1687) N. 397.
178 Estébanez Calderón, *De la conquista y pérdida de Portugal*, vol. II, p.68.
179 ASV, Segreteria di Stato 1026, *Avvisi*, *Avvisi di Napoli*, 4 May 1676.
180 Reconstruction after contemporary painting (private collection, Münster).
181 *Ibid.*
182 AHNOB, *Osuna, Estado de la fuerza*, Ct.197, d.82.
183 Reconstruction after contemporary painting (private collection, Münster).
184 *An Exact List of the Royal Confederate Army in Flanders*, 1691.
185 Reconstruction after contemporary painting (private collection, Münster).
186 Reduced to one company in 1669.
187 AHNOB, *Osuna, Estado de la fuerza*, Ct.197, d.82.
188 *Ibid.*
189 *An Exact List of the Royal Confederate Army in Flanders*, 1691.
190 AHNOB, *Osuna, Estado de la fuerza*, Ct.197, d.82.
191 *An Exact List of the Royal Confederate Army in Flanders*, 1691.
192 AHNOB, *Osuna, Estado de la fuerza*, Ct.197, d.82.
193 *An Exact List of the Royal Confederate Army in Flanders*, 1691.
194 AHNOB, *Osuna, Estado de la fuerza*, Ct.197, d.82.
195 'List of Our Army as it was drawn up at Tillroy Camp, 1689', in *A Journal of the late motions and actions of the Confederate Forces against the French, written by an English Officer who was there during the last campaign* (London, 1690).
196 AHNOB, *Osuna, Estado de la fuerza*, Ct.197, d.82.
197 *An Exact List of the Royal Confederate Army in Flanders*, 1691.
198 AHNOB, *Osuna, Estado de la fuerza*, Ct.197, d.82.
199 *An Exact List of the Royal Confederate Army in Flanders*, 1691.
200 AGS, *Estado – Flandes*, leg. 1353, d. 3.
201 AHNOB, *Osuna, Estado de la fuerza*, Ct.197, d.82, *Tercio del Ducque de Ariscole*.
202 *An Exact List of the Royal Confederate Army in Flanders*, 1691.
203 AHNOB, *Osuna, Estado de la fuerza*, Ct.197, d.82.
204 *An Exact List of the Royal Confederate Army in Flanders*, 1691.

205 AHNOB, *Osuna, Estado de la fuerza*, Ct.197, d.82.
206 *An Exact List of the Royal Confederate Army in Flanders*, 1691.
207 AHNOB, *Osuna, Estado de la fuerza*, Ct.197, d.82.
208 *An Exact List of the Royal Confederate Army in Flanders*, 1691.
209 Antonio José Rodríguez Hernández, 'La caballería hispánica, Un arma al alza', in *Los Tercios, 1660–1704, Desperta Ferro*, special issue XIX (June–July 2019), p.45.
210 *Ibid.*
211 *An Exact List of the Royal Confederate Army in Flanders*, 1691.
212 *List of Our Army as it was drawn up at Tillroy Camp*, 1689.
213 *An Exact List of the Royal Confederate Army in Flanders*, 1691.
214 AGR, Contadurie et Pagadorie des Gens de Guerre (1675) N. 334.
215 AHNOB, *Osuna, Estado de la fuerza*, Ct.197, d.82, Ducque de Ariscole.
216 AGR, Contadurie et Pagadorie des Gens de Guerre (1676) N. 349.
217 Jean-R. Cayron, 'La véritable histoire de Jacques Pastur dit Jaco', p.553.
218 AGR, Contadurie et Pagadorie des Gens de Guerre (1676) N. 350.
219 AHNOB, *Osuna, Estado de la fuerza*, Ct.197, d.82.
220 AGR, Contadurie et Pagadorie des Gens de Guerre (1676) N. 350.
221 BNC, *Codice Rossi-Cassigoli*, BNC 199, fol. 245.
222 ASV, Segreteria 1026, *Avvisi, Avvisi di Napoli*, 6 October 1688.
223 AGS, *Estado – Flandes*, leg. 1337, d. 3
224 Cayron, 'La véritable histoire de Jacques Pastur dit Jaco', pp.65–69.

Colour Plate Commentaries

Plate A: Hispanic Infantry, 1660s

1. Officer, unknown unit, Flanders 1665–1668

The painter Gillis van Tilborgh (1620–1678) was active in Flanders until the year of his death, and in his paintings he makes almost a visual chronicle of the military clothing in the Low Countries. Tilborgh portrayed officers and soldiers since the 1660s, including militiamen. This officer wears a short coat with sleeves reaching the elbow, as was typical in the Netherlands and France, over a panelled *Rhinegrave* breeches. Senior and junior officers tailored their dress privately and practically every colour could be employed, grey and other undyed clothes being the most common for private soldiers, but in this and other Tilborgh's paintings the officers wear coats of grey cloth with the usual high-ranking accessories such as ribbons and laces.

2. Musketeer, *tercio fijo provincial de Toledo*, 1665

According to the classic Spanish military historiography, the uniforms issued to the permanent provincial infantry were established by Don Juan of Austria in 1663. The clothing comprised a tailored coat lined and faced in different colours, in the *carlino* style. Some nineteenth-century illustrations depicted these uniforms with further details, such as laced pocket flaps, wide breeches of straw-yellow fabric, white cotton cravats and a wide-brimmed hat in a pale material with plumes. Contemporary images relating to these *tercios* are very rare and our current knowledge is limited to what can be found in the archives. As far as the *tercio* of Toledo is concerned, the blue coat with white facing and lining is confirmed in a document preserved in the city's archive. The coat was lined with a double layer of *fustán* (fustian), with eight buttons for each cuff; breeches, probably of the same colour as the coat, were lined with *lienzo ordinario* (canvas).

3. Arquebusier, unknown Spanish or Flemish Walloon unit, Flanders mid 1660s

Several contemporary eyewitnesses confirm the use of *pardo* (tanned brown) cloth for the manufacturing of the infantry uniforms in Flanders and Spain. Further sources, like the paintings of the aforementioned Tilborgh and other artists, depict infantrymen wearing a very simple *vestido de munición* of grey or *pardo* cloth, sometime with flap cuffs, and broad-brimmed headgear with plumes. Equipment was reduced to the essential items. Similar clothing and colours are also confirmed for the uniforms of the Army of Extremadura since the 1650s. According to the opinion of Don Juan of Austria, the appearance of the soldiers dressed in the rough tanned brown clothes 'would have disgusted the most miserable of shepherds', but despite this bitter comment, *pardo* remained a common colour of the Monarchy's armies in the following decades.

Plate B: Hispanic Infantry, 1670s

1. Musketeer, unknown Spanish tercio, Flanders 1672–73

Seventeenth-century Flemish Walloon painters offer a wide range of images relating to soldiers in the Spanish Low Countries. This infantrymen is portrayed in a painting of David Theniers (1610–1690), datable to the early 1670s. Grey coats are confirmed in the news published in the *London Gazette* of 1671. The journal reported that the governor Count of Monterrey had ordered all the Spanish infantry in Flanders to be dressed in grey with red facings, and he wanted to extend this uniform to all the infantry in the country, Walloons and Italians included, probably with different linings and facings.

2. Arquebusier, *tercio de Zaragoza* (EI-242), Catalonia 1678

The uniform established for the Aragonese infantry represent one of the most interesting and accurate testimonies of the 'dawn of the uniform' in Spain. The choice of this colour was preceded by a long debate and involved the highest authorities of the Kingdom. Blue was the colour that identified the Aragonese troops serving in the Monarchy's armies since the early 1670s, but the definitive decision to employ this colour occurred in 1678. The investigation conducted by Luis Sorando Muzas and Antonio Manzano Lahoz in the *Archivo de la Corona de Aragón* has produced an accurate study on this matter. Thanks to their efforts, this figure has been reconstructed following contemporary drawings and prints.

3. Artilleryman, 1680–90

Little is known about the uniform of the Hispanic artillery in the late seventeenth century, but probably the Spanish private gunners wore the same colour coats as the infantry: grey in Flanders and red in Italy, while the Italian artillerymen in Milan and Naples possibly had blue coats. In one of the rare illustrations of Spanish artillery, a gunner is represented wearing a coat with a zigzag pattern on the breast, and this suggests he is wearing a buff coat. The upper part seems to be tailored with a double layer, like the coat issued to the heavy cavalry. The use of leather in artillerymen's dress was a measure used for saving the gun crews from flames and sparks when firing the cannon. Leather coats were very popular among gunners in the first half of the century, and wearing this type of clothing may have continued longer in Spain. Source: *El perfecto bombardero y pratico artificial*, by Sebastián Fernández de Medrano (1691).

Plate C: Hispanic Infantry, 1680s

1. Officer, unknown Spanish unit, Madrid 1683

In a painting by Francisco Rizzi of an *auto-da-fé*, dating from the early 1680s, several officers and NCOs are portrayed wearing coats of different colours. The style of their dress is close to the French one, as is clearly shown by the *justaucorps* coats with wide flap cuffs. Some of the figures are wearing particularly elaborate coats, embroidered and lined with a multitude of lace, and broad-brimmed hats with coloured plumes. This officer wears a French-style coat made with brocade cloth and he is typical of aristocrats and senior officers in Spain and Italy. In this period, Hispanic military dress reached its peak in the use of luxurious clothes, and decorative accessories such as ribbons and lace.

2. NCO, unknown Flemish Walloon unit, Flanders early 1680s

In a painting of an unknown Flemish Walloon artist preserved in the Castello Sforzesco's antique art collection in Milan, a group of soldiers, NCOs and officers are depicted resting after a march. The red scarves of the officers identify them as Hispanic soldiers. Despite the poor condition of the painting, it is possible to distinguish soldiers wearing grey coats with blue facings, a mounted officer in dark blue, an ensign in red, and a couple of NCOs with red coats with blue lining and cuffs. One of them, possibly a veteran *sargento*, wears a fashionable coat with wide double silver lace. The variety of colours shows that there was no specific regulation regarding the clothing of NCOs, who were usually dressed differently from soldiers and their coats were marked with lace anticipating the rank markings distinctive of the following century.

3. Drummer, unknown Neapolitan unit, 1684–88

This figure is a reconstruction from a painting of the Neapolitan school, dating from the 1680s, which is preserved in the collection of the Museo di Capodimonte. It illustrates a group of soldiers in the foreground, before San Vincenzo's tower in Naples. The level of detail is low, but some features may be guessed at using information from other sources. The archives of the Vatican nunciatures in Italy are a very useful source for many details of the armies operating in the Italian Peninsula. Together with these documents, the *Avvisi* from the major cities of the Papal States add valuable information regarding the movements of troops, the composition of the garrisons and also the colours of the uniforms. Although the descriptions are often limited to a few brief notes, certain details have helped in the reconstruction of the first Hispanic uniforms. In the 1680s, the *Avvisi* of Naples and the Italian nunciatures often report on the purchasing of *panno turchino* (blue cloth) for the coats of the Italian infantry quartered in the Kingdom. The blue coat had been one associated with Italian troops since the previous decade, but it is interesting to note that no further colours are recorded in the contract. It is therefore probable that even NCOs and musicians wore coats of the same colour, with just the usual accessories such as ribbons and laces.

Plate D: Hispanic Cavalry, 1660s

1. Coracero, lifeguard company of the Kingdom of Naples' viceroy, mid 1660s

Lifeguard heavy cavalry companies formed to escort governors and other high officers of the kingdoms are often depicted wearing armour. This figure is a reconstruction from a print illustrating the arrival in Naples of Spanish Viceroy Pedro Antonio de Aragón, Duke of Segorbe and Cardona in 1666. Heavy cavalry lifeguards wear corselets with pauldrons and gauntlets, and their appearance is very similar to that depicted by the Neapolitan artist Carlo Coppola in some of his paintings, except for the headdress, which is a plumed broad-brimmed hat.

2. Officer, unknown Spanish unit and 3. Trooper, unknown Spanish or Flemish Walloon unit, Flanders late 1660s

The Flemish artist Lambert de Hondt the Younger (1645–1709?) left several paintings depicting military scenes dating to the late 1660s and early 1670s. Some subjects are portrayed in a generic way, but some details are very accurate and allow us to get a good idea about the clothing of the Hispanic cavalry in these years. The officer wearing the red coat does not wear any armour, a feature that could identify him as an officer of a company or *trozo* of *jinetes* – light horsemen. Cavalry warfare in Flanders, characterised by incursions and raids into enemy territory, favoured the reduction of armour protection by the cavalry. Moreover, in this period even the French horsemen had progressively renounced the use of armour.

Plate E: *Alférez* – standard-bearer, Spanish *tercio De Puy* (EC-57) Flanders 1684–89

The cavalry was the best part of the Army of Flanders and it some important victories against the French in the War of Devolution, and in subsequent conflicts did not reduce its value as a useful instrument for facing the French on the battlefield. By the 1680s the dress and equipment of the cavalry had been standardised throughout Western Europe with only minor features distinguishing the different nationalities. This standard-bearer still retains the breastplate as is typical of the Hispanic officers' dress in this period. The protection could be increased with a buff leather waistcoat worn under the coat. The saddle cover was often used for displaying elaborate and precious textiles, as depicted in several portraits of Spanish, or foreign cavalry officers.

Plate F: Spanish Cavalry and Dragoons, 1680s

1. Trooper, Spanish unknown unit, Lombardy, 1684–1688

By the 1670s, Spanish cavalry no longer distinguished between 'light' *jinetes* and 'heavy' *coraceros* specialties, being the seventeenth-century precursor of the line cavalry trooper. In this period, 'horse' is a generic term that covered several kinds of cavalry, and the equipment and armament issued to the horse varied considerably from decade to decade. Details of equipment remained subject to local variations, vagaries and mere regimental whims to a remarkable degree. The Monarchy's cavalry retained varying amounts of body armour, although the tendency was for this to diminish rapidly as the period wore on. A backplate and breastplate could be worn beneath the coat, but their use seems to have fallen out of favour after the 1680s. This figure is based on a horsemen depicted on a painted settle decorated with cavalry battle scenes by an unknown Milanese artist which dates to the early 1680s. All the mounted figures wear full grey coats, officers included, and they are engaged in action without breastplates. The equipment of the troopers comprises a cavalry carbine and a pair of pistols, as was usual for the 'heavies' in this period.

2. Private Dragoon, Spanish *tercio de dragones del Estado de Milán* (ED-8), Greece 1686

There were relatively few Hispanic dragoons in the last quarter of the seventeenth century. For example, in 1684 there were only five dragoon *tercios* in Flanders and two in Lombardy, one of which was made up of Spanish nationals and the other locally recruited. The Spanish *tercio* formed the contingents gathered in 1684 to join the Venetians in Greece. Some dragoons were described in the works of the Tuscan Knight of Saint Stephen Ignazio Fabroni, who volunteered to join the campaign against the Ottomans from 1684 to 1688, and is today preserved in the Biblioteca Nazionale Centrale of Florence. The yellow coat with red facings remained the same until the next century. According to contemporary testimonies, the dragoons in Flanders wore a dress more similar to their French counterparts and like them, the Hispanic dragoons wore gaiters instead boots.

Plate G: Spanish Coats, 1650–1670

1. Infantry *casaca*, late 1650s

Since the 1630s the *vestido de munición* usually comprised the jacket manufactured with *pardo* (tanned brown) cloth and *hungarina* (cassock) of the same colour. In the following decade the latter item disappeared, replaced by the short coat tailored in various patterns, which became the universal dress of the Spanish infantry. In the early 1660s this kind of coat was the most common garment of the Hispanic infantry before the introduction of the French style *justaucorps*, in the version known as *carlino*-style coat.

2. *Chamberga* coat for private soldier, infantry *tercio Guardias del Rey* (EI-181), 1669–78

Yellow was the traditional distinctive colour of the Spanish household troops, and the *Coronelia del Rey* (EI-15), also wore coats manufactured with this colour between 1634 and 1664. King Carlos II and his stepbrother Don Juan introduced the *justaucorps* at court following the influential French fashion, and this style was known in Spain as *carlino*. This kind of coat presumably derived from those introduced in 1663 after the formation of the permanent provincial *tercios*, and it appears in Clonard's *Memorias para la historia de las tropas de la Casa Real de España*.

3. *Chamberga* coat for musician, infantry *tercio Guardias del Rey*; a: detail of the royal livery; b: alternative pattern for Household units (after Pedro de Valpuesta's *Felipe IV swears to defend the doctrine of the immaculate concession* dated 1655–60).

4. Coat for private soldiers, infantry *tercio provincial de Sevilla* (EI-15), 1670s

Los Morados from Seville popularised this colour within the Monarchy's armies, retaining their bright uniforms until the first years of the eighteenth century. According to classic Spanish sources, in 1663 each provincial *tercio* received a distinctive colour, and these would not have changed in the following decades; when 10 new provincial *tercios* were raised in 1694, receiving uniforms similar to those of the existing units, the old corps continued to be recognised by their colour, adding the qualifying title of *viejos*.

Plate H: Foreign Soldiers in Spanish Service

1. *Guardia Alemanna* of the Naples Viceroy, 1650–60

Germans made up the largest non-Spanish nationality among Hispanic armies, including among the lifeguards such as the *guarda tudesca* of the Spanish kings in Madrid, and the *Guardia Alemanna* of the viceroys of Naples. According to some scholars, the German guards in Madrid were dressed like the Spanish guards, but in white. The German foot guards in Naples are shown in a 1650s painting wearing red-yellow clothing with red headgear similar to that of their Spanish counterparts. They formed a company of 60–70 halberdiers to serve as an escort for the viceroy and to guard his residence.

2. Pikeman, Irish *tercio O'Byrne* (EI-31), Flanders, 1678

Since the 1660s Irish infantry in Spanish service was dressed in red, and this colour continued to identify this nation in the following decades. The Irish infantry *tercios* and companies were organised like a Spanish one, and comprised musketeers, arquebusiers and pikemen. These latter wore the same uniform as the soldiers equipped with firearms, and stored the armour and helmet, usually a morion, in the garrisons. Contemporary accounts report that the pikemen of the Hispanic armies on campaign were usually *picas secas* (unarmoured pikemen). With the improvement of the range and accuracy of firearms the use of the pike declined, but its use in Spain, Italy and Flanders was only officially abolished between 1702 and 1704.

3. English Musketeer, Regiment *Porter* (EI-14) Flanders 1680–1685

Juan Luis Sánchez Martin, in his article *Tropas Británicas de la Casa de Austria*, published in 1999 in the magazine *Researching & Dragona*, gives valuable information on the Irish, Scottish and English regiments in Spanish service. He states that the English infantry was dressed in blue with red facings and lining, while the Scots wore yellow coats faced and lined in red. There is little archival information concerning the dress of the soldiers from the British Isles, and some reconstructions are conjectural, however, the author is an authoritative researcher on this matter. English presence in the Hispanic armies had begun in the sixteenth century, and lasted until 1692, when the last existing regiment in Flanders was disbanded.

Plate I: Spanish Infantry Ensigns

1. Infantry company ensign, 1670–1680, attributed to the marine tercio, *Mar de Napoles* (EI-4)

According to some scholars, the marine infantry had an ensign with a blue background, however in a 1630 painting depicting this *tercio* in Naples, the ensigns are in white with the red *aspa*.

2. Infantry company ensign, 1660–70, *tercio provincial de Sevilla* (EI-15)

Ensigns with the monochrome background belong to the oldest *tercios*, and this yellow flag is attributed to the *morados viejos*, the provincial infantry of Seville, originally formed in 1634 as the king's guard infantry regiment.

Plate J: Spanish Infantry Ensigns

1. Infantry company ensign, 1683, unknown Spanish unit

This flag is depicted in the painting of an *auto-da-fé* by Francisco Rizzi. As for most of the infantry ensigns, the colours could suggest some heraldic correspondence with a province or a captain. However, this ensign has been attributed to both the *Guardias del Rey* (or *las Chambergas*, EI-118), and the *tercio Provincial de Madrid* (EI-70). The former is improbable, since the *Chambergas* had been disbanded in 1678.

2. Infantry company ensign, last quarter of the seventeenth century, Navarre regular infantry or militia

This flag is one of the rare original ensigns still existing, and it is preserved at Elizondo, in Navarre. Possibly, this ensign belonged to a militia company, but design and colours are typical of the infantry ensigns in the age of Felipe IV and Carlos II. The size of the ensign is also considerable, measuring approximately 200x200 cm.

Plate K: Spanish Infantry Ensigns

1. Infantry company ensign, 1663, *tercio provincial de Asturias* (EI-118)

Reconstruction after José Luis Calvo Pérez, 'El tercio fijo del principato de Asturias', 1663, in *Researching & Dragona*, n.20, 2003.

Another flag with a geometrical pattern, lost in 1693 at the battle of the Ter. Compared to the previous flag, in 30 years the design had changed little.

Plate L: Spanish Infantry and Cavalry Ensigns, Early 1690s

1. Infantry colonel ensign belonging to an unknown Milanese tercio
2. Infantry company colour, *tercio Casco de Granada* (EI-46)
3. and 4. Infantry ensigns belonging to unknown German regiments in Spanish service
5. Cavalry standard belonging to an unknown Milanese unit
6. Cavalry standard belonging to the German regiment *Lorrena* (EC-113)

Plates M and N: Spanish Infantry Ensigns Belonging to Unknown Units, Early 1690s

These and the previous ensigns were captured by the French in the early 1690s in Catalonia and Piedmont and are a good example of style and design of ensigns carried by the Hispanic infantry and cavalry in the period 1660–1690. These and other trophies were displayed in the church of Saint Louis of Versailles, but were removed in the 1790s, because they were a symbol of the deposed Monarchy. After *Les Triomphes de Louis XIV* (Bibliothèque nationale de France, Paris).

Plate O: Guardroom Scene

Guardroom by Gillis van Tilborgh, Flanders, 1664–68 (Hermitage Museum, St Petersburg). Note in centre the officer wearing an overcoat with 'Brandenburg' button laces. In the last quarter of the seventeenth century, many artists depicted Hispanic soldiers, but less than compared to the previous years when the Monarchy's armies were extensively depicted by Peter Snayers or Diego Velásquez. In this painting, there are a several examples of soldiery's clothing in the early phase of the formation of the Spanish military uniforms, although as for concerns the army of Flanders in the 1660s.

Plate P: Carlo IV Borromeo

A portrait of Carlo IV Borromeo, dating 1680–82, wearing an elaborate blue coat lined and faced red with floral embroidery in silver and gold and red-white lace. Ribbons and bow are also in red and white. This is a good example of the late 'Spanish *carlino* style' in the version introduced in Italy in the last decades of the seventeenth century.

Select Bibliography

Archival Sources

Archivo General de la Corona de Aragón (Barcelona)
>   *Consejo de Aragón*
Archivo General Militar de Madrid (Madrid)
Archivo General de Palacio (Madrid)
Archivo General de Indias (Seville)
>   *Indiferente*
Archivo General de Simancas (Valladolid)
>   *Consejo y Juntas de Hacienda*
>   *Estado*
>   *Guerra Antigua*
>   *Guerra Moderna*
>   *Guerra y Marina*
>   *Contaduría Mayor de Cuentas*
>   *Secretarías Provinciales*
ASVe Archivio di Stato di Venezia
>   *Stato da Mar, Provveditori sopra le Camere*
Archivo Histórico Municipal de Barcelona
>   *Consell, Deliberacions*
Archivo Histórico de la Nobleza (Toledo)
>   *Bornos*
>   *Osuna*
Archivo Histórico Nacional (Madrid)
>   *Consejos Suprimidos*
>   *Estado*
>   *Órdenes Militares*
Archives Générales du Royaume (Brussels)
>   *Contadurie et Pagadorie des Gens de Guerre*
>   *Secretaire de Guerre*
Archivio di Stato di Milano
>   *Militare parte antica*
>   *Dispacci Reali*
Archivio di Stato di Napoli
>   *Museo*
>   *Scrivania di Razione e Ruota dei Conti*
Archivio Storico Siciliano
>   *Documenti*

Biblioteca Nacional de España (Madrid)

Sucesos

Archivio Segreto Vaticano

Avvisi

Nunziatura

Contemporary Printed Works and Manuscripts

Anon., *Journal de ce qui s'est passé entre l'Armée d'Espagne, & celle de Portugal, du coste de Galice, entre le Duero & le Minho.* (Lyon, 1662)

Anon., *De la guerra de Portugal, sucessos del año MDCLXIII* (manuscript dated 1664, Bibliothèque nationale de France)

Anon., *Memoría de los accidentes mas notables succedidos en la guerra pasada durante el Gobierno del Ducque de Villahermosa* (manuscript dated 1681, Biblioteca Nacional de España)

(Author not stated) *Noticias y documentos relativos a la organización del Ejército de Flandes, entre 1535 y 1661*(manuscript without date, Biblioteca Nacional de España)

Agurto, Francisco de, *Tratado y reglas militares* (Madrid, 1689)

Arrieta Arandia, Juan Antonio de, *Resumen de la verdadera destreza y modo fácil para saber los caminos verdaderos en la batalla* (Pamplona, 1688)

Davila Gastón Orejón, Francisco, Excelencia *del arte militar y varones ilustres* (Madrid 1683)

Di Rampone, Guglielmo, *Esercitio Militare generale della fanteria e cavallaria* (manuscript dated 1662, Biblioteca Nacional de España)

Fernández de Medrano, Sebastián, *El Perfecto Bombardero y Artillero* (Antwerp, 1723)

Filamondo, fra' Raffaele Maria, *Il Genio Bellicoso di Napoli. Memorie Historiche d'alcuni Capitani Celebri Napolitani c'han militato per la Fede, per lo Re, per la Patria nel secolo corrente* (Napoli, 1694), Vols I–II

Grana del Carretto, Ottone Enrico, Marchese del, *Despachos para Su Majestad del Gobierno de Flandes, en tiempo del Excmo. Sr. Marqués de Grana, desde primero de abril 1682* (manuscript 9888, Biblioteca Nacional de España)

Gualdo Priorato, Galeazzo, *Relatione della città e stato di Milano sotto il governo dell'eccellentissimo sig. Don Luigi de Guzman Ponze de Leone* (Milan, 1666)

Gualdo Priorato, Galeazzo, *Teatro del Belgio ò sia Descritione delle Diciassette Provincie del Medesimo* (Frankfurt am Main, 1683)

La Peña, Narcíso Feliu de, *Annales de Cataluña*, vol. III (Barcelona, 1709)

Mascarenas, Geronimo, *Campaña de Portugal per la parte de Estremadura el Año de 1662* (Madrid, 1663)

Samaniego, Juan Antonio, *Disertación sobre l'antiguedad de los Regimentos de Infanteria, Cavalleria y Dragones de España* (Madrid, 1738)

Ventura de la Sala y Abarca, Francisco, *Después de Dios la primera obligación y glosa de Ordenes Militares* (Naples, 1681)

Villahermosa, Carlos Aragón y Borja, Duque de, *Correspondencia de Carlos de Gurrea y Aragón, Duque de Villahermosa, relativa a su gobierno en Flandes*, BNE, Manuscript 2412, vols I–VIII.

Villahermosa, Carlos Aragón y Borja, Duque de, *Correspondencia de Carlos de Gurrea y Aragón, Duque de Villahermosa, relativa a su gobierno en Cataluña*, BNE, Manuscript. 2398, vols I–X.

General Documentary Sources

Aleo, Jorge, *Storia cronologica del Regno di Sardegna dal 1637 al 1672* (Sassari: Francesco Manconi, 1998)

De Santiago y Gómez, José, *Historia de Vigo y su Comarca* (Madrid, 1896)

Di Bella, Saverio (ed.), *La Rivolta di Messina (1674–78) e il mondo mediterraneo nella seconda metà del Seicento*, in 'Acts of the International Conference, 1975' (Cosenza: Luigi Pellegrini, 1979)

Elliot, John, *Imperial Spain, 1496–1716* (London: Penguin Books, 2002)

Giannini, Massimo Carlo & Signorotto Gianvittorio (editors), *Lo Stato di Milano nel XVII secolo. Memoriali e relazioni* (Rome: Ministero per i Beni e le Attività Culturali – Dipartimento per i Beni Archivistici e Librari – Direzione Generale degli Archivi, 2006)

Israel, Jonathan I., *The Dutch Republic: Its Rise, Greatness and Fall, 1477–1806* (Oxford: Clarendon Press, 1995)

Israel, Jonathan I., *Conflict of Empires: Spain, the Low Countries and the Struggle for World Supremacy 1585–1713* (London: The Hambledon Press, 1997)

Kagan, Richard L. and Geoffrey Parker (eds), *Spain, Europe and the Atlantic World: Essays in honour of John H. Elliott* (Cambridge: Cambridge University Press, 1995)

Kamen, Henry, *Spain's Road to Empire: The Making of a World Power, 1492–1763* (London: Penguin, 2002)

Maura y Gamazo, Gabriel, *Vida y Reinado de Carlos II* (Madrid: Aguilar, 1990)

Pernot, François, *La Franche-Comté espagnole. A travers les archives de Simancas, une autre histoire des Franc-Comtois et de leurs relations avec l'Espagne, de 1493 à 1678* (Besançon: Presses Universitaires de Franche-Comté, 2003)

Rodriguez Zamora, Francisco, *La pupilla dell'occhio della Toscana y la posición hispánica en el Mediterráneo occidental (1677–1717)* (Madrid: Fundación Española de Historia Moderna, 2013)

Sánchez Prieto, Ana Belén, *La Adninistración Real bajo Los Austrias y la expedición de títulos nobiliarios*, in S. Cabezas Fontanilla and M. del Mar Royo Martínez (editors) 'V Jornadas Científicas sobre Documentación de Castilla e Indias en el siglo XVI' (Madrid, 2005), pp.379–407

Stradling, Robert A., *Spain's Struggle for Europe, 1598–1668* (London: The Hambledon Press, 1994)

Military History

Barado, Francisco, *Historia del Ejército Español. Armas, Uniformes, Sistema de Combate, Instituciones, Organización del mismo, desde los tiempos más remotos hasta nuestros días* (Barcelona, 1889), vol. III.

Chardon, Carlos Fernando, *Reseña historica del origen y desarrollo de las Milicias Puertorriqueñas bajo el regime español* (Puerto Rico: Puerto Rico National Guard, 1978)

Chiaramonte, Socrate, *La rivoluzione e la guerra messinese del 1674–8: appunti e documenti* (Palermo, 1899)

Clonard, Serafín María de Soto y Abach, Conde de, *Memorias para la historia de las tropas de la Casa Real de España* (Madrid, 1824)

Clonard, Serafín María de Soto y Abach (conde de), *Historia orgánica de las armas de infantería y caballería española desde la creación del ejército permanente hasta nuestros días*; vols I–XV (Madrid, 1851–62)

Clonard, Serafín María de Soto y Abach (conde de), *Album de la Infanteria española desde sus primitivos tiempos hasta el día* (Madrid 1861)

Clonard, Serafín María de Soto y Abach (conde de), *Album de la Caballeria española desde sus primitivos tiempos hasta el día* (Madrid 1861)

Cortés, Fernando, *El real ejército de Extremadura en la guerra de la restauración de Portugal, 1640–1668* (Badajoz: Servicio de Publicaciones de la Universidad de Extremadura, 1985)

Estébanez Calderón, Serafín, *De la conquista y pérdida de Portugal*, vols I–II (Madrid, 1885)

Espino López, Antonio, *Cataluña durante el reinado de Carlos II. Política y guerra en la frontera catalana, 1679–1697* (Barcelona: Bellaterra – Universitat Autónoma de Barcelona, 1999)

Espino López, Antonio, *Guerra, fisco y fueros la defensa de la corona de Aragón en tiempos de Carlos II, 1665–1700* (Valencia: Universidad de Valéncia, 2007)

Espino López, Antonio, *Las guerras de Cataluña. El Teatro de Marte* (Madrid: EDAF, 2014)

Giménez González, Manuel, *El Ejército y la Armada* (Madrid, 1862)

Girbal, Enrique Cláudio, *El sitio de Gerona en 1684* (Gerona, 1882)

Ligresti, Domenico, *Le armi dei Siciliani. Cavalleria, guerra e moneta nella Sicilia spagnola (secoli XV–XVII)* (Palermo: Mediterranea Ricerche Storiche, 2013)

Maffi, Davide, *La cittadella in armi. Esercito, società e finanza nella Lombardia di Carlo II 1660–1700* (Milan: Franco Angeli, 2011)

Maffi, Davide, *En defensa del Imperio. Los ejércitos de Felipe IV y la guerra por la hegemonia europea (1653–1659)* (Madrid: Actas, 2014)

Maffi, Davide, *Los últimos tercios. El ejercito de Carlos II* (Madrid: Desperta Ferro, 2020)

Manzano Lahóz, Antonio, *Las banderas históricas del Ejército español* (Madrid: Ministerio de Defensa, 1996)

Martínez de Merlo, Jesús – Álvarez Abeilhé, Juan, *La heráldica y la orgánica de los Reales Ejércitos* (Madrid: Ministerio de Defensa, 2015)

Martínez Ruiz, Enrique, *Los soldados del rey. Los ejércitos la Monarquia hispánica (1480–1700)* (Madrid: Actas, 2008)

Picouet, Pierre, *The Armies of Philip IV of Spain 1621–1665* (Warwick: Helion & Company, 2019)

Ribot García, Luis Antonio, *La Monarquia de España y la guerra de Mesina (1674–1678)* (Madrid: Actas Editorial, 2002)

Rodríguez Hernández, Antonio José, *España, Flandes y la Guerra de Devolución (1667–1668). Guerra, reclutamiento y movilización para el mantenimiento de los Países Bajos Españoles* (Madrid: Ministerio de Defensa, 2007)

Rodríguez Hernández, Antonio José, *Los Tambores de Marte. El Reclutamiento en Castilla durante la segunda mitad del siglo XVII (1648–1710)* (Valladolid: Universidad de Valladolid, 2011)

Rodríguez Hernández, Antonio José, *Breve historia de los ejércitos. Los tercios de Flandes* (Madrid: Nowtilus, 2014)

Rooms, Etienne, *De organisatie van de troepen van de Spaans-Habsburgse monarchie in de Zuidelijke Nederlanden* (Brussels: Koninklijk Legermuseum, 2003)

Samaniego, Juan Antonio: *Disertación sobre la antigüedad de los regimientos de Infanteria, Cavalleria, y Dragones de España* (Madrid, 1738)

Articles and Essays

Álvarez-Ossorio Alvariño, Antonio, 'The State of Milan and the Spanish Monarchy', in Thomas James Dandalet, *Spain in Italy: Politics, Society, and Religion 1500–1700* (Leiden–Boston: Brill, 2007), pp.99–131

Alvarez-Ossorio Alvariño, Antonio, 'La Chamberga: el regimiento de la guardiea del rey y la salvaguarda de la majestad (1668–1677)', in *Gobierno de corte y sociedad politica: continuidad y cambio en el gobierno de la Monarquia de España en Europa en torno a la Guerra de Sucesión (1665–1725)* (Madrid, 2012), pp.21–103

Álvarez-Ossorio, Alvariño Antonio, 'The Legacy of Carlos II and the Art of Government of the Spanish Monarchy', in A. Álvarez-Ossorio, C. Cremonini and E. Riva (eds), *The Transition in Europe between 17th and 18th Centuries, Perspectives and case studies* (Milan: Franco Angeli, 2016), pp.23–34

Blanco Núñez, José María, 'Presencia italiana en la milicia española', *International Review of Military History* N. 94 (Madrid: International Commission of Military History, 2016)

Bragado Echevarría, Javier, 'El sitio y defensa de Valencia De Alcántara durante la Guerra de Restauración (1664)', *Caminos de la Historia de Valencia de Alcántara*, Año 1, N. 4 (January 2014), pp.5–38

Calcagno, Paolo, *La 'puerta a la mar' del Ducato di Milano: il Marchesato del Finale nel sistema imperiale spagnolo (1571–1713)*, Thesis of Doctorate Research (Verona: Dipartimento di Discipline Storiche, Artistiche, Archeologiche e Geografiche – Università di Verona, 2011)

Calvo Pérez, José Luis, 'El tercio fijo del principato de Asturias, 1663', *Researching & Dragona*, n.20, 2003, pp.31–38

Caro del Corral, Juan Antonio, 'La frontera cacereña ante la Guerra de Restauración de Portugal: Organización defensiva y sucesos de armas (1640–1668)', *Revista de Estudios Extremeños* (2012), Tomo LXVIII, Número I, pp.187–226

Cayron, Jean-R., 'La véritable histoire de Jacques Pastur dit Jaco', *La Fourragère*, N. 3 (December 1951), pp.533–592

Contreras Gay, José, 'La reorganización militar en la época de la decadencia española (1640–1700)', *Millars. Espai i Historia*, XXVI (2003), pp.131–154

Cortés, Fernando, 'Extremadura a mediados del siglo XVII. El real ejército de Extremadura y su presión sobre la región', *Alcántara: revista del Seminario de Estudios Cacereños*, n. 11 (1987), pp.7–20

De Mesa Gallego, Eduardo, 'Los tercios en combate (III). Organización y tácticas de los ejércitos de la Monarquia Hispánica (1660–1700)', *Los Tercios, 1660–1704*, Desperta Ferro, special issue XIX (June–July 2019), pp.32–38

Echevarría Bacigalupe, Miguel Angel, 'El ejército de Flandes en la etapa final del régimen español', in E. García Hernán and D. Maffi (eds), *Guerra y sociedad en la monarquía hispánica: política, estrategia y cultura en la Europa moderna (1500–1700)* (Madrid: Fundación MAPFRE, Laberinto; Consejo Superior de Investigaciones Científicas, CSIC, 2006), vol. I, pp.553–578

Espino López, Antonio, 'Las tropas de Granada en las guerras de Cataluña, 1684–1697: una visión social', *Chronica Nova*, n. 20 (1992) pp.129–151

Espino López, Antonio, 'Las tropas italianas en la defensa de Cataluña, 1665–1698', *Investigaciones Históricas* n. 18 (1998), pp.51–74

Espino López, Antonio, 'El esfuerzo de guerra de la Corona de Aragón durante el reinado de Carlos II, 1665–1700. Los servicios de tropas', *Revista de Historia Moderna Anales de la Universidad de Alicante*, N. 22 (2004), pp.7–90

Espino López, Antonio, 'El ocaso de la maquinaria bélica hispánica', *Los Tercios, 1660–1704*, Desperta Ferro, special issue XIX (June–July 2019), pp.14–20

Estrella, Antonio Jiménez, 'Mérito, calidad y experiencia: criterios volubles en la provisión de cargos militares bajo los Austrias', J.F. Pardo Molero and M.L. Cortés (eds), *Oficiales reales. Los ministros de la Monarquía Católica (siglos XVI–XVII)* (Valencia: Universitat de València, 2012), pp.241–264

Fernández Izquierdo, Francisco, 'Los caballeros cruzados en el ejército de la Monarquía Hispánica durante los siglos XVI y XVII: ¿anhelo o realidad?', *Revista de Historia Moderna – Anales de la Universidad de Alicante*', n. 22 (2004), pp.7–131

Dentant, Arnaud, *Van ridders tot militaire entrepreneurs? Een analyse van de Zuid-Nederlandse adel in het Ejército de Flandes. 1598–1701*, Ghent University, History Examination Board (Academic year 2010–2011)

Jiménez Estrella, Antonio, 'Las milicias en Castilla: evolución y proyección social de un modelo de defensa alternativo al ejército de los Austrias', Javier Ruiz Ibáñez (ed.) *Las milicias del rey de España. Política, sociedad e identidad en las Monarquías Ibéricas*' Fondo de Cultura Económica, Madrid (2009), pp.72–103

Jiménez Moreno, Augustín, *Nobleza, Guerra y Servicio a la Corona. Los caballeros de hábito en el siglo XVII*. Thesis of Doctorate Research (Madrid: Departamento de Historia Moderna, Facultad de Geografía e Historia-Universidad Complutense de Madrid, 2010)

Maffi, Davide, 'L'Amministrazione della Finanza Militare nella Lombardia Spagnola: I Veedores e i Contadores dell'Esercito (1536–1700)', *Storia Economica* V (2002), n. 1, pp.54–106

Maffi, Davide, 'Una epopeya olvidada. Los flamencos/valones al servicio de la monarquía española (siglo XVII)', in E. Martínez Ruiz (ed.), 'Presencia de flamencos y valones en la milicia española', *International Review of Military History* N. 96 (Madrid: International Commission of Military History, 2016), pp.53–72

Maffi, Davide, 'Asentistas del rey. Il mondo degli appalti militari nella Monarchia spagnola durante il XVII secolo', *Storia Economica* XIX (2016), pp.135–158

Maffi, Davide, 'Fieles y leales vasallos del rey. Soldados italianos en los ejércitos de los Austrias hispanos en el siglo XVII', J.M. Blanco Núñez (ed.), 'Presencia italiana en la milicia española', *International Review of Military History* N. 94 (Madrid: International Commission of Military History, 2016), pp.39–60

Martínez de Merlo, Jesús, 'La caballería entre Los Austrias y Los Borbones', *Revista de Historia Militar* N. 121 (2017), pp.138–197

Morales, Óscar Recio, 'When Merit alone is not enough. Money as a "Parallel Route" for Irish Military advancement in Spain', *Irish Immigration Studies in Latin America – Society for Irish-Latin American Studies* (Burtigny, Switzerland, 2012), pp.121–124

Quirós Rosado, Roberto, 'La fiel nación. Una aproximación al servicio militar borgoñón bajo los últimos Austrias españoles (1674–1714)', E. Martínez Ruiz (ed.), 'Presencia de flamencos y valones en la milicia española', *International Review of Military History* N. 96 (Madrid: International Commission of Military History, 2016), pp.73–96

Ribot García, Luis Antonio, 'El ejército de los Austrias', *Temas de Historia Militar*, vol. I, *Ponencias del Ier Congreso Historia Militar* (Estado Mayor del Ejército, Madrid 1983), pp.157–203

Ribot García, Luis Antonio, 'El ejército de los Austrias, aportaciones recientes y nuevas perspectivas', *Revista d'Historia Moderna*, n. 3 (1983), pp.89–126

Ribot García, Luis Antonio, 'Las Provincias Italianas y la defensa de la Monarquía', *Manuscrits* n. 13 (1995), pp.97–122

Ribot García, Luis Antonio, 'Milano, piazza d'armi della Monarchia spagnola', *Millain the great. Milano nelle brume del Seicento* (Milan: Cassa di Risparmio delle Province Lombarde-Federico Motta Editore, 1989), pp.349–363

Riccobene, Emanuele, 'La difesa della Sicilia nella seconda metà del XVII secolo ossia la storia militare come chiave di lettura dei rapporti tra Sicilia e Spagna in età moderna', *Instituto Cervantes* (Palermo, 2015), pp.1–12

Rodríguez Hernández, Antonio José, 'El Reclutamiento de españoles para el Ejército de Flandes durante la segunda mitad del siglo XVII', E. García Hernán and D. Maffi (eds), *Guerra y sociedad en la monarquía hispánica: política, estrategia y cultura en la Europa moderna (1500–1700)* (Madrid: Fundación MAPFRE, Laberinto; Consejo Superior de Investigaciones Científicas, CSIC, 2006), Vol. II, pp.395–434

Rodríguez Hernández Antonio José, 'La contribución militar del reino de Granada durante la segunda mitad del siglo XVII: la formación de los Tercios de Granada', A. Jiménez Estrella and F. Andújar Castillo (eds), *Los nervios de la guerra. Estudios sociales sobre el Ejército de la Monarquía Hispánica (siglos XVI–XVIII): nuevas perspectivas* (Granada: Editorial Comares, 2007), pp.149–189

Rodríguez Hernández, Antonio José, 'Poner una pica vallisoletana en Flandes. Reclutamiento y costes del transporte de tropas a los Países Bajos (1665–1700)', *Investigaciones Históricas*, n. 28 (2008), pp.55–78

Rodríguez Hernández, Antonio José, 'Financial and Military Cooperation Between the Spanish Crown and the Emperor in the Seventeenth Century', in Peter Rauscher (ed.) *Die Habsburgermonarchie und das Heilige Römische Reich vom Dreissigjährigen Krieg bis zum Ende des habsburgischen Kaisertums* (Vienna: Aschendorff Verlag, 2010), pp.575–602

Rodríguez Hernández, Antonio José, 'La venta de títulos nobiliarios a través de la financiación de nuevas unidades militares durante el siglo XVII', F. Andujár Castillo and M. Felices de la Fuente (eds), *El poder del dinero. Ventas de cargo y honores en el Antiguo Régimen* (Madrid: Biblioteca Nueva, 2011), pp.274–302

Rodríguez Hernández, Antonio José, 'Al servicio del rey. Reclutamiento y transporte de soldados italianos a España para luchar en la guerra contra Portugal (1640–1668)', in D. Maffi (ed.), *Tra Marte e Astrea. Giustizia e giurisdizione militare nell'Europa della prima età moderna* (Milan: Franco Angeli, 2012), pp.229–275

Rodríguez Hernández, Antonio José, 'Miedos de Guerra y Ecos de Frontera: la posición de España ante una alianza franco-lusa durante la Guerra de Holanda (1672–1679)', *Historia Moderna*, Serie IV, vol. 25 (2012), pp.117–149

Rodríguez Hernández, Antonio José, 'De Galicia a Flandes: reclutamiento y servicio de soldados gallegos en el ejército de Flandes (1648–1700)', in *Obradoiro de Historia Moderna* N. 16 (December 2012), pp.213–251

Rodríguez Hernández, Antonio José, 'El reclutamiento de asturianos para el ejército de Flandes durante el reinado de Carlos II', in E. Martínez-Radio Garrido, *Entemu* N. 17, Aportaciones a cinco siglos de la Historia Militar de España (2013), pp.7–47

Rodríguez Hernández, Antonio José, 'Los hombres y la guerra. El reclutamiento', in *Historia Militar de España – III Edad Moderna. II Escenario Europeo* (Madrid: Comisión Española de Historia Militar – Real Academia de Historia, 2013), pp.187–222

Rodríguez Hernández, Antonio José, 'Asientos y asentistas militares en el siglo XVII: el ejemplo del pan y la pólvora', in *Comercio y Finanzas Internacionales en una España en Transición, 1680–1721* (Universidad de Salamanca, 2013), pp.61–98

Rodríguez Hernández, Antonio José, 'La presencia militar alemana en los ejércitos peninsulares españoles durante la guerra de restauracion portuguesa (1659–1668)', in L. Ruiz Molina, J.J. Ruiz Ibañez and B. Vincent (eds), '*Yakka. Revista De Histudios Yeclanos*', vol. 10 (2015), pp.269–288

Rodríguez Hernández, Antonio José, 'Evolución o innovación? Los cambios técnico-tácticos en el armamento del ejército español durante el relevo dinástico: nuevas consideraciones', *Cuadernos de Historia Moderna*, 41-2 (2016), pp.273–294

Rodríguez Hernández, Antonio José, 'Guerra y alianzas en la lucha por la hegemonía europea durante la segunda mitad del siglo XVII. El papel de España', in L. Ribot and J.M. Iñurritegui (eds), *Europa y los tratados de raparto de la Monarquia de España, 1688–1700* (Madrid: Biblioteva Nueva, 2016), pp.247–275

Rodríguez Hernández, Antonio José, 'La evolución del vestuario militar y la aparición de los primeros uniformes en el ejército de la Monarquía Hispánica, 1660–1680', *Obradoiro de Historia Moderna* N. 26 (2017), pp.179–206

Rooms, Etienne, 'Bezoldiging, bevoorrading en inkwartiering van de koninklijke troepen in de Spaanse Nederlanden (1567–1700)', *BMGN* 118, afl. 4 (2003), pp.545–566

Sánchez Martin, Juan Luis, 'Apuntes para una reconstrucción histórica de los tercios del siglo XVII' (part one), *Researching & Dragona*, vol. I, n. 2 (June 1996), pp.4–24

Sánchez Martin, Juan Luis, 'El último ejército de Flandes', *Researching & Dragona*, vol. II (1997), n. 3, pp.17–45

Sánchez Martin, Juan Luis, 'La cadena de mando del tercio de la Sangre, hasta después de Rocroi (1645)', *Researching & Dragona*, Vol. VIII, n. 19 (2003), pp.4–29

Sánchez Martin, Juan Luis, 'Tropas Británicas de la Casa de Austria', *Researching & Dragona*, vol. IV, n. 8 (14a) 1999), pp. 4 11

Saavedra Vázquez, María del Carmen, 'La situación militar de Galicia tras la guerra de Portugal (1669–1677)', in *Obradoiro de Historia Moderna*, N. 26 (2017), pp.207–235

Sorando Muzas, Luis and Manzano Lahoz, Antonio, 'El tercio de Aragón: notas sobra su Evolución, indumentaria y emblematica (1678–1698)', *Emblanata – Revista Aragonesa de Emblemática* N. 1 (1995), pp.153–165

White, Lorraine, 'Guerra y revolución militar en la Iberia del siglo XVII', *Manuscrits* 21 (2003), pp.63–93

White, Lorraine, 'Los Tercios en España: el combate', *Studios Historicos'* (Ediciones Universidad de Salamanca, 2009), pp.141–167